THE CAMBRIDGE HISTORY
OF THE ENGLISH LANGUAGE

GENERAL EDITOR Richard M. Hogg

VOLUME VI English in North America

THE CAMBRIDGE
HISTORY OF THE
ENGLISH LANGUAGE

VOLUME VI   *English in North America*

EDITED BY

JOHN ALGEO
Professor Emeritus, University of Georgia

CAMBRIDGE
UNIVERSITY PRESS

PUBLISHED BY THE PRESS SYNDICATE OF THE UNIVERSITY OF CAMBRIDGE
The Pitt Building, Trumpington Street, Cambridge, United Kingdom

CAMBRIDGE UNIVERSITY PRESS
The Edinburgh Building, Cambridge CB2 2RU, UK
40 West 20th Street, New York, NY 10011-4211, USA
10 Stamford Road, Oakleigh, VIC 3166, Australia
Ruiz de Alarcón 13, 28014 Madrid, Spain
Dock House, The Waterfront, Cape Town 8001, South Africa

http://www.cambridge.org

First published 2001

Printed in the United Kingdom at the University Press, Cambridge

Typeface Monotype Garamond 11/13pt   *System* QuarkXPress™   [SE]

A catalogue record for this book is available from the British Library

ISBN 0 521 26479 0 hardback

CONTENTS

Contents

CONTRIBUTORS

JOHN ALGEO *Alumni Foundation Distinguished Professor of English Emeritus, University of Georgia*

RICHARD W. BAILEY *Professor of English Language and Literature, University of Michigan*

LAUREL J. BRINTON *Professor of English, University of British Columbia*

RONALD R. BUTTERS *Professor of English and Cultural Anthropology, Duke University*

†FREDERIC G. CASSIDY *Professor Emeritus of English, University of Wisconsin; Chief Editor,* Dictionary of American Regional English

MARGERY FEE *Professor of English, University of British Columbia*

EDWARD FINEGAN *Professor of Linguistics and Law, University of Southern California*

JOHN HURT FISHER *John C. Hodges Professor Emeritus of English, University of Tennessee, Knoxville*

JOAN HOUSTON HALL *Chief Editor,* Dictionary of American Regional English

WILLIAM J. KIRWIN *Professor Emeritus of English Language and Literature, Memorial University of Newfoundland*

JONATHAN E. LIGHTER *Research Associate Professor of English, University of Tennessee, Knoxville*

MICHAEL MONTGOMERY *Professor Emeritus of English, University of South Carolina*

SALIKOKO S. MUFWENE *Professor and Chair of Linguistics, University of Chicago*

LEE PEDERSON *Charles Howard Candler Professor of English, Emory University*

SUZANNE ROMAINE *Merton Professor of English Language, University of Oxford*

RICHARD L. VENEZKY *Professor of Educational Studies, Linguistics, and Computer and Information Sciences, University of Delaware*

† Frederic G. Cassidy died on June 14, 2000, before the final editing of this volume; his colleague and successor at the *Dictionary of American Regional English*, Joan Houston Hall, proofed their joint chapter. We are proud to include his share of this chapter as a final contribution of one of the great American scholars of English language and literature.

GENERAL EDITOR'S PREFACE

Although it is a topic of continuing debate, there can be little doubt that English is the most widely-spoken language in the world, with significant numbers of native speakers in almost every major region – only South America falling largely outside the net. In such a situation an understanding of the nature of English can be claimed unambiguously to be of world-wide importance.

Growing consciousness of such a role for English is one of the motivations behind this History. There are other motivations too. Specialist students have many major and detailed works of scholarship to which they can refer, for example Bruce Mitchell's *Old English Syntax*, or, from an earlier age, Karl Luick's *Historische Grammatik der englischen Sprache*. Similarly, those who come new to the subject have both one-volume histories such as Barbara Strang's *History of English* and introductory textbooks to a single period, for example Bruce Mitchell and Fred Robinson's *A Guide to Old English*. But what is lacking is the intermediate work which can provide a solid discussion of the full range of the history of English both to the anglicist who does not specialize in the particular area to hand and to the general linguist who has no specialized knowledge of the history of English. This work attempts to remedy that lack. We hope that it will be of use to others too, whether they are interested in the history of English for its own sake, or for some specific purpose such as local history or the effects of colonization.

Under the influence of the Swiss linguist, Ferdinand de Saussure, there was, during the twentieth century, a persistent tendency to view the study of language as having two discrete parts: (i) synchronic, where a language is studied from the point of view of one moment in time; (ii) diachronic, where a language is studied from a historical perspective. It might therefore be supposed that this present work is purely diachronic. But this is not so.

One crucial principle which guides The Cambridge History of the English Language is that synchrony and diachrony are intertwined, and that a satisfactory understanding of English (or any other language) cannot be achieved on the basis of one of these alone.

Consider, for example, the (synchronic) fact that English, when compared with other languages, has some rather infrequent or unusual characteristics. Thus, in the area of vocabulary, English has an exceptionally high number of words borrowed from other languages (French, the Scandinavian languages, American Indian languages, Italian, the languages of northern India and so on); in syntax a common construction is the use of *do* in forming questions (e.g. *Do you like cheese?*), a type of construction not often found in other languages; in morphology English has relatively few inflections, at least compared with the majority of other European languages; in phonology the number of diphthongs as against the number of vowels in English English is notably high. In other words, synchronically, English can be seen to be in some respects rather unusual. But in order to understand such facts we need to look at the history of the language; it is often only there that an explanation can be found. And that is what this work attempts to do.

This raises another issue. A quasi-Darwinian approach to English might attempt to account for its widespread use by claiming that somehow English is more suited, better adapted, to use as an international language than others. But that is nonsense. English is no more fit than, say, Spanish or Chinese. The reasons for the spread of English are political, cultural and economic rather than linguistic. So too are the reasons for such linguistic elements within English as the high number of borrowed words. This History, therefore, is based as much upon political, cultural and economic factors as linguistic ones, and it will be noted that the major historical divisions between volumes are based upon the former type of events (the Norman Conquest, the spread of printing, the declaration of independence by the USA), rather than the latter type.

As a rough generalization, one can say that up to about the seventeenth century the development of English tended to be centripetal, whereas since then the development has tended to be centrifugal. The settlement by the Anglo-Saxons resulted in a spread of dialect variation over the country, but by the tenth century a variety of forces were combining to promote the emergence of a standard form of the language. Such an evolution was disrupted by the Norman Conquest, but with the development of printing together with other more centralizing tendencies, the emergence of a standard form became once more, from the fifteenth century on, a major characteristic of the language. But processes of emigration and colonization then gave rise to new regional varieties overseas, many of which have now achieved a high degree of linguistic independence, and some of which, especially American English, may even have a dominating influence on British English. The structure of this work is designed to reflect these different types of development. Whilst the first four volumes offer a reasonably straightforward chronological account, the later volumes are geographically based. This arrangement, we hope, allows scope for the proper treatment of diverse types of evolution and development. Even within the chronologically oriented volumes there are variations of structure, which are designed to reflect the changing relative importance of various linguistic features. Although all the chronological volumes have substantial chapters devoted to the central topics of semantics and vocabulary, syntax, and phonology and morphology, for other topics the space allotted in a particular volume is one which is appropriate to the importance of that topic during the relevant period, rather than some pre-defined calculation of relative importance. And within the geographically based volumes all these topics are potentially included with each geographical section, even if sometimes in a less formal way. Such a flexible and changing structure seems essential for any full treatment of the history of English.

One question that came up as this project began was the extent to which it might be possible or desirable to work within a single theoretical linguistic framework. It could well be argued that only a consensus within the linguistic community about preferred linguistic theories would enable a work such as this to be written. Certainly, it was immediately obvious when work for this History began, that it would be impossible to lay down a 'party line' on linguistic theory, and indeed, that such an approach would be undesirably restrictive. The solution reached was, I believe, more fruitful. Contributors have been chosen purely on the grounds of expertise and knowledge, and have been encouraged to write their contributions in the way they see most fitting, whilst at the same time taking full account of developments in linguistic theory. This has, of course, led to problems, notably with contrasting views of the same topic (and also because of the need to distinguish the ephemeral flight of theoretical fancy from genuine new insights into linguistic theory), but even in a work which is concerned to provide a unified approach (so that, for example, in most cases every contributor to a volume has read all the other contributions to that volume), such contrasts, and even contradictions, are stimulating and fruitful. Whilst this work aims to be authoritative, it is not prescriptive, and the final goal must be to stimulate interest in a subject in which much work remains to be done, both theoretically and empirically.

The task of editing this History has been, and still remains, a long and complex one. One of the greatest difficulties has been to co-ordinate the contributions of the many different writers. Sometimes, even, this has caused delays in volumes other than that where the delay arose. We have attempted to minimize the effects of such delays by various methods, and in particular by trying to keep bibliographies as up-to-date as possible. This should allow the interested reader to pursue very recent important work, including that by the contributors themselves, whilst maintaining the integrity of each volume.

As General Editor I owe a great debt to many friends and colleagues who have devoted much time and thought to how best this work might be approached and completed. Firstly, I should thank my fellow-editors: John Algeo, Norman Blake, Bob Burchfield, Roger Lass and Suzanne Romaine. They have been concerned as much with the History as a whole as with their individual volumes. Secondly, there are those fellow linguists, some contributors, some not, who have so generously given their time and made many valuable suggestions: John Anderson, Cecily Clark, Frans van Coetsem, Fran Colman, David Denison, Ed Finegan, Olga Fischer, Jacek Fisiak, Malcolm Godden, Angus McIntosh, Lesley Milroy, Donka Minkova, Matti Rissanen, Michael Samuels, Bob Stockwell, Tom Toon, Elizabeth Traugott, Peter Trudgill, Nigel Vincent, Anthony Warner, Simone Wyss. One occasion stands out especially: the organizers of the Fourth International Conference on English Historical Linguistics, held at Amsterdam in 1985, kindly allowed us to hold a seminar on the project as it was just beginning. For their generosity, which allowed us to hear a great many views and exchange opinions with colleagues one rarely meets face-to-face, I must thank Roger Eaton, Olga Fischer, Willem Koopman and Frederike van der Leek.

The preface to the earlier volumes acknowledged the considerable debt which I owed to my editors at Cambridge University Press, firstly, Penny Carter, and subsequently Marion Smith. Since then the History has seen two further editors, firstly Judith Ayling and now Kate Brett. Both have stepped into this demanding role with considerable aplomb, and the project has been extremely fortunate in obtaining their help and advice. I am very grateful to both. In particular we should all like to express our gratitude to Kate Brett for ensuring that this long trail is now at its end.

Richard M. Hogg

VOLUME EDITOR'S PREFACE

From small beginnings sometimes come big consequences. When the first Indo-Europeans began the trek from their Urheimat, wherever it may have been, an observer could hardly have predicted the spread of Indo-European languages and cultures over the world. When the first Anglo-Saxons crossed the sea to settle in Britain, an observer could not have anticipated that a millennium and a half later much of the globe would be colored pink. And when the first scraggly colonists stepped off the boat onto Virginia soil, no observer could have foreseen French airline pilots talking English to Turkish controllers, Japanese and Arab businessmen negotiating in English, or jeans-clad teenagers all over the world singing English lyrics to raucous music.

American English has lately played a role in those unanticipated consequences and has itself been continually changed in the process. This volume seeks to trace both of those facts: primarily the way the English language in its American variety has changed, from its exceedingly small beginnings to its role as a world force, but also how it has affected others during that historical transformation.

All living languages change constantly. Language change has no simple cause but is the result of changes of two broad kinds. First, changes in the speakers' environment – physical, social, cultural, and intellectual – are responded to by changes in the language. Second, the language system itself undergoes certain internal fluctuations and adjustments (by processes called assimilation and dissimilation, drift, pull-chain and push-chain effects, analogy, and so on). The results of such causes are cumulative differences in the use of a language from one generation to another and, over long stretches of time, shifts so great that the resulting system is a different language from the original one. So Latin transformed into Italian, Spanish, Portuguese, French, Romanian, and other Romance tongues; and

Anglo-Saxon transmogrified into the English of stockbrokers, rappers, and computer nerds.

As long as all the members of a speech community are in frequent contact with each other, their language changes in parallel ways. The reason is obvious. If one speaker, for whatever reason, begins to change the way he or she talks, three sorts of responses by other members of the community are possible. First, they may not notice the change (either consciously or unconsciously), or if they do, they may choose to ignore it. In that case, the change has no effect on the language of the community. Second, they may notice the change, dislike it, and respond negatively. In that case, the one who has introduced the change may be induced to correct it; or if not, the negative reaction toward it will reinforce the unchanged use by the community at large, and again there is no effect on the language of the community. Third, the change may be noticed, consciously or unconsciously, and not rejected but responded to favorably and imitated by those who hear it, thus reinforcing the change in the one who introduced it and spreading it through the community, thereby changing the language.

Whether an incident of change is suppressed or reinforced and extended, the language of the community remains relatively homogeneous. There is, to be sure, no completely uniform speech community anywhere. Every language has internal variation, and every language community has varieties. But some variation and some degree of varieties can be institutionalized, that is, accepted by speakers generally and accorded a place within the total system of the language. The speakers will then regard the different ways of talking they hear around them as "one language," and we can speak of a "relatively homogeneous" speech community.

If, on the other hand, the members of a single speech community are divided into two groups with severe impediments to free communication between them, a quite different result ensues. The impediments may be physical separation by oceans, mountains, deserts, or merely distance. Or they may be social separation by ghettos, castes, occupations, economics, education, clubs, or cliques. In either case, when people do not talk together, they come to talk differently. When there is no mutual correction and reinforcement between the members of two groups, their ways of talking drift apart, becoming increasingly different over time. After some generations of such uncoordinated drift, the result is two distinctively different varieties of language: two dialects or two standards, or ultimately two languages.

The process of differentiation between the English of Britain and that of America began with the first settlement in America. The colonists were divided from their fellows in the British Isles by a wide ocean, whose crossing by sail took weeks or months, and so not many persons made it often. No other means of communication was available. Contact with the mother country continued, but it was not easy or convenient; and its frequency and intimacy varied from one colony to another and from one social group or class to another.

The English used in America and the English used in Britain began consequently to drift apart. This process was not (as it is sometimes erroneously described) one of American English becoming different from British English. It is rather one of the English used by American speakers and the English used by British speakers both changing, but in unlike ways. So American English and British English became different from each other and both became different from the English of which they were mutual descendants. As a result, these two varieties must be considered synchronically by comparison with each other and diachronically by comparison with their common ancestor – a distinction that is sometimes confused.

American English and British English are the two major national varieties of English today, in terms of number of native speakers, volume of texts, and influence. Consequently, the most convenient way to describe either of these two present-day varieties as distinct from general English is to compare them with each other. In effect, what is distinctively American is what is not British, and what is distinctively British is what is not American. Other varieties – which are minor by the same factors of number of speakers, volume of texts, and influence – are conveniently described by comparing them with either British or American, whichever they are most like.

The synchronic descriptive convenience of comparing British and American with each other does not imply, however, a corresponding diachronic description. That is, present-day American English can no more be appropriately derived from British than present-day British English can be derived from American. They are equally derived from their common ancestor, the English of the sixteenth century, which was neither American nor British because American usage had not yet begun to develop and the English spoken in the British Isles had at that time nothing to define it by comparison.

Before English speakers began to spread around the world, first in large numbers in America, there was no British English. There was only English. Concepts like "American English" and "British English" are defined by comparison. They are relative concepts like "brother" and "sister." A single offspring cannot be a sibling, which is a category that requires more than one member. So language dialects or varieties cannot be spoken of until there are at least two of them, being mutually defining.

All languages have internal variation ranging in scope from idiolects (the particular ways different persons use the language) to national varieties (standardized forms of the language used in a particular independent political unit). Those two categories on the cline of language variation are major terminuses, although below the idiolect there are variations in the way a single person uses the language system and beyond the language itself there are families (Germanic, Indo-European, and perhaps Nostratic or even common Human). Between the idiolect and the national variety are dialects, regional and social, of various dimensions.

Pre-seventeenth-century English certainly had variations of many kinds. There was even a period, before the 1707 Act of Union subsumed the Scottish government under the English parliament, when it is appropriate to speak of two national varieties within the British Isles: Northern (Scottish English) and Southern (England English). But Scots ceased to exist as a separate national variety after the Act of Union. It then became a regional variety with strong local attachment and pride.

The colonists in America spoke dialects of the mother tongue, for in the early eighteenth century there were no contrasting national varieties of English. But with the American Revolution, the variations that had developed in the colonies became a new national variety, contrasting with what from that point can be called the British national variety. The year 1776 is the conventional beginning, not just of American English, but also of its correlative, British English.

A language does not exist in a landscape, but in the brains and on the tongues of its speakers. Neither the land of England nor the British Isles has a privileged position with respect to the identity of English. The speech-ways we now call English were used in prehistoric times on the continental European shores of the North Sea; they are used today around the globe, from Barrow, Alaska, on the north to the Falkland Islands on the south. For more than a millennium, between the middle of the fifth and the end of the sixteenth centuries, they were used primarily in the British Isles. But that long period of local use does not confer tenure on the locality.

The American variety of English is the language used by English speakers in America. It is just as continuous with the English of Cædmon and Ælfric, of Chaucer and Langland, of Shakespeare and Milton, as is the language of English speakers between Land's End and John o' Groats. The process of differentiation between the English spoken in America and that spoken in Britain went on for about three hundred years. It began with the first English colonization of America at the start of the seventeenth century, and continued until about the time of World War I. Thereafter the improved means of transportation and communication that developed in the twentieth century seem to have arrested and even reversed the process. Because of the complexities of linguistic systems, it is impossible to speak with confidence about how much alike or how different two speechways are or to compare two dialects with respect to their overall rate or degree of change. Only general impressions are possible. However, it is clear that the two national varieties have been growing closer together since the beginning of the twentieth century. As Albert Marckwardt (Marckwardt and Quirk 50, 55) remarked:

> Ultimately, I suppose, the unifying forces slowly began to outweigh those making for separation. If we must give dates, I suppose we'd have to say that between 1900 and 1920 the trend towards separation was really reversed. . . . What we see here, instead, is really an increasing unification of English, resulting in a steady, almost relentless, march towards the status of a world language.

Indeed, this process of reunification points out the danger of taking our metaphors too seriously. We talk about varieties of a language, such as British and American, as though they were well-defined objects in space. We speak of them as "separating" or "splitting." We talk about mother languages and sister languages and language families, and we depict the relationships between languages by a family tree, on the analogy of a human family with parents and offspring. To talk in that way is to reify language, that is, to treat an abstract system as though it were a physical thing. To talk about language in such metaphors is useful and not to be avoided. But it is wise to remember that such talk is metaphorical, not literal.

Because a language is not a thing, but an abstract system in human brains, it does not behave in a thingy way. The system is constantly being modified in the brain of every person, and the modifications in the brain of one person affect those in the brains of other persons by way of the messages sent between them by air vibrations or light waves. Concepts like "a dialect," "a language variety," or "a language" are further abstractions – classes of the already abstract systems in the brains of a number of persons, which are in some ways alike. But the systems in all those individual brains are ever changing, and so consequently are the classes of them that we call British English and American English.

New differences continue to arise in the way English speakers use English all over the world – including Britain and America. Those differences reinforce the status of British and American as different varieties. But the spread of new uses from one country to the other, often with surprising speed, now preserves and promotes the fundamental unity of the English language.

The focus of this volume is on how English in North America, that is, the United States and Canada, got to be the way it is as a result of inevitable changes in the ways Americans and Canadians use the abstract language systems in their brains.

• Chapter 1 ("External History," by John Algeo) surveys the political and social history of Americans from the first settlement at Jamestown, Virginia, to the present day, as background to the language Americans use and the ways their language has changed during those four hundred years. It divides that history into three great periods. During the Colonial period (1607–1776), settlers brought the English language to America, where it began to change in ways not fully parallel with changes underway in Britain. In the National period (1776–1898), the sense of a distinct variety arose, which was standardized especially in dictionaries and spelling books and spread over the continent during the westward expansion of the nation. Throughout the International period (1898 onward), Americans became increasingly involved with the world overseas, and American English gradually became a variety of the language used around the world.

The chapter focuses on events relating to several major themes. The English-speaking population of America had notable mobility, beginning with the colonists and extending through the pioneers to present-day business people, tourists, scientists, and scholars. Americans have been innovative in their response to the new environment, in technology and in language. Although clearly derived from English roots, American society developed a sense of discontinuity with the past and of newness as a correlate of its self-identity. American government and culture was decentralized, so that no single standard of style or language developed. Democracy or social mobility accompanied geographical mobility and reinforced the resistance to centralized authority and models. The large land area of the American continent provided a range of topography from arctic tundra to tropical swamp and a richness of resources. The American population, regionally varied among the first colonists, has been continually diversified by the immigration of new ethnic groups.

• Chapter 2 ("British and American, Continuity and Divergence," by John Hurt Fisher) emphasizes the actual continuity of British and American English, not only on the basis of historical derivation from a common source, but because of the continual interaction between the two national varieties throughout the time of their separate existences. The basic identity of the two national varieties balanced the patriotic and sometimes chauvinistic celebration of differences.

The institutions that both defined American as a distinct variety and preserved its links with changing British English – sometimes by influencing the latter – included Noah Webster's dictionaries as authorities, the educational system, the literary tradition, and prestige models of pronunciation as well as other aspects of language. The chapter also surveys the relationship between American and British dialects and their role in creating a recognizably American speech.

• Chapter 3 ("British and Irish Antecedents," by Michael Montgomery) deals in some detail with the complex question of the sources of American English in the dialects of the British Isles and four issues involved in identifying those sources (reconstruction, demography, data, and generalization). It identifies the sources of our knowledge of Colonial English as popular observations by outsiders, comments by grammarians and lexicographers, literary attestations, rhymes, and records and manuscripts.

The chapter surveys the history of attempts to relate American English to its roots in the British Isles and summarizes the perceived connections by both region and linguistic feature. The regions of Colonial America whose British roots have been investigated are New England, Pennsylvania, Appalachia or the Upper South, Virginia and the Lower South. Irish, Scottish, and regional British influences affected all of these regions in varying proportions. Prominent linguistic features are vowel mergers and shifts, rhotacism, *wh-* aspiration, verb inflection, and pronoun forms.

The chapter concludes that dialects from the British Isles were not replicated in America, but were mixed with each other and with indigenous developments in a process combining "cultural transference and cultural re-creation."

• Chapter 4 ("Contact with Other Languages," by Suzanne Romaine) surveys the extensive language contacts that have existed between English and a variety of other languages in America from the earliest explorations and colonization until the present day. Those languages include potentially all 350 to 500 Amerindian languages spoken within the boundaries of what became the United States. The most influential were languages of the Algonquian family, but the Iroquoian, Siouan, Uto-Aztecan, Athabaskan, and Penutian families were also to be reckoned with. Lingua francas like Mobilian Jargon and Indian pidgin Englishes were also contact languages for the European settlers.

European colonizing languages in North America other than English were Danish, Dutch, French, German, Russian, Spanish, and Swedish. The most important immigrant languages between the middle of the nineteenth century and the Immigration Act of 1921 were French, German, Italian, Polish, and Spanish. African languages, Chinese, and Yiddish were also to make significant contributions, and Hawaiian Creole English is taken as a typical instance of its type.

• Chapter 5 ("Americanisms," by Frederic G. Cassidy and Joan Houston Hall) treats the most innovative and influential aspect of American English, its vocabulary. The term *Americanism* dates from 1781, when it was coined by analogy with *Scotticism* by John Witherspoon, himself a Scotsman. The term has, however, been used in two principal senses, one historical or diachronic and the other synchronic.

The earliest diachronic Americanisms were loanwords of Amerindian origin relating to New World flora, fauna, and artifacts, which antedate the English settlement of North America. Colonization, however, produced a situation of dialect split that resulted in the retention or promotion of some native English options in the colonies that were lost or marginalized in the mother country. The latter terms thus became synchronic Americanisms, although historically they were part of general English.

Americanisms did not spring into existence all over the colonies at once. They were often regional in origin and use, specifically Southern, New England, Middle Atlantic, and Appalachian, each with subregions, such as south central Pennsylvania, the site of German influence known as "Pennsylvania Dutch." The westward moving frontier was another significant factor in the creation of Americanisms, including the most successful of all Americanisms, *OK*, whose origin and early spread has been documented in detail by Allen Walker Read.

If we were to identify a single person who influenced the adoption of Americanisms in the United States, it would be Noah Webster through his dictionaries and spelling book. In addition, however, John Bartlett documented Americanisms and promoted pride in their use. The Civil War and the succeeding Reconstruction were important sources of new Americanisms, as were the experiences the pioneers and cowboys had on the Great Plains, especially through contact with Spanish speakers in the south central and southwestern parts of the nation.

The urbanization and technological advances of the later nineteenth and early twentieth centuries were other productive sources for American vocabulary, as were both World Wars and the social changes that followed them. The non-Anglo ethnic group that has made the most pronounced contribution to Americanisms is doubtless the African-American. Subjects that have been prolific include religion, sports, and foods. Taken all together, Americanisms constitute a mighty and pervasive contribution to the vocabulary of English.

• Chapter 6 ("Slang," by Jonathan E. Lighter) covers the aspect of American vocabulary that is arguably both the most prolific and the most characteristic. The term *slang* has been used both widely and imprecisely. A definition of the term is stipulated in this chapter as a kind of vocabulary that is informal, nonstandard, nontechnical, novel-sounding, associated with youthful, raffish, undignified persons, connoting impertinence or irreverence. On the one hand, slang is a form of pop poetical language, but on the other hand, unlike poetry, it is untraditional and anti-introspective.

The origin of the term *slang* is uncertain, and the history of its use is as complex as the attitudes toward it, which have varied from outraged condemnation to rhapsodic celebration. Twentieth-century scholarship on slang blossomed as that type of vocabulary came to be regarded as an important object of study. Although the term does not appear until the middle of the eighteenth century, American colonists of the seventeenth century were using language that can fairly be characterized as slang, and the subsequent history of slang in American English is rich and complex.

The semantic domains most productive of slang are sex, intoxication, violence, death, deception, and weaknesses of mind or character. Ethnicity, crime, the military, sports, and entertainment are also prolific sources. Slang is especially associated with teenagers and college students and their concerns.

Of foreign contributors, Spanish and Yiddish have been especially important. Slang can be regarded as a particularly characteristic feature of American English, so it is appropriate that this chapter closes with a consideration of "why Americans should revel in this style of expression, even as many of them decry it as frivolous, offensive, or corrupting."

• Chapter 7 ("Dialects," by Lee Pederson) surveys American pronunciation and other dialectally variable features. Dialects are often divided into regional and social, but that division is more a reflection of scholarly approaches than an objective distinction between kinds of dialects. Dialect variation is typically both regional and social in a complex set of interrelated patterns. It has been studied by linguistic geography, derived from European dialectology as developed in the United States through the Linguistic Atlas program and the *Dictionary of American Regional English*, as well as by the techniques of sociolinguistics.

American regional dialects are distinguished primarily by phonological and lexical features, and secondarily by grammatical ones, both morphological and syntactic. Of those features, the phonological ones are especially noteworthy because they are distinctively linked to dialects. There is no "General American" pronunciation, parallel with British "Received Pronunciation." That is, America has no nonlocal pronunciation as a national standard. So American pronunciation can be adequately described only in terms of dialect patterns.

Present-day American dialects are the historical descendants of the speech patterns of the colonists, modified by several hundred years of development. Their systematic study began with the formation of the American Dialect Society in 1889. American English exists in four major geographical patterns, each including a number of subpatterns. These areas are characterized by settlement patterns and topography determining economic uses, which channeled their settlement:

(1)   Northern, including New England, New York, and the northern part of the country extending westward from New York State;

(2)   Southern, including the area along the Atlantic Coast from Virginia southward and along the Gulf Coast;

(3)   Midland, in two major parts: the North Midland, from Pittsburgh westward to Cincinnati, Indianapolis, Saint Louis, and Kansas City; and the South Midland, from Philadelphia southward through the Appalachian and Ozarks and the piney woods areas from north Georgia to east Texas; and

(4)   Western, a large area including the Mississippi Valley, Great Plains, Rocky Mountains, and the Pacific Coast.

• Chapter 8 ("African-American English," by Salikoko S. Mufwene) deals with the major ethnic dialect of the United States, associated with Americans of African descent, and approaches it particularly from the standpoint of sociolinguistics. The chapter begins by defining its subject and specifying the features that characterize the dialect: phonological, grammatical, semantic, and pragmatic. It is notable that, unlike the regional patterns of American English, grammatical features are very significant in identifying African-American English, and lexical ones are less so.

A major question about African-American English concerns its origin and historical development, whether it began in or developed through a creole stage, or whether it was a development of the regional and social variety of Anglo-American English that the African slaves were exposed to. That question is considered at length, and the assumptions behind the dichotomy are examined in an evenhanded manner.

The chapter also recognizes subvarieties of the dialect, and considers the history and uses of their study.

• Chapter 9 ("Grammatical Structure," by Ronald R. Butters) looks at the distinctive features of American English grammar, that is, those aspects of morphology and syntax that serve to identify the American variety of the language as distinct from other national varieties, particularly British English. This is, not surprisingly, one of the shortest chapters in the book, for grammar is the aspect of English in which the various national varieties differ least and in which the standard language is most uniform worldwide.

The chapter is devoted to three matters: first, grammatical features found in nonstandard American dialects; second, grammatical features of standard American English that match regional and social nonstandard dialects of Britain; and third, grammatical features of standard American English which appear to be independent developments.

The focus of this chapter, as determined by that of the whole volume, is on grammatical features that are distinctive of American English. There are, however, also negative features, that is, grammatical features of British English lacking in American (Algeo 1988a), but their specification pertains properly to a description of British English.

• Chapter 10 ("Spelling," by Richard L. Venezky) describes the patterns of spelling that distinguish American English from the other major national variety, British. At the first settlement of America in the seventeenth century, English spelling was still far more variable than it is today. The differences between present-day American and British spelling patterns, summarized in this chapter, result mainly from different choices among seventeenth-century options. The chapter traces the history of those choices and of the forces that influenced them, as well as periodical but largely unsuccessful efforts at more radical spelling reform. American spelling, although distinct in style, is different from British in only a few ways. It is likely that those ways will decrease in number and importance.

• Chapter 11 ("Usage," by Edward Finegan) opens with a demonstration that linguistic prescriptivism is common even among descriptive linguists, who differ from traditional prescriptivists mainly in the object of their prescriptions. The chapter traces the history of grammar (which has been the chief focus of usage study) and of usage study itself in America from Noah Webster through nineteenth-century school grammars to the conflict with linguistic scholarship that generated modern usage study. As a result of the *Oxford English Dictionary*'s publication and various usage surveys, a relativistic view of correctness became dominant in the second half of the twentieth century. A negative reaction, however, was generated by work of the National Council of Teachers of English and especially *Webster's Third*, which evoked a usage furor that highlighted the difference in values between professional linguists and language traditionalists.

• Chapter 12 ("Canadian English," by Laurel J. Brinton and Margery Fee) surveys the English language in Canada and its study. Except for Newfoundland, which had a different history, English settlement of Canada was a consequence of the American Revolution. At the end of that war, many Loyalists, who opposed the separation of the colonies from the mother country, emigrated northward. Thus the roots of Canadian English are American, although the subsequent history of the variety was independent, responding to both stimuli from within Canada and influences from British and American English.

Distinctive Canadian features include phonological ones like the "Canadian raising" of [aʊ] and [aɪ] before voiceless consonants (a feature shared, however, with several eastern areas of the United States), grammatical features like "narrative *eh?*" used to mark boundaries in narrative discourse, and distinctive Canadian words such as *heritage language* 'a language spoken in Canada other than French or English.' Quebec English has a distinctive vocabulary, heavily influenced by French, including loanwords like *autoroute* 'highway' and calques like *conference* 'lecture.'

• Chapter 13 ("Newfoundland English," by William J. Kirwin) treats English in Newfoundland, which was quite different in origin from that of mainland Canada or the rest of the Atlantic Provinces. Newfoundland for much of its early history was a commercial fishery rather than a colony like the rest of Canada and America. The English language began separate development in Newfoundland considerably before it did in the rest of Canada, and the area did not enter the Canadian Confederation until 1949.

Newfoundland English has a strong strain of West Country English in its phonology and grammar. But Anglo-Irish influence is also strong in both those aspects. As with mainland Canadian and American English, independent distinctive features are most notable in the regional vocabulary.

• Chapter 14 ("American English Abroad," by Richard W. Bailey) observes that the response to American English from abroad – whether from Britain or other parts – has always been variable. The response of foreigners, especially from the motherland, to the English of America is regularly confused with their response to other aspects of American culture (a phrase sometimes regarded as a contradiction in terms). Indeed, it is not unusual for educated and otherwise linguistically sophisticated English men and women to assume that any new linguistic feature they encounter is American in origin, and therefore objectionable on two grounds.

From the earliest days, long before permanent English-speaking settlements were established, British writers commented extensively and often unfavorably on words borrowed from languages of the New World and later on the varieties of English used in it. Americans replied with boosterism for their own usage and scorn for that of England. So Noah Webster contrasted the pure language of the New England yeoman with the effete usage of foreign capitals and courts. There were, to be sure, exceptions on both sides: Britons who recognized the inevitability of change in the colonies and Americans who respected the linguistic standard of England. Yet on the whole, the attitudes of speakers on each side of the Atlantic to the speech of those on the other can be matched only by those of fans and supporters of present-day rival sports teams.

After the middle of the nineteenth century, British amused disdain for the language of the erstwhile colonies turned into a widespread alarm at "creeping Americanisms." In fact, British and American English are each strongly influenced by the other. The chief difference is that Britons tend to be conscious of influence from America, even imagining it where it does not exist, whereas Americans tend to be unaware of the corresponding influence from Britain, assuming all innovations to be homegrown, if they think about their origin at all.

Although it is difficult to measure the influence of any language variety on others, it seems clear that the influence of American English on other forms of English around the world, and particularly on the English of England, has been growing. The role of American English on the world stage has at the same time become more prominent. A continued alarm at the cultural and economic consequences of increasing American prominence has been sounded on such high levels as that of Charles, Prince of Wales, who declared American English to be "very corrupting." Yet the declaration by Robert Burchfield, editor emeritus of the *Oxford English Dictionary*, can hardly be refuted, that American is now "the dominant form of English."

ACKNOWLEDGMENTS

The contributors to this volume are grateful for the help and advice they have received from friends, colleagues, and students, as well as from their fellow contributors and the editors of and contributors to other volumes. We wish especially to thank the following.

Adele S. Algeo, Judith C. Avery, Julia Huttar Bailey, Barbara Beaton, Connie Eble, William Kretzschmar, Merja Kytö, Marcyliena Morgan, Lisa McNair, National Endowment for the Humanities, Patrick O'Flaherty, Allen Walker Read, John Rickford, Lil Rodman, Deaver Traywick, Bernard van't Hul, Luanne von Schneidemesser, Patricia Wells, and Donald Winford.

In addition, we are grateful for assistance from the General Editor, Richard M. Hogg, and a number of staff members of the Cambridge University Press, present and past: Penny Carter, Judith Ayling, and especially Kate Brett for her continued help.

EXPLANATORY NOTES

A work by multiple authors that has been long underway is bound to be in some respects uneven in its report of scholarship. Some chapters of this volume were completed several years before others and could not be completely revised. But the historical facts of American English, although they increase, do not change their nature with the passage of time, even if scholarly interpretation of them fluctuates. The volume as a whole presents scholarship on the history of American English at the turn of the century.

References in all chapters are to a single combined bibliography at the end of the volume.

Abbreviations for titles of publications are entered and explained in the bibliography at the end of the volume. Other abbreviations are entered and explained in the glossary of linguistic terms preceding the bibliography.

Spellings, punctuation, and style generally follow common American usage, for example, as in *Merriam-Webster's Collegiate Dictionary*, 10th ed. The spellings of English loanwords from Hawaiian in chapter 4 consequently do not follow the orthography adopted for the spelling of modern standard Hawaiian by 'Ahahui 'Ōlelo Hawai'i in 1978, which indicates the glottal stop and vowel length with diacritics.

In accordance with usual practice, citation forms are italicized and their glosses put in single quotation marks (*interstate* 'highway'), and morphemes are put in curly brackets (third person singular {-Z}, the ending spelled *-s* or *-es* and pronounced /s/, /z/, or /əz/). An asterisk preceding a form indicates that the form does not occur or is ungrammatical in a particular variety (**I sick*). Conventions for writing sounds are explained on the next three pages.

PRONUNCIATION SYMBOLS

Various styles of the phonetic alphabet are used to write the sounds of American English. The symbols below are ones used in chapters of this volume to represent sounds, either phones (indicated by writing the symbol between square brackets: [u]) or phonemes (indicated by writing the symbols between slashes: /u/). Other styles for writing these sounds are also common. Symbols grouped together in the list below are primarily differences in writing styles rather than representations of differences in pronunciation. Sequences of symbols not listed here are combinations of their parts.

[ɑ]   cot, father, for most Americans; a low, central to back, unrounded vowel

[æ]   cat; a lower mid, front, unrounded vowel

[æy]   bad, hand, in parts of the South; a diphthong with a palatal off-glide

[ɑ:]   father, car, path, in New York City, parts of the South, and RP; a low, back, unrounded vowel

[a]   father, car, path, in eastern New England; a low, front, unrounded vowel

[aɪ], [ai], [ay]   cry

[ɐ]   a lower mid, central, unrounded vowel

[ɐɪ], [ʌɪ]   before voiceless consonants, as in *bite*, for some Americans

[aʊ], [aw]   now

[ɐʊ], [ʌʊ]   before voiceless consonants, as in *bout*, for some Americans

[b]   bay; a voiced bilabial stop

[β]   a voiced bilabial fricative

[č], [tʃ]   chin; a voiceless palatal affricate

[d]   day; a voiced alveolar stop

[e], [eɪ]   day; a higher mid, front, unrounded vowel, typically with a palatal off-glide

[ɛ]   bet; a lower mid, front, unrounded vowel

[ə]   above, sofa; a mid, central, unrounded vowel occurring in unstressed syllables

Pronunciation symbols

['ə], [ʌ]   cut; a mid to lower mid, central to back, unrounded vowel

[ɜ]   bird, in parts of the South; a lower mid, central, unrounded vowel

[ɜɨ]   bird, in New Orleans

[f]   fee; a voiceless labiodental fricative

[g]   go; a voiced velar stop

[h]   hot; a voiceless glottal fricative

[i], [iː]   beet; a high, front, unrounded vowel, typically with a palatal off-glide

[ɪ]   bit; a less high and front, unrounded vowel

[ɨ]   a high, central, unrounded vowel

[ǰ], [dʒ]   joy; a voiced palatal affricate

[k]   kit; a voiceless velar stop

[l]   like; an alveolar lateral

[l̡]   a palatal or "clear" [l], produced with the blade of the tongue raised toward the palate

[m]   may; a bilabial nasal consonant

[n]   no; an alveolar nasal consonant

[ŋ]   sing; a velar nasal consonant

[o], [ou], [ow]   no; a higher mid, back, rounded vowel, typically with a velar off-glide

[ɒ]   caught, for some Americans; a low, back, rounded vowel

[ɔ]   caught, for some Americans; a lower mid, back, rounded vowel

[ɒɪ], [ɔy], [oi], [oy]   toy

[p]   pay; a voiceless bilabial stop

[r], [ɹ]   red, borrow, far; a retroflex semivowel or one produced with the blade of the tongue bunched in the center of the mouth

[ʈ]   a retroflex flapped r-like consonant

[ɚ]   a central r-colored vowel or vocalic glide, as in *beer* [biɚ]

[s]   so; a voiceless alveolar sibilant fricative

[š], [ʃ]   shy; a voiceless palatal sibilant fricative

[t]   toe; a voiceless alveolar stop

[ɾ]   latter and ladder; a flap consonant

[θ]   thin; a voiceless interdental fricative

[ð]   then; a voiced interdental fricative

[u]   rule; a high, back, rounded vowel

[ʊ]   pull; a less high and back, rounded vowel

[ʉ]   a high, central, rounded vowel

[ɵ]   a less high, central, rounded vowel

[ɯ]   a velar vocalic glide, a high-back unrounded vowel

[v]   vie; a voiced labiodental fricative

[w]   wail; a velar semivowel

[hw], [ʍ]   whale, for those who distinguish it from *wail*; a voiceless [w]

[x]   as in Scottish lo**ch**; a voiceless velar fricative

[y], [j]   you; a palatal semivowel

[ʸ]   a palatal glide

[yu], [jʉ], [ju] [iu], [ɾu]   mute

[z]   zoo; a voiced alveolar sibilant fricative

[ž], [ʒ]   vision; a voiced palatal sibilant fricative

[ᵉ], [ᵊ] and other superscript vowels indicate a vocalic glide in a diphthong

[˜] indicates nasalization of the vowel under it

[:] indicates that the preceding sound is long

['] indicates the onset of primary stress, as in 'sofa, a'bove

[ˌ] indicates the onset of secondary stress, as in 'tele,phone, ,tele'phonic

[ˇ ˆ] indicate lowering and raising, respectively, of a preceding vowel

[˃ ˔] indicate backing and fronting, respectively, of a preceding sound

I   EXTERNAL HISTORY

John Algeo

1.1   History, external and internal

The history of a language is intimately related to the history of the community of its speakers, so neither can be studied without considering the other.

The external history of a language is the history of its speakers as their history affects the language they use. It includes such factors as the topography of the land where they live, their migrations, their wars, their conquests of and by others, their government, their arts and sciences, their economics and technology, their religions and philosophies, their trade and commerce, their marriage customs and family patterns, their architecture, their sports and recreations, and indeed every aspect of their lives. Language is so basic to human activity that there is nothing human beings do that does not influence and, in turn, is not influenced by the language they speak. Indeed, if Benjamin Lee Whorf (1956) was right, our very thought patterns and view of the world are inescapably connected with our language.

It is, of course, possible to view the history of a language merely as internal history – a series of changes in the inventory of linguistic units (vocabulary) and the system by which they are related (grammar), quite apart from any experiences undergone by the users of the language. We can describe how the vocabulary is affected by loanwords or how new words are derived from the language's own lexical resources. We can formulate sound laws and shifts, describe changes that convert an inflected language to an isolating one, or a syntax that puts an object before its verb to one that puts the verb before its object. That is, we can describe a language purely as a formal object. But such a view will be abstract, bloodless, and often lacking in explanation for the linguistic changes.

Because language is a human capacity, the history of a particular language is linked with that of its speakers. As a part of a total culture, a language

1

cannot be completely separated from the culture of which it is a part. To extend Meillet's dictum cited by Salikoko Mufwene (at the end of § 8.3), a culture is a system in which everything hangs together. Therefore to understand the whole culture, we must understand the language; and vice versa, to understand the language, we must understand the culture. The effort to trace the history of a linguistic system and its units (lexical, phonological, morphological, and syntactic history) is the diachronic aspect of microlinguistics. The effort to trace the history of the speakers of that language is the diachronic aspect of macrolinguistics.

This chapter does not offer a history of America, but rather a brief account of political and social events that can reasonably be seen as having had a significant influence on the English language. Some events of great moment in other ways are therefore treated lightly or not at all, and other events of small import in themselves, but with consequences for the language, are treated at greater length. The difference between the two kinds of events is, to be sure, a matter of judgment.

With respect to the events it reports, the aim of this chapter is that of Max Lerner (1987, xvi) in his cultural history of America – not to present either "a rosy and euphoric picture seen in a haze of promise or an unsparing indictment" but rather "to avoid both these sins . . . the sin of complacency and the sin of self-hatred."

The external history of American English has involved a number of factors with profound effects on the language: population mobility, innovation, discontinuity with the past, decentralization, democracy, a large land area, and a large and ethnically diverse population.

First among those factors is mobility. The colonists were by definition a moving population, but as settlers they did not simply settle in. Rather they continued moving. Americans have consequently always been a peripatetic population. The history of America has been described as one of an expanding frontier, from the first settlements along the Atlantic coast to "a small step" for a man onto the surface of the Moon.

The second factor follows from the first: mobility requires adaptability and innovation. Change of location requires change of lifestyle. The first colonists could not live in the New World just as they had in the Old. They had to adapt. Later immigrants likewise had to adjust to the new conditions they found. Change and adaptation became hallmarks of American life. Innovation became the norm of American life – in social structures, technology, and attitudes.

Innovation led to a third factor: a sense of discontinuity with the past and of perpetual youth. We can never be actually separated from our past, but a perception of separation affects our view of ourselves. American life and language are, to be sure, unmistakable continuations of the life and language of England. And, indeed, in certain respects, Americans have been more conservative than Britons. But in other respects they are less bound to former ways. The emphasis of the "New" World has been on its newness and its break with the Old World. Immigrant populations typically retain a sentimental attachment to the "old country," but assimilate into the new pattern of life, while inevitably changing that pattern by their assimilation. The result is a perpetual sense of newness. In Oscar Wilde's bon mot, "The youth of America is their oldest tradition. It has been going on now for three [today four] hundred years."

Another consequence of mobility has been decentralization. The very structure of American government is one of a federal union of states, which retain certain prerogatives and rights. On many matters, there is no single American law, but fifty different laws. So also, though Washington, DC, is the governmental capital of the nation and New York City is a commercial capital, there is no cultural capital in the nation. No location in the United States corresponds to London as the center of the United Kingdom.

A related factor is that of democracy or, perhaps more accurately, "social mobility." The latter term's first recorded use in the *OED* is from 1925, by Pitirim A. Sorokin, founder of the Department of Sociology at Harvard: "We used to think that in the United States . . . social mobility was greatest." Equality of life in America can be and has been exaggerated. Class differences certainly exist, based on wealth, fame, education, profession, connections, and other such factors, although they may be less clearly defined and more permeable than in some other places. But there is no inherited American aristocracy to rule or serve as a model. It is part of the American myth that the only aristocracy in the land is one of merit. Myths may be untrue, yet they are powerfully influential.

In physical size, the United States is nearly as large as the entire European continent, with even greater variability in climate and topography. The sheer size of the country presents English speakers with a wide environment to respond to and with extensive resources to draw on. The major stages of territorial expansion of the United States after the post-Revolutionary settlement with Britain at the Treaty of Paris (1783) were the Louisiana Purchase from France (1803), the Florida cession by treaty with Spain (1819), the admission of the Republic of Texas (1845), the Oregon acquisition by treaty with Great Britain (1846), the Southwestern cession by conquest from Mexico (1848), the Gadsden Purchase of territory in southern

Arizona and New Mexico from Mexico (1853), the Alaska Purchase from Russia (1867), and the annexation of the Republic of Hawaii (1898).

In population, the United States is nearly five times as large as the United Kingdom, having grown from a little under 4 million in the first census of 1790 to just under 250 million in 1990. The more people who use a language, the more opportunity there is for the language to change in diverse ways.

Moreover, the mixture of ethnic groups, which began in Colonial times and has never ceased, constantly brings diverse foreign influences to bear on American English. America has always been a land of diverse immigrants. The Amerindians were early immigrants from Asia, and the process of migrating and mixing has never ceased. English has always been, and continues in Britain today to be, heavily influenced by other languages. But the diversity of such influence and the common level on which it operates are probably greater in America than in any other native-English-speaking land.

1.2   Periods in the history of American English

The history of American English can be conventionally but usefully divided into three periods whose beginnings are marked by critical events in the history of Americans (Algeo 1991). Those periods are –

• The Colonial period, initiated by the establishment of the first permanent English-speaking colony at Jamestown, Virginia, in 1607. Though English speakers had established contact with the New World, both directly or indirectly, before this time, the Jamestown colony began the creation of a new variety of the language. Three factors brought this new variety into existence: the exposure of English speakers to new experiences on the American continent that required new ways of talking about them, the begetting of a native population to whom those experiences and the new ways of talking were normal, and the obstacle that distance made for communication with their fellow English speakers in the motherland. The result is what might metaphorically be called the gestation period of American English.

• The National period, beginning with the American Declaration of Independence from England in 1776. Political independence brought with it inevitably – and in the case of the new United States, swiftly – a quest for cultural independence that included linguistic self-awareness. Many American colonists had from the beginning displayed independence and self-assertion. Indeed, their desire for independence – economic, governmental, and ecclesiastical – was a factor in the foundation of several of the colonies, though economic ambition on the part of the sponsors of various colonies also played a prominent role. After the American

Revolution, the heady feeling of freedom from King and Parliament led to an assertion of other sorts of independence. During this period, English-speaking Americans spread over the continent from the Atlantic to the Pacific, in the process absorbing and being influenced by the cultures of other settlers. To continue the metaphor, this period might be called the childhood and adolescence of American English.

• The International period, beginning with the Spanish-American War of 1898. Though the Spanish-American War was hardly more than a skirmish – a "splendid little war," as it was called at the time – it was the turning point between some historical needs and the means of satisfying those needs. The needs were for new frontiers, new markets, and a new sense of purpose.

America had begun as a frontier land; when the first settlers arrived, the entire eastern seaboard was frontier. As the settlers spread inland, the frontier continually receded to the west. By the end of the nineteenth century, the continent had been spanned and the expansion-minded and expanding population looked for new frontiers to absorb its surplus restlessness. In addition, after the Civil War, the successfully cohesive nation underwent an explosion of economic power. America had always been a supplier to other countries, but now it needed new markets to serve and be supported by.

Perhaps most important, America's sense of national purpose, defined very early in its history and adhered to faithfully, was one of "manifest destiny." Although that catchphrase is now often regarded with irony as chauvinistic hubris, a sense of social and collective calling has been basic to the national consciousness. It underlay the foundation of the earliest New England colonies, whose members listened to the words of the Sermon on the Mount (Matt. 5.14): "Ye are the light of the world. A city that is set on an hill cannot be hid." Today, we may regard the Puritans' belief that they were that "city set on a hill" as self-righteous arrogance, but it was a motivating force for them. The Founding Fathers also went about their task of creating a new nation with a sense of historical inevitability and purpose. The nineteenth-century belief that it was America's "manifest destiny" to expand over the continent from east to west was only one expression of a much wider sense of national purpose. But when that expansion had been accomplished, the nation felt called upon to look for its destiny elsewhere.

The immediate results of the Spanish-American War included the independence of Cuba, the acquisition of the territory of Puerto Rico by the United States, and the forced sale of the Philippines by Spain. But the long-range result was the movement of America into international politics. The Spanish-American War was followed by the nation's late entry into World War I, critical entry into World War II, and decisive role in bringing about the fall of the Iron Curtain, thus ending the division of the world into two evenly balanced power camps.

The spread of the English language and its culture over the world is a major event in human history. That spread was effected chiefly by two impulses: the creation of the British Empire, which was at its height in the nineteenth century, and the spread of American technological and economic hegemony, which reached an apogee at the turn of the twentieth into the twenty-first century. The worldwide dissemination of English, most recently in its American variety, affects other languages around the globe, but it also affects English, which is changed by its contacts with other languages, just as it changes them. So one sequel to that "splendid little war," lasting only a few months, was the influence that American English has come to exert on other languages and the reciprocal influence they exert on English through its American variety. The otherwise minor Spanish-American War marked the maturity of American English and its entrance onto the world stage.

The future is always uncertain. It is practically certain that other English-speaking countries will come to play an increasing role in the world history of English, and it is probable that some of them will in time become principal players on that field, joining or perhaps displacing Britain and America. It is also possible that the English language will one day be replaced as the dominant means of communication for science, technology, commerce, and world culture generally. But that day gives no sign of dawning soon. During the foreseeable future, world culture (as distinct from local, national, and ethnic cultures) is being expressed through the English language, and increasingly through its American variety.

How the big consequence of the present-day role of American English on the world stage developed from the small beginnings of colonial settlement and how English was changed in America during the process is the subject of this book. The focus of this chapter is on the experiences of Americans during the four hundred years of their history as those experiences impacted the language they speak.

1.3   The Colonial period

The English language began to be influenced by the New World long before any English speakers settled there. That influence came partly from the exploration of North America by English adventurers, and partly indirectly from contacts between English speakers and other Europeans with experience in the New World. But such influences were on English generally; they did not create a new variety of the language. For the latter to come into being, it was necessary that communities of English speakers should settle in America and be cut off from easy and frequent contact with their fellows in the motherland.

The process of diversification between British and American English began with the settlement of Jamestown by about a hundred colonists in 1607. That colony was also the site in British America of the first cultivation of tobacco, the first representative governmental body (which evolved out of the 1619 House of Burgesses), the first African slave population, and the first Anglican Church. It was, however, never a thriving colony, partly because it was built on unhealthful marshland and partly because the first settlers were not self-sufficient. They were "gallants" faced with an inhospitable landscape and none of the amenities of civilization they had known (Kraus 40).

The first permanent New England colony was Plymouth, settled in 1620 by Pilgrims. They, unlike the Puritans, had left the Anglican Church and sought to establish their own separatist theocracy in America after having spent a dozen years in Leiden, Holland. The Pilgrims were a closely organized minority in the colony, who controlled it during its early decades. Plymouth Colony was not chartered, but became part of the Massachusetts Bay Colony in 1691.

The major English colonization of America started about 1630. David Hackett Fischer (1989) has proposed a history of settlement of the American colonies in four major waves, involving different places of origin, classes and customs, places of settlement, and times. His argument is that the total life of the colonists falls into four cultural patterns, embracing dialect, housing styles, attitudes toward life, religion, superstitions, food, dress, education, entertainment, government, naming, childcare, family customs, values, and indeed folkways and mores generally. He further postulates that these four patterns of culture continued after the Colonial period, assimilating new immigrants from non-English countries, and that they still exist in contemporary forms marking basic differences in the national life. Fischer's is the most ambitious theory of American cultural history ever put forward.

There were, to be sure, other movements of settlers and other cultural complexes than Fischer's four primary ones, but the latter were these:

(1) Puritans from eastern England to Massachusetts Bay, 1629–41.
(2) Gentry and their servants from southern England to Virginia, 1642–75.
(3) Quakers from the North Midlands and Wales to the Delaware Valley, 1675–1725.

(4)   Common people from northern England, northern Ireland, and Scotland to the Appalachians, 1717–75.

Fischer's overview of the settlement and subsequent history of America is subject to the flaws of all grand generalizations and can be criticized in various of its details and as an oversimplification. Nevertheless, it provides a useful schema for tracing and relating together the external and internal history of America.

1.3.1   Puritans in New England and the northern colonies

The first great wave of settlement was the Puritan migration, which took place during a decade (the 1630s) of great social uncertainty in England. King Charles I was attempting to rule without Parliament, and Archbishop William Laud was trying to purge the Anglican Church of its Puritan faction and to require high-church practices like genuflection and chanting, anathema to the Puritans. In addition, the cloth industry, in which nearly a fourth of the early New England colonists had worked, was depressed. During the decade, more than 20,000 Puritans emigrated to Massachusetts, leaving some English towns half depopulated. At the end of the decade, the migrations suddenly stopped and even reversed, with Puritans returning to England. In the 1640s the Civil War broke out which was to result in the establishment of the Commonwealth and the temporary dominance of Puritan interests in England.

The primary motive for the Puritan emigration was religious and political, although the settlers included some economic refugees as well. The Puritan leaders came to Massachusetts to found a new Zion on the new continent. They were largely educated and middle class, with a notable absence of lower-class members, and they came not singly but by families. Although they came from all over England, East Anglia was their principal place of origin. The typical Puritan leader was well-educated, a graduate of Cambridge, with a strong religious and social commitment. The typical Puritan follower was a craftsman – literate, urban, disciplined, and pious. The Massachusetts colony was remarkably homogeneous, especially in its leadership.

The institutions and attitudes of the New England colonies were very influential: "Their heavy reliance on the Bible, and their preoccupation with platforms, programs of action, and schemes of confederation – rather than with religious dogma – fixed the temper of their society, and foreshadowed American political life for centuries to come" (Boorstin 1958, 19). The

Puritan insistence on written laws and agreements, rather than on an oral common law, foreshadowed the American Constitution as a secular bible.

The colonists brought with them the speechways of their native counties. The "Norfolk whine," associated with a high-pitched nasality, was the forerunner of the "Yankee twang" of eastern New England (Fischer 57–62). From Massachusetts, the New England colonists ultimately migrated southward to New Jersey, eastward to Maine and Nova Scotia, northward to Canada, and westward to upper New York and on to the Pacific coast. In doing so, they took with them their customs and dialect, which became the basis of the Northern dialect of American English.

New Hampshire's first settlement was established in 1623, although the region was not named after the English county until 1629. Between 1641 and 1679, the region was under the government of Massachusetts. In 1679, it was made into a royal province.

Rhode Island was settled by dissidents from the Massachusetts Bay Colony – by Roger Williams and his congregation in 1636, by William Coddington and Anne Hutchinson in 1638, and by others later. A confederacy of the settlements was established in 1647, and a royal charter issued in 1663 became the foundation of the colony's government well into the nineteenth century.

Connecticut was also first settled from the Massachusetts Bay Colony between 1633 and 1638. Settlements in that region were united under a single government in 1665.

1.3.2 Catholics in Maryland

In one of the minor emigrations, the English settled Maryland in 1634 under the leadership of Leonard Calvert, younger brother of Cecil Calvert, Lord Baltimore. The colony was intended as a haven for Roman Catholics, but because of a lack of Catholic colonists, Protestants were in the majority from the beginning. The economic base of the colony was tobacco farming, using indentured servants from England and, after the late 1630s, African slaves. Religious tolerance was established by law, but applied only to those professing a belief in the divinity of Jesus, and denial of the Trinity was a capital crime. The city of Baltimore was founded in 1729.

1.3.3 Cavaliers and others in the South

The second great wave of English settlement, to Virginia, took place during the Civil War and the resulting Commonwealth and Protectorate

(1642–60), when Royalists were not in favor in England. The nickname of the state, "Old Dominion," may allude to the loyalty of its colonists to the exiled Charles II. The dominance of the Puritan oligarchy in England during the Commonwealth and Protectorate sent large numbers of cavaliers to Europe and Virginia. Virginia's elite, many of whom were younger sons of English gentry, were Royalist in politics and Anglican in religion. Two-thirds of them were from the south or west of England; and a third had lived for some time in London.

Whereas the New England settlers were primarily middle class, Virginia settlers were mainly lower and upper class, or at least would-be upper class: "In England in the later 17th century the ambition of a prosperous tradesman was to become a country gentleman" (Boorstin 1958, 99), and Virginia offered that possibility. The ruling elite, of whatever origin in the motherland, were only a small fraction; 75 percent of all immigrants were indentured servants. Most of the Virginia colonists were rural rather than urban, farmers or unskilled laborers rather than craftsmen, and illiterate. Three quarters of them were males between the ages of fifteen and twenty-four. They came from the same southern and western counties as the elite.

Features of Virginia speech have been traced to the dialects of southern and western England (Fischer 256–64). Citing such scholars as Bennett Wood Green (1899) and Cleanth Brooks (1985), as well as Hans Kurath (1972, 66) and Raven McDavid (1967), Fischer (259) concludes:

> Virtually all peculiarities of grammar, syntax, vocabulary and pronunciation which have been noted as typical of Virginia were recorded in the English counties of Sussex, Surrey, Hampshire, Dorset, Wiltshire, Somerset, Oxford, Gloucester, Warwick or Worcester.

The upper classes of Virginia, and later South Carolina, maintained a closer and more sympathetic connection with the establishment in the motherland than did those of any of the other colonies (Fisher in §§ 2.8.3, 2.9). The speechway that developed in these colonies blended upper-class and lower-class British usage with later influences from the African slave population. It became the basis of the Southern dialect of American English.

Following earlier efforts by the Spanish and the French to settle the Carolina coast, in the 1650s Virginia settlers began moving into the territory that had been called Carolina as early as 1629. In the 1660s a royal grant established the colony of Carolina and settlers from England arrived in 1670. The colony was governed from Charleston, founded in 1680. North Carolina was set apart and governed by a deputy from Charleston, and eventually North Carolina and South Carolina were established as separate colonies. In 1731, Georgia was created from the southern part of the area.

Georgia was the last of the original thirteen colonies to be established. The first English settlement was in Savannah in 1733. James Oglethorpe, a philanthropist, obtained a charter for the colony to provide a refuge and new opportunity for the economically depressed of England. The colony was to be a buffer between the other English colonies to the north and the Spanish to the south. It was also to produce silk and other commodities for England through a system of small villages inhabited by yeoman farmers. Slavery was outlawed to avoid large plantations. The utopian scheme failed, partly because the land was unsuited for the type of agriculture envisioned, and in 1752 the proprietors turned the colony back to royal control.

1.3.4   Quakers and others in the Middle states

Of all the American colonies, those on the middle of the Atlantic coast were, from the time of their first settlement, the most mixed in origin. Because of that very fact, they developed into the typical American culture of later times.

The third great wave of migration began as the second was tapering off after the Restoration of King Charles II. The third wave consisted mainly of Quakers and Quaker sympathizers and was so substantial that by the middle of the eighteenth century the Society of Friends was the third largest religious group in the colonies. From that high point, the relative strength of the Quakers precipitously declined, but in Colonial days, they were a major force in America. The Quakers settled in the Delaware Valley, chiefly in Pennsylvania, but also in nearby West Jersey, northern Delaware, and northern Maryland. Non-Quakers also settled in the region and by the middle of the eighteenth century came to outnumber the Quakers.

The motive for Quaker migration was similar to that of the Puritans – to escape persecution at home and to find a place where they could put their religious principles into practice. But the Quaker principles were in contrast with the Puritan. Quakers relied on the "inner light" and eschewed professional clergy, as well as sacraments and ceremonies. They were, at least during a critical phase of colonization, socially active and engaged, and dedicated to religious freedom and social pluralism. Their ideals embraced the work ethic, education, and simplicity of life.

Although Quaker immigration to the Delaware Valley had begun earlier, the founder of the Pennsylvania colony was the Quaker William Penn, who in 1681 received a grant of land to the west of the Delaware River from

Charles II in compensation for a debt the king had owed to Penn's father. Penn aspired to found there a commonwealth inspired by the Quaker ideals of life, referring to it as "a holy experiment." In 1682 Penn wrote a governing plan for the colony, guaranteeing personal rights and freedom of worship, and including a formal provision for amendments to the plan, presaging the amendment provision of the American Constitution. In 1696, the foresighted Penn even drafted a plan for uniting the American colonies, a concept that had to wait nearly a century for its realization.

In ethnic origin the Quaker colonists were mainly English, Welsh, Scotch-Irish, and German. They were generally of the lower middle class, being husbandmen, artisans, manual workers, and shopkeepers. Although they came from all over England, the main source of English Quaker immigrants was the North Midlands, especially Cheshire, Derbyshire, Lancashire, Nottinghamshire, and Yorkshire.

Because the Delaware Valley settlement was more mixed in origin than Massachusetts Bay or Virginia, its dialect may be presumed also to have been more mixed. It became, however, the ancestor of the contemporary North Midland dialect of American English, which is arguably the most typically "American" of all contemporary regional dialects (Fischer 470–5).

The area of New Jersey had come under English control in 1664, although the Dutch continued to claim it for some years afterwards. In 1676 the area was divided into two colonies, East Jersey and West Jersey (a Quaker settlement); in 1702 the two colonies were reunited. New Jersey and New York shared the same governor until 1738.

New York was first colonized as New Netherland by the Dutch. In 1624 they settled Fort Orange (later Albany) and in 1625 established New Amsterdam (later New York City). The Dutch governor, Peter Stuyvesant, surrendered to an English invasion of New Amsterdam in 1664, and by 1669 the whole colony had become English and was renamed for the Duke of York, the future King James II. Dutch influence was prominent, however, in both Albany and New York City, and was memorably described by Washington Irving in his satirical *History of New York*.

Although the Dutch colonization was modest, it had significant effects on American life, many prominent families, including the Roosevelts, being descended from Dutch colonists. Its linguistic influence is also apparent from terms like *boss, coleslaw, cookie, Santa Claus,* and *Yankee*. Upstate New York was settled heavily by colonists from Massachusetts and Connecticut, and Germans established several settlements there as well.

Delaware was settled by Swedes in 1638 as the colony of New Sweden. The colony was captured by the New Amsterdam Dutch in 1655, and by the English in 1664. It was governed as a part of New York until 1682, when it was transferred to William Penn, who wanted to unite it with Pennsylvania. In 1704, however, Delaware acquired its own legislative assembly, although it shared a governor with Pennsylvania. The colony was called *Delaware* after the bay, which had been named for Sir Thomas West, Baron De La Warr.

1.3.5   The Scotch-Irish in Appalachia

By the end of the seventeenth century, the population of the American colonies was about 220,000: 95,000 in the southern colonies, 80,000 in New England, and 45,000 in the middle colonies (Kraus 92). But major immigration was still to come.

The settlers of the fourth great wave, unlike the others, were not united or motivated by religion or politics. What they had in common was that they were marginalized, geographically and economically. They came from the north of England, from Scotland, and from Northern Ireland and have traditionally been referred to in America as Scotch-Irish. Their immigration was a folk migration, rather than a movement inspired by a cause or directed by a leader.

This migration lasted longer than any of the others, stretching over much of the eighteenth century, and it involved more immigrants. They traveled in families, women were well represented, and so were all age groups except the elderly. Their social backgrounds were diverse, but only a few were of the higher classes, though also few would have been of the lowest orders simply because the poverty stricken could not afford travel. Few came as indentured servants, because there was little demand for the services of the Scotch-Irish.

The Scotch-Irish came to escape economic privation and in quest of a better material life, but the reality they came to was often one of prejudicial discrimination. They were, along with Amerindians and African blacks, an underclass in Colonial society. In turn, they were themselves xenophobic, clannish, conservative, and given to feuds. But they were also loyal to family and friends, respectful of individual rights, and believers in the necessity of "elbow room."

Some came into Boston and moved to the western frontier of New England. Many arrived in the port of Philadelphia but were immediately encouraged by the Quakers to move westward. They passed into the interior of Pennsylvania, and into the mountainous regions of Maryland, Virginia, and Carolina. From about 1760, the Scotch-Irish settled the inland parts of the Carolinas. They became frontiersmen, the inhabitants of Appalachia, and later expanded into Arkansas, Missouri, Texas, and on to the far southwest. Their speechways became the South Midland dialect (Fischer 652–5).

1.3.6   Late migration

During the fifteen years between 1760, when the French and Indian War ended in America (1.3.8), and 1775, when the American Revolution began, a great immigration to the colonies took place (Bailyn 1986b): 125,000 from the British Isles (55,000 Northern Irish, 40,000 Scots, 30,000 English), 12,000 from Germany and Switzerland, and 84,000 from Africa. The immigration from Britain was so great that Parliament considered a bill banning emigration to North America (Bailyn 1986b, 29–66). Whereas the Europeans came mainly into ports in the middle colonies, the bulk of them as part of the fourth great wave from Britain, the Africans came mainly as slaves to the southern colonies.

Not all of the British immigrants during this late period were Scotch-Irish. Of those entering the colonies on the eve of the Declaration of Independence, nearly a fourth were from metropolitan London and a sizable number from the Home Counties. They were predominantly young, male, unmarried, and indentured (Bailyn 1986a, 11–13). They were not necessarily London natives, however, for the capital city was a magnet attracting the mobile and ambitious from all over the island.

The chief motive for migration was economic – the quest for better living conditions by those who came voluntarily and the need for cheap labor by those who bought the services of bound workers. Bound workers were of four types. Indentured servants contracted themselves before immigrating to serve for a specified period of time. Redemptioners after arriving in America offered themselves as workers in return for the payment of their transportation. Convicts were freed from prison in return for their labor. Slaves were involuntary workers whose servitude had no terminal date. The treatment of indentured servants, redemptioners, and convicts from Britain was not significantly different from that of slaves from Africa. And all such bound workers often sought to escape the bonds of servitude by running away from their masters to make a new life for themselves (Bailyn 1986b, 324–52).

The intense immigration from abroad was accompanied by an extensive in-migration. The result was a mixture of populations that inevitably affected their speechways. The cultural continuity that doubtless linked various of the American colonies to counties and regions of Britain was balanced with a jumbling of regional cultures. The result was not a homogeneous blend, but a mixture ensuring that American local differences cannot be traced back to the motherland by any simple direct line. Individual features and, in some cases, even complexes of features have been so traced, but on the whole, the colonies were the breeding ground for a new variety of English language and culture.

1.3.7   Contacts with non-English populations

When European settlers arrived in the New World, they found it already inhabited by the native Amerindian populations. They were not a single people, but a large number of different tribes. It has been estimated that North America held as many as 2,000 different Amerindian languages and consequently cultures. The history and relationships of these languages are not well known and have been a matter of scholarly dispute. Many of the Amerindian languages became extinct as their speakers died out after European colonization of the continent, and today some of them are imperfectly known, attested only by sketchy word lists or descriptions.

The English settlers along the Atlantic coast were cheek by jowl with a variety of tribes, such as the Delaware, Massachusett, Mohegan, Nanticoke, Narraganset, Pamlico, Pennacook, Pequot, and Powhatan. From these groups they borrowed names for the landscape and terms for flora, fauna, and Amerindian cultural features. The influence of Amerindian languages on American English was exclusively lexical, although the influence of native tribes on American culture was not insignificant. The early settlers learned much about coping with their new environment from their Amerindian neighbors despite the violence and antagonism that typically characterized their relationships.

The non-Europeans who were to have the greatest influence on American English were, however, African slaves. The Southern colonies were the last of the slave economies to develop in the New World, Brazil and the Caribbean being earlier. The first Africans were brought to the American colonies in 1619 by Dutch slave traders, who sold twenty slaves in Jamestown. Between that event and the abolition of the slave trade by Congress in 1807, an estimated 400,000 Africans were brought to the English colonies. Many of them were brought directly from the Caribbean; that area and Brazil contained the largest number of African slaves in the hemisphere.

The height of the slave trade to America was the eighteenth century, when the development of plantation culture in the South created a demand for cheap labor. The typical American sense of the word *plantation* arose at that time: "an estate or farm . . . on which cotton, tobacco, sugar-cane, coffee, or other crops are cultivated, formerly chiefly by servile labor" (*OED*, in which the first citation for the sense is dated 1706).

Slaves were used to raise the cash crops on which the colonial economy rested: tobacco in Virginia and Maryland, rice in Carolina, and cotton in Georgia. The African population in America consisted of three broad groups. The first were field hands, generally newly imported slaves who grew the cash crops and the need for whose services created the "peculiar institution," so much at variance with the religious and later Enlightenment ideals that otherwise framed American society. The second were house servants, who often lived in intimate relations with their white owners. The third were craftsmen or skilled workers. The latter two groups were usually native born in the colonies.

The extent and exact nature of the African influence on early American English and culture are matters of scholarly dispute (see ch. 8), though its reality is generally accepted. This influence continued throughout later periods in the history of the national variety and remains a potent force in present-day America.

During the Colonial period, however, the most noted contacts were with other European powers. The English had competition in America: the French to the north in Canada and the Spanish to the south in Florida and to the far west in Mexico and later California. And other nations were also seeking to colonize the same general area as the English, as noted above. The Dutch moved into what is now New York, founding the colony of New Netherland in 1624. That colony lasted until 1664, when the English took control of it. Through this colony, Dutch had some influence on American English. There was moreover a short-lived Swedish colony in the area that became Delaware.

Settlers also came from other European countries, such as Germany, notably the Palatinate, without establishing a colonial base in America, but significantly influencing American language and customs. French Huguenots settled throughout the colonies, but especially in Carolina; a notable early descendant of Huguenot forebears was Paul Revere, whose family name had been remodeled from *Rivoire* (Kraus 104). Smaller contingents of Scandinavians and Jews came as well.

1.3.8   Colonial wars

A consequence of the mixture of European colonial powers in North America was that European conflicts had their echoes on the American continent. Four colonial wars had increasing effects on the American colonies. The names of these differ between Europe and America. In the colonies the first three were called by the names of English monarchs, the implication being that they were the doings of overseas kings and queens – of little concern to the American colonies.

The European War of the League of Augsburg (1689–97), known in the colonies as King William's War, had little effect in America, producing no territorial changes there.

The War of the Spanish Succession (1702–13), known in America as Queen Anne's War, was brought to an end by the Treaty of Utrecht, which gave Britain the French colonies of Newfoundland and Acadia (renamed Nova Scotia) and the territory around Hudson Bay.

The War of Jenkin's Ear with Spain merged into the War of the Austrian Succession with Prussia, France, and Spain (1740–48), called King George's War in America; it ended with the Treaty of Aix-la-Chapelle. In that war, New England troops took the French fort of Louisbourg, which controlled the approach to the St. Lawrence River. The fort was, however, returned to the French by the treaty, a severe disappointment to the colonists.

The French and Indian War (1754–63) was a different sort of conflict, being more important to the colonists and following a reverse geographical pattern from that of the three earlier wars. It began in America and spread to Europe as the Seven Years War (1756–63). France, in an attempt to control the land west of the Appalachians into which English colonists had begun to penetrate, built a line of forts including Fort Duquesne on the location of present-day Pittsburgh. The governor of Virginia sent George Washington, who was then a young surveyor, to negotiate. But the French rejected him. A second mission in which Washington was accompanied by a small force of 150 fared no better. The British then sent an army of Redcoats, accompanied by Washington and a small colonial troop to enforce their claims. But they were ambushed near Fort Duquesne and driven back. The war then spread to Europe. Under the direction of William Pitt, the Elder, the British were successful, and the treaty ending the war gave Britain the territory of Canada and all land east of the Mississippi River, including Florida.

As a result of the Seven Years War, Britain became the premier colonial power in Europe. In the colonies, however, the French and Indian War had mixed consequences for both the British and the Americans. Removal of the French threat to the west eliminated the colonists' need for defense by the motherland. Gratitude to the British, and especially Pitt, for whom Fort Duquesne was renamed, was coupled with elation at the prospect of an unimpeded opening to the west. However, there was also a dark side.

Subsequent British attempts to impose taxes raised a resentment that fed upon the disaffection which had arisen between Redcoats and the colonial forces during the war.

While admiring the Redcoats' professional skills, the colonists found their behavior in other respects to be objectionable, particularly their profanity and crudeness and the hauteur and severe discipline enforced by the British officers. On the other hand, the British regarded the American colonials as incompetent soldiers, undisciplined, insubordinate, cowardly, and unkempt. The scorn with which the British officers viewed colonial troops led them into a grave misjudgment during the later Revolutionary encounters, when they assumed that the ragamuffin colonial forces would break and run at the sight of Redcoats marching in close ranks with bayonets.

> Such opinions reflected the degree to which English and colonial
> values and traditions had diverged, and they suggest that separation of
> the two societies was not merely possible but probably inevitable.
>
> [Garraty 207]

1.3.9 *The development of English in Colonial America*

The Colonial period of American history was the foundational one for American English. It began with the isolation of groups of English speakers from their fellow countrymen in Britain. The ocean separating the colonies from the motherland was a grave impediment to frequent and free intercommunication. Transportation and communication across the Atlantic were by sailing vessel, relatively slow and costly. Consequently, although intercourse with Britain was maintained, it was not on a mass scale or of an intimate, everyday type. Consequently the language of the colonies and that of the mother country began to drift apart.

The drift between American and British usage was widened by the fact that in the new land the colonials had to cope with a new environment – new topography, new flora and fauna, new economic and social conditions. Their response to that challenge was inevitably reflected in their language, most apparently in the vocabulary. New words were borrowed and coined. Old words changed their meanings and uses under the pressure of the new environment.

In addition, on the North American continent the English colonists encountered speakers of other languages – French, Spanish, Dutch, German, Amerindian, African, and so on – under conditions that differed greatly from the contacts Britons had elsewhere with foreigners. Although English throughout its history has been heavily influenced by other languages, the foreign influences on it in America were unique and not shared directly by other English speakers.

As the first colonists settled in and begot families, their descendants accepted the New World – its environment, culture, and language – as their native inheritance and as the natural state of affairs. The colonists became native Americans, and that fact was a powerful psychological factor molding their attitudes toward their own language and the English of Britain. Though the British standard was still held up, on both sides of the Atlantic, as the defining variety of correct English and exerted a powerful influence on Colonial English, the base of the latter became American during the Colonial period.

The foregoing developments are the factors that produce dialect split. And during the Colonial period they created a split between English in America and English in Britain, which also was continuing to change and evolve in new directions – but not in the same directions as the English of the colonists. The American vocabulary had expanded significantly, drawing on both foreign and native resources. The fact that Englishmen expressed disapproval of American lexical innovations helped to consolidate a sense of Americanness among the colonies.

On the other hand, roads and stagecoaches, weekly newspapers and almanacs, and Benjamin Franklin's postal service, all increased the ease and frequency of communication among the colonies. As a result, the colonies grew closer together in culture, opinion, and language, just as they were collectively growing farther apart from and less dependent on the motherland.

The colonists had brought with them a diversity of British cultural patterns, from various regions and classes of the motherland. They were motivated by various visions. But from the first settlement of America, the colonists found that practical concerns of survival and adaptation outweighed whatever intellectual assumptions they may have brought with them. The result was a shared pragmatic attitude (Boorstin 1958, 149–58).

Differences there certainly were among the colonies and the classes of colonists. But the perception of difference depends on a standard of comparison. British visitors to the colonies in the eighteenth century remarked on the uniformity and propriety of American English (quoted by Boorstin 1958, 274–5):

> The Planters, and even the Native Negroes generally talk good English without Idiom or Tone.
>
> The propriety of Language here surprized me much, the English tongue being spoken by all ranks, in a degree of purity and perfection, surpassing any, but the polite part of London.

> In North America, there prevails not only, I believe, the purest
> Pronunciation of the English Tongue that is anywhere to be met with,
> but a perfect Uniformity.
>
> A striking similarity of speech universally prevails; and it is strictly
> true, that the pronunciation of the generality of the people has an
> accuracy and elegance, that cannot fail of gratifying the most judicious
> ear.

The impression of uniformity may be explained, at least partly, by a comparison with the diversity to be encountered in Britain. But it may also be partly a consequence of communication between the colonies and of a common response by the colonists to their environment.

1.4   The National period

1.4.1   *The American Revolution*

The French and Indian or Seven Years War created conditions that led on to the American Revolution by a series of escalating reactions. The Seven Years War had been very expensive for Britain. Government expenditures more than doubled during the war, and consequently taxes in Britain were at an all-time high. Those taxes fell heavily on the landed and ruling classes, who not unnaturally thought that the colonies should share the burden of a war that had started in America. Defense of the colonies was going to be an on-going and costly need because of the threat of the Indians and the Spanish, to whom France had ceded the Louisiana territory west of the Mississippi, as well as of a potential revived threat by the French. Moreover, the civil administration of the colonies was costly; for example an inefficient customs service cost three and a half times as much to maintain as it raised in revenue (Kraus 183).

Consequently the British government began a policy of finding ways to tax the colonists, who until that time had been taxed only slightly. In addition, Britain sought to exploit the fur and other trade with the Indians in the area between the Appalachians and the Mississippi, a trade that had been largely a French monopoly before the war. Consequently a royal proclamation of 1763 defined a line through the Appalachians that separated eastern and western areas. To the east of the line colonists were free to settle; to the west, British commissioners were to have exclusive rights to Indian trade and Indians were to be free of encroachment by colonial settlers. The limitations did not sit well with the colonists, who looked to the trans-Appalachian territory for future settlement and who objected to Britain's intervention.

Of a number of taxes levied by Parliament, the Stamp Act of 1765 evoked the strongest response. The Act put a tax on a variety of paperwork, such as bills of lading for shipping, legal documents, and newspaper advertisements. This tax affected most directly colonists like merchants, lawyers, journalists, and bankers, who were also the most powerful of the colonists. It was, in addition, the first entirely domestic tax put upon the colonists by Parliament. All earlier taxes had been import duties, which could be justified as regulating commerce between the mother country and its colonies. The Stamp Act had no rationale other than raising revenue for Parliament.

Because this kind of tax was normal in Britain, its government did not anticipate the violence of the American response. Riots broke out in Boston and elsewhere, complaints against taxation without representation were articulated, and representatives from nine states met in New York to write a statement of rights and grievances and to petition Parliament for the repeal of the Act. The Stamp Act was repealed, but at the same time Parliament affirmed its unconditional right to tax the colonies. It asserted that right by imposing tariffs on a large number of basic commodities that were imported, including tea.

The position of many colonials was that Parliament could pass laws governing the empire as a whole and the relationships between its various constituents, but had no right to control internal matters of the individual colonies. They also invoked their rights as Englishmen not to have taxes imposed on them by a Parliament in which they had no representation and thus no voice concerning the imposition of the taxes. The colonies therefore responded by adopting a policy against importing any commodities that were taxed. In 1770, the British government rescinded the tariffs, except that on tea, which it kept as a token of its right to tax. The colonials engaged in a policy of noncooperation with customs officials, with consequent frequent skirmishes, in one of which British troops killed five persons, an event known as the Boston Massacre.

In 1773, the British government gave the East India Company, which had fallen on hard times, the exclusive right to sell tea directly to the colonists, rather than through colonial merchants – thus cutting out middlemen and their profits. This would have made available good quality tea at reasonable cost to the consumer, to compete favorably with the untaxed inferior tea that was being smuggled in. But it would also have cut out the colonial merchant. Colonial commercial sentiments were outraged. When the tea shipments arrived in Charleston, they were impounded. When they arrived in New York and Philadelphia, they were returned to England. But when they arrived in Boston, they had a reception that became a national symbol.

A group of Bostonians, dressed as Indians, stormed the tea-bearing ships at anchor in Boston Harbor and threw tea worth £10,000 into the water. In reprisal, the British closed the Boston port, set aside the colony's charter, appointed a government with broad powers to replace the elected body that had been functioning for more than eighty years, forbade the traditional New England town meeting, and quartered troops in the houses of the citizenry. They also punitively joined the territories along the Mississippi River to Canada for administrative control, blocking the prospect of colonial advancement westward.

The colonial response to these "Intolerable Acts" was to convene the first general representative body, the Continental Congress, in Philadelphia in 1774. Thomas Jefferson prepared a statement asserting that colonies such as the American ones were separate entities, with the King as their head, but not under the legal control of Parliament. This first Continental Congress did not envision violence but aimed at using economic pressure to achieve its goals. By the time of the second Continental Congress in 1775, however, skirmishes had taken place at Lexington and Concord, which accordingly became emotionally charged symbols of colonial resistance to British tyranny. The Congress began to raise an army. The King declared a state of insurrection to exist and banned commerce with the colonies. An American army invaded Canada and captured Montreal but could not hold it.

Early in 1776, Thomas Paine's pamphlet *Common Sense* was published and was highly influential in turning sentiment in the colonies toward independence from Britain. Congress urged the colonies to form governments independent of Britain and appointed a committee to write the Declaration of Independence, which was drafted by Jefferson. That document based itself, not on the common-law rights of Englishmen, but on a theory of natural rights, affirming that any government exists only by the consent of those whom it governs.

The American Revolution or War of American Independence, as the British call it, began as a civil war, in which about a fifth of the colonists remained loyal to the British government. It expanded, however, to an international war when France, which had been supporting the colonies earlier, entered the war formally in 1778, Spain in 1779, and the Netherlands in 1780. The Revolution succeeded because the Americans had a high stake in winning, the British generals were ineffective, and other nations, particularly France, assisted.

In 1781, the British General Cornwallis surrendered his army of some 8,000 soldiers at Yorktown, Virginia, in the last major campaign of the war. An exodus of upwards of 80,000 colonial loyalists fled their homes for Britain, Canada, or the West Indies. Many more remained, some converting to the sentiments of the new nation, but others having a difficult time with resentful neighbors.

A preliminary treaty was signed at Paris in 1782 between Britain and America, and the following year all participants agreed upon a comprehensive series of treaties known collectively as the Peace of Paris. In those treaties, Britain recognized the independence of the colonies and ceded all territory between them and the Mississippi to the new nation. Britain kept Canada but gave Florida back to Spain.

The American Revolution began, as Emerson said, at Concord with "the shot heard round the world." It was the first in a series of uprisings that were to sweep the globe from the Bastille to Latin America, Greece, the Kremlin, China, and Vietnam, and it was to transform social and political structures. It established the first large-scale democratic government anywhere (Bushman 944).

But just as the British Empire was not only the greatest, but also the most enlightened and humane of colonial powers, so the American Revolution was the most conservative and least radical of revolts in its social consequences. And the linguistic consequences of the Revolution were also in many ways conservative. The colonies had begun lexical innovation early, but they were also old-fashioned and conservative in many aspects of grammar (such as the participle *gotten*) and pronunciation (such as rhotacism and "flat" *a* in words like *path*), as well as in some word choices (*fall* for the season).

1.4.2   The Constitution

The Revolution successful, the independent colonies had to figure out how they could become a nation. The process of doing so was to be a gradual one, for their history had been one of squabbling among themselves, and their traditions were diverse, in spite of their all being English. Until the formation of the Continental Congress, the colonies had not worked together and had little sense of national unity. They had no tradition of shared or common institutions. They had no means of financing collective governmental operations, no common systems of transportation or communication. On the other hand, newspapers in the various colonies had drawn on common sources, and so provided a relatively consistent view of events. And the American colonists had long experience in self-government. They knew very well how to form representative bodies and conduct business through them.

In 1787 a convention was held in Philadelphia to correct the flaws in the weak Articles of Confederation, which had been adopted in 1781 as a stopgap fundamental law for the independent colonies. The representatives from Virginia urged a radical replacement of those Articles to create a unified national government. The Constitution that was written in response established a three-fold government with separate powers: a presidential executive with veto power over actions of the legislature; a bicameral legislature, one house having representation proportional to population and the other equal representation for each state; and a federal judiciary to hear cases between states or involving federal law. Despite being a written Constitution, the document has evolved by both amendment and interpretation. Thus, although the Constitution does not explicitly give the federal judiciary the right of judicial review over the constitutionality of laws passed by the Congress or state legislatures, the Court early assumed that right, which has become institutionalized as a key element in the separation of powers.

The Constitution represented a striking new view of America as a unified nation, rather than a collection of separate states. Its opening seven words articulated the vision of a single people:

> *We the People of the United States*, in Order to form a more perfect Union, establish Justice, insure domestic Tranquility, provide for the common defense, promote the general Welfare, and secure the Blessings of Liberty to ourselves and our Posterity, do ordain and establish this Constitution for the United States of America.

The Constitution was ratified by the requisite number of states and took effect in 1789, when George Washington was unanimously chosen as the first president. The adoption of the Bill of Rights (the first ten amendments to the Constitution) in 1791 completed the fundamental law of the land by guaranteeing certain freedoms derived from English common law and from the concerns of Americans over what they had seen as abuses under British sovereignty.

1.4.3 Westward expansion

Thomas Jefferson, who became the third president in 1801, more than doubled the land area of the United States by the Louisiana Purchase from

France in 1803. Spain had ceded the territory west of the Mississippi back to France, and James Monroe, Jefferson's representative in France, arranged for its purchase from Napoleon without authorization or prior approval by Congress. Jefferson sent Meriwether Lewis and William Clark on an expedition lasting from 1804 to 1806 to explore the territory and discover what the purchase consisted of.

The United States remained neutral during Britain's wars with Napoleon (1803–14), but both combatants engaged in naval activities restricting trade between America and the other side. In addition, Britain impressed men into naval service, sometimes seizing Americans for that purpose. Old hostilities and resentments flared, and in 1812 Congress declared war on Great Britain. Hostilities lasted through 1814. The most positive outcome of the War of 1812 was the establishment of a boundary commission to settle disputes about the border between Canada and the United States, which subsequently became known as the longest unguarded border in the world.

The War of 1812, a conflict that many even at the time thought should have been avoided, was the last hostility between Britain and America. Thereafter, although the two nations have disagreed from time to time about specific policies, a "special relationship" has in fact existed, largely perhaps because of a coincidence of views and interests.

National expansion was furthered by the acquisition of Florida by President James Monroe in 1819 after the first Seminole War (1817–18), which responded to runaway African slaves seeking asylum with the Seminoles. Monroe went on to articulate what has been called the Monroe Doctrine, which reaffirmed George Washington's advice to steer clear of European affairs and accordingly warned European powers against interfering in the Americas. The Doctrine was a statement of general national views rather than a specific formulation of policy, but it was in keeping with the tenor of the times.

In the 1820s American settlers began moving into Texas under a grant from the Mexican government. In 1836 the Republic of Texas was established with the support of many Mexicans in Texas. After an earlier unsuccessful effort to be annexed, Texas was finally admitted as a state in 1846.

The annexation of Texas and a dispute over its border with Mexico led to the Mexican-American War (1846–48). The result was that the United States acquired half a million square miles of Mexican territory stretching all the way to California. The 1849 gold rush brought adventurers and settlers to the West Coast to exploit the gold strike made the year before at Sutter's Mill, near the Sacramento River.

The Gadsden Purchase of 1854 (named for James Gadsden, minister to Mexico, who negotiated it) acquired some 30,000 square miles of Mexican territory, in what is now southern Arizona and New Mexico, as a passage for a railroad line across the Southwest. The purchase price was $10,000,000.

Americans began moving into the Pacific Northwest in the 1830s, and in 1846 the Oregon country became American territory by treaty with the British.

After the murder of Joseph Smith near the Mormon settlement of Navoo, Illinois, Brigham Young led a mass migration of Mormons on the 1000-mile trek to Utah, where they settled in 1847. An early petition for statehood was denied, but Utah was admitted as a territory in 1850, and statehood was delayed until near the end of the century.

In 1867, Alaska was purchased as the result of a tender by Russia, in spite of widespread opposition in the United States. The purchase at a price of $7,200,000 was arranged by the Secretary of State, William Seward, and was consequently nicknamed "Seward's Folly."

The expression "manifest destiny" was coined in 1845 by the editor of the *United States Magazine and Democratic Review*, John L. O'Sullivan, as an expression of his belief that divine providence had called Americans to settle the continent from coast to coast. It became a catchphrase invoked in practically every westward territorial expansion thereafter.

1.4.4   Technological and social expansion in the early nineteenth century

The nation underwent a series of economic and technological revolutions in the decades following the War of 1812. In 1812 Robert Fulton and Robert Livingston began a steamboat service between New Orleans and Natchez, Mississippi; it was the beginning of a system that provided the dominant commercial transportation in the central part of the country until after the Civil War. The Erie Canal, a project of the New York governor DeWitt Clinton, was constructed between 1817 and 1825. It was the largest public works project in the United States until the construction of the Interstate Highway system after 1956. By connecting the Great Lakes with New York City through the Hudson River, the canal opened the upper Midwest to settlers by providing a cheap route for shipping raw material eastward and manufactured goods westward.

Railroads appeared in the 1820s and became a national network of 30,000 miles by 1860 and of 164,000 miles by 1890 (Stover 906–7). In 1859, George Pullman introduced the sleeping car. Roads were also constructed to satisfy the mobile population and hotels sprang up to accommodate them. Anthony Trollope in his travel book on America in the 1860s commented on the abundance of hotels (cited by Boorstin 1965, 141):

> Hotels in America are very much larger and more numerous than in other countries. They are to be found in all towns, and I may almost say in all villages . . . Whence are to come the sleepers? . . . The hotel itself will create a population, – as the railways do. With us railways always run to the towns; but in the States the towns run to the railways. It is the same thing with the hotels.

Telegraphy became a significant means of communication as lines were strung across the nation during the 1840s, following Samuel Morse's invention of the technique of the electric telegraph and the Morse Code in the 1830s. Other inventions included Goodyear's vulcanizing of rubber, the Colt revolver, and the McCormick reaper. In addition, the factory system was developed, and labor unions came into existence, beginning with the Federal Society of Journeymen Cordwainers in Philadelphia in 1794.

The population was increasing at the rate of a third every ten years. That increase was fueled during the 1830s and 1840s by a flood of immigrants, especially from Germany and Ireland. German immigrants settled especially on farms in the Ohio Valley, but the Irish were poor, unskilled, and Catholic, which made them unwelcome in much of the country. They tended therefore to concentrate in urban centers, where they were low-paid menial workers. During the thirty years between 1815 and 1845, a million Irish came to America (Kraus 392). By the middle of the century New York City had a population of half a million, of whom 45 percent were foreign born.

A myth sprang up about American life, abetted by the report of Alexis de Tocqueville, whose *Democracy in America* (1835–40) painted a portrait of the land and its society as idealistically egalitarian. American society was comparatively open, but by mid century there were more millionaires in America than in Europe. In the large cities of the Northeast, 1 percent of the population owned half the wealth. Still America lacked a hereditary nobility. And American manners tugged the forelock for no squire, so an aura of egalitarianism pervaded the land. The myth, or ideal, was also held by Americans themselves, who believed that self-reliance, in the Emersonian sense, or a more materialistic ideal of the self-made man was possible for everyone. The very expression "self-made man" was originally an Americanism, the first recorded use in the *OED* being from a Congressional Register of 1832: "In Kentucky, . . . every manufactory . . . is in the hands of enterprising self-made men."

Another aspect of the American myth was that Classical values and ideals were being reembodied in the New World. Greek Revival architecture swept over both Europe and the United States in the first half of the nineteenth century, but in America the revival was not limited to columned mansions, though there were enough of those, especially in the South. It extended to place names as well. Classical names like Athens, Rome, Sparta, and Troy were reused in Alabama, Georgia, New York, North Carolina, Ohio, South Carolina, and Texas from the late eighteenth through the nineteenth century. The revival also extended to behavior. George Washington consciously followed the model of the Roman general Lucius Quinctius Cincinnatus, who assumed command of the Roman forces at a crisis in the history of the republic but returned to his farm when the crisis was past. In 1783 officers of the Continental Army formed the Society of the Cincinnati, with Washington as its first president. Cincinnati, Ohio, was named for them in 1790.

Public education received increased attention in the nineteenth century. The *McGuffey Readers*, first published in 1836, became the most widely used elementary textbooks in the nation, selling two million copies a year. Called "the most influential volumes ever published in America" (Dulles 104), they propagated such legends as the story of young George Washington and the cherry tree. In 1839 Horace Mann, "the father of the American common school," founded the first state normal school for the education of teachers. Land-grant colleges were started all over the country as a result of the Morrill Act (1862). Johns Hopkins University, founded in Baltimore in 1876, introduced graduate education on the German model.

Established as a library for legislators in 1800, the Library of Congress grew during the nineteenth century to be the major cultural repository and the national library.

In the 1830s, the "penny press" made its appearance – four-page daily newspapers written for mass appeal, the forerunner of twentieth-century tabloids. They were balanced by such quality magazines as *Harper's* (1850) and the *Atlantic Monthly* (1857).

American politics of the period became more egalitarian as the right to vote was expanded. In the early part of the century, in many states it was necessary to own land and to be a taxpayer in order to be qualified to vote, and most states used their legislatures to choose electors who would vote for the president of the country. In the course of a few decades all that changed: the franchise was extended to adult white males generally (extension to blacks and women was to come considerably later), and the presidential vote became in fact a popular election.

The two decades leading up to mid century were called an "age of reform," not in politics alone, but in a variety of social movements. Groups were dedicated to the betterment of working conditions, public education, prison reform, the humane treatment of the insane and the handicapped, an end to capital punishment, pacifism, women's rights, and the temperance movement. The abolition movement to support the end of slavery became a political force.

Utopian communities were founded, such as the Transcendentalist-inspired Brook Farm, Massachusetts, the scientifically oriented New Harmony, Indiana, and the messianic and sexually unconventional Oneida, New York. More conventionally religious enterprises included Bible and tract societies, home missionary societies, and the Sunday School Union. Some reform was not collective and social, but individual and inward directed, of which that inspired by Ralph Waldo Emerson was the most notable. He drew on such sources as Neoplatonism, Swedenborg, and Hindu philosophy in developing his view of the potential of the human spirit to rise above material limitations.

1.4.5 Slavery and abolition

The most pressing concern during the first two-thirds of the nineteenth century and the least amenable to a generally acceptable solution was the problem of slavery. It was an ethical, economic, and political dilemma.

During the Colonial period and the first years of the new nation, slavery was not a major economic factor anywhere in North America. Slave holding was most common in the areas where a cash crop was the basis of the economy, but in the normal course of events, the early demise of slavery might have been expected because of the growing sentiment against it. As early as 1816, the American Colonization Society was formed to resettle freed slaves in Africa, and for the next thirty years it repatriated Africans to an area on the coast of West Africa that in 1847 became Liberia.

However, at the end of the eighteenth century, a technological advance was made that radically changed the role of slavery in America: Eli Whitney's invention of the cotton gin in 1793. The gin was a machine for separating the fibers of the cotton boll from the seeds, a task which, if done by hand, was slow and laborious. The gin greatly increased the production of cotton fiber and made commercially viable the use of short-fiber plants to produce cheaper and thus more salable cotton fabric.

Cotton culture became highly profitable as the main export commodity of the Southern states, and thereby increased the need for cheap field labor. "King Cotton" ruled the South (the catchphrase derived from *Cotton Is King*, an 1855 book by David Christy). As new territories in the South were settled – Alabama, Mississippi, Louisiana, and Texas – cotton culture was extended westward, and the demand for slave labor likewise increased. By the middle of the nineteenth century, two-fifths of the population of the South were African slaves, and two-thirds of them worked the cotton fields. The economy of the South had come to depend on slavery.

In the North, on the other hand, where slavery provided no significant economic benefit, most of the states had abolished it by the first decade of the century. The result was a sharp divergence between the cultures of the North and the South. Yet all was not well with Northern blacks. Although they were freemen, their condition was comparable to that of the new Irish immigrants, with whom they competed for unskilled jobs. As an underclass, they were discriminated against economically, educationally, politically, and socially, with no effective means for correcting the injustice. But at least they could not be bought and sold.

Most of the free states had less than 1 percent of blacks in their population (New Jersey was the highest at 4 percent). Of the Deep South states, none had less than 25 percent black population (South Carolina was the highest at nearly 60 percent). That difference created sharply different views of the issue. In the North it was almost solely an ethical question. In the South it was, in addition, an economic and social dilemma.

The issue of slavery became bitterly divisive. Several churches, including Methodists and Presbyterians, underwent schisms over it in the 1840s. From the 1830s on, the abolitionist movement became a crusade aimed at the immediate end of slavery and racial discrimination. It was based partly on religious conviction and partly on intellectual and social conscience, but included radical and violent activists like John Brown.

The diverging economic and cultural orientations of North and South affected politics. The North wanted new states coming into the Union to be free; the South wanted them to be slave-holding in order to maintain balance in the Senate and thus prevent or at least stave off the inevitable end of slavery, which would revolutionize the Southern economy. The result was an ongoing contest over new western territories, with a series of political accommodations. The most influential of these, the Missouri Compromise (1820), allowed for the admission of Maine as a free state and of Missouri as a slave-holding state, but otherwise restricted slave-holding west of the Mississippi to the area south of Missouri's southern border.

1.4.6   The Civil War and Reconstruction

Eventually it became clear that the nation could not continue divided between free and slave-holding states. The South's response to this realization, crystallized by the election of Abraham Lincoln, was to form a new nation. Accordingly in early 1861, just before Lincoln's inauguration, delegates from the Deep South met in Montgomery, Alabama, to form the Confederate States of America. In April of that year, Confederate forces besieged Fort Sumter, South Carolina, and the Civil War began.

It was an unequal contest. The Union had twenty-three states: all nineteen of the free states (California, Connecticut, Illinois, Indiana, Iowa, Kansas, Maine, Massachusetts, Michigan, Minnesota, New Hampshire, New Jersey, New York, Ohio, Oregon, Pennsylvania, Rhode Island, Vermont, and Wisconsin) and four "border" states, which were slave-holding but remained with the Union (Delaware, Kentucky, Maryland, and Missouri). The Confederacy had eleven states (Alabama, Arkansas, Florida, Georgia, Louisiana, Mississippi, North Carolina, South Carolina, Tennessee, Texas, and Virginia). Population in the Union was 21,000,000; in the Confederacy, 5,500,000 whites and 3,500,000 black slaves. Manufacturing plants in the Union numbered 100,000; in the Confederacy, 18,000. The Union had more than 70 percent of the railroads; the Confederacy, less than 30 percent.

What the Confederacy chiefly had was passion. But in addition the South had skilled military leaders, a long coastline that was difficult to blockade, and the hope of foreign support, which, however, never materialized.

The war lasted four years and was a turning point in military history. Among the features it introduced to warfare were ironclad warships, a submarine, machine guns, land and water mines, balloon reconnaissance, photographic records, newspaper reportage, telegraphic communication, and organized medical care for troops.

The Civil War was a disaster, whose positive outcomes were both the abolition of slavery and the establishment of the inviolability of the Union. Although slavery was at the heart of the conflict, it did not figure as the primary motive on either side. The North fought the war primarily to preserve the Union, and only secondarily to abolish slavery and secure civil rights for African-Americans. The South fought the war mainly to establish state autonomy and cultural independence, and only secondarily to maintain the institution of slavery. In fact, it was clear on both sides that slavery would eventually have to end; the questions were when and under what circumstances.

31

Lincoln's 1863 Emancipation Proclamation had no basis in Constitutional law. It was four things: a statement of principle, a tactic to put pressure on the Confederacy (the threat to issue it in 1862 was an unsuccessful attempt to induce compromise on the part of the South), a successful foreign relations move to make support of the Confederacy by European powers more difficult, and a means of bringing black troops into the Union army (some 180,000 enlisted between the Proclamation and the end of the war). The actual emancipation was accomplished by the thirteenth amendment to the Constitution, ratified in December 1865.

The Confederacy, on the other hand, in early 1865 had communicated with European powers, offering to emancipate the slaves in return for diplomatic recognition and support. But the offer came too late and was not accepted. It was, however, evidence that the South recognized the need to abandon its "peculiar institution."

The period of Reconstruction, the process of governing the Southern states after the war and of reintegrating them into the Union, was confused and contentious. Some Northerners sought to use Reconstruction as a means of punishing the South for its insurrection. Some Southerners sought to find ways of bypassing the effects of the thirteenth amendment freeing the slaves and of the subsequent fourteenth (1868) and fifteenth (1870) amendments, guaranteeing civil and voting rights.

1.4.7 Technological and social expansion in the later nineteenth century

As the nation recovered from the trauma of the Civil War and its aftermath, a period of remarkable growth and development followed. The population increased by 50 percent during the last two decades of the century, much of it from the 9,000,000 immigrants who entered the United States then. The majority of these immigrants, like earlier ones, came from western and northern Europe. At the end of the century, however, that pattern changed to immigration from eastern and southern Europe, and with that change was to come a shift in attitudes toward immigration generally.

North American territorial expansion had been completed with the purchase of Alaska in 1867. By the end of the century, forty-five states had entered the Union, with Arizona, New Mexico, and Oklahoma to follow shortly thereafter. The continental frontier – an aspect of American life for 300 years – had disappeared. The westward movement was being replaced by urbanization. During the last two decades of the nineteenth century, the urban population of the United States increased from 28 to 40 percent. In

1850 there were eighty-five cities with a population greater than 8,000; in 1900 their number increased sevenfold (Dulles 89).

Part of the new wealth of the nation came from the discovery of mineral deposits. The California gold rush of 1849 was followed by the discovery of the Comstock Lode of silver in Nevada in 1859 and more gold fields in the Black Hills, South Dakota, in 1874 and at Cripple Creek, Colorado, in 1891.

Cattle raising dominated the life and economics of a central portion of the country from Texas north to the Great Plains in the 1870s and 1880s (Boorstin 1973, 5–41). It gave rise to the mystique of the hard-riding, straight-shooting cowboy, clad in sombrero, chaps, and spurred boots, who herded cattle on the open range. Killing freezes in 1886 and 1887 depleted the herds and ended that way of life, leaving only a myth behind.

The first transcontinental railroad was achieved by the joining of the tracks of the Central Pacific, running eastward from Sacramento, California, and those of the Union Pacific, running westward from Council Bluffs, Iowa. They met in Utah in 1869. Railroads spread out across the country, a web of transportation binding the states into one network.

The Brooklyn Bridge was built between 1869 and 1883, with the longest span in the world. Nearly fifty years later it inspired Hart Crane's visionary poem *The Bridge*, about the human ability to unite past and future.

A period of economic prosperity beginning in 1878 lasted for twenty years. Manufacturing, factories, and factory workers all doubled during the period. The iron and steel industries boomed. Public utilities were established for electric, gas, and telephone service, and transportation by streetcars came to the cities. Inventions that were to transform American life included the air brake (George Westinghouse, 1869), typewriter (Christopher Latham Sholes, 1867, marketed 1874), telephone (Alexander Graham Bell, 1876), refrigerator train car (Gustavus Franklin Swift, commissioned 1877), phonograph (Thomas Alva Edison, 1877), practical incandescent lighting (Thomas Alva Edison, 1879), linotype (Ottmar Mergenthaler, 1884), and calculating machine (William Seward Burroughs, 1885, patented 1892).

The end of the century saw the growth of big labor, big business, and big government. The first major national labor organization was the Knights of Labor, founded in 1869; the American Federation of Labor followed in 1881. The end of the century saw a series of labor actions, such as the national 1893 Pullman Strike, led by Eugene V. Debs and Louis W. Rogers. The move to megabusiness was made by Andrew Carnegie in steel and John D. Rockefeller with the foundation of the Standard Oil Trust in 1882.

J. P. Morgan's name became a byword in banking. The United States Civil Service Commission was established in 1883 to take career government jobs out of the patronage system. The Interstate Commerce Commission, established in 1887, was the first government regulatory agency in the United States. The Sherman Antitrust Act of 1890 dealt with monopolistic practices interfering with open competition.

The game of baseball became the national sport during the last part of the century. Developed from the English game of rounders, also called "base ball," the American sport has been misattributed to an 1839 invention of Abner Doubleday, the Union commander of the troops that fired the opening shots of the Civil War at Fort Sumter. The game was popular with the army during that war, and afterwards evolved from an amateur to a professional sport. The National League was formed in 1876.

1.4.8   *The development of English in the National period*

The Revolutionary War had won political independence for the United States, but cultural independence had yet to be gained. Movement in that direction came almost immediately. The Founding Fathers of the body politic had their linguistic counterpart in Noah Webster (1758–1843).

Webster's *American Spelling Book* or "Blue-Backed Speller" (part 1 of *A Grammatical Institute of the English Language*, 1783) was amazingly successful. With total sales of perhaps 100,000,000 copies, it taught literacy to generations of early Americans and provided a standard for American spelling. Webster is often called a spelling reformer. It is true that he tried to introduce a number of reforms into American orthography, but they were unsuccessful. What are often thought of as Webster's "reforms" were for the most part spelling variants found on both sides of the Atlantic but popularized in America through Webster's enterprise and prestige.

During the seventeenth century, when America was first settled, English spelling was far from standardized. During the eighteenth century, it became relatively stable, but with a number of variations, between which English writers vacillated. They included options like *center/centre, honor/honour, magic/magick, paneling/panelling,* and *realize/realise.* In the case of such options, Webster chose the one he thought simpler, more historical, or analogous, and that one generally became the American preference, whereas in many cases British English went in a different direction.

Webster was an American patriot. He called the language of the new country "Federal English" and praised it as the use of American "yeomen." He scorned what he thought were the affected uses of the

English royal court and society. His highly didactic reader for schools, first published in 1785, preferred selections by American authors or about American themes.

A nation that committed itself to a written Constitution might also be expected to turn to a written standard of language. Although some of the early Founding Fathers toyed with the idea of an American Academy, a fancy they inherited from their British cultural forebears, the idea came no more to fruit on the American side of the Atlantic than it had on the British. Instead, for a source of linguistic authority, Americans came to rely on a semi-mystical book, "the dictionary." So far as that archetype had a physical realization, it was in the lexicographical work of Noah Webster.

Webster is best remembered as a lexicographer, and much of his life work was devoted to recording in dictionaries the English language used in America, from his 1806 *Compendious Dictionary of the English Language* to his two-volume 1828 *American Dictionary of the English Language*. Webster's dictionaries became the most influential works on the English language in America, and they gave rise to the longest continuous lexicographical tradition in the English-speaking world: the Merriam-Webster dictionaries. Webster's name became a synonym for dictionaries, appropriated by others for its talismanic merchandizing value.

Webster's "Blue-Backed Speller" and his dictionaries were the symbols of language authority in the United States. Language attitudes in America have always been Janus-like. On the one hand, there has been a concern for purity in language, defined by the authority of dictionaries. So John Pickering (1816, in Mathews 1931, 65) observed: "The preservation of the *English language* in its purity throughout the United States is an object deserving the attention of every American, who is a friend to the literature and science of his country." On the other hand, Walt Whitman, speaking as the American Everyman, could boast in "Song of Myself": "I sound my barbaric yawp over the roofs of the world" and write an essay in defense of slang (1885) at a time when it was widely considered to be a disease of language.

American English was more distinctive from British in vocabulary and pronunciation than in grammar. But it was also distinctive in style (Boorstin 1965, 275–324). Thomas Pyles (1952, 125–53) called the nineteenth-century style "tall talk, turgidity, and taboo," and Daniel Boorstin (1965, 296–8) referred to "booster talk," for example the euphemistic use of *home* instead of *house*. The declamatory style of oratory, both political and religious, was also mocked by the conscious illiteracy and homespun anecdotes of the cracker-barrel philosophers. They sprang from Benjamin Franklin's

Poor Richard and ranged through the apocryphal writings of Davy Crockett, James Russell Lowell's Hosea Biglow, Charles P. Browne's Artemus Ward, Henry Wheeler Shaw's Josh Billings, Finley Peter Dunne's Mr. Dooley, and on to the twentieth-century Will Rogers and Al Capp's Mammy Yokum.

Another aspect of cultural independence was the development of a distinctive American literature written by American authors who were acknowledged internationally for their contributions to English literature. American belletristic authors productive during the National period included:

- Washington Irving (1783–1859)
- James Fenimore Cooper (1789–1851)
- William Cullen Bryant (1794–1878)
- Ralph Waldo Emerson (1803–82)
- Nathaniel Hawthorne (1804–64)
- Henry Wadsworth Longfellow (1807–82)
- Edgar Allan Poe (1809–49)
- Oliver Wendell Holmes (1809–94)
- Henry David Thoreau (1817–62)
- James Russell Lowell (1819–91)
- Herman Melville (1819–91)
- Walt Whitman (1819–92)
- Emily Dickinson (1830–86)
- Samuel Langhorne Clemens, pen name Mark Twain (1835–1910)
- William Dean Howells (1837–1920)
- Henry James (1843–1916)
- Stephen Crane (1871–1900)

The English of America, especially its vocabulary, was constantly changed by the events of the National period. The development of improved means of communication and transportation served to make American English more uniform. Likewise, the great migrations westward, in which settlers from various regions of the East mixed in the Far West, promoted a homogeneity of language. On the other hand, the large size of the continent created barriers to communication that promoted the formation of new dialects. And the tendency to urbanization gave the first indications of a future replacement of purely geographical dialects by a rural-urban split.

The National period saw the creation of a new nation, its preservation under the threat of division by civil war, and its expansion geographically, socially, and economically to the cusp of the twentieth century. It likewise saw the development of the language used by Americans into a standard form, distinctively different from any of the regional and social dialects of the first settlers and likewise different from the standard form that had developed in Britain from the same roots as those of the first American colonial speech. At this point, British and American English, each changing separately and divergently, seemed on the road to becoming different languages, as Italian and Spanish had 1,500 years earlier. But that divergence was not to continue.

1.5   The International period

1.5.1   The Spanish-American War

The Spanish-American War lasted a bare four months in 1898. It was hardly more than a skirmish and merits only passing concern in the military history of the United States. But it had very great political and social consequences because it was a turning point in the history of the country, directing the nation's attention outside its own borders to the world stage. Internationalists and isolationists have vied with each other throughout the history of the nation, but after the Spanish-American War, the turn was to internationalism.

The history of the United States during the twentieth century was one of interlinked expansion on two fronts: international and economic. That expansion was not consistent but was moderated by periodical deflation on both fronts – some minor blips and two major retrenchments, one on international expansion in the years following World War I and the other on economic expansion during the Great Depression. But on the whole, the country moved from a focus within its own borders on the American continent to a global perspective and from a prosperous agrarian society with developing industry to an economic superpower.

Throughout the nineteenth century, the nation had followed, more or less closely, George Washington's advice to steer clear of foreign entanglements. But toward the end of the century a number of factors combined to change American attitudes. Following the Civil War, the United States had become powerful economically, and policy makers in the country felt the urge to wield that power. Moreover, a concern for the defense of the nation seemed to require a sizable navy, which in turn required bases in other parts of the globe for its effectiveness.

At the same time, the end of the continental frontier created a need, both psychological and economic, to look for new worlds. Americans were motivated by a vision of the nation's destiny inherited from some of the earliest settlers (Boorstin 1973, 557):

> The nation's view of its future and of its relations to the world never
> lost the mark of its earliest past. The Puritans were sent on their
> "Errand into the Wilderness" not by a British sovereign or by London
> businessmen, but by God Himself. Whatever names later Americans
> used to describe the direction of their history – whether they spoke of

"Providence" or of "Destiny" – they still kept alive the sense of mission. "We shall nobly save or meanly lose," Lincoln warned, "the last best hope of earth."

The end of the frontier also created a commercial need to find new territories to expand into. As Bernard Bailyn (1986a, 67) remarked apropos of westward expansion during the Colonial period: "There was never a time in American history when land speculation had not been a major preoccupation of ambitious people." The lack of fresh land on the continent directed the attention of Americans abroad.

The emergence of America on the international stage in a significant way placed the country in a role that Americans as a whole were unprepared for, but which Theodore Roosevelt defined for them (Dulles 157):

> In foreign affairs, we must make up our minds that, whether we wish it or not, we are a great people and must play a great part in the world. It is not open to us to choose whether we will play that great part or not. We have to play it. All we can decide is whether we shall play it well or ill.

The entrance on that role was the Spanish-American War. In 1895 a revolution begun by Cubans against Spanish rule provoked violence on the island, with exaggerated reports in sensationalist American newspapers. Public opinion in the United States was aroused against Spain. Then in 1898 the USS *Maine* exploded and sank in Havana harbor. A naval court of inquiry attributed the explosion to a mine. When Spain refused to accept an American demand for Cuban independence, the war began.

The conflict was "a splendid little war" – in the memorable phrase of John Hay, the Secretary of State – "begun with the highest motives, carried on with magnificent intelligence and spirit, favored by the fortune which loves the brave" (Dulles 168). Later assessments have been less self-congratulatory, but the importance of the war as a symbolic turning point is clear. At the settlement, less than four months after the declaration of war, Spain gave Cuba its independence, transferred Puerto Rico and Guam to the United States, and passed control over the Philippines into American hands in return for $20,000,000.

1.5.2 Imperialism and progressivism

Its new Caribbean and Pacific territories launched the United States as an imperialist power, although more economic and cultural than political. However, the die of internationalism had been cast. Hawaii, which had been an independent kingdom, became a republic controlled by American commercial interests in 1893 and was annexed by the United States in 1898, during the Spanish-American War. It became a territory in 1900 and was finally admitted to statehood in 1959.

It is notable that all of the territorial expansion of the United States proper took place during the nineteenth century, before the end of the Spanish-American War. Territorial acquisitions after that war were few and mostly small, and a number of them, notably the Philippines, were granted independence or, notably the Canal Zone, returned to the country from which they had been acquired. Puerto Rico by repeated popular vote has retained its special commonwealth status rather than change to statehood or independence. The American "empire" has been commercial and cultural, rather than territorial.

At the end of the century, the United States proposed to Britain, France, Germany, Italy, Japan, and Russia an "Open Door" policy to control the monopolizing of Chinese trade or the colonization of China by any of the great powers. American interest was not altruistic but centered on the exporting of cotton goods to China. Despite violations by Japan, the Open Door policy generally held until World War II, after which the communist rise to power in China ended traditional trade arrangements. Theodore Roosevelt's mediation, ending the Russo-Japanese War of 1904–5, at a peace conference in Portsmouth, New Hampshire, won him the Nobel Prize for Peace in 1906.

After an abortive French effort to build a canal across Panama, the United States purchased the French assets in 1902, but Colombia, which was then sovereign in the Panamanian isthmus, balked at a proposed treaty. Panama, with American support, declared independence in 1903. In 1904, a treaty was signed with Panama creating the Panama Canal Zone, and construction of the canal was begun – the greatest engineering project up to its time. The sovereignty exercised by the United States over the Canal Zone was a continuing source of annoyance to Panama; in 1977 the Panama Canal Treaty abolished the Zone, recognizing Panamanian sovereignty there but retaining the American right to operate the canal until the end of 1999.

The dissatisfaction of several European powers with the failure of some Latin American countries to honor their debts led to the 1904 Roosevelt Corollary to the Monroe Doctrine. Whereas the latter warned European nations against intervention in the Americas, the former asserted the intention of the United States to require Latin American countries not to give cause for European intervention. The first instance was Theodore Roosevelt's 1905 appointment of a financial manager for the Dominican Republic to oversee its revenue collections when it defaulted on obligations.

William Howard Taft introduced a foreign policy dubbed "dollar diplomacy," which was an extension of the Roosevelt Corollary. It was intervention in the affairs of other nations, especially in Latin America, for the purpose of maintaining their fiscal stability and of protecting American financial interests. The policy naturally generated resentment where intervention occurred, and the term came to be used pejoratively.

Woodrow Wilson, while publicly abjuring dollar diplomacy, continued the policy by imposing a government on Haiti in 1915, occupying the Dominican Republic in 1916, and intervening in Nicaragua during that time. He also bought the Virgin Islands from Denmark in 1916 to prevent their being acquired by Germany.

While the nation was expanding its spheres of influence abroad, at home a complex of reform movements collectively called progressivism took shape. Progressivism was a movement responding to the social changes following the urbanizing and industrializing of the country. Religious leaders began to preach the Social Gospel. Journalists turned to yellow journalism – banner headlines, illustrations, and human-interest stories – and to "muckraking," an old term given a new sense by Theodore Roosevelt – the reporting of corruption and exploitation. Writers like Upton Sinclair became social critics with works like his 1906 novel, *The Jungle*, an exposé of the stockyards and meat packing, which helped to pass the Pure Food and Drug Act.

The sixteenth and seventeenth amendments to the Constitution were ratified in 1913. The sixteenth amendment authorized an income tax by the Federal government. The seventeenth provided for the direct election of senators by popular vote, instead of their selection by state legislatures. Its effect was to make the Senate more responsive to the will of the electorate and less reactionary.

1.5.3   World War I and its aftermath

The outbreak of hostilities in Europe in 1914 inevitably engaged American interests, initially through the efforts of the British to establish a blockade of the Continent and of the Germans to control shipping by submarine warfare. The German sinking of American ships led to a declaration of war in 1917. By 1918, more than a million men of the American Expeditionary Force reached France. They and the US Navy's assistance in overcoming the German submarine threat helped to bring the war to a close in November of that year.

President Woodrow Wilson, a practical idealist, envisioned the war as one to "make the world safe for democracy." He hoped for general agreement among the powers, but when the other Allied governments showed no interest in his idealistic plans, Wilson presented those plans to Congress in January 1918 as fourteen points: (1) reliance on open diplomacy rather than secret agreements, (2) freedom of the seas, (3) free trade, (4) disarmament, (5) adjudication of colonial claims with respect for the sovereignty of the colonial peoples, (6) assistance to Russia, (7) respect for the integrity of Belgium, (8) restoration of French territories, (9) adjustment of the border of Italy based on ethnicity, (10) autonomy for the peoples of Austria-Hungary, (11) guarantees for the independence of the various Balkan states, (12) self-determination for the peoples of the Ottoman Empire and free passage through the Dardanelles, (13) independence for Poland, and (14) the formation of a League of Nations to guarantee independence for all countries, large and small. The Germans opened armistice talks on the basis of those fourteen points, but later held that the Treaty of Versailles undermined their principles.

After the war, sentiment for isolationism rose in the United States. Opposition to the treaty, especially the establishment of the League of Nations, was waged by a group of conservative Republican senators. In the course of campaigning for his vision, Wilson suffered a stroke. He was succeeded by Warren Harding, under whom American approval of the treaty and membership in the League became a dead issue. The United States concluded a separate peace with Germany in 1921. A benefit of the isolationist sentiment was the improvement of relations with Latin America through a policy of nonintervention that culminated in Franklin Roosevelt's Good Neighbor Policy and lasted through World War II but then lapsed during the anticommunist activities of the Cold War.

The postwar revival of isolationism coincided with xenophobia, social reactionism, a Red scare, racial unrest, and labor troubles. Immigration was restricted both in numbers and by country of origin. During the 1920s the Ku Klux Klan became a political and social force with an estimated membership of five million. Christian fundamentalism offered emotional security, especially in rural areas and small towns, by emphasizing moral values and a literal interpretation of Scripture. The eighteenth amendment to the Constitution, prohibiting the manufacture, sale, and transportation of alcoholic drinks, was passed in 1919 and was repealed by the twenty-first amendment in 1933. During the fourteen years of its existence, national Prohibition was probably the most widely violated law the country has ever had.

The height of fundamentalist influence was exemplified by the trial of John T. Scopes, a Tennessee teacher of biology who challenged a 1925 state law forbidding the teaching of evolution. The resulting Scopes Trial pitted William Jennings Bryan as prosecutor against Clarence Darrow as defending lawyer and was widely reported, notably by the social critic H. L. Mencken. Scopes was found guilty and fined $100 but was acquitted on appeal because the fine was judged excessive.

The dozen years following the end of World War I were a temporary, though not unique, reversal of the usual twentieth-century movement toward greater international involvement and intellectual sophistication. On the other hand, they also saw a number of social and technological changes that undermined the resurgence of isolationism and social reaction. Those changes caused the period to be dubbed the Roaring Twenties and the Jazz Age. The passage of the nineteenth amendment in 1920, giving women the right to vote, was a critical factor leading to increased efforts for sexual equality later in the century.

The year 1927 saw the last of the Ford Model T cars and the first of the Model A. In 1929, four and a half million passenger cars were sold in America, one car for every twenty-seven persons in the country, a rate not to be surpassed until after World War II. The mass-produced and widely available automobile brought personal mobility on a scale never before known, with consequent social change.

The telephone had been developed in the last quarter of the nineteenth century, but during the Roaring Twenties, significant technological improvements were made. For example, in 1927, AT&T (American Telephone and Telegraph) developed a handset combining transmitter and receiver elements.

Commercial radio began with one station in 1920. Two years later there were 564 stations in the nation. The first radio network was NBC (National Broadcasting Company), which acquired a New York station in 1926 and began producing daily programs for other stations. In 1927, the FCC (Federal Communications Commission) was established to regulate the growth of broadcasting.

Motion pictures were shown in France as early as 1895, but the form is especially associated with America (Lear). In 1905–8, cheap nickelodeons attracted more than 25 million viewers each week. D. W. Griffith's 1915 *Birth of a Nation* was the first popular feature film. During the 1920s, motion pictures became a significant industry in America and a major form of entertainment. *The Jazz Singer* of 1927 was the first film with spoken dialog, and the 1920s also saw the introduction of the first Technicolor, although full-color Technicolor did not appear until the 1930s. Weekly attendance at the movies rose to forty million persons, half that number being minors. By the late 1930s weekly attendance had doubled to eighty million. The fact that the movies appealed especially to the young, coupled with a drift toward sexually suggestive content, led to self-censorship through the Hays Office, an advisory group that established guidelines for acceptability in content and presentation. The Hays code did not forbid innuendo or violence, but prescribed the manner in which they could be depicted and the context in which they were shown. As Hollywood movies were shown around the world, they depicted American values and standards.

The print media saw the birth of a number of influential magazines during the 1920s: Henry R. Luce's *Time* (1923), H. L. Mencken's *American Mercury* (1924), and Harold Ross's *New Yorker* (1925).

The alternative name for this period, the Jazz Age, reflects a new improvisational musical style. Jazz music has its roots in African rhythms and grew from early nineteenth-century plantation and later minstrel band music, as transmitted through a syncopated musical style of the late nineteenth century known as ragtime. The word *jazz* is of unknown etymology, but is perhaps derived from a creole sexual term applied to dance movements. Jazz developed in New Orleans about the turn of the century and developed into what is called the "Chicago style" during the 1920s and later into a style called "swing." Jazz, which became the music of Prohibition speakeasies (clandestine places serving alcohol illegally), featured a series of solo variations on a musical theme, performed on various instruments.

The history of jazz is one of social amelioration and geographical spread. It began as the music of New Orleans brothels, became more sophisticated in Prohibition speakeasies all over the country, developed as the respectable orchestral music of swing, and finally appeared in concerts around the globe. Jazz as a distinctive style has, however, retained its association with the African-American community. Its later developments, such as swing, bebop, and rock, became part of world pop culture.

1.5.4 The Great Depression and World War II

After the stock market had reached an all-time high in August 1929, on October 29, known as "Black Tuesday," a record sixteen million shares were traded, and the market collapsed, sending the nation into the longest and most severe economic depression in its history. The depression quickly spread internationally since the United States had become the principal creditor for European recovery after World War I. Four years later, stock

John Algeo

prices averaged only a fourth or fifth of their 1929 value, many financial institutions and other businesses had declared bankruptcy, a quarter of the work force was unemployed, and wages were halved.

Major political and social repercussions followed. In 1932 Franklin Delano Roosevelt was elected President of the United States, to become the longest-serving holder of that office. Government control of financial matters became common in order to regulate economic stability. New agencies were established, such as the TVA (Tennessee Valley Authority) to build dams and power plants and the WPA (Works Progress Administration), PWA (Public Works Administration), and CCC (Civilian Conservation Corps) to employ workers. The Social Security Act of 1935 began the creation of a safety net for the elderly, unemployed, handicapped, and dependent.

In Germany, Adolf Hitler rose to power in 1933. The depression ended in Germany with increased production of armaments, and in the United States with a similar increase in industrial production after the outbreak of hostilities in Europe.

World War II began with Germany's 1939 invasion of Poland, following an unsuccessful 1938 policy of appeasement that acquiesced in Hitler's occupation of Austria and annexation of the Sudetenland from Czechoslovakia. In early 1941, the Lend-Lease Act made it possible to support the Allies by giving them supplies on credit. In August of that year, Roosevelt and Churchill met on shipboard off the coast of Newfoundland to promulgate the Atlantic Charter, whose principles echoed some of those of Woodrow Wilson: self-determination, free trade, open seas, disarmament, and international cooperation to promote economic and social well-being.

By November 1941, American intelligence knew that the Japanese were planning imminent military action, but expected it in the Philippines. The December 7 surprise attack on Pearl Harbor, Hawaii, put out of commission the American battleship force, as well as nearly 350 airplanes, and caused more than 3,500 personnel casualties. That attack united public opinion in the United States and for the remainder of the century ended the policy of isolationism as a dominant force in the nation.

In 1941 the Office of Scientific Research and Development was created to enlist scientists and academics, whose assistance proved crucial to the conduct of the war. Wartime production and mobilization geared up in the United States and by early 1944 was twice as great as that in all of the Axis powers taken together. On June 6 of that year, American, British, and Canadian forces landed on the beaches of Normandy and a push was begun into Germany. Eleven months later, the German forces formally surrendered.

In the Pacific theater, American strategy was to move gradually from island to island toward Japan. By mid 1945, enough island bases had been captured to permit heavy bombing of Japan in preparation for an invasion. However, the development of the atomic bomb resulted in its first test on July 6, and on July 26 Truman issued Japan a demand for surrender, with the alternative of "prompt and utter destruction." On August 6 and 9, atomic bombs were dropped on Hiroshima and Nagasaki, bringing about the surrender of Japan and obviating the need for a land invasion whose cost was estimated at a million American lives.

The United Nations Organization was founded in 1945 to be a peace-keeper following the war, and other international organizations also came into existence to foster world welfare, such as the cultural organization UNESCO, the International Monetary Fund, and the World Bank.

1.5.5   Foreign political engagement in the last half of the twentieth century

As they had in the years following World War I, an isolationist movement and a revived Red scare gained some support after World War II but did not rise to the effectiveness of the earlier reaction. The new reaction began during the final years of the war, when Vice President Henry Wallace was removed from the ticket because of his liberal position on social and economic issues and was replaced by a relative unknown, Harry Truman. Later Senator Joseph R. McCarthy's campaign to find communists in the American government led to the introduction of a new word, *McCarthyism* – 'the use of unsupported accusations and inquisitorial investigation to label political opponents as traitors' – but the campaign was discredited during his lifetime.

The Cold War, however, developed soon after the conclusion of World War II. The term had been used by George Orwell in 1945 and was popularized in the title of a 1947 book by Walter Lippmann. It referred specifically to political, economic, and propagandistic competition between the United States and Soviet Russia for hegemony and in response to the Iron Curtain. The latter expression derives from British use of a movable firewall between the auditorium and the stage of theaters from the late eighteenth century onward. Metaphorical extensions to other barriers, especially of communication, soon followed. The term was applied to Russia as early as 1920, but what the *OED* calls its locus classicus was a 1946 speech by Winston Churchill at Westminster College in Fulton,

Missouri: "From Stettin, in the Baltic, to Trieste, in the Adriatic, an iron curtain has descended across the Continent."

Soviet dominance of Eastern Europe and the threat of Soviet expansion elsewhere governed much of American foreign policy from 1947 until the collapse of the Soviet superstate in the early 1990s. During the Cold War, Russia intervened in East Germany (1953), Hungary (1956), Czechoslovakia (1968), Afghanistan (1979), and elsewhere. The United States responded in Guatemala (1954), the Dominican Republic (1965), Grenada (1983), and elsewhere.

When economic pressures led Britain to withdraw its aid from eastern-Mediterranean countries in 1947, the United States stepped in to provide support for the noncommunist governments of Greece and Turkey with the Truman Doctrine of using economic aid to support foreign policy aims. That same year saw the inauguration of the European Recovery Program, popularly called the Marshall Plan after its architect, Secretary of State George Marshall. It was the most extensive system of foreign aid in human history and was designed to restore Europe to economic health.

The first major engagement of the Cold War was the Soviet ground blockade of West Berlin in 1948–9, which resulted in an airlift to supply the Allied-governed sectors of the city. In 1949 NATO (North Atlantic Treaty Organization) was formed as an alliance against potential Russian aggression. It survived its immediate genesis to play a role in the Balkans crisis of the Serbian province of Kosovo in the late 1990s.

The year 1950 saw the invasion of South Korea by communist North Korea, to which Harry Truman promptly responded by securing a resolution from the United Nations Security Council calling on member states to oppose the aggression. The resolution could be passed then because Russia, which had veto power, was boycotting the Council. The operation was technically a police action taken under UN auspices and conducted under the UN flag. It included troops from a number of UN members, though the United States was the most prominently represented nation. An armistice was signed in 1953, essentially restoring the status quo ante.

The Peace Corps was the 1961 creation of John F. Kennedy to help developing countries by providing assistance in agriculture, community development, education, health, and technology. Volunteers – at first typically new college graduates – spent two years abroad, speaking the native language and living on the level of their counterparts in that culture. In 1966, more than 15,500 such volunteers were serving in some fifty countries. Later the volunteers tended to be older and more specialized in their expertise.

Another turning point in the Cold War was the Cuban missile crisis of 1962, in which the Soviets were discovered to be installing in Cuba ballistic missiles capable of reaching American cities. The resulting confrontation ended with Russia withdrawing the missiles and was followed by the Nuclear Test Ban Treaty of 1963 but also generated a continuing arms race of conventional weapons and forces.

The United States had been supplying aid to Vietnam since 1954, when the French withdrew. In 1964 an attack on American warships in the area led to the active involvement of the United States in the civil war of that country. The war lasted ten years, divided public opinion, and had severe political repercussions domestically. The consequent desire to restrict American involvement in foreign fields resulted in a policy of détente with Russia and the SALT (Strategic Arms Limitation Talks) agreements of 1972 and 1979, ending a race for antiballistic missile development.

The presidency of Jimmy Carter (1977–81) had the goals of improving human rights in friendly nations by diplomacy, particularly in Argentina, Iran, Rhodesia, South Africa, and South Korea, and of brokering peace agreements, notably the 1979 Camp David accord between Egypt and Israel. His efforts in Iran backfired, however, with the overthrow of the Shah and the establishment of a fundamentalist, anti-Western Islamic Republic.

Ronald Reagan's presidency (1981–9) included several unsuccessful or controversial foreign-affairs initiatives: aid to the rightist Contras in Nicaragua; a marine peacekeeping force sent to Lebanon, which fell victim to a terrorist attack; a comic-opera invasion of Grenada; and the sale of arms to Iran in exchange for American hostages. His most substantive achievements were improved relations with China and the INF (Intermediate-range Nuclear Forces) treaty with Russia.

In 1989, George Bush reverted to an interventionist policy in Latin America, when he sent American troops into Panama to capture General Manuel Noriega on charges of trafficking in drugs and racketeering. The following year, he responded to Iraq's invasion of Kuwait by organizing a coalition of NATO and Arab countries under UN auspices. The resulting Gulf War in 1991 repulsed Iraqi forces, but left the Iraqi government of Saddam Hussein in power as a continuing threat to stability in the Middle East.

The overthrow of communist governments in eastern Europe in 1989–90 was followed by the breakup of the Soviet state into Russia and fourteen other autonomous nations in 1991 and so marked the end of the Cold War.

Regional and ethnic conflicts continued to break out around the world, and under the presidency of William Jefferson Clinton, the United States attempted, with varying success, to play the role of peacemaker or peacekeeper in several of them. A 1993–4 effort to supply relief to Somalia, plagued by famine and torn by civil strife, ended after the slaying of eighteen Americans. In 1994, Yasir Arafat of the Palestine Liberation Organization and Prime Minister Yitzhak Rabin of Israel met in Washington to sign an agreement on the West Bank and the Gaza Strip. In 1995, the presidents of Croatia, Serbia, and Bosnia met near Dayton, Ohio, to conclude a treaty settling their territorial disputes in the Balkans. In 1997, three former members of the Soviet block – the Czech Republic, Hungary, and Poland – were admitted into NATO.

An agreement to resolve the longstanding troubles in Northern Ireland between Catholic Republicans who want to join with the Republic of Ireland and Protestant Unionists who want to remain part of the United Kingdom was reached in 1998 with American mediation. The long-range success of the agreement rested on the willingness of both parties to compromise, an issue much in doubt even at the time the negotiations were successfully concluded.

In 1999 the festering situation in the Balkans came to a head with a program by Slobodan Milosevic of Serbia for the ethnic cleansing of Albanian Muslims from the province of Kosovo. NATO responded with an air war that established two new principles: the effectiveness of air power without ground troops and the right of the international community to intervene in the internal affairs of a country on behalf of a persecuted minority.

1.5.6   *Domestic social developments in the last half of the twentieth century*

The need for personnel, both military and civilian, during World War II had important consequences. Two economically underprivileged groups had made significant contributions to the war effort: blacks and women. Those contributions resulted in advances in their status that continued after the war. The wartime prohibition of racial discrimination in employment and training programs was to be followed by a variety of civil rights programs for minorities in general and blacks in particular.

The 1954 Supreme Court decision in the case of *Brown versus Board of Education of Topeka* ended segregation in the public schools of the nation. At the time the decision was handed down, of 4,355 Southern school districts, only three were integrated, and eight Southern states had no schools enrolling both blacks and whites. In 1955, Martin Luther King, Jr., led a boycott of segregated buses in Montgomery, Alabama, beginning the civil rights movement that led to the Civil Rights Act of 1964, which has been called the most important law of its kind since Reconstruction. It outlawed discrimination in voting, public accommodations, education, employment, and unions, and created the EEOC (Equal Employment Opportunity Commission) to oversee fairness in the workplace for minorities and women.

The entry of women into the work force during World War II (symbolized by the figure of Rosie the Riveter) broke down sexual barriers in employment and led to greater opportunities for women in a variety of occupations. The women's liberation or feminist movement became especially powerful and successful from the 1960s on, resulting in changes in employment and social patterns. The *Roe versus Wade* Supreme Court decision of 1973 legalized abortions. That coupled with new contraceptive measures, such as "the pill," contributed to the revolution in sexual mores and family patterns.

Service personnel returning after World War II were assisted with their reentry into civilian life by a number of programs, such as the GI Bill of Rights, providing loans and educational opportunities for veterans. New housing was constructed on a massive scale, thereby creating jobs in the building and allied industries. And a baby boom swelled the population, creating demands for new schools and facilities for children.

Postwar domestic events included the most extensive public works program ever undertaken, the building of a vast system of interstate highways starting in 1956 under Dwight Eisenhower.

Lyndon B. Johnson's Great Society programs started in 1965; they included Medicare and Medicaid health insurance, federal housing programs, federal funding for education on all levels, the Voting Rights Act, the Immigration Act eliminating quota preferences against some countries, and a host of domestic social programs.

Immigration patterns changed significantly between the nineteenth and twentieth centuries (Carnes and Garraty 134–5). In 1850, the ten states with the largest number of foreign-born were Illinois, Indiana, Massachusetts, Michigan, Missouri, New Jersey, New York, Ohio, Pennsylvania, and Wisconsin. The main countries of birth of the foreign-born in those states were Ireland, Germany, Britain, and Canada.

In 1910, California and Minnesota had replaced Indiana and Missouri as states with the largest number of foreign-born residents, and the main countries of origin were, in addition to the four of 1850, Austria, Hungary,

Italy, Japan, Norway, Russia, and Sweden. Japanese were prominent in California; Swedes in Minnesota; Norwegians in Minnesota and Wisconsin; Russians and Italians in Illinois, New Jersey, New York, and Pennsylvania; Hungarians in Ohio.

In 1980, the top ten states for foreign-born residents included Texas and Florida in place of Minnesota and Wisconsin. Ireland was no longer a major source country, though Britain, Germany, and Canada continued. Of other European sources, Italy remained; Poland and Portugal were added. The principal new sources were Cuba, the Dominican Republic, Mexico, the Philippines, and Vietnam. Mexican immigration was heaviest in California, Texas, and Illinois; Cuban in Florida; Dominican in New York; Italian in Massachusetts, New Jersey, New York, and Pennsylvania; Portuguese in Massachusetts; Polish in Illinois; and Canadian in California, Florida, Michigan, and Massachusetts.

The number of immigrants to the United States declined precipitously between 1900 and 1940 (Carnes and Garraty 258–9), because of restrictive immigration laws. The second half of the century saw a steady increase, but also a diversification. Before 1960, Europe provided more immigrants than any other area; after 1960, Latin America and Asia became the chief sources. Spanish speakers came into every state of the Union, with concentrations of Mexicans in the border states of Texas, New Mexico, Arizona, and California, but also in Illinois (principally the Chicago area). New York and New Jersey received large numbers of Puerto Ricans (who are not counted as immigrants because of the special governmental status of the island). Florida was heavily settled by Cubans and Puerto Ricans.

These changes in immigration patterns will certainly have a significant effect on American society, culture, and language; but it is too early to know the extent and exact nature of that effect.

1.5.7   Technological changes by the end of the twentieth century

The economic policies of the Reagan administration (1981–9) were domestically popular, but created the largest budget deficit in the nation's history. By the end of his second term, the United States had ceased to be a creditor nation and had become the largest debtor nation in the world. By the end of the century (1997), however, the five nations with the largest gross domestic product were the United States ($7,834 billion), Japan ($4,190 billion), Germany ($2,092 billion), France ($1,392 billion), and the United Kingdom ($1,296 billion), the US gross domestic product being larger than that of the next three countries combined. The economic strength of the nation was reflected in and partly resulted from its technological accomplishments and the popular appeal of American culture. The effect of commercial and technological expansion on American society and language has been profound (Boorstin 1973).

Although television broadcasting dates from the 1930s, the widespread use of television came after World War II. In 1949, the United States had a million television sets; in 1951, ten million; in 1959, fifty million.

Cable television transmits signals by means of coaxial or fiber-optic cables. It began in the United States in the 1950s to provide service to areas that otherwise had poor reception because of interference from natural features or tall buildings. In addition to improving reception, cable television offers an increased number of channels, some specializing in weather, news, financial reports, sports, or films. By 1997, the share of the viewing audience held by the three largest networks – ABC, CBS, NBC – had dropped to 49 percent. Three smaller networks – Fox, UPN, Time Warner – had 21 percent. Cable networks such as TNT, ESPN, and PBS (Public Broadcasting Service) had 30 percent.

In 1962, AT&T (American Telephone and Telegraph Company) first relayed television signals overseas by satellite, from the United States to England and France. The Moon landing in 1969, transmitted by satellite, was watched by an estimated one hundred million persons. By the 1970s practically the whole inhabited surface of the planet could receive television signals from any point on Earth relayed by satellites in geostationary orbit, that is, in a fixed position above the earth's surface. An example is CNN (Cable News Network), founded in 1980 to provide live broadcasts of twenty-four-hour news reports. Headquartered in Atlanta, Georgia, CNN has bureaus all over the world, with coverage transmitted by satellite. It gained widespread recognition for its coverage of the Gulf War in 1991, which included broadcasts from inside Iraq during hostilities.

The popularity of VCRs (videocassette recorders) in the 1970s gave new life to old movies. By 1990, the profit from videocassette sales was double that from movies in theaters (Lear 757).

The first electronic digital computers were developed in the 1930s and 1940s. The first generation of commercial computer in the United States was the UNIVAC (Universal Automatic Computer), which used vacuum tubes and was produced in 1951. The second generation of computers used transistors and appeared about 1960. Later in that decade and on into the 1970s, third-generation computers used integrated circuits, miniaturized transistors on a silicon chip that made possible the mass production of faster and cheaper computers. Fourth-generation computers used even more compressed transistors, the microprocessor, produced in 1974, and RAM (random-access memory) chips, which made possible the desktop computer.

Further technological advances produced ever faster and cheaper computers, making them household items for many Americans and expanding their range of uses. By the end of the century, the growth of CDs (compact disks) containing texts, including reference works like dictionaries and encyclopedias, and the reality of electronic books raised prospects of a readjustment in the use of print media.

The Internet developed from a 1969 Department of Defense communications program, ARPANET (Advanced Research Projects Agency Network), for organizations doing defense work. Academics supported by the NSF (National Science Foundation) adapted it as a connection of many computer networks, which then developed commercial and personal uses. The World Wide Web is an information retrieval service of the Internet that gives access to many Internet sites by a graphical interface. In the 1990s it became a major communication tool and the most important part of the Internet.

One of the earliest activities of the Internet was e-mail (electronic mail), which remains one of its most popular and widely distributed uses. By the end of the century, however, e-commerce, that is, the offering of commodities for purchase on the Internet, became increasingly common.

Fax (from *facsimile*) is a system of transmitting texts and images electronically in digitized form by telephone circuits. It became common in the 1980s.

The development of electronic communication in various forms impacted the print media, and particularly the press – newspapers and magazines. The press has been an influential factor in American life since Colonial days (T. Leonard). Local publications have always abounded; Cincinnati had a newspaper in 1793 serving fewer than 500 citizens. After the Civil War, large urban newspapers grew more prominent; the *New York Times* began before the war as a penny paper, but after the turn of the century became the United States' newspaper of record. The number of dailies peaked in the 1920s, when about 2,600 were published, declining at the end of the century by more than a third.

Automobiles were developed at the end of the nineteenth century in Europe, but quickly spread to the United States, where they were to have their greatest impact (Flink 64). Early European cars were expensive and so primarily for the wealthy; American cars were more primitive but also cheaper, so more affordable. By 1898, 50 companies in the United States were manufacturing cars, and ten years later that number had increased to 240. One of those was that of Henry Ford, who in 1908 produced his black Model T, popularly dubbed the "tin lizzie," a standardized, assembly-line produced automobile, cheap enough for the mass market. Twenty years later, the automobile had become a normal means of transportation in America and other industrialized countries.

The passenger car became the principal means of transportation for families and ended rural isolation. By the 1990s Americans were driving more than 150 million vehicles for more than 1.5 trillion miles a year. This explosive growth of automotive traffic jammed streets and roads, and led to the creation of the superhighway and the Interstate Highway system. It also produced a new type of accommodation, the motel (the term being first recorded in the *OED* in 1925), a temporary lodging for travelers, usually located on a highway, with parking spaces near the rooms.

Wilbur and Orville Wright built a double-winged plane with an engine and propellers, and in 1903 made the first powered heavier-than-air flight at Kitty Hawk, North Carolina. The World War I military use of airplanes gave impetus to the further development of aviation. After the war, commercial mail-carrying flights were introduced, and further improvements led to the first solo nonstop flight across the Atlantic from New York to Paris by Charles A. Lindbergh in 1927. Improved monoplanes with metal bodies were developed in the 1930s, and jet-engine military aircraft appeared during World War II. In the 1950s, the jetliner became the norm for commercial aircraft, as air travel grew to be the principal form of long-distance transportation in the second half of the twentieth century.

The possibilities of space travel by means of rockets received serious consideration during the early part of the twentieth century. World War II and the preparations leading up to it included research into rocket propulsion for military uses. After Russia launched the first artificial satellite in 1957, the United States followed with the second in 1958. Manned space flights were launched by the Russians and the Americans in 1961. A lunar flight was made in 1969, when Neil Armstrong and Buzz Aldrin became the first humans on the surface of the Moon. During the 1960s to 1980s, unmanned landings, orbitings, and flybys were made to Venus, Mars, Jupiter, Saturn, and Uranus. In 1973, the first American space station was launched; in 1981, the first space shuttle, named *Columbia*, went into operation.

Some way of cooling living space artificially has long been practiced, but not until the twentieth century did air-conditioning become common. The first theater to be air-conditioned was Graumann's in Los Angeles in 1922;

the first fully air-conditioned office building was constructed in San Antonio, Texas, in 1928. Trains were air-conditioned in the 1930s. It was not until the 1950s, however, after World War II that domestic air-conditioning became common through room units and central systems.

Air-conditioning had important effects. It helped to make possible the construction of the glass-walled skyscraper, of which the United Nations Secretariat in New York City (1949) was the paradigm. It also eliminated the need for windows that open, interior courtyards, and air-shafts for ventilation. It permitted the construction of enclosed shopping malls, which have transformed retail business in America. It changed domestic architecture, eliminating a need for porches, overhanging eves, awnings, high ceilings, basements, and upper floors, thus promoting the single-level ranch-house style. It changed the design of automobiles by allowing them to be sealed; factory-installed air-conditioning in cars increased from 10 percent in 1955, to 23 percent in 1965, to 54 percent in 1969, to a standard feature in all cars by 1990. It made possible lunar exploration through the air-conditioned space suit, without which Neil Armstrong would never have stepped onto the surface of the moon and delivered his famous line, "That's one small step for [a] man, one giant leap for mankind."

But air-conditioning especially changed the in-migration patterns of population movement in the United States. Before air-conditioning, summers in the South were steamy with heat and high humidity, and equally hot in much of the West. Air-conditioning reversed the migration of people from the South to the North and created the Sun Belt. In 1910, a net out-migration from the South of 1 million persons a year is estimated, and by 1940, a net out-migration of 2.5 million a year. In the 1960s, the net loss declined to 1 million a year, and in the 1970s and 1980s, the South received a net increase by in-migration from the North of 2.5 to 3 million persons a year. Between 1950 and 1995, the population of Florida increased by 411 percent, that of Texas by 142 percent, and that of Georgia by 109 percent, compared with 36 percent for Illinois and 15 percent for Pennsylvania. Air-conditioning changed the population patterns and thus affected the dialect patterns of America.

Mechanical lifts are ancient; the Roman architect Vitruvius (1st century BC) described them as construction devices. However, the modern passenger elevator became feasible when in 1853 Elisha Otis produced a safety device that prevented the elevator compartment from falling. The first such elevator, driven by steam, was installed in a department store in New York City in 1857. The next major improvement was the use of electric power to drive the elevator, followed by a series of other technical advances for safety, convenience, speed, and height. The fast, automatic, and reliable elevator helped to make the modern skyscraper possible.

The term *skyscraper* has a first recorded use in 1883 to denote the many-storied, tall building that advances in construction technology had made possible and the growth of urban population and commercial activity called for. The first buildings to be so called were structures of ten to twenty stories, but the term came to be used mainly for buildings at least four times that height. Architectural styles have fluctuated, but the typical image of a skyscraper is the International Style, with simple, straight lines, glass walls, open spaces, and vertical emphasis, which dominated design from the middle of the twentieth century until a reaction to the style set in by the end of the century.

Coca-Cola, one of the products that symbolize America around the world, came into existence in Atlanta, Georgia, in 1886, when a pharmacist developed it as a cure-all tonic and created the script trademark that has identified it ever since. The name reflects the plants that originally furnished ingredients for the drink: the coca leaf and the kola nut. (Coca leaf extracts were omitted after 1905.) Beginning as a tonic sold in local soda fountains, often located in drugstores or pharmacies, Coca-Cola became, through skillful advertising and marketing, the best-known soft drink in the nation. About mid century the nickname *Coke* was trademarked and the drink had become internationally known.

The McDonald's fast-food restaurants are a franchise enterprise whose "golden arches" logo is another visual symbol of American business around the world. Beginning in San Bernardino, California, the name and concept were packaged as a chain with the first branch in Des Plaines, Illinois, in 1955. By the mid 1980s, 7,500 McDonald's outlets were operating around the world. The company continued its expansion, for example by moving into the Czech Republic, Hungary, Poland, and Slovakia in the 1990s, and at the same time announcing it would open branches in India, where it would abandon its staple, the beef hamburger, in deference to Hindu dietary customs. A 1997 collection of anthropological studies, *Golden Arches East*, describes the East Asian use of McDonald's restaurants as community and family centers.

Another American pop culture symbol is the garment variously called jeans, blue jeans, denims, dungarees, and Levi's (a trademark). They were originally workmen's trousers with seams reinforced by copper rivets, manufactured by the San Francisco firm of Levi Strauss in the nineteenth century. Associated with cowboys, jeans became a popular item of apparel by the middle of the twentieth century and, in various forms, are now worn internationally by both men and women.

The technological developments sketched above resulted in what has been called the "globalization" of culture. Diverse native cultures exist all over the world, and will continue to do so as far into the future as we can imagine, just as diverse regional cultures exist in the United Kingdom and the United States. Yet, also just as a national culture overlies the regional differences of Britain and America, so the global culture is an overlay to the various folkways and mores of native cultures. That global culture has been long in the making and combines diverse influences from many cultures, but its dominant form at the end of the twentieth century was pronouncedly Anglo-American.

1.5.8 *The development of English in the International period*

The internationalization of American interests during the twentieth century had a predictable influence on and by American English. On the one hand, American English became a channel for influences from other languages on English. On the other hand, American joined British as a source of influences from English on other languages. The influences in both directions are most obvious in loanwords. However, the adoption of English as a foreign language or a language of special purposes has the potential of affecting both phonology and grammar by the adopters. The result is an increase in the varieties of nonnative English.

Also significant have been the use of American English as an international language and its influence on other national varieties of the language during the twentieth century. In 1780, John Adams, the second president of the United States, wrote a letter to the president of the Continental Congress, in which he said (Mathews 1931, 42):

> English is destined to be in the next and succeeding centuries more generally the language of the world than Latin was in the last or French is in the present age. The reason of this is obvious, because the increasing population in America, and their universal connection and correspondence with all nations will, aided by the influence of England in the world, whether great or small, force their language into general use.

As improbable as Adams's prediction might have seemed at the time, it was accurate. The combined influence of Great Britain and the United States, not just political, but technological, economic, and cultural, has advanced the use of the English language beyond that of any other language in human history. The widespread adoption of English is not due to any inherent superiority of the language, but to its practical usefulness in ways that matter to those who adopt it.

An article in the *Chicago Tribune* (February 15, 2000, 1–8/4–5) reported that in Japan

> a government panel released a report called "Japan's Vision for the 21st Century." It concluded that all Japanese should have a practical mastery of English by the time they finish middle school, and that Japan should consider establishing English as its second official language.

The impact of the American variety of English internationally is based heavily on the technological, scientific, commercial, and industrial capacities of the United States. It is also, however, reinforced by cultural considerations. The latter are chiefly pop and youth culture, but in addition include the considerable body of literature the country produced during the twentieth century. American authors whose literary reputation has traveled well beyond the borders of the nation include the following:

- Robert Frost (1874–1963)
- Sinclair Lewis (1885–1951)
- Ezra Pound (1885–1972)
- Eugene O'Neill (1888–1953)
- T. S. Eliot (1888–1965)
- F. Scott Fitzgerald (1896–1940)
- John Dos Passos (1896–1970)
- William Faulkner (1897–1962)
- Ernest Hemingway (1899–1961)
- Vladimir Nabokov (1899–1977)
- Thomas Wolfe (1900–38)
- John Steinbeck (1902–68)
- Isaac Bashevis Singer (1904–91)
- Richard Wright (1908–60)
- Eudora Welty (1909–)
- Tennessee Williams (1911–83)
- Bernard Malamud (1914–86)
- William S. Burroughs (1914–97)
- Ralph Ellison (1914–94)
- Saul Bellow (1915–)
- Arthur Miller (1915–)
- Walker Percy (1916–90)
- Carson McCullers (1917–67)
- J. D. Salinger (1919–)
- Jack Kerouac (1922–69)
- Truman Capote (1924–84)
- James Baldwin (1924–87)
- Flannery O'Connor (1925–64)
- William Styron (1925–)
- Edward Albee (1928–)
- John Barth (1930–)
- Toni Morrison (1931–)
- Sylvia Plath (1932–63)
- John Updike (1932–)
- Philip Roth (1933–)
- Thomas Pynchon (1937–)
- Joyce Carol Oates (1938–)
- Alice Walker (1944–)

As different as some of those authors are from one another, they all expressed themselves in the English of America, and they all reflect qualities of Americanness through that English.

In the decade after mid century, Max Lerner (805) assessed the status of American English:

> American speech is surely one of the richest products of the American experience, at the base of much else that is creative in American popular culture. Abrupt, inventive, muscular, irreverent, it expresses with striking fidelity the energies and rhythm that have gone into the making of the national experience.

American English has variations within it that reflect the variety of sources from which it derives and of experiences that Americans have gone through. Yet, considering the size of the nation in area and population, it is remarkably homogeneous. American English marks off the people of the United States as a separate community in the Anglophone world, with their own characteristics, values, and assumptions. Yet, despite a multitude of differences between it and British English, the two are remarkably similar in their standard forms.

FURTHER READING

An overview of American history by topics is *The Reader's Companion to American History* (Foner and Garraty 1991). The settlement history of America is traced by Bernard Bailyn in *The Peopling of British North America* (1986a) and *Voyagers to the West* (1986b) and by David Hackett Fischer in *Albion's Seed* (1989). Critical surveys of American social history have been made by Max Lerner in *America as Civilization* (1957, 1987) and by Daniel J. Boorstin in the three volumes of *The Americans* (1958, 1965, 1973). A popular, opinionated, and readable social treatment is *A History of the American People* by Paul Johnson (1998).

2 BRITISH AND AMERICAN, CONTINUITY AND DIVERGENCE

John Hurt Fisher

2.1 The continuity of English

British antecedence to American English is reflected first of all by the fact that the language of the United States of America is called "English." Language is the soul of a nation, as Solzhenitsyn expressed it in his Nobel lecture. Cultures are universally identified with languages, and this has been especially true since the emergence of nation states in the Renaissance. The English language is inextricably associated with England. When the American colonists separated from the mother country, it would have been natural for them to adopt another designation for their language. But the separation of the American nation from England after 1776 was schizophrenic, characterized on the one hand by violent rejection of English tyranny, as it was regarded by the American revolutionaries, and on the other by acute nostalgia for their English culture.

The rejection was mirrored by the provisions in the United States Constitution against aristocracy and autocracy. The anti-English sentiment of the Founding Fathers has been treated by all historians of the American Revolution, but best from our point of view by David Simpson, *The Politics of American English, 1776–1850* (1986). At the meetings of the Continental Congress there were half-hearted suggestions that the new nation should adopt another language, such as Hebrew, French, or Greek. But these suggestions were never taken seriously and were capped off by the observation of the Connecticut representative, Roger Sherman, that "it would be more convenient for us to keep the language as it was, and *make the English speak Greek*" (Baron 13).

2.2 Settlement history

More than 95 percent of the immigrants to the original colonies were from Great Britain, having arrived in four migrations, described in most detail by David Hackett Fischer in *Albion's Seed* (1989):

59

1. 20,000 Puritans largely from East Anglia to New England, 1629–41, to escape the tyranny of the crown and the established church that led to the Puritan revolution;
2. 40,000 Cavaliers and their servants largely from the southwestern counties of England to the Chesapeake Bay area and Virginia, 1642–75, to escape the Long Parliament and Puritan rule;
3. 23,000 Quakers from the North Midlands and many like-minded evangelicals from Wales, Germany, Holland, and France, to the Delaware Valley and Pennsylvania, 1675–1725, to escape the Act of Uniformity in England and the Thirty Years War in Europe;
4. 275,000 from the North Border regions of England, Scotland, and Ulster to the backcountry of New England, western Pennsylvania, and the Appalachians, 1717–75, to escape the endemic conflict and poverty of the Border regions, and especially the 1706–7 Act of Union between England and Scotland, which brought about the "pacification" of the Border, transforming it from a combative society in need of many warriors to a commercial and industrial society in need of no warriors, with the consequent large-scale displacement of the rural population.

Fischer's scenario documents the conclusions about American settlement patterns and the connections between American and British regional dialects that have been drawn by Hans Kurath, George Philip Krapp, Allen Walker Read, Albert Marckwardt, Raven McDavid, Cleanth Brooks, and other historians of American English. His presentation enriches, but does not materially alter, the familiar picture of Colonial settlement. His extrapolation of the influence of the four migrations upon the development of American culture after 1800 has been criticized both for generalizing too broadly and for failing to take account of the influences of Native Americans, eastern and southern Europeans, the Celtic Irish, Africans, and Asians.

J. L. Dillard's *All-American English* (1975), written in response to the work of the earlier historians, presents the most direct attack upon the familiar scenario of settlement and linguistic transfer. It brings together contemporary statements about the maritime pidgins the English emigrants encountered, the heterogeneity of their American settlements, and the uniformity of Colonial language. From this, Dillard infers the existence of a koiné created in the colonies out of which the American dialects subsequently developed under the influence of isolation and non-English immigrants, with little reference to British antecedents. The basis of this impressive argument is considered elsewhere in this volume (ch. 8), but the argument is obviated by chronology. The non-English influences Dillard brings forward are nearly all post 1800. Fischer's superbly documented study, the most comprehensive compendium so far produced of the British antecedents to American culture up to 1800, delineates the disposition of the earliest settlers, which made it inconceivable for them not to continue to think of English as their native language.

2.3   Nationalism, American English, and Noah Webster

Nevertheless, the American Revolution produced self-consciousness about the fracture with the mother country and a consequent impulse to define the language of the new nation as "American English." In 1781 John Witherspoon introduced the term "Americanism." In 1782 Robert Ross produced an *American Grammar*. In 1787 Noah Webster renamed his *Accurate Standard of Pronunciation* the *American Spelling Book*. In 1788 Benjamin Rush argued in his "Plan for a Federal University" that instruction in "philology" should be stressed because "our intercourse must soon cease with the bar, the stage, and the pulpits of Great-Britain, from whence we received our knowledge of the pronunciation of the English language. Even modern English books should cease to be the models of stile in the United States" (Read 1936, 1148). In the same year some young men of New York organized themselves into a Philological Society "for the purpose of ascertaining and improving the *American Tongue*" (Read 1936, 1148; Baron 9–11). In 1793, William Thornton made the nationalist claim very directly (D. Simpson 25):

> You have corrected the dangerous doctrines of European powers, correct now the languages you have imported, for the oppressed of various nations knock at your gates, and desire to be received as your brethren. As you admit them, facilitate your intercourse, and you will mutually enjoy the benefits. – The AMERICAN LANGUAGE will thus be as distinct as the government, free from all follies of unphilosophical fashion, and resting upon truth as its only regulator.

But the sense of cultural independence was always muted. More common was an awareness of the generally unsettled character of English that was leading dictionary makers and grammarians in England to create tools for "ascertaining" and "fixing" the language (Baugh and Cable ch. 9). Hobbes, Locke, Burke, Johnson, and others associated order in language with order in society (D. Simpson 32–51). John Adams's 1780 proposal for an American academy to improve and fix the English language is only one item in a movement traced from 1721 to 1925 by Allen Walker Read. This movement was motivated more by the European neoclassical desire to ascertain and refine all language than by any desire to distinguish American from British English. The literati in Boston and Philadelphia were as aware as Swift and Johnson of the variations in eighteenth-century English and of the British failure to establish an academy on the French model to standardize the language. They felt, quite simply, that America could succeed where the mother country had failed, by creating an academy to choose among variations and enforce uniformity in English worldwide.

Noah Webster is an important figure in this tradition. His first foray into the regulation of language, *The Grammatical Institute of the English Language* (1783–5), had no nationalistic agenda. It argued that the adoption of a single textbook would help to achieve uniformity, and its first part, called *A New and Accurate Standard of Pronunciation*, followed closely the spelling in Johnson's dictionary. By 1787, however, Webster had been drawn into the nationalistic movement. His *American Spelling Book* (a revision of part 1 of *The Grammatical Institute*) promoted several forms that today distinguish American from British spelling: preference for *-or* rather than *-our* in unstressed syllables (*honor, favor*) and preference for final *-er* rather than *-re* (*center, theater*). In his 1789 *Dissertations on the English Language* he wrote, "As an independent nation, our honor requires us to have a system of our own, in language as well as in government" (20). But it is hard to know the extent to which his spelling reform was intended to distinguish American English, and the extent to which it was merely a play in the international game of rationalizing English spelling. Baron (69–98) lists sixteen proposals for spelling reform, beginning with Benjamin Franklin's of 1768 (written in England) down to the proposals of the British-American Spelling Board of 1906. Krapp (1925) has a chapter on American spelling (1: ch. 6), as does Mencken (1963, ch. 8), and chapter 10 in this volume.

The titles of Webster's books reveal his ambivalence about the relations between the British and American languages. His 1806 dictionary, designated *A Compendious Dictionary of the English Language*, promoted many more simplifications than *The American Spelling Book*, for example, omission of silent letters (*determin, altho, crum, ile, fashon*), use of single letters rather than digraphs and double letters (*economy, traveler*), *k* for [k] (*aker*), *oo* for [u] (*soop*), *e* for [ɛ] (*fether*), and various other simplifications. His 1828 dictionary, called *An American Dictionary of the English Language*, introduced many new words but eliminated most of the simplified spellings except for those found in the 1787 speller. In 1830, when the dictionary was reprinted in London as *A Dictionary of the English Language*, Webster spoke of British and American English as one language, and in 1829 he had reissued his *American Spelling Book* as *The Elementary Spelling Book, Being an Improvement on the American*

Spelling Book. Webster was more absolute in his essays than in his reference books about the existence of distinctively American forms, and he ended up espousing the notion of a clarified, simplified international language.

2.4 Education and culture norms

Respect for the language and culture of England was reinforced by the development of education in America. This respect, of provincials for a central authority, was shared with Scotland and the Border regions from which Fischer's fourth great migration emanated. London and the Home Counties were the seat of British power and prestige. Both North Britons and Americans sought self-consciously to emulate and absorb the sophisticated manners and language of London. In the eighteenth century, domestic manners and language were supposed to be inculcated by family and associates, not taught in school. English grammar schools – "public schools" in the British sense of the term – did not teach English composition or English literature until the nineteenth century. Literacy was taught in school through the *literae humaniores*, the Latin and Greek classics. But the Scottish schools could not assume that polite usage in English language and culture would be absorbed at home. After the seat of government moved to London with the Act of Union in 1706, Scottish schools began to teach English composition and English literature (Davie).

The Scottish system of municipally supported elementary and secondary schools and a four-year arts curriculum in the universities, controlled by secular authorities rather than by the church, was the model upon which American education developed (Martin). The first college textbook of English rhetoric and literature in Scotland was Hugh Blair's *Lectures on Rhetoric and Belles Lettres* (1783). Blair, Professor of English Rhetoric at the University of Edinburgh, appointed in 1762 by the Town Council (as the governing body of the university), was the first professor of English in Great Britain. His two volumes of *Lectures*, the published form of versions he had been delivering at the university for twenty years, argued that literary excellence was mirrored as much in English as in classical literature. Most of his authorities were still the classics, especially Quintilian, Cicero, and Demosthenes, but he cited modern rhetoricians like Fenelon and especially Lord Kames's *Elements of Criticism.* Many of his illustrations were likewise translations from Latin and Greek, but, in four lectures, he analyzed Addison's style in *The Spectator*, and he devoted a lecture to the style of Jonathan Swift and part of a lecture to Milton's *Paradise Lost.* In addition, he took many examples from Shakespeare, Dryden, Pope, and Samuel

Johnson. Among the poets, he cited examples from Akenside, Cowley, Ossian, Mackenzie, Prior, Allan Ramsay, and Edward Young; among the novelists, Defoe, Richardson, Fielding, and Smollett; among the dramatists, Beaumont and Fletcher, Cibber, Congreve, Farquhar, Ben Jonson, Otway, Sheridan, and Vanbrugh. He cited some thirty contemporary writers of expository prose, among them Hooker, Locke, Sir William Temple, Bishop Berkeley, and Lord Clarendon, and both Robert Lowth's *English Grammar* and his Latin *De Sacra Poesi Hebraeorum*. Blair's *Lectures* remained for a hundred years the most influential introduction to composition and literature in both England and America. Yale introduced a course using Blair in 1785, and Harvard did so in 1788 (W. Parker).

The "dissenting academies" began teaching English in England at the same time as the Scottish common schools. The dissenting academies were, like the Scottish schools, created largely for the disadvantaged. They were created by ministers for students who would not take the oath of conformity to the Church of England after 1662 (Palmer ch. 1). All of the immigrants to America except for those in Virginia came from these nonconforming factions in England. Nonconforming students were barred from universities and public schools in England until the end of the nineteenth century, so the dissenting academies had to provide elementary, secondary, and advanced education. While the traditional public schools catered largely to the gentry, the dissenting academies catered largely to the commercial and industrial classes. As such, their curricula were, like those of the Scottish schools, directed to "useful knowledge": arithmetic, economics, science, modern history, modern languages, and English composition and literature.

Joseph Priestley, tutor of language and belles lettres in such a school, Warrington Academy, compiled one of the earliest textbooks for teaching English, *Rudiments of English Grammar Adapted to the Use of Schools* (1761). This included extracts from the Bible, from Addison, Young, Bolingbrok, Hume, Swift, and Pope, and Wolsey's farewell speech from *Henry VIII*. The year after Priestley's book, Robert Lowth, a clergyman in the established church who eventually became Bishop of London, published his *Short Introduction to English Grammar* (1762, printed in Philadelphia in 1775). Like Samuel Johnson, Lowth was a self-appointed guru on usage. He cited grammatical errors in the Bible, Shakespeare, Donne, Milton, Swift, Dryden, Pope, Addison, and other prominent writers, but these very citations enhanced the canonical status of the English classics.

The Scottish common schools and the dissenting academies of England were the models for the earliest schools in the United States. To take only one denomination as an example, by 1744 Presbyterian ministers and synods were creating parochial schools, and in 1758 the New York and Philadelphia synods enjoined every presbytery to establish within its bounds one or more free academies (Fisher 1946). By 1857 there were more than a hundred such academies – the exact number cannot be ascertained because autonomy in operation was a cardinal principle of the evangelical sects as they established themselves in the new country. Many of the Presbyterian academies developed college departments from which important colleges (such as Coe, Hanover, Lafayette, Maryville, Oberlin, Occidental, Trinity, Tulsa, Wabash, Washington and Jefferson, Whitworth, Wooster) and universities (Indiana, New York, Ohio, Tennessee) eventually developed. And those are only the Presbyterian foundations. The Congregationalists, Methodists, and eventually the Baptists founded many more academies that grew into colleges.

A principal characteristic of the American academies and colleges was their cultural conservatism. David Hackett Fischer describes (55–6) the "aching sense of physical separation from the European homeland [that] became a cultural factor of high importance in Colonial settlements. The effect of distance created feelings of nostalgia, anxiety, and loss. The prevailing cultural mood became profoundly conservative." Nowhere did this conservatism manifest itself more clearly than in the central place given to the study of English composition (rhetoric, as it was called until the 1930s) and English literature. This fixation upon English literature lasted for 150 years. American literature did not begin to be studied in American schools and colleges until the 1920s.

Lindley Murray's *English Grammar, Adapted to Different Classes of Learners*, first published in 1795, was the most popular textbook in the early academies. Murray, an American-born merchant, had studied at Franklin's English Academy in Philadelphia. He practiced law in Pennsylvania and amassed a large fortune in commerce before moving to England in 1785. Murray's grammar, written at the request of friends for use in a girls' school in England, sold more than a million copies in America by 1850. It was based upon Lowth's grammar, but was even more conservative and pietistic, characteristics that appealed to the mission of the American academies (D. Simpson 50). All of its authorities were British, and the grammar it purveyed was Murray's interpretation of cultivated English usage.

Until the middle of the nineteenth century, Murray was the most popular grammar in American secondary schools as Blair was the most popular rhetoric in American colleges. Thirty-nine editions of Blair's *Rhetoric* were published in the United States before 1835. It became the standard text for the first-year college courses in English composition; by 1835 it had been adopted at Columbia, Pennsylvania, Brown, North Carolina, Middlebury, Williams, Amherst, Hamilton, Wesleyan, Union, and many other colleges (Martin 22–4). Murray and Blair maintained the prestige of British writing and British literature, and the American textbooks that replaced them after the middle of the century were equally centered on the imitation, elucidation, history, and biography of British authors.

2.5 Literature, writing, and the standard

Supported by – and supportive of – the practice in the schools, Americans from their first settlement through the nineteenth century acknowledged the authority of British writers (Krapp 1925, 1: ch. 2). Many who are considered pioneer American authors actually did much of their writing in England and abroad, as much for British audiences as for American: Benjamin Franklin, John Adams, Philip Freneau, David Humphreys, Joel Barlow, James Fenimore Cooper, Washington Irving, not to mention such later icons of American letters as Henry James and T. S. Eliot. The Scotsman John Witherspoon made the first collection of Americanisms (1781) as examples of solecisms and peculiarities. He asserted that "the language of Great-Britain [is] the pattern upon which we form ours" (Mathews 1931, 15).

John Pickering began collecting material for his *Collection of Words and Phrases Which Have Been Supposed to Be Peculiar to the United States of America* (1816) while he was secretary to the American ministry in London. In its introduction he observed, "It is true, indeed, that our countrymen may speak and write in a *dialect* of English, which will be understood in the *United States*; but if they are ambitious of having their works read by Englishmen, they must write in a language that Englishmen can read with pleasure" (Mathews 1931, 66). Cooper thought that the best British speakers could not be rivaled (D. Simpson 151; Mathews 1931, 123–9). Irving espoused British genteel language and values (D. Simpson 112–13).

Once government and law come to rest on written documents, authority in language resides in writing rather than in speech. Grammatical structures and lexicon that enable clarity and specificity are determined by precedent. The principles set forth in the Declaration of Independence and the American Constitution would have been meaningless had they not been in language expressing the philosophical and legal concepts of an expository tradition that had been developed in England since 1400 by the Chancery and behind that the Latin and Greek upon which Chancery English was founded (Fisher 1996).

David Simpson (33–40) is at some length to establish the extent to which the writing of Hobbes, Locke, Burke, and other British authorities informed the writing of Jefferson, Adams, Hamilton, and the other Founding Fathers. There are no "Americanisms" in the Declaration of Independence nor in the writings of such literary figures as Bryant, Poe, Emerson, Whittier, or Longfellow. An article in *The Monthly Anthology* (1807) attacks Webster's *Grammar* for its "notion of an American tongue, or gaining our idiom from the mouths of the illiterate, rather than from the pages of Milton, Dryden, Swift, Addison" (D. Simpson 78). Jefferson thought of American English, indeed all American law and culture, as descended from Anglo-Saxon, and proposed that Anglo-Saxon be a required subject in the curriculum of the University of Virginia, but in his *Essay on the Anglo-Saxon Language* (1798) he remained wonderfully open, foreseeing the eventual development "of an American dialect in every way as poetic and rich as that of the parent island" (Hauer 892).

2.6   Vocabulary

The sense of British English as the written standard persisted, but after 1800 (D. Simpson 123 would say after the War of 1812), recognition began to emerge that the evolution of American culture required its own lexicon. Noah Webster was quite circumstantial in the introduction to his *American Dictionary* (1828):

> It is not only important, but in a degree necessary, that the people of this country, should have an *American Dictionary* of the English language; for, although the body of the language is the same as in England, and it is desirable to perpetuate that sameness, yet some difference must exist. Language is the expression of ideas; and if the people of one country cannot preserve an identity of ideas, they cannot retain an identity of language. Now an identity of ideas depends materially upon a sameness of things or objects with which the people in the two countries are conversant. But in no two portions of the earth, remote from each other, can such identity be found. Even physical objects must be different. But the principal difference between the people of this country and of all others, arise from different forms of government, different laws, institutions, and customs. Thus the practice of hunting and hawking, the institution of heraldry, and the feudal system of England originated terms which formed, and some of which now form, a necessary part of the language of that country; but in the United

States, many of these terms are no part of our present language – and they cannot be for the things which they express do not exist in this country. They can be known only as obsolete or foreign words. On the other hand, the institutions of this country which are new and peculiar, give rise to new terms or to new applications of old terms, unknown to the people of England; which cannot be explained by them and which will not be inserted in their dictionaries, unless copied from ours. Thus the terms *land-office, land-warrant, location of land, association of churches, regent* of a university, *intendant* of a city, *plantation, selectman, senate, congress, court, assembly, escheat,* etc., are either words not belonging to the language of England, or they are applied to things in this country which do not exist in that.

Jefferson's and Webster's observations derive from looking at national requirements for expression and communication. What they regard as an inevitable, natural evolution, British observers tended to designate as barbarous "Americanisms." M. M. Mathews (1931, 13) quotes as the earliest reflection on American English the remark of a British traveler, Francis Moore, in 1735:

> When he was gone, I took a view of the town of Savannah.
> It is about a mile and a quarter in circumference; it stands upon the flat of a hill, the bank of the river (which they in barbarous English call a bluff) is steep and about forty-five foot perpendicular.

The term "Americanism" was introduced by John Witherspoon, who in 1768 was called from Edinburgh to become president of the College of New Jersey, which eventually became Princeton University. Witherspoon published three articles in 1781 on the characteristics of American English. He observed that the vulgar in America spoke more uniformly than the vulgar in Great Britain because they were more mobile and that educated people in England used colloquial language as freely as educated people in America.

> But there is a remarkable difference in their public and solemn discourses. I have heard in this country, in the senate, at the bar, and from the pulpit, and see daily in dissertations from the press, errors in grammar, improprieties, and vulgarisms, which hardly any person of the same class in point of rank and literature would have fallen into in Great-Britain. Curiosity led me to make a collection of these.
>
> [Mathews 1931, 16]

Witherspoon discusses these differences under eight headings: (1) Americanisms, or ways of speaking peculiar to the country, (2) Vulgarisms in England and America, (3) Vulgarisms in America only, (4) Local phrases or terms, (5) Common blunders arising from ignorance, (6) Cant phrases, (7) Personal blunders, (8) Technical terms introduced into the language. Of these, categories 2, 3, 5, and 7 are essentially deviations from polite usage in England as systematized by grammarians like Lowth and Murray. It is interesting how many of the idioms that Witherspoon lists as British vulgarisms (for example, *this here*, *that there*) would now be listed as American vulgarisms. Categories 4, 6, and 8 are the terminology occasioned by new conditions like those cited by Webster and discussed by Krapp (1925, 1: chs. 2–3). Of the first category Witherspoon writes:

> The first class I call Americanisms, by which I understand an use of phrases or terms, or constructions of sentences, even among persons of rank and education, different from the use of the same terms or phrases, or the construction of similar sentences in Great-Britain. It does not follow, from a man's using these, that he is ignorant, or his discourse upon the whole inelegant; nay, it does not follow in every case, that the terms or phrases used are worse in themselves, but merely that they are of American and not of British growth. The word Americanism, which I have coined for the purpose, is exactly similar in its formation and signification to the word Scotticism. [Mathews 1931, 17]

He goes on to observe that many Scotticisms are inherently as good as or better than the equivalents used in England, yet because the government and court have moved to London, Scottish "speakers and writers must conform to custom." But he presciently concludes that Americans, "being entirely separated from Britain, will find some center or standard of their own, and not be subject to the inhabitants of that island, in receiving new ways of speaking or rejecting the old."

Dictionaries of Americanisms were compiled more for entertainment and social criticism than for practical use. David Humphreys's glossary to his play *The Yankee in London* (1815, 103–10) is the next list after Witherspoon's. John Pickering in his *Vocabulary of Words and Phrases Which Have Been Supposed to Be Peculiar to the United States* (1816) notes with satisfaction that "there is a general and increasing disposition to regulate our pronunciation by that of Walker" (Krapp 1925, 1: 356). William Cullen Bryant drew up a list of thirty words of the New York dialect in about 1818, unpublished, left among his papers (D. Simpson 137). Mathews (1931, 99–112) prints a list of Americanisms from the *Virginia Quarterly* 1829–30. All of these are clearly considered provincialisms, of as much interest to American as to British sophisticates. W. A. Craigie (27), editor of the *Dictionary of American English*, observed that until 1820 the passage of new words and senses across the Atlantic was regularly westward, the only exceptions being objects peculiar to the New World. But after 1820 a reverse traffic set in. One half of the 7,000 senses of the 4,800 words under letters *A* and *B* in the *DAE* are of American origin and thus form additions to the international English vocabulary.

2.7   Style

It is more difficult to compare the British antecedents to American style than to grammar and lexicon because there are so many styles in both countries. Krapp devotes a chapter to the subject (1925, 1: ch. 5), in which he quotes Stuart Sherman to the effect that British style is more structured because it derives from study of the classics, while American is more free and impulsive. He remarks on the "grandiloquent" American style in oratory and the emergence after 1830 of the "Kentucky spirit" of the frontier, which Marckwardt (ch. 6) designates as "glorification of the commonplace." David Simpson (237–8) avers that in comparison to Hazlitt and Carlyle, Emerson and the Transcendentalists wrote in an informal colloquial style, while Henry Kahane (230–1) finds that the distinctive feature of American English is its democratization:

> The decolonized society of the New World represents a most
> interesting linguistic experiment. It tries to be a society for Everyman,
> and its language develops into a language for Everyman. . . . The
> essential developments of American English consist of a decline of
> Anglophilia, the standardization of informal speech, the leveling of
> social dialects, the integration of foreign elements.

Marckwardt and Quirk assert that until World War I, nearly all American writers subscribed to the central tradition of classical British literature. Mark Twain and Whitman are regularly cited as the first to break with this tradition; but after 1920 or thereabouts, with the advent of motion pictures, jazz, and writers with large British audiences, like Sinclair Lewis and Ernest Hemingway, British writers began to imitate American writers, and an increasing number of American words began to appear in British writing. Mencken (1963, ch. 6) also deals with this reversal.

American and British writing has always been and continues to be a common language. Except for a few idioms and typographical conventions, it is impossible to tell whether a writer is American or British. There are more differences between the styles within each tradition than between the two traditions. Fred Newton Scott's observation (quoted by Bridges 1925) is as good a summary as any:

I suggest . . . that the degree of divergence [between British and American English] varies inversely with the degree of importance of the subject-matter. That is, where the ideas to be expressed are trivial or facetious the two vernaculars differ so widely that they may almost be said to be foreign languages to each other. When the subject-matter is purely practical or commonplace, the divergence, though noticeable, is of secondary importance; and, finally, when the subject matter is of the highest quality, being concerned with ideal values and fundamental concepts, the divergence is so slight as to be almost negligible.

2.8   Pronunciation and class accent

Although it may not be possible in a collection of formal written documents to discern, except by spelling, which are by British writers and which by Americans, it is easy in any gathering of speakers to distinguish the British from the American. The pronunciation by which British speakers are distinguished is Received Pronunciation (RP), Oxford English, Public School English, BBC English, or standard British English, as it is variously designated. Teachers of English as a second language regularly point out that there is a standard pronunciation of British English, whereas American English has no such standard (Svejcer 27).

The two great studies of British and American dialects are posited on different assumptions. Orton's *Survey of English Dialects*, assumes the existence of standard pronunciation and usage and so records only the language of informants using the "purest local types of speech." Kurath's *Linguistic Atlas of New England* and its followers, on the other hand, assume no standard, and so record the language of educated and intermediate as well as folk speakers in each locality (McDavid 1979, 352). Usually British linguists are silent about the proportion of the population that use RP, but a recent estimate is 3 percent (Hughes and Trudgell 3). This is a small proportion, and it would have been even smaller in 1800.

Received Pronunciation developed at the end of the eighteenth century, during the period of the American Revolution. At that time there was no pronunciation by which people in America could be distinguished from people in England (Burchfield 36, Marckwardt and Quirk 61). In the impressment controversies of the 1790s, naval officers on both sides found it so difficult to tell whether sailors were British or American that the American government considered providing certificates of citizenship (D. Simpson 108).

Until the eighteenth century everyone in both Britain and America spoke a local dialect (Brooks 1935, 1–2). Gentlefolk, however, spoke differently from commoners, and, in a society stratified by birth, there was no more thought that the commoners could adopt gentle language than that they could adopt gentle blood. From the time dialects begin to appear in British novels and plays, like those of Fielding and Goldsmith, they have been markers of class and region and seldom, except by Dickens, used for comedy, whereas in America dialects have always been used for comic effect.

In the eighteenth century, British society began to shift from caste determined by birth to class determined by wealth and occupation (Fisher 1996, 147), and tools began to be provided for upward mobility. London had long been the political and cultural focus of Britain, so the language of London was recognized as the prestige dialect.

2.8.1   Orthoepists, lexicographers, and elocutionists

London grammar and lexicon were propagated by grammarians and lexicographers like Lindley Murray and Samuel Johnson. London pronunciation became the prerogative of a new breed of specialists – orthoepists and teachers of elocution. The orthoepists decided upon correct pronunciations, compiled pronouncing dictionaries and, in private and expensive tutorial sessions, drilled enterprising citizens in fashionable articulation. (Boswell took this sort of tutoring when he came to London.)

The two most influential orthoepists were Thomas Sheridan, father of the dramatist, and John Walker. Sheridan published a pronouncing version of Johnson's dictionary, *A General Dictionary of the English Language* (1780), and Walker a much more influential *Critical Pronouncing Dictionary and Expositor of the English Language* (1791). Walker's *Dictionary* appeared in an American edition in 1803, and combinations of Johnson's dictionary for spelling and Walker's for pronunciation were common in America throughout the nineteenth century. Walker introduced the term "Received Pronunciation." London pronunciation, he wrote, "is undoubtedly the best . . . that is, not only by courtesy, and because it happens to be the pronunciation of the capital, but best by a better title, that of being more generally received" (xvi). For both Sheridan and Walker, London pronunciation meant the pronunciation of the London elite. "Received" in the sense that Walker used it, means (*OED* sense 1a) "generally adopted" or "approved." It later developed the more specific meaning in "Received Standard English" (*OED* sense 1b) of "the spoken language of a linguistic area (usu. Britain) in its traditionally most correct and acceptable form."

In his *Course of Lectures on Elocution* (1762, 46–7) Sheridan distinguished the class basis of Received Pronunciation:

> Thus not only the Scotch, Irish, and Welsh, have each their own idioms, which uniformly prevail in those countries, but almost every county in England, has its own peculiar dialect. Nay in the very metropolis two different modes of pronunciation prevail, by which the inhabitants of one part of the town, are distinguished from those of the other. One is current in the city, and is called the cockney; the other at the court end, and is called the polite pronunciation. As amongst these various dialects, one must have the preference, and become fashionable, it will of course fall to the lot of that which prevails at court, the source of fashions of all kinds. All other dialects, are sure marks, either of provincial, rustic, pedantic, or mechanic education; and therefore have some degree of disgrace annexed to them. And as the court pronunciation is no where methodically taught, and can be acquired only by conversing with people in polite life, it is a sort of proof that a person has kept good company, and on that account is sought after by all, who wish to be considered as fashionable people, or members of the beau monde.

The first pronouncing dictionaries were published and the orthoepic movement began during the Revolutionary period, while social intercourse between England and America was at a minimum. When Americans began to return to England after 1800, they were surprised at the change in fashionable pronunciation (Van Schaak 162–3). James Fenimore Cooper observed that though Americans pass for natives every day in England, "it is next to impossible for an Englishman to escape detection in America." There is "a slang of society [with a] fashion of intonation . . . which it is often thought vulgar to omit." This is the pronunciation of "the higher classes in London . . . whose manners, birth, fortune, and political distinction make them the objects of admiration" (cited by Krapp 1925, 1: 13).

Both Johnson and Webster in the introductions to their dictionaries asserted that pronunciation should follow spelling. Krapp (1925, 2: 26) cites Southern American colloquial as preserving relaxed pronunciations that have been eradicated in cultivated American by spelling pronunciations, and Burchfield (40–2) lists eighteenth-century colloquial pronunciations that have been replaced in RP by spelling pronunciations: [n] by [ŋ] in words ending in -*ing* like *hunting*; initial aspiration in French words like *hotel, humble, herb* (he cites the pronunciation "erb" as an Americanism); pronunciation of *w* in words like *swore, woman, toward, Edward* (but not *sword*); pronunciation of silent consonants in words like *husban(d), so(l)dier, fa(l)con, Ra(l)ph*. There are other spelling pronunciations in American

English that may either show the influence of RP or represent parallel developments.

Webster's reaction is reflected in his criticism of "the practice of the [London] court and stage," which he saw subverting the "general practice" of the American nation (D. Simpson 68). He deplored fashionable metropolitan pronunciations that he transcribed as *edzhucation*, *natshure*, *keind*, *guyde* and so forth.

2.8.2   Intonation and stress

The intonation pattern that in the nineteenth century came to characterize RP is unique. Most of its other pronunciations are shared with one or more dialects in Britain today. When pronunciations and usages different from RP occur in Britain, they are called "dialect"; when they occur in English spoken in former colonies, they are sometimes described as "colonial lag," according to the theory propounded by A. J. Ellis (1: 19) that the development of English was arrested in the colonies. Krapp (1925, 2: 25) accepts the theory, but most recent commentators discount it. Krapp (1925, 2: 28) and Kurath (1928b) observe that all features of American pronunciation can be found in one or another of the British local dialects.

Received Pronunciation involves both intonation and segmental phones, but especially intonation. Until the end of the seventeenth century, textbooks indicate that the approved pronunciation continued to preserve fairly even stress on all syllables, with secondary and tertiary stress on the unaccented syllables of words with three or more syllables, like *secretary*, *satisfactory*, *temperament* (Dobson, 2: 445–6), which is still the characteristic American pattern. But the third edition of Sheridan's *Dictionary* (1780, liv–lv) indicates that the plosive accentuation and suppression of secondary accents had already begun to appear in elite London pronunciation. Sheridan criticized the "too great precipitancy of utterance that leads to indistinct articulation": "This fault is so general, that I would recommend it to all who are affected by it, to pronounce the unaccented syllables more fully than necessary, till they are cured of it."

This staccato stress pattern made the intonation more peremptory. It affected Webster's attitude toward Virginia pronunciation. In his *Dissertations* (1789, quoted by Krapp 1925, 2: 18) he writes:

> People of large fortunes, who pride themselves on family distinction, possess a certain boldness, dignity and independence in their manner, which gives a corresponding air to their mode of speaking. Those who

are accustomed to command slaves, form a habit of expressing themselves with a tone of authority and decision.

In New England, where there are few slaves and servants, and less family distinctions than in any part of America, people are accustomed to address each other with diffidence, or attention to the opinions of others, which marks a state of equality. Instead of commanding, they advise.

Webster was here defending New England pronunciation against what he perceived as the more peremptory intonation of the Virginia elite. The Virginia elite were, however, British aristocracy, often educated in England, who preserved the intonation patterns of RP (Fischer 226, 263).

2.8.3   Rhotacism and nonrhotacism

Of the eighteenth-century developments, loss of postvocalic [r] (nonrhotacism) is the most interesting. This is a very obvious dialect marker both in America, where it distinguishes the pronunciation of eastern New England, New York City, and the Tidewater South from that of the rest of the country, and England, where it distinguishes the pronunciation of RP classes and all classes in rural dialects in East Anglia (Wells 1: 104, 220; Kurath 1965, 105–7).

In England nonrhotacism is the prestige norm, whereas in America rhotacism is the majority pronunciation in prestigious use. There is disagreement among historians as to when and under what circumstances the [r] was dropped in England. Dobson in the most authoritative history of pronunciation up to 1700 has little to say about [r]-dropping because "it is seldom recorded before 1700 and then only in sources that reflect vulgar speech" (2: 992). The dropping is first recorded, with lengthening of the preceding vowel, in John Walker's rhyming dictionary of 1775, and discussed in his pronouncing dictionary of 1791. However, Dobson (2: 967–8) finds [r] lost before [s] and [š] without lengthening of the vowel (*burst/bust, curse/cuss, horse/hoss*) from 1300 onwards, and Krapp (1925, 2: 222) finds this early loss without lengthening a vulgarism that continues into present English. In the subsequent eighteenth-century development, [r] was not simply dropped but was replaced by lengthening of the preceding vowel followed by schwa (Dobson 2: 992); and this is the pronunciation that became characteristic of RP.

Krapp (1925, 2: 219–24) finds many instances of the early loss of [r] without lengthening in seventeenth-century Colonial records, so there is no question of British influence. The immigrants brought the vulgar *hoss, cuss* pronunciations with them when they arrived. The question is whether the second loss of [r] with lengthening is a native development in those areas of

America where it occurs or was adopted in imitation of fashionable London pronunciation. Krapp (1925, 2: 227) denies a diffusion of non-rhotic pronunciations from England, but Kurath (1928b; 1972, 70, 126–9) and subsequent historians argue that the loss of [r] with lengthening spread from the American port cities most closely in touch with England at the end of the eighteenth century (Kurath 1964, 16; Wells 1: 220). They find it characteristic of upper-class pronunciation in Boston, New York, and Philadelphia, and all classes in Alexandria, Charleston, and Savannah.

Labov finds pronunciation in New York City of [r] as in *hard* increases as one moves down the social scale from high- to low-class informants, and from formal to colloquial style – half of his informants being bilingual in Yiddish or Italian, in which [r] is always pronounced (Kurath 1972, 169). McDavid (1979, 139) finds that the loss of [r] spread from Charleston to the backcountry along with the spread of plantation culture. Van Riper (126–7) finds that in the Tidewater area "cultured speakers consistently lack [r]. . . . This variant has prestige. . . . Middle class speakers fluctuate uneasily." Loss of [r] is also characteristic of African-American English. There is argument about the reason for that loss. One hypothesis is that slaves learned their English from nonrhotic upper-class speakers in the Tidewater and, not being literate, accentuated this aspect of their pronunciation.

Preservation of [r] in American dialects other than eastern New England and the Tidewater thus represents a form of linguistic "lag" (Marckwardt 72) shared by most of the regional dialects in Great Britain. Wells finds [r]-dropping characteristic of accents in "the east and north of England" (1: 220), but Scotland and Ireland are rhotic (2: 407, 432) and it appears that the disappearance of [r] in the north of England is a recent, on-going phenomenon under the influence of urbanization (2: 367–70). Guy Lowman (Kurath 1939, 20) finds [r] pronounced in the western part of England from the Bristol Channel to London. East Anglian and RP are thus the only dialects in Britain that have consistently dropped [r]. By the end of the eighteenth century, nonrhotic became the prestige pronunciation in England. Dialect history and geography suggest that this prestige pronunciation may in turn have been imitated by the elites in the American port cities, and from them spread more broadly within their areas (Kurath 1972, 68–9; Wells 1: 230). The broader spread of nonrhotic pronunciation in the Tidewater area reflects greater prestige of the elite there. Kurath (1939, 17) finds postvocalic [r] still pronounced in Maine coastal towns, such as Marblehead and Rockport, where the Boston elite had less influence, and in western New England, which was settled from the northern Border areas of Britain.

The emergence of the rhotic dialect as more prestigious in the United States is a post-Civil-War phenomenon. Before the Civil War, the wealthiest and most politically powerful regions in America were nonrhotic Boston and Virginia, which were under the strongest influence by the British elite. After the Civil War, wealth and political power passed to New York, Pennsylvania, and the trans-Appalachian Middle West, which had been least under influence of the British elite. The trans-Appalachian Middle West had been settled originally by Border immigrants, whose dialects retained [r]. New York City had begun nonrhotic in the Colonial period, and that remains the pronunciation of old New York families, but the Hudson Valley was populated by the Dutch, and western New York State by settlers from inland New England, whose pronunciation retained [r] (Kurath 1972, 45).

By 1870, New York City had become a national center for entrepreneurs from all parts of the country and the portal for an enormous immigration from Europe and Ireland of speakers whose native languages were all rhotic. The economic and political leaders in New York City were increasingly self-made; its Colonial elite had much less influence than in Boston or Virginia, so that nonrhotic pronunciation lost its prestige. The fact that the Civil War was lost by nonrhotic speakers no doubt assisted in this denigration. By the time radio and television began to establish a norm of pronunciation, they favored the rhotic Middle Western pronunciation rather than the nonrhotic of Boston and Virginia.

2.8.4 Other segmental contrasts

In addition to [r]-dropping, other developments in RP and the prestige dialects of eastern New England and the Tidewater South are not found in the Appalachian and Middle Western dialects, which preserve their seventeenth-century pronunciations. One of these is lengthening of [æ] in words like *glass* and *bath*, which is advocated in Webster's 1828 dictionary. Another is the loss of initial aspiration in words like *why, whip* (Kurath 1939, 23; McDavid 1979, 182–8). A third is the loss of distinction between [ɑ] or [ɒ] and [ɔ] in words like *cot/caught*, and [ɔ] and [o] in words like *horse/hoarse*. Krapp (1925, 2: 33) accepts the development of [ty] to [č] in *future, nature, creature*, which has become general in America, as due to the influence of RP, although I would prefer to think of it as an aspect of the natural drift towards palatalization before a front vowel or glide that led to [š] in *action, nation* in early English. There are other choices made by RP that have not been adopted in American English, such as the weakening of secondary accents treated above (*secretary/sect'ry*), "smoothing" of diphthongs produced by loss of [r] (*shire* and *shower* to "sha," *tower* to "ta"), change to [aɪl] in *ile* spellings like *fertile*, *missile*. American has also had changes that are not dependent on developments in RP, like unrounding of [ɑ] in *cot* and loss of the palatal vocalic element in *duke* and *tube*.

The pronunciation of [u] rather than [yu] or the like in *duke* and *tube* is not characteristic of all American dialects. Wells (1: 247) gives [u] as a "general American" pronunciation, whereas Kurath (1939, 35) maps its area as about the same as that of rhotacism. This raises the question of how the dialects in the United States should be treated. Until work began in the 1920s on the Linguistic Atlas of the United States, only three dialects had been recognized: New England, Southern, and Midland.

2.9   Diversity and uniformity

In 1795, James Carrol observed that "the pronunciation of the Southern states of English America is almost as different from that of the New England states, even among the learned, as any two dialects of any illiterate nation" (Baron 79). James Fenimore Cooper (cited by Krapp 1925, 1: 34) thought that the best English was that used by the people of the "middle states," implying a difference from that of the northern and southern states. Allen Walker Read observes that in Colonial records every British dialect except East Anglian is recognized.

Against early recognition of dialect diversity must be set the frequent assertions by both natives and travelers of the uniformity of American colloquial English (Krapp 1925, 1: 46; Mencken 1963, 448; Dillard 1975, ch. 2). Krapp (1925, 2: 34), in contrast to later assertions by Fischer, finds that all of the seaboard settlers came from the Southern and Midland regions of England and had similar speech patterns; whatever differences there are between the Tidewater and New England today would, therefore, have developed after settlement.

These differing judgments reflect the expectations of the observers and must be compared with the judgments of Lee Pederson and others in this volume. Even today, rural dialects show much greater variation in England than in America. But Kurath, Marckwardt, and Fischer have all remarked on how few of the early British immigrants to America were rustic. Most, even the poverty-stricken Scotch-Irish, were of the artisan class or above, with some education (Fischer 614). As such, their language tended to use standard grammar and to be influenced by spelling pronunciation.

As early as 1758, the *American Magazine* advocated the teaching of English to preserve standards. It argued that, since Americans "are so great a mixture of people, from almost all corners of the world, necessarily speaking a variety of languages and dialects, the true pronunciation and writing of our language might soon be lost" (Baron 8). Marckwardt (140), Dillard (1975, ch. 2), and Francis (1961), have also argued that the communities in America were dialectal melting pots. In contrast, Kurath and especially Fischer see the dialects on the Atlantic seaboard as determined directly by the settlement history of each area. Marckwardt's generalization (Marckwardt and Quirk 64) is the most useful: that the British regional dialects are reflected in the dialects of the Atlantic seaboard, but level out almost completely west of the Appalachians. From this leveling comes the popular concept of "General American" as the dialect of the Middle West and points westward (Van Riper).

Krapp (1925, 1: 19, 35) says that, in the Colonial period and for sometime after, New England was the cynosure for American pronunciation but that now "if one were seeking what is generally apprehended as the general type of American speech one would not seek for it in New England but somewhere between the Alleghenies and the Rockies." John Kenyon took as the standard for his *American Pronunciation* (1924) the pronunciation of his native Hiram, Ohio. Fischer (888), writing in 1989, says that TV broadcasters are trained in the accent of Salt Lake City, Utah. (The movement westward from Massachusetts to Ohio to Utah is significant.)

Van Riper gives rhotacism and the "flat a" in *ask*, *grass* as the principal characteristics that distinguish "General American" from the seaboard dialects. Kurath (1972, 70) observes that these phones and the other vowels of "General American" are those of British English before the planting of the colonies. The changes of pronunciation that occurred in England after 1650 "are confined to the coastal areas: eastern New England, metropolitan New York, eastern Virginia, South Carolina, and the Gulf states."

Krapp (1925, 1: 36, 2: 29) and other commentators (Brooks 1937, 139–40; Kurath 1928b) find the dialects of New England and the Tidewater most nearly like those of "Southern England," and the rest of America most like those of "Northern England." These broad generalizations have been refined by Kurath and other dialectologists, as summarized in the sections on dialects in David Hackett Fischer's history, *Albion's Seed*. Fischer has tried to specify parallels in language (pronunciation, vocabulary, and grammar), as well as food, dress, architecture, religion, and other folkways between the areas in Britain from which the four great migrations emanated and the areas in America where they settled.

Fischer points to the significance of the name "New England." The 20,000 immigrants who settled in that area were very homogeneous; most came from a hundred-mile circle in Essex, Suffolk, and Cambridgeshire – the heart of East Anglia. Less than 10 percent came from London, and they tended to be transplanted East Anglians. Fischer examines the homogeneity of their education, intermarriages, and employment. They were highly literate: two-thirds of the males were able to sign their names as compared with one-third in the rest of England (Fischer 28–9). Most were urban and middle class; only one-third were agricultural. Their literacy would have been that of the London-based educated class; they would have spoken in a relatively homogeneous East Anglian dialect.

Krapp (1925, 2: 24) quotes contemporary sources that compare the New England drawl with that of Essex, and Fischer has a long comparison of the "Yankee twang" and "Norfolk whine." This twang, however, must have been modulated in cultivated New England speech by the tendency of the elite to adopt the voice quality of RP as it developed. Indeed several of the characteristics Fischer lists for the New England dialect are those that became characteristic of RP: dropping of [r] in "Haava'd"; loss of aspiration in *whale*; staccato reduction of *Sweden* to "Swed'n." In this connection, it is interesting that Dobson (1: 149) cites documents written in Norfolk, Suffolk, and Essex as providing the earliest evidence of "Modern English sound-changes" (that is, RP changes). Clearly the immigrants to eastern New England brought with them tendencies that in England, 100 years later, led to the British prestige pronunciations.

Some of the Colonial New England misspellings listed by Fischer, *har* for *hair*, *hev* for *have*, *yistidy* for *yesterday*, *kiver* for *cover*, are Colonial spellings also found in Virginia and Appalachian records. This generally distributed evidence led Krapp (1925, 2: 25–35) to infer a widespread, relaxed Colonial pronunciation that was made more precise in the eighteenth century under the influence of spelling and elocution.

Fischer describes the settlers in the Chesapeake Bay area and Virginia as very different from those of Massachusetts. The 40,000 to 50,000 immigrants to the middle colonies were led by a small handful of Cavaliers from families that had lived within a day's drive of London or Bristol. These Cavaliers were deeded large tracts of land in Virginia on which they established a culture as close to the British manorial system as they could. As late as 1860, the South had one-third of the white population of the United States but two-thirds of the richest people in the country (Fischer 854) and some of the best educated. The Cavalier elite stayed very closely in touch with England. The reason they had no need to create prestige academies and universities like Groton or Harvard was that, as Episcopalians, they could and did enroll in the British public schools, universities, and Inns of

Court. Very few evangelical academies were established in the Tidewater area. As a result of their continuing connections with England, the dialect of the Tidewater elite developed along the same lines as that of the London governing class. As Mathews points out (1931, 88), the Southern Colonial records are less useful to students of the language than those of New England because they were kept by people educated in England or in the British manner.

Virginia was a nearly feudal, agrarian society. Its cradle in England was the ancient territory of Wessex, comprising Wiltshire, Dorset, Somerset, Gloucestershire, Devon, Hampshire, West Sussex, Surrey, Berkshire, Oxfordshire, and Buckinghamshire. This area of England was agricultural and lightly populated, composed of large estates cultivated by tenant farmers but one step removed from serfdom (Fischer 240–3). Virginia established the same sort of society, composed of a few (perhaps 1,000) plantation owners and a mass (perhaps 30,000) of indentured servants (Fischer 210–28), who were largely illiterate field workers. The rural areas from which they came had different dialects, but the servants were not sufficiently cohesive or self-conscious for their British regional dialects to become distinguishable in the Tidewater.

Both Fischer and Kurath (1972, 68–9) describe the Tidewater as a culture in which the elite set the standards, including the standard language, which was emulated with increasing variation as it went down the social scale. That emulation led to the loss of the postvocalic [r] as a regional trait more widespread than in New England, but also to the retention of Colonial pronunciations cited by Krapp (1925, 2: 34–5) like "bust" for *burst*, "gjarden" for *garden*, "ceow" for *cow*, "min" for *men*, "haid" for *head*, "Sairy" for *Sarah*, "feller" for *fellow*, "hant" for *haunt*, "bile" for *boil*, "far" for *fire*, "runnin" for *running*, "lan" for *land*, "pos" for *post*. Such pronunciations were replaced in RP and the cultivated dialects in America by spelling pronunciations, but retained by the illiterate classes so that they have come to characterize Southern colloquial speech. Actually, according to Krapp (1925, 2: 35), they represent general English colloquial speech of the sixteenth and seventeenth centuries, which the immigrants brought over with them from the rural counties of South England. Because of class distinctions in education and living standards, the differences in the dialects of the elite and nonelite were more marked in the Tidewater than in other areas of the United States.

The North Midland dialect area, as it has been defined by the Linguistic Atlas, corresponds to the Delaware Valley and Pennsylvania destination of Fischer's third migration (470), led by the Quakers. This was ethnically the

least homogeneous of the migrations to America. It began fairly homogeneously: as many as 23,000 colonists settled in the Delaware Valley between
1675 and 1725, largely from the North Midland area of England. But of
these, only about 2,000 were Quakers "in good standing," and the rest were
sympathizing "attendants" (Fischer 423). The Quakers were much more
comfortable with ethnic pluralism than were settlers in New England and
Virginia. From the first they welcomed sympathizers from Wales, Ireland,
Holland, Germany, and France. Philadelphia never had a majority of
Quakers, but attracted the "human flotsam and jetsam that washed ashore
in every seaport" (Fischer 424) – like Benjamin Franklin, no doubt. By
1760, settlers from southern England were in a minority, having been outnumbered by the influx from the Continent and North Britain.

Despite being a minority, the Quakers controlled the government
in Pennsylvania until 1755, and their economic and political views shaped
the colony and eventually the Constitution of the United States. Most of
the Quakers came from the artisan class, lower than the Puritans and the
Virginia elite, but higher than the Virginia servants. Their view of order
rejected social hierarchy (Virginia) and obligatory unity (New England) in
favor of personal independence and mutual forbearance. The Quakers'
refusal to take the oath of conformity and pay tithes to the Church of
England had led to 60,000 imprisonments and 5,000 executions in England
after the Restoration (1661–85), and it was this milieu they had come to
America to escape. They did not encourage tenancy; their laws favored the
distribution of wealth; property was evenly distributed among children;
they were the first to abolish slavery (1758); their ideal of liberty was reciprocal: do unto others as you would have others do unto you. This was their
chief contribution to the philosophy of justice in the United States. They
were able artisans and merchants but had little interest in education or
higher culture. They contributed little to the American Revolution itself,
but a great deal to the establishment of the new order after the Revolution
was over (Fischer 828).

This culture, particularly after it was inundated by the North British
immigration (1717–75), was the cradle for typical American speech – that
often called "General American." Fischer's section (470–5) on the parallels
between the British and American Midland dialects is the least persuasive
of his linguistic discussions. The parallels in pronunciation are those that
Kurath asserts were established in England before the planting of the colonies, before the changes that began to occur in England after 1700, which
influenced the coastal areas of New England and the Tidewater. The
vocabulary Fischer cites tends, likewise, to be nondistinctive.

The final migration from Britain to America is that of the northern Borderers to the trans-Appalachian back country, 1717–75. This was the most numerous migration, some 275,000, versus 20,000 Puritans, 40,000 Cavaliers, and 23,000 Quakers. Of course, by the time Britons from the north arrived, the other three groups had increased greatly in number. Nevertheless, the immigrants from the north of England, the north of Ireland, and Lowland Scotland formed the nucleus of the populations in those parts of the United States whose speechways are typically American. Fischer goes to some length to explain the unsettled situation in Britain that caused this mass exodus. He rejects the usual designation for these people as Scotch-Irish, arguing with persuasive demographic evidence (608–9) that as many departed from Merseyside, Clydebank, and other ports in North Britain and Scotland as from Belfast, Londonderry, and other ports in Ulster.

Unlike the earlier emigrants from the Midlands and south of England, who were on the whole people of substance, motivated by religious and social ideals, the Borderers were economic refugees who felt no nostalgia for the old country. They were the most disorderly inhabitants of areas in Britain that had been disordered for 700 years. They came from the crofter class, which had never had property and so, unlike the emigrants from south Britain, they had no property to bring with them. But they were extremely proud and self-reliant; less than 20 percent came as indentured servants. Their poverty and pride set the tone for Middle America.

Most of the Borderers entered the country through Philadelphia, which was at that time the most receptive port for refugees of any kind. But the good land was already taken, so the new arrivals were not welcomed as settlers in the Delaware Valley. They were immediately shuffled through to the backcountry of Pennsylvania and New England – and especially down the Shenandoah Valley to the backcountry of Virginia and North and South Carolina, which at that time comprised West Virginia, Tennessee, and Kentucky. In the census of 1790, 60 percent of the surnames in Appalachia were Scotch-Irish (Fischer 634).

Upon arrival in Philadelphia, the Borderers must have spoken various dialects (Merseyside, Cumberland, Northumberland, Westmorland, Dumfrieshire, and Ulster, which is today much like Dublin), but there is no evidence of any of these accents in the American koiné they very quickly adopted. In 1722, the *Virginia Gazette* advertised for the whereabouts of an African slave named Jack who spoke "the Scotch-Irish dialect" (Fischer 652). The question is whether this meant simply *not* Tidewater, or whether there was, in 1772, a distinguishable Scotch-Irish accent. Fischer (653–5) cites parallel archaisms found in Appalachian dialect glossaries and in dialect glossaries of Cumberland and Westmorland, which may point to some direct connection, but the grammatical forms are widespread in the Southern vulgate, and, significantly, Fischer has nothing at all to say about pronunciation in this section. Later in his book (831–2) he refers to the similarities between Appalachian English and the southern British English of Cromwell's time – which is not Border dialect.

We may safely conclude that the Colonial koiné posited by Dillard was created by the migrant population of British Northerners, together with the English, Welsh, Germans, and other immigrants who moved westward from Philadelphia and the Tidewater in the eighteenth century. They felt no nostalgia for a British culture with which they had had little connection. They had never had any but unpleasant relations with the British ruling class that was creating RP. Their frontier life provided little incentive or opportunity for education. By 1860, 94 percent of the population in the northern United States was literate and the school year was 135 days, whereas in the Appalachian region 54 percent were literate and the school year was 80 days (Fischer 855). The backcountry libraries were elementary compared with those on the seaboard. Their common language was not controlled by the written tradition but was strictly oral.

2.10   British and American interrelations

This, then, is the society in which American dialects evolved. These dialects have, essentially, the intonation pattern and pronunciations of colloquial dialects of the commercial classes in England before 1700. Their grammar is essentially that of Chancery English, which had been standardized in the fifteenth century by the governing and commercial classes and used by creative writers who were members of these classes (Fisher 1996). Written Chancery English began to be ascertained and fixed in dictionaries and textbooks as English began to be taught in schools. This standard written language was, and still is, taught in American schools with greater or less effect, depending on the length of the school year and the literacy of the population.

In the eighteenth century the ruling class in and around London began to standardize an oral dialect which, in the nineteenth century, became the prestige oral English dialect throughout the world. This Received Pronunciation influenced the elite populations of the seaboard cities in America, and produced distinguishable dialects in eastern New England and the Tidewater South – especially the dropping of the postvocalic [r]. But these prestige influences did not affect the common dialects of the backcountry settlers, who continued to develop their pre-1700 pronunciations and intonation patterns.

Important early arguments about the continuity versus discontinuity of American and British English are the works of George Philip Krapp (1925) and H. L. Mencken (1919 through 1963), whose theses are stated in the titles of their books, respectively: *The English Language in America* and *The American Language*. Arguments for the continuity of British and American English are set forth by Cleanth Brooks (1935, 1985), Hans Kurath (1928b, 1965), Kurath and Raven I. McDavid (1961), and David Hackett Fischer (1989). John Hurt Fisher (1996) has treated the common origin of British and American standard English. Allen Walker Read (1933, 1935, 1938, 1979, 2001) has examined the historical relationship between the two national varieties. John Algeo (1986, 1988a, 1989a, 1989b, 1990, 1995, 1996) has treated contemporary differences and interrelations. Albert H. Marckwardt and Randolph Quirk (1964) present an overview of the issue in dialog.

3 BRITISH AND IRISH ANTECEDENTS

Michael Montgomery

3.1 Introduction

From the time it became a secure sea-lane following the collapse of the Spanish Armada in the late 1580s until well into the twentieth century, the North Atlantic brought people from all parts of the British Isles to a new life in what became the United States. Emigrants represented a broad sampling of lower and middling ranks, but few at either extreme of the social spectrum, as the latter lacked either the motivation or the means to come. These emigrants usually came voluntarily and were often accompanied by fewer material possessions than such intangibles as their hopes and beliefs. They included tens of thousands of indentured servants who sold years of labor for passage and sometimes training in a trade. Involuntary emigrants included London paupers and orphans and Irish military transportees in the seventeenth century and convicts in the eighteenth, but in proportion far fewer than to Australia and other British colonies.

Whatever their station and however meager their belongings, all emigrants brought their speech habits, usually untutored ones. Some were bilingual in a Celtic language, but with few exceptions and in ways reflecting the distinct history and culture of their regional origins, these people spoke either English or Scots (the latter being the close sibling to English that achieved national, autonomous status as the literary and governmental language of Scotland in the sixteenth century). In the American Colonial period, these newcomers arrived along a 1,200-mile seaboard, establishing beachheads and slowly beginning to penetrate the interior in a process that constituted, according to Bernard Bailyn (1986a, 4–5):

> . . . a mighty flow that transformed at first half the globe, ultimately the whole of it, more fundamentally than any development except the Industrial Revolution. This transforming phenomenon was the

86

movement of people out from their original centers of habitation – the centrifugal *Völkerwanderung* that involved an untraceable multitude of local, small-scale exoduses and colonizations, the continuous creation of new frontiers and ever-widening circumferences, the complex intermingling of peoples in the expanding border areas, and in the end the massive transfer to the Western Hemisphere of people from Africa, from the European mainland, and above all from the Anglo-Celtic offshore islands of Europe, culminating in what Bismarck called "the most decisive fact in the modern world," the peopling of the North American continent.

Emigrants embarking at major ports (especially London, Bristol, and later, Liverpool) came from large catchment areas and were quite heterogeneous, the result of internal migration from the countryside that involved far more people in early modern times than those who sailed west. Though often prompted by economic cycles or political and religious conditions at home, the transoceanic movement was near continuous, driven constantly by a desire for land. It varied widely in destination and in point of origin. Seldom did people from one part of the British Isles head to only one region of North America; even less often did any part of the continent newly opening to Europeans receive settlers from only one or two areas of the old country. Most colonies saw migrants converging from many parts of the British Isles and elsewhere, the result of which was a multilingual, multidialectal landscape that linguists and historians are only gradually coming to understand. Emigrants saw themselves as participants in local or regional streams, often heading where networks of compatriots or family could provide contact and support. Movement in and out of communities was frequent, especially in the middle colonies of New York, New Jersey, Pennsylvania, and Delaware, in cities, and in interior parts that came to be known collectively as the "backcountry." Early settlers were nothing if not mobile – indeed, a desire for mobility had usually motivated their coming.

Within this highly fluid and varied frame of reference we can begin to appreciate the complexities that accompanied the transplantation of English to North America, a long-term process in which the input of different elements and influences, along with ensuing social dynamics and contacts with other languages, had profound and formative effects on American speech patterns and produced new varieties of the language that together became identified as American English. Understanding the character and evolution of American English, as well as its regional differences and much else of interest to linguists, cultural historians, and others, rests, among other things, on an adequate account of its antecedents from the British Isles. But while emigrant language habits must have contributed to the development and differentiation of American English in crucial ways, scholars have found this difficult to establish in great detail or to relate to later varieties. Indeed, the extent of antecedents has been debated vigorously and some scholars have doubted that regional British English had any significant role in producing varieties of American English as we know them today.

Americans, academicians and laypeople alike, have had a long interest in the history and diversity of their speech, evidence of a desire to trace their ancestors and to establish their roots. This interest has often manifested itself in less than objective ways, as in the wistful seeking of "Elizabethan" or "Shakespearean" elements in the English of the Southern mountains or elsewhere. Identifying the sources of American English occasionally captures popular attention.

Presentations have usually relied on traditional scholarship, especially such works of linguistic geography as Kurath's *Word Geography of the Eastern United States* (1949), which offers the broadest picture of American speech regions. His formulation was visionary (§ 3.5.3), but provided only a tentative outline. That it remained dominant for so long testifies to its comprehensiveness and the fact that for years other American scholars gave little attention to the antecedents of American English. Rather than furthering Kurath's efforts to map features of American English and associate them with settlement history, other dialect geographers turned their energies to collecting, collating, and editing material, realizing that much basic description was necessary before systematic comparisons could be attempted.

As more was learned about the dynamics of dialect contact, socially motivated language change, and the quantitative analysis of language variation, even Kurath's attempts to specify transatlantic connections seemed piecemeal and lacked an adequate conceptual framework. To formulate a fuller and more adequate account of antecedents, scholars needed new tools and reference works, more sophisticated methodological and analytical approaches, and more data from earlier periods. These might enable what Kurath envisaged: the description of English close to the Colonial period and then the tracing of it along the emigrant trail to seventeenth- and eighteenth-century British English. However, over the past two decades scholars have again taken up the challenge of identifying antecedents and assessing their role in the formation of regional and social varieties of American English.

3.2 Background

3.2.1 Emigrant streams and their languages

An understanding of emigrants and their speech requires that the entire British Isles be taken as the proper compass and the many streams within the larger flow of emigration be seen. In the seventeenth and eighteenth centuries, English, Scottish, and Irish emigration was often independent, as colonization schemes were launched from Ireland and Scotland to compete with England or to circumvent English restrictions. Emigrants were rarely ambiguous about their nationality: they were English, Welsh, Scottish (from either the Lowlands or the Highlands), or Irish (from either Ulster and usually Protestant or the south of Ireland and usually Catholic). Each group had distinct cultural traditions, religious tendencies, and so forth. The common practice of lumping them together as "Anglo" or "Anglo-Saxon" or citing only England and the English in statements about American cultural and linguistic antecedents reflects not Colonial reality, but twentieth-century misconceptions about the regional diversity of the British Isles. However unintentional, such a point of view prevents a valid assessment of the subject.

A majority of European emigrants in the Colonial period were indeed English, but perhaps as many as one-fifth were Irish (D. Doyle) and tens of thousands were Scottish. Because of restrictions on Scottish commerce until the Union of the Parliaments in 1707 and on Irish commerce until the Act of Union in 1801, much emigration from outside England was unofficial and undocumented, not always discernible within the larger British movement to North America. Moreover, because Irish and Scottish emigrants often had English names, their numbers have routinely been underestimated in the literature, which is usually based on surname research (*Surnames in the United States Census* 1932).

With few exceptions, emigrants from the British Isles had one of six different linguistic profiles: English, Lowland Scottish, Highland Scottish, Irish, Scotch-Irish (Protestants from Ulster mainly of Lowland Scottish background), and Welsh (Thernstrom). Of these, the English (who were sometimes distinguished by region, as "west country," "Yorkshire," etc.) and the Scotch-Irish came in greatest numbers in the Colonial period and influenced American English most significantly. The contributions of the English were the most general and have been the longest recognized; though hypothesized by Kurath, the contributions of the Scotch-Irish have been identified only recently, but it is not too much to say that they shaped the linguistic geography of the United States more than any other group from the British Isles.

Lack of awareness of how greatly Irish and Scotch-Irish varieties of English differed from British ones derives from a paucity of research and reference works on them, along with much greater awareness of varieties from England, especially as attested in literature. Even the *English Dialect Dictionary* (J. Wright) provides a relatively faint picture of the diversity of English in the British Isles, especially in grammar. For all these reasons, the present essay surveys British (English and Scottish) and Irish antecedents of American English. Not only can Irish streams of English be distinguished, but they had a significant impact on American varieties of the language, contributing items directly from Ireland, through Ireland from Scotland, and as loan translations from Irish Gaelic.

The English emigrated to North America most frequently and for the longest time, and the greater part of British emigration for the first century of settlement was from southeast England, including London. They settled everywhere and were seldom in the minority anywhere (Pennsylvania and the backcountry of Virginia and the Carolinas in the eighteenth century were the principal exceptions). They were also the most internally heterogeneous; significant numbers originating in southern, eastern, midland, and northern England brought their speech to the colonies and contributed to new varieties of English being formed. The influence of English emigrants was especially profound on American English pronunciation (Lass 1990) and generally on the speech of New England and the Lower South, particularly Virginia.

Emigrants from Ireland, Scotland, and Wales came in extraordinary proportion to their home populations – 6 to 7 million from Ireland in the course of more than three centuries (K. Miller), 1.5 million from Scotland (G. Donaldson 908), and perhaps 150,000 from Wales (Berthoff), all conservative estimates. The trickle of settlers from each of these lands in the seventeenth century enlarged to a flow in the eighteenth, when they found coastal areas largely settled and tended to move inland. The bulk of each of these groups came in the nineteenth century, when passage to North America became much cheaper, easier, and quicker. Those from Ireland and Scotland were linguistically as well as regionally diverse. Some were Celtic monolinguals (such as nineteenth-century famine emigrants from southern and western Ireland), but most were either monolingual in English or Scots or bilingual in a Celtic language and a Celtic-influenced variety of English or Scots (Montgomery 2000a). Except for the Welsh, their literacy was only in English.

Scots have emigrated to North America since the seventeenth century in two broad divisions, Scots-speaking Lowlanders and Scottish Gaelic-speaking Highlanders. Their arrival often overlapped after the 1730s but differed in other respects, with the more numerous Lowlanders often coming as individuals and settling throughout the colonies (Graham). At its extreme, the vernacular Scots spoken by Lowlanders differed markedly from English – used throughout Scotland for official purposes – but the two language varieties formed a continuum that emigrants would already have mastered to one degree or another. This allowed them to shift easily to English and, with few exceptions, eroded any awareness of Scottish linguistic identity within a short time of migration.

Highland Scots, who often had Scottish Gaelic as their mother tongue but were usually bilingual in English, formed the most concentrated group of Celtic-language speakers to come to mainland North America. They tended to emigrate together, facilitated by their clan or extended-family system. Tens of thousands began settling the Cape Fear Valley of southeastern North Carolina in 1739 in a migration that lasted well after the American Civil War, with the last Gaelic speaker dying in the 1950s. The unique settlement and linguistic history of this area has long been recognized (MacLean; Meyer; J. MacDonald; Kelly), but the influence of Scottish Gaelic on the local English appears to have been minimal.

It was the trauma of the mid-nineteenth-century potato famine that spurred the most intense and memorable exodus from Ireland, but in no decade of the last three-and-a-half centuries have Irish emigrants not come, voluntarily or involuntarily, to North America (K. Miller). Almost anywhere one examines the Colonial labor force in North America, the Irish can be found. The earliest, such as Cromwellian transportees to Virginia in the 1650s, were most likely Irish monolinguals and few in number. Those going to more northerly areas in Colonial days were more numerous and were usually speakers of Ulster-Scots or Ulster-English.

Historians usually divide Irish emigration from the beginning of the eighteenth century into two broad streams. A quarter of a million people, mainly from Ulster, came between 1718 and 1776 (Leyburn; R. Dickson). Most of them (called "Ulster Scots" or "Scots-Irish" in Ireland and "Scotch-Irish" in America) were of Lowland Scottish ancestry and culture, their forebears having crossed the channel from southwestern Scotland to the Plantation of Ulster, which began in 1610 (a settlement that also brought numbers from northern and western England). In America the great majority of Scotch-Irish landed in Delaware or Pennsylvania and soon headed to frontier areas, reaching the interior of Virginia in the 1730s and the Carolinas in the 1750s. They and their descendants settled and were culturally dominant in much of the interior or Upper South – the Carolinas, Georgia, Tennessee, and Kentucky – within two generations.

After the American Revolution ended in 1783, emigrants came more broadly from throughout Ireland and were increasingly Catholics from the south and west. By the 1830s large numbers were settling in Boston, New York City, Philadelphia, and other metropolitan areas. They spoke English, Irish, or often both, their English heavily influenced by Irish. Though it numbered in the millions, the second stream of Irish had far less influence on American English than that from Ulster, because nowhere did it have cultural dominance.

Like the Irish and Scots, the Welsh came as early as the seventeenth century. In 1681 a group of Welsh Quakers was assigned a tract of land outside Philadelphia, but not until the mid 1800s did compatriots arrive in appreciable numbers, in organized parties to New York, Pennsylvania, and the Midwest. Because the Welsh language was maintained more vigorously than other Celtic languages in the British Isles, a larger proportion of Welsh emigrants were monolingual (and also literate) than were their Irish and Scottish counterparts. Except as a language of the church, Welsh rarely outlasted the first generation of settlers. Of the six emigrant streams, the Welsh was the smallest and the latest, and it had the least impact on American English. Where possible, the *Dictionary of American Regional English* (Cassidy and Hall) indicates the etymological or geographical provenance of its entries, relying mainly on the *English Dialect Dictionary* (J. Wright) and the *Scottish National Dictionary* (Grant and Murison). In the first three volumes of *DARE* (letters *A–O*), 147 items are identified as from Ireland, 519 from Scotland, more than 1,400 from England, but only one from Wales (*flummery*, from Welsh *llymru* 'a gelatinous porridge made from oatmeal or flour'). A further assessment of Irish and Scottish contributions to American English is in § 3.6.6.

3.2.2   Early relations between British and American English

Varieties of English from the British Isles have been antecedents of American English from the first permanent planting of English colonists in Virginia at Jamestown in 1607, continuing into the nineteenth century, when British and American usage competed in educated circles and among the literati, and until the present day, when Briticisms still find their way into mainstream American speech (Algeo 1990–5). Even so, American English began to be distinguished in the early days of Colonial life, particularly in its lexical borrowings from Amerindian languages. Mathews (1936, 4) states that these began as early as 1619, when a London schoolmaster commented on American use of *maize* and *canoe*. In 1754, an Englishman suggested that a glossary of such Americanisms should be compiled (Read 1933, 313). After the American Revolution, regional and social varieties from the British Isles had only minor influence on American popular speech.

American English has four principal components. The largest is the core of American English – its common vocabulary, principal grammatical paradigms, and basic sound system – corresponding for the most part to the general or standard English of the British Isles. On the other hand, much of American English, especially its vocabulary, is traceable to contact with African, Amerindian, or other European languages in the Colonial period and after, making it, with little doubt, the variety of English with the most varied constituency. A third component consists of internal developments not resulting from contact with other languages, to be found especially in word-stock, word formation, phraseology, semantics, and the like. A fourth component of American English is the particular domain of this chapter: features originating in regional or social varieties of Britain or Ireland, many of which continued evolving in North America.

Commentators identified two main aspects of the recently settled continent's English (Read 1933). Some cited (sometimes with curiosity, more often with hostility) its novel and innovative vocabulary. Others noted (with wonder or admiration) its apparent uniformity and purity of accent. Novelties included borrowings from Amerindian tongues and European languages with which English speakers had contact, such as French and Dutch, new coinages, and extensions of words to new senses (Mencken 1936 remains the best general treatment of this subject).

These additions came about for utilitarian reasons, most being nouns for topographical, zoological, botanical, and other items for which no other ready label was available. Newcomers marveled at the exotic fauna of the North American fields and forests, but commentators as early as John Smith in Jamestown were also intrigued by the un-English sounding names given such objects by native tribes. Among early adoptions from Amerindian languages were *raccoon*, *wampum*, and *tomahawk*; fully "half of all the 300 or so American Indian loanwords current today entered the language in the seventeenth century" (Carver 1992, 134). Emphasis on the uniformity and purity of American English is more surprising, and scholars have not reached consensus on interpreting commentary like the following by the Englishman William Eddis in 1770 (cited by Read 1933, 323):

> In England, almost every county is distinguished by a peculiar dialect;
> even different habits, and different modes of thinking, evidently
> discriminate inhabitants, whose local situation is not far remote; but in
> Maryland, and throughout adjacent provinces, it is worthy of note that a

striking similarity of speech universally prevails; and it is strictly true, that the pronunciation of the generality of the people has an accuracy and elegance, that cannot fail of gratifying the most judicious ear. . . . This uniformity of language prevails not only on the coast, where Europeans form a considerable mass of the people, but likewise in interior parts, where population has made slow advances.

3.3 Research questions and considerations

Answering the research questions "What are the British and Irish antecedents of American English?" and "What role did these play in the formation of American dialects?" is prerequisite to investigating many other issues in the development and differentiation of American English, such as "How did varieties of American English originate?" "How and why do they differ today?" "What are the distinctive features of American English in comparison to other extraterritorial varieties of the language?" and even "What components of Anglophone creoles can be traced to British or Irish input?" Because it involved many varieties of English and extensive, long-term contact with other languages and cultures, the transplantation of English to North America represents one of the most fertile, yet relatively uncultivated, fields for exploring processes of language contact. Such extraordinarily broad research questions have prerequisites of their own, similar to other areas of historical and comparative linguistics. Before examining what is known about British and Irish antecedents of American English, we will identify four issues with which all researchers must deal.

(1) The Reconstruction Issue: What historical data is used? What earlier form or forms of English are reconstructed for the purpose of transatlantic comparison? Not infrequently popular commentators take the simplest approach to antecedents by comparing modern speech from Britain or Ireland (F. Griffith) directly to American speech (a given variety or, in general) and asserting that commonalities between the two represent influence from the former on the latter. Valid connections require data approximating the Colonial period – optimally documentation of input varieties brought by emigrants and of the persistence of features thereafter. To the extent possible, then, careful internal reconstruction should precede comparative reconstruction. Reconstruction is a two-sided issue, requiring evidence of earlier varieties of British and Irish English as well as American ones.

(2) The Demography Issue: What demographic and historical information on migration and settlement supports the transatlantic comparison of

English? How is this information evaluated? Research on antecedents of American English requires that reconstructed data be understood within proper sociohistorical contexts (specific communities) and, to support the transmission of language, that the right people be in the right place at the right time. In identifying the settlers of an area, especially its dominant groups, and in profiling which languages and dialects were used (for many of which evidence may be circumstantial), the researcher seeks to reconstruct speech communities from an earlier period. This requires drawing on the often vast and disparate literature of social history, demography, and other disciplines to establish a historical connection between groups having the linguistic features at issue.

(3) The Data Issue: How is data for transatlantic comparison selected and validated? What are the best features to analyze? How are the sources of that data evaluated? The investigator of possible connections between British or Irish English and American usage should first attempt to "regionalize" or "localize" each linguistic item or feature in the British Isles as appropriate for comparison, that is, determine the extent to which it is characteristic of, but also is confined to and diagnostic of, a regional or social variety there. This involves establishing its currency and dominance in a particular variety or region. What area or varieties is the data characteristic of or distinctive to? To what extent were seventeenth- and eighteenth-century dialects identifiable as geographical or social entities? The researcher should rule out possibilities, consistent with demographic information, that an item came from elsewhere; the more closely it can be regionalized, the easier and better the comparison.

(4) The Generalization Issue: How can generalizations be drawn from comparisons of individual features? What inferences does the comparison permit? Addressing the Reconstruction and Data Issues ensures that a researcher has data that, although inevitably fragmentary and imperfect, is as valid as possible for comparison. The Demography Issue requires a researcher to adduce detailed, authoritative support from population movement for a transatlantic connection. The Generalization Issue concerns the extent to which a researcher, having addressed the other three, is in a position to make a statement about British and Irish antecedents. Correlations of individual features are sometimes easy (second-plural pronoun *yous*, found mainly in the northeastern urban United States, is traceable to nineteenth-century Irish emigrants), but correlations of varieties is a different matter, a long-term goal achievable only with many qualifications, if at all. How does a researcher move from the atomistic comparison of specific forms to assembling seemingly unrelated data into a coherent picture?

These issues present fundamental challenges for any scholar working on what Wakelin (1988) terms the "archaeology" of English. In theory, research on antecedents begins inductively by identifying the complexities with specific linguistic features and communities, with the goal of framing these within a general, comparative picture. Detailed description precedes comparison (research has often examined individual features, but rarely using extensive data from emigrant varieties of English reconstructed from the Colonial period). Data is evaluated with caution and its status or currency identified, if possible. Too often, however, researchers have posited transatlantic connections from superficial similarities between later varieties, rudimentary knowledge of migration and settlement, or meager data of doubtful merit. Too rarely do they discuss and justify their methodological principles (Montgomery 1989; Clarke 1997).

3.4   Sources of Colonial American English

Identifying British and Irish antecedents presupposes knowledge of seventeenth- and eighteenth-century spoken English from the British Isles and the American colonies or an approximation of it. Evidence from this transitional period comes in many written forms, none of which can be discounted if scholars are to tackle successfully "the most acute problem of all language historians, namely the lack of evidence of the spoken language of the past" (Rissanen 1994, 183). Any attempt to describe the English of the Colonial period must carefully evaluate different sources, identify their strengths and limitations, and use them advisedly to piece information together. Internal reconstruction is complicated by the fact that the farther back the researcher travels, the fewer are the materials revealing anything of speech; this is reflected in Mitford Mathews's anthology *The Beginnings of American English* (1931), an invaluable compilation of early essays, reports, and glossaries, but all postdating the Colonial period. Scholars should seek consistencies between sources and examine the total weight of evidence when possible, but many linguistic forms occur in only one type of source, as in a grammarian's proscriptions, and they present a conundrum for interpretation.

All written sources veil speech in one way or another. This section examines five types of sources for reconstructing Colonial American speech (H. Alexander 1925; Sen 1978; Jacob Bennett; Cooley 1992). Sources not surveyed include dictionaries having eighteenth-century material (Grose 1790, *EDD*, and *DARE*) and such early American linguistic works as treatises on spelling reform and attempts at phonetic alphabets (Grandgent 1899;

Stevens; F. Johnson). The first three types of sources (observations of travelers, comments of lexicographers and grammarians, and literary representations of speech) are secondary, the last two (poetic rhymes and texts) are primary. The first three are self-consciously produced, containing only forms salient to their authors, who tend to cite the unusual and the archaic rather than the typical, even when generalizing. Texts – municipal records, private letters, and the like – are less useful for lexical comparison, but sometimes reveal widespread patterns of grammar and pronunciation. When they come from less skilled writers, their language is least self-conscious, closer to speech, and therefore of the highest value. A problem with all sources, but less so with texts, is determining the currency of the features they show.

3.4.1 Popular observations by outsiders

An extraordinary variety of people (clergymen, journalists, explorers) toured or sojourned in the American colonies or the newly developing nation and then wrote of their experiences and impressions of local people, occasionally commenting also on the speech they heard (Read 1933; Mathews 1936). Usually from the mother country and reflecting a decidedly British frame of reference, they cited the unexpected in what they encountered, most often novel vocabulary or the relatively uniform accents of Americans in contrast to their homeland. To Eddis's comment that "the pronunciation of the generality of the people has an accuracy and elegance" (§ 3.2.2) we may add two others, the first from the journal of the Derbyshireman Nicholas Cresswell, who wrote on July 19, 1777 (Read 1933, 323):

> Though the inhabitants of this Country are composed of different
> Nations and different languages, yet it is very remarkable that they in
> general speak better English than the English do. No County or
> Colonial dialect is to be distinguished here, except it be the New
> Englanders, who have a sort of whining cadence that I cannot describe.

The second is from Jonathan Boucher, an Anglican priest in Maryland who, in a glossary of American terms published in 1800, wrote to British readers (Read 1933, 328):

> I ought perhaps to except [from the universal prevalence of dialect] the
> United States of America, in which dialect is hardly known; unless some
> scanty remains of the croaking, gutteral idioms of the Dutch, still
> observable in New York; the Scotch-Irish, as it used to be called, in

some of the back settlers of the Middle States; and the whining, canting drawl brought by some republican, Oliverian and Puritan emigrants from the West of England, and still kept up by their unregenerated descendants of New England – may still be called dialects.

From such observers we can but glimpse Colonial speech. Their comments are brief, vague, sweeping, and subjective, almost never identifying features, but revealing perceptions and an earlier day's attitudes about which groups were stigmatized. They suggest less about the observed than the observers' expectations, less about variation in North America than in Britain, where dialects would have been much more divergent in the eighteenth century, as they are today. To what do their observations about "dialect" pertain? Because visitors to a new locale often notice the intonation of speakers first, the comments of Colonial observers are, not surprisingly, often of this kind and doubtless refer to the cadence and more monotonic quality of American speech when compared to that of the old country. In singling out the "whining cadence" of New England speech, Cresswell apparently perceived other varieties as not distinctive from one another.

Though limited and often reflecting prejudices and misconceptions, commentary from observers provides contemporary evidence on differences in speech and deserves closer and more systematic scrutiny from scholars. Dillard (1975) has used it, but only to cite comments about uniformity in arguing that dialect differences were, for all intents and purposes, leveled in Colonial North America. In implicit rebuttal to Dillard, Cooley (1992, 184) resolves "the apparent contradiction in the evidence asserting simultaneous uniformity and diversity in early American English ... without having to question or evaluate the observational powers of any commentator or having to dismiss any kind of evidence" and concludes that "it seems likely that incipient language varieties were developing throughout early American English; they simply were consciously recognized by some people and not by others" (§ 3.5.4).

3.4.2   Commentary of grammarians and lexicographers

Commentary from contemporary language specialists (grammarians, orthoepists, compilers of spelling books and pronouncing dictionaries, and other self-professed authorities) also reveals attitudes toward language. With commentary from observers, this represents the principal source of evaluative and interpretive evidence on the language of the period. But these specialists cite linguistic forms and details more often than travelers and other outsiders, usually in condemning "provincialisms" or "errors." This material in America paralleled and followed a much larger stream of work in Britain (the latter being used in the colonies before American independence). Its chief aims were to draw up a canon of good, "correct" speech and inculcate this among the upwardly mobile and less secure classes, often by identifying usages (especially from Scotland) to avoid (Sundby, Bjørge, and Haugland). Only in the 1820s did a remotely comparable American tradition commence.

Noah Webster traveled widely in America and observed his compatriots' language closely, occasionally even castigating fellow New Englanders in his *Dissertations on the English Language* (1789, 104):

> Another very common error, among the yeomanry of America, and particularly in New England, is the pronouncing of *e* before *r*, like *a*, as *marcy* for mercy. This mistake must have originated principally in the name of the letter *r*, which, in most of our school books, is called *ar*. This single mistake has spread a false pronunciation of several hundred words, among millions of people.

Webster disliked provincial speech and sought uniformity in American English as a matter of national honor. Less an observer than a reformer, he usually described language to show how it could be improved, including how to "remedy the evil" cited above. He was seriously mistaken in describing that pattern, not recognizing an older pronunciation that must have been common in his day. Webster (1789, 110–11) wrote that the "middle states" had a distinct pattern of pronunciation that linguists were not to discuss again until the twentieth century:

> It is a custom very prevalent in the middle states, even among some well bred people, to pronounce *off, soft, drop, crop*, with the sound of *a, aff, saft, drap, crap*. This seems to be a foreign and local dialect; and cannot be advocated by any person who understands correct English.

Such comments as Webster's are infrequent, appearing only in the late eighteenth century. They reveal something about the social status of forms and the variants that competed with one another. Presumably any form they condemned must have been fairly widespread or had social salience, being associated with a group not esteemed by the writer. While commentary of grammarians and lexicographers about earlier American English is not voluminous, it reveals regional differences, as do explicit comments about speech in other eighteenth-century documents such as newspaper advertisements for runaway indentured servants and runaway slaves (Read 1938, 1939).

3.4.3   Literary attestations

Evidence for eighteenth-century English also comes from literary dialect, in portrayals of the speech of stock characters in drama and fiction. Literary depictions tend to have less variation than actual speech, but in contrast to the two previous types of evidence, they provide forms in linguistic contexts and offer the highest concentration of dialect features, as in this excerpt from a 1737 letter representing the speech of an Ulster-Scot emigrant to New York (Montgomery 1994a):

> Read this Letter, and look, and tell aw the poor Folk of your Place, that God has open'd a Door for their Deliverance; for here is ne Scant of Breed here, and if your Sons Samuel and James Boyd wad but come here, they wad get mere Money in ane Year for teechin a Letin Skulle, nor ye yer sell wad get for Three Years Preeching whar ye are. Reverend Baptist Boyd, there ged ane wee me in the Shep, that now gets ane Hundred Punds for ane Year for teechin a Letin Skulle, and God kens, little he is skill'd in Learning.

Study of eighteenth-century ethnic varieties of American English relies largely on such material, which is especially extensive for African-American and Irish characters, but because it lacked real-life models and for other reasons, its reflection of actual or contemporary speech is uncertain, if not doubtful. Even by the mid 1700s, when it began to be produced in the American colonies, dialect writing drew on British traditions of comic stereotypes, usually from the stage (Duggan; Bliss 1979; Blake). The extent to which American character types were distinctive from British ones – especially for the Irish – has yet to be investigated. Many renditions were made by authors not native to or personally acquainted with the variety they represented (Cooley 1997), or they were constrained by audience expectations. Literary dialect was a code to be manipulated for literary effect, mainly for parody and burlesque. Because their models may have been neither real nor contemporary, the dating and value of literary representations for linguistic reconstruction are uncertain. Portrayals of native American regional speech, in contrast to emigrant English, began only late in the century. Cooley has identified ten character types in Colonial American literature, including Irish, German, French, Scottish, African-American, Quaker, Yankee, Amerindian, Yiddish, and Fops, for several of which a standard set of linguistic features was employed. This repetition suggests that portrayals of ethnic and social character types took on a life of their own.

Scholars have often studied nineteenth- and twentieth-century American literary dialect to gauge its validity as compared to speech, to examine the practices and purposes of authors in portraying and differentiating characters, and to gain insight into local speech. Primarily because they recognize it as conventionalized speech, most scholars have shunned it in reconstructing earlier American English. Amateur linguists, usually antiquarians, have not been so reluctant, often taking Joel Chandler Harris's (1883) Uncle Remus stories and other local color fiction to reflect earlier African-American or Southern white speech (Brooks 1937; Polk). They have also compared it to British speech, judging Harris's dialect to be archaic, even "Elizabethan" (§ 3.5.1). Stewart (1967, 1968, 1970), Dillard (1972, 73–138), and Brasch have used attestations from three centuries of literary dialogue and historical accounts to reconstruct and trace the history of African-American speech from an Anglophone pidgin that developed in West Africa to a more recent decreolizing variety of American English. In constructing a case that the antecedents of many African-American grammatical features were not British at all, Stewart and Dillard adduce an impressive range of citations.

Like commentary from outsiders and language specialists, eighteenth-century literary dialect reveals perceptions and attitudes toward speech probably as much as speech itself. For this reason the first three types of evidence are appropriate for sociolinguistic as much as, if not more than, linguistic analysis. According to Cooley (1992, 180): "Authors who represent literary characters as speaking identified language varieties are reflecting their own attitudes and those of their perceived audiences about standard and other dialects and about the people who speak each one." A comprehensive account of nineteenth-century American English potentially useful for reconstruction is that by Edwin Ray Hunter, drawn mainly from literary materials with genuine American characters.

3.4.4 Poetic rhymes

A fourth resource for the language of the Colonial period is end rhymes from poetry. With evidence from pronouncing dictionaries, these are particularly useful for reconstructing vowel pronunciation, as Kökeritz demonstrated for Shakespeare's verse. The sizable body of distinctively Colonial American poetry that was produced, especially in the late eighteenth century, raises the prospect of detecting early American pronunciation. What makes poetic evidence so valuable is that it was contemporary with the emigrant and following generations (for New England) and was produced by identifiable individuals whose social, regional, and educational backgrounds are often known.

Unfortunately, pronunciation contemporary with the poet is only one possibility revealed in the diverse spellings of poetic rhymes. More than other types of evidence, rhymes cannot be taken as transcriptions of speech. In the seventeenth and eighteenth centuries, English vowels were in considerable flux, as the Great Vowel Shift worked its way to completion. Given their heterogeneity, emigrants would have brought various stages and versions of the overall pattern. Rhymes from Colonial poetry, especially from seventeenth-century New England, exhibited a considerable lack of uniformity (Tjossem). An apparent rhyme may represent any of several possibilities: (1) older pronunciations superseded in popular speech by sound changes, that is, rhymes conventionalized to poetic diction, having little if any existence in pronunciation (*good:flood, love:move*), (2) orthographic rhymes intended for the eye rather than the ear (*anger:danger, know:how*), (3) near or approximate rhymes, or (4) actual pronunciation.

Their early date and range of variations make rhymes valuable if interpreted cautiously. Whether they reflect speech directly and attest to alternative pronunciations can be determined by confirmation from pronouncing dictionaries, which appeared toward the end of the eighteenth century, and by evidence from texts. The principal scholars analyzing poetic rhymes are Krapp (1925), Bigelow, Tjossem, and Russell, all of whom interpret rhyme with appropriate caution but only Tjossem consults manuscript versions when possible, especially for Edward Taylor's poetry. As he concludes: "The rhymes in their verse offer the only opportunity we have to study the relationship between the language of the colonists and the seventeenth-century England which they left, or between their speech and some aspects of modern American pronunciation" (14).

3.4.5   Texts: original records and manuscripts

Evidence from nonliterary texts (public and private documents that are often unpublished) is fundamental to reconstructing Colonial American English and investigating its antecedents. These are uncolored by personal prejudice and provide more concrete and direct inferences about speech than other sources do. Their advantages are many: they are more extensive than all other types combined; they are contemporary to the Colonial period and usually datable; they come from individuals whose names and locations are usually known and about whom social information can sometimes be learned. They exist in a range of genres; they have continuous discourse, which provides contextual information and permits quantitative analysis; and they are usually not produced with the intention of publication. Texts are the earliest of the five source-types, dating from the beginning of the seventeenth century and often produced by emigrants themselves.

Among texts of potential interest are records of town, court, and church proceedings, petitions, wills, and especially private letters, whose language is more often colloquial and whose authors are more often identifiable. Texts of the greatest value are those having the naive, unstudied writing of unlettered individuals, as revealed in departures from conventional spelling and standard grammar; these "illiteracies" usually have a basis in speech. A researcher's paradox comes into play, however. The quality of writing most desired is the most difficult to find because most colonists were marginally literate (if at all) and left few documents, while the small number who were literate wrote more and had descendants who more often preserved their writing (Montgomery 1997c).

Linguistic analysis and reconstruction, especially of grammatical features, relies on texts reflecting the spoken language; a quantity of these is needed to reveal variant forms and their productiveness in different contexts. Since the time of Krapp's study *The English Language in America* (1925), which systematically sketched early American pronunciation using unconventional spellings in New England and New York town and court records, linguists have recognized the value of texts (many of which have been transcribed and published) for documenting Colonial American English. According to Krapp (1925, 2: 5), "Local records as a source of information are of exceptional importance because in many instances they go back almost to the very beginning of colonization in North America. This is especially true of the local records of town affairs in the towns of Massachusetts, Connecticut, and New York." Following his lead, others undertook intensive studies of individual colonies: Orbeck and Rath for Massachusetts, Gibson for Connecticut, C. Simpson for Rhode Island, Sen (1973) for New Jersey, and Hewitt for Maine. Hewitt, who analyzes early Maine court records to identify vowels, diphthongs, and consonants differing from present-day speech, is apparently the only one to take the additional cautionary step of consulting the unpublished originals.

More recently Kytö has built a computerized corpus of "Early American English," arranging types of written documents along a "literacy-orality" scale based on their proximity to speech (Kytö and Rissanen 1983, 1987; Kytö 1991; Rissanen 1994). The project began by assembling only New England materials, although it aims to expand to Virginia.

Work on texts from other parts of America has proceeded unevenly. Krapp (1925, 2: 7) stated, quite reasonably, that "it is unfortunate that these naive [town] records are abundant only for New England," and Orbeck (vii) justified his use of only Massachusetts materials in that "the farther south we go the fewer such sources of information." In seventeenth-century New England, town clerks and court clerks had little conventional training, but by the early eighteenth century the language written for official purposes was approaching uniformity throughout the English-speaking world and only written conventions are detectable from public records except in rare cases or in newly settling communities. But this did not apply to private documents. A generation after Krapp, Stephenson (1956, 271) objected to his predecessor's "assumption that the plain citizen in the South had little occasion for written expression and in his further assumption that naive records useful for linguistic research were lacking in the South," and he produced a detailed study of North Carolina pronunciation before 1800 using data from arithmetic books, school papers, court records, wills, letters, and other manuscripts (Stephenson 1958). Eliason used these and church records, legal papers, and other manuscript materials to study language attitudes and differences, vocabulary, and pronunciation of North Carolina from Colonial days through 1860.

Studies using Colonial manuscripts remain few, because linguists have spent insufficient time locating, assessing, comparing, and interpreting them. They are indispensable for establishing the input varieties of language of newly arrived emigrants (who often generated correspondence or other documents) and addressing the Reconstruction Issue. Montgomery (1997c) analyzes the language of an eighteenth-century Ulster-born Indian trader in South Carolina and Georgia. Letters written home by Ulster and English emigrants are examined by Montgomery (1995, 1997a) and Giner and Montgomery. In studies of the "Ship English" of logbooks and other records from transatlantic vessels, W. Matthews (1935, 1937) and G. Bailey and Ross capture the heterogeneous pronunciation and grammar of English sailors three centuries ago. Much of the manuscript evidence for Colonial America is to be found in archives in the British Isles.

3.5 Historical development of the field: paradigms of comparison and reconstruction

With continuing migration and association between Britain and the United States, not to mention cultural rivalry after the American Revolution, differences between their varieties of English have provoked commentary for more than two centuries. As Americans became aware of the divergence of their speech, they began to monitor its relation to its parent. Its continuity became a concern as early as Pickering's *Vocabulary or Collection of Words and Phrases Which Have Been Supposed to Be Peculiar to the United States of America* (1816). What kind of offspring was American English? While English commentators often saw it as a degeneration, those in the new nation sometimes took the view that Americans were "more English than the English" in speech. American comparison of their language with the mother country has progressed through five general paradigms distinguished by their objectives and methodologies.

3.5.1   American English as archaic British English

That American English conserved older British usage was mentioned as early as 1789 by Noah Webster (108), who cited "the surprising similarity between the idioms of the New England people and those of Chaucer, Shakespear, Congreve, &c." In his glossary examining the historical authority for more than 500 items of debatable usage, Pickering concluded that American English was sometimes more archaic than the language he found during a sojourn in England from 1799 to 1801: "We have formed some *new* words; and to some *old* ones, that are still used in England, we have affixed *new significations*; while others, which have long been *obsolete* in England, are still retained in *common use* with us" (11). Among other items, he identified "antiquated words, which were brought to this country by our forefathers nearly two centuries ago; (some of which too were in that day *provincial* words in England)" (20), an example being the finite use of *be*, which he associated with New England, Somersetshire, and the King James Version. Although willing to defer to English authority when justified, Pickering also aimed to "expose the calumnies of some prejudiced and ignorant writers" (17) in England who condemned American uses without proper cause.

Since Pickering, many have promoted the view that American English is in part or in whole more conservative than British English. Schele de Vere (427), an early authority on Americanisms, stated that "the largest part of so-called Americanisms are nothing more than good old English words, which for one reason or another have become obsolete or provincial in England, while they have retained their full power and citizenship in the United States." The lead article (McKnight 1925) of the inaugural issue of *American Speech*, later to become the journal of the American Dialect Society, argued that Mencken's view that independence and innovation were the hallmarks of "the American language" was at best half true. Numerous American grammatical "misuses" condemned by the British were long established in the old country, according to McKnight.

3.5.1.1 Colonial lag hypothesis

That American English is markedly conservative, preserving forms no longer found in Britain, has found expression with reference to American speech in general and to specific American varieties. That a colony's language was routinely more conservative than that of its parent country was early formulated by A. J. Ellis (1869–89, 1: 19), who argued that when a language is transplanted,

> ... there is a kind of arrest of development, the language of the
> emigrants remains for a long time at the stage in which it was at when
> emigration took place, and alters more slowly than the mother tongue,
> and in a different direction. Practically the speech of the American
> English is archaic with respect to that of the British English, and while
> the Icelandic scarcely differs from the old Norse, the latter has, since the
> colonization of Iceland, split up on the mainland into two distinct
> literary tongues, the Danish and the Swedish. Nay, even the Irish
> English exhibits in many points the peculiarities of the pronunciation of
> the XVIIth century.

By the end of the century, Ellis's theory had become a common, even facile explanation for older forms in American varieties, as in the speech of Charleston, South Carolina (Primer 1887), Fredericksburg, Virginia (Primer 1889), and Ithaca, New York (Emerson). Eggleston argued for the general antiquity of American folk uses by comparing them to sixteenth- to eighteenth-century British literature. Not surprisingly, McKnight (1925, 1) could refer to the "long-recognized conservatism in transplanted languages."

Critics had argued that the archaicness of American English was overstated, applied simplistically and too broadly, and supported by little external evidence other than the alleged "isolation" of American speakers, but the idea that a colonial variety preserves items lost by its parent received a vigorous defense by Marckwardt in *American English* (59–80). Coining the term "colonial lag" and using case histories of vocabulary, pronunciation, inflectional forms, and syntax, he acknowledged that many archaisms reflected not items completely lost in the British Isles, but older senses of terms still current there. Others were British regionalisms: "The archaic survivals in America, though not current in standard British English, may be found still firmly entrenched in the English local or regional dialects" (63). Marckwardt (80) articulated more fully than his predecessors the forces preserving the archaic element in language and cited analogous cultural elements in America that had largely disappeared in the homeland, including the blood feud, the patchwork quilt, the folk ballad, and Calvinism:

> These post-colonial survivals of earlier phases of mother-country culture, taken in conjunction with the retention of earlier linguistic features, have made what I should like to call a colonial lag. I mean to suggest by this term nothing more than that in a transplanted civilization, as ours undoubtedly is, certain features of which it originally possessed remained static over a period of time. Transplanting usually results in a time lag before the organism, be it a geranium or a brook trout, becomes adapted to its new environment. There is no reason why the same principle should not apply to a people, their language, and their culture.

In the most recent investigation, Görlach (48) concludes that colonial lag is not supported by historical dictionaries and is at best relative and partial: "Of the more convincing cases of survival, most differences between word pairs relate to meaning, frequency, and style." Full assessment of the hypothetical archaicness of American English remains to be made. Most proponents of colonial lag have had little conception of the heterogeneity of Colonial English and have generalized from only a few examples. The evidence cited for colonial lag is selective, often ambiguous or tendentious, and far from indicating that American English in any of its varieties is more archaic than innovative. Even for putatively archaic Appalachian English, neologisms abound, according to *DARE*. The evidence for colonial lag may reveal more about Britain, that is, how some uses maintained in the United States have been displaced by fashions of the court, stage, or media and relegated to local or nonstandard varieties. Often British English has been more innovative.

3.5.1.2 Elizabethan hypothesis

When writers identify items from geographically or socially "isolated" American speech found also in sixteenth- and seventeenth-century English literature, they are apt to label these "Elizabethan" or "Shakespearean." James Russell Lowell (36) took this approach in *The Biglow Papers*: "Any one much read in the writings of the early colonists need not be told that the far greater share of the words and phrases now esteemed peculiar to New England, and local there, were brought from the mother country. . . . Shakespeare stands less in need of a glossary to most New Englanders than to many a native of the Old Country."

Motivated by local pride, a desire for cultural affirmation, or curiosity about their roots, enthusiasts sometimes cloak the matter of antecedents in romanticism or myth by thus characterizing American English as "Elizabethan" or "Shakespearean." This version of the colonial lag hypothesis most often applies to the Appalachian or Ozark Mountains, but it has also been associated with the English of African-Americans, the Outer Banks of North Carolina, and the Chesapeake Bay Islands of Virginia and Maryland. The language of the mainstream has changed, it is said, not that of these "isolated" areas.

The case for one or another variety of American English being Elizabethan dates from the late nineteenth century. Dozens of articles claiming Elizabethan, Shakespearean, or Chaucerian English in the Southern mountains have appeared since Calvin Brown, who identified thirty-nine items in Tennessee speech with identical parallels in Shakespeare. William Goodell Frost (313), president of a small Appalachian college, was most responsible for propagating the idea that mountain speech and culture were legitimate survivals from older times, in taking issue with the prevailing view of their being degenerations:

> The rude language of the mountains is far less a degradation than a survival. The Saxon pronoun "hit" holds its place almost universally. Strong past tenses, "holp" for helped, "drug" for dragged, and the like, are heard constantly; and the syllabic plural is retained in words in -st and others. The greeting as we ride up to a cabin is "Howdy, strangers. Light and hitch your beastes." Quite a vocabulary of Chaucer's words which have been dropped by polite lips, but which linger in these solitudes, has been made out by some of our students. "Pack" for carry, "gorm" for muss, "feisty" for full of life, impertinent, are examples.

For proponents of this view, "Elizabethan" rarely means more than "old-fashioned" or "two or three hundred years old." A typical statement is that of C. M. Wilson (238–9):

> The speech of the Southern mountains is a survival of the language of older days, rather than a degradation of United States English. . . . [In it] a surprisingly large number of old words have survived, along with a surprisingly large number of old ways. . . . The most casual of listeners will become conscious of the preponderance of strong preterits in

mountain speech: "clum" for "climbed," "drug" for "dragged," "wropped" for "wrapped," "fotch" for "fetched," and "holp" for "helped" – all sound Elizabethanisms to be found in Shakespeare, Lovelace, or King James Bible. The Southern uplander says "fur" (for) with Sir Philip Sidney, "furder" with Lord Bacon and in common with Hakluyt, "allow" for "suppose." Like Chaucer, he forms the plurals of monosyllables ending in "st" by adding "es" – "postes," "beastes," "jystes" (joists), "nestes," and "ghostes."

The idea has taken on a life of its own and become a hardy myth in American culture, part of a popular view that the southern mountains have remained static in time and its people have maintained a cultural repository of balladry and other music, traditional story cycles, traditional dancing, and quilting.

3.5.2   Transatlantic regional comparisons

Other studies match a regional variety on each side of the Atlantic chosen on the basis of migration, thus recognizing the Demography Issue and using settlement history to focus their investigation. This paradigm takes as its premise that, if early settlers can be traced to their point of origin in the British Isles, the dialectal sources of their language should be discoverable. Its proponents place great weight on identifying the British source population of an American colony and often cite place-names, surname patterns, and ethnological similarities as corollary evidence for migration.

Studies in this paradigm have usually considered Massachusetts (sometimes New England more generally), Virginia (or the South more generally), or Appalachia and paired them with southeastern England, southern or southwestern England, and Ulster respectively (for the linguistic influence on the three American regions: §§ 3.6.1, 3.6.4, and 3.6.3). The early British settlers of Massachusetts and Virginia, who have been researched exhaustively, were not as mixed as those who entered most other colonies. The Puritans (who began coming to the Massachusetts Bay Colony in 1629 and dwarfed the Pilgrims, who preceded them) originated mainly in East Anglia. Settlers coming early to Virginia (founded in 1607) were of diverse origin, but at mid century they were joined by a much larger number of compatriots from southwestern England, many of them Cavaliers supporting the monarchy. Those settling Appalachia beginning in the latter half of the eighteenth century were largely of Ulster extraction or their descendants.

Accounts of the New England to East Anglia connection began before the last third of the nineteenth century (Chester) and usually identified

Essex as the main source for New England speech, basing their arguments largely on settlement history. Orbeck (87–119) faulted all such studies for failing to regionalize their material; using the *EDD*, he showed that purported Essex items were found in much of England. Wakelin (1986b) profiled six early Massachusetts colonists (only one of whom was from southeastern England) and identified prominent phonological and grammatical features that must have occurred in their speech, concluding that "the most impressive aspect of the present-day New England dialect is its freedom from traces of the dialect features mentioned in this article" (33). But neither Wakelin's nor anyone else's evidence will refute an idea that has passed into folklore and is promoted in the region's living history museums.

In Virginia, the ancestral connection to southern and southwestern England has become part of the Cavalier myth of the Old Dominion's origin. For speech, the case was broadened to encompass the Lower South region (much of which was settled from Virginia) and both whites and blacks there. One of its most prominent advocates was the poet and literary critic Cleanth Brooks (1935), who compared the Uncle Remus stories and a 1908 Alabama word-list with the *EDD* and concluded that the English of blacks and whites along the Alabama-Georgia border derived more from the south and southwest of England than any other source. Citing "pronunciation resemblances" between the Lower South and the English of Essex, Kent, Dorset, and Somerset, he maintained the same view half a century later: "The language of the South almost certainly came from the south of England" (Brooks 1985, 13).

According to Horace Kephart (280), "Since the Appalachian people have a marked Scotch-Irish strain, we would expect their speech to show a strong Scotch influence. So far as vocabulary is concerned, there is really little of it. A few words, caigy (cadgy), coggled, fernent, gin for if, needcessity, trollop, almost exhaust the list of distinct Scotticisms." Josiah Combs (296) also concluded that "Scotch and Irish survivals are negligible. They occur here and there, but rarely." Both men could have had little but earlier English literature for comparison, so inevitably they both decided that mountain speech was strongly Elizabethan and Chaucerian. Not until decades later did the Scottish element merit examination again. Lester Berrey and Wylene Dial made the familiar case for the antiquity of mountain speech, but in addition to Elizabethan usages noted Scottish items, including *fornenst* 'next to' and *ingern* 'onion.' A substantial Scotch-Irish component was first argued by Cratis Williams (174): "Appalachian speech was determined by the predominance of the Scotch-Irish in the settlement of the Mountain region prior to and following the American revolution."

Because of reliance on settlement history rather than linguistic evidence, the connections of New England, Virginia, and Appalachia with corollary regions in the British Isles have had, from a research point of view, the status of hypotheses. As part of constructed American memory, however, they have achieved a life of their own.

3.5.3   Comprehensive transatlantic comparisons

Studies using a third paradigm investigate antecedents more objectively and comprehensively, by comparing multiple regional varieties on both sides of the Atlantic or by assessing the contributions that different regional British varieties have made to an American one. Most make a serious attempt to regionalize their data and to address the Reconstruction Issue in a princi-pled way.

As early as the eighteenth century, commentators (Witherspoon 1781, Webster 1783–5) perceived a three-way regional division in American speech having different ethnological and social bases, these regions being New England, the Middle states, and the South. Krapp's study *The English Language in America* (1925), produced in part to refute Mencken's claim of a distinctive "American language," is the most authoritative work on the history of American (especially New England) pronunciation and the first to address the Reconstruction Issue thoroughly, by exploiting commentary from language specialists, poetic rhymes, and texts. It focuses broadly on relations between American and standard British pronunciation. Like other scholars of his day, Krapp believed that American English originated from early Modern English, and he stressed its continuities with British English rather than its archaisms.

Krapp (1925, 1: 35) identified three broad dialects: "In America three main types of speech have come to be recognized, a New England local type, a Southern local type, and a general or Western speech covering the rest of the country." He stressed the continuities everywhere between American and British varieties: "In every case the distinctive features of American pronunciation have been but survivals from older usages which were, and in some cases still are, to be found in some dialect or other in the speech of England" (2: 28). In particular, Krapp linked the variety of American English spoken in the Middle Atlantic states and the Midwest (which he called "General American") to Northern English in its intona-tion, its preference for postvocalic /r/, and its phonetically short diph-thongs for long mid vowels (the longer diphthongs in New England and the South being similar to those of London and southern England).

Investigation of speech boundaries had begun a generation earlier with the work of George Hempl. The first to employ a survey, he distinguished and named the Midland region and marked its northern edge through central Pennsylvania in a landmark 1896 essay, *"Grease and Greasy"* (R. Bailey 1992). Though saying nothing about antecedents, his work pointed a way for future investigators and introduced "Midland" to American dialectology.

Hans Kurath took up Krapp's challenge to lay a principled, scientific foundation for transatlantic linguistic comparisons, one that became the point of departure for later scholarship. The first and longtime director of the Linguistic Atlas of the United States and Canada project, Kurath sought the broadest possible picture of American speech regions and their historical foundations, a goal that required a systematic survey of all English-speaking areas of North America. The aims of Kurath's atlas were to map the continent's main speech regions, establish their basis in settlement and migration, and identify their diagnostic regional features. By seeking their antecedents in the British Isles, Kurath hoped they could be used to reconstruct the settlement history and evolving cultural geography of the country. Transatlantic comparisons were a goal, but not an immediate one. Neither his questionnaire nor those of British linguistic atlases – the *Survey of English Dialects* (Orton and Dieth) and the *Linguistic Atlas of Scotland* (J. Mather and Speitel) – were designed with such comparisons in mind and this made their data incompatible in many ways.

Kurath identified three principal regional dialects (Northern, Midland, Southern) and thirteen subregional ones. Each of these was a "unique blend of British types of speech" (Kurath 1949, 1) rather than a reflex of one British variety or another. Kurath came to believe that factors other than settlement history (migration and the influence of cultural centers) accounted in large part for the development of American regional dialects. The items most useful for mapping American regional dialects, he found, were not archaic forms preserved from the British Isles, but Americanisms unknown there.

After Kurath, transatlantic comparisons using atlas data examined individual features. Kurath and his associates may not have sketched transatlantic connections as firmly or comprehensively as they aspired to do, but to their great credit they produced reference works that regionalized bountiful data for later scholars (Kurath 1949, Atwood, Kurath and McDavid, Pederson 1986–92).

When *SED* material became available, W. Nelson Francis used it to compare regional patterns between England and America. After cautioning against interpreting data too strictly, Francis (1959) identified types of correlation between lexical variants, ranging from a term having general distribution in both England and the Atlantic states (*gutter*) to one having broad currency in England but narrow local distribution in America (*cade*, found only in New England), with perhaps the most interesting pattern being regional distributions in England and America, but of different terms for the same referent (thus for a stream, *burn* from the north of England and *beck* from the Midlands are unknown in America, where Southern *branch* and Midland *run* appear to be innovations). Francis (1961) took up the challenge issued by Atwood (42) to compare verb forms transatlantically, finding that the preterit *see* had a British East Midlands and American New England correlation and that *growed* was found in southern and western England and predominantly in the Middle and South Atlantic states. Rather than inferring correlations between regions, Francis showed that items should be examined individually because they patterned independently in the twentieth century. He also cited the necessity of adducing settlement-era data to confirm apparent relationships based on twentieth-century data. Comparisons using linguistic atlases are difficult for practical reasons, the most serious being the lack of overlap between the *SED*, the *Linguistic Atlas of Scotland*, and American atlases. Surveys for these projects were conducted in very different ways and collected different items, and their results were published in quite different formats. As a result, relatively little material from them can be used for transatlantic comparison (M. Ellis 1992).

The work of one historian has received wide attention and makes the broadest and perhaps most provocative case yet for transatlantic cultural and speech connections. Like Kurath, David Hackett Fischer seeks to use the transatlantic comparison of speech to identify the origin of American regional cultures. In *Albion's Seed: Four British Folkways in America*, he weaves what is known about British and American vernacular building patterns, marriage patterns, views of freedom, speech, and twenty other cultural "ways" into a tapestry that attributes the continuing distinctive character of four regional American cultures to the dominance of settlers from four regional cultures in Britain (evaluations by Joyner; M. Ellis 1992). Three of these cultural links are traditional ones: East Anglia with New England, southern and southwestern England with Virginia, and north Britain (which Fischer calls "Borderlands" and interprets as comprising northern England, all of Scotland, and Ulster) with the American backcountry (the interior South from Virginia south to Georgia). To Kurath's formulation Fischer adds English north Midlanders (mainly Quakers), who were the first English speakers to people the Delaware Valley in significant numbers and to leave their imprint on its speech. Fischer (473) applies Kurath's term "Midland" to this fourth region and "South Midland" to that founded by north Britons: "The speech of England's north midlands became the primary source of the midland American dialect." This distinction was earlier reflected in Kurath's North Midland versus South Midland and Carver's Lower North versus Upper South (1987, 248), but neither of those scholars attributed the speech of the northern region to Quakers from the English north Midlands.

Fischer undertakes comparison by citing lengthy sets of lexical items, phonological variants, and occasionally a grammatical form, culled from American and British sources from the regions he has twinned. Like many correlational approaches of the first two paradigms, the model on which his is based is a static one, presuming that geographical groupings of people in the Colonial period had distinct, more-or-less homogeneous speech varieties that persisted into the twentieth century. More problematical is his uncritical use of sources. He does not regionalize or otherwise analyze his material before comparing it (most of his items are not confined to his British and American regions), and he makes little use of the *EDD*, Kurath's *Word Geography*, or *DARE*. His material on demography may be his strongest, as his volume features many maps and quantitative analyses of Colonial emigration and settlement. He sees speech as embedded within cultural transfer, and his emphasis on the regional diversity of seventeenth-century settlers provides an effective picture of the heterogeneity of English-speaking cultures in the settlement period. His sometimes incautious use of sources, static conception of regional speech, and undigested presentation of material will justify some skepticism about the integrity of his connections, but his synthesis does generate testable hypotheses for linguists and other scholars.

Carver's *American Regional Dialects: A Word Geography* (1987), a comprehensive extension of Kurath (1949), aims to establish the integrity of regional varieties of English in the continental United States and to map them. Carver provides a statistical basis for speech regions using lexical data from *DARE* and linguistic atlases, positing a fundamental North-South regional divide, and rethinking Kurath's Midland (161): "The broad expanse between the Upper North and the Lower South – Kurath's 'Midland' – is not a true unified dialect region. And although a small set of features, the Midland *layer*, characterizes the area as a whole, Kurath's 'Midland' is split by the North-South linguistic divide into two dialect regions, the Upper South and the Lower North."

Krapp, Kurath, and Carver provide comprehensive accounts of American regional pronunciation and vocabulary. Their interest in antecedents is to one degree or another secondary, because they recognize the priority of description. Along with *DARE*, their work addresses the Reconstruction and Data Issues for other researchers and provides the primary tools for regionalizing American linguistic features to match works available for the British Isles.

3.5.4   *Language contact and the koinéization hypothesis*

The question of British antecedents is viewed quite differently by Dillard, one of the few linguists to have attempted a comprehensive account of American English and one of the fewer to have envisioned the linguistic landscape in Colonial America in a fresh light. He argues that regional British English contributed virtually nothing to American varieties. His scenario for the Colonial period differs markedly from Kurath's, with whom he takes issue on many points. In stressing that the origin of American English involved types of dialect and language contact ignored by other scholars, Dillard questions previous assumptions and beliefs about the early history of American English. According to him, British regional varieties were often modified before being brought to North America, were leveled to a koiné by the mid eighteenth century after arriving, and were not the only varieties of English brought. As a result, he argues (1992, 30), modern regional varieties in America have little to do with the input of seventeenth- or early eighteenth-century settler English, but arose instead in the early National period: "If it was true that the English-speaking immigrants became astonishingly unified in their use of English . . . levelling the dialects they brought from England, the seeds of a new diversity would have been sown by interaction with the Indians and the other groups which made up the extremely polyglot environment of the colonies, the new nation and especially the frontier."

While Kurath emphasizes the formation of settler communities, Dillard stresses their unsettled nature demographically and linguistically. Because many emigrants did not leave rural homes in the British Isles to come straight to North America, they often spoke modified and contact varieties acquired along the way, such as Maritime Pidgin English, which originated in the earliest days of English overseas expansion. Colonial contact vernaculars are not well attested, but Dillard argues that Kurath and Krapp overlooked evidence for them because they did not fit traditional models for reconstructing American English.

3.5.5   Sociohistorical and corpus-based comparisons

The past two decades have seen a growing body of work in a fifth paradigm, one which uses quantitative analysis of texts and other sources to reconstruct relations between American and settler varieties of English from the British Isles. Its researchers identify the sociohistorical contexts of their data (by dating it, detailing how it was collected, describing the language community that produced it, and situating its speakers or writers historically) and specify explicitly their methodological approaches. They consider antecedents within larger issues of language variation and change, usually for grammatical features because their distribution can be analyzed in terms of syntactic constraints and semantic qualities according to recognized principles of accountability.

Quantitative approaches were not unknown earlier (Abbott), but they gained general acceptance only recently because researchers previously lacked appreciation of the orderly variability of Colonial American English. Most studies in the first two paradigms have used an idealized, uniform version of their variety based on a few items (especially from older individuals). Those in the third and fourth paradigm use a taxonomic approach that permits comparison of items based on their categorical presence or absence and have considered variation to be evidence of dialect mixing (due especially to the influence of "standard English" or the written code). The fifth paradigm recognizes that inter- and intra-speaker variation is typical and attempts to describe that structured variation.

Recognizing that the transplantation of English to North America occurred while standard English was emerging in Britain, researchers in this paradigm have sought material from nonelite classes reflecting the spoken language as much as possible, thereby expanding our knowledge of how spoken vernaculars diverged from more standard, writing-based varieties. Studies such as those by G. Bailey and Ross, G. Bailey, Maynor, and Cukor-Avila, and Montgomery (1997c), using sixteenth-, seventeenth- or eighteenth-century material, show that nonstandard varieties often followed variable rules quite different from those in literary texts. The frequent focus of this paradigm on emigrant language provides a much richer view of the transitional period than was previously possible.

Exemplifying the research in this paradigm are three research initiatives, each of which seeks a critical method for addressing the Reconstruction and Data Issues. Merja Kytö and Matti Rissanen's work on the roots of American English investigates the language of early New England, from where an extraordinary range of datable, mainly published documents survive, including diaries, sermons, private and official letters, legal depositions, scientific and historical prose, and public records. Kytö (1989, 163) states that "the roots of American English lie in the new geographical variety of English that emerged in the seventeenth century as a result of migration, isolation and socio-demographic contacts" and calls this New England-based variety "Early American English." Whether this represents a single variety or is also valid for colonies such as Virginia and Carolina is not yet determined. With a corpus of several hundred thousand words composed of representative text types, the researchers' method is descriptive, but also "consists of comparisons between texts that stand in different relations to spoken language and of the quantitative analysis of the results of these comparisons" (Kytö and Rissanen 1987, 221). Recognizing that comparisons effectively pursued one feature or segment of language at a time, they have analyzed periphrastic *do* (Rissanen), modal verbs (Kytö 1986, 1989, 1990, 1991), and verbal concord (Kytö 1993).

For the past decade, Montgomery has pursued transatlantic comparison of English and Scots in Scotland and Ulster with English in America (especially in the American South and Appalachia), a line of research heavily supported by demographic data (§ 3.2.1). The primary settler groups in Appalachia were descendants of the Scotch-Irish, who arrived in Pennsylvania from Ulster, and the English, who mainly moved west from the coastal South. Montgomery's "Roots of Appalachian English" project (reported in 1989) articulates methodological and analytical standards for an effort that has assembled material from fourteenth-century Scotland to seventeenth-century Ulster to twentieth-century Appalachia in order to track the historical development of prominent grammatical features in two related strands of research. "The Roots of Appalachian English" takes grammatical features of Appalachian English, seeks their regional sources in the British Isles, and has established that the Scotch-Irish ancestry is dominant (1991, 1997b; § 3.7.2). A second strand of the project seeks to assess the influence of Scots and Irish English on American English, using literary texts and private correspondence from Scotland (fourteenth–seventeenth centuries), church records, legal documents, and private correspondence from Ulster (seventeenth–nineteenth centuries), correspondence of working-class Americans from the nineteenth century, and twentieth-century recorded interviews from Appalachia. Because many features of interest are rarely reflected in written documents, other methodologies, including syntactic elicitations of native speakers in Ulster and Scotland, have also been exploited. This research has in particular sought letters of emigrants written to relatives in Britain and Ireland.

Though they rarely date from earlier than the late eighteenth century, such letters hold the greatest interest for scholars of antecedents because many were written by individuals with little formal education. Originally focused on emigrant letters to Ulster (Montgomery 1995, 1997c), the project has expanded to analyze letters to Highland Scotland and to England (Giner and Montgomery).

Over the past decade, Poplack and Tagliamonte (1989, 1991) have pursued the project "Early African American English," whose goal is to reconstruct and identify the sources of African-American English by examining three of its varieties, including two modern ones in Nova Scotia and the Samaná Peninsula of the Dominican Republic, whose ancestors left the American mainland in the early nineteenth century. This project has conducted sociolinguistic interviews with older members of these "enclave" communities and analyzed their grammatical features within a statistically based framework. It addresses the Reconstruction Issue by preparing comparable descriptions of the varieties under study rather than by establishing the internal development of each variety or using texts, when available, to clarify the time depth that the speech of older individuals can be taken to have (Montgomery 1999). The researchers address the problem of validation by comparing their interviews with the speech of elderly African-Americans recorded in the United States in the 1930s and by arguing the isolation of the two expatriate communities.

This project contends that the three varieties of African-American English, all of which are purported to have changed little since the early nineteenth century, are fundamentally similar in grammatical detail and different from English-based creoles. Early in their work the researchers assumed that the primary language contact of African-Americans was with standard English (Poplack and Tagliamonte 1989), but more recently they have turned to possible transatlantic connections with regional British varieties. Tagliamonte has proposed that the speech of conservative communities in northern England (Yorkshire) and Scotland (Banffshire) typify varieties that were brought to the Southern colonies in the eighteenth century and served as models for the ancestors of Nova Scotia and Samaná African-American speech. These "isolated British communities" are said to represent a "much needed and logical extension of the study of early AAE" and their "relic varieties provide the critical time depth for comparison to early AAE." Tagliamonte and Smith (149) argue further that "settlement of the American colonies was actually highly circumscribed in the seventeenth and eighteenth centuries. British southerners went to the northern US and British 'northerners' went to the southern US."

The assumption by these researchers that present-day speech from British communities reflects language that might have been transported two or more centuries ago is essentially that proposed by Kurath decades earlier and remains debatable. Moreover, the assertion that emigrants from northeastern England and northeastern Scotland could have influenced the language of African-Americans in the eighteenth-century American South appears questionable on a number of demographic grounds. (1) Little, if any, evidence indicates emigration from these areas to North America. (2) Most "British northerners" emigrating in the eighteenth century went to the backcountry or interior South (western parts of Virginia and the Carolinas) of North America, not to the lower or coastal South, where the vast majority of African-Americans were to be found in that region's plantation society. (3) The coastal South (Virginia and South Carolina) had been settled in the seventeenth century by speakers largely from southern England, most likely minimizing formative linguistic influences of northern Britons, who came later. Poplack's (1999, 2) argument that the comparison of "*older* and *non-standard* varieties of English furnishes a diachronic perspective on the relevant features" addresses with only partial adequacy the Demography Issue (because one or more earlier appropriate British input varieties to which African-Americans were exposed are not documented) and the Reconstruction Issue (because Colonial-era speech is extrapolated from that of today).

The methodology of the "Early African American English" project takes inherent variability into account and examines the distribution and conditioning of linguistic variables before cross-variety comparison. It shows the value of using quantitative analysis when possible and develops one of the strongest hypotheses in comparative linguistics for showing that two varieties are related historically: "Neither the existence of a form, nor even its overall rates of occurrence, can suffice to determine its provenance ... the prior and current status of a form can only be ascertained by examining its distribution in the language, as evidenced by the hierarchy of variable constraints conditioning its occurrence" (Poplack 17). The language varieties investigated meet this high standard of resemblance, leading the researchers to conclude not only common ancestry, but direct input from British varieties to American ones. Clarke (1997) tests this comparative hypothesis by examining varieties known to be related (Newfoundland Vernacular English on the one hand and southern Irish English and southwestern British English on the other). Finding them to have different constraint hierarchies, she concludes that Poplack's standard may be too high and not able to account for internal changes within one variety or the other.

3.6 Drawing regional and social connections

American dialects as they exist today are products of many factors beyond input from British or Irish source varieties, but antecedents did play discernible roles in shaping them, contrary to arguments for complete leveling in Colonial English. The United States has long been recognized as having regional and ethnic cultures dating from the Colonial period, and scholars seeking to account for their distinctiveness have sought evidence of regional language and culture brought from the British Isles. A comprehensive account of the input to Colonial American English remains a distant goal, but for many individual features transatlantic connections can be identified, though not unambiguously or exactly.

The connections posited by Kurath and McDavid and other researchers can be classified into four broad categories (in which "general" means "widespread, occurring beyond one region"): (1) general British to general American (usually of little interest except to document "colonial lag"); (2) regional British to general American (the preference for *will* over *shall*, often taken to have been contributed by Irish and Scottish emigrants); (3) general British to regional American (the glide in *new*, now superseded in some American varieties); and (4) regional British to regional American. This section focuses on the fourth and, to a limited extent, on the third category.

British and Irish varieties thus had diverse roles and fortunes. None of them survived largely intact. No American variety inherited features from only one of them, and the linguistic input to all American colonies was complex and heterogeneous. Many features were lost in the transition or shortly thereafter. The southeastern England to New England and southern and southwestern England to Virginia connections are often treated in scholarly and popular literature, but these are not as substantial as implied. "What we can be surest of" according to McDavid (1985, 19–20), who spent decades considering the matter, "is that in every community the English-speaking settlers were of mixed origin, however convenient it is to associate New England with East Anglia, the Delaware Valley with northern England and the southern colonies with the Southwest. It is best to assume dialect mixture from the beginning in each colony, in every colony, with different results." Few items that sharply discriminate dialects in the British Isles do so as well in America, and few occur uniquely in any one region. Even Appalachia, widely considered a distinct region in the United States, "has rather few unique regional and local expressions," at least for vocabulary (Kurath 1949, 36).

Beyond the outlines sketched by Krapp and Kurath, most work on ante-cedents has been for an individual region or variety. Only for New England is there a profile of Colonial speech approaching some detail. Not only was this region settled early, with its speakers almost entirely from southern (especially southeastern) England, but it had less later emigration and pro-duced abundant seventeenth-century documentation, especially for study-ing pronunciation. The plentitude of New England local records contrasts with the scarcity and lateness of those from elsewhere (Stephenson's earli-est North Carolina material dates from 1750). The lack of Colonial sources is especially acute for social varieties like African-American English and for more vernacular elements of language. If early regional data is preferred for comparison, the paucity of sources identified outside New England places very practical limits on an accurate account of antecedents. Sometimes it also necessitates using nineteenth- and twentieth-century material and comparative reconstruction to investigate antecedents, though comparative reconstruction has constraints and limitations of its own.

As discussed earlier, regionalization is an important goal, but even if achieved, a complicating factor in tracking a feature is that not all varieties of British English or their speakers came directly to North America. The pairing of regions for comparison, as practiced by the second paradigm, is simplistic in that many people removed from rural parts to cities before emigration or from one rural region to another, complicating the cultural and linguistic geography of early Modern Britain and Ireland. One promi-nent internal migration occurred when tens of thousands from Lowland Scotland and several areas of England went to Ulster in the seventeenth century (many of their descendants later going to North America), in the process forming a colonial situation within the British Isles, with Scots, Irish Gaelic, and several varieties of English in linguistic contact (Montgomery and Robinson). Though an extreme case, this shows that even from a fairly small part of the British Isles the input was likely to have been quite complex and is in need of careful sorting out. The mix of vari-eties brought to Ulster from Britain must have been similar to that intro-duced to middle and southern American colonies somewhat later, and because of this, some constructions could have been introduced by more than one emigrant stream. While making regional comparisons more difficult, such problems can be addressed if they are properly recognized and if pertinent linguistic and demographic data can be found.

This section gathers research (some previously cited in §§ 3.5.1–3 and 3.5.5) on those American regions and varieties whose antecedents have received the most scholarly attention. Specific features are dealt with either here or, if they have broader or superregional interest, in § 3.7. These sections focus on items that can be regionalized, but they represent only part of the story of the transplantation of English to a new hemisphere. Fuller consideration must include items of a social character that were contributed to American English or one or more of its dialects.

3.6.1   New England

An awareness of their early settlement history and the maintenance of later cultural ties gave New England and Virginia, more than other sections of the country, a sense of connectedness with England. The Pilgrims who established the Plymouth Colony in 1620 came from many areas (Wakelin 1986b), but because they were few compared to the 21,000 Puritans who settled the Massachusetts Bay Colony between 1629 and 1640, New England culture and speech are traditionally linked to London and southeastern England, especially East Anglia, the heartland of the Puritans. An early historian (Fiske 63) stated that, "while every one of the forty counties of England was represented in the great Puritan exodus, the East Anglian counties contributed to it far more than all the rest. Perhaps it would not be far out of the way to say that two-thirds of the American people who can trace their ancestry to New England might follow it back to the East Anglian shires of the mother-country."

New Englanders produced and kept local records from the beginning, many produced by the hands of semitrained clerks, and most scholarship on seventeenth-century American English is based on the wealth of this surviving documentation. New Englanders were increasingly literate, and the language in these documents neared standardization by 1700, reducing variation markedly and effectively concealing underlying pronunciation. Because the settlement of New England is better documented than that of the middle and southern colonies and its communities were more static and homogeneous than elsewhere in English-speaking North America (Kurath 1939–43, 62–121), identifying the antecedents of the region's speech would seem to hold particular promise.

Early treatments (Chester, Hoar, Noel-Armfield) identify Essex as the main source for New England speech but cite very general features and are based more on emigration patterns and place names than on linguistic evidence. Higginson dissents, claiming Britain's north country English to be the true source. Later linguists either find it difficult to make a specific transatlantic link to New England or avoid the question: Krapp (1925),

Orbeck, H. Alexander (1928), and others compare early pronunciation to seventeenth-century English literature and commentary, not to East Anglian materials from any period. The most thorough account is by Orbeck, who finds in the records of four Massachusetts towns some northern British features, but a general uniformity of language common to southern and southeastern England, reflecting London speech. In their studies of grammatical features, Kytö and Rissanen do not consider East Anglian sources, but compare New England material to that from London and southern England in general.

Both specific and general correspondences are to be found, however, between the pronunciation of New England and southeastern England, reflecting their ancestry, according to Kurath and McDavid: lack of postvocalic /r/ (108); *bristle* with /ʌ/ (130); *nothing* with /ɑ/ (145–6); *loam* with /ʊ/ (158); and *blew, new* with /iu/ (168). On the other hand, they point out that some common East Anglian pronunciations are found in the United States only outside New England: *broom* with /ʊ/ (152), *law and order* with an intrusive *r* (170), and *greasy* with /z/ (178). It is commonly held that New England is somewhat closer to England in orientation than other American regions and that in the early days of the country, New England (especially Boston) saw itself as closest in culture and speech to London, the center of fashion. This apparently accounts for the rise of /a/ in eastern New England as a post-Revolutionary development in *half* and *aunt*.

One possible link to East Anglia is a feature of intonation cited frequently in the eighteenth and nineteenth centuries; this is variously called the New England "twang," "drawl," or "whine." Noah Webster (1789, 104, 108) reviled "the singular drawling pronunciation of the eastern people" and their "drawling, whining cant," and Read (1933, 326) cites a 1792 comment about a "twang peculiar to the New Englanders." According to Schele de Vere (427), "[The first generation in Massachusetts] brought not only their words which the Yankee still uses, but also a sound of voice and a mode of utterance which have been faithfully preserved, and are now spoken of as the 'New England drawl' and the high metallic ring of the New England voice . . . is nothing but the well-known 'Norfolk whine.'" Krapp (1925, 2: 13–20) examined numerous references to this characteristic, which commentators have associated with all or parts of New England, without deciding what it is, the possibilities including lengthening of short vowels, prolongation of long vowels, insertion of a glide, nasality, or rising or falling intonation.

British sources for New England vocabulary have been examined by Carver (1992, 141), who cites farming, fishing, and shipping terms brought from East Anglia. The modest linguistic support for the East Anglia to New England connection, despite the common association of the two regions, may be due in part to a lack of information about early East Anglian and other regional British speech.

3.6.2 Pennsylvania

As the seventeenth century approached its end, European migration to North America increased and diversified because of improvements in shipping, development of trade, increased land speculation, and other factors. The bulk of migrants came from outside southern England, and it was to Pennsylvania, with its cultural hearth in Philadelphia and the Delaware Valley, that many headed. Already populated with communities of Swedes and Dutch when it formally opened in 1681 – later than other Atlantic colonies except Georgia and advertised as a haven for religious dissenters seeking a new and unfettered life – the Pennsylvania colony grew rapidly, attracting substantial numbers of Quakers from the English Midlands and Welsh by the century's end and larger numbers of Germans (mainly from the Palatinate) and Scotch-Irish from Ulster shortly thereafter. Quakers were concentrated in the environs of Philadelphia, the capital, and dominated the colony's politics for a century. Germans (who came to be known as "Dutch," an anglicization of *Deutsch*) and Scotch-Irish found their way into the interior, and their descendants were among the most mobile in American history, moving westward and southwestward, reaching northern Virginia and then the piedmont of North and South Carolina by the mid eighteenth century. Their expansion westward created a major dialect boundary across northern Pennsylvania.

With the influx of Germans, Pennsylvania's population was one-third German-speaking at the time of the Revolution. Not surprisingly, most items labeled "Pennsylvania" by *DARE* are borrowings or loan translations from German, but a few came from Scottish or Ulster settlers: *bealed*, *diamond* 'town plaza,' *drouth* (pronounced like *tooth*), *flitting* 'moving one's household,' and *hap* 'quilt.' In analyzing the speech of Pennsylvanians whose ancestral language was German, Tucker found numerous syntactic constructions based on a German substratum, but also forms of Scotch-Irish ancestry. The two sources reinforced one another in some cases, as with *leave* 'let' and *want* + preposition (as *want in* 'want to go or come in'), according to Michael Adams.

Kurath considered Pennsylvania the seedbed for a larger region (which he called the "Midland"). He was responsible for articulating and propounding this idea, but decades earlier a little-known study made a similar case for Pennsylvania. Using observations of Princeton University students, N. C. Burt (413) delineated many of the nation's speech habits by region, but associated only Pennsylvania and its derivative areas with emigrants from the British Isles: "The dialect of Pennsylvania is mainly Scotch-Irish . . . Their dialect is broadly defined, both against the people of New York and the people of old Virginia on the south and east. . . . [There is] general agreement of dialect between the Pennsylvanians and the North-Carolinians." He first and alone cited *whenever* in its Ulster meaning 'as soon as.'

Frederick Jackson Turner (1920, 104) notes, "It was in Pennsylvania that the center of Scotch-Irish power lay," and it is there that their influence on vocabulary can most easily be identified. Crozier documents the Ulster ancestry of thirty-three items in Pennsylvania, including *piece* 'distance,' *dornick* 'small round stone,' *fireboard* 'mantel,' and *redd up* 'prepare, tidy up.' The influence of the Scotch-Irish was greatest in western Pennsylvania, where they were dominant in Pittsburgh. In the generation after the American Revolution, newspapers around the city featured poetry in Ulster Scots on local political topics, especially by David Bruce, who wrote under the name "The Scots-Irishman" (Newlin 1928; Montgomery 1996a, 2000b). Today the speech of Pittsburgh ("Pittsburghese") is noted for such uses as *you'uns* or *yinz* 'you (plural)' and *need* + past participle (as *needs washed*), both brought from Ulster.

According to Kurath and McDavid, a number of Pennsylvania pronunciations reflect ancestry from Ulster and north Britain: *calm* with vowel /ɒ/ or /ɔ/ (142); *food* with /ʊ/ (156); *daughter* with /ɑ/ (161); and *drouth* with /u/ (167). A more general feature, merger of the vowels in *caught* and *cot*, which encompasses western Pennsylvania and a widening corridor westward, is discussed in § 3.7.1. The only study of early Pennsylvanian English using texts is that of Montgomery (1997c), who examines the grammar and pronunciation of an Irish-born Indian trader on the pre-Revolutionary frontier.

3.6.3   Appalachia and Upper South

The settlement of the upland interior of Virginia, the Carolinas, and Georgia (often called the "backcountry," "Upper South," or "South Midland") and the coastal areas of these colonies (the "Lower South") differed broadly (§ 3.2.1, Wertenbaker, Bridenbaugh, Fischer). According to Kurath (1949), supported by much of Carver's (1987) evidence from

DARE, the Upper South and Appalachia form a region largely derived, beginning in the middle third of the eighteenth century, from Pennsylvania demographically and linguistically. This region is here considered under a heading separate from Pennsylvania because the literature usually treats Appalachia as an autonomous, distinct region. Its antecedents have attracted more attention than those of any other regional variety, because the presence of archaisms, added to the persistence and attraction of the Elizabethan myth, has compelled many to postulate its antiquity. The model still most prevalent considers the variety homogeneous across a broad region and pays no attention to the four research issues; it relies on a few correspondences between mountain speakers anywhere and Elizabethan or earlier literature to make its case, without regionalizing or gauging the currency of items on either side of the Atlantic (§ 3.5.1.2). Early commentary was often accompanied by claims of the racial purity of mountain natives, as in this statement from a well-known folklorist (J. Combs 283): "The Southern mountaineers are the conservators of Old, Early, and Elizabethan English in the New World. These four million mountaineers . . . form the body of what is perhaps the purest Old English blood to be found among English-speaking peoples. Isolated from the outside world, and shut in by natural barriers, they have for more than two centuries preserved much of the language of Elizabethan England." Among the few serious assessments of the Elizabethan issue are those by Mona Combs, who compares the vocabulary of Shakespeare with that of older Kentucky mountaineers and lists 100 Middle English words and presents statistical data on informants' knowledge and use of them, and Montgomery (1998a), who examines and assesses the principal arguments put forth by advocates of Elizabethan English in southern Appalachia.

Most of the quarter million Scotch-Irish who arrived in North America in the Colonial period debarked at Delaware Valley ports and headed inland. A few settled in Appalachia, but a great many of their children and grandchildren migrated there; no group of Europeans came directly to the mountains, though the modern myth of "Scotch-Irish" emigration claims otherwise (Kennedy 1995). By many accounts, these descendants were the predominant white settlers in the backcountry from central Pennsylvania south to Georgia, spreading throughout the region between 1750 and 1850 (§ 3.2.1), as a result of which Appalachia was one of the last areas east of the Mississippi to be fully populated, the mountains being settled gradually from the valleys and piedmont below.

The possibility of a significant Scottish or Scotch-Irish element in mountain speech was mentioned as early as 1891 and occasionally thereafter

(§ 3.5.2), but it could muster little evidence and failed to make much headway against the more popularly reputed Elizabethan origin. Although (or perhaps because) it is the variety of American English most often cited as preserving older forms, commentary on the antecedents of Appalachian English remained anecdotal; there was no serious attempt to determine its historical background and regional sources – to test the Elizabethan and Scotch-Irish hypotheses – before Michael Ellis (1984, 1992) for vocabulary and pronunciation and Montgomery (1989) for grammar. In comparing thirty-two lexical items from contemporary east Tennessee with the *SED*, Ellis (1984, 41–2) found that "only one is an English Southern form. Eight are basically English Northern forms and five are Midland forms," but that of seventy-six phonological forms compared, "twenty-eight show a greater similarity with English Southern and West Midland forms, and only four share a greater similarity with Northern forms." Though he found many specific correspondences (Appalachian *waspers* 'wasps' to the English West Midlands), no convincing overall pattern emerged. Ellis (1992, 293) demonstrates effectively that Appalachian English has connections with more than one region of the British Isles and concludes that "the mixture of British regional influences in Appalachian English suggests that the southern British element must be taken into account." Schneider (1994, 509) compares Appalachian speech more extensively, using a present-day glossary (Fink) and the *EDD*. He finds strongest correlation with Yorkshire and Northumbrian, secondarily with Lincolnshire and the central and west Midlands, and concludes that "the North of England and Scotland are the most important donor varieties for the Appalachian vocabulary [but] that the preoccupation with Scotch-Irish elements has led to a certain neglect of the role of the English English."

Comparisons of Appalachian or Upper South vocabulary (as labeled by *DARE*) with Ulster and Scottish works reveal more extensive connections: *airish* 'chilly, cool,' *back* 'to endorse a document, letter,' *backset* 'a setback or reversal (in health),' *bad man* 'the devil,' *barefooted* 'undiluted,' *beal* 'suppurate, fester,' *biddable* 'obedient, docile,' *bonny-clabber* 'curdled sour milk,' *brickle* 'brittle,' *cadgy* 'lively, aroused,' *chancy* 'doubtful, dangerous,' *contrary* 'to oppose, vex, anger,' *creel* 'to twist, wrench, give way,' *discomfit* 'to inconvenience,' *fireboard* 'mantel,' *hippin* 'diaper,' *ill* 'bad-tempered,' *let on* 'to pretend,' *muley* 'hornless cow,' *nicker* 'whinny,' *poor* 'scrawny,' *swan* or *swanny* 'to swear,' and *take up* 'begin' (Carver 1992, Montgomery 1996c). One of the more intriguing Ulster contributions is *cracker* 'white Southerner' (Otto).

As Ellis and Schneider indicate, for vocabulary we must expand the contributing varieties to include those of the north and west of England; items from these regions were probably transported directly as well as through Ulster. The antecedents of Appalachian pronunciation remain unassessed, but any investigation would find many traditional pronunciations once widely current in eighteenth-century British English (*join* /dʒayn/, *oblige* /oblidʒ/, J. S. Hall) and little, if any, evidence of Scotch-Irish influence (forms cited for Pennsylvania do not occur farther south). The Appalachian vowel system, like that of other American varieties, is southern British (Lass 1990). For grammar, however, the Scotch-Irish element is quite broad and deep (§ 3.7.2). Though often considered the most distinctly regional speech in America, Appalachian English is actually mixed in origin.

3.6.4   *Virginia and Lower South*

More research has been published on the English of the South than on any other American region (McMillan and Montgomery). The American South is usually taken to have a broad geographical and cultural division between the Upper South (linguistically part of the Midland, § 3.6.3) and the Lower South (encompassing lowland areas of Virginia and the Carolinas and their extensions westward). Much literature on Lower South speech emphasizes its conservativeness and its dialect survivals, but little attention has been given to the actual tracing of antecedents.

The basic characteristics of traditional Southern speech are in most respects clear. Blacks and whites share most features, especially those originating in the British Isles, which are of two broad types. Lower South speech retains many items of vocabulary and pronunciation (and some of grammar) that were "widespread at various stages in the settlement of the country, but which over two or three centuries' time eroded away in the North surviving only in the South" (Carver 1987, 104). Some of these were regional in England, but most were general usage, former or current (the glide in *new* and *had liked to*, now reduced to *liketa* 'nearly'). Lower South speech also shares a sampling of Scotch-Irish features, especially grammar, with the Upper South (§ 3.7.2). Because of historical and geographical differences, the Upper South versus Lower South cultural distinction remains very real more than two centuries after settlement (Fischer), but it has been somewhat blurred by internal migration in the nineteenth and twentieth centuries.

Early settlement of the Lower South began with the formation of coastal communities and preceded that of the Upper South by three-quarters of a century or more. Its first several generations of settlers were mainly from England and very early also from Africa; the latter's stamp on

Lower South speech – white as well as black – was to be indelible. Despite geographical and social diversity within the region (which has far less uniformity than commonly believed), Virginia and the Lower South constitute an extended cultural belt sharing many speech characteristics (Kurath 1949, Kurath and McDavid, Carver 1987). As Pennsylvania was the seedbed for the Upper South, so tidewater and piedmont Virginia and coastal South Carolina, with their cultural hearths of Richmond and Charleston, were for the Lower South. With the growth of plantation agriculture, the Lower South expanded west to Texas by the mid nineteenth century. The earliest settlers were more diverse than New England's, in part because Virginia attracted adventurers seeking economic gain rather than settled communities in which to practice their religion. Those sponsored by the London Company to found Jamestown in 1607 were English, mainly from the south and London, but like the Pilgrims in Massachusetts, early Virginian settlers were soon outnumbered by a much larger second wave, one coming from southwestern England and London. Fischer (226) estimates that "in the range of 40,000 to 50,000 [came] during the period from 1645 to 1670," and that Virginia's population nearly quadrupled between 1640 and 1660. South Carolina, founded in 1670, was the most heterogeneous of the Southern colonies, peopled by English (many from southwestern England by way of Barbados) and Africans (mainly from Barbados or Africa), as well as Jews, French Huguenots, Scots, and others in its first half century. The British sources of its speech have never been explored, perhaps because it was regarded as having a foundation different from other mainland colonies, not directly from England.

As with Appalachia and the Upper South, much interest in Virginian and Lower South speech has been antiquarian, emphasizing its conservative character and focusing on correspondences with seventeenth- and eighteenth-century England. However, the terms "Elizabethan" and "Shakespearean" have almost never been applied to the speech of Virginia, although as the only American colony founded before the Bard's death, it can lay some claim to those designations. Views on its precise English regional source have varied, but all writers have stressed its conservative nature and the southern British roots of Virginia speech. For instance, Primer (1889) identifies peculiarities of northeast Virginia pronunciation, which has "preserved to a remarkable degree the older English sounds brought over in the seventeenth century by the early settlers of this region." B. W. Green discusses the character, ancestry, and contributing streams of Virginia speech and concludes that "there seems to be a distinctly southern, southwestern and east midland character in the speech of the Virginians, little or none of the East-Anglian or Norfolk" (8). Using English Dialect Society glossaries, he also identifies "standard" words that were brought and describes Virginia English as a "survival of archaic forms that have been lost in England" (8).

Among other factors, the South's rural society, later development of public schooling, and relative lack of contact with outsiders (other than Africans, few emigrants came in the nineteenth century compared to the North) have been proposed to account for the region's conservative speech (Kurath 1928a, 292). Brooks (1937) argues that isolation and a strong oral tradition were in addition responsible for Southerners preserving older speech. Brooks (1935) concludes that the English of blacks and whites of the Alabama-Georgia border region and the South in general derived primarily from the south and southwest of England, a position that he continues to maintain (1985, 13): "The language of the South almost certainly came from the south of England."

Krapp (1925, 2: 34–5) holds that "the speech of Virginia and the speech of New England at the period of colonization were essentially the same. . . . The colonists were contemporaries, they came from the same regions of England, in the main from London and Midland and Southern regions, and they represented the same social classes, a sprinkling of gentry in a large body of artisans, farmers, and laborers. . . . It is remarkable how many details of a popular dialect in the South may be paralleled by similar details in present or earlier New England speech. . . . they are to be explained as having a common origin." Among eleven features of pronunciation he cites are [æ] in *haunt*, [aɪ] in *boil*, and the loss of *t* in *post*. Kurath (1928a, 295) agrees with Krapp: "The local dialects of the South have preserved features that we know to have existed or to survive in secluded places also in New England (and in the British Isles)." Krapp took pains to document many a "survival of a custom in speech which was formerly more general" and to show its historical basis; *gwine* 'going' was an older pronunciation that had become associated with African-American speech but whose uniqueness to that variety Krapp was determined to discount. He also made some regional associations, as in likening the off-glides of long mid vowels in the American South to those in London and southern England.

Lucke (1949) undertakes a systematic comparison of the pronunciations of Virginia and England. Using Joseph Wright's *English Dialect Grammar* (1905) and Guy Lowman's maps (Kurath and Lowman), she drew isoglosses for seven features. While recognizing that the territory for some had no doubt changed since the seventeenth century, she concludes that Virginia speech (and we may say that of the Lower South, since all her features extend well beyond Virginia) most resembles, and most likely originated in, the English East Midlands. That region had three features not coinciding anywhere in southern England: a vowel distinction between *morning* /ɔ/ and *mourning* /o/; centralization of the vowel nucleus in *twice*; and /æ/ in *marry*, most likely the source of the three-way contrast with *merry* /ɛ/ and *Mary* /e/. She says (183), "The lack of these three special Virginia characteristics in London establishes the Virginia dialect as essentially non-London." It is noteworthy that features specific to the English southwest are difficult to identify in Virginia, contrary to expectations from settlement history.

Other antecedents of Lower South pronunciation (merger of *pen* and *pin*, loss of postvocalic /r/) are treated in § 3.7.1. According to Kurath and McDavid, the following Southern pronunciations reflect ancestry from southern England: *deaf* as /dif/ (132); *yesterday* with /ɪ/ in the first syllable (134–5); *yeast* as /ist/ (174–5); and *car, garden* with an initial palatal (175). The last feature is, according to Krapp (1925, 2: 208), "a local survival from a time when this pronunciation was not only more general but also highly commended as an elegant accomplishment in speech," especially in southern and eastern counties of England. In America, Kurath and McDavid (175) find it "from the Potomac to the Savannah . . . on all social levels, although it is clearly recessive." *DARE* (s.v. *garden*) finds it also in the Upper South.

Distinctive Southern words tend to be either Americanisms or retentions of earlier general English; very few have antecedents in specific dialects of the British Isles. Of eighteen Southern terms (Kurath 1949, 38) compared with *EDD* evidence, four (*haslet, turn of wood, whicker* 'whinny,' and *goop!* 'call to animals to come') are general British dialect; the other fourteen are either old, nondialectal terms (*low* 'to moo') or American innovations (*press peach, johnny cake, woods colt* 'illegitimate child').

With few exceptions, mostly attributable to African-American influence, the grammatical features of the Lower South are shared with the Upper South. Features having British antecedents include possessive pronouns in *-n* (*hern, hisn*), plural pronouns *you all* or *y'all*, and combinations of modal verbs (*might could*). Occurring mainly in the Lower South are *were* with singular subjects, zero marking on third-singular present-tense verbs, and finite use of *be*. All of these are discussed in § 3.7.2. Whether features are shared with the Upper South as the result of Scotch-Irish settlement, later internal migration, or diffusion is largely unexplored. Analysis of Colonial Lower South grammar is severely hampered by the lack of documents, which forces researchers to use early nineteenth-century material such as letters from plantation overseers for reconstruction.

Islands in two parts of the coastal South that have maintained conservative English sometimes prompt the label "Elizabethan." These are the
Outer Banks of eastern North Carolina and Tangier and other islands of
Virginia and Maryland in the Chesapeake Bay. All of these were settled
from the mainland in the eighteenth century. For the Outer Banks, early
commentators like Cobb cite relic vocabulary (*couthy*, *fleech*) and pronunciations preserved from Middle and early Modern English, but later writers
(L. Morgan, Shores 1989b) stress that the islands in some respects have
maintained Colonial speech: the *a*- prefix on present participles, as well as
postvocalic /r/ and other features lost elsewhere in the coastal South in the
eighteenth century. Another study (Wolfram and Schilling-Estes) finds the
English of Ocracoke, the largest island, to be quite mixed in its American
and British antecedents. Tangier Island, Virginia, is also notable for its old-
fashioned pronunciation. Shores (1985, 1989a) finds it to have maintained
/r/ in all positions.

3.6.5   African-American English

In the 1960s interest in the genesis of African-American English motivated renewed interest in antecedents from the British Isles. Greater
understanding of the structure of creole languages and the discovery of
commonalities between them prompted comparisons with African-
American, which is usually treated as a nonregional, monolithic variety,
except for Gullah. Scholars had long argued that, because it shared numerous features with white folk speech in the South, African-American
English had, with perhaps trivial exceptions, its ultimate sources in earlier
British dialects; even though it was always differentiated from white
English in literary portrayals, scholars viewed the English of blacks and
whites as having a common ancestry. Resemblances in certain grammatical
patterns between creoles and African-American, however, suggested that
some similarities between the latter and other varieties of English might be
only superficial.

Views on historical relations between the English of whites and blacks
and the affinities of the latter with creole or African languages have evolved
radically over the past century, reflecting the progression of paradigms
sketched in § 3.5. They have ranged from the idea that African-American is
a static variety preserving Elizabethan or Colonial white English – preserved by isolation from mainstream culture and by disadvantaged formal
education – to most recently one seeing multiple sources and factors as
responsible for its current dynamic form.

3.6.6   Irish, Scottish, and regional British influence

Most literature on antecedents identifies southern England as the primary source for Colonial American speech and cites few, if any, possible alternatives. This apparent consensus reflects the failure of investigators to consider material from Ireland and Scotland or the inaccessibility of such material. Irish emigrants to America formed the third largest national group after the English and Germans, and the surnames they and their Scottish counterparts contributed to the American populace are innumerable. English and Scots were brought in well-documented emigrant streams from Ireland and Scotland, yet accounts of American English are virtually silent about their relevance as input varieties or their possible linguistic influence.

In pronunciation this influence is apparently slight (§ 3.6.2 treats Ulster Scot contributions to Pennsylvania). Krapp (1925, 2: 97) believed that American English pronunciation exhibited nothing from Ireland or Scotland not brought earlier by English emigrants and that Irish English reinforced existing features but contributed nothing new to American English, including anything derived from Irish Gaelic. He identified [e] in *reason* and [ɪ] in *friend* and *chest* in Irish and American English as both derived from seventeenth- or eighteenth-century British English, even though these pronunciations were later lost in Britain (or at least the standard English of southern England).

Mencken (1936, 160–2) believed that the Irish had a more diverse and decisive impact on American English, taking the view that "[Irish emigrants] gave American [English], indeed, very few new words; perhaps *speakeasy*, *shillelagh*, and *smithereens* exhaust the list. . . . [But] of more importance . . . than these few contributions to the vocabulary, were certain speech habits that the Irish brought with them – habits of pronunciation, of syntax, even of grammar." These include *bile* 'boil' and *rench* 'rinse' (older British pronunciations), use of the definite article with names of languages (*the Latin*) and diseases (*the measles*), intensifying expressions such as *no-siree* and *yes-indeedy*, the greater currency of the *a-* prefix (*a-running*) in American English than in British English, and a preference for *will* over *shall*. Further, Mencken agreed with Patrick Joyce (cited by Mencken 1936, 162) that "many locutions [of Irish origin] . . . are now often mistaken for native inventions, for example, *dead* as an intensifier, not to mention many familiar similes and proverbs," which suggests that the Irish ancestry of some constructions was discernible only with systematic exploration and a familiarity with both Irish English and Irish Gaelic.

DARE's identification of 147 items with Irish ancestry and 519 with Scottish ancestry (in the *A–O* range) suggests considerably more lexical influence than even Mencken believed. Most of these were etymologically English, but a few were Gaelic borrowings (Carver 1987): *dauncy* (< *donas* 'evil, harm'), *sugan* (< *suggan* 'saddle made of straw or rushes'), *clabber* (< *clabbar* 'mud, thick milk'). Hamilton examines the maintenance of Scottish items in America and finds them to be concentrated in certain lexical domains, such as food (*bannock*, formerly of oats, now of flour or corn meal) or children's games (*Antony over*). Many have shifted meaning. Their loss probably reflects the general attrition of traditional cultural practices in America more than anything else. That they have persisted, often into the late twentieth century, is attributable to their unique semantic reference; indeed, in a particular lexical domain, such as body parts (Macafee forthcoming), where Scottish and English equivalents have competed, very few of the Scottish items survive.

The disproportion between Irish and Scottish items reflects the reference sources that *DARE* used (Scottish dictionaries are quite comprehensive but no dictionary of Irish English was published until recently). Scrutiny of *DARE*'s Scottish items in dictionaries of Irish English and Ulster Scots (Macafee 1996; Fenton; Dolan 1998) would doubtless find them often attested in Ulster; it is from there that they were most likely brought to North America (aligning the *DARE* items more closely with the numbers of Irish and Scottish emigrants). Of the 519 Scottish items, 60 are assigned one or more regional labels, most commonly Midland (25), South (19), Appalachia (16), Pennsylvania (5), Northeast (7) and Midwest (4); the largely Midland distribution indicated by these labels is consistent with Kurath's hypothesis of half a century ago about the influence of the Ulster Scots. Braidwood (31–2) identifies 13 items Ulster contributed to the American vocabulary, including *aftergrass*, *granny* 'midwife,' *hap* 'quilt,' and *mooley* 'hornless cow.' Crozier's study (§ 3.6.2) is the most extensive examination of Scotch-Irish vocabulary. Ulster Scot emigrants influenced another language in America according to Reed (1953), who identifies archaic pronunciations and vocabulary the Pennsylvania Germans borrowed from their Ulster Scots neighbors in an earlier day.

As an identifiable language variety, Scots apparently survived the emigrant generation only as a conscious poetic idiom in New Hampshire and Pennsylvania communities settled predominantly by Ulster Scots (Montgomery 1996a, 1998b, 2000b), but its influence on American English grammar, through Ulster Scot emigrants, is remarkably broad and deep (Montgomery 1997b; § 3.7.2). On the other hand, Scottish Gaelic survived for a century as a language of the home and the church among Scottish Highlanders in southeastern North Carolina, but their Gaelic-influenced English, also brought to North America in Colonial days (Millar), contributed little to American English, perhaps because Highland Scots were far less numerous or widespread than Ulster Scots. Donald MacDonald identified two dozen "pure Gaelic" lexical items in the English of Highland Scot descendants in North Carolina, including *brogan* 'heavy shoe,' *clabber* 'curdled milk,' and *poke* 'small bag, sack,' but these occur in a much larger territory today and were attested among the Ulster Scots as well, so their existence in Highland English played primarily a reinforcing role. On the other hand, the *r*-fulness of Highland settlements may have resisted the encroachment of *r*-lessness from surrounding areas. The Cape Fear Valley forms the only corridor along the Atlantic coast to exhibit distinctly Upper South features, such as the monophthongal [a] in *twice* (Kurath and McDavid 109) and such lexical items as *quarter till ten*, *big house*, *fire board*, *jacket* 'vest,' and *little piece* (Kurath 1949, 47). Partial influence from Highland English cannot be discounted for some of these, but one or two place names appear to constitute the unique contribution of this emigrant group.

The only feature of Irish English to draw significant attention is the habitual use of *be*, because it resembles African-American English. More than one scholar has proposed that the verb's use in Irish English has a Gaelic substratum. Even if true, however, that does not mean it was brought to America by early emigrants from Ireland. For example, Rickford (1986a) examines six hypotheses for the diffusion of Irish-English habitual forms into Anglophone creoles and African-American English. Although stating that "details about the socio-historical context in which such diffusion is presumed to have occurred are almost non-existent" (246), he conjectures about close contact between African and Irish laborers and about the languages and features used by early Irish emigrants. He concludes that a hypothesis involving decreolization from creole *does* + *(be)* and incorporating possible influences from Irish and British English most likely explains the development of habitual verbs, and he rejects on structural rather than demographic grounds their diffusion through contact between Irish emigrants and Africans in the seventeenth century.

A mixed or combined British and Irish English origin may be possible, but establishing the diffusion of habitual verbs in North America calls for more than circumstantial evidence of early Irish-African contact and for attestations from Ireland or from Irish emigrants in the Colonial period. Rather than providing these, Rickford and other American linguists infer seventeenth-century Irish English from late-nineteenth- and twentieth-century citations, assuming that varieties of Irish English were static for more than two centuries.

Irish English today has three habitual forms of the copula (*be*, *bes*, and *does be* or *do be*), and their distribution appears consistent with the most likely avenue of input to African-American English: *be* and *bes* are primarily Ulster forms, while *does be* and *do be* dominate elsewhere in Ireland. Unfortunately, neither the linguistic literature nor the documentary record attests these verbs in Ireland before the mid nineteenth century. Emigrant letters, in which there is evidence of many other vernacular forms, suggest that Irish English habitual *be* and *bes* arose in the early nineteenth century, produced by transfer from Irish Gaelic to English. The earliest documented occurrence in a letter is from 1860, and evidence is absent from literary dialect until the latter half of the nineteenth century (Montgomery and Kirk). Despite remarkable formal and functional parallels, habitual *be* almost certainly developed too late in Ireland to have influenced American varieties of English. The verb in African-American English most likely derives either from a creole or from independent, more recent development in America (G. Bailey and Maynor 1987, Montgomery and Mishoe). The proposed diffusion from an Irish source is also called into question by the absence of habitual *be* in present-day or historical Appalachian English, in which Ulster influence is considerable.

Regional British grammatical features have been linked to American English by John Harris, who compares habitual markers in southwestern England, Ireland, and New World creole varieties (including African-American English); Hancock (1994), who identifies a range of similarities between the English of west Cornwall and Gullah and postulates a significant southwestern English formative component in that creole; and Trudgill (1997), who finds remarkably parallel use of the conjunction *do* in East Anglia and North Carolina.

3.7 Linguistic features

The previous section dealt with features that can be regionalized. However, much of the English brought by emigrants was nonregional in character (not confined to an identifiable area, most likely because its dimensions were social, either standard or nonstandard), and much of it became super-regional in America. The present section considers features of pronunciation and grammar of the latter type. It does not consider vocabulary for three reasons. First, vocabulary is the most mobile part of language, traveling through the printed word and other means that often make it more problematic to regionalize in America than pronunciation or grammar (M. Ellis 1984 and Schneider 1994 show how mixed is the traditional vocabulary of Appalachia). Lexical items can be regionalized in the British Isles somewhat more successfully (some of these are discussed in § 3.6). Second, the researcher must employ late nineteenth- and early twentieth-century reference works such as the *EDD* in seeking lexical antecedents; material from the Colonial period does not exist in a usable form. Third, American English is vastly more innovative in vocabulary. Establishing an inventory for transatlantic comparison is especially difficult because only a very small portion of British and American regional lexical items can be compared directly. As Kurath (1949) discovered, the most revealing words for American linguistic geography grew out of native American life (*shuck* versus *husk*, *snake doctor* versus *mosquito hawk*, *chigger* versus *red bug*). These stop at the shore of the Atlantic and have no history in the British Isles, much less a regional one there. Only a small proportion of American lexical items can be traced other than to general British English (§ 3.6.4 treats Lower South vocabulary). Many of these are of individual etymological interest (*hoosier*, *antigoggling*), but are dealt with adequately in *DARE* and elsewhere and reveal little in the way of a general pattern. The findings of Francis that regional terms for streams in England (*burn*, *beck*) and America (*branch*, *run*) are entirely different can no doubt be replicated in many domains.

3.7.1   Pronunciation

Krapp (1925) provides the most comprehensive description of early (primarily New England) American pronunciation, using Colonial and early National material. He examined the relations of early American vowels, diphthongs, and consonants with those of British English and documented the persistence of English pronunciations in early American records. Many of those pronunciations later disappeared in standard use in both Britain and America. He evinced no doubt that characteristics of modern American pronunciation in all their diversity were traceable to England. Nor did Kurath (1928a, 282) in an early statement: "One must not forget that most of the American colonists doubtless spoke the dialect of their home-counties, or a more or less strongly dialectal variant of the Southern English Standard, and it is from the speech of these men that American pronunciation of the present day, in all its varieties, has received its present form," a point reiterated frequently in *The Pronunciation of English in the Atlantic States* (*PEAS*, Kurath and McDavid). Krapp and Kurath and McDavid base transatlantic connections on individual segmental correspondences and make few references to settlement history. Among emigrant groups, Kurath and McDavid mention only the Ulster Scots by name, and they offer frequent blanket statements that all British variant pronunciations for given words were brought to North America. Kurath's 1928 statement is one he pursues throughout *PEAS,* demonstrating that his phrase "in all its varieties" does not imply dialect-to-dialect correspondence but accounts for dialect mixing (albeit not in a systematic way). Kurath's statement has the status of a continuing hypothesis: for some prominent features of American pronunciation (the drawling of front lax vowels in the American South) a plausible transatlantic source has yet to be identified.

Lass (1990) compares the vowel systems of American and other "extraterritorial" varieties of English to those of northern and southern Britain. He concludes that, in whatever respects the demography of American settlement may have differed from one region to another, the vowel systems of all American dialects are essentially that of southern, especially southeastern, England and that "non-southern features that do occur are generally unabsorbed relics" (1987, 275). Completely absent from American English, for instance, are many northern British patterns that characterized the speech of Scottish and Ulster emigrants, such as the nonshifting of /u/ to a diphthong in *house;* the nonlowering of /ʊ/ in *but;* and the lengthening of vowels before /r/, voiced fricatives, or a morpheme boundary. Two exceptions to this general statement are the merger of the vowels of *caught* and *cot* and the maintenance of postvocalic /r/; in both cases the speech of Ulster Scots settlers reinforced or served as the basis for a similar pattern in American English. Kurath (1972, 69) believes that variation in American English pronunciation reflects variation in British English and that "all varieties of American English largely conform to the phonemic pattern of Standard British English," by which he meant southern British English.

The Pronunciation of English in the Atlantic States has the strengths of linguistic atlas material (broad systematic coverage and detailed phonetic information on individual vowels and consonants) but also its weaknesses (difficulty in gauging currency of variable forms or in converting material to indexes for comparison, in part because of its complexity). The presentation and segmental approach of Krapp (1925) and Kurath and McDavid make their volumes easy, but not entirely adequate, to use for transatlantic comparison. *PEAS* is a compilation of twentieth-century material that entails assumptions about the time period represented by its data. It uses mainly Wright (1905) for regionalizing British pronunciations and comments from Walker for their social status in eighteenth-century England.

Like many other scholars, Kurath and McDavid use only the modern dialects of England for comparison. For instance, they state (162), "There is at present no evidence in English dialects for the /e/ [in the second syllable of *because*] in our Southern folk speech." This pronunciation is documented in Ulster sources they did not consult, rendering their (138) statement that "the distinctive features of the dialect of the northern counties of England, of Scotland, and of Northern Ireland rarely survive in American English" somewhat suspect. Kurath and McDavid worked before the publication of data from the *SED* and could not employ it.

Nonetheless, Krapp (1925) and *PEAS* (129–79) enable us to identify and understand much about the complex and varied diachronic relations between British and American English (summarized by Laird 163–74). Few American pronunciations today do not correspond somehow to British ones. Some of these form discernible, if not always sharp, regional patterns (§ 3.6), but others are current widely in popular speech, without regional patterns on one or both sides of the Atlantic (/ŋ/ for final *-ing* in *singing*). Some American pronunciations that are recessive or restricted to folk speech or to individual lexical items reflect general (often standard) British usage of a former day: /kæg/ 'keg,' /yo/ 'ewe,' /aɪ/ in *joint, boil* (except *rile*, a standard variant of *roil*), /ɑr/ in *mercy, service* (except in *sergeant, varsity*, a clipping of *university*, and *varmint*, a former variant of *vermin*). Others are now universal or nearly so in American English but marginal in Britain, suggesting a once general currency in the mother country (the medial flap in *matter, metal*). Some that doubtless occurred in emigrant speech show no apparent trace in North America: fricative /x/ in *daughter*, from Scotland and Ulster, or the voicing of initial fricatives /f, s, θ, ʃ/, from southwestern England. Still others, including later stages of the Great Vowel Shift, appear either in individual lexical retentions (*drouth* with vowel /u/ in Pennsylvania) or only sporadically in American English (/rel/ 'real') but broadly in northern England, Scotland, and some parts of Ireland.

Antecedents from the British Isles often provided raw material from which many independent, ongoing developments took place in American English. Among the more prominent features that have drawn commentary about possible antecedents are the following, each of which has geographical and social dimensions.

3.7.1.1 Merger of /ɛ/ and /ɪ/ in pen and pin

According to Krapp (1925, 2: 34), these vowels often fluctuated in eighteenth-century British and American English and "the pronunciation of *e* before *n* as *i*, that is *men, ten, tennis*, as *min, tin, tinnis*, prevalent in Georgia, Alabama, and other regions of the South, is but a survival of a Colonial pronunciation that probably passed current on all levels of society." Evidence from the Colonial period comes from Benjamin Franklin, who transcribed *get* and *friend* as *git* and *frind* in his proposed phonetic notation, and from Sen (1974, 42), who finds variation common in eighteenth-century New Jersey regardless of social class and traces it back to the fourteenth century. How and when the merger of the vowels to [ɪ] before nasal consonants arose is not clear. This is the general pattern in the American South today, the process having spread rapidly in the past century (V. Brown), but its earlier history and its antecedents are unclear. Sen states that the merger before nasals was especially common in initial unstressed syllables and spread to stressed syllables from this environment, but her evidence is far from the South, as is that of Montgomery (1997c), who finds the merger occurs only before nasals in the language of a Dublin-born Indian trader in Pennsylvania. An Irish source is possible – indeed, Krapp noted the pronunciation in Irish English but believed that its occurrence was "so old and so general in American speech as to make it unnecessary to call in the aid of the Irish immigrant to explain its presence" (1925, 2: 97). An origin in America is at least as likely.

3.7.1.2 Loss of /r/

Because naive spellings reveal it so often and so clearly, we know as much about the loss of /r/ as any other feature of English pronunciation in recent centuries. The lack of constriction became prestigious in England and America at about the same time (the late eighteenth century), which suggests a historical connection – either contemporary British influence or an earlier inheritance brought by emigrants. The loss of postvocalic /r/ was, however, a multistage process. The consonant weakened and disappeared before alveolars long before the period of emigration, which accounts for forms such as *cuss* and *bust* in American popular speech today and *hoss* 'horse' and *passel* 'parcel' in conservative American English in the Southern mountains and elsewhere outside the coastal areas usually associated with /r/-lessness.

3.7.1.3 Vowels in *fast, calf, bath, can't*

In the early Modern period, such words as *fast, calf, bath*, and *can't* had [æ], but in eighteenth-century England their vowel retracted, producing a pronunciation that was stigmatized well into the nineteenth century before becoming standard in the twentieth. Sheridan's (1780) pronouncing dictionary gave no indication of [ɑ] in England for words of this group, but Webster (1789, 124) noted the divergence in vowels and, not surprisingly, condemned British practice. Both vowels are found in Britain and America today, but the much wider prevalence of American forms with [æ] confirms its earlier general currency in Britain.

For words in which the vowels are contrasted, their incidence is conditioned phonologically (occurring usually in words in which a voiceless fricative or *n* follows the vowel) or lexically (Laird 165–7; Lass 1990, 258–62). In America the retracted or "broad" *a* (varying between [a] and [ɑ]) has very limited distribution, exemplified in Kurath and McDavid's (135) statement about *aunt*: "In two areas, Eastern New England and Tidewater Virginia, *aunt* has predominantly the vowel occurring in *car, garden*, etc.; that is, low-front . . . in New England, low-back to low-central . . . in Virginia." In those areas "broad" *a* prevails in educated, rather than folk speech, indicating that the retracted vowel must have been adopted in the post-Revolutionary period under the influence of British fashion (its limited occurrence in the Outer Banks and other peripheral coastal areas also indicating later superimposition of the vowel in American English). Consistent with this is the argument of Carver (1992, 135) that [æ] in *fast, bath, aunt* is a colonial lag reflecting earlier emigration, and that alternative pronunciations gained currency in the eighteenth century as New Englanders and Virginians attempted to keep pace with English speech, facilitated by the contact of coastal American cities with England, which was closer than that of the hinterland. Grandgent (1920) and Krapp (1925, 2: 36–86) provide the most extensive treatment of historical developments in New England.

3.7.1.4 Merger of /ɔ/ and /ɑ/ in *caught* and *cot*

Open *o* [ɔ] is sometimes fronted slightly to the rounded vowel [ɒ], and sometimes unrounded to [ɑ]. This merger in *caught* and *cot* or *dawn* and *don*, is spreading rapidly in urban America but has traditionally been confined (except for part of eastern New England) to western Pennsylvania and a band of territory widening westward from it through the Ohio Valley and encompassing most of the western half of the country (Kurath and McDavid 17). Webster noted /ɑ/ in *soft, drop* (§ 4.2) and associated it with the middle colonies (1789, 110–11) and the Scotch-Irish (389). Krapp (1925, 2: 142) ascribes /ɑ/ in *crop* to dialects from England, especially from the southwest, but the merger is usually attributed to Scotch-Irish influence: "Despite its recent spread into new areas, the merger itself is clearly an old one and ties in well with settlement geography. The most likely source is Ulster Scots" (Lass 1990, 273). Complicating this scenario are two things, however. The merger is to a different vowel in American English, /ɑ/ or /ɒ/, from that in Scotland and Ulster today, /ɔ/ (Lass 1987, 286), and evidence is lacking that it spread into the Upper South, as many other Pennsylvania features did.

3.7.1.5 Remnants of vowel shifts

In the seventeenth and eighteenth centuries, English vowels were in considerable flux, as the Great Vowel Shift (which in simplest terms raised historically long vowels and diphthongized /i/ and /u/ to /aɪ/ and /aʊ/) worked its way toward completion. In southern England its last stages were being sorted out, while more peripheral areas of the British Isles were in the midst of earlier stages of a shift that has never been completed. Given their heterogeneity, emigrants to the American colonies would have brought to America various stages of the overall pattern. The spellings *plase* 'please' and *schame* 'scheme' in eighteenth-century letters indicate that Irish emigrants brought the "*meat-mate* merger," in which /e/ had not raised to /i/ (Montgomery 1997c). Krapp (1925, 2: 125–8) finds evidence of this alternation in seventeenth-century New England and considers it a common inheritance by Irish and American English from British English. The unraised vowel in modern American English appears in only isolated lexical forms (/rel/ 'real'), as do other manifestations of the uncompleted shift (/druθ/ 'drought').

It is the modern reflexes of Middle English *i* and *u* that most likely reveal the uncompleted shift in American English. In several American (and Canadian) varieties, the vowel nucleus of diphthongs derived from the historic vowels are centralized, but usually only before voiceless consonants. The details are complex (Whitehall). Kurath and McDavid (110) found this pattern in discontinuous Atlantic areas: (1) coastal Maine, southern New Hampshire, and upstate New York, (2) tidewater Virginia and adjacent parts of Maryland and North Carolina, and (3) coastal South Carolina and Georgia. When and by whom the centralized diphthongs were brought to America has not been established convincingly. According to Kurath (1928a, 292), the centralized onset before voiceless consonants "has its parallel in northern England" today, and more recently Lass (1987, 285) agreed that the tendency was "very like the Aitken's Law alternation . . . in Scots." Further comparative research is needed on the

142

phonetic characteristics of these and other diphthongs to establish their history and antecedents.

3.7.1.6 Loss of aspiration in *what, while*

At the time of emigration, the initial aspirate was rapidly losing ground in Britain socially and geographically. Walker (xiii) cited Londoners as having the fault of "not sounding *h* after *w*," indicating that educated classes had lost the consonant by the end of the eighteenth century, if not long before. The process began in the south and spread northward, so that by the late nineteenth century the prevalence of aspiration had shrunk to the northernmost counties (J. Wright 1905, 240). Krapp (1925, 2: 245) found variable aspiration in eighteenth-century America and considered it "one more of the many characteristics which American English has inherited from Southern British." Kurath and McDavid (178), in noting more frequent aspiration in America than in England, disagreed: "The widespread use of /hw/ in the Eastern States points to a rather extensive preservation of this initial cluster in parts of England at the time the American colonies were established, since the widespread use of /hw/, especially in the South, cannot be attributed to the influence of this spelling."

The extent to which /h/ has been preserved (or perhaps restored) as a spelling pronunciation remains to be established. Unlike in Britain, in America initial aspiration has no discernible regional pattern, but it is not inconceivable that eighteenth-century emigrants from areas other than southern England had a role in establishing it in American speech. A related feature in England was the general loss of initial aspiration in *home, help*, which Sheridan (42) labeled a common provincialism that had reached the higher classes; by the mid nineteenth century the territory of initial /h/ had receded to northernmost England except for small pockets elsewhere. Krapp (1925, 2: 206) found no evidence of /h/-dropping "at any time or in any region" in American English. Another feature prevalent in eighteenth-century England that did not survive transfer was the medial glottal stop in *metal, bottle*. Possibly these features disappeared because they were stigmatized; the latter would not likely be detectable in misspellings.

3.7.1.7 Later British influence

That British English might have influenced American pronunciation with respect to the loss of postvocalic /r/ and the use of "broad a" raises larger questions of whether later emigration, American perceptions of British speech, or commercial and other ties of American cities with Britain contributed to American pronunciation following the Revolution. C. K. Thomas (193) believed that the lack of contact kept the speech of the mid-Atlantic area (including Baltimore) "the closest of any of the coastal types to the speech of the interior." Krapp considered a possible British role in the development of /tʃ/ in *future*, *nature*, but decided that the change was too general to have been more than slightly reinforced by a British model. He (1925, 2: 33) cautioned that "questions of direct and determining influence of British upon American speech since the period of migrations must always be stated with many qualifications and limitations." Whatever the fashions from Britain and their influence, they were counterbalanced by anti-English sentiment in many parts of the new nation.

3.7.2 Grammar

The generally accepted picture of American regional dialects, both present-day and Colonial, is based on word geography (Kurath 1949; Carver 1987) and to a lesser extent on pronunciation (Kurath and McDavid; C. K. Thomas). Traditional dialectology investigates few grammatical features other than inflectional morphology and verb principal parts, and relatively little is known about the morphology and syntax of eighteenth-century English because of the infrequent and uneven use of texts. Much of what is believed about Colonial grammar is inferred from later material, especially dictionaries and linguistic atlases. While this is to some degree inevitable, many patterns of regional and nonstandard grammar are recoverable from earlier texts (§ 3.5.5). This section considers selected features of American English morphology and syntax whose British or Irish ancestry has been posited, relying as far as possible on documentary research.

In one sense, eighteenth-century sources do not throw an especially interesting light on the question of grammatical antecedents. Many non-standard features (double negation, variant principal parts) in early American texts, and virtually all of those drawing comment from early grammarians and lexicographers, are demarcated socially rather than geographically on both sides of the Atlantic today and apparently were two centuries ago as well. These must have been transplanted from many parts of the British Isles, especially London, producing a general colloquial grammar in America (what Mencken termed "the Vulgate"). The region-to-region correlational approach for examining grammatical antecedents often does not work well, both for this reason and because many features continued to evolve in America (as indeed they did in Britain and Ireland).

That grammatical features have more often been socially diagnostic is shown by Atwood (40), who analyzed data from *LANE* and *LAMSAS*; he is able to regionalize twenty-five verb forms roughly, but finds the overwhelming majority of these and others patterned by the social class and educational level of speakers both within and across regions. Grammatical features have many potential advantages for investigating antecedents, however, not the least of which are that grammar generally changes more slowly than vocabulary or pronunciation (making it a better indicator of a speaker's affiliation) and that grammatical features often permit more sophisticated types of comparison (between rules and constraints rather than items or categories).

Regionalization of items in the British Isles is more problematic than in America because it must pertain to a somewhat earlier period. However, a careful assessment of the *EDD* and other sources indicates that a broad "southern British" versus "Scotch-Irish" distinction is valid (Montgomery 1991, 1997b) for many grammatical features and represents a first step toward regionalization of antecedents. Here "southern British" is a convenient cover term for the south and the Midlands of England. "Scotch-Irish" refers collectively to the northern half of Britain, as well as Ulster (future research may extend its application to southern Ireland). It is used mainly for the language variety brought by Ulster Scots, which was itself a mixed Colonial variety having components of Scots and Northern and West Midland English (brought to Ulster in the seventeenth century), and influences from Scottish Gaelic and Irish Gaelic. Because of British settlements in Ulster and the linguistic influences they brought, the two labels are not mutually exclusive. Some southern British features (*a*-prefixing, finite *be*) could have come to America directly as well as through Ulster. However, it is not too much to say that the speech of Ulster emigrants is responsible for much of the diversity of present-day American English grammar. Kurath suspected such an influence on Midland speech but was unable to detect it (§ 3.5.4) because his linguistic atlas survey was designed to elicit few grammatical patterns. Solving "Kurath's puzzle" requires focusing more intensively on morphology and syntax and including possible source varieties in Ireland and Scotland only partially accessible in the *EDD* and not at all in the *SED*.

3.7.2.1   Verbal features

Subject-verb concord is a grammatical subsystem that has been extensively reconstructed from earlier periods and scrutinized in varieties throughout the British Isles, as a result of which reliable transatlantic connections can be sketched. Besides the standard paradigm based on number and person of the subject, which marks concord only in the third singular, three other agreement patterns can be documented (Klemola 2000). Suffixal *-s* generalized across the present-tense paradigm occurs in the southwest, and generalized zero in the southeast of England. The Scotch-Irish pattern prevailing in northern England, Scotland, and much of Ireland marks concord when the verb has a third-plural subject other than *they* (as *soldiers goes* versus *they go*) or when the verb is separated from its subject, especially by a clause (as *they come and goes*). This system, in which the person, number, type, and proximity of the subject all govern concord, is ultimately based on a substratum from the variety of Old Welsh spoken in Northumbria and has sometimes been referred to as the "northern present-tense rule" (J. Murray; Ihalainen; Montgomery 1994b, 1997a; Klemola 2000). Its southern limits are the English northern Midland (McIntosh; Giner and Montgomery). Montgomery (1997a) traces the concord rule from fourteenth-century Scotland to twentieth-century Appalachian English and finds that the proximity constraint has been lost but that the type of subject constraint has not. This modified Scotch-Irish pattern is found in modern American English in the South and especially in Midland speech (Atwood 29).

Both American and British English have shown change and variation over the past three centuries in the patterning of the past-tense copula and auxiliary forms *was* and *were*. (1) Leveling to *was* in all plural contexts is a strong tendency in the twentieth century. *LAE* maps M22 and M23 show it in the English Midlands and the South, except for small pockets; Atwood (28–9) finds plural *were* common in America only in southern New England and attributes it to modern education. Regularization to *was* is so prevalent in regional and colloquial English in both Britain and America that it must have come with many emigrants in the eighteenth century, but it was not the only pattern brought. (2) In seventeenth-century Scotland (Montgomery 1994b) and eighteenth-century Ireland (Montgomery 1997c), *were* was used only with plural personal pronouns, meaning that variation between *was* and *were* followed the Scotch-Irish concord rule outlined above. (3) In southern England, *were* sometimes regularized in the singular: according to the *SED* (*LAE* map M21), *she were* occurs in parts of the South and the Midlands. An early nineteenth-century South Carolina document (Montgomery and Mishoe) shows *war* or *ware* in eighteen of twenty-two singular contexts. The first pattern has become the dominant nonstandard form in American English, however, as the second and third have receded, except apparently in eastern North Carolina, where *weren't* has been regularized for both singular and plural contexts (Wolfram, Hazen, and Schilling-Estes). Lack of concord marking in the third singular, producing *he do*, is southern (more specifically, southeastern) British. Trudgill (1996) has documented it in late Middle English in East Anglia; and G. Bailey, Maynor, and Cukor-Avila, in the Cely Letters of a prominent sixteenth-century Essex family. According to the *English Dialect Grammar* (J. Wright 1905, 435), "the ending is often dropped, especially in the s.Midl., eastern, and southern dialects," and *LAE* map M34 shows the lack of -*s* in East Anglia as well as the South, southwest, and West Midlands of England. Its historical and regional status in England, if not its exact currency, would seem clear, and a connection with the American South would seem plausible, given that Atwood (27) finds it used "fairly commonly" from coastal Virginia to Georgia.

This lack of third-singular concord marking has played a role in debates over the sources of present-day African-American English (in which zero marking is dominant), but its historical currency in American English is in question. In contrast with -*s* on plural verbs, -*s* on singulars is almost never mentioned in the literature on white speech as being variable, presumably because it occurs categorically. One study of early nineteenth-century white English finds the rate of the suffix to be 96 percent in the singular, but only 60 percent in the plural, figures that closely approximate evidence from black letter-writers a generation later (Montgomery, Fuller, and DeMarse). The lack of third-singular -*s* in African-American English may ultimately have a source in British English, but it undoubtedly has other, probably more recent ones that account for the pattern today.

Finite *be* is southern British but probably has one or more other sources in American speech. It is well documented in English folk speech: *LAE* map M28 shows it in the South, southwest, and the West Midlands. This present-day descendant of the Old English copula *beon* was, according to the *OED*, "widely spread in south. and midl. dialects" at the time of the dictionary's first volume in 1888. Emigrants from southern and southwestern England must have brought it to Southern colonies, New England, and elsewhere in the seventeenth and eighteenth centuries. This is consistent with *DARE*'s label, "chiefly NEast, Sth, somewhat old-fashioned," but the dictionary's citations show the verb to have once been general in American English, perhaps testifying to how widely the southern British settled in the colonies. Habitual *be* in African-American English most likely has its source not in Irish English, but in later, independent developments (§ 3.6.6).

The prefix *a-* on present participles (*a-blowing*) is southern British. Its source, identifiable as far back as Middle English, was usually a reduction of the preposition-prefix *on-* (still seen in *afire*). A century ago, the *EDD* found the prefix in the South and Midlands of England but not beyond the north Midlands (J. Wright 1898, 3). More recently the *SED* (Upton, Parry, and Widdowson 491) found it in every English county but three in the extreme southwest. Its historical and geographical presence in England argues English folk speech as its primary source in other varieties. In the twentieth century, American literature has widely associated the prefix with Appalachian English (Wolfram 1980), but *DARE*'s citation evidence and label ("throughout US, but esp frequent SW, Midl") indicate that it is far more extensive, in the past even more so. A remarkable similarity to the verbal noun construction in Gaelic has led some (Dietrich; Mencken 1936) to attribute its existence in Irish English to an Irish substrate. The currency of *a*-prefixing there is problematic, however, as mention of it is conspicuously absent from the literature on Irish English. Montgomery (1997c) found fifteen examples in the letters of two Irishmen, one from the north and one from the south, who emigrated from Ireland about 1740; it was indisputably brought from Ireland, though this could hardly have been its only source or its primary one. Most likely it was taken to Ireland in the seventeenth century from southern Britain (Montgomery and Robinson). Nonetheless, this feature highlights the possibility of multiple sources and their structural convergence.

The combination of modal verbs (such as *might could, might would*) is another Scotch-Irish feature. Because *LAMSAS* found these combinations in Pennsylvania, Atwood (35) suggested that they were derived from German, but their modern occurrence in Scotland, northern England, and Ulster indicates they are of Scotch-Irish provenance (Montgomery and Nagle; Fennell and Butters). In America they are found in the Midland and South (Mishoe and Montgomery) as well as in African-American English, but in more combinations and with different pragmatic functions.

Variant principal parts of verbs are uncommonly numerous in both America and Britain, especially in folk speech. Some of the variants reflect ongoing changes in verb paradigms in the early Modern period (this being evidence against the leveling hypothesis). Most of them are socially rather than geographically marked; indeed, relatively few can be regionalized in either the British Isles or North America. The only efforts at transatlantic comparison are by Francis (1961) and Viereck, both using present-day linguistic atlas records. Neither makes inferences about antecedents, but some correlations are apparent, and research using eighteenth- and nineteenth-century texts may well reveal others. According to the *SED*, Southern and Midland preterits *seen* and *growed* contrast with Northern and northeast Midland *saw* and *grew*. According to Atwood (40), in America *seen* is "chiefly Midland," and according to *DARE*, *growed* is "chiefly Sth, S Midl." Atwood also finds *boilt* to be "chiefly Midland," suggesting that American preterits in *-t* may be predominantly Midland forms reflecting the northern English and Scots tendency to devoice the final consonant.

Among other verbal features investigated for possible antecedence is the auxiliary verb *done*, found in the Upper and Lower South, as well as in African-American English. (Feagin, Schneider 1989, and Winford 1998 believe this feature is likely to have a Scotch-Irish source, but it needs further investigation.) More definitely Scotch-Irish is the combination of *need* and a past participle, as in "That thing *needs washed*," from Scotland and Ulster (T. Murray, Frazer, and Simon; Montgomery 1997b).

3.7.2.2 Pronouns

American English has several second-person pronouns to express plurality in addition to *you*, all but one of which are either American innovations (*you guys*) or contributions from Ireland (the Southern *y'all*, the Southern and Midland *you all*, the Midland *you'uns*, and the Northern urban *yous*, which has compounded to *yous guys*). *Amongst you* or *mongst-ye*, which occurs marginally in Virginia and Maryland, is documented in Suffolk by the *EDD*. British *you lot* and *you together* are attested as common phrases on their way toward pronominalization in England, but there are few plural forms there in comparison to Ireland. This is explainable on one or more counts. *Yous, yez, yiz*, the pronoun most common in Ireland today, is apparently a late eighteenth- or early nineteenth-century development through language transfer, as Irish Gaelic speakers attached *-s* to an English root to reflect a grammatical distinction in Irish. In England the *thou*-versus-*you* second-person pronominal distinction remained vigorous in traditional speech, while in more formal and standard varieties phrases have always been available to convey plurality. Further, not all American forms of Irish ancestry functioned as pronouns before leaving the Emerald Isle. For instance, *y'all* was apparently derived from the phrase *ye aw* in Ulster Scots speech (Montgomery 1992), but its many uses in American English (plurality by association, a collective pronoun, and others) are unknown in Ireland today, indicating that American developments are of greater significance than any facts of etymology. *You'uns* has its roots in Scotland, where *one* is frequently encliticized in a general process that also came to America, spawning *we'uns*, another double-barreled pronoun, as well as *young'un* 'child' and other forms. In America, *you'uns* (often written *yinz* or *yunz* to indicate its monosyllabic pronunciation) has currency in the upper Ohio Valley as far north as Pittsburgh. *DARE*'s yet unpublished citations support Kurath's summary statement of half a century ago, that its distribution is a Midland one.

The possessive pronouns *hisn*, *hern*, and *theirn* are southern British, occurring throughout the Midlands and to a less degree in the South (*LAE* maps M77–9), but not in the North. According to *DARE*, their distribution in America is "Chiefly Sth, S Midl, N Engl." The reflexive pronoun *hisself* is also southern British, showing up throughout the South and Midlands of England (*LAE* map M80) and characterized as "chiefly Sth, S Midl" in America. Both it and possessive pronouns in -*n* must formerly have been more widespread in America.

3.7.2.3   Miscellaneous grammatical items

Other forms attributable to the Ulster migration and found today predominantly in the American Midland (Montgomery 1997b) include prepositions *fernent* 'opposite, next to' and *till* 'to' (especially in expressing time: "quarter *till* eight"); the conjunctions *whenever* 'when, at the moment when' (as in "*Whenever* I heard about it, I signed up right away"), *till* 'in order that, so that' (as in "Drop me a card *till* I'll know you got it"), and *and* to introduce an elliptical clause without a verb (as in "He would steal the hat off your head *and* you [would be] lookin' at him"); and the adverb *anymore* 'nowadays' (in positive sentences, as in "Government jobs are about all they have *anymore*").

3.7.3   Redevelopments

The majority of British and Irish antecedents remained intact after arrival, but permeating many transatlantic connections identified in this chapter are processes of later structural, functional, or semantic shift. Continuing developments in grammatical and other features of American dialects have rarely been explored outside African-American English, but they resemble what has been found for creole languages (indeed, an understanding of such phenomena rests on insights from creole linguistics; Mufwene 1997a). If they have taken new senses or functions in American English or have modified their form substantially, items that migrated represent both antecedents and Americanisms, and their ancestry may be of secondary significance to their subsequent evolution. In fact, their modern manifestation may disguise their source. An example is *y'all*, the second-person plural pronoun widely used in the American South. It quite likely derives from *ye aw* 'you all, all of you' brought by Ulster Scots in the eighteenth century (Montgomery 1992), a form grammaticalized from a phrase in emigrant speech. In Ulster today it remains a phrase, though a rare one, with none of the many pragmatic and semantic characteristics of American *y'all* (Montgomery 1996b). As Mufwene (1994c) argues, researchers have progressed much farther in understanding African-American English than white varieties of American English as a product of contact, but the same considerations probably explain how many North American varieties have developed (indeed, he believes that the terminological distinction between creole and other vernaculars is a sociopolitical one). Other grammatical features that continued to develop after emigration include the following: *fix to* 'prepare to,' which has evolved to the auxiliary phrase *fixin' to* 'be preparing to, be intending to' in the American South; the combination of modal verbs, which has developed new patterns (Montgomery and Nagle) and new pragmatic functions to express uncertainty or indirectness (Mishoe and Montgomery); and *all the far* 'as far as,' a construction from Ulster and Scotland that has developed comparative and superlative forms *all the farther, all the farthest* having the same meaning (E. Thomas). Guy Bailey identifies many phonological and grammatical features that have arisen or spread in Southern American speech since the nineteenth century, some of which have a basis in British or Irish antecedents.

3.8 Research needs and conclusions

The input from Britain and Ireland complemented other influences in shaping the distinctive character of many varieties of American English. Certainly no variety of British or Irish English found itself replicated in North America, and no American dialect, however conservative, derives largely from the British Isles. In all types of American English the indigenous character is dominant, especially in vocabulary. Of the items diagnostic of American varieties today, more were homegrown than were transported or modified from abroad. Existing sources may never permit exact estimation of the British and Irish component in American English, though that component is substantial and unmistakably indicates the general origin of American varieties in the British Isles, even if precise origins are often not easy to isolate.

As the field has worked toward establishing antecedents, many research needs have become apparent, all of which will persist for the foreseeable future. Descriptions of Colonial English and input varieties are far from adequate, as much historical work is needed on earlier, nonstandard varieties from all parts of the British Isles. The field has many simplistic statements and assumptions about what must have occurred in new dialect formation in the American colonies, rather than documentation of input varieties and the extent to which these were maintained. This research must be informed by the expectation that such varieties are likely to be highly dynamic and to exhibit orderly variability.

Arguably the eighteenth century was as important as the seventeenth for the foundation of American English. It brought more people from more language groups to North America and into contact with one another. It saw far greater expansion of English-speaking territory and the rise of sectional differences. However, the eighteenth century remains relatively uncharted linguistically, and texts have been less frequently analyzed than for the previous century because fewer are published. This should prompt researchers to search for manuscript documents, and it highlights the need for case studies analyzing them (Montgomery 1997c). A firm understanding of the areas of the British Isles from which Colonial American speech derives remains elusive because of the diversity of early settlers, the uncertain social dynamics of colonial settlements, and the intrinsic difficulties of proving dissemination of a linguistic feature. Our knowledge of British and Irish varieties should inform, but not limit, our study of American English. Overemphasis on antecedents obscures the fact that American English is fundamentally innovative.

Establishing antecedents of American English requires internal and external evidence, documentation of both the language and its users. We must know when and from where emigrants came. That they spoke English is easy to determine, but precisely what varieties of English often is not. Regionalization of their language in the American Colonial period is an immense scholarly challenge. Modern regionalization is relatively easy, but it cannot be extrapolated unguardedly to the Colonial era. It needs support from earlier sources. For vocabulary, *DARE* can sometimes fill this gap. Research indicates that earlier sources will provide only a partial view of Colonial English and that little evidence will be found for many features, because they are too vernacular or too subtle. We may not be able to tell whether they are innovations or have British or Irish antecedents. When possible, internal reconstruction is a necessity, but in many cases comparative linguistics will be required and will, along with modern regionalizations, be useful for generating hypotheses for investigation and for informing research questions such as dialect obsolescence (Schilling-Estes and Wolfram).

The hypothesis of an American Colonial koiné is questionable on both philosophical and linguistic grounds, but we need better data and better informed conceptions of Colonial American English to test it. Examination of individual features of newly forming Colonial varieties suggests that koinéization was only part of the picture, hardly encompassing all the internal and external dynamics. Dialect diversity, especially as reflected in style shifting, was likely the rule, but this needs empirical investigation with more sophisticated and refined models for dialect contact than have heretofore been employed for American English (such as that in Trudgill 2000).

Because the occurrence of identical forms in two varieties is easily taken for transmission and because independent or analogical developments are always possible, evidence from demography is imperative to support a linguistic connection. Undoubtedly many regional forms were brought (and were sometimes used in literature) and only gradually disappeared. The advent of *DARE* and other tools has opened new possibilities for transatlantic comparison, but researchers must avoid a simple correlational approach. Correlation does not equal transmission.

The Colonial era was a period of both cultural transference and cultural re-creation. Many factors formed American English dialects, including selective retention of items from general British English and new terms that arose and became associated with a region. Understanding antecedents of American English is one element of understanding American cultural formation and change, an important part of understanding the linguistic diversity of North America and of gaining insight into the nature of language change.

FURTHER READING

Hans Kurath dealt most widely with transatlantic connections, and his numerous articles and two books (1949, 1961 with McDavid) remain the point of departure for many issues. Laird (1970) synopsizes and evaluates Kurath's evidence for phonological features. Within broader issues of language and dialect contact, the American Colonial period has received increasing consideration in the works of Dillard (1992), Mufwene (1997a, 2001), Winford (1998), and Trudgill (2000). Lass (1987, 1990) most capably deals with the formation of American English in comparison to other colonial varieties. Krapp (1925) and Carver (1987) are comprehensive descriptions of American pronunciation and vocabulary, respectively, and are indispensable tools for exploring connections between American and British-Irish English.

4 CONTACT WITH OTHER LANGUAGES

Suzanne Romaine

4.1 Pre-contact: languages before English in North America

English speakers were relatively late participants in the expansion of European colonialism. Long before English was much used outside the British Isles other European languages such as Portuguese, Spanish, and Dutch had reached around the world. The first signs of the global expansion that was to characterize the development of English in subsequent centuries and bring it into contact with many other languages appeared in the sixteenth century. Before that time English was little used abroad, and languages outside Europe had hardly any direct influence on it.

The waves of settlement and immigration that brought the first settlers to the North American continent covered an enormous time span and involved widely scattered settlements. Initially, there was little two-way contact between the first English settlers and the indigenous people in North America (R. Bailey 1991a, 62). English speakers had come explicitly as colonists, unlike the French, for instance, who came to trade. The English settlers lived in self-contained communities dependent on Britain for supplies until necessity drove them to seek help locally. The earliest words to make their way back to England came in travelers' reports and were more usually from European rather than indigenous languages. Even many of the indigenous words such as *tobacco* that eventually were to become part of international English came in via another European language first (§ 4.2.2.2).

The pre-contact aboriginal population had considerable physical, linguistic, and cultural diversity. The American Indian population of what is now the United States is estimated to have ranged from one to seventeen million at the close of the fifteenth century, when the Spanish and Portuguese were engaged in intensive exploration of the New World. These various Indian groups spoke some 350 to 500 languages belonging to twenty-five different language families. The total number of speakers of many of these languages was small, and the English-speaking settlers as well as other European explorers and colonists encountered a large number of different languages.

These languages have, however, been in continual decline since their speakers have come into contact with European settlers. Leap (1981, 116) estimates there are some 200 distinct language traditions (grouped into seventeen language families) among the surviving American Indian tribes in the United States, many of them concentrated in particular parts of the country such as the Southwestern and Northwestern states through policies of forced removal. There is, however, considerable disagreement over the number of distinct linguistic families in the Americas. According to some scholars there may be as many as sixty families in North America, while others such as Greenberg recognize only three families for all the languages of North and South America. At issue is the origin of the similarities among these languages and whether they are the result of diffusion from one family to another, or are due to common genetic inheritance.

The Algonquian language family is the largest of the American Indian language stocks, in both geographical spread and number of speakers. It includes languages such as Arapaho, Blackfoot, Cheyenne, Cree, Delaware, Fox, Micmac, Ojibwa, Chippewa, Narragansett, Pottowatomi, Powhatan, Virginian, and Penobscot. The first loanwords in America (called "wigwam" words by the settlers) were taken from these languages, many of them even before the arrival of the Pilgrims in 1620 (e.g. *moose, persimmon, terrapin, raccoon*), and the founding of the Massachusetts Bay Colony in 1630 (e.g. *powwow, wigwam*). Other language families of the North American continent before the arrival of Europeans include Iroquoian, Siouan, Uto-Aztecan, Athabaskan, and Penutian. The Iroquoian family includes Cherokee. The Uto-Aztecan languages are found in the Southwest. The Siouan languages are found mainly in the plains area west of the Mississippi (§ 4.2.2.1).

Long before Europeans arrived, many American Indian groups solved the problem of communication across tribal boundaries through lingua francas, such as Mobilian Jargon, a pidginized form of Choctaw-Chickasaw in widespread use across the Mississippian Complex from at least the beginnings of French colonial times and continuing until the mid twentieth century, or Plains Sign Language, used by various Indian groups in the Great Plains. Pre-contact use of indigenous lingua francas has, however, been little investigated (but see Crawford; Drechsel 1976, 1996). A greater variety of American Indian contact languages probably once existed than is suggested from the available evidence.

155

Historical documents report some complex multilingual transactions involving different groups of Indians and Europeans carried out in intertribal pidgins such as Mobilian Jargon. In 1742, the Frenchman Antoine Bonnefoy reported an encounter with the northern Alabama tribe, British traders, and Chickasaw Indians near present-day Memphis. Interestingly, Bonnefoy reports using Mobilian Jargon with the British, which he says they knew (Drechsel 1996). In the Southwest, Europeans used Trader Navajo, a simplified form of Navajo (Werner). More often, however, a contact variety of English was used (see § 4.2.1).

Early European observers no doubt often mistook intertribal pidgins as full-fledged American Indian languages. For their part, many Indians used their true tribal languages only among themselves and never in front of Europeans. In about 1908, a Congregationalist minister named Paul Leeds unwittingly employed Mobilian Jargon (which he believed to be Koasati) in his efforts to convert the Indians in southwestern Louisiana.

It is not always possible to determine how long a particular variety was in use and whether its existence predates the advent of Europeans. Linguists are not agreed, for instance, on the history of Chinook Jargon; some believe that it was already in existence before Europeans arrived (Thomason 1983) and others, that it is the product of contact between Europeans and Indians (Samarin). In many cases there was a "double illusion of communication," as suggested in this report from a French Missionary, Paul Le Jeune, who in 1663 commented on the use of a jargonized Montagnais in what is now Canada: "When the French use it, they think they are speaking the Savage Tongue, and the Savages, in using it, think they are speaking good French" (cited by Allan Taylor 183).

Similar arguments arise about the origins of Mobilian Jargon. Drechsel (1996) argues that the very word *bayou*, which has come to be so closely identified with the French colonization of Louisiana, is actually Choctaw in origin (< *bayuk* 'river, creek') and entered both French and English through Mobilian Jargon. Other words which came into English through a circuitous route are *pecan* (< *pacini*), and *moccasin* (< *manggasin*), which are probably Algonquian loanwords in Mobilian Jargon. The latter was noticed by Ezra Stiles, a Connecticut minister and later president of Yale, who recorded it from a surveyor named Selden, a former captive of the Osage Indians on the Missouri River.

Drechsel (1996) points out, however, that Selden's Indian vocabulary was at least in part Mobilian Jargon rather than an Algonquian language, as Stiles had believed. Since the use of Mobilian Jargon extended as far northwest as 500 miles upstream on the Missouri River, where the Osage lived, it could have served as the direct medium for Algonquian loanwords. Crawford (1978) suggests that the French had picked up these words from Algonquian Indians in Canada or from their Algonquian guides and interpreters who accompanied them on their explorations down the Mississippi River. When they arrived in Louisiana, they used these terms in their interactions with local Indians. The term *papoose*, also in Selden's list, to refer to an Indian child or baby is, however, found in both Mobilian Jargon (*papos*) as well as Algonquian languages (cf. Narragansett *pápu:s*), and, of course, in Louisiana French and English.

In many other cases it is not possible to determine the origins of certain words or phrases unequivocally. One famous case concerns the term *kemo sabe*, with which the Indian guide Tonto addressed the Lone Ranger in the famous radio and television program. While it has been traditionally derived from Spanish *quien no sabe* 'whom no one knows' or the Portuguese equivalent, some have suggested an origin in various American Indian languages with the meaning 'white man.'

A pidginized form of the Unami variety of Delaware was used during the seventeenth century in parts of what are now New Jersey, Delaware, New York, and Pennsylvania. It emerged from contact between Europeans and Indians and was used by the Swedish, Dutch, and English. The most extensive record of this pidgin is found in the *Indian Interpreter*, a collection of traders' vocabulary of words and phrases (Prince; Thomason 1980). There were also pidginized forms of Massachuset, Powhatan, Eskimo (Stefánsson), and Navaho (Werner), as well as a Tidewater Pidgin in Virginia (E. Alexander). A report about what may have been a lingua franca Creek in the early 1870s came from George Stiggins, an agent of part-Natchez descent raised among the Creek.

An increasing interest in pidgin and creole studies in the 1970s has stimulated a growing concern in American Indian contact media and in questions about the extent of pidginization and creolization in the history of American Indian languages (Barnhill and Reinecke). Brief sketches of six of the major American Indian contact languages (Afro-Seminole Creole, American Indian English, Chinook Jargon, Delaware Jargon, Eskimo Jargon, and Mobilian Jargon) can be found in Holm (1989).

4.2 Language in post-contact North America

4.2.1 Pidgins based on English and other European languages

Both European and Indian languages were pidginized and probably repidginized in the ongoing contacts between indigenous people and Europeans.

Allan Taylor (180), for instance, notes that contact between European fishermen and American Indians goes back at least to the beginning of the sixteenth century, and probably earlier. Pidginized forms of Breton, Portuguese, Basque, English, and French may have been used for communication. Certainly, pidginized French and English are well attested in other regions and for later periods.

There are numerous attestations of a pidgin English used by the Indians from the seventeenth century (Leechman and Hall; Dillard 1972; Goddard). English became a lingua franca for a few Indians who served as interpreters between the Indian communities and Europeans. One of the early examples of such intermediaries was Tisquantum (or Squanto), a Patuxet Indian who was captured on the Massachusetts coast in 1615 and then sold into slavery in Spain. He subsequently got to England in 1617 and returned to America in 1619. As an accidental exile in England, he gained sufficient knowledge to act as an interpreter between the Plymouth colonists and the Massachuset tribe. From 1620 until the time of his death in 1622 he played a crucial role in relations between the colonists and the Indians (Allan Taylor).

When Squanto returned from England, however, he found that his tribal group had been exterminated by disease, and so he attached himself to the Massasoit and Wampanoag. The English colonists were told about him by another Indian named Samoset, who was on hand almost immediately after the Mayflower arrived. William Bradford's *History of Plymouth Plantation* records the surprise of the Plymouth settlers when "about 16th March [1621], a certain Indian came boldly among them and spoke to them in broken English, which they could well understand but marvelled at it.... At length they understood by discourse with him, that he was not of these parts, but belonged to the eastern parts where some English ships came to fish, with whom he was acquainted and ... amongst whom he had got his language" (cited by McCrum, Cran, and MacNeil 120). It was largely thanks to interpreters such as Samoset and Squanto that the colony endured, for it was Samoset who directed the Pilgrims, in the words of William Bradford (81) "how to set their corn, where to take fish, and to procure other commodities, and was also their pilot to bring them to unknown places for their profit, and never left them till he died."

As Richard Bailey (1991a, 69) points out, however, contact with the settlers and their technology, which was in certain respects superior to that of the Indians, was beneficial to Squanto too. His access to the settlers enhanced his own power with people among whom his own status was marginal.

Interestingly, these interpreters were first called *linguoa* (Portuguese 1554) and later *linguisters* in New England (1649) and *linguists* (1711). They were apparently to be found on most expeditions as members of polyglot crews. Other American Indians such as Manteo, a Croatoan, and Wanchese, a Roanoke, were also brought to England and learned English. Long voyages provided opportunities for mutual language learning and intercultural contact. Thomas Heriot (1560–1621), who was given charge over these two men, was the first to elicit directly from native speakers a word list of an indigenous language. Only a few terms such as *skunk* and *manitou* survive from his 1588 *Briefe and True Report of the New Found Land of Virginia*. Heriot also prepared a dictionary and phonetic alphabet of the Algonquian language of Roanoke. It was unfortunately destroyed in the Great Fire of London in 1666 (R. Bailey 1991a, 63–7).

Some short examples of Indian Pidgin English are recorded in *Remarkable Adventures in the Life and Travels of Colonel James Smith*, printed in Lexington, Kentucky in 1799. Smith was captured by a war party of Delaware and Iroquois Indians in western Pennsylvania in 1755 when he was eighteen years old and remained with the Indians for four years. One instance occurs when Smith was looking at a piece of fat meat and a Delaware said to him, "What meat you think that is?" When Smith replied that he thought it was bear, the Indian said, "Ho, all one fool you, beal now elly pool," that is, "Ho, you're a complete fool; bears are very poor [thin] now" (Allan Taylor 180).

The spread of settlers westward beyond the Mississippi resulted in similar pidgin English varieties arising from contact with the Indian tribes. Not surprisingly, in the Southwest such contact languages are mixed with Spanish (Dillard 1975, 119). Pidginized Spanish was probably used in Florida, Texas, and the Southwest. Allan Taylor (181–2) mentions Chileno, which was used by Indians from the Bodega Bay areas north of San Francisco. The few recorded examples display a predominantly Spanish lexicon, but with little morphology.

The first systematic exposure of Southwestern American Indians to English probably occurred in boarding schools during the nineteenth century. Removed from the influence of their home communities, the students were educated in an environment where their native language was forbidden. The intertribal mixture among the school children meant that English served as a lingua franca.

A very early and little known study on this so-called "boarding school English" was done by Schuchardt. His main concern was to raise the question of whether the features he found amounted to more than an idiosyncratic collection of learner errors. In other words, had a stabilized and distinct variety of contact English developed among American

Indians? Later researchers such as Leechman and Hall and Mary Miller used the term "American Indian Pidgin English."

Schuchardt examined letters written by Indian schoolchildren at the Carlisle School, which Albert Gatschet sent to him. The Carlisle Indian School, which ran from 1879 to 1918, enrolled Indian children from the Western and Midwestern tribes. It offered vocational training and taught the children to read and write in English. No further studies have thus far been conducted on these and other Indian school newspapers, which seem likely to be rich sources of information on the nature of the early contact variety of English in use around the turn of the twentieth century.

Despite its many shortcomings, Schuchardt's evidence from papers published in 1881 and 1882 shows many elements characteristic of a stable pidgin: coalescence of masculine and feminine pronouns ("two Cheyenne boys, one she name Little Elk, one she name Kise"), pronoun repetition of a nominal subject ("that was my friend he is died; one girl she afraid; Philadelphy it is a large city, where ladies they learn"), variable deletion of the copula ("I very happy in Carlisle school"), and coalescence of personal and possessive pronouns ("he name").

Schuchardt does not take his analysis further and there were no other studies of Indian English for three quarters of a century (Leap includes modern discussions). Subsequent studies have shown that the English spoken by those of American Indian origin is not a homogeneous sociolect, but varies according to the differing substrate influences of the first or former languages of its speakers (Bartelt). This raises questions about whether it was a "true" pidgin or just a "broken" English, foreigner talk register, largely a second language learner variety.

Dillard (1972, 139–85) has documented the use of a pidgin English spoken by the Seminole Indians and runaway black slaves, which he relates to Gullah. (The term *Seminole* derives from Spanish *cimarron* 'runaway, wild.') Hancock discovered that this Afro-Seminole Creole, as he called it, was spoken until recently in Bracketville, Texas, and across the border near Naciemento, Mexico. This may be one of only a few cases in which a pidgin with a partial base in a native North American language actually creolized. Most of the Native American pidgins were never adopted as native languages. Indians who were not forced onto reservations often merged with poor white or black populations. Another case where Indians adopted African-American ways of speech can be found among the so-called Brandywine people in southeastern Maryland (Gilbert).

As continued westward expansion took Americans to the Pacific, they encountered different forms of pidgin English, such as Chinese Pidgin

English used in ports such as Canton, Shanghai, and later in California through Chinese immigration. During the first half of the nineteenth century some form of makeshift communication drawing on Hawaiian and English, referred to as *hapa haole* (Hawaiian 'half foreign'), was used for trading purposes by foreign sailors and traders during their brief stopovers in the Hawaiian islands in search of sandalwood, and later whales. Hapa haole was probably also used during the early years of the plantations when most of the workers were Hawaiians. A pidginized variety of Hawaiian was also used in early maritime contacts. The extent to which hapa haole was distinct from a pidginized form of the Hawaiian language is not yet clear (Bickerton and Wilson).

Hawaiian islanders were among the first Pacific islanders to travel in large numbers, they being willing crew members and recruits for labor on the North American frontier and later on whaling vessels. By the late 1780s Hawaiians had been to Canton and Vancouver Island. On the North American west coast they served as trappers and canoeists. A typical trapping party described in 1818 was made up of twenty-five Canadians, thirty-two Owhyhees (Hawaiians), and thirty-eight Iroquois.

Through the whaling trade, which became a largely American dominated enterprise centered in New England, Hawaiian Pidgin and hapa haole spread. By the 1820s groups of Hawaiians could be found in New England ports such as Nantucket and along the coast of California. The *Boston Recorder* reported twenty Sandwich Islanders residing in Nantucket. An early convert to Christianity, Henry 'Ōpūkaha'ia, who died in Connecticut in 1818, had traveled extensively at sea before being converted. Although he lived there some years, his English apparently retained its broken character.

By the 1840s more than a thousand Hawaiians left the islands each year for employment. In his book *Two Years before the Mast* Richard Henry Dana, Jr., a young New England gentleman, gave a detailed account of his experiences as a common seaman in the years 1834–5, when he was in his twenties. Among the people he met when his ship, the *Pilgrim*, stopped at San Diego, were a group of Sandwich Islanders (as Hawaiians were then called), who had set up temporary residence in a bread oven left behind by the crew of a Russian ship. The oven became known as the Kanaka Hotel. Pacific Islanders were called *kanakas* by whites. The term comes from Hawaiian and other Polynesian languages and means a 'man' or 'human being.' The Kanaka Hotel had a door at the side, a vent hole at the top and was big enough to hold eight or ten men. The Hawaiians had covered the floor with mats they had carried with them from the Hawaiian Islands and covered up the vent hole so they could use the oven as a refuge from bad weather. Inside they played cards, drank, and sang.

These Hawaiians overseas were part of a much larger group, as many as 3,000, who served on foreign vessels, many never to return to Hawaii. Having made enough money from the last job to support themselves for a while, nothing could induce them to take another job until their money ran out. Dana (176) tells how his own Captain Thompson tried to get three or four of them aboard the *Pilgrim* since he was short of men. Although the Captain offered them fifteen dollars a month, their spokesman, a Hawaiian known all over California as Mannini, declined by saying, "*Aole! aole make make makou i ka hana.* [no, no we don't want work]. Now got plenty money; no good, work. *Mamule* [after], money *pau* [gone] – all gone. Ah! very good, work! – *maikai, hana hana nui!*" [yes, work a lot]. When the captain replied, "But you'll spend all your money in this way," Mannini said, "Aye! me know that. By-'em-by money *pau* – all gone; then Kanaka work plenty."

Later Hawaii Creole English developed as a native language among the children of the plantation workers during the early part of the twentieth century. Although locally called "pidgin," it is technically a creole since it functions as the native language of most of its users rather than as a second language.

Pidginized French was also used in the seventeenth century. One case is the French-based jargon in use between fishermen and Micmac Indians in Nova Scotia. A partially French-based variety still serves as the language of persons of mixed blood resulting from intermarriage between French traders and Amerindian women in the late eighteenth and early nineteenth centuries. These people are called Métis 'mixed' and their language, Michif, is spoken in the Canadian provinces of Manitoba and Saskatchewan as well as in the states of North Dakota and Montana. In Montana there may be as many as 2,000 speakers, while in Canada perhaps fewer than 1,000. There may also be isolated pockets of Michif speakers elsewhere in the two countries. While the Métis were in contact with Indian nations, their primary language was an American Indian one, but it became French after the frontier moved further west and left them stranded among a European majority (Allan Taylor 180–1). Many Michif nouns are of French origin, as are some grammatical elements such as articles, adjectives, possessive pronouns, and prepositions. However, the verbs and verbal inflections are Cree (Bakker).

4.2.2   Languages of colonization

There were three great waves of European immigration to North America. It was during the first of these that English was transplanted by colonists who settled in Jamestown in 1607 and elsewhere along the Atlantic seaboard in the seventeenth century. An earlier attempt by Sir Walter Raleigh to establish a colony on Roanoke Island in 1585 had to be abandoned because of tensions between the settlers and the Spanish, on the one hand, and the Indians on the other. Yet it was with Raleigh that colonization began in earnest.

The second period occurs during the expansion of the original thirteen colonies west of the Appalachians and closes roughly with the outbreak of the Civil War in 1860. During this time fresh immigrants, mainly from Ireland and Germany, arrived. Before the Civil War, and even as late as 1890, most of the immigrants came from the British Isles and northern European countries, but during the third period and particularly after 1890, people from southern European and the Slavic countries entered in great numbers.

Immigrants came to escape religious persecution, the turmoil of wars, and economic misery. Indeed, emigration to the colonies became so massive that European countries were alarmed and some passed edicts against emigrating. It is estimated that around one fifth of the total population of Sweden and Norway left. In addition, the slave trade began a forced immigration in the seventeenth century, which ended about the middle of the nineteenth. Each of these periods of immigration left an impact on the English that was to emerge in the United States. In the rest of this chapter, colonial languages (primarily English, French, German, and Spanish) will be distinguished from the languages of subsequent immigration, although some languages, such as Spanish, played a role both in colonization and immigration. Black English is dealt with in chapter 8, rather than here, but some of the contributions from African languages are noted below (§ 4.3.5).

Colonization dates from the seventeenth century, although individual settlers and explorers had preceded English-speaking colonists such as the Pilgrims in New England and the Jamestown settlers. As the seventeenth century ended, the sparsely settled and geographically and politically separate English colonies had developed not only distinctive social and cultural traits, but also linguistic differences. These were due in part to the regional backgrounds of the settlers in particular areas, to new terms created in particular areas (fishing terms in New England versus tobacco-farming terms in Virginia), and to whatever localized borrowings had entered the speech through contact with Indians and other colonial languages.

Different languages provided sources for American words at different stages. Borrowings from American Indian languages, for the most part, entered the language during the seventeenth century, whereas French words appeared mainly during the eighteenth and nineteenth centuries. In fact, the English language in America borrowed more words from Continental French than at any other time since the Middle Ages (§ 4.2.2.2).

By 1700, Welsh Quakers, Swiss Pietists, Finns, Danes, and Germans had established flourishing settlements in Pennsylvania. The eighteenth century was a period of consolidation, during which the scattered areas of settlement along the eastern seaboard were gradually joined together and settlers began to push westward into the interior. By 1750 there was an unbroken chain of English-controlled settlement, extending from the Penobscot in Maine to the Altamaha in Georgia. This area was the heartland of what was to become American speech. Within it developed all the regional types of Colonial English, which were to spread westward after the Revolution.

By the middle of the eighteenth century the English colonies of the Atlantic seaboard were an enclave bounded by the French to the north and west and by the Spanish to the south and west. Yet these English-speaking colonies extended their control over continental America until they absorbed the former French and Spanish colonies into the present political entity of the United States.

4.2.2.1 Contact between Native Americans and English speakers

Not surprisingly, the first Americanisms in vocabulary were probably borrowed from the Indian languages spoken by the indigenous tribes with whom the first settlers had their earliest contacts. Most of these words indicate natural and cultural objects with no counterparts in England. In 1608, Captain John Smith, for instance, mentioned a strange animal referred to variously as a *rahaugcum* or *raugroughcum* (from Algonquian meaning 'scratcher'), which later, in 1624, he calls a *rarowcun*. It was not until 1672 that the word became conventionalized in the form we know today as *raccoon*. In popular speech it is reduced to *coon* and is often seen in colloquial phrases such as a *coon's age* 'a long time' or *coon cat* 'a large cat with coloring similar to that of a raccoon.' Similarly, *squash* emerged from *isquontersquashes* 'vegetables eaten green' (1674). In fact, it was John Smith who introduced many of these terms into English in his role as explorer, administrator, and scientific observer. He had more extensive contact with American Indians than any Englishman before him and was the first Englishman to attempt a systematic rendering of many of these terms. *Persimmon* and *muskrat* (first recorded as *musquash* before the founding of the Massachusetts Bay Colony) also first made their appearance in John Smith's writings.

Siebert (290) claims that Powhatan was the source of more loanwords in English than any other Algonquian language, including, for instance, *chinquapin, chum, hominy, matchcoat, moccasin, muskrat* (a loanblend), *opossum, persimmon, raccoon, terrapin, tomahawk,* and others. Apart from Algonquian, only a few words from the Muskhogean languages in the south entered during the Colonial period, such as *catawba* (also *catalpa*). Among these languages were Creek, Seminole, and Choctaw.

Some words were also borrowed from Pacific Northwest languages, for example, *muckamuck* ('food') and *potlatch* (from *patshatl* 'gift'). These may have been adopted via Chinook Jargon, a contact language spoken along the northwest coast, from Oregon to the Alaska panhandle and inland along the major rivers. The term *chinook* means a warm, moist or dry wind that blows intermittently from the sea to the land or down the eastern slopes of the Rocky Mountains. *Muckamuck* has come to mean an important person, especially in *high muckamuck*. In contemporary American English the term *potlatch* means an ostentatiously expensive party with a vulgar display of wealth. Cassidy and Hall also cite the use of *euchalon* in the Pacific Northwest to refer to a smeltlike fish food, from Chinook Jargon *ulâkân*.

In what appears to have been the first proposal for a Dictionary of Americanisms, Richard Owen Cambridge (*World* 1754) commented that it was "high time to publish an interpretation of West India phrases, which soon will become so current among us, that no man will be fit to appear in company, who shall not be able to ornament his discourse with those jewels" (cited by Read 1933). Among the jewels displayed by Cambridge were expressions such as *make the war-kettle boil, scalp, speech-belt, string of wampum,* and *take up the hatchet.*

Mencken and other historians of American English give many examples of early borrowings such as *raccoon.* The term *moose,* for instance, is derived from the Narrangansett Indian word *moosu* meaning "he trims or cuts smooth," referring to the animal's habit of stripping the lower branches and bark from trees when feeding. Other words in this category include *caribou, hickory, opossum* or *possum, pawpaw,* and *skunk. Woodchuck* is from Cree *wuchak* 'fisher, weasel' via folk etymology. The original forms of many of these terms are obscure since early spellings are highly variable. Hodge (1907–10), for instance, lists sixty-four spellings for *Iowa.* It is also often hard to determine the precise language of origin of a particular item because a comparison of different scholars will produce slightly different sources and spellings for a number of words. For instance, Marckwardt (29–30) says that *squash* is a clipped form of Narragansett *askutasquash* and *mugwump* is a Natick word meaning 'great chief,' but other historians cite other sources.

In addition to names for flora, there were also place names and names for objects of Indian culture. Twenty-six states have Indian names, as do more than a thousand rivers and streams and many towns and counties: From Algonquian and Iroqoian languages come *Massachusetts* ('place of the great hills'), *Mississippi* ('big river'), *Monongahela* ('rolls with venison richness on the palate'), *Ohio* ('beautiful water'), and *Shenandoah* ('daughter of the skies'). Among the objects of Indian culture are *moccasin, papoose, powwow* (from *powan* from a root meaning 'he dreams' used to refer to a priest presiding over ceremonies), *squaw, tomahawk* (from *tah-mahgan* 'a beating thing'), *wampum* (from *wampumpeag* 'shell money'), and *wigwam*. All of these were in common circulation by the mid eighteenth century.

Other new words and expressions entered by loan translation or calquing: *to bury the hatchet, fire water, medicine man, paleface* (first used by James Fenimore Cooper), *peace pipe, to speak with forked tongue,* and *warpath*. The term *fire water* for alcohol is thought to be a literal translation of Algonquian *scoutiouabou*, and *paleface* of Ojibwan *wabinesiwin* (Marckwardt 33). Many of these words may have existed and first been used in Amerindian pidgins such as Mobilian Jargon (Drechsel 1996, who cites *oke lowak* 'water' + 'fire' for 'brandy, spirit'). Others, however, are likely the product of imagination, created by the settlers as stereotypes of Indian speech: *happy hunting ground, heap big chief,* and the like.

The Louisiana Purchase in 1803 prompted President Thomas Jefferson to commission the Lewis and Clark expedition, which while ostensibly economic in purpose, also had scientific goals. The leaders were to find out about the geography of the newly acquired French territory between the Mississippi River and the Rocky Mountains, the customs of the Indians who inhabited it, and the natural resources of the region. In notebooks of members of the expedition, many loanwords are found to name the new things that were discovered. Marckwardt (27) reports sixty-seven in these journals, although many of them did not endure in the language.

The total number of borrowings from Indian sources is difficult to estimate since many of the items in use in earlier times have since been lost. For instance, Clapin (1902) lists 110 Indian loanwords, but according to Mencken (1963, 106) only twenty-four of them had any currency at the time he was writing in the early part of the twentieth century. The rest survived only as proper names, such as *Tupelo* and *Tammany*, or had become obsolete altogether. Marckwardt (24–5) lists about fifty words which he believed were still current in the latter half of the century. The largest number of loanwords in his list are those concerning Indian culture and institutions, and the second largest group comprises flora, fauna, and food. Three quarters derive from Algonquian.

Other terms which spread more generally to other varieties of English include *caucus* (probably from Algonquian *caucauasu* 'one who encourages or advises'). The Indians of the Far West apparently made few contributions to the American vocabulary, although *hogan*, a Navajo term for a dwelling built from earth and supported by upright or slanting timbers, is one, and *tepee*, a term used by the Plains Indians to refer to a conical-shaped dwelling constructed of skin, is another. Most of the new borrowings that entered the language through contacts between settlers and Indians west of the Mississippi came via Spanish, such as *coyote* (which is probably Nahuatl) or through Chinook Jargon, such as *cayuse* 'horse.' It is possible, however, that the latter came from the French *cailloux* 'pebbles.' *Maize* came into Colonial speech from some West Indian speech variety by way of Spanish. From English it spread to French, German, and other European languages but became obsolete in American English, where it was replaced by *corn*.

As is often the case with borrowed items, some underwent semantic shift. For instance, *catawba* (also *catalpa*) meaning 'separated' was applied to a Siouan tribe living in Carolina. Then it referred to a grape grown in that area, later to wine made from that grape, and finally to the color characteristic of the wine. Similarly, *Chinook*, which was also originally a term for a tribe (as in Chinook Jargon), later referred to two different kinds of winds and a variety of salmon. In British English it can also refer to a type of helicopter. Another such example is *mackinaw*, which was the name given to the island at the junction of Lakes Huron and Michigan. According to one explanation, it is derived from *Michilimackinac* meaning 'great turtle' (Marckwardt 30). It became the site of an Indian agency where the United States government issued brightly colored plaid and checked blankets, which were then known as *Mackinaw blankets*. After the northern part of Michigan became a lumber center, the blankets often were used to make short jackets worn by the lumbermen. These were called *Mackinaw coats* and finally just *mackinaws*.

Another result of contact between American Indians and European settlers was the formation of a number of compounds with the word *Indian* as first element: *Indian corn* (brightly colored corn), *Indian giver* (one who gives what is ostensibly a gift and then takes it back), and *Indian summer* (an extended warm period into the early autumn) being some of the most common (Marckwardt 32–3). The origin of some of these combinations is obscure. Pyles (36), for instance, suggested that *Indian summer* may be so named because Indians predicted its occurrence to the early settlers or that Indians were responsible for lighting the brushfires common in the late autumn or early winter, or even that the period constituted a last chance for the Indians to attack the settlers. It is also possibly related to *Indian giver* because the settlers thought of the Indians as fickle and false and therefore termed the sham summer weather similarly. Although the term does not in fact appear to have been used by the early settlers, by 1830 it was used in England by Thomas De Quincy in the figurative sense of 'declining years' and much later by John Galsworthy in his *Forsyte Saga*. By the eighteenth century, when American English had already become a target of derision by the British, one of its aspects singled out for criticism (along with various perceived innovations and archaisms) was the borrowing of terms from American Indian languages, which were widely believed to be corruptions.

Many early borrowings made their way back to England in the reports of explorers, travelers, and settlers and were well established in written American English by the time Dr. Johnson published his dictionary in 1755. Since Johnson compiled his dictionary in an age when anything provincial or dialectal was heavily criticized, it is not surprising that he excluded slang, dialect (including Scottish), and "unnecessary" foreign words. Johnson never visited America, but his negative attitude toward it and its use of English is well known. In his review of Lewis Evans's *Geographical, Historical, Political, Philosophical and Mechanical Essays* (1755), he noted, for example, that the treatise was "written with such elegance as the subject admits tho' not without some mixture of the *American* dialect, a tract [trace, trait] of corruption to which every language widely diffused must always be exposed" (cited by Read 1933, 317).

4.2.2.2 Contributions to English from other colonial languages

At least seven European languages in addition to English were introduced into North America as languages of colonization: Danish, Dutch, French, German, Russian, Spanish, and Swedish. They differed widely in their impact on American English.

A Swedish colony, for example, disappeared before Swedish gained any importance as a colonial language, though it does also later figure as a language of immigration. The New Sweden or New South Company was organized in 1633 by capital from Sweden and Holland. A Dutchman, Peter Minuit, entered the Swedish service and was granted a charter for settlement on the Delaware River. The first expedition arrived in 1638 and set up Fort Christina at the present site of Wilmington. Despite the subsequent buying out of Dutch interest, the Swedes had a short-lived stay there from 1638 to 1655. In the latter year, Peter Stuyvesant took Fort Casimir which controlled the approaches to New Sweden.

The log house was an early Swedish contribution to the emerging pioneer culture, which gave rise to the term *log cabin*, which has since secured a place in the American pioneer ethos. Probably the most frequently used word of Swedish origin is *smorgasbord*, both in its literal sense of a table laid with food (originally Scandinavian open faced sandwiches called *smörgås*, and *bord* meaning table) and also in an extended sense of a large variety of anything, as in a "smorgasbord of opportunities."

Russian served as a lingua franca in the Aleutian Islands and the nearby Alaskan mainland between 1750 and 1867, but was of little importance after the purchase of Alaska. Danish had no lasting impact as a language of colonization outside Greenland. That leaves four main colonial languages with an influence on the development of American English: Dutch, French, Spanish, and German. Each had its largest influence in those areas where many settlers spoke it as their first language.

4.2.2.2.1 Dutch

In 1626, Peter Minuit purchased the island of Manhattan (Algonquian *manah* 'island' *atin* 'hill') from the local Indians for sixty guilders worth of trinkets. The small town of New Amsterdam established there became a gathering place for traders. When the Dutch West India Company opened the New Netherlands to non-Dutch settlers from Europe, Welsh, Huguenot French, Swiss, and Sephardic Jews began to arrive. New Amsterdam became a cosmopolitan town where many languages, both European and Indian, were spoken, particularly at the annual Dutch festival called the *kermis*, as well as at bazaars and auctions called *vendues* (a Dutch borrowing from Middle French *vendre* 'to sell'). A town officer called the *schout*, who combined the roles of mayor and sheriff, was in charge of keeping order at these fairs. The title still survives in the English term *scout*.

Relations between the Dutch and English were generally friendly in New Amsterdam, but in outlying areas there were conflicts of interest over boundaries. The English regarded the Dutch as an impediment to their further westward expansion. After prolonged English and Dutch warfare, the English confiscated all the holdings of the Dutch West India Company. New Netherlands became an English colony in 1664, and New Amsterdam was renamed New York.

Suzanne Romaine

Dutch was taught in the schools of New York until the end of the Dutch occupation and used in the city's Dutch Reformed churches for a century thereafter. In the upper reaches of the Hudson River valley, where Dutch trading posts had been located since 1610, it survived longer. Noah Webster reported the use of Dutch in sermons in Albany as late as 1786. Along the Hudson in the countryside of Nieuw Nederlandt, Walloon settlers built their *boueries* ('farms'). The *bowery* of the Dutch governors survived as a place name in later New York.

Dutch, as spoken in the colony of New Amsterdam, contributed the following terms to American English: *boss* (from *baas* 'master'), *coleslaw* (from *koolsla* 'cabbage salad' often folk etymologized to *cold slaw*), *cruller*, *Santa Claus* (from *Sinter Klaas*), *smearcase*, *stoop* (from *stoep*), and *waffle*. The term *boss* was apparently borrowed as a euphemism for *master*, as noted by James Fenimore Cooper, who also pointed out the subterfuge behind this substitution, since Dutch *baas* meant precisely the same as *master* (Marckwardt 50). Mencken (1963, 108) says that the Dutch probably established the use of the term *bush* (from *bos* 'uncleared woods or forest') as a designation for backcountry. The word also appears in South African English and has been borrowed into Australian English from American English. In American English it also appears in new formations such as *bushwhacker* and *bushranger*. Many Dutch terms are still found in the place names of the Hudson River region, e.g. *dorp* 'village' in *New Dorp*, *hook* 'hook' in *Sandy Hook* from Dutch *Zandt Hoek*, and *kill* 'channel' in *Catskill mountains* and the *Schuylkill River*. Other surviving names are less obviously Dutch in origin, e.g. *Flatbush* (from *Vlacht Bos*) and *Gramercy* (from *De Kromme Zee*).

Of the forty-six Dutch loanwords listed by Clapin, only a dozen or so remain in general use, but one of the most notable loanwords in American English is probably also Dutch: *Yankee*, originally a nickname for Dutch buccaneers. Although earlier etymologists sought an Indian origin for the term, Mencken (1963, 110) is convinced that it is to be derived either from *Janke*, a diminutive form of the name *Jan (John)* or from *Jankees* (where *kees* means 'cheese,' the term being thus *John Cheese*). However, no satisfactory answer has been given to the question of how this alleged nickname for Dutchmen came to be applied to Englishmen, and particularly to the settlers of New England, both male and female. It was already in use in 1765 as a term of derision, but by 1775 Yankees began to take pride in it. During the Civil War it became a term of disparagement again when applied by Southerners to all people from the Northern states. In 1917 the English began using it and its shortened form *Yank* to refer to all Americans.

Another legacy of the Dutch influence in American English can be found in expressions such as *Dutch door* and *Dutch oven*. Despite the fact that the surviving Dutch element is much smaller than that contributed by either French or Spanish, Marckwardt (48) claims that the Dutch words are in more general use.

4.2.2.2.2 French

Frenchmen from Normandy were fishing the cod banks of Newfoundland a century before the founding of the English colony at Jamestown in 1607 or the founding of Quebec by Champlain in 1608. During the sixteenth century, French explorers and traders made forays into the northern wilderness and established scattered trading posts that were to presage the French colonial empire. Early explorers in the West frequently depended on the experience of French guides called *engages* and the French word *portage* was already in use before the end of the seventeenth century. The French traveled freely along the border between New France and Maine, trapping and trading their furs at markets in Montreal and New Amsterdam. By 1700 they controlled virtually all the strategic posts along the St. Lawrence and Mississippi Rivers and many important sites on the Great Lakes as well.

French settlement was not limited to the North. French Huguenots fleeing religious persecution in France sought refuge in the Carolinas during the sixteenth century and attempted settlement twice, stirring up the Spaniards in St. Augustine. The English united with the French against the Spanish and allowed the Huguenots asylum in their colonies. The presence in colonial records of names such as *Faneuil*, *Bowdoin*, and *Bayard* are the result of Huguenot influence in New England. New Orleans was the center of French influence in the United States and still occupies that position today.

The extensive and earlier contact between the French (especially the missionaries) and Indians brought French versions of Indian names into English. *Caribou*, for instance, came into English from Algonquian via French. Noah Webster complained about the French spellings of some of these: "How does an unlettered American know the pronunciation of the names *ouisconsin* or *ouabasche*, in this French dress?" (Dohan 132). He succeeded in anglicizing some words, but others such as *Sioux*, *Iroquois*, and *Illinois* are still spelled in French fashion and pronounced without a final /s/, as they would be in French. There are also many terms associated with Indian life that are French in origin: *brave* 'warrior' and *lodge* (from *loge*) 'Indian dwelling.'

French loanwords, mostly nouns, fall into two main categories: terms for food and terms pertaining to exploration, travel, and landscape, such as *chowder* (from *chaudière* 'caldron') and *cache*. Before the Revolution, *bureau*, *bateau*, and *prairie* were borrowed and soon afterward, *gopher*, *bogus*, and *flume*. *Prairie* has given rise to compounds such as *prairie dog*, *prairie hen*, *prairie fire*, and *prairie schooner*. Other French terms, such as *bayou*, *depot*, *crevasse*, *picayune* (from *picaillon*), *levee*, and *butte*, came in after the Louisiana Purchase was ratified in 1803. The term *carry-all* is also French in origin (from *carriole*) via folk etymology. Food terms such as *jambalaya* and *praline* were associated with French high culture in New Orleans. Furthermore, three monetary terms, *mill*, *cent*, and *dime*, were borrowings from French.

Many French names were anglicized via folk etymology; thus, *Bob Ruly* was once *Bois Brulé* ('burnt forest'), and *Bob Low* was formerly *Bois Blanc* ('white forest'). The French coined *brulé* to describe burnt over ground on which grass had grown. The term *bois brulé* was also used as a pejorative description for the skin color of a person of mixed European and Amerindian origins such as the Métis (see § 4.2.1).

Despite these local adaptations, Marckwardt (37) is of the opinion that French borrowings were not as "distorted in form or pronunciation" as were American Indian terms. Of course, since French and English were related languages to begin with, less adaptation would have been required to bring French loanwords into conformity with English phonological patterns. French does not have series of pharyngealized and glottalized consonants as many of the Indian languages do. Marckwardt notes too that French loanwords show much less semantic deviation than do borrowings from the Indian languages.

Nevertheless, there are changes in meaning, often because many of the words previously borrowed were reborrowed later with a somewhat different sense. The term *portage*, for example, had already existed in English for several centuries with a number of meanings, some of which were already archaic when it was adopted in its American sense. Similarly, *dime* had come into British English as early as 1377, but dropped out long before it was taken into American English. *Picayune* was originally the name of a small coin, but became extended to refer to anything trifling. There are also cases where a French term was borrowed by both British and American English, but earlier by the American variety, e.g. *crevasse*, which in American English refers to a break in a levee and in British English, to a fissure or chasm in a glacier (Marckwardt 38). The term *bureau* in the sense 'a chest of drawers' is rare in British English, in which the word denotes what Americans call a *writing desk*, *escritoire*, or *secretary*. Today there are also significant differences in the degree of assimilation undergone by French borrowings in British compared with American English. Generally speaking, the British versions are more assimilated as can be seen in the differing pronunciations of British *fillet* /ˈfɪlɪt/ and American *filet* /fəˈle/.

Among the common items that show semantic drift is *depot*, which entered English in the late eighteenth century. It originally meant the act of depositing and then the deposit itself until finally it became a term for a place where anything was deposited, both goods and passengers, on American railroads. In the early twentieth century, however, Marckwardt (39) says that the term became regarded as old fashioned and countrified and a great deal of effort was made to substitute *station* in its place, resulting in such inconsistencies as the Pennsylvania Railroad Station located on Depot Street. Then the term later enjoyed a revival and was applied to bus terminals. The term *depot wagon* for a horse-drawn vehicle, completely gave way, however, to *station wagon*. Now the term refers to a particular model of car with ample rear seating and storage space.

Marckwardt (34) observes that French had a generally acknowledged prestige value for the early settlers. The language was important in New England because Calvin had written in it, while in the South, gentlemen were expected to have some knowledge of French. During the last half of the eighteenth century, prominent Americans such as Benjamin Franklin and Thomas Jefferson were important figures in the transmission of the language. Another factor favoring the survival of French in North America was that the French-speaking settlers (unlike, say, the Germans) arrived under the protection of an official plan of French colonization to establish a New France. Even after the loss of Canada to the British and Louisiana to the Americans, memories of New France died hard, and French retention in Louisiana is still high, where Cajun or Louisiana Creole is spoken. The Cajun (from *Acadia*) variety of French is of Canadian origin, while Creole is descended from the plantation pidgin and creole French spoken by black slaves and whites in the French Caribbean Islands. Although French-speaking communities may still be found in New England, particularly in Maine, New Hampshire, and Massachusetts, they lack the high status of the French-speaking culture associated with New Orleans and the language has been less well maintained.

4.2.2.2.3 German

Since Colonial times, Germans have been the largest group of non-British immigrants in America, and until recently they were the largest body of non-English speakers in the United States. Along with the Scotch-Irish, they constituted the dominant element in the Colonial frontier population. There were three or four major waves of German migration to America, and the

German component of American English was the first to come from an immigrant people rather than a conquered colonial rival. As early as 1683, immigrants from southwestern Germany had begun to settle in Pennsylvania, notably in Germantown, and after 1700 in German Flats, a region in Herkimer county near Utica, New York. The Westricher variety of German spoken in the Palatinate became known as Pennsylvania Dutch (from *Deutsch* 'German') and continues to be spoken today, particularly by the Old Order Amish and Mennonites, among whom it has survived through their maintenance of traditional lifestyles and religious conservatism.

The second wave of German migration, begun as early as 1830, was concentrated mainly in Midwestern metropolitan centers such as Milwaukee, Chicago, Cleveland, Detroit, and St. Louis, but also in Buffalo and New York. German-language daily newspapers flourished in all the large cities of the Midwest until 1917, and many communities had their own German schools. In Colonial days, signs appeared in both English and German, and often only in German (to Benjamin Franklin's disgust). Given the size of the German population, one would expect the language to have had a significant impact on American English. Unlike other groups such as the Irish and Scotch-Irish, the Germans, however, did not assimilate easily in heavily populated German-speaking areas and they contributed little except regional terms to the vocabulary. Later influxes of German immigrants aroused similar negative reactions to those voiced by Franklin (§ 4.2.2.3).

Most of the German elements in American English, such as *lager, kindergarten, wiener, pumpernickel, delicatessen,* and *frankfurter,* date from after the Revolution, although *sauerkraut, noodle,* and *pretzel* are probably older. The term *hamburger* gave rise to many new combinations: *hamburger stand, hamburger bun, hamburger steak.* The suffix *-burger* has made new creations possible via folk etymology, e.g. *chickenburger, pizzaburger, cheeseburger,* and even *mooseburger* and *buffaloburger.* Originally the term referred to a food associated with a geographical area, in this case, Hamburg (so also *frankfurter,* associated with Frankfurt). However, the meat of the hamburger suggested to some speakers a connection with *ham* and *burger* came to denote what surrounded it, or the way in which the food was made into a patty in a sandwich. The suffix *-fest* has been used productively in compounds such as *songfest, gabfest,* and *funfest.* The prefix *ker-,* used to form expressions (often onomatopoeic) like *kerplonk* and *kerflop,* is probably derived from the German prefix *ge-.*

4.2.2.2.4 Spanish
Contributions from colonial and immigrant Spanish to American English are greater than those of any other Continental European language. Until

California was annexed to the United States in the late 1840s, Spanish had been a prestige language associated with the Spanish Conquest. Nevertheless, even today Spanish speakers continue to have an important influence on the English language in the United States through successive waves of immigration from Mexico, Puerto Rico, and Cuba (in order of relative chronology and numerical importance). These immigrations have, to a certain extent, re-Hispanized parts of the United States that were once Spanish borderlands and injected an element of Spanish language and culture in urban focal points such as Miami, Los Angeles, and New York City. Most of the varieties of Spanish brought with the immigrants are nonstandard and now show heavy influence from English (Amastae and Elias-Olivares).

Of the nearly 9 million persons of Hispanic ancestry in the United States, 60 percent reside in five states: Arizona, California, Colorado, New Mexico, and Texas. With 6.5 million of them claiming to speak Spanish at home, Spanish is clearly the most important immigrant language in the country. The significance of the Hispanic element in the United States population has never been greater than in the latter part of the twentieth century. In the twenty-first century, Hispanics alone may constitute over 30 percent of the total population of the United States. In Los Angeles, for example, a city with almost 50 percent of the Hispanic population of California, the 1990 census reported during a ten-year period an increase of 2 million persons five years or older who claimed to speak Spanish at home.

Most of the Spanish loanwords date from after the Louisiana Purchase in 1803 because there was very little contact between the first English-speaking settlers and the Spaniards in the Southwest until Zebulon Pike's expedition in 1806 provided impetus for Anglo expansion across the plains. The Spanish empire was thinly spread out in the Southwest, apart from St. Augustine, Florida, which was a target of both the French and the English from the time of its founding in 1565. Some Spaniards also went north to New France to compete in the lucrative fur trade.

The first Spanish loanwords were primarily adaptations of Indian terms picked up by early explorers in the West Indies. For example, the first word of North American origin to be used in English in 1533, *guaiacum* (a Caribbean tree whose resin was used as a medicine), was borrowed by the Spanish from the Taino language of the Bahamas (R. Bailey 1991a, 60). Other terms from indigenous languages that made their way into English via Spanish include *barbecue, canoe, chocolate, potato, tapioca, tobacco,* and *tomato.* The word *barbecue* is from Haitian *barbacoa,* meaning a frame set up to lift a bed off the ground, which later acquired the meaning of a frame for roasting meat. There are, however, some genuine Spanish words dating from the sixteenth and seventeenth centuries, such as *alligator* (1568), *creole* (1604), *key* ('islet' 1697), *pickaninny* (1657), and *sarsaparilla* (1577). *Sassafras* (1577) may also belong in this list. The *OED* says that its Spanish origin is unclear; it may be American Indian. Richard Bailey (1991a, 60), however, believes it entered English via French. Other Spanish loans from the sixteenth century include *banana*, *cannibal* (from *Cariba*, a tribal name meaning 'strong men'), *cockroach* (derived from *cucaracha* by folk etymology), and *mosquito*. *Hurricane*, also from a Taino word meaning 'storm,' was introduced from both Spanish and Portuguese.

In many parts of the United States, Spanish was and still is the first language of large segments of the population. Today there are two principal Hispanic communities which are direct survivors of the Spanish colonial era. These are the Isleños ('islanders') of Louisiana and the Spanish settlements in New Mexico and southern Colorado. Major contributions to the English language from Spanish were not made until another century had passed and the English colonies had become one nation. In the Southwest, the Spanish borrowed terms such as *avocado* (probably from Aztec *ahuacatl* folk-etymologized by the Spanish into *avocado* 'lawyer') and *mesquite* from the local Indians, and those terms along with many others such as *canyon*, *mustang*, *arroyo*, *sombrero*, and *siesta* entered into English. Terms connected with ranching and the cattle industry come mainly from Spanish: *bronco*, *buckaroo* (*vaquero*), *chaps* (*chaparejos*), *corral*, *lariat* (*la reata*), *ranch* (*rancho*), and *rodeo*. Terms associated with Spanish architecture were also borrowed: *adobe*, *hacienda*, *patio*, and *plaza*. Expressions such as *adios* and *vamoose* 'to make a quick departure' (from the first person plural form *vamos* 'let's go') and its possible derivative form *mosey* 'to move slowly' entered popular speech. Other common terms such as *burrito*, *chili* (probably ultimately from Nahuatl), *taco*, *tamale*, and *tortilla*, popularized by fast food chains, are now familiar to most Americans outside the Southwest. Spanish also had an impact on American Indian languages in the surrounding area.

A prolific source of Hispanic place names can be found in Southwestern toponyms such as *canyon*, *mesa*, and *pueblo*, many of which would strike Spanish speakers as inappropriate. For instance, Spanish *pueblo* means simply 'town' but the English word refers to an Indian settlement. Similarly, *Nevada* was a Spanish adjective extracted from *Sierra Nevada*. Many current Spanish street names have been created by developers with no knowledge of Spanish. An example is *Monte Vista* 'mountain view,' possibly modeled on the probably authentic *Buena Vista* 'good view' but containing an ungrammatical noun + noun construction. Similarly, *Bayo Vista* 'bay view' is a hybrid formation of the kind often referred to as Spanglish (Craddock

198–9). The term *cafeteria* was adopted in 1893 at the Chicago World's Fair, and the suffix *-teria* has been used productively in formations such as *washeteria* and *luncheteria*, suggesting an element of self-service.

4.2.2.3 Attitudes to colonial languages other than English

Benjamin Franklin's negative reaction to the use of German in public has already been mentioned. It was he who queried why the "Palatinate boors" should be "suffered to swarm into our settlements and, by herding together, establish their language and manners to the exclusion of ours? Why should Pennsylvania, founded by the English, become a colony of aliens, who will shortly be so numerous as to germanicize us instead of our anglifying them?" (Dohan 145).

There were reactions against other colonial languages, too. For example, in South Carolina when the admission of new counties with predominantly French populations changed the representational proportion in the Assembly, some Englishmen asked whether "the Frenchmen who cannot speak our language should make our laws?" (Dohan 142). In New York the persistence of Dutch and French as languages of trade and commerce and of Dutch in church and school, prompted Anglican missionaries to appeal to the Bishop of London to forbid the use of either Dutch or French in churches and classrooms.

Today a renewed backlash against languages of immigration is making itself felt in so-called English Only laws, which establish English as the official language. While its advocates have failed to get English Only accepted at the federal level, a number of states have adopted it, including three states in the Southwest with large Hispanic populations (California, Arizona, and Colorado).

4.3   Major languages of immigration

A great flow of European immigration to the United States began with the Irish potato famine of 1847 and continued until the passage of the Immigration Act of 1921 and subsequent legislation, after which the influx was greatly reduced. Of the five chief languages of immigration, three (French, Spanish, and German) were also important as languages of colonization. The other two are Polish and Italian. Varying degrees of language loss are now reported for all these groups, and those languages that have been studied in detail, such as varieties of Spanish and Norwegian, reveal dialect leveling, code-switching, and interference from English. In recent years, however, languages that had been on the verge of disappearing have been revitalized as part of a phenomenon which Joshua Fishman et al. term "the ethnic revival." Only those languages not discussed in section 4.2 are treated here. Also omitted are contributions made by the Scots, Scotch-Irish, and Irish, since these immigrants were largely already English-speaking peoples. Contributions to American English from their original Celtic languages are few and their origins often disputed, for example, *shenanigan*, first recorded in America in 1855 or *shebang* in 1879. Here only Italian, Yiddish, Slavic, Chinese, and African elements are treated.

4.3.1 Italian

The Italians are near in importance to the Spanish as an immigrant population in the United States. Every state has identifiable Italian American communities resulting from the massive immigration that reached a peak between the years 1900 and 1910, when over 2 million Italians arrived. The direct influence of the Italian language on American English is not commensurate, however, being most notable in cooking. Many common food terms such as *fettucine*, *pasta*, *pizza*, *ravioli*, *spaghetti*, *spumoni*, and *tutti-frutti* are familiar to most Americans. Although *paparazzi* was probably not first used in English by Americans, the extension of that term in such forms as *video-razzi* and *rumorazzi* is American. *Mafia* and *mafiosa* acquired distinctive uses in America, and a number of related terms, such as *don* 'high-ranking member of the mafia,' *capo* 'head of a local unit,' and even *family* 'a local unit of the mafia,' are probably Americanisms.

4.3.2 Yiddish

Yiddish in the United States has had a brighter history than other immigrant Jewish languages, but the language remained strong only as long as new immigrants continued to arrive. Now it is in decline and has, in many areas, largely given way to Yiddish-influenced varieties of English called Jewish English or sometimes "Yinglish," filled with expressions such as "I need it like a hole in the head," a calque from Yiddish "kh'darf es vi a likh in kop" (D. Gold 288). Many of the following words are in regular use in New York by Jews and non-Jews alike: *kibitzer* 'one who offers unsolicited advice,' *mishuggah* 'crazy,' *schickse* 'female Gentile,' *schlemiel* 'fool,' *schlepp* 'carry, drag,' and reduplications like *money schmoney*. Formations of the latter type are productive morphological processes in the speech of many Americans of non-Jewish ethnicity with no knowledge of Yiddish. Popular books have made the Yiddish element in American English more widely known and appreciated by those of non-Jewish origin. The prominent novelist, Isaac Bashevis Singer, who died in 1991, was responsible for making Yiddish-speaking culture accessible to a wider audience since his works were translated into English.

4.3.3 Slavic

Although it is customary to refer to the Slavs as a new immigration, Slavic settlers were already in America before the arrival of the *Mayflower*. The only full-fledged colonizers, however, were the Russians, who after the discovery of Alaska in 1741, moved down the Pacific coast towards San Francisco. Economic factors were primarily responsible for later immigration. With the exception of the Czechs, who were for the most part educated, many of the Slavs were peasants who became a source of cheap labor, particularly in the large industrial cities of the East and Midwest (especially Chicago and Pittsburgh), where they went to make quick money, often with the intent of returning to their homeland rather than settling permanently. Slavs of the professional classes, especially those who left their homelands for political reasons, were later émigrés. Polish ranks along with Spanish, German, Italian, and French as one of the top five immigrant languages in the United States. Today Chicago contains the largest group of people of Polish ancestry. As with Italian, the impact of Polish has been primarily in the domain of food, e.g. *kielbasa* (a type of sausage).

4.3.4 Chinese

Chow in the slang sense of 'food' is probably from Chinese Pidgin English *chowchow*. *Chop suey*, *joss*, and *chow mein* may also have come via Chinese Pidgin English. *Yen* in the sense 'craving, yearning, longing' is from Chinese by way of earlier meanings including 'opium' and 'a craving for a drug.' *Brainwash* was introduced to American English during the Korean War as a loan translation of a Chinese term. More recent loans are *chi-kung* or *qigong* 'a meditative type of movement related to the martial arts,' *chi* 'the vital energy necessary to maintain health,' *kombucha* 'a mushroom or a tea made from it to which various health benefits are attributed,' and loan translations like *little emperor* or *little empress* 'an only and therefore spoiled child' and *barefoot doctor* 'a country doctor.' Recent loans disseminated by the popular press are often international rather than distinctive of any one English-speaking country.

179

4.3.5   African languages

Even before the Pilgrims landed on Plymouth Rock, slaves from the west coast of Africa were being transported to North America. The English language itself had already reached Africa by the sixteenth century, where it began to be used as a lingua franca over half a century before it became established in North America. In 1554 the first West Africans visited England in order to learn the language (Dalby 170). Most of the Africanisms survive in creole varieties such as Gullah (Turner) rather than in mainstream American English and are not widely known even in present-day African-American varieties of English.

Some of the words traceable to African origins may have entered English via other colonial languages. For instance, *gumbo* appears to be derived from Angolan *'ngombo*, but may have been introduced by way of Louisiana French. Likewise *bogus* has been attributed to Hausa *boko, boko-boko* 'fraud, deceit,' but compare Louisiana French *bogue* 'fake, fraudulent'; and *gris-gris* 'a charm, spell' is from Louisiana French Creole though ultimately of African origin (Cassidy and Hall). *Okra* (perhaps from Akan) was first used in the West Indies and may have come into English via Spanish. Similarly, *voodoo* (and *hoodoo*) from Fon *tovodoun* probably came through French. The status of *goober* (perhaps from Congo *nguba* 'peanut') and of *juba* as African loanwords is uncertain. Dalby (173) lists a few other food items such as *banana* and *yam* from both Mandingo and Wolof.

In addition, Dalby provides a list of more than eighty probable Africanisms (most from Mandingo and Wolof) in semantic fields other than the food and ethnobotanical terminology illustrated so far. Some of these are not borrowings, but calques, such as the expressions *bad eye* and *bad mouth* in Black English, alleged to be derived from Mandingo *nye-jugu* and *da-jugu* respectively (Dalby 177). Quite a few of these terms relate to music: *banjo* from Kimbundu *mbanza* 'stringed musical instrument' and *boogie (-woogie)* from Hausa *buga* and Mandingo *bugo* 'to beat.' Some of these may have been taken into African languages from Arabic, such as the interesting expression *obladee-oblada*, which appeared in one of the Beatles' songs in a refrain 'Obladee, oblada, la la la la, life goes on.' Dalby (184) says this is Arabic in origin (*abandan, abada l-abadin* 'forever') but is found in Mandingo as *abada* and in Hausa as *abadaa, abadaa-aabaadi* with the same meaning.

More controversial, however, is Dalby's attribution of *OK* and *uh-huh* to African sources. There has been repeated speculation over the source of what may be one of the most widespread of all Americanisms. Mencken

(1963, 173–4) lists quite a number of the foreign etymologies fancifully proposed over the years. In evaluating the considerable literature on the topic, Cassidy (1981) supports the explanation offered by Read, who published a series of articles in the journal *American Speech* during 1963 and 1964. Read shows that the earliest attested use of *OK* was as a playful acronym for the comic misspelling *oll korrect*, then used as a pun for Old Kinderhook, a nickname given to Martin Van Buren in his election campaign of 1840. Cassidy (1981, 270) points out that unlike other proposed etymologies, Read's furnishes an exact time, place, and reason for the creation and spread of *OK*. Cassidy also reminds us that the "discovery" of Africa as a possible source for Americanisms is associated with the Black Power movement of the 1960s.

4.4   Conclusion

English displaced most of the languages it came into contact with as it expanded and consolidated its influence. Later waves of immigrants found the English language already in place for the most part and adapted to it. In assessing the impact of other languages on English, it is important to remember that most discussions of borrowing (and, for that matter, most treatments of the history of English) assume a standard variety of English as their point of reference. It is then all too easy to lose sight of the fact that contact existed between local varieties of English and other varieties and languages. Thus, when we read that such and such a language exerted little influence on English, we must bear in mind that the impact of contact would probably have been much greater in certain areas than others. Yiddish, for instance, can be expected to have had little impact on varieties of English spoken, say, in South Dakota, while it has had a large influence on those spoken in the New York and Los Angeles areas, where there are large concentrations of Yiddish speakers. (Dorian discusses this point with reference to the alleged influence of Celtic languages on English.)

Similarly, if one wants to look for influence from the Hawaiian language on English, one would look first to local forms of English in Hawaii rather than to the mainland United States. The impact of Hawaiian on standard English is indeed negligible; *aloha, lei, hula, ukulele*, and a few other terms like *aa* (a particular kind of lava often figuring in crossword puzzles) are the only items generally known outside Hawaii. Reinecke (36), however, estimates that about 1,000 Hawaiian words may have been in use at one time in Hawaii, of which 250 to 350 were in fairly common use colloquially but not in writing (also Reinecke and Tsuzaki). Although this number is now fewer, many still persist in local English and many more in the Hawaii Creole English of older speakers.

Americans from the mainland United States would be as puzzled as non-American tourists by the following: "Go ewa one block, turn makai at the traffic light, go two blocks Diamond Head, and you'll find the place on the mauka side of the street" (from "Which Way Oahu?" *National Geographic*, November 1979). Understanding of these directions depends on a familiarity with Hawaiian traditional terms of direction relating to geography rather than to points of the compass. *Mauka* means 'towards the mountains' and *makai*, 'towards the sea.' The other directions are derived from landmarks such as Diamond Head to the east and Ewa Beach to the west on the island of Oahu, where the capital, Honolulu, is located. While virtually all local residents would understand the meanings of *mauka* and *makai*, a survey which I and some students conducted on one of the outer islands showed little familiarity among its residents with the term *ewa*.

A number of terms in Cassidy and Hall's *Dictionary of American Regional English* are labeled "Hawaiian Pidgin" (for what is technically Hawaii Creole English). Many of them would be familiar only to local residents, e.g. *hemo* 'to take off,' *hapai* 'to carry,' *hanahana* 'work hard,' and *haole* 'foreigner, now usually Caucasian.' They include both current words and some that are obsolete or obsolescent. The word *hemo*, for instance, does not seem to be widely known among younger people nowadays, whereas virtually everyone resident locally would know *haole*. The tourist industry now actively promotes the use of some Hawaiian words. As the Hawaiian language and culture undergoes revitalization, we can expect that more words may come in to replace those that now seem to be disappearing. Among the new words recorded by Algeo and Algeo (1993) is indeed *kahuna* 'priest.'

The Hawaiian example also shows that the impact of other languages on English is likely to affect certain speech styles and genres more than others, in that case, colloquial speech rather than writing. In the case of Yiddish, borrowings are more likely to occur when the topic is humor. Lexicographers and historians generally pay much less attention to these styles since their interest is focused largely on the standard written language, often in its most formal and literary styles. Marckwardt (56), for instance, devotes only one paragraph to the contribution made by Yiddish to American English, and mentions just three words that have passed more generally into the language, one of which he says is outdated. Otherwise, he acknowledges that many people in metropolitan centers might passively recognize five to seven others. Pyles and Algeo (304–5) treat Yiddish in a single paragraph under loanwords from High German. They mention twenty-two words of Yiddish origin and a number of others with the suffix *-nik*. They also list *goy* 'gentile' and four other Yiddish words of Hebrew origin (306).

Most historians of the language also take little note of more recent influences on English through post-colonial contact, such as that between Hawaiian and English. The influence of more recent languages of immigration such as Vietnamese also awaits detailed treatment.

FURTHER READING

Most histories of English have chapters discussing foreign loanwords and Americanisms in particular. Among the useful histories of American English are *All-American English* by J. L. Dillard (1975), *American English* by Albert H. Marckwardt (1958), *The American Language* by H. L. Mencken (1963) as edited by Raven I. McDavid, Jr., and *Words and Ways of American English* by Thomas Pyles (1952). Frederic G. Cassidy and Joan Houston Hall's *Dictionary of American Regional English* (1985–) is a source for vocabulary whose use is restricted by area or social group.

5 AMERICANISMS

Frederic G. Cassidy and Joan Houston Hall

5.1   Introduction

The use of English as the de facto, though unofficial, language of the United States is a natural consequence of history. English, the language of the settlements from which the present nation grew, continued at first to be used just as it was in the motherland. But a gradual loss of contact between that motherland and the colonies and, more important, the natural growth of the language in the new land from the experiences of its speakers there produced many differences, which the Revolution and new nationhood were greatly to increase. So in four centuries a new growth has developed on the "family tree." The aptness of the arboreal metaphor for the English language, with British English as the trunk from which American, Canadian, Australian, South African, and other branches have grown, has been questioned by John Algeo ("What Is a Briticism?" 1992b), who rightly points out that until the development of American English, there was no "British" English against which to compare it, there was simply English. That is, British English, as surely as American English, was born in 1776. Algeo goes on to say:

> A language is not a landscape, a tree, a river, or any of the other
> metaphors we use as concrete visualizations of what a language really is
> – an abstract system of relationships contained in the minds of people
> and expressed by sounds and marks. We must remind ourselves that
> when two "branches" of a language grow apart, they are not
> categorically distinct like the branches of a real tree, but continue to
> exchange influences and may grow back together.   [289]

With that caveat in mind, the tree metaphor can still be useful in terms of understanding American English as rooted in the already established and thriving varieties of language spoken in England before colonization. That the "trunk" was far from a homogeneous core is understood, as is the fact that over time, the relationships between the earlier and later varieties (the trunk and the branches) have altered as political and demographic balances have shifted. Yet the changes in vocabulary, grammar, and pronunciation between the English of the Old and New Worlds justify the terms *American English* and *Americanism*.

As applied especially to language, *Americanism* was first used by non-American observers – and critics – to whom America was a world different from their own. It was not "here" but "out there" at the other end of the telescope. This view was natural enough in the eighteenth century, when the word was coined after the American colonies had won their independence from Britain and had thereby become a new force to be reckoned with, pretending to go its own way, presuming to be different in its own way. With such pretensions, it had to be looked at quizzically in Britain as a rebel, its differences judged and neither easily welcomed nor uncritically accepted.

Americanisms – variances from what was considered good English usage – had to be carefully noted and judged, certainly not adopted unaware. In short, the word *Americanism* at first implied a certain critical caution on the part of the observer. Later it came to be used neutrally and even, with a transatlantic shift in the point of view, favorably or, as by H. L. Mencken, with overtones of manifest destiny.

5.2   Definitions

The first use of *Americanism* in reference to language dates from 1781, when John Witherspoon, a Scot and then president of Princeton College, coined and defined it (Mathews 1931, 17):

> Americanisms, by which I understand an use of phrases or terms, or a construction of sentences, even among persons of rank and education, different from the use of the same terms or phrases, or the construction of similar sentences, in Great-Britain. It does not follow, from a man's using these, that he is ignorant, or his discourse upon the whole inelegant; nay, it does not follow in every case, that the terms or phrases used are worse in themselves, but merely that they are of American and not of English growth. The word Americanism, which I have coined for the purpose, is exactly similar in its formation and signification to the word Scotticism. By the word Scotticism is understood any term or phrase, and indeed any thing either in construction, pronunciation, or accentuation, that is peculiar to North-Britain. There are many instances in which the Scotch way is as good, and some in which every

person who has the least taste as to the propriety or purity of a language in general, must confess that it is better than that of England, yet speakers and writers must conform to custom.

Coming at a time of vigorous debate about standards in language, when attempts to "fix" a literary form were at their height, Witherspoon's remarks are unusually dispassionate and judicious. The emergence of a vigorous new nation feeling its linguistic independence and having already begun to differ in some particulars from the mother tongue had sharpened the question. Witherspoon writes further about the conditions leading to change (Mathews 1931, 15):

> The English language is spoken through all the United States. We are at a great distance from the island of Great-Britain, in which the standard of the language is as yet supposed to be found. Every state is equal to and independent of every other; and, I believe, none of them will agree, at least immediately, to receive laws from another in discourse, any more than in action. Time and accident must determine what turn affairs will take in this respect in future, whether we shall continue to consider the language of Great-Britain as the pattern upon which we are to form ours: or whether, in this new empire, some center [sic] of learning and politeness will not be found, which shall obtain influence and prescribe the rules of speech and writing to every other part.

In short, Witherspoon, an educated leader, admitted the need for some focus of uniformity. He must have been aware of the several attempts already made in Britain to form an academy on the Continental pattern, none of which had succeeded. He must also have been aware of Samuel Johnson's prefatory remarks in his *Dictionary* of 1755 to the effect that change in language cannot be prevented: that the best one can hope for is to slow the process of change and guide its direction. This hope, though still alive among traditionalists, is weakened by the enormously increased complexity of modern life.

More recent definitions of Americanisms have been offered by our two historical dictionaries, made on the pattern of the *Oxford English Dictionary*. The *Dictionary of American English* of William A. Craigie and James R. Hulbert, though preferring *American English* to *Americanism*, sought to include "those features by which the English of the American colonies and the United States is distinguished from that of England and the rest of the English-speaking world" (v). Craigie therefore included "not only words and phrases which are clearly or apparently of American origin, or have greater currency here than elsewhere, but also every word denoting something which has a real connection with the development of the country and the history of its people" (v). This recognizes American differences as new growths branching naturally from the English trunk. (A convenient classified list of hundreds of Americanisms may be found in the introduction to each volume of the *Dictionary of American English*.)

Second, Mitford M. Mathews's *Dictionary of Americanisms* makes a much narrower distinction – certainly one easier to apply – which relies on the dates at which new words, phrases, and meanings came into use. In Mathews's view, " 'Americanism' means a word or expression that originated in the United States. The term includes: outright coinages, as *appendicitis, hydrant, tularemia*; such words as *adobe, campus, gorilla*, which first became English in the United States; and terms such as *faculty, fraternity, refrigerator*, when used in senses first given them in American usage" (v). This distinction relies flatly on the history of the forms and senses, specifically the dates of their origin in America.

For the present discussion, it is useful to recognize the validity in both Craigie's and Mathews's stances. The two points of view have been nicely reconciled by John Algeo (1992b, 287). He uses the term *synchronic Americanism* for any "expression with characteristic form or use in America, whatever its origin may have been," and the term *diachronic Americanism* for an "expression that originated in America, whatever its current use may be." We have adopted Algeo's terminology here, including in our discussion both those words native to US soil and those that were imported but which grew and developed here in ways they did not in other English-speaking lands. This inclusive stance admits as synchronic Americanisms a wide range of terms important in their reflection of America's development as a nation and a people.

In the generally chronological discussion that follows, historic trends and events provide opportunities to mention specific Americanisms illustrative of or emerging from those historic contexts. No discussion of this length can attempt to do more than sample the tremendous number and variety of such terms, however, and readers are urged to consult the dictionaries by Craigie and Hulbert and by Mathews for Americanisms up to the middle of the twentieth century, and to peruse such sources as *Fifty Years Among the New Words* (Algeo and Algeo), a compilation of articles from the journal *American Speech*, for recent additions to American English.

Americanisms began to enter the English language in the "Age of Discovery," when the "brave new world" of America was just beginning to count on the English scene – the late sixteenth and early seventeenth centuries. The language by this time had found something like a standard form for use in such public matters as politics, commerce, literature, and learning. The heavy inflow of French words, sounds, and sentence forms had moderated; the well of Latin and the new-found spring of Greek furnished a strong current in education.

Spoken upper-class English, based on that of the London area and the southeast Midlands, dominated. In popular speech, the language of geographical sections was distinct and well known. Stereotypes had developed, of which Shakespeare made good humorous use in *Henry V.* In that patriotic play he sets against the French a mixed, but unified, English military force with outlander captains – Jamy, a Scot; Fluellen, a Welshman; and Macmorris, an Irishman – all speaking their provincial forms of English but fighting side by side under the English king, whose language is the accepted "right" kind of English used at the court.

The American colonists a generation or two later, especially their leaders, tacitly acknowledged the prestige of standard English centered in London. They were also fully aware, however, of the considerable variety of provincial differences that existed, many of which were to make their contributions to American Colonial speech.

5.3   First additions

The earliest Americanisms, using the term broadly, were those picked up from the indigenous "Indians" by explorers. In Captain John Smith's accounts of his voyages, especially to the Jamestown colony in Virginia (1607 and after), the words *moccasin, tomahawk, raccoon, opossum, persimmon, chinquapin,* and *puccoon* are recorded for the first time, as also *cawcawwassough* 'priests and their assistants among the Chickahominy Indians,' the probable source of our word *caucus* (Arber 51).

New World Indian words had begun entering general English indirectly after 1492 by way of other European explorers, giving the language hundreds of names for indigenous animals, plants, fish, birds, and topographical features: *potato, cacao, tarpon,* and *quinine* via Spanish; *bayou, pemmican,* and *caribou* via French. These are Americanisms only because they name things found in the New World. Direct borrowings from the Native Americans, such as Smith's, were made at first contact and have continued to enter American English down the years as the frontier moved west and new tribes and languages were encountered, for example: *powwow* (1624), *wigwam* (1628), *squaw* (1634), *wampum* (1636), *terrapin* (1672), *catalpa* (1731), *tamarack* (1805), *mugwump* (1832), *cayuse* and *chipmunk* (1841), *sequoia* (1869), *hogan* (1871), *hoochinoo* (1877).

Probably the most valuable thing the colonists learned about from the Indians was maize or *Indian corn*, as they first called it, immediately simplifying that to mere *corn*. In England the latter word meant grains generally – wheat, barley, oats – and still does. In America it soon came to mean maize alone. The settlers learned how to grow corn, store it, and prepare it in various ways: *samp, supawn, nocake, apoquinimink, piki*. But of the many Indian-corn words almost the sole survivors today are *pone, hominy*, and *succotash*. *Corn*, an English word, came more naturally. The common foods now made with maize are *corn bread, grits, spoon bread, Indian pudding* – all English words, but given new meanings in America. *Maize* (from Spanish, which borrowed it from the Caribbean language Taino) is a largely unknown term, but Mathews's *Dictionary of Americanisms* lists more than 150 words and phrases using *corn*.

Proof that a foreign word has been fully adopted comes when it acquires transferred and metaphorical meanings. Indian words of this kind in American English include *hickory* – the tree, the nut, and the wood with its special sturdiness. The persuasive hickory switch or stick became the mark of the stern schoolmaster with "readin' and writin' and 'rithmetic, taught to the tune of the hickory stick." Andrew Jackson, the tough frontiersman, later president, earned the nickname "Old Hickory." Similarly, the weasel-like animal whose foul-smelling secretion is most difficult to get rid of, the *skunk*, has become a symbol of disgust and the lowest kind of behavior in human beings. The *woodchuck*, from Algonquian *wejack*, a marmot regionally called *groundhog*, has evoked in jocular folklore the unanswerable question: "How much wood would a woodchuck chuck if a woodchuck could chuck wood?" And throughout the country, February 2 is unquestioned as "groundhog day."

5.4   First colonization

Colonization from Britain, once it began, came in waves throughout the seventeenth and into the eighteenth century to four chief foci: Virginia, Massachusetts, Pennsylvania, and Appalachia. These colonies differed, however, in many ways – in the purposes that lay behind them, the kinds of people who composed them, the way they were governed, and the natural conditions the settlers had to face. All these differences are reflected today in regional variations in language and have contributed to the creation of Americanisms. The chart in Fischer's *Albion's Seed*, 787, concisely lists the characteristics of the four English folk migrations, summarized below.

The Virginia colony, begun at Jamestown in 1607, was sponsored and governed as a Royal colony, a piece of England abroad with the established Church of England, where the younger sons of the gentry and aristocracy might hope to acquire property and position. Settlers came generally from the East Midlands of England, with family connections in London and the Southwest. The common folk were farmers, artisans, servants, the men greatly outnumbering the women. The land was known to be fertile, and once the colony expanded up the James River and began to flourish there was hope of enrichment by the export of tobacco, indigo, and other crops to Britain. But growth at first was slow, with much quarreling among the men and few families to furnish stability. Indian resistance was also strong.

The New England colonies were better organized, both the Plymouth Colony with its single purpose of escaping religious persecution, and the Massachusetts Bay Colony, also a corporate body seeking religious freedom. Settlers came mostly from London and the East Midlands and were led by Congregational ministers and magistrates. There were, on the whole, fewer farmers and more artisans and tradesmen. Women were nearly as numerous as men, and the settlers came largely in family groups, with few elderly people. The land was relatively fertile. They had the good luck not to be much opposed by the Indians, who had suffered from a serious epidemic shortly before the colonists' arrival. But it was chiefly their good organization and self-dependence that made them flourish.

The Pennsylvania and Delaware Valley settlement came chiefly in the last quarter of the seventeenth century, its focus being Philadelphia and the Delaware River. Settlement was chiefly from the North and North Midlands of England. With the famous grant of land to William Penn in 1681, it was settled by Quakers – traders, artisans, and farmers – and thanks to Penn's peaceful methods, it was not troubled by Indians for nearly a century. It attracted many non-English settlers – Germans, Dutch, Scots, Irish, and French Huguenots – though it remained under government of the Penn family until the Revolution.

Early in the eighteenth century and continuing for half a century more, a great influx of settlers from Scotland and Northern Ireland moved from southeastern Pennsylvania down along the Blue Ridge into the southern Appalachian chain of mountains. Coming from highlands, these settlers preferred mountainous territory where independent small farms could be cultivated but the "plantation culture" of the eastern piedmont was impossible. Presbyterians and Anglicans, they settled in family groups, keeping ties with Britain and Protestant Ireland. Today their speech is the most distinctive regional type of American English, retaining more archaisms in vocabulary and grammar than other varieties have preserved.

5.5 English redistributed

These four chief migrations shared English as their common language, but it was never homogeneous. Even the members of leading classes differed in geographical origin and the "commons" spoke their various home dialects. The London type of English accepted and required in education was probably "more [often] honored in the breach than the observance." Especially in the rural areas of America, old terms continued in use after they had fallen out of use in Britain; later English visitors heard them first in America and took them to be "Americanisms." By our definition they are indeed synchronic Americanisms, though historically survivals rather than innovations.

For example, in England *autumn* – a French word based on Latin – had been introduced by at least the fourteenth century for what was popularly the *fall of the leaf* (recorded from the sixteenth century but probably much older). That English popular form became established in America – characteristically abbreviated to simple *fall* – and is now the regular spoken form throughout the United States though *autumn* has some formal written use. Thus a split developed: since *autumn* grew to be the term favored in England, *fall*, though British in origin, can be taken as a synchronic Americanism.

The same kind of development may be seen in the name for the last letter of the alphabet, *z*. Though *zed* is now the regular English form, *z* had also been pronounced *zee* from the seventeenth century in England. Both forms were taken to America, but evidently New Englanders favored *zee*. When, in his *American Dictionary of the English Language* (1828), Noah Webster wrote flatly, "It is pronounced *zee*," he was not merely flouting English preference for *zed* but accepting an American fait accompli. The split had already come about and continues today.

A more complex example of English variants being retained but reshuffled in American English is the case of *drought* and *drouth*. Both words descend from Old English *drugath*, but *drought* became the preferred form in southern England and the influential London area, whereas the conservative *drouth* hung on in the North and in Scotland. The immigrants to Virginia and Massachusetts, for the most part from southern and Midland England, kept *drought*, while the Quakers and Scots from the North brought in *drouth*. Interestingly, today, as the *Dictionary of American Regional English* (Cassidy and Hall) shows, *drouth* is more frequently the spoken form than *drought* (373 examples versus 327 in the *DARE* sample); it is widely used in nonurban areas in the central states. *Drought*, however, is more frequently the written form.

It is probably significant that *drought* was chosen by the King James Bible translators; to them *drouth* would have seemed provincial. There has been a geographical switch with the American Northern form coming from the British South and Midland, whereas the British Northern form has gone to the American South and Midland. *Drouth* is still alive in Britain in "relic areas" in the outer corners of Northumberland, Kent, Somerset, and Cornwall, and in a fairly solid area around Worcester stretching into Stafford, Warwick, Hereford, and Gloucester in the West Midlands (Orton, Sanderson, and Widdowson 249). But *drought* is the standard form in England.

Yet another English word that is an Americanism in a synchronic sense is *creek*. In England it means a narrow estuary or inlet on the seacoast, and in this sense it continued early in New England. As settlement moved inland, however, *creek* came to mean a small tributary to a river, and this is now its prevailing sense throughout the United States. In the North, except in New England, it is usually pronounced "crick." Though *creek* was in use in England from the sixteenth century, the change in meaning in the US qualifies it as an Americanism.

Competing with *creek* in the US are the regional terms *brook*, *run*, and *branch*. *Brook*, the New England term, has retained its English meaning, so cannot be counted among the Americanisms of either type. (Its use is now being artificially spread by government departments of natural resources for streams they stock with trout.) *Run*, however, found especially in Pennsylvania, Ohio, West Virginia, and Maryland, has a stronger claim to the label. Although its first occurrence in the *OED* is from Scotland in 1581, and the first American instance is from Massachusetts in 1605, *run* has remained an infrequent northern dialect form in England while it has maintained strength as a wider regional term in America. *Branch* is unquestionably an Americanism, which also maintains a strong regional distribution throughout the South and South Midland today. Although the word itself goes back to the thirteenth century, its application to a creek or stream has been traced to 1663 in a North Carolina government record, making it a good example of a diachronic Americanism.

Two semantically similar terms referring to intermittent streams and their channels can also be considered Americanisms in that, though they were adopted from other languages, they came into English through American use. Both terms are, predictably, regional in the US: *arroyo*, from Spanish, is found in the extreme Southwest; and *coulee*, from French, occurs both in the Upper Midwest, where French explorers left their mark, and in French Louisiana. (The distributions of all these words are set forth in *DARE*.)

5.6   Regional differences

As they grew, the four focal Atlantic colonies expanded northward, westward, and southward with their distinctive ways of life and speech. As the southernmost focal area grew, both from internal increase and external migration, the colonies of Maryland, the Carolinas, and Georgia were created, all ultimately with signers of the Declaration of Independence. Westward expansion later resulted in the creation of West Virginia, Kentucky, and Tennessee. But the coastal and piedmont areas of Virginia preserved some differences. Among the Americanisms that were born and tended to remain there were *ash pone* 'a type of cornmeal cake,' *chamber* 'a sitting room (rather than a parlor),' *cowpen* 'to manure a field by enclosing cattle on it,' *cuppen* 'an enclosure for cows beside the barn,' *dining day* 'a large dinner party,' and *frenchman* 'a tobacco plant that grows straight up instead of producing broad leaves.'

The Massachusetts colonies spread northward, creating New Hampshire, Maine, and Vermont, and southward, forming Connecticut and Rhode Island. Americanisms from this region include *apple slump* 'a type of deep-dish apple pastry,' *catouse* 'an uproar,' *conquedle* 'a bobolink,' *cymbal* 'a doughnut,' *dooryard* 'the grounds around a house,' *flummadiddle* 'a type of bread pudding' or 'nonsense,' *full chisel* 'at top speed,' *gam* 'a sociable visit, especially between whaling crews at sea,' *intervale* 'an area of low-lying land along a stream,' and *nocake* 'parched corn crushed into meal.'

The Massachusetts colonies also spread westward and southwestward into New York and in the process overran the New Netherland settlement begun in 1613. This overrunning resulted in the adoption of quite a number of Dutch words which, coming into English through American usage, legitimately count as Americanisms. They include *dominie* 'a pastor,' *vendue* 'a public sale or auction,' and *scow* 'a flat-bottomed boat,' all from the seventeenth century, and in later years *clove* 'a ravine,' *coleslaw* 'cabbage salad' (later folk-etymologized into *cold slaw*), *cruller* 'a twisted doughnut,' *mossbunker* 'the menhaden fish,' *poppycock* 'nonsense,' *Santa Claus* 'St. Nicholas,' *spook* 'a ghost,' *stoop* 'a small porch,' *vly* 'low ground,' and *waffle* 'a battercake with deep indentations.' One of the most successful borrowings from Dutch was *boss* 'an employer, master,' one of the small number of Americanisms that would be carried around the world.

But even more productive than *boss* has been *Yankee*. The word is almost certainly Dutch, but beyond that, the particulars of its origin are uncertain. It seems to have begun as a nickname applied by the English to the Dutch, in which *Janke* would be no more than a familiar form of *Jan* 'John.' Another proposal derives it from *Jan Kees* 'John Cheese' in derisive allusion to the Dutch dependence on cheese in many forms – as in the New England regional name *Dutch Cheese* for homemade cottage cheese, once the prevailing term throughout western New England, where the product, though universally known, was often considered a low form of food.

The *Yankee trader* became a proverbial figure in New England wherever he traveled, selling all kinds of small goods or *notions*, household necessities, tinware and clocks, needles and thread, and mechanical devices like the *egg-beater*. Yankees became known as sharp traders, hard to beat in a bargain, tricky enough to pass off wooden nutmegs as real. Connecticut became the *Nutmeg State*, and Mark Twain presents the "Connecticut Yankee at King Arthur's Court" as a modern, sharp, practical, material-minded, tricky figure, the antithesis of the romantic or chivalrous. Even before the Revolution, the New England Yankee had already achieved the proverbial character of a type who depended on his wits, was likely to overreach others if he could, and was in general *'cute*, or pretty sharp.

After the Revolution, *Yankee* was identified as a New Englander of any kind. During the Civil War, the term was extended to include all Northerners and, in the First World War, became for Europeans simply equivalent to *American*: "The Yanks Are Coming" in the words of the song that accompanied the American Expeditionary Force to Europe – a transmogrification that did not please American Southerners. And south of the US border, the phrase "Yankee Go Home" later typified the distrust of Latin Americans for the Norteamericanos.

The Philadelphia and Delaware colony was much influenced by topography, the Delaware River being navigable well into the agricultural lands and the mountains cutting diagonally from northeast to southwest, dictating the natural direction of movement. Settlement was prevailingly from the northern counties of England, especially by groups of Quakers, who settled eastern Pennsylvania, named *Philadelphia* the City of Brotherly Love, and dominated the state politically for more than a century. A few Americanisms from this area include *after night* 'in the evening,' *apee* 'a kind of gingerbread,' *corn pudding* 'a baked pudding of corn, eggs, milk, and sugar,' and *dough tray* 'a wooden trough.'

The area of south central Pennsylvania is much better known, however, as the source of a different kind of Americanism: words that came into

English through the German spoken by the immigrants who came during the seventeenth and eighteenth centuries from southwestern Germany and Switzerland. Pennsylvania German (or Pennsylvania "Dutch") words characteristic of the area include *all* 'all gone, used up,' *already yet* 'previously, before, ago,' *elbedritsch* 'an imaginary creature used in a "snipe hunt,"' *get awake* 'to wake up,' *hex* 'to bewitch,' *pannhaas* 'scrapple,' *snits* 'sliced dried fruit,' *spritz* 'to sprinkle,' and *what for a* 'what kind of a.'

The Appalachian migration, beginning in the early eighteenth century and continuing for sixty years or more, was the last of the large migrations from Britain. Some distinctive diachronic Americanisms from Appalachia include *bald* 'a bare mountaintop,' *boomer* 'a mountain squirrel,' *brogue* 'to walk, trudge,' *county site* 'county seat,' *gum* 'a beehive, or a trap for small animals,' *hardness* 'ill will, resentment,' *poke-sallet* 'the cooked greens of pokeweed,' and *project (around)* 'to saunter, loiter, or to experiment, meddle.'

But the Appalachian region is probably better known for its synchronic Americanisms, in this case relics – words and forms that have been retained in that relatively isolated area after having fallen out of use in Britain and in other parts of North America. Examples include *alongst* 'alongside of,' *antem* 'anthem,' *as* 'like, such as,' *coast* 'an area or region, such as a part of a mountainside,' *devise* 'to tell, narrate,' *disgust* 'to detest, be disgusted by,' *dunt* 'stupid,' *farce* 'to stuff (poultry),' *hit* 'it,' *'oman* 'woman,' *soon* 'early,' *whatsomever* 'whatever,' and *whindle* 'to whine.'

5.7   The westward movement

Before the Revolution and independence, exploration of the western parts of the early colonies was hampered by the Appalachian chain of mountains. But when, in 1750, the Cumberland Gap in northeastern Tennessee was discovered and in 1775 Daniel Boone led pioneer settlers through it to the site of Boonesborough, a new era began – the "Opening of the West." The Louisiana Purchase of 1803 added a huge, largely unexplored territory stretching from Louisiana to the Canadian border, which led in 1804–6 to the famous expedition to the Pacific by Meriwether Lewis, William Clark, and their party. In their journals they recorded for the first time the names of hundreds of animals, birds, fish, and geological features, as well as terms for practices of the Native Americans they encountered. Some of these words were ephemeral or remained quite local; others have entered firmly into the vocabulary of Americanisms and into the life of the nation. Among bird names are *rain crow, sapsucker,* and *duckinmallard;* among animals, *prairie dog, horned lizard,* and *yellow-jacket;* among trees and plants, *tamarack, simlin,* and *camas* or *quamash.* Very important for dealing with the Indians were the *calumet* or 'peace pipe,' *medicine* 'the magical power of the *medicine man,' medicine bag* 'a container in which the materials of medicine and its powers were believed to reside,' and *lodgepole,* 'a type of pine, from its use in constructing Indian lodges.'

The opening of the "Wilderness Road" to the West just before the Revolution added enormously to the feeling of elation, the sense of escape from conventional society, its laws and limitations. The success of the Revolution only served to increase those feelings. Hopes for freedom, adventure, political careers, and fortunes to be made, are all reflected in an outburst of the popular language that characterized the late eighteenth century and continued through the nineteenth. Among the Americanisms that mirror this spirit are a number of quite colorful phrases, many of which have survived to the present: *all talk and no cider, eat crow, dog eat dog, put on the dog, not dry behind the ears, keep one's eyes peeled, run one's face, easy as falling off a log, make the feathers fly, get even, get the hang of (something), bury the hatchet, hornswoggle, nip and tuck, paddle one's own canoe, root hog or die, take a shine to, keep one's shirt on, spoil for a fight, break for tall timber,* and *pull the wool over one's eyes.*

The American tradition of "log cabin to White House," illustrating the tremendous force of political democracy, began with Andrew Jackson, a man of the frontier who rose by his own efforts and personal powers to be a military hero and ultimately president for two terms and whose financial and governmental politics drew the nation decisively away from more traditional forms of leadership. Some words introduced in the Jacksonian era and after were *know-how, populist party, popular sovereignty, land poor* (as Jackson was in his early years), *locofoco, know-nothing,* and others now only historical. Under Jackson's successor, Martin Van Buren, however, the most successful of all Americanisms was invented and launched into popular use, now adopted around the world: *OK.*

The origin of *OK,* subject of many guesses and much debate, is now at last certainly established (Read 1963, 1964). It is the jocular offspring of popular journalism, fostered by political ballyhoo. By no means the first initialism, it nevertheless happened along at a time when the language of ordinary people and the use of abbreviations was getting more and more attention in the press.

OK's career began in Boston and New York in 1838, when a sort of journalistic game of using initial letters, often of comically misspelled phrases, came into vogue. To condemn an opponent, one had only to say he was *N.G.* (no good) or *K.Y.* ("know yuse" – no use). If a debtor disappeared overnight with all his assets, it was taken for granted that he had *G.T.T.*

(gone to Texas). One could satirically refer to an opponent as one of *O.F.M.* (our first men). Many common phrases were given the same jocular treatment, among others "oll korrect" which was claimed by political opponents of Andrew Jackson to be the way he spelled it – supposedly a proof of his illiteracy.

Later, when Jackson's successor, Martin Van Buren, was seeking reelection, a favorable slogan was fashioned from "oll korrect," and Van Buren was proclaimed to be *OK*. Further, his partisans created for Van Buren the nickname *Old Kinderhook* in allusion to his birthplace, Kinderhook, New York: thus he became twice OK. Not many of these jocular acronyms have survived, but *OK*, blazoned throughout the nation in a hard-fought presidential contest, apparently caught the popular fancy. Ironically, Van Buren lost the election and his opponents gleefully reversed the slogan, saying he was *"KO"* (knocked out). It may be that *Old Kinderhook* is patterned in part on Jackson's nickname, *Old Hickory*, or on Henry Clay's, *Old Kentuck*.

In any case *OK* survived conspicuously. Part of its success may be due to its simplicity and utility. Though other related senses have developed, its original sense of 'all correct' is still the basic one. *OK* is now found worldwide as a colloquialism, though it has never quite been accepted in formal discourse.

The movement to the West was a sort of outburst, manifested as much in language as otherwise. The spoken language was often the only language – schooling was scanty and not for everybody: the useful arts and crafts were mostly learned on the job in the traditional way. But the unexplored West held out such possibilities that book-learning often seemed unnecessary. Frontiersmen could live off the land through hunting and the fur trade, through Indian fighting, through guiding settlers to new lands ready for settlement, and later through the cattle trade, mountaineering, prospecting, and mining. What schooling Andrew Jackson and Abraham Lincoln got was elementary: they were largely self-taught, reading for the law on their own. To emerge as leaders they had to acquire the language of education, the rhetorical models of their day. But they also had to hold their own at the popular level with the people's language, as both men did.

The language of the frontier has perhaps best been represented by Mark Twain in *Roughing It* (1872, 330):

> As all the peoples of the earth had representative adventurers in Silverland, and as each adventurer had brought the slang of his nation or his locality with him, the combination made the slang of Nevada the richest and the most infinitely varied and copious that had ever existed anywhere in the world, perhaps, except in the mines of California in the "early" days. Slang was the language of Nevada.

In his famous story of the frontiersman Scotty's attempt to arrange a funeral for his friend Buck Fanshaw, Twain presents a colloquy in which the frontiersman's Western slang is as unintelligible to the minister as the minister's overblown clerical language is to Scotty (331–2):

> But to return to Scotty's visit to the minister. He was on a sorrowful mission, now, and his face was the picture of woe. Being admitted to the presence he sat down before the clergyman, placed his fire-hat on an unfinished manuscript sermon under the minister's nose, took from it a red silk handkerchief, wiped his brow and heaved a sigh of dismal impressiveness, explanatory of his business. He choked, and even shed tears; but with an effort he mastered his voice and said in lugubrious tones:
>
> "Are you the duck that runs the gospel-mill next door?"
>
> "Am I the – pardon me, I believe I do not understand?"
>
> With another sigh and a half-sob, Scotty rejoined:
>
> "Why you see we are in a bit of trouble, and the boys thought maybe you would give us a lift, if we'd tackle you – that is, if I've got the rights of it and you are the head clerk of the doxology-works next door."
>
> "I am the shepherd in charge of the flock whose fold is next door."
>
> "The which?"
>
> "The spiritual adviser of the little company of believers whose sanctuary adjoins these premises."
>
> Scotty scratched his head, reflected a moment, and then said:
>
> "You ruther hold over me, pard. I reckon I can't call that hand. Ante and pass the buck."
>
> "How? I beg pardon. What did I understand you to say?"
>
> "Well, you've ruther got the bulge on me. Or maybe we've both got the bulge, somehow. You don't smoke me and I don't smoke you. You see, one of the boys has passed in his checks and we want to give him a good send-off, and so the thing I'm on now is to roust out somebody to jerk a little chin-music for us and waltz him through handsome."

Another Western phenomenon was "tall talk," the kind of elaborate boasting that gun-toting bullies, encouraged with drink, could burst forth with. The following sample is from Twain's *Life on the Mississippi* (1883, 45), representing the period before 1850:

> Whoo-oop! I'm the old original iron-jawed, brass-mounted, copper-bellied corpse-maker from the wilds of Arkansaw! – Look at me! I'm the man they call Sudden Death and General Desolation! Sired by a hurricane, dam'd by an earthquake, half-brother to the cholera, nearly related to the small-pox on the mother's side! Look at me! I take nineteen alligators and a bar'l of whiskey for breakfast when I'm in

robust health, and a bushel of rattlesnakes and a dead body when I'm ailing! I split the everlasting rocks with my glance, and I squench the thunder when I speak! Whoo-oop! Stand back and give me room according to my strength! Blood's my natural drink, and the wails of the dying is music to my ear! Cast your eye on me, gentlemen! – and lay low and hold your breath, for I'm bout to turn myself loose!

Though the picture is exaggerated, it well represents some extremes of Americanism to which the language was subjected in the raw West.

5.8 The Webster impact

Although the frontiersman had little use for formal education, people in the established communities in the East had from the beginning evinced real interest in popular education. That interest produced one figure of great importance to Americanism, in both the cultural and the linguistic senses of the term: Noah Webster. Webster, a New Englander, was eighteen years of age at the time of the Revolution. He fought briefly in the War of Independence and as a patriot always looked toward a brilliant future for America and things American.

Webster considered the language used by the English to be "effete" and sought to improve it in various ways. Devoted to the education of the nation, he published between 1783 and 1785 the famous "Blue-Backed Speller," as well as a grammar and reader that became staples of popular education – the speller, especially, selling by the millions and serving throughout the country for *spellers, spelldowns,* or *spelling bees* (all Americanisms).

Though generally conservative, Webster was not afraid of change if it led to improvement. He worked out his own, not always consistent, orthographic principles (set forth in his introductory section, "Orthography," in *An American Dictionary of the English Language,* 1828). He is certainly responsible for establishing (though not inventing) the common differences between traditional British and American spellings – the final *-or* versus *-our* in *color, labor, savor,* and the like; *-er* versus French *-re* in *theater, center, meter;* and the simplification of final *-ck* as in *physic, music, logic.*

With Webster's lexicographical competitors Lyman Cobb and Joseph Worcester attacking and vilifying him, it is surprising that Webster's reforms succeeded so well, for they have become standard American usage. Probably it was his persistence as a forward-looking educator, pursuing his patriotic goal of showing that America could equal and in some ways excel in things intellectual, that ultimately won national admiration, for his name has become synonymous – certainly in the United States – with the word "dictionary," an accolade that not even Samuel Johnson was accorded in Britain.

Webster's enthusiasm for things American might well have influenced another champion of American speechways, John Russell Bartlett, whose first edition of the *Dictionary of Americanisms* was published in 1848. Like other glossarists of the time, Bartlett took pains to demonstrate that many supposed Americanisms were actually relics or provincialisms traceable to British English sources. He declared, "In fact it may be said, without exaggeration, that nine tenths of the colloquial peculiarities of New England are derived directly from Great Britain" (preface to the 1848 edition). His criteria for inclusion were not clearly spelled out in 1848, but when the second edition came out in 1859, its preface (viii) included an added note making explicit his intent:

> The term "Americanism," as used in this Dictionary, may then be said to include the following classes of words:
>
> 1. Archaisms, i.e. old English words, obsolete, or nearly so, in England, but retained in use in this country.
> 2. English words used in a different sense from what they are in England. These include many names of natural objects differently applied.
> 3. Words which have retained their original meaning in the United States, although not in England.
> 4. English provincialisms adopted into general use in America.
> 5. Newly coined words, which owe their origin to the productions or to the circumstances of the country.
> 6. Words borrowed from European languages, especially the French, Spanish, Dutch, and German.
> 7. Indian words.
> 8. Negroisms.
> 9. Peculiarities of pronunciation.

Bartlett's criteria were much like our own, admitting Americanisms on both diachronic and synchronic grounds. The 1848 edition, however, also included many terms common to the colloquial language of both countries, and these, numbering nearly 800, were "rejected to make way for pure Americanisms" in 1859 (iv). Those "pure" Americanisms included "the singular words occurring in prairie and frontier life as well as those common to Texas, New Mexico, and California" (iii) that Bartlett had collected while serving as Commissioner on the Mexican Boundary; they also included other words and phrases peculiar to the United States, and many common terms for plants, trees, and fruits. So the second edition was a much better reflection of the kinds of changes in the English language that had actually occurred in the United States. It included such characteristically American terms as *boss* (noun and verb), *bushwhacker, cahoot, callithumpian, canyon, corduroy road, cut didoes, dicker, fandango, filibuster, gallinipper, gerrymander, gopher* (a land turtle), *killdeer, lickety split, mulatto, no-account, paddle one's own canoe, pale-face, papoose, ring-tailed roarer, rub out, shooting-iron, apple slump, nothing to be sneezed at, stamping ground, tight squeeze, water-witch, worm fence,* and *Yankee.*

Bartlett's dictionaries met with great popular success, reflecting a growing inclination toward pride in American linguistic ingenuity rather than shame over any "corruption" of the British model.

5.9   The Civil War

In 1877, Bartlett published a fourth edition of his dictionary, this one "Greatly Improved and Enlarged." By this time Americans had suffered through a long Civil War, and the *Dictionary* included quite a number of Americanisms arising from that conflict. Some of them have persisted to the present: *doughboy* 'an infantryman,' attested before the Civil War but made popular during that conflict, was still common during World War I; following that war, soldiers-turned-politicians did not hesitate to advertise themselves as "former doughboys."

The origin of *doughboy* is not known for certain, but there have been some interesting speculations. Mitford Mathews suggests that it might have come from *adobe*, applied to Army personnel by Spaniards in the Southwest in the mid nineteenth century. However, Elizabeth Custer, widow of General George Custer, speculated differently in 1887 (516). As she understood it, "A 'doughboy' is a small round doughnut served to sailors on shipboard, generally with hash. Early in the Civil War the term was applied to the large globular brass buttons on the infantry uniform, from which it passed, by a natural transition, to the infantrymen themselves." Still a third conjecture is found in the *Dictionary of American History* (2: 365): "The word 'doughboy'. . . can be traced [with certainty] as far back as 1854. . . . The explanation then was that the infantrymen wore white belts and had to clean them with 'dough' made of pipe clay." Whatever its origin, *doughboy* was not only an Americanism in a diachronic sense, but has remained so synchronically as well, never escaping to be used for British or any other soldiers.

A similar term, *doughface*, referred to a Northerner who did not oppose the institution of slavery and later to one who actually sided with the

Confederacy during the War. This Americanism has a more explicable origin, probably coming from *doughface* in reference to a (presumably pasty-looking) face mask which would hide one's true identity. Though not as widely known as *doughboy*, *doughface* has stayed alive by transferring or generalizing its sense so that it can refer to anyone who wears a "false face" or shares the principles of an opposition group.

Other military and political Americanisms from the Civil War era include *bummer* 'a deserter who became a raider or plunderer,' *Butternut*, *Grayback*, and *Secesh*, all used to refer to a Confederate soldier, *copperhead* 'a Northerner who sympathized with the South,' *contraband* 'a former slave put under the protection of the US government,' *monitor* 'any ironclad vessel similar to the original *Monitor* of 1862,' *double-quick* 'a rapid march' or as a verb 'to march at a double-quick pace.' The War period saw the issuance of *greenbacks*, a rise in *inflation*, and the resulting call for *remonetization*. It was also the era of *emancipation* in its specifically American senses and connotations, and the emergence of *equal rights* as a concept of equity between men and women as well as between blacks and whites.

Ironically, it was also at this time that the term *Ku Klux Klan* emerged, denoting a terrorist group dedicated particularly to persecuting blacks who attempted to stand up for their newly granted *civil rights*. The cultural impact of this organization is reflected in the very rapid assimilation of the term *Ku Klux Klan* into the American vocabulary and the speed with which the noun was adapted to other functional uses. The entries in the *Dictionary of Americanisms* illustrate the process: The earliest citation for the organization is from 1868, but in the same year the *New York Herald* (July 30, 3/2) could publish a headline, "A Bill To Punish Ku-Kluxism," and the editor of the Fayetteville, North Carolina, *Eagle* could say, "We are inclined to think he is somewhat disloyal and may be in sympathy with the Ku Kluxes" (T. D. Clark 62). The abbreviation *Klan* was also well established in 1868.

By 1871 the verb had emerged (at least among the members themselves): "I considered that I had done nothing to be Ku-Kluxed for" (*Report of the Joint Select Committee on the Condition of Affairs in the Late Insurrectionary States*, 1872, 6: 364); by 1882 it was in mainstream publications: "It made the Ku-Klukers feel sorter solemn when the niggers tuck to Ku-Klukin' them" (*Atlantic Monthly* July 106/2). In 1872 the initials *KKK* were widely understood, and in 1873 (June 5, 3/4) the *Newton Kansan* reported the arrival of a "Ku Kluxic looking stranger." *Ku-kluxery* occurred in *Harper's Weekly* in 1876, and by the 1880s *Ku-Kluxer* (also appearing in the variant form *Ku Klucker*) could be used without comment in a novel by Albion Tourgee and in the *Century Magazine* respectively. Both the words and the organization have persisted. Although David Duke tried to downplay his former association with the group in his failed 1991 *gubernatorial* bid in Louisiana, the label *Klansman* was one he could not shake; it probably shaped more voters' opinions than anything he said on the campaign trail.

Closely associated with the *KKK*, though not spawned by it, were the Americanisms *lynch*, *lynching*, *lynch mob*, and other combinations. Probably based on a 1780 law named after Virginian William Lynch, which was enacted in response to intolerable lawlessness in Pittsylvania County, *lynch law* originally referred to the infliction of punishment such as whipping, without the amenities of prior legal process. By the end of the Civil War, however, the punishment had escalated so that *lynching* usually meant hanging, especially by white-robed and pointy-hatted mobs, and the flouting of law was reflected in the oxymoronic terms *lynching bee* and *lynching party*.

The Civil War and its aftermath were also the source of the Americanisms *the man on the horse* 'the person in charge,' *bulldoze* 'to intimidate by threats or violence,' and *reconstruction*, with its optimistic connotations among Federal advocates and its equation with submission by many Confederate defenders. Although the policies of the Reconstruction were largely unsuccessful, the term was later adopted outside America and used in reference to the rehabilitation of war-damaged areas in Europe after both World Wars (*OED* 2). The word has escaped from the purely political arena and is often used with more than a tinge of irony: "Now – in this reconstructional mood – Professors are no longer Scholars or Professors, but 'Heads of Depts.'" (Gordon 133).

On a par with *reconstruction* in terms of its propensity to antagonize Southerners was the term *carpetbagger*. Though it had been used before the War in reference to adventurers who went to Kansas when it was opened for settlement, the word gained virulence after the War as thousands of Northerners went south, their worldly belongings in carpetbags. Some would make legitimate contributions toward the healing of the South; too many others would make their own fortunes at the expense of people already traumatized by years of conflict. Although *carpetbagger* has undergone some amelioration over the years, it is still generally opprobrious. Like *reconstruction*, it has crossed the ocean, as this 1955 quotation from the *London Times* (May 26, 4/3) illustrates: "In this carpet-bagging age, a home-grown politician is as rare as a home-grown professional footballer."

The *bloody shirt* was also a legacy of America's most deadly conflict, symbolizing any attempt to reignite regional hostilities in the postwar period. One who *waved the bloody shirt* was unwilling to let anyone forget what had been known variously as the *Civil War, Confederate War, Rebellion, Rebel War, Southern War, War between the Blue and the Gray, War between the North and the South, War between the States,* or *War of Secession* – or simply *the War* – or in ironic euphemism *the Late Unpleasantness.*

Cessation of the War, the end of Reconstruction in 1876, and overall eagerness to get on to better ways of living encouraged both westward migration and the development of pre-existing industrial bases in the North and the South. With the withdrawal of Federal troops from the South, many black Americans decided not to trust their safety to those who had previously held them in bondage to the *peculiar institution* (slavery). Those who left, particularly those who went in large numbers to Kansas, became known by the Americanism *Exodusters.*

For those who stayed in the South, a new system of farming needed to be devised, accommodating large numbers of new farmers on land still owned by a relatively small number of landlords. The system that prevailed was *sharecropping,* by which a family farmed land belonging to someone else, giving the owner a share of the harvest. Those who provided *furnish* 'seed, food, and supplies' often did so at inflated prices, so that farmers were perennially in their debt, with no choice but to commit each succeeding year's crop to them. By 1880, over one-third of the South's farmers were sharecroppers or tenant farmers (Norton et al. 488). By 1920 the proportion had soared to 67 percent and by 1930 had grown to 80 percent. Census data for succeeding decades show a steady decline from that high point, the numbers sinking to 30 percent by 1959, after which time sharecroppers were no longer separately classified (US Department of Commerce 465).

Suffering from a lack of draft animals and farm equipment after the War, Southern farmers tended not to try to diversify their system but to continue to rely on cotton. The dominance of cotton both in the plantation and the sharecropping systems is reflected in the number of Americanisms resulting from its cultivation and manufacture. The *DA* devotes nine columns to *cotton* in its various compounds, from *cotton belt* to *cotton futures, cotton rock* to *cotton candy, cotton caterpillar* to *cotton rat.* Not surprisingly, many of these Americanisms remain regional in American English today. *Cotton-eyed,* for instance, meaning 'having the whites of the eyes especially prominent' is cited in *DARE* from Alabama, Arkansas, and Texas; *cottonhead* meaning 'towhead' is found especially in the South and South Midland; *cotton-picking* as an adverbial intensifier ("I was so cotton-picking mad") is especially common in the South and Southwest, though *cotton-picking* as a disparaging adjective is found throughout the country; and in the South, to warn a woman that her slip is showing, many folks still whisper "Cotton is low," or some variant of the phrase.

Tobacco production, the other dominant agricultural industry of the South and South Midland, also contributed a large number of Americanisms, particularly compounds dealing with cultivation and preparation of the *Virginia weed*. The *DA* has more than four columns devoted to them.

The need to get both cotton and tobacco from Southern textile mills and tobacco warehouses was one spur to the development of railroads in the South. In other parts of the country, coal mining, steel production, timbering, grain production, and gold and silver mining had already provided incentives for railroad expansion. The 1869 linking of the Central Pacific with the Union Pacific Railroad at Promontory Point, Utah, symbolized the interconnectedness of the nation's economic system. The railroad industry itself was a powerful generator of occupational jargon, much of it specifically American, as numerous glossaries of the lingo have attested. A small sample of such terms includes *boomer* 'a drifter,' *cow catcher* 'the frame on the front of a locomotive,' *crummy* 'a caboose,' *deadhead* 'a nonpaying passenger,' *gandy dancer* 'a section hand,' *highball* 'a signal telling the engineer to proceed,' *parlor car* 'a passenger car with luxurious accommodations,' and *zulu* 'an emigrant car.'

5.10   Settling the West

The last decades of the nineteenth century saw the largest migrations in American history, as the Plains states and the vast American West drew many hundreds of thousands of new settlers, many of them coming directly from European countries. Between 1870 and 1900, more land was settled and farmed than during the preceding 250 years (Norton et al. 481). The success of agricultural expansion in the Plains and the West is attributable in large part to the determination and stamina of the immigrants; but it could not have been achieved without the concomitant transformation of agricultural practices based on increased mechanization.

A sampling of Americanisms dealing with agricultural production explains why American farmers could vastly increase the acreage tilled, and do it at lower cost than before. This was the era of the *combine*, which could head, thresh, and clean grain in one operation; the *binder*, which could both cut grain and tie it in bundles; improved *seeding plows*, *mowing machines*, and *harvesters;* the *wheel cultivator* and *walking cultivator*, the *chain harrow*, *disk harrow*, and *cutaway harrow;* and, early in the twentieth century, the *tractor*. *Elevators* allowed farmers to store their grain, either until it could be transported or until it could be sold more advantageously. *Experimental farms* were established, and techniques of *dry farming* were developed to allow tillage of hitherto unusable regions of the West.

In areas where the existing water sources could be *channelized*, *irrigation ditches* were dug, and *irrigation districts* became politically as well as economically powerful governing units. In much of the West it was the *water master* or *ditch rider* who controlled access to water and monitored conditions of the irrigation system. In the Southwest it was the *mayordomo* who was in charge of the *acequia*. Where water was scarce, those in charge of its distribution were sometimes targets of manipulation or blackmail, as this 1859 quotation from the Salt Lake City *Mountaineer* (August 27, 2/4) suggests: "If the water-masters of our district or ward will see that we have a double portion of water during the ensuing week for our garden, we will now agree not to mention them again."

In many parts of the West, it was ranching rather than farming that was suitable on the land, and it was ranching that gave rise to one of the most potent figures of romance in American history, the *cowboy*. From Owen Wister's *The Virginian* through John Wayne's heroes of the 1950s, the cowboy had glamor and allure based on a sense of freedom and independence, of opportunities to prove one's skills, endurance, and manliness. Novels, movies, and television, which tended to highlight the adventure and to downplay the sheer exhaustion of the work, also spread many of the Americanisms associated with cowboy life.

A large number of cowboy terms came into American English through Spanish, whether adopted largely intact, or altered almost beyond recognition. Those in the first group include *bronco, caballero, calaboose* (Spanish *calabozo*), *caramba, chaps* (abbreviated from either *chaparajos* or *chaparreras*), *cinch* (Spanish *cincha*), *corral* (as both noun and verb), *lariat* (Spanish *la reata*), *lasso* (Spanish *lazo*), *lobo, loco, mañana, pinto* (in reference both to the spotted horse and the spotted bean), *pronto, ranch* (Spanish *rancho*), *remuda, rodeo* (now often pronounced ['rodio] as well as [ro'deo]), *stampede* (Spanish *estampida*), and *vamoose* (Spanish *vamos*). In the second category belong *buckaroo*, which evolved via a large set of variants from *vaquero* (Cassidy 1978); *cavy-yard* and variants, which come from *caballada*; *dally welter*, from Spanish *dale vuelta* 'give it a twist' (imperative); *hackamore*, from *jaquima*; *hoosegow*, from *juzgado*; *McCarty*, from American Spanish *mecate* 'a rope'; *mustang*, from *mesteño*; and *wrangler*, from *caballerango*.

Other cowboy Americanisms have come from Native American languages: *cayuse* and *Chickasaw*, names for an Indian pony (from tribal names).

Some derive from surnames: *maverick* 'an unbranded stray animal,' after Samuel A. Maverick; *stetson* 'a broad-brimmed hat,' after John B. Stetson. And many have come from the general stock of English words, gaining new senses in this context: *Boot Hill, broomtail, buck, bulldog* 'to throw (a running steer) by grabbing its horns and twisting its neck,' *bunkhouse, bust* (hence *bronco buster*), *cattle boss, cattle drive, chuck wagon, drag* 'the tail end of the herd,' *flying* or *lazy brands* 'those with wavy lines' or 'those lying on their sides,' *outfit* 'the cowboys, horses, and equipment associated with a particular ranch,' *outlaw* 'a vicious horse,' *paint* 'a piebald horse,' *range, rawhide, roundup, six-shooter, tenderfoot,* and *trail drive.* For one Americanism made popular through the song "Get Along Little *Dogie*," we simply have to admit, "origin uncertain."

The topography of the West, so different from the verdant and rolling terrain familiar to many of the immigrants, yielded a large number of Americanisms related to the land and the climate. Through French, American English had already accepted *bayou* 'a sluggish or stagnant stream' (ultimately from Choctaw), *chenière* 'a grove of live oak trees' (later altered to *shinnery*), *coulée* 'a small stream or dry stream bed,' *levée* 'an embankment to protect low farm lands from high river levels,' *marais* 'a swamp or slough,' and *prairie* 'a meadow, especially the flat, grass-covered lands in the central part of the country.' The English term *plain*, used in the plural, had also been specialized in America to refer to this vast area.

As *landlookers* scouted the region and immigrants started settling it in the nineteenth century, *prairie* and *plains* compounds flourished, indicative of the attempts to make the lands amenable to cultivation and civilization: *plains wagons* brought settlers out across the *prairie ocean*, past villages of *prairie dogs; prairie breakers* were developed to cut a wide but shallow furrow in the *plains lands; prairie chips* (or *prairie coal, prairie fuel*, also known as *buffalo chips*) provided fuel for cooking and for heating the *soddies* and *prairie cottages; prairie fires*, which had historically revitalized the prairie grasses and flowers each spring, came to be feared rather than welcomed when homes and crops stood in their path; they led to the phrase *spread like prairie fire*, used of anything (such as a rumor) that spread very quickly. A similar fear attended the destructive *twisters, prairie twisters*, or *tornadoes* (in the specifically American sense of the rotating storm under a funnel-shaped cloud). Those who could, took refuge in their *cyclone cellars, fraid holes*, or *scared holes*.

Further to the Southwest, meeting an entirely different set of landforms, settlers simply adopted the Spanish terms already in use. Coming into the English language through American use, these too can legitimately be considered Americanisms: *acequia, adobe, arroyo, barranca, bosque, canyon, chaparral, malpais, mesa, patio, temblor.* A small sampling of plant and animal names from Spanish in the Southwest suggests the magnitude of the difference between the new landscape and what most of the settlers were familiar with: *ajo, alegria, alfilaria, amole, chamiso, cholla, chuckwalla* (Spanish *chacahuala*), *coyote, huisache, javelina, madrone, manzanita, mariposa, mesquite, ocotillo, pinon, saguaro.*

5.11 Urbanization

As the American West was being "won," dramatic changes were occurring in urban America as well. Between 1870 and 1920, the population of America's cities increased from 9.9 million to 54.3 million, and the number of cities with more than 100,000 people grew from fifteen to sixty-eight (Norton et al. 529). While many of the new urban dwellers came from the American countryside, many more came from Europe and, to a smaller extent, from Asia, Mexico, and Canada.

As a rule, people tended to try to live near others from their homelands, creating ethnic neighborhoods within the cities. Because they encouraged separatism, such neighborhoods contributed to the "us" and "them" distinctions. Ethnic epithets abounded. In addition to older terms such as *cousin Jack, frog, Hun, Ike, Jap, Mike, Paddy, Polack, squarehead,* and *Yid,* new Americanisms were also created: *dago, greaseball, Hike, spaghetti (eater),* and *wop* for Italians or Spaniards; *bohunk, Hunk(y), Hunyak,* for Eastern Europeans; *hebe, kike,* and *sheeny* for Jews; *beaner, chili eater, cholo, greaser, pepper belly, spic, spigotty,* and later *wetback* for Latin Americans; *chocolate drop, coon, jig(aboo), shine, spade,* and later *spook* for blacks; *chink, slant-eyes,* and later *slopy* for Orientals; *harp* and *Mick* for Irish immigrants; *jickey* for English people; and *heinie* for Germans. In turn, members of racial and ethnic minorities retaliated with such designations as *anglo, buckra, gringo, honky, ofay, paleface,* and *whitie* for members of the dominant culture.

But the solidarity of ethnic neighborhoods also contributed to the retention of native customs, especially ways of preparing food, that eventually escaped the neighborhoods and were adopted both in word and in substance by the general community. Thus English has been enriched by such Americanisms as *bratwurst, butter bread, fasnacht kuche, frankfurter, hamburger, kaffee-klatsch, lager beer, lebkuchen, pretzel, sauerkraut, schnitz, smearcase,* and *zwieback* from German; *chili relleno, enchilada, frijole, garbanzo, guacamole, taco, tamale, tomatillo,* and *tortilla* from Spanish; and *flatbread, fruit soup, julekake, kringle, krumkake, lefsa,* and *lutefisk* from Norwegian, to name just a few.

Urban populations not only provided the labor pool for commercial enterprises – factories, offices, warehouses, department stores, banks – and for the building of infrastructure, particularly roads and mass transit systems, but they also functioned as consumers, thereby fueling more commercial and industrial growth (Norton et al. 529). A small sample of the Americanisms of the late nineteenth and early twentieth centuries reflects some of the changes taking place as Americans moved from a largely rural to an increasingly urban society.

Technological advances yielded *air brake, air conditioner, kerosene, Kodak, mimeograph, oleomargarine, phonograph, radiator, telegram;* medical research, *appendectomy, chiropractor, halitosis, inhalator, urinalysis;* advertising, commercial enterprises, and manufacturing concerns, *bargain basement, big business, cut rate, department store, dry goods, emporium, fire insurance, general store, real estate agent, sky scraper, variety store;* industry and inventiveness, *ice box, ice cube, fire hydrant, rayon, reduction works, refinery, refrigerator, sawmill, sewing machine, Thermos, zipper;* improved transportation systems, *belt line, cable car, commute, commuter, elevated* and its abbreviation *L, interurban* (as both an adjective and a noun), *Pullman, subway,* and *trolley,* as well as *trolley bus* (also *car* and *line*).

Once the *automobile* had established itself (the term was adopted from French, but soon became the quintessential symbol of twentieth-century America), a spate of terms associated with it also came forth: *flivver, Model T, Model A, jalopy,* and later *hoopy* and *hot rod,* all referring to the car itself, while *antifreeze, headlight, hitchhike, hit on all four (cylinders), muffler, parking lot* (also *meter, space,* and *ticket*), and *traffic artery* (also *cop*) were ancillary automobile Americanisms. Though *smog* actually originated in Britain, its early and lasting association with Los Angeles and the automobile qualifies it as a synchronic Americanism.

America's relatively short involvement in World War I, as well as the fact that the war was fought in other lands, meant that fewer Americanisms were generated by that conflict than by the long Civil War. While Americans became all too familiar with new terms from the front – such as *battle front, battle zone, mustard gas, shell shock,* and *trench warfare* – these were shared by speakers of British English. Americanisms tended to arise from domestic political reaction to the War, with such terms as *Hooverize, Liberty Bond, Wilsonian democracy,* and, as the Industrial Workers of the World or IWW became increasingly vocal in its antiwar as well as its anticapitalist position, *wobbly.*

The decade of the 1920s, known both then and later as a period of excess, was a time of *consumerism* made possible by a rise in wages and salaries coupled with a stable cost of living. A few Americanisms of that time are suggestive of the atmosphere of freedom, acquisition, and loosening of social mores. It was the *jazz age* and the decade of the *Charleston* and the *shimmy*; young folks, exposed to *sloganeers* and to the *quickie* films of Hollywood, yearned to have *sex appeal*, while hotels and dance halls tried to be *ritzy*. Consumers became accustomed to having their own *checking accounts*, and *time payment* plans made major purchases easier for manual as well as *white-collar workers*.

After the stock market crash in 1929, however, when Wall Street was declared in *Variety* magazine to have *laid an egg*, the merchant's preference was for *cash on the barrel head* rather than any installment plan. The period of the Great Depression yielded terms descriptive of the hardships people suffered: *Okies* and *Arkies* moved West, fleeing the *Dust Bowl*, and times were described as *iffy*. Herbert Hoover was given the blame for many of society's ills, as Americans joked of *Hoover beans* 'pinto beans' or 'black-eyed peas,' *Hoover buggy* (*cart* or *wagon*) 'a horse-drawn vehicle,' *Hoover cat* 'catfish' (increasingly important as a food source), *Hoover dust* 'a cheap grade of tobacco,' *Hoover hog* 'a rabbit,' *Hoover pork* 'sowbelly,' *Hoover steak* 'turtle meat,' and *Hooverville* 'a settlement of shacks and shanties.'

The decade was not altogether one of despair, as other Americanisms attest. The emergence of such words as *bathinette*, *blacktop*, *burp*, *carhop*, *carport*, *curvaceous*, *double parking*, *fellow traveler*, *four-letter word*, *motor court*, *New Dealism*, *newsworthy*, *nylon*, *parking meter*, *prefab*, *sanforized*, *soap opera*, *tourist court*, *whodunnit*, and *winterize* suggests the range of social and political activities occurring during that period.

5.12   World War II

In contrast to World War I, World War II generated a large number of Americanisms. The nation's long and intense involvement was inevitably reflected in the language of both those staying home and those fighting abroad. It was a period ripe for initialisms, as government agencies were formed, re-formed, and replaced (A. M. Taylor). The *CAA* (Civilian Aeronautics Administration) of 1939 was reorganized in 1940 into both the CAA and the *CAB* (Civilian Aeronautics Board); the *CPT* (Civilian Pilot Training) branch of the *WTS* (War Training Service) of the CAA trained civilian volunteers, though it was not a part of the *OCD* (Office of Civilian Defense), while the *DFD* (Dogs for Defense), with its nickname *Wags*, concentrated its efforts on providing trained dogs for use in the armed services; the *EDB* (Economic Defense Board) was started in 1941, but in 1943 the *OEW* (Office of Economic Warfare) was created, subsuming the responsibilities of a third agency, the *BEW* (Board of Economic Warfare).

To help keep all this straight, there were the *OGR* (Office of Government Reports) and the *OFF* (Office of Facts and Figures), the latter merging with the *OWI* (Office of War Information). For a person actually doing the fighting – known as a *GI* or *GI Joe* – perhaps the most important of the initialed agencies was the *USO* (United Service Organization), which provided places of respite and touches of home for millions of lonely service people. For the cynical, war situations were often summed up by one acronym that found a permanent place in civilian as well as military slang – *snafu* (situation normal, all fouled – or fucked – up).

While many of the alphabet agencies passed out of existence after the war, other Americanisms generated then have stayed in our vocabulary, including *A-bomb, atomic bomb, bazooka, blood bank, boot camp, genocide, Jeep, nerve gas, pattern bombing, walkie-talkie,* and *white noise.*

Although World War II was followed by the Korean War and by *McCarthyism, containment,* the *CIA, loyalty oaths,* and political witch hunting at home, the period of the late 1940s through the early 1960s was generally one of economic prosperity and social calm, which allowed Americans to turn their attention to personal satisfactions. It was the era of suburbia, shopping malls, and emphasis on the nuclear family, symbolized on television – the new American fascination – by such shows as "Father Knows Best" and "Leave It to Beaver." A short list of Americanisms from that period suggests the prevailing atmosphere: *babysit, blue-collar, bobby socks, bop(per), car pool* (noun), *catbird seat, cook with gas, dee-jay, deep freezer, disposable income, do-it-yourself(ism), high rise, influence peddler, jet set, litter bug, meter maid, ranch house, ranchette, soft sell, swing shift,* and *take-home pay.* Technological development and the satisfaction of consumer demands yielded *agribusiness, automation, cortisone, fax* (widely known only in the 1990s but recorded by Algeo and Algeo from 1948), *genetic engineer, industrial park, niacin, printed circuit, simulcast, telecast, teleprompter,* and *xerography.*

The decade of the 1960s saw "more economic, political, and social reform than any period since the New Deal" (Norton et al. 936) and included Lyndon Johnson's *War on Poverty* and *affirmative action* legislation. The time was also one of discontent, however, stemming from imbalances of wealth and power, lack of opportunity for minorities despite significant civil rights legislation, and growing opposition to the undeclared war in Vietnam. In terms of Americanisms, these attitudes were expressed by the popularization of such phrases as the *arrogance of power, Black Power, credibility gap,* and *long, hot summer.* The coinage of such terms often antedates their popularization; J. William Fulbright's book *The Arrogance of Power* (New York: Random House, 1966) made people aware of how the United States was viewed in other parts of the world, but he was not the first to use the title, *The Arrogance of Power: A Drama of 1925* having been published by Naunton Covertside as part of the Welsh Drama Series of 1920.

The Vietnam War itself spawned *Charlie*, *draft dodging*, *fragging*, *medevac*, *napalm* (though this word was coined in 1942), *post traumatic stress syndrome*, and *Vietnamization*. For many of those who opposed the war, the *hippie counterculture* and back-to-the-land movements were alternative lifestyles of choice. But even many of those who derided those choices gained a new recognition during the late 1960s and early 1970s of the need to respect the natural environment. That recognition is exemplified by such Americanisms as *biodegradable*, *carpool* (verb), *endangered species*, *energy crisis*, and *gas guzzler*.

Changes in American society during the 1970s and 1980s, with a political shift toward *supply side* economics and a concomitant rush by students to get MBA degrees, encouraged the phenomenon of the *yuppie* 'the young urban (or upwardly mobile) professional.' Coined by analogy with the preceding *hippie* and *preppie*, *yuppie* generated its own fleet of *spinoffs*: *buppie* 'a black yuppie,' *suppie* 'a Southern yuppie,' *skippie* 'a school kid with income and purchasing power,' and *dumpie* 'a downwardly mobile middle-aged professional.' In the same jocular vein, Americans recognized both *dinks* 'those with double income, no kids,' and their unwitting *podwogs* 'parents of dinks without grandchildren.'

Having two incomes allowed many young couples to buy things their parents would never have dreamed of, including *condos*, *microwaves*, and cars with *cruise control*. *Flextime* in the workplace afforded them time to enjoy their acquisitions. Some of these people became interested in *aerobics*, attending *sensitivity groups*, enjoying *New Age* books and music (though popularized in American use during the 1970s and 1980s, the term goes back to the last century in Britain), and philosophizing about the *harmonic convergence*. But at work, many business women also began to discover the corporate *glass ceiling* and, if they chose to have children as well as careers, found themselves on the *mommy track*.

The decade of the 1980s also saw the emergence of the *couch potato*, the *dweeb*, and the *wannabe*; and it saw a distressing increase in what came to be called *date rape* or *acquaintance rape*, as well as the inexplicable phenomenon of *wilding* 'random violence by a gang of youth.' On a larger scale, the prospect of a *nuclear winter*, the emergence of the *ozone hole*, and spread of *computer viruses* and *AIDS* caused grave concern, while a glimmer of hope was provided by the prospect of some measure of a *peace dividend*.

Perhaps the largest category of new words to enter the English language since the late 1970s is that related to technology, particularly to *personal computers* in both their commercial and recreational applications. The tremendous impact of a *wired* world has meant that in a very short period of time, words or senses that were originally technical, such as *byte, crash, database, diskette, download, floppy disk, hacker, interactive*, and *software*, have become part of the common coin. And children as well as (or even more than) adults are incorporating *browsers, chat rooms, e-mail, home pages, search engines, spell checks*, and the notion of *virtual reality* into their everyday realities. The rapid spread of such words and phrases has already invited numerous dictionaries of computer terms; this brief mention of the topic only suggests the wealth of computer-related Americanisms. The very nature of electronic communication, however, means that terms that originate in America are not claimable as Americanisms for very long; seemingly instantaneously, the *internet* spreads vocabulary not just throughout the English-speaking world, but throughout most of the world. The quick dissemination is true of vocabulary related to other topics as well, with the result that many of the Americanisms of the last decades are Americanisms only in a diachronic sense – that is, they were coined in America, but have been adopted wherever else in the English-speaking world they are applicable.

For lexicographers, one result is that dictionaries now have more and more labels of the type *orig. US* and fewer of the type *chiefly US*. But even determining whether a word originated in the United States is often difficult, as such a determination depends on the keen eyes of readers who watch for neologisms. Nowadays, a word might well appear in the *Times* of London on the same date as in the *New York Times*. So increasingly, the more interesting Americanisms will be the synchronic ones, words that characterize American society as different from other English-speaking societies.

This roughly chronological survey of Americanisms has not included a number of subjects with distinctly American characteristics that have contributed important Americanisms to the English language: race, religion, sports, and foods. A brief look at those topics will round out the discussion.

5.13   Black contributions

Of all the immigrants to America, the Africans brought as slaves have, for obvious reasons, taken the longest time to become acculturated. The condition of slavery is a hard one to escape: emancipation did not come till late in the nineteenth century, and only after a sanguinary civil war, whose wounds are not yet healed. As unwilling immigrants, blacks lost their home languages without being in a position to learn well the language of their masters. They were deprived of education and, being easily identifiable racially, formed a racial caste. Despite these handicaps, they progressed from speaking some marginal "pidgin" form of English in the seventeenth century to creole forms, when the conditions of life on isolated plantations led to that, or to language modeled on dialectal forms of English superimposed on relics of West African sounds, intonations, and syntax. The way they spoke English was inevitably African-influenced, yet recent studies of black speech in the American South show that, there, it does not differ notably from the speech of whites at the same social level (Troike 184–5).

Among Americanisms owing to blacks are the names of several plants and foods brought from Africa. *Gumbo* is basically a soup thickened with *okra*, a plant of the genus *Hibiscus* best known for the mucilaginous quality of its pods. (*Gumbo* has also been transferred to describe a heavy, sticky kind of soil.) Peanuts are known by the African terms *pinders* (chiefly in the South Atlantic and Gulf states), *goobers* (throughout the country but particularly in the South), and *goober peas* (chiefly in the South Midland, but spreading through use in a popular song).

Cooter, a freshwater turtle, is well known in the South Atlantic states, especially in coastal areas of South Carolina and Georgia. *Buckra*, from Efik *mbakara* 'one who governs,' until this century used for 'master,' acquired derogatory meanings and is now pretty much displaced by *boss*, though the Southern blacks' derisive term *poor-buckra* for ignorant, lower-class whites still has some currency. Other black Americanisms referring to whites include *ofay* or *fay*, which may be African, *honky*, probably a variant of *hunky* (see *DARE*), and *(Mister) Charlie*. The verb *badmouth* 'to speak ill of,' has become widely known in the last few decades. Less well known are *bloody-noun* 'a bullfrog,' probably an African word of imitative origin, *cush* 'a cornmeal dish,' and *day clean* 'daybreak.'

Hoodoo, the US variant of West African *voodoo*, is now pretty much limited to underground witchcraft practices among blacks, though it was used among Western miners in the form of a divining rod or *hoodoo stick* (1850 onward) in prospecting for ore. (European whites have introduced beliefs similar to *hoodoo*. A common and now widespread Americanism of German origin is *hex*, both as a noun, a magical practice to get power over others, and as a verb, to exert this power against others. In the Pennsylvania German area one sees barns painted with *hex marks* to protect them.)

In the twentieth century especially, blacks have come into their own in the field of music, and a preeminent Americanism is *jazz* – once thought to be of African origin, but used in the lingo of San Francisco sports writers (Cohen 2000). Like the music it names, the word *jazz* has gone abroad as one of the most successful Americanisms, and has acquired a whole gamut of additional meanings. Associated with it are such terms as *dig, hip, jive*, and *rap* – perhaps not Africanisms, but certainly Americanisms.

The world of African-Americans, like that of other Americans, is considerably mixed: geographically between the South and North, rural and urban, generationally between older conservative and younger radical, educationally between professional and *dropout*, and economically between entrepreneurial and welfare-assisted. The language of American blacks is also highly diverse. Among teenagers and young adults Black English is often cultivated as a self-protective, even clandestine idiom (Folb; Smitherman 1977).

5.14   Some subject categories

5.14.1   *Religion*

The prospect of religious freedom that had inspired some of the earliest settlements in the future United States continued over the next three centuries to be attractive to people with unconventional religious ideas, and many new religious organizations were formed. Some were relatively short-lived, for example, the *Campbellites*, the *Christian Connection*, the *Harmonists*, the *Rappists*, the *Rogerenes*, the *Schwenkfelders*, the *Second Adventists*, the *Separatists*, and *United Zion's Children*. Others, such as the *Methodist Episcopal Church*, the *Seventh-Day Adventists*, and the *United Brethren*, have continued to the present.

Some members of mainstream denominations took advantage of the free religious atmosphere by splintering into various subgroups, such as the *Shouting Methodists, Free Methodists, Republican Methodists*, and numerous Baptist groups: *Dunkers, foot-washing Baptists, hard-* and *soft-shell Baptists, old Baptists, seed-* (or *two-seed*) *Baptists, snake Baptists, United Baptists, water Baptists*, and *whiskey Baptists*. A few well established Americanisms deriving from nineteenth-century religious traditions include *amen corner, anxious bench, camp meeting, circuit preacher* (or *rider*), *holy roller, jerking exercise, mourner*, and *mourner's bench*.

Two American religions, *Christian Science* (also known as *metaphysical healing*) and *Mormonism* (the *Church of Jesus Christ of Latter-Day Saints*), gained enough adherents and support to become relatively major denominations. In many predominantly Mormon communities in the West, the influence of the Church is pervasive enough that Americanisms specific to Mormonism are widely recognized throughout the community: *elder* 'a member of the Melchizedek priesthood,' *home evening* 'a weekly family gathering,' *jack*

Mormon either 'a non-Mormon who is favorable toward Mormons' or 'a lapsed Mormon,' *Melchizedek priesthood* 'the higher order of priesthood in the Church,' *prophet* 'a high official in the Church,' *saint* 'a Mormon,' *Seventy* 'an elder who performs missionary service,' *stake* 'a Mormon district,' *tabernacle* and *temple* 'a place of worship,' and *tithing house* 'a place where members of the Church pay their tithes.'

5.14.2   Sports

In the sports arena, Americans can take credit for *basketball, lacrosse, softball,* and *volleyball,* and have even contributed such words as *gridiron* to football and *swan dive* to swimming. But the greatest contribution, one whose terminology permeates our general vocabulary, is *baseball.* Not only are the terms of the game (such as *bull pen, diamond, earned run, error, first base, fly-ball, force play, foul,* the *majors, out* (noun and adjective), *outfielder, pitch, sacrifice, shut out, single, southpaw, spit ball, steal, strike, triple, walk*) widely known throughout American culture, but many phrases have been so thoroughly absorbed that they are easily transferred to other situations or are used metaphorically. Thus we use such phrases as *in the ballpark, keep one's eye on the ball, play ball, have something on the ball, throw one a curve, out in left field, pinch hit, in there pitching,* and *squeeze play* almost without realizing their origin in America's favorite sport.

5.14.3   Foods

The favorite foods at the ballpark have traditionally been *frankfurters* or *franks* (better known as *wieners* or *hot dogs*) and fresh roasted *peanuts,* washed down with a nice cold *Coca-Cola* or *Coke.* Early in the twentieth century the *hamburger* (and later the *cheeseburger*) also graced the menu. While these terms have spread worldwide, their association with things American makes them continue to be synchronic Americanisms as well as diachronic ones. Other food terms that were coined in America include *apple butter, club sandwich, cobbler, coleslaw, condensed milk, cupcake, doughnut, eggnog, grits, gumbo, hopping john, hot cake, hush puppy, jelly bean, malted milk, Manhattan, martini, pie plant, shoofly pie, slapjack, slumgullion, snap bean, switchel,* and those traditional American favorites *banana split, milk shake, peanut butter, popcorn, roasting ear, sundae,* and *tollhouse cookie.*

5.15   Conclusion

It is tempting to say that many of the Americanisms discussed above are "as American as apple pie." The phrase itself illustrates the tension between the notions of diachronic and synchronic Americanisms. *Apple pie* was not coined in America, yet it is so much a part of the culture – with connotations going far beyond a particular fruit-filled pastry – that surely it is a linguistic Americanism in a synchronic sense as well as a cultural symbol. If we were to insist that only those words and phrases that originated in America were legitimately Americanisms, we might feel obliged to say "as American as *apple cobbler* (or *apple pandowdy*, or *apple grunt*)."

Having accepted as Americanisms those terms with characteristic form or use in America, whatever their origin, we have, however, been able to show widely varied influences on American English and to get a sense of the cultural diversity that has shaped the language as well as the communities of the United States. Consider again such words as *moccasin, raccoon*, and *hoochinoo*; *arroyo, Yankee, smearcase,* and *kringle*; *hornswoggle, OK, sharecropping, maverick*; *sex appeal, smog, babysit, flextime*. In one way or another, all of those are Americanisms. Taken together they suggest the growth and development of Americans as an English-speaking people and of a language that is obviously English, yet uniquely American.

FURTHER READING

The classic works on Americanisms have, in general, stood the test of time quite well, though recent electronic databases have made it easy to antedate many of the headwords as well as document new terms that qualify as Americanisms. Bartlett's *Dictionary of Americanisms* (1848) was an admirable attempt to break new ground, with each subsequent edition providing refinements in terms of criteria for inclusion as well as additional headwords; Richard H. Thornton's *An American Glossary* (1912) was particularly valuable in that it provided copious and better-documented illustrations of actual use (a third volume largely prepared by Thornton was published posthumously in the journal *Dialect Notes*, 1931–9); Craigie and Hulbert's *Dictionary of American English* and Mathews's *Dictionary of Americanisms* both followed the model of the *Oxford English Dictionary* in their historical treatment and their careful documentation, with Mathews bringing the illustrative quotations up to mid century (the *DAE* had included quotations only up to 1925).

Americanisms of the second half of the twentieth century are recorded by Algeo and Algeo (1991), based on the column "Among the New Words," a regular feature in the journal *American Speech*. A somewhat unorthodox but very lively treatment of Americanisms is *America in So Many Words*, by Barnhart and Metcalf (1997), which features a word for each year since 1750 (plus selected others as well); often the word is assigned to the year of first attestation, but it can also be linked to the year of significant prominence. The explanatory paragraphs provide colorful vignettes of the social history of the American nation.

A new dimension has been added to the study of Americanisms with the debut of the CD-ROM (1994) and online (2000) versions of the *Oxford English Dictionary*. Their searching capabilities allow one to collect all the headwords and senses that include the labels "*U. S.*" or "*orig. U. S.,*" in effect creating a new compilation of Americanisms. Other electronic databases, such as *The Making of America* (University of Michigan, 1996, and Cornell University, 1999) and the Library of Congress's *American Memory* (1998), have search capacities that invite one to start with known examples of Americanisms and search for antedatings. As the editors of the *Dictionary of American Regional English* have discovered, the results can be extremely rewarding.

6 SLANG

Jonathan E. Lighter

Buckaroo and *megabuck, glitz* and *glam, tightwad* and *uptight* – all are slang. Since the days of the fast clippers, thousands of similar idioms have raced from home shores to be recognized everywhere as particularly "American slang." Thanks partly to the telegraphers of the Atlantic cable, the laconic *OK* (1839 *OED*) had reached England by 1866 and turned up as "an Americanism" in a subsequent edition of Hotten's British slang dictionary (*OED;* Hotten 1874); in the twentieth century it became probably the most widely recognized Americanism on earth. The common noun *guy* took two or three generations to overhaul the earlier *bloke* in Britain, Australia, and elsewhere, but the American term (ultimately traceable to the name of Guy Fawkes) is now familiar wherever English is spoken. American slang has circled and recircled the globe.

In spite of its worldwide influence, the significance of American slang has been long slighted. Except for Richard Bailey (1996), Gerald Cohen, Connie Eble, and Karl Sornig, trained linguists have rarely given slang more than a quick hello. Indeed, the word *slang* itself may be on the decline as a term of art; the four heavy volumes of the *International Encyclopedia of Linguistics* (Bright), for instance, do not offer an article on the subject and mention slang in passing only. Yet the increasing perspicuity of critical thought about language is what resulted in the recognition of slang in the first place, and slang's rise to prominence is a salient fact in the history of American English. The introduction to volume 1 of *The Random House Historical Dictionary of American Slang* (Lighter) amplifies a number of points in this discussion and provides further general information.

Word-lovers and journalists – Eric Partridge and H. L. Mencken being the best known – have shown more interest in slang than have linguists; diverting communiques on "the latest slang" – typically "GI jargon," "jazz (or rock or rap) chatter," "street lingo," "CB slanguage," "surfer talk," and

219

the "hot new teenspeak" – have brightened the nation's newspapers and magazines for decades. But linguists are wary: they are put off by the convoluted array of competing and overlapping senses attached to the word *slang* during its 250-year history. The equivocal nature of the term *slang* encourages facile and uninformed commentary in the classroom as well as in print. Textbooks on composition have assiduously warned students against the use of slang for a hundred years though the warnings have become less categorical. What such warnings mean by *slang* is not always evident; among clearer examples like *grody* and *spaced out*, one current guide cites *lifestyle*, *sexist*, *gentrification*, *Watergate*, and even *glasnost* as examples of recent slang (Kirszner and Mandell 275).

6.1   A definition of *slang*

To employ the useful heuristic label *slang* as a broad synonym for most lexical innovation only perpetuates the confusion surrounding the subject. So taking into account the various definitions in dictionaries as well as the more detailed treatments of such authors as Henry Bradley, Stuart Flexner (preface to Wentworth and Flexner), H. L. Mencken, and Eric Partridge, the following definition will be stipulated (based on Dumas and Lighter, summarized by Landau 189):

> *Slang* denotes an informal, nonstandard, nontechnical vocabulary composed chiefly of novel-sounding synonyms (and near synonyms) for standard words and phrases; it is often associated with youthful, raffish, or undignified persons and groups; and it conveys often striking connotations of impertinence or irreverence, especially for established attitudes and values within the prevailing culture.

Like Samuel Johnson's celebrated definition of *network*, this one is cumbersome, but it has the virtue of matching common perceptions of slang. Despite disagreements over the slanginess of specific words and phrases, all speakers of English are presumably familiar with slang; to a native speaker, any assertion to the contrary would be astonishing. There is no acid test for slang; but neither is there much doubt about its intersubjective reality.

Slang can also be distinguished from both formal and colloquial usage on the basis of style, context, function, and emotive association. Slang deviates stylistically from other sorts of English; its hallmark is its undignified or indecorous tone. Indeed, this is the critical distinction between slang and the merely informal. Whereas the merely informal or

colloquial imparts a natural, unstilted tone to discourse, slang is conspicuously divergent, taking the place of words that lie near the familiar core of
standard English. The aim and chief function of slang is to lower and
disavow the dignity of discourse. Thus characterized, slang may exist in all
languages, but it is not clear that all cultures share an equal interest in undermining dignity or, if they do, that all have evolved extensive and widely
known deflationary slang vocabularies. Indeed, it may be that widespread
cultural awareness of such a vocabulary as a deviant subcategory of the
lexicon belongs exclusively to highly stratified, literate societies having a
strong tradition of standard language (Lighter 1: xviii).

Slang has a distributional as well as a stylistic aspect. Typically absent
from settings where standard English is the norm – edited serious discourse, for example – it is found in contexts where standard English is not
cultivated: work environments, military and naval bases, high school and
college campuses, prisons, sporting arenas, neighborhood taverns, and
locations for leisure-time activities.

The social and psychological functions of slang appear also to differ conspicuously from those of most other registers of English. Bradley (207)
and others have suggested that slang is typically "a means of concealing
secrets." The vocabulary of criminals has often been supposed to serve
chiefly to mask their intentions from prospective victims (or *marks*); similarly, teenagers are often supposed to affect exotic lexicons as a means of
expressing taboo thoughts in front of their innocent and uncomprehend-
ing parents (or *rents*). This theory of teen slang was advanced in the 1811
Lexicon Balatronicum (vi), which avers that young men "of spirit . . . may now
talk bawdy before their papas, without fear of detection." While such secre-
tive, colorful dialogues may sometimes play themselves out, the usual social
functions of slang (as opposed to deliberately created secret codes) are
considerably more subtle.

Often out of simple playfulness or else to express the insider's wry appraisal of a linguistic referent, slang renames (and thus radically reorients) familiar concepts. In its social role, slang serves to test, establish, or reinforce
nonconformist attitudinal bonds between peers. Slang is certainly "socially
isolative" when it flies past "outsiders" to discourage their attention. The
uncomprehension of a bemused addressee also boosts the slangster's ego; he
knows something the addressee doesn't, and he may explain it or not, as he
pleases. But, equally to the point, slang is also "socially cohesive"; in a minor
way, the regular use of slang reminds the young, in particular, of shared out-
looks and a social identity that is to some extent consciously developed and
fostered. Slang thus emphasizes one's independence of antagonistic or

uncongenial people – authority figures generally – and of their values as well (Drake).

Not surprisingly, slang flourishes in same-sex groups composed of peers of comparable age and social status. Controlled studies have yet to be done, but men have traditionally appeared to use more slang than women (Jespersen 1921, 248; Wentworth and Flexner xii; Lighter 1: xxxii). A study by de Klerk indicates that South African schoolgirls know about as many slang terms as the boys; but one cannot deduce from this that they *use* as many. Some awareness that one shares a slang vocabulary with peers must enhance, perhaps in a small way, a satisfying sense of group distinctiveness. That is unquestionably true for those sizable, loose-knit, often youthful groups whose members have most affected slang, especially over the past century: military personnel, lawbreakers, inner-city youngsters, and high school and university students. Youthful speakers especially may express irritation when they hear their most characteristic slang taken over or poorly imitated by the larger culture, which happened about 1970 to such now familiar Americanisms as to *freak out*, to *cop out*, to *do one's (own) thing*, and to *blow one's mind*, which are of varied origins but all were popularized through press coverage of the hippie movement of the sixties. Few speech situations in English are more ridiculous than the violation by adults (worse yet, parents) of role expectations and generational distance through using teen slang to impress teenagers.

Not violation but shortening of social distance accounts for the rise, over the past half century, of identifiable Black English in the general slang vocabulary. This rise of black slang came about through the interplay of several major factors. The most publicized was the big-band heyday of about 1935–50, which circulated a number of African-American slang terms like *cat* 'fellow, jazzman,' *dig* 'to understand,' *beat up your chops* 'to talk,' and *knock yourself out* 'to enjoy yourself' among young swing fans (*jitterbugs* and *alligators*) of all ethnic groups. Later developments in pop music, most recently the emergence of rap or hip-hop in the 1980s, have periodically reinforced the trend. *Hype* and *dope* 'wonderful' and *wack* 'no good' are examples.

The role played by American slang in what Bronislaw Malinowski (in Ogden and Richards 1923) called "phatic communion" is important. But the emotive and rhetorical features of slang are equally so. Indeed, as the definition of slang above suggests, all these contributory elements are intertwined. To recognize the often marked emotive and rhetorical (or, taken together, "tonal") difference between American slang and ordinary colloquialisms, fluent speakers have only to make some simple comparisons.

Compare colloquial *mess up* 'to make a mess or muddle of, botch' with the slang synonyms *bitch up*, *screw up*, and *fuck up*; colloquial (and mostly feminine) *goose* 'silly person' with the slang *dingaling* and *jerk*; colloquial *get mad* 'become angry' and *blow up* 'fly into a rage' with slang *get steamed* and *blow one's top*.

Slang impacts middle-class sensibilities as undignified or aggressive for a number of reasons. The sheer novelty of slang is often a source of comment. Examples include *spondulix* 'money,' *gizmo* 'peculiar object, contrivance, or mechanism,' *slugfest* 'boxing match in which many hard blows are exchanged, (hence) bitter debate,' *blizzard* 'gunshot, volley of shot' (hence the now-standard meaning 'violent snowstorm'), *humongous* 'gigantic,' *skag* 'heroin,' *nerd* 'socially inept person,' *skedaddle* 'to run away,' *barf* 'to vomit,' *goon* 'stupid person or thug,' *scuzzy* 'scruffy, grimy, unsavory,' *snafu* 'bungled or confused situation.'

The expressive, sometimes intriguing, figurative associations of much slang are also notable: *bones* 'dice,' *rotgut* 'vile liquor,' *dogs* 'feet,' *clink* 'jail or prison,' *broad* 'woman,' *wimp* 'weak or cowardly person,' *pot* 'marijuana,' *pissed off* 'angry,' *the Rust Belt* 'heavily industrial areas of the Ohio Valley,' *pass the buck* 'to shift responsibility,' *shoot the breeze* 'to chat or converse idly,' *fuzz* 'police,' *snow job* 'soothing, flattering, insincere talk,' *the Big Apple* 'New York City.' Slang is also witty in a playful or derisive way: *birdman* 'aviator,' *lamebrain* or *knucklehead* 'simpleton,' *suds* 'beer,' *wise-ass* 'impertinent individual, know-it-all,' *salt horse* 'pickled beef,' *tightwad* 'miser,' *snot-locker* 'nose,' *flatfoot* 'police patrolman,' *give the boot* 'to dismiss or discharge abruptly,' *hit the hay* 'to go to bed,' *slap-happy* 'dazed,' *knowledge box* 'head,' *shit on a shingle* 'creamed chipped beef on toast,' *do the bone dance* 'engage in sex.'

In the final analysis, however, the decisive factor in the emotive impact of slang rests in the cultural need to distinguish "proper" from "improper" diction. Certain expressions become "improper" chiefly through their association, real or imagined, with various disesteemed kinds of speakers, especially the young, the disreputable, the irreverent, the callously cynical – speakers, whatever their group membership, whose linguistic license exceeds their concern for dignity (some would call it pretentiousness) of either speech or self.

The matrix of sociolinguistic responses giving rise to this perception of slang comes in large part from the fundamental requirement among educated speakers for decorum in responsible speech. Much of the often cited "raciness" or "vitality" of slang comes, moreover, from this awareness of its social context: slang is most at home in face-to-face settings where decorum is at a discount, where subtle values of "social deference and reverence for the past," often conveyed by exclusive use of standard diction, are irrelevant (Sechrist). Slang must also occur in writing (fiction, drama, and reportage in particular) that seeks to evoke or recreate such settings.

Because the slang element in English is limited almost entirely to content words, and because few speakers seem to compartmentalize their active slang vocabulary as one might a foreign language, no one "talks in slang" for more than a phrase or two at a time. People who have most thoroughly internalized anti-establishment attitudes probably use the most slang, and it can take conscious effort to *kick the habit*, a phrase that entered colloquial use in the mid 1960s from the slang of drug addicts (Haertzen, Ross, and Hooks). Thus at the end of World War II (or so the story goes), Navy personnel were admonished before leaving the service:

> Now, when you get home, and you're a hero, and you're wearin' civvies again, and the whole family's gathered round the table – Mom and Dad and your brother and sister and all your aunts and uncles and cousins and maybe that cute little gal next door who's been waitin' for you all these years – and Mom's cooked up a turkey dinner in your special honor, and old Dad says grace and thanks the good Lord you're back home safe and you didn't get drowned or blown up by a big Jap torpedo, and everybody's smilin' and startin' to hoist in some of Mom's terrific home-cookin' – don't *you* say, "Hey, Baldy! Pass the fuckin' red lead!"
>
> [Related by a naval veteran in New York City in 1974. *Red lead*, an ingredient of weather-resistant paints used on shipboard, means 'ketchup.']

True or not, this anecdote implicitly identifies habit, socialization, social roles, and an antagonism of norms as bearing on the psychology and impact of slang usage.

6.2   Slang and poetry

A less hard-bitten impression of slang than that underlying the "red lead" story is now common among academic observers. S. I. Hayakawa (194–5) has characterized slang as "the poetry of everyday life"; another writer (Gaston) has called it "the poetry of group dynamics." Eble (1987) has compared the phonology, syntax, and lexicon of college slang with that of poetic language and finds that, though used for different purposes, the two share many lexical and phonological devices. In comparison with ordinary English, it might well be said that slang works at a heightened intensity, like a kind of negative poetry. Certainly slang employs many of the same figurative devices found in poetic language, as shown by the following examples:

ANTIPHRASIS: *bad* 'very pleasing; extremely impressive,' *winner* 'that which is disappointing or useless,' *son of a bitch* 'remarkable fellow'

ANTONOMASIA: *John Wayne* 'a foolishly daring fellow,' *Romeo* 'a man noted for his many love affairs,' *[Uncle] Tom* 'a black man who behaves subserviently toward whites'

BURLESQUE METAPHOR: *crowbait* 'an old or poor horse,' *sing* 'to turn informer,' *Arkansas toothpick* 'hunting knife,' *gasbag* 'boastful or loquacious speaker,' *apple* 'baseball,' *rock* 'basketball,' *doughnut* 'automobile tire,' *cowboy Cadillac* 'pickup truck,' *lung-duster* 'cigarette,' *Oreo* 'a black person aligned with white political interests'

HYPERBOLE: *super* 'quite pleasant or satisfactory,' *rotten* 'quite unpleasant or unsatisfactory,' *annihilated* 'very drunk,' *slaughter* '(in a game) to defeat decisively,' *slam* 'to criticize,' *chew someone's ass out* 'to rebuke or scold someone sharply,' *knock dead* 'to impress very favorably'

MEIOSIS: *kid* 'child,' *berry* 'dollar,' *lettuce* 'money,' *peanuts* 'a small or inadequate amount of money,' *pig* 'police officer,' *hide* 'racehorse,' *heap* 'automobile,' *crate* 'aircraft,' *tin can* 'naval destroyer'

METAPHOR: *bread* 'money,' *sconce* 'head,' *pill* 'a cannonball,' *hooks* 'fingers, clutches,' *grass* 'marijuana,' *paws* 'hands,' *chick* 'young woman,' *frost* 'a failure,' *peach* 'a very fine example,' *pegs* 'legs,' *gravy* 'profit,' *vines* 'clothing,' *spook* 'intelligence agent'

METONYMY: *skirt* 'young woman,' *kraut* 'German,' *macaroni* 'Italian,' *badge* 'police officer,' *flicker* 'motion picture,' *nose* 'a wine's bouquet,' *tube* 'television programming,' *suit* 'business executive,' *the Big Smoke* 'Pittsburgh'

ONOMATOPOEIA: *sock* or *biff* 'to hit hard,' *buzz* 'telephone call,' *zing* 'to pitch [a fastball],' *boomer* 'a heavy ocean billow; a thunderstorm,' *splash* 'to shoot down (an enemy aircraft) over water'

PERSONIFICATION: *Uncle Sam* 'US Government,' *Johnny Bull* 'the British Empire,' *Johnny Crapeau* 'the French,' *Johnny Reb* 'Southern Confederate forces,' *Jerry* or *Heinie* or *Fritz* 'German forces,' *Ivan* 'Soviet forces,' *GI Joe* 'an ordinary US soldier during and since the Second World War,' *Joe College* 'a typical male college student,' *Suzie Sorority* 'a typical member of a Greek-letter sorority'

SYNECDOCHE: *wheels* 'automotive transportation,' *southpaw* 'left-handed baseball pitcher,' *piece of ass* 'act of copulation,' *the tube* 'television set,' *fender-bender* 'minor automotive collision'

Some of the foregoing examples may be figuratively ambiguous, but the observation that slang resembles literary expression must be taken seriously. Both, for example, are highly connotative, and both are in the business of defamiliarizing the mundane. But their differences are also important. We expect poetic language (as opposed to Augustan poetic diction) to be original and unique to the poem; slang, on the other hand, must enjoy some degree of currency to be distinguishable from nonce terms and idiosyncrasies. Poetic language strives for subtle emotional and conceptual effects; slang settles for the jocular and the startling. Like modern poetry in particular, slang implies the inadequacy of ordinary language to deal with new conditions of real life.

Yet even at its most radical, poetry celebrates continuity with the past; poets, after all, recognize poetry itself as a venerable artistic pursuit and place themselves somewhere within (or sometimes at the end of) that tradition. Slang, in contrast, rejects tradition: the lay public experiences slang idioms as novel (one of the chief reasons for using them) and thinks of slang as a twentieth-century phenomenon. When American college students are told that Dickens, for example, used slang in his novels, they are mildly surprised and cannot identify that slang; when it is pointed out to them, they express disappointment that Victorian slang is "so nothing." "It's just – I don't know – why is *governor* ['father'] slang if *'orse* and *'orrible* aren't?" Their disappointment reminds us that slang is expected to be entertaining and that "outsiders" have a hard time appreciating it. The South African schoolgirls and boys mentioned earlier reacted to de Klerk's questionnaire with "astounding enthusiasm . . . delight at being able to let go of linguistic inhibitions anonymously, and at the fact that some people are interested in the language of youth."

More tellingly, a central purpose of poetic language is to prompt introspective reflection; a central function of slang is to short-circuit reflection and to exalt snap judgments and habitual attitudes among social peers. Indeed, each time a slang term is repeated, unthinking evaluative norms are reinforced. Irrationalism has always had its voice in civilized life, and this frankly anti-rational function of slang is what underlies the objections so often expressed by educators and essayists.

6.3 Radiations of the meanings of the term *slang* and of attitudes toward slang

In 1987, a reviewer for the *Times Literary Supplement* endorsed American slang as "the one untrammelled glory" of the United States. Britons of other days had more than once assailed American slang, and neologisms of all kinds, as so much ignorant vulgarity; but from the postmodern landscape of the 1980s the *TLS* reviewer concluded that American slang was an asset to international English, a valuable rejuvenating force, "a gift to a greyer, older world" (H. Williams).

To critics of the eighteenth and early nineteenth centuries, British or American, approbation of slang from a quarter so august as the *Times* would have seemed incredible, a stinging insult to decent English speech. The critical aim, unattainable and often unexpressed, was steadily to evolve a cogent and civilizing diction suitable for all human purposes; slang, almost by definition, was antithetical to such an aim. From the days of Swift and Defoe, an article of faith for critics and grammarians alike was that unregulated, unstandardized speech served only to corrupt language, to undermine the human capacity for rational thought, and thus ultimately to hinder the wise exercise of free will. Slang was seen as both emerging from and sustaining an undisguised baseness of mind that must lead to the coarsening of both language and civilization.

Users of slang in this view might sometimes be persons of wit but never of merit. The English belletrist J. P. Thomas observed in 1825 that "men of discretion will not pervert language to [slang's] unprofitable purposes of conversational mimicry." "Slang," he wrote, "is the conversation of fools" (quoted in Partridge 1933, 7). Americans like the Harvard-educated Richard Henry Dana, Jr., shared this perspective. After expressing his admiration for the novels of Dickens, Dana confided to his journal in 1842 that Dickens' *American Notes* was another matter altogether, "careless, pretentious, & with a kind of off-hand, slang-ey [sic], defying tone, which a man with a well-balanced mind & the delicate perceptions & self respect of a gentleman could not fall into" (Dana 1968, I: 103). Already in 1828 Noah Webster had become the first lexicographer to enter the word *slang* in a standard dictionary, defining it unceremoniously as "low, vulgar unmeaning language."

The word *slang* itself is of uncertain origin and has had a curious history. Despite the evidence of the *OED*, its earliest recorded occurrences did not apply to language at all. Partridge demonstrates the existence of the word *slang* in several obscure senses as part of the argot of English vagabonds, swindlers, and thieves as early as 1740–1, more than a decade before the *OED*'s primary citation (Partridge 1949, s.v. *slang-madge*, *slang-mort play*, *slang upon the safe*, *slanging the gentry-mort rumly*, etc.). The early examples of usage allude uniformly to criminal deception. Earliest of all and especially curious is the appearance of the unexplained form *slango* in *The Amorous Gallant's Tongue* of 1740 (date according to Burke 68): "You, Fellow-traveller, what do you do for a living? *You, Cole, what Slango do you go upon?*"

The sense 'underworld occupation' in the 1740 citation recurs a half century later, now in the familiar form *slang*, in George Parker's invaluable description of English criminality, *Life's Painter of Variegated Characters* (140): "'How do you work now?' . . . 'O, upon the old *slang* [of impersonating a mute], and sometimes a little *lully-prigging* ['stealing wet linen off the hedges' (Parker's gloss)].'" Here the word *slang* clearly denotes a hoodwinking trick. It is tempting to fancy a connection between *slango/slang* and the name of the servant Slango, an important character in Henry Carey's comic opera *The Honest Yorkshire-Man*, first performed in 1735. Not only is the plot driven by Slango's strategy of disguise, he being described as "an arch fellow" among a cast that includes characters significantly named Gaylove, Muckworm, Sapscull, and Blunder, but also his speeches are identified throughout by the printed abbreviation *Slang*.

Merriam and Oxford are equally at a loss for an etymology of the word. A possibility – though no more than that – is that it may be a borrowing with transferred meaning of the Dutch *slang* 'snake, serpent,' a word known to have become the late eighteenth-century prisoners' *slang* 'a chain.' A connection with ideas of cheating and fraud may have come from an original association with the serpent of Genesis, a creature often cited as the first and most successful of deceivers. But intriguing as it may be, this is mere conjecture.

At any event, the principle of etymological parsimony leads the *OED* to wonder whether its first citation, from 1756, really designates language; it could as well refer to deceptive practice: "Thomas Throw had been upon the town, knew the slang well." The earliest unequivocal application of *slang* to a kind of diction occurs two years later in a minor satirical pamphlet by the pseudonymous "Henry Humbug." In a Swiftian attack upon thoroughly corrupt London thief-takers (professional apprehenders of thieves), Humbug (lxxix) advises that their orphaned brats be fully instructed in the "Slang Patter" of malefactors so as better to prepare them for their own lives of crime. Humbug's referent is quite specific: *slang patter* means the obscure, exclusionary, and socially restricted jargon of a mostly itinerant criminal class.

First noted in the sixteenth century by Copland (1535–6, 24), who believed it to be of recent introduction into England, this mystifying jargon was often known as *pedlar's French* or *pedlyng Frenche* and later as *cant*, the designation favored throughout most of the eighteenth century by both the canters and the commentators. The *OED* favors a derivation of *cant* at some remove from Latin *cantare*, but does not dismiss the likelihood – recently reasserted by Hancock (1984, 385) and more appealing on sociolinguistic if not on phonological grounds – that it comes directly from Irish and Gaelic *caint, cainnt* 'speech.' *Patter* was long a generic cant synonym for 'talk' or 'speech,' so Humbug's *slang patter* literally means 'hoodwinking talk.' When Captain Grose defined *slang* in 1785 (its first appearance in a dictionary of any kind), his definition was succinct and specific: "SLANG. Cant language."

Grose's practice throughout his humorously titled *Classical Dictionary of the Vulgar Tongue*, edited by Pierce Egan for its fifth edition in 1823 and known in the United States by 1805 (*Port Folio* 261), shows that by "cant" he meant rogues' language specifically. Grose's definition of *canting* is "a kind of gibberish use by thieves and gypsies, likewise pedlar's French, the slang, &c. &c."

Once it had surfaced in the speech of relatively upright citizens, the word *slang* almost immediately took on a predictable extended sense, virtually the same secondary sense that decades earlier had attached itself to *cant*. In 1762, the playwright Samuel Foote (5) portrayed Oxford students using the noun *slang* as a new synonym for 'empty or deceptive language, rubbish,' a sense of the word which survived for several decades. Similarly, the *Britannica* in 1801 condemned "that sentimental slang of philanthropy" (cited in *OED*), and the American glossarist Pickering (159) in 1816 referred to "that sort of political or other cant ['insincerity'] which amuses the rabble, and is called by the vulgar name of *slang*." Washington Irving (216), the first significant American author to use the word, reports in the voice of "Pindar Cockloft" that his nieces "complain of that empty sarcastical slang / So common to all the coxcombical gang, / Who . . . boast of themselves, when they talk with proud air / Of man's mortal ascendancy over the fair."

Additional senses of *slang* had developed by the end of the eighteenth century, including one of the longest-lived, that of "abusive or vituperative language, offensive talk, invective." In 1786, the wry versifier William Woty (2) asked, "Did ever Cicero's harangue / Rival this flowing eloquence of slang?" A note explains the neologism as "A cant word for vulgar language." Washington Irving (364) also rhymed "slang" with "harangue." The anonymous biographer of Congressman David Crockett observed in 1832 that "Colonel Crockett . . . has been exposed to the wrath of the [press, couched in] every style, from the most chaste and sedate language, to the most violent slang of modern party spirit" (*Sketches* 129). An Irish-American music-hall song of the 1870s tells of a young tough who "told the old woman . . . to shut up her giving him . . . slang" (R. L. Wright 595). A derivative based on the sense in question is *slangwhanger*, employed by both Cooper and Irving (who may well have coined it), and meaning 'a carping journalist or politician given to invective or verbal abuse.' As late as 1927, former private Elisha Stockwell (156) recalled the reaction of a New Orleans woman to his Wisconsin comrades in arms during the Civil War:

> She swore like a man and called the soldiers nigger thieves and said if they touched those vegetables she would come over there. They . . . told her they didn't want her truck. But she kept on with slang, and told them to come up there two at a time and she would lick the whole bunch.

A trace of this sense of 'verbal abuse, offensive talk' lingers among the many Americans of the present day for whom the word *slang* means mainly profanity and "four-letter words" outside of any framework of standard versus nonstandard.

The next sense to develop, common in the United States between the 1830s and perhaps the 1920s, had a subliterary reference: 'an extravagant style of verbal humor employing grotesque comparisons, nonstandard or newly coined words, and often dialect or eccentric spellings.' The "Crockett almanacs" of 1833–60 typify the style, which also exploited (and largely invented) the "tall talk" vocabulary of "mouth-filling words" like *explaterate, killniferously*, and *exflunctify* (a list of which is given by Mathews 114–5). "Ben Harding," the fictive boatman-author of the 1839 *Almanac* (2), promised ironically to "keep all your low slang out of the book, and make it read as slick as a greasy bed-blanket, and as strait [sic] as a frozen nigger. All the stories will be as beautiful as a red eel or a painted monkey."

The works of Charles F. Browne ("Artemus Ward") were thus said to be "written in slang," as were those of the early dialect humorists Joe Strickland, Seba Smith, Thomas Haliburton, George Washington Harris, and others. After 1871 the best-known example of this limited genre was undoubtedly the episode of Buck Fanshaw's funeral in chapter 47 of Mark Twain's *Roughing It* (1872, 299): "Are you the duck that keeps the gospel-mill next door? . . . the head clerk of the doxology-works." The humor of such efforts turns chiefly on the pretense that the uneducated have their own funny language, chock-full of ludicrous wonders, which they speak incessantly. Writers could have fun experimenting with nonstandard English while their ironic sensibility simultaneously condemned it. No linguistic condemnation, however, is evident in the short stories of journalist Damon Runyon (1884–1946), written mostly in the 1930s and 1940s. Owing to the difficulty of collecting or manufacturing ad hoc an offbeat vocabulary sufficient to sustain interest for its own sake, most writing of the "slang" sort is mercifully brief. Ephemeral modern examples occur now and again, often thrown together to introduce newspaper fillers on the "latest" teen lingo.

Inspired by Harlem slang or "jive" and encouraged by the writers Langston Hughes and Zora Neale Hurston, the African-American editor Dan Burley (1944) hoped to foster a lexically contrived but culturally authentic "jive literature" during World War II to reflect the innovative energy of the black urban vocabulary. As editor of the *New York Amsterdam News*, Burley sought to popularize jive both as a means of black self-expression and as an instrument of racial harmony, as its humor might appeal to anybody. Much of the vocabulary collected or coined by Burley eventually found its way into a tour de force of American biography, *Really the Blues* (Mezzrow and Wolfe 1946). A decade later the jive style was revived as parodic farce by the "beat" comedian Lord Buckley (15) as in his redaction of the Gettysburg Address:

> Four big hits and seven licks ago, our Before daddies Swung forth upon this sweet groovey Land, a jumpin', Swingin', stompin', wailin' NEW NATION! Hip to the cool sweet groove of Liberty and solid sent upon the Ace Lick that all Cats and Kitties, Red, White, or Blue! are created *LEVEL*, in *FRONT.*

Buckley's eccentric capitalization may reveal a debt to the canny satirist George Ade (1866–1944), the past master of "slang writing." Set beside Buckley's avalanche of figuration and lexical invention, however, Ade's many "fables in slang," still effective though written between 1897 and 1920, seem measured and muted in comparison.

Other important developments in the semantic career of the word *slang* also reach back 200 years. In the early nineteenth century, English writers extended the semantic range of the word considerably. Soon slang came to include any nonstandard idiom in popular, particularly in urban, use, which, to the fastidious ear of the intelligentsia, could mark an individual as ignorant, vulgar, or disreputable.

Next to the baffling (and thus especially degenerate) cant of criminals ("Flick me some panam and caffan," "Twig the cull, he is peery," from Grose 1785), the litterateurs of the late Georgian era and thereafter found catch phrases, vogue words, and the cliches of commerce to be the most pernicious of nonstandard idioms, and to these also they freely applied the scornful epithet of "slang." Doubtless speaking for many, Lady Louisa Stuart lamented early in the century, "Slang has superseded language" (quoted by McKnight 1923, 409). The youthful Carlyle (1: 53) in 1815 sought escape from "the cant & slang of the coxcombs, the bloods, the bucks, the boobies with which all earth is filled." His elder contemporary Coleridge (4: 359) in 1818 indiscriminately equated "what we now call *slang*" with "vulgarisms."

De Quincey (120) showed just how far the label could be stretched, when he confessed in 1821, "Reading is an accomplishment of mine; and, in the slang use of the word *accomplishment* as a superficial and ornamental attainment, almost the only one I possess." Here the adjective *slang* means something like '(of diction) fashionable though imprecise,' an attenuated usage which, owing to the later associations of the word, has now an eccentric or pedantic ring, at least in this case. But insofar as they were pretentious, unfamiliar, or obscure, even the jargons of the arts and professions might be stigmatized as slang. The *OED* cites Bentham's contemptuous allusion before 1813 to "lawyer's slang" (not just words, but the whole mystifying legalistic style). Later in the century Hotten freely categorized as slang the words *aesthetic, transcendental,* and *chiaroscuro,* fine arts terms just entering the mainstream of educated usage after mid century. Any specialized vocabulary, high, low, or nondescript, could thus be dismissed as slang. In America, the *Somerset* (NJ) *Messenger* reproved President elect Lincoln for humorously applying the "slang phrases" *free-love affair* and *passional attraction* to the state of the Union; these he drew from the idiom of the notorious "free-love" movement (Feb. 21, 1861, cited by Siegal 19).

At one time the label *slang* connoted the general style and content of a discourse about as often as it did specific words and phrases. The appearance in 1823 of a duodecimo volume called *Slang*, compiled by "Jon Bee" (a pen name for the Englishman John Badcock), helped tip the scales further in the direction of words and phrases. As the first publication to carry the word *slang* in its title, Badcock's catchpenny production justified itself as "a dictionary of the turf, the ring, the chase, the pit, of bon-ton, and the varieties of life." It meant to elucidate "words and phrases that are necessarily, or purposely, cramp, mutative, and unintelligible, outside their respective spheres." These chiefly urban spheres were markedly undignified: pugilism, sports betting, crime, street life, and the habits of dandies and their university epigones. For Badcock, the chief devotees of slang were those we would today call "street people." The natural habitat of slang was very much the teeming city, an idea emphasized by the American philologist G. P. Krapp nearly a century later (quoted by I. Allen 1994). Many others have shown a similar orientation: nonstandard urban vocabulary is "slang" and vulgar; country ("dialect") words of unusual formation or use may be inelegant, but are in contrast felt to be earthy, provincial, redolent of quiet, old-time ways.

In 1848, the American John Russell Bartlett drew a sharp, if implicit, distinction between "slang" and "provincialisms" on the one hand and, on the other, "words found in the dictionaries of Drs. Johnson and Webster," with the remark that slang and provincialisms "are low, or vulgar, or only to be heard in familiar conversation." Bartlett, whose *Americanisms* was preeminent in its field for fifty years, did not specify what he meant by "slang words" except to say that he had included those "not noticed by lexicographers, yet so much employed as to deserve a place in a glossary" (iv). One infers that he meant "low," "vulgar," and "familiar" expressions unnoticed by the great lexicographers, plus new items not obviously "provincial" or regional, and of varying degrees of respectability.

Before the 1850s the word *slang*, as applied to language, was fraught with negative connotations, but during that decade a benchmark was reached in the amelioration of the word. In 1853 came the appearance in *Household Words* of an approving article, written anonymously by the English journalist George Augustus Sala, which commended the expressiveness and utility of many recent idioms not yet, or not likely to be, recognized by standard dictionaries. The *Living Age* of New York reprinted the piece later that year. Sala urged the creation of a new "slang" dictionary to replace the outdated collections of Francis Grose, Pierce Egan, and "Jon Bee." In 1859 it appeared, reportedly put together largely by Sala and others, but edited, introduced, and published by John Camden Hotten (Burke 21).

A Dictionary of Modern Slang, Cant, and Vulgar Words, commonly referred to simply as *The Slang Dictionary*, was in its way a British counterpart to Bartlett, but its vocabulary was more extensive and more decidedly urban. Hotten, the editor, was twenty-seven years old in 1859 and a keen publisher of popular literature. He had come to America at the age of sixteen and lived eight years with American English; his book quotes on occasion from Bartlett. Hotten took a favorable view of what he called for convenience "slang," defining it epigrammatically as "the language of street humour, of high, low, and fast life." Hotten's relatively limited conception of slang has directly and indirectly influenced most serious collectors since.

But in practice Hotten still welcomed material of a very general nature. As the contents of his book show, Hotten wished to treat as slang those vernacular expressions unrecorded in standard dictionaries, informal neologisms, and notable figurative meanings of every kind that did not originate in the works of established authors and which did not develop to fill clear-cut technical needs of the learned professions. There was also a generous amount of underworld lingo, as there had been in Grose, and, of course, there were those words of the street, the alehouse, the prize ring, the music hall, and the university, as well as some of the affected diction of high society, that Hotten had chosen as the real core of slang.

Nevertheless, any current word or phrase that had ever undergone a notable change or extension of meaning was likely to be called slang or "formerly slang," regardless of the circumstances surrounding the change.

Hotten's dictionary did not effect a revolution in the meaning of the label *slang*, but, by extending the word's range to include the usefully colloquial or figurative as well as the substandard, Hotten mitigated some of the word's unfavorable connotations and encouraged scholars to show greater tolerance of the phenomenon. Slang was no longer a simple pejorative term specific to the lexicon of human foibles and discreditable pursuits. Hotten's eighty-six page history of slang and criminal cant, the roughly 5,000 entries in the first edition (which grew to more than 10,000 in the fourth), and the closely printed thirteen-page bibliography made Hotten's the most substantive book on slang that had yet appeared. The third edition received an extended favorable review in the American *Harper's Monthly* (Nordhoff) in 1865.

Enthusiasts like Hotten were discussing the nature of "slang" at a time when academic scholars had yet to rationalize the category. The associations of the word itself were beginning to improve. The change, however, was still incipient. In 1877, nearly thirty years after his brief allusion to "slang" in the first edition of his *Dictionary of Americanisms*, and eighteen years after the first appearance of Hotten's slang dictionary, Bartlett (4th ed., iii–iv) turned to the subject in greater detail:

> The vocabulary of slang . . . may be divided into several classes. First are
> the terms used by bankers and stock-brokers. . . . These may be classed
> among the more respectable slang. . . . Next we have "College Slang," or
> words and expressions in common use among the students in our
> colleges and pupils in our higher schools. . . . Then there is the slang of
> politicians, of the stage, of sportsmen, of Western boatmen, of
> pugilists, of the police, of rowdies and "roughs," of thieves, of work-
> shops, of the circus, of shop-keepers, workmen, &c., which taken
> together form a rich mine from whence new words are derived; some of
> which, after a struggle, . . . finally obtain places in "Webster's
> Unabridged."

Bartlett's listing of the social classes most likely to use and create slang suggests one trait in common: all were more or less unrefined and undignified in an age when dignity of manner was a centrally held value among upstanding citizens. Richard Meade Bache (128) had succinctly stated this social fact in 1869: "Familiarity is insulting and all slang is familiar." Whereas Hotten (47) had tried to distinguish "slang" from criminal "cant" and subscribed to the concept of "learned slang" (jargonesque terms of art used by lawyers, critics, and theologians), Bartlett more cogently subsumed the vocabularies of rowdies, roughs, and thieves under the more general heading of slang, which he then confined to the unlearned classes. Bartlett also recognized that there could be degrees of slanginess, the limited slang of investment and finance being more respectable (because closer to mainstream values and closer to being a technical vocabulary) than that of socially less accepted pursuits.

Meanwhile, Hotten's fourth edition of 1874 had occasioned a substantial and generally favorable discussion of "The Philology of Slang" by the great English anthropologist E. B. Tylor. Probably the first academic to publicly acknowledge the subject as worthy of study, Tylor emphasized the fact that semantic change in English and other languages was generally unpredictable, and that figurative usage, unbound by formal rules and not confined to poets, was of great importance in semantic evolution. His examples of "slang" chosen from Hotten, Grose, and others, as usual, comprehend idioms from all levels of diction and from all social strata. Tylor's ambivalence toward the subject makes itself felt in his concluding paragraph: he has deliberately omitted some of slang's "proper topics" as being "too repulsive. Much of the slang-maker's skill is spent on foul ideas, which make the Slang Dictionary, at its best, an unpresentable book; while short of this limit, there is an ugly air about lists of words so largely coined by vagabonds and criminals." Yet more significant than these reservations are Tylor's opening words:

> Slang, despised and ignored until lately by the lexicographers, is a genuine and influential branch of speech. It is one of the feeders of what may be called standard language, which with little scruple adopts and adapts the words it happens to want, whether from the technical terms of shopmen and artisans, or out of the quainter vocabularies of costermongers and prize-fighters, schoolboys and fops. This practical importance entitles it to be treated linguistically, like any other working dialect.

Slang was now being taken seriously by a few scholars of greater note than Hotten. In 1875, Yale's William Dwight Whitney expressed his cautiously favorable opinion of slang in the broad context of metaphor and simile. Whitney (112–13) acknowledged:

> The mind not only has a wonderful facility in catching resemblances and turning them to account, but it takes a real creative pleasure in the exercise, and derives from it desirable variety and liveliness of style. . . . So far as this is odd or undignified, it forms the largest element of what we call "slang," and we frown upon it; and properly enough, but yet it is only the excess and abuse of a tendency which is wholly legitimate, and of the highest value, in the history of speech. . . . [I]n the . . . natural

delight of language-making, slang is a necessary evil, and there are grades and uses of slang whose charm no one need be ashamed to feel and confess; it is like reading a narrative in a series of rude but telling pictures, instead of in words.

For Whitney, slang was chiefly "odd or undignified" metaphor, but, once seen from the perspective of rhetoric rather than that of pathology, it could please us as a "charming" entity going directly to some prelinguistic level of the mind. In Whitney's view, slang was not decay: it was instead a catalyst for the growth of language.

One might even call it poetry, which is essentially what Walt Whitman did just a decade later. In his paean to "Slang in America," Whitman rhapsodizes over a mode of speech he defines only as "indirection." Whitman moreover regards the creation of slang as a liberating process, "an attempt of common humanity to escape from bald literalism and express itself illimitably," a universal tendency of mind which "in highest walks produces poets and poems, and doubtless in pre-historic times gave the start to, and perfected, the whole immense tangle of the old mythologies." Still widely regarded in 1885 as little more than an eccentric, Whitman was unlikely to persuade his learned contemporaries that slang was beneficial to anything at all, but his literary apotheosis a generation later lent credibility to his extravagant praise of the virtues of American slang. And Whitman had held this opinion for a long time. Even before the Civil War he had written, "Many of the slang words among fighting men, gamblers, thieves, prostitutes, are powerful words. These words ought to be collected – the bad words as well as the good; – Many of these bad words are fine" (1856–?, 735–6).

It was the lexicographer Whitney, who as editor-in-chief of the great *Century Dictionary* (1889–91) prepared what is perhaps the first modern, specialized definition of slang as a narrow subclass of nonstandard English:

> *Slang* . . . In present use, colloquial words and phrases which have originated in the cant or rude speech of the vagabond or unlettered classes or, belonging in form to standard speech, have acquired or have had given them restricted, capricious, or extravagantly metaphorical meanings, and are regarded as vulgar or inelegant.

With its etymological discussion combined with illuminating citations and an extended descriptive note, the *Century's* article on *slang* runs to about a thousand words. As the preceding discussion of the historical context makes clear, the *Century's* superior treatment comes not from greater insight into the nature of an empirically existing "slang" but from a professional awareness of how such commentators as Hotten, Bartlett, Tylor, Whitman, and Whitney himself had employed the term.

Thus, before the end of the nineteenth century, the modern lexicographical understanding of slang had emerged. Yet to the ordinary user of English, the word remained useful primarily as a wonderfully flexible term of dispraise. The Boston surgeon Oliver Wendell Holmes, Sr., had unforgettably warned that "the use of *slang*, or cheap generic terms, as a substitute for differentiated specific expressions, is at once a sign and a cause of mental atrophy" (1870, 275). Even Greenough and Kittredge of Harvard, the first American academics to address the place of a broadly defined slang in the overall development of English, echoed Holmes's warning in 1901 (73), admonishing that "the unchecked and habitual use of slang (even polite slang) is deleterious to the mind."

In their condescension toward the subject, Greenough and Kittredge call to mind a past when academics could avoid much exposure to Whitman's "blab of the pave." Finding "nothing abnormal about slang," the Harvard professors nonetheless advise, "The prejudice against this form of speech is to be encouraged" (55). Part of the reason for their distaste is that, since

> ... it is not the accepted medium of communication, [slang] has a taint of impropriety about it which makes it offensive. Again, the very currency of slang depends on its allusions to things which are not supposed to be universally familiar or generally respectable; and hence it is vulgar, since it brings in associations with what is for the moment regarded as unknown or in bad repute. [72]

Slang words, too, "are evanescent, counting their duration by days instead of decades, and becoming obsolete even while one is speaking them." Indeed, because "slang . . . has no fixed meaning" and "tends to level all those nice distinctions of meaning . . . which the consensus of the language has been at so much pains to build up," its use "must gradually reduce one's thought to the same ignorant level from which most slang proceeds" (73).

6.4 Twentieth-century scholarship on slang

Evanescent or not, slang was becoming ever more prominent. In response to the increasing amount of slang in mainstream print, H. L. Mencken's thoughts on the subject ballooned from fewer than ten pages in *The*

American Language of 1919 to well over 150 by 1948. Less straitlaced than most earlier observers, Mencken keenly appreciated the amusement afforded by transitory slang expressions; moreover, he became especially careful in his 1936 revision to discriminate between *slang*, occupational and professional *cant* (in the sense of a vocabulary of any kind – technical or otherwise – limited to a professional or vocational group), and criminal *argot* (a word covering the various heterodox vocabularies associated with habitual criminals). In terms of the material Mencken actually chose to address, his distinction between "slang" and "cant," at least, became rather moot: copious but uncritical lists of subcultural vocabularies appear in the 1948 *Supplement*, ranging alphabetically from "Actors" to "Union men in general."

Mencken's wry but superficial essay, with its theoretical and historical overview and its colorful word lists, remained the standard reference on American slang until 1960, the year that saw the appearance of Harold Wentworth and Stuart Flexner's ambitious *Dictionary of American Slang*. This was the first painstaking lexicographical attempt to do justice to American varieties of slang. Though it suffered from the inevitable shortcomings of a pioneering work (including a definition of *slang* that was as broad as any from the nineteenth century), Wentworth and Flexner greatly surpassed in coverage and sophistication the few earlier general dictionaries of American slang (Maitland 1891; Weseen 1934; Weingarten 1954). Still partially expurgated but unusually frank for its day, *DAS* was the first American dictionary of any kind to deal forthrightly with sexual and scatological slang, though later research shows that such terms exist in even bawdier profusion than *DAS* might suggest. The collections of Partridge and of Farmer and Henley indicate that the production of coarse vocabulary is equally vigorous elsewhere in the English-speaking world.

Flexner's extensive analytic comments stress the various social and psychological aspects as fully as the formal features of the slang vocabulary. Echoing the impression of Jespersen earlier in the century, Flexner also observed that "most American slang is created and used by males," for the primary reason that American men belong to more identifiable subgroups than do women and because American culture has encouraged men to be coarser and more hyperbolic in informal speech (xii; Jespersen 1921, 248; Lighter 1: xxxii; but cf. Risch). Wentworth and Flexner's dictionary was twice revised before being thoroughly revamped and retitled by Robert L. Chapman in 1986.

Solid specialized studies in an area where careful scholarship has been a rarity must not go unmentioned. All of these significant works on

American slang have been published since the 1930s, the earliest of them soon after Mencken in America and Partridge in Britain had revealed something of the extent and importance of slang in the English lexicon. All demonstrate a serious interest in the subject, an interest that would have been seen as morbid and improper in the days of Dr. Holmes.

W. J. Burke's meticulous annotated bibliography, *The Literature of Slang* (1939), covered informal vocabulary of all kinds, but its great scope only enhances its value. Surveying the entire history of English from the sixteenth century, Burke's annotated inventory of sources remains a primary reference work in the field, and it is unfortunate (if entirely understandable) that no scholar has taken up the challenge of providing a sequel to cover the years since its publication. Many additional sources are listed in the bibliographies of the "Second Supplemented [i.e., third] Edition" of *DAS* (Wentworth and Flexner 1975).

Col. Elbridge Colby's necessarily discreet *Army Talk* of 1942 has been importantly supplemented by the equally informal but larger and quite unexpurgated *Dictionary of Soldier Talk* (1984) by John R. Elting, Dan Cragg, and Ernest Deal. The prodigious *American Thesaurus of Slang*, edited by Lester Berrey and Melvin Van den Bark, appeared in 1942 and was revised twice in the next ten years. A later thesaurus, organized alphabetically, has been compiled by Lewin and Lewin (1988, 1994). Both works have been fattened by the assiduous inclusion of very uncommon terms.

The prison chaplain Hyman Goldin, along with Frank O'Leary and Morris Lipsius, compiled a *Dictionary of American Underworld Lingo* in the early 1940s (but not published till 1950), a work especially notable for the clarity and precision of its definitions. David Maurer's sociolinguistically oriented *The Big Con* (1940), *Whiz Mob* (1955), and *The American Confidence Man* (1974) will not soon be surpassed as discursive studies of the language and livelihood of American swindlers and pickpockets; his collected shorter articles, augmented by new introductions, were ably edited in 1981 as *Language of the Underworld*.

Edith Folb's in-depth examination of street vocabulary among African-American teens and gang members in Los Angeles in the 1960s and 1970s, called *Runnin' Down Some Lines*, is likewise a landmark in slang study. Robert S. Gold's *A Jazz Lexicon* (1964, revised as *Jazz Talk* in 1975) applies historical lexicography to the slang of jazz musicians. Thomas L. Clark of Las Vegas has done much the same thing for gamblers' lingo in his *Dictionary of Gambling and Gaming*. Popular word-collector Paul Dickson has compiled a useful *Baseball Dictionary*, which gains authority from drawing on the unpublished collections of the indefatigable word-collector Peter Tamony.

239

The journal *American Speech* has long been the chief outlet for well-informed articles on American slang. Rooted in meticulous documentary research, the contributions of Gerald L. Cohen (1982, 1985–97, 1991), Barry Popik and Cohen (1995, 1997), and David Shulman (1986) have been especially enlightening concerning such salient terms as *shyster* 'an unethical attorney,' *dude*, *hot dog*, *jazz*, and *the Big Apple*.

6.5 The historical development of American slang

Although it has stimulated great curiosity in the twentieth century, American slang, for reasons that should now be apparent, scarcely drew notice in the seventeenth and eighteenth centuries. The earliest slangy Americanism that we have good evidence for is undoubtedly the New England word *netop*. This was a borrowing from the native Algonquian languages of the northeast coast that persisted in New England for 250 years. In his description of Algonquian speech written in 1643, Roger Williams included the phrase "*Netop machage*," which he translated as "Friend, not so." This was hardly English language slang. But later citations (*DAE*, *DA*) show that some of the English settlers picked up the word, perhaps via pidgin, and began using it in contexts that had nothing to do with Indians. As late as 1898, New York State novelist David Westcott wrote in his contemporary novel, *David Harum*, that "Mr. Harum and I are great 'neetups,' as he says . . . It means, 'cronies,' I believe, in his dictionary" (cited in *DA*).

Clearly there was no urgent need for the seventeenth-century settlers of Massachusetts and Connecticut to adopt a Native word for 'friend' and then pass it on for two centuries and more; their own English had perfectly good equivalents, including *friend*, *companion*, and *brother*. Similarly there was no obvious need for the undergraduates of Cambridge to coin *crony* at roughly the same time, or for Westerners to coin the synonymous *sidekick* late in the 1800s. The word *netop*, serving no purpose in English but to add a little pioneer swash to one's image and a breezy sense of place to conversation, presumably carried similar emotive associations. A parallel adaptation, transforming Choctaw *itibapishili* 'my brother' into regional English *bobbasheely*, occurred later on the Alabama frontier (*DARE*). *Kid* 'a child or young person,' was often applied in the colonies to the generally youthful indentured servants who had frequently been enticed or stolen (in thieves' lingo, *napped* or *nabbed*) from their homes in Britain; hence *kid-napper* and, via back-formation, to *kidnap*, words accepted into formal English only after their employment in condemning the activities of His Majesty's press gangs in the latter 1700s.

Other durable expressions in use in America as well as in Britain in the eighteenth century and probably deserving the name of slang were *bones* 'dice' and *booze* 'liquor,' both having declined in acceptability from Middle and early Modern English, *grub* or *belly-timber* 'food, victuals,' *widgeon* or *gudgeon* 'a simpleton,' *kill-devil* 'rum,' *blackcoat* 'a clergyman,' *flam* 'a hoax,' *pins* 'the legs,' *phiz* 'the face,' *sconce* 'the head,' *save one's bacon* 'to save oneself,' *Adam's ale* 'water,' *give the bag* 'to escape from or evade,' *roger* 'to copulate with,' *punk* 'a prostitute,' and *scab* 'a contemptible fellow.' In addition to formerly offensive oaths like *zounds!* and *blood and wounds!* most of our current vulgar epithets were in use among the less decorous population long before the Revolution, particularly the plosive set *bitch, bastard, bugger,* and *son of a bitch.* The epithet *bloody,* extended unremarkably from its seventeenth-century sense of 'bloody-minded, cruel,' developed its offensive modern use as a mere epithet during the eighteenth century. Redcoats were jeered at in the streets of Boston as *bloodybacks, lobsters,* and *lobsterbacks,* insults that helped precipitate the "Massacre" of March 5, 1770.

Of more than passing interest is the fact that the first American known to have commented on slang as we would understand it today was Benjamin Franklin, inventor, philosopher, statesman, and, at the age of sixteen, collector of slang synonyms for being drunk. In Boston in 1722, the teenaged Franklin (writing as "Silence Dogood," 37) published an essay on the virtues of temperance that included the following interesting passage:

> It argues some Shame in the Drunkards themselves, in that they have invented numberless Words and Phrases to cover their Folly, whose proper Significations are harmless, or have no Signification at all. They are seldom known to be *drunk,* tho they are very often *boozey, cogey, tipsey, fox'd, merry, mellow, fuddl'd, groatable, Confoundedly cut, See two moons,* are *Among the Philistines, In a very good humour, See the Sun,* or, *The Sun has shone upon them;* they *Clip the King's English,* are *Almost froze, feavourish, In their Altitudes, pretty well enter'd,* &c. In short, every Day produces some new Word or Phrase which might be added to the Vocabulary of the *Tiplers.*

Richard Steele had complained in issue no. 12 of *The Tatler* (1709) that the vocabulary of London chocolate-house loungers changed every "half year." Noteworthy in the light of this and of countless later, similar comments on slang are Franklin's observations that new words and phrases concerning drunkenness are invented "every day" and his imaginative inference that tavern habitues deliberately created new locutions so as to screen from others their conversations about drink. Fifteen years later, in his own paper, the *Pennsylvania Gazette,* Franklin published an expanded list running to 228 items. Not all the items Franklin assembled can equally be called "slang," a word and, to some extent, a concept he did not know: in large part they are allusive descriptions of the effects of alcohol. Some are probably idiosyncratic, though Edward Seeber (104) claims to have discovered 138 expressions from the later list independently entered in various dictionaries. Nevertheless Franklin's lists prove that intoxication and its effects have been domains unusually productive of slang for a long time. As might be expected, few of Franklin's terms for being drunk have survived into the twentieth century; exceptions, from the list of 1737 (1), are *stew'd*, *jagg'd*, *boozy*, *cock'd*, and *cock-ey'd*.

The Rev. John Witherspoon's essays on the state of British and American English in 1781 mention a few slang items, all long established in Britain and America; of special interest for us are *bamboozle*, *bilk*, *bite* 'to cheat,' and *sham Abraham* 'to malinger.' Witherspoon calls these "*cant* phrases, introduced into public speaking or composition." But, as we should expect, Witherspoon includes "under the head of cant phrases" not just slang in a narrow sense but "all proverbial or common sayings introduced into the language, as well as trite and beaten allusions" (Mathews 1931, 27–8), in other words, all cliches that might blunt the effectiveness of formal diction. Witherspoon comments that most such idioms are "in their nature temporary and sometimes local." Yet he also makes the important observation that "a cant phrase" may ultimately establish itself as "an idiom of the [standard] language." *Mob*, he finds, though despised and condemned by Swift decades earlier, is now "established for ever" (29).

A second American slang glossary, very different from Franklin's and the only other extended list known to have appeared during the eighteenth century, is a valuable list of criminal cant appended to William Smith's *The Confession of Thomas Mount*, dated May 20, 1791, at Newport, Rhode Island. Mount, born in Middletown, East (i.e., New) Jersey, about 1764, had been a criminal for nearly fifteen years at the time of his execution for burglary. The Rev. Smith, who actually wrote the as-told-to confession, was primarily concerned with the salvation of Mount's soul; nevertheless, in the days before the execution, he secured from the unrepentant Mount and his condemned cell mate James Williams a list of well over a hundred words and phrases of thieves' cant, which the two thugs themselves referred to as "the flash language" (W. Miller 1929). Among the most typical and longest-lived examples on the list are *cove* 'a man,' *blowen* 'a woman,' *peepers* 'eyes,' *quod* 'jail,' *wheel* 'a dollar,' *doss* (spelled *dause* by Smith) 'a bed,' *pops* 'pistols,' *prad* 'a horse,' and *bit* 'money.' Several of these survived into the twentieth century in the United States or elsewhere.

The vocabulary of the *Confession* is doubly valuable for its authenticity; most of the terms are recorded earlier (and later) in British use, but a goodly number would seem to be Americanisms (Partridge 1949, passim). A similar list, less valuable only because less extensive, appears in Henry Tufts's probably ghost-written *Narrative* of 1807, listing about eighty cant words learned by Tufts from "flashmen as they termed themselves" (316–17) in a Massachusetts prison in 1794. A humorous anecdote of "Lord Mansfield" and "a jail bird," containing seven cant or "flash" phrases, identified as slang, appeared in *Father Tammany's Almanac for . . . 1792* (19).

By the beginning of the nineteenth century, "slang" of one kind or another had existed in American English for nearly 200 years. Owing to the dearth in early America of the breezy kind of humorous and picaresque writing commonly associated with slang, satisfactory knowledge of its complexion during this period is difficult to come by. The American slang glossaries of Franklin, Smith, and Tufts are the only ones known for the period before 1820, encompassing altogether about 400 terms. We do not know how wide a distribution many of these expressions enjoyed. Though Partridge's extensive research has shown the durability of many items of criminal cant, surely most of the flash lingo of Mount, Williams, and Tufts was unfamiliar outside of jails and the *flash kens* "underworld hangouts" of the "canting crew."

Much of the slang vocabulary included by Captain Grose, however, was indeed known in America along, inevitably, with other unrecorded terms and terms not recorded in print until the nineteenth century. If the records relied on by Craigie and Hulbert for the *DAE*, Mathews for the *DA*, and others paint a trustworthy picture of early slang in the United States, this slang did not become markedly "American" until the 1830s or 1840s. That "if" is a big one, however; the newly liberated pop culture of Jacksonian America, fueled by the explosion of newspapers (including W. T. Porter's influential *Spirit of the Times*, devoted to theatrical and sporting matters), may well have unearthed and broadcast as much slang as it actually created. Indeed, as late as 1858, Dr. Holmes could still score American slang as "commonly the dishwater from the washings of English dandyism, school-boy or full-grown, wrung out of a three-volume novel which had sopped it up" (247). But Holmes's upper-crust Boston was hardly the nation in miniature.

As we conjecture the overall state of American slang before 1800 and try to put it in perspective, we cannot overlook some basic demographic factors. In 1760 the thirteen colonies held a thinly spread population of 1.7 million persons, a number slightly smaller than the population of

Cleveland, Ohio, at the end of the twentieth century. At the time of the first federal census in 1790, the American population had boomed to 3.9 million, the size of today's Washington, DC, metro area but less than one-third that of Greater Los Angeles. Virtually everywhere in the colonies, population density was low. In an overwhelmingly agrarian society, 95 percent of Americans were living in places of fewer than 2,500 population in 1790. Only twenty-four communities identified as "cities" stood on American soil during the Washington administration as opposed to well over 7,000 in 1990. Moreover, no city in 1790 – not New York, Boston, or Philadelphia – held more than 50,000 citizens.

Today more than 330 cities and towns have populations greater than that. For every settler in the English colonies of 1700 (about 250,000) there were 1,000 American citizens in the final decade of the twentieth century (Porter 169; *Statistical Abstracts* 27; Welland 137). The voluminous increase in the size and density of the American population has brought about an even greater exponential rise in the number of social networks that encourage the production and establishment of slang, as they do of other new, nonslang, terminologies.

Associated with the increase in population, changes in the technology of communication – the development of genuinely mass-oriented, mass-circulation newspapers and magazines by 1900 and of instantaneous mass communication in the 1920s – guaranteed the national spread of slang that in earlier times must have remained of local currency only. The light fiction appearing in mass-oriented periodicals like *Collier's* and *The Saturday Evening Post* and in innumerable pulp adventure magazines before and between the World Wars frequently exploited slang as a stylistic resource, as did, even more pervasively, nationally syndicated comic strips, a phenomenon of American life dating only from the 1890s.

The twentieth-century revolution in communications dramatically abbreviated the time required for neologisms of all kinds, including slang, to gain national currency. During the few minutes of Commander Alan B. Shepard's suborbital flight on May 5, 1961, the astronauts' *A-OK* simultaneously entered millions of vocabularies, the direct result of live radio and television coverage; a generation later it retains a less conspicuous currency. The communications explosion has also indirectly stimulated the production and dispersal of slang.

In the first three or four decades of the century especially, nationally syndicated cartoonists like T. A. "TAD" Dorgan (1877–1929) and gossip columnists like Walter Winchell (1897–1972) popularized slang expressions that might otherwise have remained restricted to Broadway and sporting and gambling circles (Zwilling; Mencken 1936). Through magazine stories written mainly for *Collier's* from about 1929, Damon Runyon introduced underworld lingo to millions of readers and writers. Significantly, few of the self-conscious coinages of such popular writers ever achieved more than nonce status. Winchell's *Reno-vate* 'to travel to Reno, Nevada, for a quick divorce,' and *infanticipating* 'expecting a child' are occasionally cited as "American slang" but had no independent currency.

On the other hand, *making whoopee* 'having a good time, esp. making love,' coined by Winchell about 1929, has outlived its creator, largely because of its early adoption as the title of a popular song. Later items that gained general currency from their appearance in the media include *to be toast* 'to be doomed or done for,' introduced in the script of the film *Ghostbusters* (1984), and *babelicious* '(of a young woman) sexy,' created by comedian Mike Myers for NBC-TV's *Saturday Night Live* in the early 1990s.

Certain semantic domains have been especially productive of slang idioms. But without the enthusiasm, derision, or callous disregard that accompany those domains, the idioms would not be regarded as slang. By far the most productive of these domains are physical sexuality; intoxication by liquor or drugs; sudden, energetic, or violent action; death; deception; and weakness of mind or character. The slang-producing vitality of these domains seems to be nearly the same throughout the English-speaking world. Indeed, the continual creation of fresh slang synonyms within these domains implies that, for many speakers, no level of language adequately expresses the affective content of their ideas.

Furthermore, unconscious notions permeate certain slang metaphors. Flexner (in the preface to Wentworth and Flexner) has called attention to the way American slang often expresses a cultural-psychological association of sexual acts with victimization and contempt; the chief such idiom, *to fuck (somebody) out of (something)* 'to cheat (somebody) of (something),' is recorded as long ago as 1866 in the United States and, in the broader sense of 'to ruin or undo,' some decades earlier in the United Kingdom (Lighter 1: 834). A survey of Civil War court-martial records indicates, in the words of one historian, that "the swearing of [Union soldiers] did not differ greatly from that of [their] descendants in World Wars I and II. . . . [T]he age-old array of smutty, four-letter words, used singly and in combination, also had frequent usage" (Wiley 249, also 199, 201, 213, 248; Lighter; Lowry passim).

In a multiethnic society whose ethnic groups tend to preserve and even exalt their own distinctiveness while frequently viewing "outsiders" dubiously or with contempt, pejorative names for ethnic groups inevitably occur. In the United States these epithets multiplied in the wake of succeeding waves of immigrants, especially during the nineteenth and early twentieth centuries. Among the earliest, reflective of social and political circumstances in the late Colonial and early National periods, were *(John) Bull* 'Englishman,' *bog-trotter* or *Paddy* 'Irishman,' *Sawney* 'Scotsman,' *blackie* 'African,' *redskin* 'American Indian,' *frog-eater, frog,* or *(Johnny) Crapaud* 'Frenchman,' and, of course, *Yankee,* of obscure origin but first applied derisively to New Englanders.

As sociopolitical conditions have changed, many of these terms have either fallen from use or else lost their contemptuous force. Some have been replaced with more contemporary terms, and ethnic groups coming to prominence in the past century and a half, notably Hispanics, Germans, Jews, Italians, Slavs, and, most recently, Asians, have come in for their own share of verbal abuse, a linguistic upshot of the American tendency to xenophobia. Country people too have long been ridiculed with abusive epithets intended to reflect on their presumed gullibility and lack of cultivation: *hick* (from the seventeenth century), *hoosier* (now a neutral or affectionate nickname for an Indianan), *hayseed, rube, redneck, ridge-runner, hillbilly, shitkicker, plow jockey,* etc.

Popular interest in the exploits of outlaws has lasted since the Middle Ages. In the Prohibition era of the 1920s, modern lingo like *gat* and *rod* 'firearm,' *bigshot* 'ringleader, (hence) important or influential person,' and *flatfoot* 'police officer' became familiar to the general public through newspaper features, films, and pop fiction. The 1950s and especially the late 1960s similarly popularized the slang of narcotics addicts (*horse* 'heroin,' *reefer, pot,* and *grass* 'marijuana'). New illicit drugs get slang names almost immediately; *crack* 'free-base cocaine,' quickly moved via the news media from street slang to standard English during the mid 1980s.

American military slang (*boot, rookie* or *rook* 'recruit; trainee,' *topkick* 'first sergeant, senior sergeant,' *leatherneck* or *jarhead* 'marine,' *dogface* 'common soldier,' *swabby* or *squid* 'common sailor,' *brass* 'commissioned, esp. senior, officers,' *zoomie* 'member of the air force,' *grunt* 'enlisted combat soldier' and hence in civilian life 'low-level, hard-working employee') has proliferated since 1917 to match the tremendous growth in size and influence of the military itself. World War II undoubtedly created and broadcast more slang than any other short-term historical event. More than sixteen million Americans served under arms in World War II, over four times the population of the entire country in 1790, and probably ten or twelve times that of the limited "English-speaking world" (England) of 1066.

Coming into familiar civilian use during and after the war were such typically military expressions as *GI* 'an army enlisted man, (broadly) any serviceman,' *brass* '(in civilian use) police officials, top corporate executives,' *snafu* 'a bungled, badly confused situation,' to *hit the sack* 'to go to bed,' *grounded* '(of an airman or an aircraft) removed from flight status, (hence, of a teenager) denied the use of a car, punished by being forbidden to date,' *boondocks* 'wild, remote, or rural areas' (from Tagalog *bundok, bondok* 'mountain,' recorded in the Philippines as early as 1909 and eventually shortened to *boonies*), and the originally scatological *sad sack* 'an inept, unlucky, or unpromising person.' Unnoticed by prewar dictionaries, *sweat it out* 'to put up with anxiety, hardship or danger until it has passed' had been Midland slang for generations: "After this failure we were too closely watched to get any chance to escape, and so had to 'sweat it out' as long as the rebels could keep us in that jail" (Pike 368) and "All right, though; she'd like to see me in just such a fix – let her sweat it out!" (Twain 1876, 155).

World War II introduced this phrase to millions of Americans, often with a concretized direct object in the senses 'to endure grimly or anxiously, to worry about, to wait for anxiously or expectantly.' Kay Boyle describes the wives of servicemen in Colorado "talking G. I. talk as if they had learned it not this year, / Not here . . . 'Sweating out three weeks of maneuvers, or sweating the weekend pass, / Or sweating him out night after night,' they'll say" (6).

The contribution of sports, primarily baseball and prizefighting, to general American slang was not strongly felt until the first explosion of sports journalism before World War I (a second explosion, still in progress, began in the 1970s). Gambling, on the other hand, with cards, dice, bouncing balls, and fighting cocks has been a primarily masculine concern from the early days of settlement and has generated a good deal of slang, particularly since the mid nineteenth century when poker (formerly "brag"), euchre, and faro became the card games of choice, especially on the Western frontier. To American gambling we owe such terms as *pass the buck* 'to shift or abandon responsibility,' *buck the tiger* 'play at faro,' *snake eyes* 'a throw of two on the dice,' *boxcars* 'a throw of twelve,' the recent *crapshoot* 'a situation offering a highly uncertain outcome,' and many others.

The vaudeville stage exploited and popularized a certain amount of slang around the turn of the century. "Probably nine-tenths of this country's popular slang expressions . . . have come out of vaudeville," said the *New York Times* in 1917 ("Argot"), and the show business paper *Variety*, founded in 1905, eventually developed a characteristic style that was part slang and part wild idiosyncrasy (much of it associated at first with staffers Jack Conway and Jack Lait) that became internationally celebrated in the late 1920s. Two of *Variety*'s headlines have earned a permanent place in the history of American journalism as well as that of American English: "Wall St. Lays an Egg," announcing the stock market crash of 1929, and, later in the 1930s, the memorable "Stix Nix Hick Pix," that is, "Rural audiences reject films about country life" (Stoddart; Conway).

The slang of teenagers, high-school and college students, has exerted a special influence on national slang. The reason is simple: students are the slang-using group nearest the mainstream of American society and the largest in number. Indeed, once out of school, they themselves go to make up that mainstream. The slang of American college students received book-length treatment as early as 1851, when there were few colleges, in *A Collection of College Words and Customs*, by Benjamin H. Hall, a Harvard senior. Numerous local collections have appeared since then (for example, Babbitt 1900), particularly since the 1920s, and especially in the pages of *American Speech*. Connie Eble has published a number of interesting studies on the subject (1984, 1985, 1989, 1996), based on her research at the University of North Carolina at Chapel Hill, and Munro (1989) has compiled material from students at UCLA.

The influence of languages other than English on American slang has been relatively small. Spanish is often cited as the chief contributor to the new-word stock of American English, primarily through the nineteenth-century Southwest. Yet, other than some familiar exceptions like *calaboose, gringo, savvy, vamoose, buckaroo, hoosegow,* and *nada,* Spanish has given little to American slang, at least so far.

David Dalby has suggested that a number of slang terms connected with swing music, namely *hip, hipster, hipcat, dig,* and *jitterbug,* might have come from West African languages like Wolof and Mandingo, but the historical record makes such an origin most unlikely. The words appear far too late and, based as it is on superficial resemblances, their connection to West African cultures and vocabularies is too tenuous to be taken as any more than conjecture. American English itself is more likely to have given rise to these particular words. Nor is the word *jazz* especially likely to be of African origin: no convincing African etymon has yet been suggested, nor has the known history of the word in English been fully reviewed by proponents of an African origin (R. Gold; Tamony; Holbrook; Merriam and Garner; Lighter 1: xxxi, 2: 258–62). The *juke* of *juke joint* and *jukebox,* however, once a Gullah word of restricted currency, may well stem from West Africa.

The foreign language that has given most to American slang (and its limited contribution is about fifty words out of many thousands) is Yiddish. *Kibitzer*, which surfaced in the early 1920s, was one of the earliest, though German influence is possible here as well. Many others, *schlep*, *schlemiel*, and *megilla*, for example, were communicated directly to the upper middle class during the 1940s and 1950s by the humorist S. J. Perelman, whose writings for the *New Yorker* over four decades are a treasury of slang of all kinds.

6.6   The role of slang in American life

No brisk summary can do justice to the entire subject of American slang. But one additional question demands consideration here: why Americans should revel in this style of expression, even as many of them decry it as frivolous, offensive, or corrupting.

As is well known, American society in the past century or more has become increasingly urban, mobile, stratified, and industrialized; it has also become more competitive and impersonal. Sociologists have long held that the rapid pace of societal change, as well as the attendant weakening of confidence in other people and in the stability of one's own life, has led to increasing alienation among individuals within American society. For many decades the exigencies of a mass society have made Americans increasingly skeptical, not to say cynical, about the dependability of the social structures that are supposed to make life tolerable, not to mention the good faith and competence of the functionaries, from the President and Congress on down to the neighborhood banker and physician, on whom society depends for its stability. (Goldfarb in *The Cynical Society* discusses these phenomena in detail.)

The everyday penalties incurred by bad decisions, personal and impersonal, and by ordinary ill luck are often severe, even as the ubiquitous voice of advertising insists that all problems have quick and easy solutions and that conspicuous consumption will banish all woes. In such circumstances a markedly slangy style is a kind of whistling in the dark. It allows one to assert, with a display of self-assurance, a real or playful rejection (it is often hard to tell which) of such values as reason, tolerance, and restraint, which are essential to the maintenance of society but whose practice is less than fully evident in everyday life.

In the middle of the twentieth century, in his critical survey of American civilization, the social historian Max Lerner (626) offered the following germane and penetrating insight:

Americans can be as sentimental as any people in the world. Yet the pressures of the culture run the other way. A market economy means a market society, in which the great crime is to be taken in and the great virtue to be tough and illusionless. The nightmare of American life is to be left dependent and helpless – a greater nightmare than failing to help others when they need help. The result is the desensitized man whose language is the wisecrack and whose armor is cynicism.

In America it was the gadfly satirists Mark Twain, Finley Peter Dunne, George Ade, and Ring Lardner who, in the generation between 1884 and 1917, first exploited the potential of slang and nonstandard speech as an illuminator of character and a lance against pretense and illusion. It was Dunne's Chicago-Irish *barkeep* "Mr. Dooley" who predicted after the turn of the century, "Whin we Americans are through with th' English language, it will look as if it's been run over be a musical comedy" (quoted by E. Ellis 306). Literary maverick Jack London, writing in the first decade of this century about sailors, sourdoughs, and prizefighters, was the first bestselling American novelist to regularly present slangy characters as sympathetic protagonists. His works, published between 1898 and 1916, contain more than 600 slang expressions; his *Martin Eden* (1909) even features a coddled young woman who punctiliously corrects her working-class suitor's "slang" and cannot comprehend the word *booze*. "O. Henry" (the pen name of William Sydney Porter) gained a huge following in the same period with his slang-filled but reassuringly saccharine short stories, as did George Ade with his mordantly humorous slang fables.

Not till the 1920s, however, in the disillusioned aftermath of World War I, did very much slang appear in serious American fiction. And the fiction was *tough-guy* fiction, from Hemingway, Hammett, Farrell, and others. The war-weathered *vet*, the *wisecracking roughneck*, the *hardboiled dick*, the *cool customer* – the aggressive rather than the merely courageous and resourceful hero gradually claimed center stage as the beau ideal of American pop culture, ousting the more polite and cerebral heroes of prewar days. *Tough guy* alone was a common phrase by 1916: "I used to think everybody was a sissy who wasn't a tough guy. I was a tough guy all right, an' mighty proud of it" (Burroughs 38); *he-man* was earlier (1832, *OED*), but comparatively rare before the twentieth century.

American movies, blander than prose fiction, still paid homage to the warm heart beneath the hard-bitten exterior, but the tough style was established nonetheless. In the 1920s and 1930s, America's imagined heroes were increasingly loners, cool and cynical, who could survive no man's land and urban jungles alike, whereas the soft civilized chap could not; their character had been honed in the World War or in the badlands of Prohibition. Soon Virginia Woolf could write approvingly of Lardner's facility with America's "expressive ugly vigorous slang" (quoted by Douglas 356, with insightful comments on the role of slang passim). Louis MacNiece (102) recommended that "the American wisecrack" was "something with which the poet should stay in communion."

In 1939, innocent viewers of the film *Gone with the Wind* were shocked, then impressed, that romantic Rhett Butler really didn't "give a damn." Since the appearance of Mike Hammer in 1947 (Spillane), angrier and more brutal than any previous American popular icon, the tough-guy role model of pop culture has, if anything, become even harder, *cooler*, more alienated, more violent, and more ubiquitous (as some of the rap lyrics reprinted by Stanley 1993 show). We have a "bastard hero" to match and humiliate the "bitch heroine." (K. White 1993 provides a valuable complementary sociological perspective on some of these points.) Perhaps such fantasies (when they are fantasies) reassure writer and audience alike that, like A. E. Housman's Mithridates, they too can *take it* – and, like Edward G. Robinson in the 1931 film *Little Caesar*, presumably *dish it out* as well. (Wilkinson has examined "toughness" as an American popular ideal, though with limited reference to language.)

The conscious use of slang may mark for many speakers their wished-for, possibly media-inspired identity; it may be a rhetorical pose, an element in what Goffman calls their "presentation of self." It is no coincidence that the period beginning with Prohibition, which saw the ascendancy of the tough and illusionless fictional hero, also saw the emergence of slang as a characteristically American style of speech, recognized and often emulated around the world. The conscious use of slang may mark for many speakers their wished-for identity, may be a semantic pose, a key factor in how they present themselves to the world. For slang, owing to its associations of irreverence and cynicism, often communicates a shrewdness, real or feigned, a level of *savvy* that defends against being seen as a *wimp*, of being *ripped off*, of not being *hip* to what's really *going down*. "A *sucker* is born every minute" and "Never give a *sucker* an even break" are familiar modern adages; even more recent but just as proverbial are "Money talks, *bullshit* walks," "What have you done for me lately?" "That and a nickel [now more like $1.25] will get you a cup of coffee," and the mostly military "If you're looking for sympathy, try the dictionary between *shit* and *syphilis*."

In such proverbs, as in the use of slang, one senses exactly the kind of linguistic armor that Lerner discerned in the 1950s and earlier – the armor of the cynic, the *wiseguy*, the *cool cat*, the tough *broad*, the *bad dude*. Far more than from some mystical determination to "express group identity," the attraction of the slang style for many Americans springs from the stresses of life in a depersonalizing society, where there is plenty to be irreverent, cynical, and angry about. The startling associations of much slang warrant its value, for more than ever stridency, ridicule, and hyperbole appear to be the verbal strategies most likely to win popular attention or, indeed, to be taken seriously at all.

FURTHER READING

Partly because of the not very distinct nature of the subject, little that has been written about American slang offers significant analysis, cultural context, or theory; slang dictionaries, unless scrupulously edited, can be quite misleading as to the meaning and currency of many entries. Though now outdated, Mencken (1936, 535–89; 1948, 643–786) has long been a starting point for students. Flexner (Wentworth and Flexner 1960) provides an influential general discussion, whereas the Introduction to Lighter (1994) attempts to clarify the place of slang in American linguistic history. In the context of world English, R. Bailey (1996) treats many of the issues addressed in the present chapter. Illuminating book-length works from various perspectives include those by Dalzell (1996), Eble (1996), Folb (1980), and, for colloquial innovation in general, Sornig (1981).

7 DIALECTS

Lee Pederson

7.1   Introduction

American dialects record the contents of the English language as social facts realized in a geographic framework. As complete linguistic systems, all dialects report speech within the context of larger constructs – a language or a national variety of a language at a given point in the history of its development. American dialects transmit a national variety of Modern English in a distinctive pattern of pronunciation, grammar, and vocabulary.

The first speakers of American English received the language in a plastic state and shaped it according to their experience. Current regional and social dialects of American speech reflect the experiences of explorers and settlers on the Atlantic seaboard, of Western pioneers who followed them, and of later immigrants who energized the society as it moved across the continent. The dialects echo developments in the English language at critical historical junctures. They mirror cultural interaction – distinguishing Northern, Southern, Midland, and Western divisions of American geography, stratified according to the racial caste, sex, age, and education of American society. And they unite in the formation of American English, unmistakable to any speaker of the English language today.

The sounds, syntactic structures, and lexicon of American English unite in an integrated system. The phonology provides a system of contrastive sets (phonemes) that distinguish consonants, vowels, and units of intonation (stress, pitch, and juncture). The grammar outlines the arrangement, selection, and inflection of speech parts. And the vocabulary records a cultural index through distinctive words that identify the artifacts, ideas, and behavior of the American people. Each regional and social variety forms a contrastive set within the national pattern. Because word study lends itself most easily to written description, dialect study traditionally concentrates on vocabulary, rather than pronunciation or grammar, as

253

a matter of convenience. Dialect perception, however, invariably begins with the reception of the sounds of those words, the pronunciation of consonants and vowels realized in a distinctive intonational contour of stress, pitch, and juncture. And, as communication, dialect interpretation depends upon grammar for the organization and transmission of those words in syntactic structures. The union of these phonological, grammatical, and lexical systems forms the dialects that distinguish speakers as Northerners, as Southerners, or as members of one social group or another. And although this report concentrates on regional speech, the evidence implies social variation within every geographic construct of American English.

As integrated linguistic systems, these dialects share essential structural characteristics realized in all varieties of Modern English. This common core includes phonemes (contrastive phonological units), a basic grammar, and a general vocabulary that make communication possible among all English-speaking peoples. Their shared cultural experience has given rise to the language itself. Defined as sets of dialects within national varieties, a language reveals its organization and substance through the expression of its regional and social patterns. Within a large and complex language, such as English, national varieties form its primary divisions – specifically, British, Scottish, Irish, Canadian, Australian, and American. Within each of these political domains, dialects emerge, but all of these preserve the basic features that make them English.

As vernaculars, spoken varieties of American English, these dialects transmit social experience through patterns of pronunciation, grammar, and vocabulary. They record the cultural contributions of the earliest settlers and the migration routes established by those who followed them. They reflect old political and ecclesiastical boundaries, often coinciding with zones of physical geography and climate. And they outline cultural centers, illustrate social structure, and demonstrate the impact of later immigrants who helped reshape the English language in the New World.

7.2 History and geography

Atlantic and Gulf coastal communities form the primary settlement areas of American dialects, from Massachusetts Bay to New Orleans. Out of northeastern focal areas came pioneers who settled Upstate New York, western New England, and the Inland North westward, as well as the Shenandoah Valley through Virginia into North Carolina and east Tennessee. To the south, planters occupied the piedmont, the coastal plains, and ultimately the delta divisions of the Mississippi River. Routes south and west gained force from the religious and political influence of Puritans in New England, Quakers in Pennsylvania, and Mormons in the Middle West. Later, sectionalism divided the country, North and South, on the issue of slavery, but before that the geography of the eastern half of the continent channeled migration along practical routes.

Climate determined the northern limits of the Cotton Kingdom with the 180-day growing season. It also marked the western limits of conventional eastern agriculture with twenty-two inches of annual rainfall at the ninety-eighth meridian. Intensive settlement beyond that line, from the Red River in the Upper Midwest to the Pecos River in Texas, followed the conclusion of the Civil War, Indian removal, and specialized rural occupations unknown in the East, as, for example, large-scale cattle and sheep production, as well as "dry farming" to feed those animals.

These processes led to the development of great centers of American culture at Boston, New York City, Philadelphia, Charleston, New Orleans, Atlanta, Houston, Dallas, Phoenix, Cincinnati, St. Louis, Chicago, Minneapolis-St. Paul, Denver, Salt Lake City, Seattle, San Francisco, and Los Angeles. As focal areas, each of these controls a domain of urban influence, hosts a complex social structure, and attracts newcomers from virtually every country in the world. As a result, geographic dialects and their history record the divisions of a national language and demonstrate the impossibility of either a national standard of correctness or a descriptive simplex, sometimes posited as a fictional "General American" pattern.

Although much work remains to be done, especially in the Western states, American dialect research has outlined the principal characteristics of major regional dialects and their urban focal areas. Following the aforementioned facts of physical, social, and linguistic geography, current dialect study suggests four major speech areas in the United States: Northern, Southern, Midland, and Western.

Virtually every group of immigrants to the New World brought a substantial set of dialect features. The most complicated of these emerge from the English-speaking varieties of the British Isles – from England, Scotland, and Ireland. When these can be sorted out and identified with authority across the United States and Canada, such definition will surely clarify the geographic and social patterns of American English. Because all of these sources formed speech in the early focal areas in Massachusetts, Pennsylvania, Virginia, and the Carolinas, a convincing discrimination of British, Irish, and Scottish contributions would help outline the language that gave rise to modern dialects. For definitive identification, such description will require characterization of the rural and urban varieties of Elizabethan and Jacobean English in England and Scotland, as well as the development of English in Ireland in the seventeenth century from British and Scottish sources.

American dialects reflect the evolution of Modern English from the early seventeenth century to the present. They suggest the impact of social forces that directed several courses of development. And, most important, they illustrate the history and the contents of a major national variety of the most influential language in the world today. These dialects – regional and social lexical, grammatical, and phonological patterns – report the form and substance of American English and imply the social history from which they emerge.

American dialects originated in the seventeenth century during the most unsettled period in the history of the language. Early Modern English accepted more words into its lexicon and demonstrated more variety in its grammar and pronunciation than at any time before or since. These facts mirror a society under equally dramatic social change. Like the rest of Europe, England had undergone a cultural renaissance that brought with it a conviction that the speech of the people should be the official language of the land. England also shared the experience of its neighbors in educational, political, religious, and intellectual developments that reorganized its culture. Those social forces produced a civil war, a modification of the monarchy, large-scale immigration to the New World, and a remarkable era of experimentation with, and practical applications of, scientific theory.

Supported by the formation of modern mathematics, this era witnessed the greatest concentration of intellectual development in human history. This contribution proceeded from a belief, first, in a natural order underlying surface irregularity and confusion and, second, in the perfection of thought through rational habits of the mind. Neither assumption was new to Western thought, but, when harnessed with the idea of progress, they gave shape to a modern mindset. The emergence of New World settlements logically projected those beliefs, providing a rationale, as well as faith and courage to establish order in a wilderness through the application of reason, energy, and social reform. This legacy laid the foundations of American society.

That society and its experience gave rise to these distinctive dialects. As the realization of the English language in America, these varieties illustrate the same sensitivity to social forces found in all cultural institutions. As Frederick Jackson Turner (1894) explained:

Behind institutions, behind constitutional forms and modifications, lie the vital forces that call these organs into life and shape them to meet changing conditions. The peculiarity of American institutions is the fact that they have been compelled to adapt themselves to the changes of an expanding people, to the changes involved in crossing a continent, in winning a wilderness, and in developing at each area of this progress out of the primitive economic and political conditions of the frontier into the complexity of city life.

Those forces include reflexes not only of the Age of Reason coupled with the idea of Progress, but also of the Industrial Revolution, the theory of Manifest Destiny, and the discovery of electricity and its practical applications. All of these factors gave rise to an unprecedented development of a new society through the resources of modern transportation and mass communication.

7.3   American dialectology

Systematic American dialect research began with the formation of the American Dialect Society in 1889. Six volumes of *Dialect Notes* (1890–1939) record the contributions of its members. Later pioneering research continues to appear in the monograph series, Publication of the American Dialect Society, and the quarterly journal *American Speech*. Founded by Louise Pound and H. L. Mencken in 1925, *American Speech* remains the journal of record for American dialect studies, although the *Journal of English Linguistics* has more recently become an equally valuable resource. The early efforts of the American Dialect Society and the solid documentation of American dialect research in successive editions of H. L. Mencken's *American Language* laid the foundation for two great modern projects, the Linguistic Atlas of the United States and Canada (Kurath 1939–43; H. Allen 1973–6; Pederson 1986–92) and the *Dictionary of American Regional English* (Cassidy and Hall).

Two bibliographical essays (H. Allen 1977; Pederson 1977b) document research in American regional dialects and pronunciation since 1945. During those first two decades after World War II, research virtually completed a general regional survey of the Eastern, Northern, Upper Midwestern, and Southern United States through American linguistic atlas projects, while the *Dictionary of American Regional English* or *DARE* (Cassidy and Hall) project extended a lexical survey across the entire country. Taken together, those efforts outline a regional pattern of vocabulary, grammar, and pronunciation from the Atlantic States to the Mississippi Valley with a substantial lexical record for the Western states. In 1988, the Linguistic Atlas of the Western States (LAWS) project initiated a systematic survey of those regions beyond the Upper Midwest in the north and Gulf States in the south (Pederson 1996b). As the bibliographical essays indicate, valuable independent studies outlined much information about Western pronunciation and grammar, but the work offers no integrated record to match the authoritative information on the regional vocabulary found in the *DARE* survey. For that reason, the following summary of Western dialects is a preliminary overview.

This report summarizes available evidence that characterizes American dialects. These sources include findings of American atlas projects, collateral research, and independent sociolinguistic investigations. Specifically, these include the linguistic atlases, the *DARE* project, and the subregional surveys, all described by Harold Allen (1977). The dependence upon atlas evidence follows the fact that these efforts produce systematically contrastive data across large target areas and yield a unified data base, however limited in range and resources.

All of this research records the findings of deductive word study. Focused on the phonological word, investigations have outlined patterns of usage according to lexical, morphological, and phonological (phonemic and phonetic) distribution. The approach reflects the fact that no method has yet demonstrated either a procedure for the contrastive analysis of large linguistic units – as, for example, phrase structures or sentences – or the fact that dialect features can be usefully described at this level of inquiry. Although the immediate future of linguistic geography will probably depend upon an integrated word geography, the recorded evidence, so far, yields autonomous sets of lexical, morphological, and phonological units. As a result, the findings are suggestive at best, and a review of American dialects today can promise no more than an opaque pattern of probable distribution. Essays that promise more require close and skeptical reading.

The study of American social dialects is equally inconclusive, but its findings offer a systematic approach that promises useful results. Wolfram (1969) documents the aims, methods, and findings of research conducted from this perspective. Its most compelling arguments proceed from the study of small sets of features, but such discussions communicate little information immediately useful in the identification, analysis, and description of general regional or social patterns of American English. Such work, nevertheless, has become the central preoccupation of many dialectologists today. Their findings offer a sensitivity to sociolinguistic reality that cannot be matched in regional surveys aimed at global coverage (evenhanded representation of lexical, grammatical, and phonological features). Combined with atlas investigations, however, these narrow studies offer depth, delicacy, and internal coherence. And those resources provide an evaluation procedure that tests the adequacy of the broad-gauge regional surveys. In the present overview, sociolinguistic findings demonstrate the implications of those general surveys and contribute most in outlining the varieties of American English dialects.

7.4   Historical background

Like all varieties of Modern English, American speech has its source in the dialects of Middle English (1100–1500). And like vocabulary and grammar, pronunciation evolved from the dialects of fifteenth-century England into those of early Modern English (1500–1700). Principal developments during these two centuries include a reorganization of the vowel system and a modification of consonants to bring them virtually in line with their incidence today. Between 1400 and 1600, eighteen of the twenty stressed vowels underwent quantitative or qualitative change in the phonological process called the "Great Vowel Shift." During the same period, the resonant consonants, especially /l, r, w/, also developed sets of alternates that became crucial markers in the identification of American English dialects.

Seven of these form a basic index for American regional and social variation through early Modern English reflexes of Middle English pronunciations:

(1)   "long o" before /f, m, p, t/, realized as /u/ or /ʊ/, and least frequently /ʌ/, in *broom, cooper, hoof, hoop, roof, room, root*, and *soot* (*broom* words);

(2)   "short o" realized as /ɑ/ or /ɔ/ before stops in *hop, cob, cot, hod, rock*, and *hog* (forms with "short o" before /g/ and also some other consonants, as in *on, cloth*, and *closet*, are a special set of *hog* words);

(3)   /a/ before /r/, realized as /ɑ/ or /ɔ/, as in *barn, car*, and *park* (*barn* words), and after /w/, when before an alveolar obstruent, as in *wash, water*, and *watch* (*wash* words);

(4)   the diphthongs /ai/ and /au/, realized as [aɪ ~ aː ~ aə] and [aʊ ~ æʊ ~ æo ~ æə], especially before voiceless obstruents, as in *right* and *route;*

(5)   postvocalic /r/, realized tautosyllabically as [ə] or [ɚ], as in *beer, bear, burr*, and *boar;*

(6)   postvocalic /l/, realized tautosyllabically as [ə] or [ɯ] after back vowels, as in *pull* and *fall*, and heterosyllabically after front vowels as [ļ] or [1], as in *silly* and *belly;* and

(7)   initial /hw/, realized as /hw/ or /w/, as in *wheat, wheel*, and *white* (*wheat* words).

In addition to those sets of regionally contrastive features, several social markers distinguish American dialects, irrespective of their geographic provinces, including:

(1) alternation of tip-dental fricatives /θ/ and /ð/ as /t, f/ and /d, v/, respectively;

(2) modification of postvocalic consonant clusters /-sps, -sts, -sks/, as in *wasps*, *posts*, and *desks*, through simplification to become /wɑsp, post, dɛsk/, /wɑs, pos, dɛs/, or /wɑstɪz, postɪz, dɛstɪz/;

(3) the homophony of /ɪ/ and /ɛ/ before nasal consonants, as in *gym* and *gem* or *pin* and *pen;*

(4) the substitution of /ai/ for /oi/ in *oil, boil, hoist,* and similar words; and

(5) aberrant verb inflections, as, for example, preterits *blowed (blew), brang, brung (brought), catched (caught), clim (climbed), div (dived, dove), drownded (drowned), growed (grew), knowed (knew), riz (rose),* and *seen (saw)*; and past participles *broke, busted (broken), et (eaten), froze (frozen), gave (given), rode (ridden), stole, stoled (stolen), swam, swimmed (swum),* and *writ, wrote (written).*

The following regional summaries identify principal dialect features of American pronunciation. These include a phonemic system, most easily recognized through its relationships to British Received Pronunciation (RP), a dominant regional pattern of pronunciation, most conveniently identified with the Inland Northern dialect, and a number of recessive features, most clearly associated with social dialects, especially those of Afro-Americans and Latinos. Taken together, those consonants, vowels, and intonational contours form a distinctive national pattern.

American regional dialects share a common phonemic system, identical in most respects with that of standard British English. American English (AE) phonological segments are twenty-four consonants and fourteen vowels. Two subsets of consonants include (1) the obstruents: stops /p, b, t, d, k, g/ (as in *pill, bill, till, dill, kill,* and *gill*), fricatives /f, v, θ, ð, s, z, š, ž, h/ (as in *fill, view, ether, either, sill, zoo, shoe, pleasure,* and *hill*), and affricates /č, ǰ/ (as in *chill* and *pledger*) and (2) the resonants: nasals /m, n, ŋ/ (as in *mill, sin,* and *sing*), laterals /l, r/ (as in *lieu* and *rill*), and semivowels /w, y/ (as in *will* and *you*). Three subsets of vowels include (1) free vowels: front vowels /i, e/ (as in *peel* and *pail*), back vowels /u, o, ɔ/ (as in *pool, pole,* and *pall*), and diphthongs /ai, au, oi/ (as in *file, fowl,* and *foil*), (2) checked vowels /ɪ, ɛ, æ, u, ɑ, ʌ/ (as in *pit, pet, pat, put, pot,* and *putt*), and (3) two weakly stressed vowels /ɨ, ə/ (as in *Cody* and *coda*).

Striking differences between the two national patterns appear in the realization of postvocalic /r/ and low checked vowels, as well as in the distinctiveness of intonational contours. In tautosyllabic contexts, both RP and coastal varieties of AE, as well as some interior Southern varieties, vocalize postvocalic /r/ in both strongly and weakly stressed syllables, as, for example, *dear, dare, poor, pour, hurt,* and *water,* respectively. Both sets of dialects also have an unrounded low-back vowel before historical /r/ in *par* /ɑ/, with AE Southern dialects often including a nonphonemic centralizing glide [ə]. In RP and the American dialects of eastern New England, two phonemes, /ɒ/ and /ɔ/, occur respectively in *stop* and *straw.* In the British dialect, the rounded low-back vowel /ɒ/ occurs only before a consonant, as in *stop,* contrasting with /ɔ/ in *straw,* whereas the American dialects have /ɒ/ in both environments. Thus, in both dialects, *par* contrasts with *paw,* as /ɑ/ versus /ɒ/ or /ɔ/, on the basis of lip rounding.

Even more distinctive are the intonational features that distinguish RP and AE. These include stress (contrastive loudness of syllables) and pitch (tune or melody). The sequence of stressed syllables contrasts in many words, as, for example, the placement of primary stress in *inquiry, garage,* and *advertisement* and the presence or absence of secondary stress in *library, dictionary,* and *territory.* Daniel Jones (361–5) also identifies "three noteworthy points of difference" of pitch that distinguish American intonation in certain contours that involve flat, falling, and modulating tone in the articulation of utterances.

For the past century, Inland Northern pronunciation has provided a functional baseline for most discussions of American pronunciation. This proceeds from several historical facts. Kurath (1939, 124) took the "central values" of the Inland Northern vowel system as "a standard of reference" for the transcription of speech in New England. Subsequent American atlas projects followed Kurath's lead, as explicitly stated, for example, in the LAGS survey (Pederson 1977a, 33–4). The widely read pronouncing dictionary of Kenyon and Knott also transmitted Inland Northern features as its base form. For example, Chomsky and Halle (ix): "The dialect of English that we study is essentially that described by Kenyon and Knott... In fact their transcriptions are very close to our own speech, apart from certain dialectal idiosyncrasies of no general interest, which we omit." And earlier, three of the most influential American structural linguists, Leonard Bloomfield, Bernard Bloch, and Morris Swadesh, used their native Chicago pronunciation as the basis for their descriptions of American English.

But a descriptive convenience, a "standard of reference," should not be confused with a fictional standard American pronunciation. The inaccurate and misleading phrase "General American" is sometimes used for this regional form. Cultivated Inland Northern has no more authority as a national standard of correctness than have the parallel social dialects in

New York City, Philadelphia, Charleston, Miami, Atlanta, New Orleans, or St. Louis. All of these focal areas establish regional patterns, and, when needed, as, for example, by electronic broadcasters, cultivated speech in those cities remains the best baseline for the identification of standard, locally acceptable pronunciation. Indeed, Southerners, for example, may find Inland Northern pronunciation overly precise, self-conscious, and unnatural, whether articulated in Chicago or Nashville.

As surely as the speech habits of Germanic immigrants in the past century helped to shape the Inland Northern pattern, current ethnic dialects, especially Afro-American and Latino, complicate the structure of regional dialects across the country. On the one hand, Afro-American immigrants to Northern cities during the second half of the twentieth century brought with them Southern regional dialects that became social dialects in those urban settings. Northern isolation kept these habits in place through at least two generations. Latino immigrants modify Northern and Southern urban speech in another way. Anglo-Hispanic urban bilingualism seems to reflect current trends in pronunciation with little evidence of traditional standards of pronunciation. Current English pronunciation habits in South Florida and South Texas show the influence of the speech of younger Americans across the country, from the realization of postvocalic /r/ in virtually all situations to the emergent collapse of the low-back vowels /ɑ, ɔ/ as /ɑ/, as in *cot* and *caught*.

Regional and social dialects form the major varieties of American English today. These include four basic geographic patterns and three basic ethnic patterns. The regional dialect areas are Northern, Southern, Midland, and Western. The primary social divisions are Anglo (European extraction), Afro-American (African extraction), and Hispanic (Central American extraction). Within each of these regional and social sets, synchronic analysis can lead to consideration of every social factor at any historical juncture. A comparison of any two or more of these historical moments yields the evidence for diachronic analysis. Simply put, any summary of major varieties of American English can become quite complicated with little effort.

Dominated by the Anglo ethnic pattern, the Northern dialect area covers the Northeastern and Upper Midwestern states, extending as far south as the middle reaches of Ohio, Indiana, and Illinois and exhausting its certain domain at the Mississippi River. Another essentially Anglo domain, the Midland dialect area originates in Pennsylvania and forms a large transition area between the Northern and Southern divisions east of the Mississippi River. Although controlled by the Anglo pattern, as are all

American regions, the Southern dialect area extends below the Midland region to the Gulf of Mexico and across the Mississippi into Texas, Oklahoma, and Arkansas, combining influences of all three ethnic groups, and demonstrates the most powerful expression of Afro-American culture among rural dialects. Conversely, the Western dialect area covers the rest of the "lower Forty-Eight" states and includes a distinctive Latino force, from South Texas through southern California and through the Rocky Mountain states of Arizona, New Mexico, and Colorado. An absence of evidence makes it necessary to exclude Hawaii and Alaska from these divisions.

An analysis of these rural regional dialects depends on convention and convenience because much work remains to be done in the study of American English. Conventional divisions of Northern, Midland, and Southern dialect areas reflect contributions of American atlas projects (Kurath 1939–43; H. Allen 1973–6; Pederson 1986–92). Identification of a Western division involves four facts: (1) compared to the Eastern states, American speech north of Arkansas and west of the Dakotas has been relatively unstudied, (2) the territory is without a primary settlement area, (3) all preliminary research suggests a blend of regional dialects from the Eastern, Midwestern, and Southern United States, and (4) climate and physical geography provide a basis for the division of the American Midwest and West that reflects historical, social, and linguistic developments.

Including urban regional patterns, American social dialects require similar descriptive flexibility. Common sense recommends the possibility of as many social dialects as there are combinations of social factors within each rural regional and ethnic configuration. These include the absolute factors of ethnic identity, sex, and age, the relative factors of formal education and social class, and the secondary factors that comprise the parental and ancestral records of age, education, and social class. Each of these configurations can then be studied in regional (rural or urban) contexts to identify as many social dialects as description requires and patience allows. For those reasons, this summary concentrates first on the rural regional framework and then considers the implications of social features in major centers with attention to ethnic and other social factors.

This approach follows the fact that the base stratum of the national language is English and its culture is Anglo. Prior to World War II, the powerful influences of Afro-American and Latino forces went unappreciated because they were virtually ignored in systematic research of American English. Since then, largely through the efforts of sociolinguistic investigation, students have begun to appreciate the impact of non-Anglo ethnic groups upon American language and culture. At this time, however, the findings remain at best fragmentary and inconclusive. For those reasons, it is impossible today to provide an accurate history of American dialects, but current research also makes it impossible to ignore the implications of Afro-American and Latino-American contributions to the national language, especially in its urban centers.

7.5   Four major American dialects

The Northern and Southern dialects of American English emerged from primary settlements in the eastern United States, and the Midland and Western from secondary settlements to the south and west. The Northern dialects had their source in Massachusetts; the Southern dialects, in Virginia and the Carolinas. Originating in Pennsylvania, the Midland dialects are an extension from the Northern area. Today, these three are the strongest regional divisions in American speech, although now Midland seems everywhere to be a blend of Northern and Southern features, having lost most of its distinctiveness. In the same way, north and west of Texas, Oklahoma, and Arkansas, the Western dialect area combines features from the other three areas. The Northern and Southern dialects originated in the seventeenth century, with the Massachusetts, Carolina, and Virginia colonies reflecting the Puritan/Royalist division in England. The Midland dialect area grew with the development of the Old Frontier in the eighteenth century. The Western dialect area is a social product of the nineteenth century, following the Louisiana Purchase.

The first successful English communities in the New World, at Jamestown (1607) and Plymouth (1620), exemplify the cultural distinctiveness from which these contrasting groups came. The Virginia colonists steadily preserved Old World traditions with a dependence upon the cultural resources of the mother country. The Massachusetts colonists brought a revolutionary spirit and a determination to reform the source culture according to the beliefs that led them out of England. These social facts stand at the base of the primary regional division of American speech, Southern and Northern.

In the words of the Southern historians Simkins and Roland (13):

> The English colonists who established themselves in Virginia in 1607, in Maryland in 1634, in Albemarle [now North Carolina] region by 1653, in South Carolina in 1670, and in Georgia in 1733, possessed one common purpose. They wanted to live as Englishmen. In this ambition they succeeded in great measure. They established the Anglican church by law and at the same time tolerated other forms of Christianity

congenial to English customs. The Southern county and parish governments reproduced English concepts of local administration, and the Southern provincial governments of charter, governor, and representative assembly were reproductions on a smaller scale, of the English system. Education and architecture followed English patterns. English books were read, English clothes worn, English tools and furniture used, and English holidays celebrated. For generations correspondence was maintained with English relatives.

By contrast, the colonists in the North were determined to remain separate and free to go their own way. They established a cultural pattern that indeed came to be recognized as "The New England Way." As Boorstin (1958, 15–16) wrote of this distinctive Colonial experience:

> To the Puritans and to many who came here after them, the American destiny was inseparable from the mission of community-building. For hardly a moment in the history of this civilization would men turn from the perfection of their institutions to the improvement of their doctrine. Like many later generations of Americans, the Puritans were more interested in institutions that functioned than in generalities that glittered.
>
> The phrase "The New England Way" was an earlier version (not entirely different in spirit though vastly different in content) of the modern notion of an American Way of Life.

Consistent with those cultural facts, when American English today is discussed as a unified form, as "General American," for example, the designation identifies the Inland Northern dialect. And that is the reflex of a New England dialect. The speech reflects early westward migration, first out of Newtown (now Cambridge), Massachusetts, into Connecticut with Thomas Hooker's congregations, extending its pattern across the Upper Midwest from the Connecticut Valley and Upstate New York to Chicago and beyond.

The Midland dialect area outlines the domain of Pennsylvania influence upon the English language in the Northern and Southern states. It originated early in the eighteenth century and demonstrates the largest demographic movement in American history. During the fifty years (1725–75) preceding the Revolutionary War, that progression extended through the Shenandoah Valley to the south and the Ohio River Valley to the west. These German, Scottish, Irish, and Welsh settlers were experienced travelers, who outlined the territory of the Old West and established a large and diversified region. As illustrated by Pederson (1978, 304), the historical boundary of the Old West in 1800 corresponded perfectly with the western limits of the American dialects of the Eastern states, as described by

Kurath (1949). As the Northern area was distinguished by its predominantly English sources, the Midland area included large numbers of German settlers in its early development. It also revealed a comparatively stronger Scottish and Irish influence and a weaker English one than did the regions to the north and south.

Beyond the Mississippi River, the Western dialect area developed in the nineteenth century, with the territory delimited before the onset of the Civil War in 1861. Here, in two tiers of states in the eastern sector – Missouri, Iowa, and Minnesota, as well as the Dakotas, Nebraska, and Kansas – the immediate source of the Western area emerged. With the exception of Missouri, all American English in these states remained essentially mixtures of Northern and Midland speech throughout the era. Missouri combined Northern, Midland, and Southern features, thereby establishing a pattern that dominated American English through the Rocky Mountain states. In the rural dialects of the Pacific states, California, Oregon, and Washington, native speech preserves Northern and Midland features. In urban centers throughout the West, as well as in the Northern and Midland areas, Afro- and Latino-American ethnic dialects markedly alter regional patterns and distinguish the language of the cities. And with the great migrations of Southern poor whites and blacks into the urban centers during the present era, all Western cities, like those of the other three major regions, share substantial and pervasive elements of rural Southern dialect features.

7.6 Northern dialects

Among the oldest and most influential of American patterns, the Northern dialects extend from Maine to Northern Pennsylvania in the east and reach beyond the Mississippi across northern Iowa, Minnesota, and the Dakotas. These dialects have their primary source in New England. As Kurath (1939, 8) summarized:

> New England has two major dialect areas, an Eastern and a Western. The Eastern Area corresponds roughly to the section of New England occupied in gradual expansion from the Atlantic Seaboard; the Western, to the area settled from the Lower Connecticut Valley and from Long Island Sound west of the Connecticut River. The "seam" between these two settlement areas runs straight north from the mouth of the Connecticut River ... through both Massachusetts and Connecticut to the southern boundary of Franklin County ..., where it swerves west and follows the southern boundary of Franklin County to the

Berkshires. . . . Here it turns north again and runs along the crest of the Green Mountains to the northern boundary of Vermont.

Furthermore, as a dialect area of the northeastern United States, it must also include the broadly different and complex isolate of metropolitan New York City. Although originally most closely bound to Hudson Valley in New York State and its Dutch heritage, the metropolitan area might sensibly be regarded a major regional dialect area in itself, according to its social history of the past two centuries.

Today, this Northern area includes six principal subdivisions: in the east, (1) northeastern New England (Maine, New Hampshire, and eastern Vermont), (2) southeastern New England (the Boston focal area), and (3) metropolitan New York (the New York City focal area); and in the west, (4) southwestern New England (western Massachusetts, Connecticut, and north central Pennsylvania), (5) the Hudson Valley (south central New York and northeastern Pennsylvania), and (6) the Inland North (western Vermont, Upstate New York, and derivatives spread across the Midwest beneath the Great Lakes and beyond the Mississippi into Iowa, Minnesota, and the Dakotas).

The six subdivisions share a number of regional words. These include Northern lexical hallmarks: *angleworm* 'earthworm,' *boss, bossie,* or *co-boss* (a cow call), *brook* 'small stream,' *clapboards* 'finished siding,' *darning needle* 'dragonfly,' *eaves trough* 'gutter,' *fills* or *thills* 'buggy shafts,' *johnnycake* 'corn bread,' *pail* 'bucket,' *pit* 'cherrystone,' *stone wall* 'fence of rough stones without mortar,' *swill* 'table scraps for hogs,' *whiffletree* or *whippletree* 'singletree, wooden bar hooked to the traces of a harness.' Historically, however, many words now of general currency also originated in the northeastern quadrant of this territory, for example, *chipmunk, coal hod, firefly, gutter* 'eaves trough,' *kerosene, picket fence, salt pork, skunk, string beans, teeter(board* or *-totter), white bread.* Although no longer diagnostically useful in distinguishing regional speech, such words illustrate the influence of this geographic pattern on the national language.

Although the least productive set of discriminative features, Northern morphology also contributes to the dialect structure. Among verb forms, Atwood (40) identified these as "Chiefly Northern": *wun't* (for *wasn't*), *be* (for *am*), *hadn't ought* (for *shouldn't*), and the atypical past forms *see* (preterit), *dove,* and *et.* Like the Northern phrases — *all to once* 'all at once, suddenly' and *sick to the stomach* 'nauseated' — these forms have emerged from folk usage and diminished in currency through the passage of time and the spread of general education. Nevertheless, each helps to characterize the historical base of the regional pattern and to offer evidence for the establishment of Old World associations in the historical composition of Northern American English dialects.

Like all other major regional divisions of American English dialects, Northern speech includes few general phonological features that distinguish it from the other three patterns. Indeed, the major phonemic features of the area are common to all current dialects of the English language.

Moreover, like all other American dialects, the most striking regional features of Northern speech include the reflexes of historical /hw/, /hy/, postvocalic /r/, and the low vowels /æ, ɑ, ɔ/. Because all three of the consonant features particularize subregions of the area, none stands as a distinctive Northern marker.

General Northern features, therefore, appear in the pronunciation of a few consonants and vowels. The fricatives /s/ in *greasy* and /ð/ in *with* offer the surest old-fashioned and regionally distinctive pronunciations. Among the vowels, these features mark the region: the contrasts of /o/ and /ɔ/ in *mourning* and *morning, hoarse* and *horse, fourteen* and *forty*, and historically similar pairs; /ʊ/ instead of /u/ in *roots* (less frequently in *room* and *broom*), and /u/ for /ʌ/ in *gums*.

Coastal Northern (eastern New England and New York City) has a number of striking characteristics. From Maine to Rhode Island, words such as *apple dowdy* 'deep-dish pie,' *bonny clabber* or *clapper* 'curdled milk,' *buttonwood* 'plane tree, sycamore,' *comforter* 'quilt,' *fritters* 'fried cakes,' *hog's head cheese* 'headcheese,' *pigsty*, and *spindle* 'tassel' mark the rural vocabulary.

Virtually no subregionally distinctive morphological features recur across the territory in all varieties of coastal Northern speech. A few folk forms, however, help to reinforce the subregional pattern. These include the preterits *waked* 'woke,' *et* 'ate,' *riz* 'rose,' *div* 'dived, dove,' and *driv* 'drove,' as well as the preposition *against* or *agin* 'next to.' Although none of these has currency today, unless in the speech of the oldest and most isolated rural folk speakers, the forms identify sources of interior Northern speech, as well as the historical distribution of features generally associated with Southern or Western speech.

Coastal pronunciation provides the most distinctive forms of the subregion: a centering glide for tautosyllabic postvocalic /r/, as in *beard* [bɪəd], *bear* [bɛə], *bare* [bæə], *bird* [bɜːd], *boor* [bʊə], *boar* [boə], *barn* [bɑːn], a nonhistorical linking /r/ between vowels, as in *law[r] and order*, and the loss of the onset fricative /h/ in *wheat* words. Locally distinctive vowel pronunciations include: (1) a low-front vowel [a] before historical /r/ in *barn* words and less consistently before voiceless fricatives, as in *pasture, glass*, and *afternoon*; (2) a rounded low-back vowel [ɒ]) in *crop*, *on*, and other reflexes of the historical Middle English short *o*; (3) a shortened and centralized variant of /o/ called the "New England short o," as in *stone*, *boat*, and similar words; (4) a distinctive, noncentralized monophthong or diphthong in *Tuesday*, *new*, and *due*; (5) residual incidence of old diphthongs [ɐɪ] and [ɐʊ] especially before voiceless consonants, for example, in *bite* and *bout*, respectively; (6) a rounded low-back onset [ɒ] in pronunciations of the diphthong /oi/, as in *oyster* and *oil*, especially in eastern New England; (7) the same rounded low-back onset for the diphthong /aɪ/ in all contexts, especially in current New York City and New Jersey speech.

Inland Northern, extending from the lower Connecticut Valley, first into the New England frontier and then across the vast expanse of the Middle West, contrasts with all the aforementioned coastal forms. Whether as a result of isolation from British sources or the internal social chemistry of the frontier setting, this pattern is more typical of American usage than any other regional configuration. The typical pronunciations are most striking: (1) postvocalic /r/ is preserved in all contexts; (2) /ɑ/ is the expected vowel in *crop*, *on*, and almost all other members of this historical set, with the exception of *dog* and with divided usage in *hog* and *log*; (3) the "New England short o" steadily diminishes in incidence westward with scattered occurrences in northeast Pennsylvania; (4) the diphthongs of *Tuesday*, *new*, and *due* are ingliding in the speech of descendants of immigrants from the British Isles; among Germanic immigrants, however, the coastal relic /u/ gains reinforcement, especially in the urban centers of Chicago, Milwaukee, and Minneapolis.

Northern lexical and morphological forms are extended over the entire territory. Words such as *burlap bag*, *chipmunk*, *clapboards*, *faucet*, *fried cake* 'doughnut,' *hay cock*, *lobbered milk* 'clabbered milk,' *spider* 'frying pan' (originally with three legs), *stoneboat*, and *teeter-totter* mark the regional vocabulary. In addition to the preposition *to* in *sick to the stomach* (which is general use in Northern), the folk verb forms *clim*, *scairt*, and *boughten* outline the southern limit of the Northern territory across the Middle West.

Historically, the dialects of New York State include three principal divisions: Upstate, Hudson Valley, and metropolitan New York City speech. Although an Inland Northern subdivision (with the Connecticut River Valley and western Massachusetts, comprising eastern Inland Northern), the Upstate area shares Hudson Valley, predominantly Dutch, relics and reflects the powerful influence of New York City. From the Hudson Valley come *pot cheese* 'cottage cheese,' *olicook* 'doughnut,' *barracks* 'haystack,' *suppawn* 'mush,' and *skimmerton* 'shivaree.' Regionally distinctive morphology includes the familiar Eastern usage (wait or stand) *on line* 'in line' and (live) *in a street* 'on a street.' The Hudson Valley and New York City areas share coastal Northern pronunciations of postvocalic /r/, whereas the Upstate pattern conforms with interior Northern usage. The three agree in the homophony of stressed vowels in *mourning/ morning* and *hoarse/horse*, the loss of /h/ before /w/ in *whale, whip,* and similar words, the glottalized allophone of /t/ in *mountain* (less frequently in *bottle*). The Hudson Valley and New York City have /e/ in *Mary.*

7.7 Midland dialects

The most controversial of regional patterns, the Midland dialect area reflects the formation and influence of Pennsylvania speech. As McMillan (122) illustrates, the controversy proceeds from two definitions. The first had currency before American atlas projects were underway – "the dialects of the Middle Atlantic states." The second reported atlas findings – "the dialect lying between the Northern and Southern dialects." Eastern Pennsylvania (Philadelphia) and Western Pennsylvania (Pittsburgh) divisions of the Midland dialect extend their influence into the South respectively through the Shenandoah Valley and across the Midwest through the Ohio Valley. The historical reflex of these developments yields two primary constructs (east/west) and two secondary constructs (north/south). Some students reject these divisions on the basis of strictly synchronic evidence because they begin as transition areas between the North and South in the East and reform as part of a general geographic pattern with features of the North and South beyond the Mississippi River. But Kurath (1949, 2–3) explains the historical Philadelphia base in the east/south axis this way:

> During the last decades before the Revolution large numbers of Pennsylvanians and many immigrants from abroad who landed on Delaware Bay had occupied the fertile farm lands along the Shenandoah and pushed their way across the Blue Ridge into the piedmont of the Carolinas before coastal settlements of Virginia and the Carolinas had expanded into these areas. The Scotch-Irish and the Palatine Germans from Pennsylvania and from overseas constituted the major elements in the population of these southern uplands, but Virginians, Carolinians, and Englishmen mingled with them.
>
> The southwestward thrust from Pennsylvania through western Maryland into the Valley of Virginia and the Carolina piedmont (1725–1775) was met by a series of thrusts up the rivers from the coastal settlements of the South. Southern settlers mixed with the

Pennsylvanians along the periphery of the Southern settlement area, especially south of the James River, but the seam of these two major settlement areas is clearly reflected in a well-defined speech boundary which runs along the Blue Ridge in Virginia and then swerves out into the piedmont at Lynchburg.

After the Revolution the descendants of these southern uplanders crossed the Appalachians in large numbers by way of the Holston River and the Cumberland Gap. They occupied fertile lands of central Kentucky and Tennessee, and established themselves in southern Ohio, Indiana, and Illinois during the first decades of the nineteenth century. They also infiltrated into the narrow valleys of the Kanawha and its tributaries in West Virginia.

Kurath (1949, 3) outlines the historical Pittsburgh north/west base this way:

> Farther north the settlements in the Pittsburgh Wheeling area of the upper Ohio expanded rapidly up the Monongahela into West Virginia, up the Allegheny to Lake Erie, and down the Ohio Valley. The settlers came from Pennsylvania east of the Alleghenies, from West Jersey, and from abroad, but there were also New Englanders among them. By 1810 the downward thrust from the upper Ohio had met the northward thrust from Kentucky in the region of Cincinnati and Louisville.

Taken together, such demographic facts explain the historical region:

> This far-flung Midland area, settled largely by Pennsylvanians and by the descendants in the south uplands, constitutes a separate speech area which is distinct from the Northern area – the New England settlement area – and from the Southern area. Its northern boundary runs in a southwesterly direction along the Blue Ridge and through the Carolina piedmont. The South Midland, to be sure, exhibits a considerable infusion of Southern vocabulary and pronunciation.

Only a few general Midland lexical forms extend across the territory from Pennsylvania into the Upper Midwest. They include *blinds* 'roller shades,' *coal oil* 'kerosene,' *dip* 'sweet sauce for pudding,' *fish(ing) worm, green beans* 'string beans,' *hull* 'to shell (beans or peas),' *little piece* 'short distance,' *(paper) poke* '(paper) sack,' *side pork* or *side meat* 'salt pork,' *skillet* 'frying pan,' *snake feeder* 'dragonfly,' *sook* (a cow call), and *spouts* or *spouting* 'drainpipes (from a roof).'

More narrowly defined, the historical Midland vocabulary emerges in another set of words that are essentially confined to the state of Pennsylvania: *cruddled* (milk) 'curdled,' *fire bug* 'firefly,' *hand stack* 'hay shock,' *overden* 'barn loft,' *overhead* 'loft,' and *piece* 'to snack.'

Besides the German loan translations that dominate these lists, such as *fire bug, green beans*, and *snake feeder*, other words also occur in communities with substantial German subcultures, from Milwaukee in the north to East Texas in the south: *fat cakes, rain worm, sawbuck* or *woodbuck, smearcase* 'cottage cheese,' and *thick milk*. Other Germanisms, such as *clook* 'hen,' *paper toot* 'paper sack,' *ponhaws* 'Philadelphia scrapple,' *snits* 'dried fruit,' and *vootsie* (a cow call) are largely confined to Pennsylvania and its immediate neighbors. Conversely, the old Pennsylvania German loans *sauerkraut* and *spook* 'ghost' have gained general currency in virtually all dialects of American English.

Perhaps the most familiar feature in Midland morphology may be the preposition *till*, in the phrase "quarter till the hour." Other regional phrases include *all the further* 'as far as,' *got awake* 'woke up,' and *want off* 'want to get off.' Although now widespread in American folk speech, the following verb forms are also best associated with the Midland dialect area: *boilt* 'boiled,' *clum* 'climbed,' *dogbit* 'bitten by a dog' (originating in the Wheeling, WV, area before spreading south and west), and *seen* 'saw.' Within the primary source area, the most distinctive morphological and grammatical features originate in the Pennsylvania Dutch dialect with constructions that occur, like the vocabulary, in the German-American subcultural enclaves across the country: (the oranges are) *all* 'all gone,' *make out* (the lights) 'put out,' and (school) *leaves out* 'lets out.'

Midland speech demonstrates its clearest regional distinctiveness in the pronunciation of certain consonants and vowels. Most pervasive is the realization of a fully retroflex postvocalic /r/, setting the area apart from coastal speech to the east and interior (historical plantation) speech to the south. The Northern-Midland boundary, from Pennsylvania to North Dakota, however, emerges most convincingly in the regional reflexes of Middle English /wɑ-/ in *wash* and *wasp* and "short o" in the *hog* words. The old-fashioned eastern contrast of front vowels in *Mary* /e/, *marry* /æ/, *merry* /ɛ/ becomes a binary division of /æ/ in *marry* and /ɛ/ in *Mary* and *merry* in the Midland territory, often collapsed to general homophony with /ɛ/, especially in the speech of younger natives. Perhaps the most distinctive marker of Midland pronunciation is the widespread occurrence of intrusive /r/ in *wash* and *Washington*, most common in folk speech. Other systematic features include /ə/ in *haunted* and *careless*, /ɪ/ in *stomach*, and /θ/ in *with*.

The North Midland division extends the pattern south out of Philadelphia and west out of Pittsburgh. Marked at the south by the occurrence of /s/ instead of /z/ in *greasy*, as well as other features that divide

Northern and Southern speech, the boundary between North Midland and Northern extends the southern influence of Philadelphia speech into the great valley of Virginia in the east and follows the course of Ohio River settlements from Pittsburgh to St. Louis in the west. Here also, pronunciation offers the most reliable basis of regional distinctiveness, especially the pronunciation of low-back vowels before /r/: /ɑ/ to the north and /ɒ/ to the south in *barn* words. A western reflex of the Pittsburgh pattern, this feature extends to the south and west where it merges and helps define the South Midland pattern of Southern Missouri, Arkansas, and Texas. Those areas include the homophony of *hoarse/horse* and *morning/mourning*, the occurrence of /ɪ/ for /i/ in *creek*, and the monophthongal and diphthongal allophones of /u/ ([ʉ] or [ʊʉ]) in *due, new, Tuesday*, and similar words, instead of the centralized glides [ɪu] and [ɨʉ], which prevail to the east and south.

In addition to the German features of eastern Pennsylvania, the distinctive *baby coach* 'baby carriage' endures only in the Philadelphia area, whereas *pavement* 'sidewalk' spreads south to Baltimore and beyond. Spreading southward out of Chesapeake Bay, *snake doctor* 'dragonfly' holds an easterly course in the north, but in the south it becomes a powerful up-country Southern marker as a dominant form in the Georgia piedmont and the Cumberland Basin of middle Tennessee. From there the form extends as far south and west as interior Texas. Out of Western Pennsylvania come *baby buggy*, which replaces Pittsburgh's *baby coach* in the southwesterly realization of the form, and *gunnysack* 'burlap sack.'

The South Midland subregion extends the northeastern Philadelphia pattern deep into the southern United States, where it merges with up-country dialects in the east and delta speech to the west. Among the most powerful South Midland lexical markers are these: *dog irons* 'andirons,' *fireboard* 'mantel,' *French harp* 'harmonica,' *red worm* 'earthworm,' and *tow sack* 'burlap sack.' Especially in east Tennessee, the area preserves many general Midland lexical forms, such as *fish(ing) worm, (paper) poke*, and *snake feeder*, none of which has much currency beyond the southern boundary of the state. Morphological features include preterit and past participial *drinkt* and *shrinkt*, archaic *sot* for *sat* (preterit), and unmarked *swim* (preterit).

The most striking phonological feature is the [a] or [aᵉ] allophones of /ai/ before voiceless obstruents, as in *like, nice*, and *white*. The fully retroflex postvocalic /r/ distinguishes the South Midland region from the South more dramatically than any other features of American English. Much, if not all, of this territory otherwise might be most effectively identified as the northern and western extensions of the interior South.

7.8   Southern dialects

Historically, Southern dialects of American English begin south of the Potomac River in the east and extend across the domain of the old Confederacy, including Texas as well as the more recently settled Indian Territory (Oklahoma) and the border states of Kentucky, Arkansas, and Missouri, especially south of St. Louis. This region includes three primary speech patterns, coastal, interior, and delta. The coastal pattern extends from Richmond, Virginia, to Brownsville, Texas, including the seaboard of the South Atlantic and Gulf states. Behind this region, the interior division includes two major South Midland divisions: the full domain of the highlands and piney woods and southern plains, where the African slavery of the plantation society gave the region its most distinctive cultural forms. The delta landforms divide the area from south to north, with the lower Mississippi and Atchafalaya basins uniting in the coastal pattern and the Yazoo, Red, and St. Francis basins joining the interior.

These dialects reflect the demographic history of the region. Two of the greatest population movements in American history shaped the cultural composition of the South. First, the migration out of Pennsylvania settled the Carolina piedmont and then the upper and lower reaches of the interior and extended historical Midland forms across the territory. Second, the mass transportation of blacks from their birthplaces in Virginia and South Carolina into the New Orleans slave markets reorganized the speech patterns of the central South.

As these processes continued, the plantation systems moved steadily southward and westward, first with tobacco planters in Virginia, then with indigo developers in South Carolina, and finally with developers of cotton, rice, and cane across the plains and up the five river basins of the Mississippi delta. (As used here, the term "Mississippi delta" includes the area from Memphis to the Gulf of Mexico. It is divided into an upper delta, which includes the basins of the Arkansas, Tensas, and Yazoo rivers, and a lower delta, dominated by New Orleans, but also influenced by Baton Rouge and Natchez.)

The history and distribution of dialect features (Pederson 1996a, 13–23) recommend a tripartite division of Southern and South Midland dialects into coastal, interior, and delta regions. The coastal dialects cover the full extent of the shoreline and the piney woods subdivisions behind it. The interior dialects cover (1) the piedmont from Virginia to Alabama, (2) the eastern, central, and western plains that verge on the woods to the south, and (3) the highlands that extend from the Blue Ridge of east Tennessee to the Ozarks of lower Missouri and Arkansas, interrupted by the Mississippi Valley and the delta system. The delta dialects spread northward from New Orleans, the most powerful cultural center in the South, beginning as an essentially coastal pattern and concluding in upper Arkansas much more closely identified with interior dialects.

A number of lexical features mark the area, from the coast northward and across the entire South Midland territory. These include *baby carriage*, *bucket* 'pail,' *butter beans* 'lima beans,' *chifforobe* 'wardrobe,' *chitlins* 'hog intestines as cooked food,' *chop* (cotton) 'hoe,' *clabber* 'curdled milk,' *common* (a pejorative), *corn dodgers* 'corn bread preparation,' *(corn) shucks*, *dirt dauber* 'mud wasp,' *feist* 'small, noisy dog,' *goobers* 'peanuts,' *greens* 'boiled leaf vegetables, especially collards,' *grits* 'ground hominy,' *hoot owl*, *Irish potatoes*, *jackleg* 'an inexperienced or fraudulent tradesman or professional,' *light bread* 'white bread,' *lightwood* 'pine kindling,' *pallet* 'bed on the floor,' *peckerwood* 'woodpecker,' *polecat* 'skunk,' *roasting ears* 'corn on the cob,' *screech owl*, *seed* 'cherrystone,' *seesaw*, *singletree* 'wagon evener,' *skillet*, *skin* 'bacon rind,' *slop bucket*, *tote* 'carry,' *varmint* 'small predator,' *whetrock* 'sharpening stone,' *white lightning* 'unlicensed whiskey, moonshine,' and *yams* 'sweet potatoes.'

Morphological and grammatical features found across the entire area include verb forms, function words, and distinctive pronominal usage. Although rarest in cultivated speech, the deleted copula and auxiliary verb occur all over the South, as in *he big* and *he done it*, respectively. The negative construction *ain't* also seems indigenous to the entire area, although the fierce prejudice against this form seems at last to be taking hold even here. Other grammatical features are the preposition *at* in the phrase "sick at the stomach," the directive *yonder* 'there' as in "over yonder" or "yonder comes Nora," double modal auxiliaries *might can* or *might could* as in "I might could do it," the intensifier *right* as in "right nice," and the perfective *done* as in "I done told you that already."

Among the most familiar and widespread characteristics, the preterit and past participial form *drug* 'dragged' also spreads across the entire territory with few constraints of social distribution. Indeed, the form has a remarkably high incidence among the youngest native generation of the region. The most familiar elements of Southern word formation may, however, be the distinctive second person plural forms, *you all* or *y'all* and the less frequent possessive *y'all's*.

The general regional pattern includes several pronunciations of consonants and vowels, as well as prosodic features, that set Southern speech apart from the rest of the country. Besides extending /z/ in *greasy* across the entire geography of the South, consonant pronunciations include a "clear l" between front vowels, as in *Billy*, *Nelly*, and *silly*. In regional folk speech, an /l/ replaces /n/ in *chimney*, / ǰ/ replaces /ž/ in *rouge* and more widely in *Baton Rouge*, /t/ is pronounced in *often*, and /l/ is vocalized after a back vowel and before a consonant as in *bulb*, *cold*, *colt*, and *pulp*. Vowel features include the contrast of /o/ and /ɔ/ in *hoarse/horse* and *mourning/morning*, /ɔ/ in *wash*, the frequent alternation – especially among younger speakers – of /ɪ/ for /ɛ/ before /n/, creating such homophonous pairs as *den/din*, *meant/mint*, *pen/pin*, and *ten/tin*. Before voiced consonants, /ai/ and /oi/ are pronounced [a: ~ aᵉ] as in *ride* and [ɔᵊ] as in *oil*. Checked vowels /ɪ, ɛ, æ, ʊ, ɑ, ʌ/ tend to be raised and retracted, often with weakly realized offglides, as in *pit, pet, pat, put, pot*, and *putt*. Before a voiced velar /g/, the low-back vowel of *hog* words is often realized as an upgliding diphthong [ɔˇɔˆ]. Other distinctive phonemic features are /ʊ/ in *coop*, /ɪ/ in *Negro*, /ɑ/ in *stamp (stomp)*, and the loss of the second syllable in *Louisiana* (/ˈluzɪˌænə/), less frequently in *Mississippi* (/ˈmɪzˌsɪpɪ/). General Southern intonation includes primary stress on the first syllable of *July*, *September*, *October*, *November*, and *December* and weak stress on the final syllable of all seven days of the week, where the vowel is realized as /ɨ/ [i], rather than /e/, as in most varieties of American English.

From tidewater Virginia to the southernmost Texas coast and across the piney woods beyond that coastal strip, certain generalized features further characterize Southern speech, including lexical, grammatical, and phonological features. The general coastal lexicon includes *blood pudding*, *cat squirrel*, *gopher* 'land-burrowing tortoise,' *hog(s)head cheese*, *hoppergrass* 'grasshopper,' *live oak*, *mosquito hawk* 'dragonfly,' and *mouth harp* 'harmonica.' Words peculiar to the coastal strip include *collard greens*, *rain frog*, and *shell road*. In the piney woods, the subregional vocabulary includes *croker sack* 'burlap sack,' *mantel board*, *pinders* 'peanuts,' *piney-woods rooter* 'range hog,' *press peach* 'cling peach,' *shiner* 'minnow,' *skeeter hawk* (alongside *mosquito hawk*), *smut* 'soot,' and *splinters* 'resinous kindling.'

General coastal pronunciation includes /ɛ/ for /ɪ/ in *since*, /ɪ/ in the second syllable of *January*, loss of medial /t/ in *twenty* and of /r/ in *forward*, the alternation of /n/ for /ŋ/ in *Washington*, and weakly retroflex /r/ in unstressed syllables, as in *November*. Along the coast, pronunciation includes the loss of /h/ before /w/ in *wheel* words and the vocalization of postvocalic /r/ in all tautosyllabic environments. The old-fashioned pronunciations of /ai/ and /au/ with centralized onsets endure in old-fashioned Tidewater and extend along the Carolina coast with very little occurrence in Georgia low country today. All of these features contrast with piney woods usage, where the realization of /hw/ conforms with that in the rest of the interior South and the realization of a fully retroflex post-vocalic /r/ conforms with South Midland usage, as do the allophones of /ai/ and /au/ before voiceless obstruents.

General coastal word formations include past participial *drove* and *drank*, as well as the preposition *on* in the phrase "sick on the stomach." Elsewhere, the dominant forms of American English grammar mark the speech of the coastal strip, now dominated by urban patterns. Conversely, as a predominantly rural relic area, the piney woods preserves many old-fashioned folk forms now lost in the rest of the Lower South. Some of these are preterits *come* and *busted*, as well as past participial *blowed*, *swimmed*, and *took*.

As outlined by Pederson (1996a), the most interesting historical concordances in this division, however, unite the highlands and the piney woods as South Midland derivatives. Shared forms include *boogerman* 'devil,' *dairy* 'storage cellar,' *flitters* 'pancakes,' *granny (woman)* 'midwife,' *hoosier* 'rustic,' *liver and lights, middling(s)* 'bacon sides,' *mushmelon, ridy-horse* 'seesaw,' *rock fence, serenade* 'shivaree,' *somerset, swingletree* 'whiffle tree,' and *widow woman*. Common word formations include the preterits *drawed, drownded*, and *riz*, past participial *rode*, and the preposition *till* in phrases like "quarter till the hour." Besides realizations of historical /r/ and the /hw/ sequence, folk speech of the highlands and piney woods share these pronunciations: /o/ for /u/ in *ewe*, /č/ for /s/ in *rinse*, /š/ for /sk/ in *tusk*, /e/ for /æ/ in *chance*, excrescent final /r/ in *bellow, yellow*, and similar words, /y/ for /hy/ in *humor*, raised onsets of /au/ [æo] as in *cow* and *plow*, as well as the monophthongs and short glides of /ai/ before voiceless obstruents, as in *ripe, might, like, knife*, and *rice*. All of these correspondences suggest that piney woods was historically a South Midland dialect. It probably originated above the South Carolina piedmont in the vicinity of the old Waxhaw settlement, birthplace of Andrew Jackson. Through the powerful influences of the plains to the north and the coastal strip to the south, however, it deserves classification today as Southern dialect.

The speech of the New Orleans focal area forms one of the most influential zones in the geographic structure of American English. As a primary settlement area and perhaps the most powerful focal area of American English – extending its influence as far north as Nashville, via the Ohio and Cumberland, and across the Gulf coast from Houston, Texas, to Pensacola, Florida – it unites the coastal and interior subdivisions. As a historic cultural center, New Orleans extended influence to Mobile Bay in the east and to the South Texas coast in the west. In the interior, its domain extends up the Lower Mississippi, Atchafalaya, and Yazoo basins as far north as the Louisiana-Arkansas border. General delta features include *bayou* (for both 'backwaters' and 'creek'), *buckshot (land), buffalo fish, Catahoula cur* 'a breed of intrepid stock dog,' *coal oil* 'kerosene,' *coco grass* 'field weed,' *cush* 'mush,' *frogstool, gallery* 'porch,' *grass sack* 'burlap sack,' *gumbo (land), middlebuster* 'lister plow,' and *salt meat* 'fat bacon.' Local word forms include preterit *fitted*, past participial *did* 'done' and *hung* 'hanged, executed,' and the preposition *in* for the phrase "sick in the stomach."

Pronunciation extends the coastal treatment of postvocalic /r/ as [ɜ] as in *bird, heard*, and similar words, and the /hw/ sequence far north into the Red River and St. Francis basins. Other distinctive phonological features are /ɑ/ in *stabbed* (for /æ/) and in *sausage* (for /ɔ/) and a low-back rounded vowel [ɒ] in *garden*.

Dominated by the powerful New Orleans focal area, speech of the lower delta combines features current in the basins of both the Mississippi and Atchafalaya basins. The subregional vocabulary includes *banquette* 'sidewalk,' *beignet* 'fried cake,' *boudin* 'sausage' (particularized as *red boudin* 'blood sausage' and *white boudin* 'pork sausage'), *cush-cush* 'mush,' *gar(fish), (gasper)goo(fish), guts* 'chitlins,' *jump the broomstick* 'marry,' *lagniappe* 'something extra,' *orphan child, pave road, picket(s)* 'picket fence,' *scrape cotton* 'chop or hoe cotton,' and *shallots*.

Although only preterit *swole* (of *swell*) occurs as a distinctive grammatical feature, a substantial number of pronunciations mark the territory: /e/ in *again*, /ɛ/ in *chair* (the general vowel for this word in American English, but not general in the South), /ɔ/ in *mourning*, /ai/ in *hoist*, postvocalic /r/ usually vocalized tautosyllabically, as in *chair, church, cork, garden*, and *queer*, sometimes lost in *careless* or often weakly retroflex, for example, in *thirteen*. Most characteristic pronunciations include the loss of /h/ in *wheat* words, the vocalized upglide [ɜɨ] in *church, girl*, and *third*, and the familiar disyllabic pronunciation of *New Orleans* as /'nyɔln̩z/.

From metropolitan New Orleans, north to Natchez, Mississippi, and west to the boundary of the Atchafalaya delta, a smaller set of features marks the core of the region. These include *Cajun* 'rustic,' *irons* 'andirons,' *kyoodle* 'dog of mixed breed,' *locker* 'clothes closet,' *lord god* 'logcock (a woodpecker of striking appearance),' *(potato) pump* 'cellar' (predominantly in the rural perimeter), and *sheepshead*. In addition to past participial *ate*, the area is marked by /t/ for /θ/ as in *three*, vocalized /l/ in *wool*, /šw/ and /sw/ in *shrimp* (exclusively in folk speech), rounded low-back vowels [ɒ^ or ɒ] in the stressed syllables of *Charleston* and *Chicago* (which correspond closely to the native pronunciations of those two distant places), but the unrounded, retracted low-central [ɑ⁾] or an unrounded low-back vowel in *tassel* and *cough*.

The Atchafalaya delta centered at Lafayette, Louisiana, the heart of the Louisiana Cajun French territory, covers the domain of the Atchafalaya River. The vocabulary includes *blackjack (land)* 'poor land,' *champignon* 'mushroom,' *charivari* (French pronunciation in four syllables with uvular *r*), *choupique* (a local type of fish), *coonass* 'rustic,' *coulee* 'creek bed,' *croquignole* 'doughnut,' *flood rain* 'heavy rain,' and *sacalait* (a local type of fish). Also distinctive are the animal calls *pee* or *kee* (in various sequences to chickens) and *cho* or *choo* (in various sequences to hogs). In addition to preterit *et* 'ate,' this southwesternmost basin in the Mississippi Valley also includes /ʊ/ in the second syllable of *mushroom*, /ɛ/ in the first syllable of *syrup*, /ɑ/ in *coffee*, flapped /r/ in *thrashed*, devoiced /g/ in *eggs*, and final consonant loss (of /t/ and /d/ respectively) in *chest* and *wound*.

Beyond the Atchafalaya delta, other lower delta features extend across the Sabine River into Texas in the south and into the plains and basins of the Red and Ouachita rivers to the north and west. Here, the easternmost set of Western features emerges. They include *bellow* 'cry of a cow,' *blackland* 'prairie' or 'soil,' *cottonwood, hackberry, lunch* 'snack,' *mustard greens, passed* 'died,' *prairie* 'meadow,' and the familiar Northern markers *burlap sack* and *(corn) husks*.

Without distinctive morphological features, this tentative zone shares these features of pronunciation: a weakly stressed second syllable in *always*, /m/ for /n/ in the second syllable of *captain* "cap'm," low-back vowels in *barn* and *wash*, devoiced /d/ in *hand*, a lowered /ɔ/ in *oranges*, an unrounded low-back vowel [ɑː] in *God*, centering glides [ɑ³] and [i³] respectively in *water* and *field*, and a weakly retroflex postvocalic /r/, as in *cork*.

Dominated by the piedmont and the plains, interior Southern preserves most of the hallmarks generally associated with American Southern dialects. These are lexical features: *bateau* 'rowboat,' *battercakes* 'pancakes,' *branch* 'creek,' *counterpane* 'bedspread,' *crocus sack* 'burlap sack,' *firedogs* 'andirons,' *flambeau* 'makeshift lamp,' *galluses* 'suspenders,' *goozle* 'trachea,' *ground peas* 'peanuts,' *harp* 'harmonica,' *hunker down* 'crouch,' *lamp oil* 'kerosene,' *pulley bone* 'wishbone,' *salad tomatoes* 'cherry tomatoes,' *spring onions* 'green onions,' *terrapin* 'tortoise,' *tommytoes* 'cherry tomatoes,' *tree frog* 'small frog,' *tumbleset* or *tumblesault* 'somersault,' and *veranda* 'porch.'

Only the preposition *of* in phrases like "quarter of the hour" seems to be a locally identifying grammatical unit. From the Virginia piedmont across the Mississippi River into the upper Texas plains, interior pronunciation shares these features: (1) vocalized postvocalic /r/ and /l/, (2) strong nasality of stressed vowels, replacing nasal segmental phonemes, as in *rim, run*, and *bring* (most common in Afro-American folk speech), (3) substitution of

/s/ for /š/ before /r/ in words like *shrimp* and *shrub,* (4) tense /e/ in *Mary* and *Sarah,* (5) an unrounded low-back vowel [ɑ:] in *barn* and *wash,* and (6) strongly centralized vowels, [ʊ ʉ], [ɪʉ], often becoming [jʉ], in *new, tube,* and similar words.

Within the interior region of the South, a substantial number of forms are shared among the Nashville-Cumberland basin of middle Tennessee, the Georgia piedmont to the south and east, and the Yazoo delta to the south and west. In Mississippi, distribution follows the course of the Natchez Trace from Tennessee and Alabama to the river town. The vocabulary includes *candle fly* 'moth,' *clabber milk, sauce* 'sweet topping,' *snake doctor* 'dragonfly,' *sorghum* 'molasses,' *sowbelly* 'salt pork,' and *spoiled* 'rancid' (of butter).

With a dialect grammar similar to the rest of the interior, this subdivision has these striking pronunciation features: complete loss of /r/ in *car* and of /y/ in *Matthew* [mæθu], the lax high-back vowel /ʊ/ in *bulk,* a fully realized diphthong /ɪu/ in *student,* and a rounded low-back vowel in *wasp.* The incidence of such features may reflect historical facts of interior movement and may help to explain the complex patterns of dialect distribution in the Southern states.

7.9   Western dialects

Beyond the Mississippi River, Western dialects consist of three large divisions: (1) the Mississippi Valley and western Midwest plains, (2) the Western plains and Rocky Mountains, and (3) the Pacific Coast. As social products of the nineteenth century, all major varieties in this large speech area developed from Eastern sources. Western extensions of Northern, Midland, and Southern patterns reach to the Rocky Mountain states, where Spanish influence and cross currents of settlement reshaped the dialects as distinctive regional composites. The linguistic atlases of the North Central States, the Upper Midwest, and the Gulf States offer empirical data to outline the territories to the east, north, and south, respectively. The crucial central area, however, in Missouri and Kansas remains uninvestigated by a general dialect survey. Thus, the dialect composition of the central Mississippi Valley must be extrapolated from data available in atlas sources.

Although exploration of the West began before the Louisiana Purchase (1803), settlement followed the establishment first of overland trails and later of railroads that united the full expanse of the region with the staging areas to the east, especially at St. Louis and Kansas City. The Mississippi Valley, however, is the primary source of Western dialects;

there regional speech extended and reformed the three primary eastern patterns.

Immediately west of the Mississippi River, the eastern pattern of Northern, Midland, and Southern is modified. The northern third of Iowa preserves a basic Northern pattern. The Southern pattern extends northward to the Louisiana-Arkansas border. But between these reasonably well-differentiated areas, western reflexes of Midland dialects merge in a large graded area that combines Northern and Southern features with the west Pennsylvania pattern. Northern speech then extends westward across eastern South Dakota and southwestern North Dakota, where it enters the Rocky Mountain region in the Black Hills. Besides the delta subdivision that reaches up the Mississippi, Red, and St. Francis river basins to the Missouri bootheel, interior Southern speech extends westward across the Louisiana and East Texas piney woods to merge with plains Western beyond Dallas and Forth Worth.

At the center of this zone, St. Louis became the primary source of Western dialects that developed following express routes, wagon trails, and later railways, east to west. Much of the West, however, was settled through the establishment of pioneer speech communities directly from eastern sources in a process Robert Hall (1964, 256) described this way:

> With ever increasing mobility, innovations are likely to travel very fast and far, and to be diffused first to secondary and then to tertiary centers of radiation, often by-passing many geographically intermediate but more isolated places, in a manner reminiscent of military "island hopping" and capture of advanced outposts by parachute troops before the "mopping up" operations carried out by the main body of the army.

For example, the pervasive Inland Northern features in Rocky Mountain enclaves in Utah and Colorado, as well as on the Pacific Coast in California and Washington, demonstrate this pattern most dramatically. But similar extensions of Mississippi Valley speech out of Missouri and Texas demonstrate more deliberate extensions that followed roadways without much development of intervening territories. The Mississippi Valley region includes two subregions that divide north and south in Iowa. The northern sector, centered at Minneapolis and Saint Paul, is a western extension of the Inland Northern dialects, and the southern sector, centered at St. Louis, combines Northern with Midland features. Although both subdivisions include dialects that extend well into the plains, where distinctive Western forms first emerge, the easternmost varieties are of paramount importance because they form basic centers of communication for the transmission of Eastern forms into the West.

From eastern Minnesota to north central Iowa, a small but distinctive set of features outlines the Northern core of features in the upper Mississippi Valley. These include lexical forms *belly flop* 'a dive in which the front of the body lands flat,' *boulevard* 'grass strip at the side of a road,' *(devil's) darning needle* 'dragonfly,' *Dutch cheese* 'cottage cheese,' *gopher*, *spider* 'frying pan,' *stone boat* 'a flat sledge for dragging heavy objects,' *swill pail*, and *whiffletree* 'a pivoted swinging bar to which harness traces are attached and by which a vehicle is pulled.'

Pronunciation includes the preservation of /h/ before the semivowels /w/ as in *whip* and /y/ as in *humor*. It also has /ɪ/ in *creek*, /ɑ/ before /r/ as in *barn* words and in most reflexes of Middle English "short o," including the *hog* words, and, less regularly, /ʊ/ in *broom* words.

As the cradle of Western dialects, the speech of the west central Midwest spread from Iowa to Arkansas along the river in the east and to the Ozarks and Oklahoma hills in the west before ranging across most of Nebraska and Kansas. Centered in Missouri, the major staging areas – with St. Louis in the east and Independence and Kansas City in the west – transmitted an essentially western Midland pattern over the lower extensions of the Great Plains and Rocky Mountains.

This Midland pattern reflects the union of two subregional sets that originated in Pennsylvania. The primary source of dialects in this area seems to proceed from Western Pennsylvania, following the course of the Ohio River in the Mississippi Valley. Nineteenth-century demographics, however, show a secondary source that proceeded into the same territory along an extended and circuitous route. The great migration out of eastern Pennsylvania first extended south through the Shenandoah Valley terminating in the Carolinas and east Tennessee. The discovery of the Cumberland Gap in 1750 offered a route first into east central Kentucky and, later, a southern access to the Midwest.

Settlement of the middle Mississippi Valley from those two sources reunited the historical Pennsylvania patterns in the middle nineteenth century with all the cultural acquisitions gathered through almost a hundred years of diverse social experience. The resultant vocabulary includes items from Western Pennsylvania and its Ohio Valley extensions, such as *baby buggy*, *green beans* 'string beans,' and *gunnysack* 'burlap sack,' and terms from eastern Pennsylvania, West Virginia, and Kentucky, such as *coal oil* 'kerosene,' *(corn) shucks* 'corn husks,' *French harp* 'harmonica,' *singletree*, *skillet*, *slop bucket*, and *snake feeder* or *snake doctor* 'dragonfly.'

Pronunciation in this area shows a predominantly Western Pennsylvania influence with rounded low-back vowels in *hog* words, as well as in the development of historical /ɑ/ in *ma* and *pa* and before /r/ as in *barn* words. Reflecting Southern sources are the incidence of /z/ in *greasy*, /č/ in *rinse*, /ʊ/ in *coop*, and /æ/ in *keg*.

An essentially Southern dialect base extends across the delta regions, the Louisiana and East Texas plains and includes the relic highland enclave of the Missouri and Arkansas Ozarks. Its distinctive contributions to Western dialects, however, emerge as the local patterns reach westward. The incidence of features such as *baby buggy*, *coal oil*, *green beans*, and *skillet*, as well as the low-back vowels mentioned above, unite the middle and lower Mississippi Valley subdivisions from the Missouri bootheel to New Orleans. The incipient Western vocabulary emerges from north of the New Orleans focal area. This includes a few Atchafalaya delta terms, such as *coulee* 'creek bed,' *prairie*, and *step* 'inside stairs.' In the Red River basin in northwestern Louisiana and the adjacent plains of Arkansas and East Texas, a distinctively mixed Southern and Western vocabulary appears, including *branch* 'creek,' *corral*, *French harp* 'harmonica,' *lariat*, *lasso*, *peckerwood*, *pulley bone*, *souse*, and *whetrock*.

Pronunciation includes strongly retroflex realizations of postvocalic /r/ and the reemergence of /h/ before /w/, both missing in territories dominated by New Orleans and the lower Mississippi delta. As the dialect of the Louisiana piney woods crosses the Sabine River to become that of the East Texas pine flats, a distinctly Western vocabulary takes shape. There the western lower Mississippi Valley pronunciation combines with Western words such as *blinky* '(of milk) turning sour,' *(blue) norther* 'fierce northern wind,' *bronc(o)* 'unbroken horse,' *dogie* 'orphan calf,' and *draw* 'dry creek.'

Beginning west of the ninety-eighth meridian and extending beyond the mountains and deserts, this large Western speech area finds unity in the physical and social facts that underlay its destiny. West of the ninety-eighth meridian, the plains become a semiarid to arid zone. The productive farming that marked the Midwest was impossible there until the advent of specialized methods such as "dry farming" and modern tools such as the Oliver plow and the spring-tooth harrow, first produced after the Civil War. When these became available, the area was rapidly settled and became a clearly defined cultural region, restricted by the absence of the twenty-two inches of annual rain necessary for productive traditional farming.

Because mobile cattlemen could move across a vast territory in search of good grasslands, making use of even the badlands in the winter months, the domain of the cowboy ultimately extended from Texas to Montana and into western Canada. Culturally, the trails from Texas into Colorado and Wyoming carried the language and artifacts through the area. Even today, such linguistic forms distinguish the West, however dominant Eastern institutions over the general development of these societies may be.

From the west central Dakotas through Texas, this area is characterized by a small set of words: *sugan* 'range blanket,' *trail*, and the previously mentioned Western terms of the Southwestern plains, such as *blinky*, *bronc(o)*, *jerky* 'dried beef or venison,' *lariat*, *lasso*, *ranch*, and *ranch hand*. All of these occur across the rural Rocky Mountain regions in old-fashioned folk speech, reinforced by *bum* 'orphan cattle or sheep,' *cavvy* 'string of horses,' *cinch* 'saddle girth' (as opposed to Southern *bellyband*), and *rope* 'lasso.' Other rural words of general currency across the West are these familiar topographic designations: *alkali (bed, flats, land, soil)*, *badlands*, *canyon*, *draw*, *gorge*, *gulch*, *ravine*, and *wash*. The region, extending from the Dakotas to the Rio Grande, combines Northern and Midland vocabulary. Striking Midland features include *baby buggy*, *coal oil*, *green beans*, *gunnysack*, *(mouth) harp* 'harmonica,' *nicker* 'gentle sound of a horse,' *pack* 'carry,' and *want off* 'want to get off.'

From Montana and Idaho through Wyoming, Utah, and upper Colorado, Western dialects preserve an essentially Northern pattern. This reflects the comparatively late settlement of the area, primary routes of travel from the east, and the large number of Americans of European birth or parentage. The Mormons, who formed the largest early settlement, had followed a course from Northern Ohio to Missouri, back to Nauvoo, Illinois, and then westward to Utah along the Mormon Trail with Brigham Young, a native of Whitingham, Vermont. Although those settlers initially staked out the entire Southwest as the State of Deseret, their domain finally narrowed to the state of Utah and the border regions of Idaho, Wyoming, Colorado, and Nevada.

Prior to 1845, the border between the United States and Mexico divided southwest and north central Colorado at the Arkansas River. Thus, the first settlers entered the northeast quadrant of the state. With the Pike's Peak Gold Rush of 1858, newcomers arrived from the east along northern and southern routes. These facts seem reflected today in the strong Northern element in the upper and central part of the state against an essentially Midland pattern elsewhere, especially in the most newly settled areas.

In Montana and Idaho, the predominant Northern pattern reflects the remarkable numbers of immigrants and first-generation Americans in both states. The population of Montana in 1930, for example, was 45 percent of these newcomers, with the overwhelming majority from Germany and Scandinavia. Because these states repeated the pattern established earlier in

Minnesota and the Dakotas and included many settlers from those states, Northern speech was extended westward across the northern Rockies.

The distinctive mountain flora and fauna of the northern Rockies were named with such terms as *quakies, quakers,* or *quaking aspen* 'indigenous poplars.' Other lexical features of the region include *basin* 'extended valley between mountains,' *butte* 'flat-topped hill,' *hole* (a Western-sized counterpart of the Eastern *mountain hollow*), *park* 'high plains meadow,' *piggin string* 'tie used in calf-roping,' and *(saddle) fender.*

Across the Western plains and mountains, as far south as central Colorado and the entire state of Utah, vocabulary and pronunciation reflect a Northern influence. Examples are *(peach) pit, teeter-totter,* and *whetstone,* as well as the pronunciation features /s/ in *greasy,* /hw/ in *whip* words, fully retroflex postvocalic /r/, which prevails across the mountains and Pacific Coast, and homophony of *Mary, marry,* and *merry.* The occurrence of /ɑ/ in *log* words also marks old-fashioned rural speech across this territory. The coalescence of /ɑ/ and /ɔ/ in all contexts among young speakers points toward the loss of the /ɔ/ phoneme in the northern Rockies, as far west as Idaho. Other striking features include /s/ in *Boise,* /æ/ in *Colorado* and *Nevada,* and a weakly stressed final syllable in *Oregon.*

Inseparable from the development and expansion of Texas after the Mexican War, the southern Rockies preserve a Spanish influence that steadily competed with transplanted Anglo-American forms from the east. Nowhere was this competition greater than in New Mexico and Arizona. When, in 1905, Congress proposed the creation of a single state across this southwestern territory, residents of both subdivisions objected. In New Mexico, citizens feared the loss of their Hispanic traditions; in Arizona, they worried that their American-English culture would be lost under Spanish influence. As a result, separate states were simultaneously established in 1912.

From central Colorado to interior Texas, as well as across the states of New Mexico, and Arizona, regional speech reflects the mingling of four cultural influences from the north, east, and south. These are (1) the extension of the general Midland pattern that marks the northern subdivision, (2) a western Midland pattern that distinguishes these lower enclaves, (3) a Southern residue that diminishes east to west, and (4) a powerful Spanish influence, which provides the southern part of the Western plains and Rocky Mountains with its most distinctive dialect features.

The general Midland vocabulary includes a number of forms that occur with decreasing incidence in the Rockies. These include *(corn) shucks, roasting ears, slop bucket,* and *souse.* From the western Midland come *baby buggy, coal oil*, and *crawdad* 'crawfish,' as well as the strongly rounded low-back vowels, both before /r/ as in *barn* words and in *hog* words.

Strongest in west Texas and southeastern New Mexico, Southern and South Midland features include *Christmas gift* (as a greeting), both *croker sack* and *tow sack* 'burlap sack,' *dog irons* 'andirons,' *gully washer* 'heavy rain,' *paper sack*, *pulley bone* 'wishbone,' *seesaw*, *snake doctor* 'dragonfly,' *toad-frog*, and *you all* (second person plural). Probably more important are the Southern lengthened free vowels and ingliding checked vowels that characterize the Southwestern drawl.

From Spanish sources come *arroyo* 'dry creek,' *calaboose* 'jail,' *frijoles* 'pinto beans,' *hoosegow*, *mesa* 'flat-topped hill,' *remuda* 'string of horses,' and *sudadero* 'saddle fender.'

In addition, an exclusive Southwestern vocabulary further defines the subregion with forms such as *hackamore* 'rope halter,' *horned toad*, *shinnery* 'oak-covered land,' *surly* (euphemistically) 'bull,' and *trap* 'livestock enclosure.'

Anglo-Americans settled the coastal west early – in the Willamette Valley of Oregon (south of modern Portland and the Columbia River) and in California at Sacramento and San Francisco. Each area was originally settled from the Midwest by the northern Oregon Trail originating at Independence, Missouri, and by the southern Old Spanish, Santa Fe, and California trails. The striking New England influence, especially in San Francisco, may reflect early connections with the merchant mariners, as well as with early settlers from New England who arrived by sea, entering the Pacific across Nicaragua and Panama or around Cape Horn. Although early settlement was accelerated by the Oregon Boom in 1847 and the California Gold Rush two years later, the most powerful influences on the speech of the Pacific Coast followed the Civil War. And these have been primarily Northern forces that shaped the development of cultural centers at Los Angeles, San Francisco, Sacramento, Portland, and Seattle.

Unlike communities in the plains and mountain states of the interior West, the subarea comprising Washington, Oregon, California, and Nevada has no direct union with the gradual westward expansion from the East. And, as no clear extension of a Northern-Midland, a Northern-Southern, or a Midland-Southern boundary emerged beyond the ninety-eighth meridian, the patterns of regional dialects in the Far West are understandably convoluted. All dialects of the Far West reflect settlement by "parachuting," with focal areas in Seattle and San Francisco antedating and surpassing in influence most of the important cultural centers of the Rocky Mountain states, for example, Boise, Casper, Denver, and Phoenix. Only Salt Lake City emerged as an important site in that region, but like other centers there, it had little influence on the development of regional speech to the north, south, and west.

For that reason, a predominantly Inland Northern pattern dominates in the states of the Pacific Coast and Nevada, but an internal subdivision seems to separate Washington, Oregon, and northern California from southern California and Nevada. This pattern reflects the major routes of settlement, by trails, railroads, and finally the highway system that united the Far West with the Middle West.

The essential regional composition of the four states reflects a mix of Northern and Midland features. But, as Elizabeth Jackson has suggested for Colorado speech patterns, virtually all Western dialect mixtures reflect processes that were well underway or completed before they were extended beyond the Middle West.

Lexical, grammatical, and phonological features form a general pattern across the Pacific states and Nevada, reflecting the preeminence of Northern dialect influence on the speech of the region with less influence from Midland sources, fewer from plains and Rocky Mountain Western, and least from the South. These Far West features include a considerable number that today approach general currency in American English. From the Northern dialects come *andirons, angleworm, chipmunk, clingstone peach, cloudburst, firefly, freestone peach, harmonica, headcheese, mantel, pail, pig pen, pit* 'cherrystone,' *ram, salt pork, stallion, string beans, to* in "quarter to the hour" and "sick to one's stomach," *whinny, white bread,* and *wishbone.* From Midland and Southern (usually south Midland) sources come *baby buggy, (barn) lot, coal oil, coal bucket, green beans, gunnysack, gutters, mush, roasting ears* 'corn on the cob,' *second crop, seesaw, shivaree, singletree, skillet, snake doctor* 'dragonfly,' *till* in "quarter till the hour," and *(window) blinds.* Specialized usage of Western words include a preference for *lasso* (with primary stress on the first syllable in the Far West and on the last syllable in the Rockies) over *lariat* and *rodeo* (with primary stress on the second syllable more often than in the Rockies, where it is invariably on the first syllable).

Washington and Oregon attracted large numbers of Eastern farmers, fishermen, and miners, drawn by the promise of abundant rainfall, access to the ocean and powerful rivers, and a long history of success in the extractive industries. As the terminus of the Oregon Trail, the Willamette Valley absorbed the first settlers who extended Northern and Midland forms across the territory now dominated by the two states. Later development of heavy industries, especially at Portland and Seattle, reinforced a dominant Inland Northern pattern. Indeed, apart from a few Cook County shibboleths, the speech of metropolitan Chicago is as nearly indistinguishable from Seattle speech as it is from that of San Francisco. And, after having little currency across the interior West, Northern terms reemerge: *(devil's) darning needle, Dutch cheese* 'cottage cheese,' *johnnycake* 'corn bread,' and *stoop* 'back porch.' Although these occur to the south in Nevada and California, they have higher incidence in the Pacific Northwest. Local speech is further marked by the occurrence of Midland *dog irons* 'andirons' and distinctly sub-regional *cayuse* 'wild horse' and *chinook* 'warm, moist southwestern wind' (in contrast with the warm, dry wind of the Upper Rockies).

Like the dialects in the southern Rockies to the east, speech in the Pacific Southwest acquires much more from Midland and Southern, as well as Hispanic, sources than does the northern coastal area. Although the combination of early and recent immigrants preserves a predominantly Northern pattern, especially in the cities of Sacramento, San Francisco, Los Angeles, and San Diego, contributions from those other three sources distinguish California and Nevada. Midland and Southern features include *bucket* 'wooden vessel,' *coal bucket* 'metal vessel,' *horned, horn,* or *horny toad, jag* 'partial load,' *lightning bug, mud dauber, mushmelon* 'cantaloupe,' *rock* 'stone,' *rock fence, side meat, singletree, skillet, sowbelly, spicket,* and *wardrobe* 'built-in closet.' From Spanish sources come *adobe, arroyo, burro, cholo* 'Mexican,' *corral* (common throughout the West except in Washington), *frijoles, mesa, peon, riata,* and *vaquero,* as well as terms such as *enchilada, patio, plaza, taco,* and *tortilla,* all of which have gained general currency in virtually all dialects of American English.

These Western dialects suggest the immediate future of the national language more reliably than any other regional pattern. As products of American social history since the Civil War, local speech of the West incorporates features from eastern sources and reforms them across the plains, mountains, and coastal subdivisions of the Western states. In this area, modern cultural influences of American life manifest themselves linguistically. These changes reflect the impact of mobility, urbanization, and social reform on the contemporary family, education, economy, and technology. All of these experiences have contributed to the development of the Western, trans-Mississippi, dialects of American English at the end of the twentieth century.

In an era dominated by the automobile, industrialization, and social integration, the American West came into its own as the national center of population reached the Mississippi Valley. The confluence of Northern, Midland, and Southern speech forms reshaped the language here in a territory that established unique relationships with European and American sources. Western society found its basis in native usage, and its dialects offer the most reliable model for American English at the beginning of the twenty-first century.

7.10   Summary: major American dialects

1. Northern
   a. northeastern New England
   b. southeastern New England
   c. metropolitan New York City
   d. southwestern New England
   e. Hudson Valley
   f. Inland North (western Vermont, Upstate New York, and derivatives spread across the Midwest beneath the Great Lakes and beyond the Mississippi into Iowa, Minnesota, and the Dakotas)
2. Southern
   a. coastal
      (1) Atlantic
      (2) Gulf
   b. interior
      (1) piedmont
      (2) Gulf plains: eastern, central, western
   c. delta
      (1) upper: Arkansas River basin, Yazoo River basin, Red River basin
      (2) lower: Atchafalaya River basin, lower Mississippi River basin
3. Midland
   a. eastern (Philadelphia)
   b. western (Pittsburgh)
   c. North (western reflexes of Pittsburgh)
      (1) eastern: Cincinnati, Indianapolis
      (2) western: St. Louis, Kansas City
   d. South (southern reflexes of Philadelphia)
      (1) highlands: eastern: Virginia, Kentucky, east Tennessee, Georgia Blue Ridge; central: middle Tennessee, upper Alabama Cumberlands; western: Missouri and Arkansas Ozarks
      (2) piney woods: Georgia and Alabama wire grass; Florida and Alabama sand hills and pine flats; Mississippi and Louisiana piney woods; East Texas pine flats
4. Western
   a. Mississippi Valley and western Midwest plains
   b. Western plains and Rocky Mountains (beyond the 98th meridian,

forty miles west of the Red River in North Dakota and fifty miles west of Fort Worth in Texas, where annual rainfall usually fails to exceed the twenty-two inches required for traditional Midwestern farming)

c. Pacific Coast (Pacific Northwest, San Francisco, southern California)

FURTHER READING

The best current resources of American dialects include William Kretzschmar's Linguistic Atlas projects site <http://us.english.uga.edu/> and William Labov's TELSUR project (Atlas of North American English) <http://www.ling.upenn.edu/phonoatlas>. Useful recent readings include Cynthia Bernstein, Tom Nunnally, and Robin Sabino (1997), *Language Variety in the South Revisited*; Ellen Johnson (1996), *Lexical Change and Variation in the Southeastern United States, 1930–1990*; William A. Kretzschmar, Jr. (1998), "Ebonics"; William A. Kretzschmar, Jr. and Edgar Schneider (1996), *Introduction to Quantitative Analysis in Linguistic Survey Data*; Rosina Lippi-Green (1997), *English with an Accent: Language, Ideology, and Discrimination in the United States*; Salikoko Mufwene, John Rickford, Guy Bailey, and John Baugh (1998), *African-American English: Structure, History, and Use*; and Edgar W. Schneider (1996), *Focus on the USA*. The most comprehensive source for lexical information about American dialects is Frederic G. Cassidy and Joan Houston Hall (1985–), *Dictionary of American Regional English*.

8 AFRICAN-AMERICAN ENGLISH

Salikoko S. Mufwene

8.1 What is African-American English?

The term African-American English (AAE) is used here for "the whole range of language [varieties] used by black people in the United States: a very large range indeed, extending from the Creole grammar of Gullah spoken in the Sea Islands [and coastal marshlands] of South Carolina [and Georgia] to the most formal and accomplished literary style" (Labov 1972a, xiii). This chapter is focused, however, on vernacular varieties characterized as basilectal or mesolectal. A basilect is a variety most different from educated, middle-class English, called an acrolect, and a mesolect is intermediate between the basilect and the acrolect.

The term AAE is used here as a general, umbrella term that must be distinguished from more specific ones such as Gullah – also known as Sea Island Creole – and African-American vernacular English (AAVE). Gullah is any of a range of creole varieties, and AAVE is any of the continental nonstandard varieties of African-American speech. Following several African-American scholars (J. Baugh 1983; M. Morgan 1989; Smitherman 1977; Spears 1988; Tolliver-Weddington) but in contrast with William Labov (1972a, cf. however 1982) and others, the term "vernacular" is used here for varieties of AAE allegedly used by 80 to 90 percent of continental African-Americans as a primary means of communication for their day-to-day intragroup communication (Smitherman 1977, 2; Spears 1988, 109; Wofford 367). That percentage is only an estimate suggesting that most African-Americans speak those varieties of AAE.

Labov, on the other hand, identifies AAVE as "that relatively uniform grammar found in its most consistent form in the speech of the [adolescent] black youth from 8 to 19 years old who participate in the street culture of the inner cities" (1972a, xiii), which prompts the question of whether the rest of African-Americans speak white middle-class English or white nonstandard

291

English. Labov's position also raises the question of whether it is legitimate to project the variety spoken by teenage members of the street culture, a subset of the youth – thus a small though visible proportion of the population – as the prototype of African-Americans' vernacular.

Given Labov's position, Gilyard (118–9) asks whether there is a reliable correlation between participation in street culture and the proportion and frequency of features associated with AAVE. Most students of AAE who have socialized informally with less-educated African-Americans of any age group will find the question justified. It is not surprising that many African-American scholars, who are most likely to socialize with the relevant African-American population in less constrained contexts, view the vernacular of African-Americans as internally diverse (such as J. Baugh 1983, despite his emphasis on "street culture"). It is assumed here that AAE as a vernacular is diverse and may vary structurally from one speaker, setting, or region to another, although the varieties are all perceived as manifestations of basically the same ethnic language variety, with perhaps the exception of the Gullah varieties.

Internal diversity is characteristic of all language varieties. For example, not all Southerners – born, raised, and living in the American South – use all the linguistic features associated with Southern English. Every Southerner uses a somewhat different subset of the features, which overlaps with other speakers' subsets. The set-theory union of these idiolects defines Southern English. So it is with African-Americans who either claim or are assumed to speak AAE. The description of any language variety is thus a useful construct, which makes it possible to situate every speaker of the variety within its range of lects. This fact implies the need for variation analysis to characterize speech as an instantiation of a system allowing more than one structural alternative for the same communicative function.

According to the studies cited above (and Dillard 1972), AAVE is spoken both in cities and in rural areas, and by all age groups of both sexes. Gullah, on the other hand, is primarily a rural phenomenon. It is also spoken by persons of all age groups and of both sexes, though not by every African-American living on the Sea Islands and coastal marshlands of South Carolina and Georgia. People speak AAE "to varying degrees. Many use some of the features included in the linguistic definition, but never all of them" (Spears 1988, 109).

The "linguistic definition" of AAVE mentioned by Spears amounts to the basilect, an "analytical construct [like] the Chomskyan idealized native speaker" (Mufwene 1987b, 98–9), which is useful in helping scholars to determine the position of speech samples on the basilect-to-acrolect continuum. For AAVE, as well as Gullah and Caribbean English creoles (Rickford 1990, 160), the mesolect is the norm.

Despite the use here of AAE as an umbrella term including Gullah and AAVE, each of these varieties has its own basilect and mesolect. No single creole basilect or mesolect occurs from one community to another because creoles and similar contact-induced varieties are not defined structurally (Chaudenson; Mufwene 1986c; Singler 1990). The restructuring that produced these varieties has no specific end. The notions "basilect" and "mesolect" simply measure how far the restructuring has proceeded in a particular community. Although Gullah and AAVE are presented here as regional varieties of AAE, the former being southeastern coastal and the latter continental, they are more or less separate in origin. This observation bears on the discussion in section 3 of AAE's development.

According to the identification of AAVE used here, the variety spoken by African-American adolescents who participate in the street culture is only one of the subvarieties of this larger ethnic variety, called "Ebonics" by some. AAVE has indeed been identified by several names in the literature, including "urban Negro speech" (Stewart 1965), "American Negro Dialect" and "Negro (nonstandard) English" (Stewart 1968), "Merican" (Fickett 1970), "American Negro English" (Loflin; Stewart 1965, 1974), "Negro nonstandard dialect" (R. Smith), "Black English" (Burling; Dillard 1972; and others), "Black English Vernacular," abbreviated as BEV (Labov 1972a, 1972b, and other quantitative sociolinguists), "PALWH" (pronounced [pælwhə]) for "Pan-African Language in the Western Hemisphere," Twiggs), "Ebonics" (Tolliver-Weddington; R. L. Williams, and many publications since 1997), and "Black Street Speech" (J. Baugh 1983). Other names include "Black Dialect," "Black Idiom," and "Black Talk" (Smitherman 1977, 1994).

Most of the terms for their vernacular reflect what African-Americans have been called at different times since the nineteenth century. Geneva Smitherman (1991, 1994) surveys the history of such terms since Colonial days, and John Baugh (1991) treats the reintroduction of "African-American." The terms "PALWH," "Ebonics," "Bilalian," "Black Talk," and "Black Street Speech" were initiated by African-American scholars but have not gained wide currency in the linguistic literature. The term "African-American English," adopted in this article and in much of the literature of the 1990s, is a response to a proposal by African-American political leaders that the term "African-American" replace "Black" in reference to Americans of African descent. The reality, however, is that most speakers of what is identified here as AAE do not have a name for their vernacular. Generally they say they speak English.

The discussion of Gullah together with AAVE in this chapter calls for justification because the former is identified as a creole in the same literature that assumes AAVE is not, or is no longer, one (see § 8.3). According to most creolists, creoles are new languages and not dialects of their lexifiers. Thus Gullah would be a different language and should not be lumped together with varieties of English.

Several reasons, however, justify a joint discussion of Gullah and AAVE. First, the assertion that creolization results in a new language is arbitrary. The restructuring resulting in a creole is not demonstrably different from that leading to a new dialect. Nor have creoles been shown not to be dialects of their lexifiers.

Second, no convincing case has been made against considering AAVE to be a creole. The characterization of AAVE as a "semi-creole" (§ 8.3) begs the question, in the absence of structural criteria defining creoles. The boundary between AAVE and Gullah is fuzzy, corresponding in part to the fuzzy geographic area that separates the marshlands of coastal South Carolina and Georgia from the rest of the mainland. The distinction between Gullah and AAVE really amounts to different degrees in their restructuring.

Third, Gullah speakers think they speak a variety of English, just as continental African-Americans generally think they do. As with other language varieties, such as Dutch and Flemish, it is safe to follow native speakers' sentiments in this matter. Accordingly, the general term AAE is used here for all vernacular varieties spoken by African-Americans more to highlight their genetic link to (American) English than to suggest that Gullah and AAVE are the same. Differences between these varieties are dealt with below. Their common features are discussed together both in the interest of economy and to show how much they share.

8.2   Features of AAE

A feature is any phonological, morphological, syntactic, semantic, or pragmatic characteristic that distinguishes one language variety from another. A question often asked about the genesis of AAVE is whether the structural features associated with it are peculiarities of African-Americans only. The question seems to be misguided, because different language varieties may share features. It would be surprising if varieties that share part of their ancestries and developed in related sociohistorical conditions, such as AAVE and white Southern English, did not share several of their structural features.

Virtually all the structural features of AAE are "variable" in the sense proposed by Labov (1972b, 72). That is, they alternate with others in the same contexts. For instance, possessive constructions may be on the pattern of either *John book*, without a possessive marker, or *John's book*, with one. Likewise, constructions such as *Mary home* "Mary is home," without a copula, alternate with *Mary's home*, with a contracted copula. What is noteworthy about such nonstandard AAE alternatives is their high frequency, compared with educated, acrolectal varieties and even some other nonstandard varieties. The peculiarity of AAE lies in both the statistical distribution of these features and the structural principles that produce them. The fact that a feature is attested in other varieties does not make it less typical of AAE, just as the interdental fricatives in *thick* and *this* are not less typical of English merely because they are also attested in varieties of Swahili.

Nonstandard features occur most frequently in casual and familiar settings. Switches toward acrolectal options are made in other settings, often resulting in hypercorrections. In extreme cases, such as Gullah, speakers simply do not talk before strangers, making it almost impossible to detect features of their vernacular systems.

8.2.1   Phonological features

One of the most common stereotypes of AAE is the variable absence of interdental fricatives in words such as *think*, *them*, *mother*, *mouth*, and *with*. In word-initial position they are often replaced by /t/ or /d/, thus producing *tink* and *dem*. In intervocalic and word-final position, they are sometimes replaced by /f/ and /v/, producing *movuh*, *mouf*, and *wiv*. The last is alternatively *wit* or *wid*. The name *Ruth* may be *roof* or may have a glottal stop, yielding *Ru'*. Some words, however, follow no consistent pattern: *three* as *free*, *through* as *troo* or *too*, and *throw* as *trow* or *tow*. The r-less pronunciation of *throw* is almost regular in Gullah.

AAE is often characterized as nonrhotic: /r/ is omitted most often in word-final and preconsonantal position, next in word-final position followed by a vowel, and least often word-medially before a vowel (Labov 1972a, 43). If nonphonological contextual factors did not help, there would be confusion between pairs such as *guard* and *god*. Because of intervocalic omission of /r/, *Carol* may be pronounced *Ca'uhl*, *interested* as *intuhested*, and *four o'clock* as *foh uhclock* (some impressionistic and eye-dialect spellings are used for convenience). The last two examples have alternative pronunciations that reduce the number of syllables by eliminating the schwa: *intested* and *foh clock*. The loss of intervocalic /r/ can extend even to words like *borrow*, *warrior*, and *arrow*, which may be *buhoh*, *wahyuh*, and *ah-ow* (Pat Wells, private communication).

The absence of linking *r* in expressions like *four o'clock* and *forever* (when pronounced *foh evuh* rather than *fehvuh*) is related to a more general phenomenon. In words such as *studying*, *however*, and *Diane*, as well as sequences such as *I ain(t)* and *you and me*, the linking glide [y] or [w] of other varieties of English does not occur. This phonological peculiarity is so strong that in constructions such as *the ear* and *the air*, the definite article is commonly pronounced *duh* (that is, /də/) rather than with [i]. Nouns such as *idea* and *invitation* are often preceded by the indefinite article *a* rather than *an*. Labov (1972a, 71) cites the construction "He is a expert."

The lateral /l/ is often omitted in preconsonantal and word-final positions, as in *help* and *toll*, although less commonly than the omission of postvocalic /r/. The omission in *help* is related to a more general simplification of consonant clusters in word-final position. Thus *guest*, *desk*, and *wasp* are often pronounced without the final stop as *guess*, *dess*, and *wass*, which are pluralized as *guesses*, *desses*, and *wasses*. This phenomenon occurs also in white nonstandard English (Michael Miller).

The consonant cluster simplification rule applies to the alveolar stops /t, d/ more frequently in monomorphemic words, such as *past* than in polymorphemic words, such as *passed* (the verb *pass* and the past tense suffix *-ed*), and more often when the following word starts with a consonant, as in *past/passed me > pass me*, than when it starts with a vowel, as in *past/passed us* (Guy 1980, 1991; Labov 1972a).

Final consonant cluster simplification may be connected with tense marking (Dillard 1972; Stewart 1967, 1968). Verbs like *pass* may have no such phonological simplification in past-tense forms because at least part of AAVE operates on a creole-like system, in which the form referring to the past is generally the same as the stem. Although omissions of past-tense marking have been statistically low (Schneider 1989), the few attestations of past-time *come* and *run* (rather than the ablaut forms *came* and *ran*) suggest a creole-like system. However, the alternative of convergence of two distinct principles, phonological and grammatical, at the level of either individual speakers or the speech community need not be ruled out. Such convergence of phonological and grammatical principles may apply also to omission of the possessive {-Z} in noun phrases, third person singular {-Z} in the present tense of verbs, and the plural marker {-Z} for nouns (discussed in § 8.2.2.1 below).

Noteworthy in some varieties of AAVE is the merger of the vowels of words such as *pen/pin* and *ten/tin*, pronounced indistinguishably as *pin* and *tin*. The merger is restricted to the prenasal environment; it does not affect pairs such as *bet/bit* or *tell/till*. There are exceptions to this rule, however, as *get* is often pronounced *git*.

In words such as *cry, toy, loud*, and *road*, the diphthongs /ay, oy, aw/ and /ow/ are frequently monophthongized or at least have very weak glides. Although the same tendency is observable among white Southerners, Dorrill shows that it is stronger among African-Americans. On the other hand, a slight diphthongization often occurs in words such as *bad* and *hand* pronounced /bæyd/ and /hæyn(d)/, a feature also shared with Southern white vernacular English.

Some speakers of AAVE also lower the vowel [ɪ] to [æ] before the velar nasal of words such as *thing, sing*, and *ring*. This tendency varies from speaker to speaker, especially regarding the specific words affected by the phenomenon. However, the progressive suffix *-ing* is usually [ɪn]. Also noteworthy in AAE is the occurrence of [o:] in words such as *sure/shore* and *poor/pour*, making the members of the pairs homophonous. The numeral *four* and the possessive pronoun *your* are commonly pronounced *foh* and *yoh*, respectively.

Some phonological peculiarities distinguish Gullah from AAVE and other varieties of English in North America, including the sporadic pronunciation of /v/ and /w/ as [β] in words such as *very* and *well*, though the phenomenon may not be as widespread as reported in the literature. The vowel of words such as *bear* and *hair* is typically pronounced [ʳɛ]. The diphthong /ay/ in *knife* and *wife* is commonly pronounced as [æʸ] and that of *oil* as [ɑʸ]. What otherwise distinguishes Gullah from AAVE is its prosody, which is reminiscent of that of the Bahamas and to some extent the West Indies.

Of all English varieties spoken in North America, AAVE is prosodically most similar to white Southern English. For instance, the following words are typically stressed on the first, rather than the second, syllable in both varieties: *police, Detroit*, and *umbrella*. Such phonological and other structural similarities have kindled two of the competing hypotheses on the genetic status of AAE (§ 8.3.1), namely that African-Americans have influenced the speech of Southern whites or that features of AAE are retentions from Colonial white English.

8.2.2   *Grammatical features*

Among the grammatical features of AAE, the most often cited are the possessive, noun plurals, subject-verb agreement, the copula and predication, time reference, negation, and complex sentence formation.

8.2.2.1   The possessive, noun plural, and subject-verb agreement markers

AAE often lacks the possessive marker in phrases such as *Nate book*, the plural marker in *two puppy*, and subject-verb agreement in constructions such as *Duane love Felicia*. Contrary to the suggestion (§ 8.2.1) that phonological and grammatical principles may converge to account for the absence of the relevant markers, Labov (1972a, 1973) observes that the tendency for consonant cluster simplification is perhaps not an important factor in the absence of the possessive marker, because this marker is also absent when the possessor word ends in a vowel, *his daddy name*. In Gullah (Mufwene 1992a) and Guyanese Creole (Rickford 1990), constituent order may be considered the primary and sufficient marker of possession. Likewise, nominal number is redundant in some contexts because of a quantifier in the same noun phrase (*two dog*) or an anaphoric context in which the number of a noun is obvious from its earlier use. Subject-verb agreement is redundant because of the presence of the subject noun or pronoun. Thus, at least for some speakers, the absence of these formal markers may be conditioned primarily by grammatical principles. Phonological environments, on which quantitative sociolinguists have focused, may simply be factors favoring or disfavoring the application of rules.

The markers for possessive, noun number, and subject-verb agreement all tend to be absent with equal frequency in casual speech between familiar acquaintances (J. Baugh 1983, 96). In such situations, their probability coefficients (the quantified likelihood that they will occur) are as follows: .601 for third person singular, .635 for possessive, and .621 for noun plural. In interactions with participants from outside the community, especially those who do not participate in the vernacular culture, the third person singular marker tends to be absent the most, with a probability coefficient of .417. That is still significant although coefficients of less than .5 are considered as "disfavoring" a particular alternative in quantitative analysis. The absence of the possessive marker has a coefficient of .249, and that of the plural a coefficient of .345.

Labov's position seems to be supported by the above figures, although they report group, not individual, statistics and therefore do not tell us how one speaker may differ from another in use of the variable features. The fact that the third person singular is a semantically empty marker should account for why it is the most omitted in controlled behavior. Lack of detailed information on where the plural marker is absent most often in AAVE, for instance whether quantifiers favor its absence, makes it difficult to verify the likely role of semantic redundancy suggested above, similar to the role of syntactic word order in possessive constructions.

The possessive constructions considered here do not include possessive pronouns. AAVE has possessive pronouns like those of other varieties of English. Except for the variable pronunciation of *our* as [aw], the pronouns are always pronounced in full form. In the Gullah basilect, a different grammatical rule applies, which simply preposes a pronoun in the subject or object form, like any other possessor noun phrase, to the head noun. Since Gullah, unlike AAVE, marks possession solely by word order, there is less justification for speaking of the absence of a possessive marker in it.

In the Gullah basilect, the marker of nominal number is a free morpheme, *dem*, as in *dem book* 'the books.' Its use is regulated by principles that are semantic and somewhat different from those underlying the distribution of the plural suffix {-Z} in AAVE and other varieties of English. For instance, the Gullah basilect allows no indefinite plurals or generic reference with an indefinite singular. Instead, a bare noun phrase, without a determiner or quantifier, is used for generic reference, as in *Clint like ooman* 'Clint likes women' (additional information in Mufwene 1986b, Rickford 1986b, 1990).

8.2.2.2 Predication and the copula

AAE differs from other varieties of American English in predication – what the subject combines with to form a sentence. Most predicates are verb phrases, but some are verbless, consisting of an adjective, a prepositional phrase, or a noun phrase: *John (very) sick* 'John [is] (very) sick,' *They with Belle sister* 'They [are] with Belle's sister,' and *Diane the girl* 'Diane [is] the girl.' The fact that the predicate *sick* can be modified by *very*, like a regular adjective, suggests that, contrary to what several creolists assume, an adjective does not become a verb in predicate function.

The copula (any form of nonexistential *be*) is most often absent before the future marker *gon*, as in *Diane gon come* (about 90 percent of possible occurrences), and before the progressive (70 percent), as in *John talkin*. It is absent with about equal frequency before adjectives (42 percent) and prepositional/locative phrases (44 percent), and least frequently (27 percent) before predicate noun phrases (figures averaged from Labov 1972a and Mufwene 1992b). This variable has been explained in two opposite ways. One is that the copula is deleted by a phonological rule operating on the contractions of the verb (Labov 1972a). The other is that the copula is added by an insertion rule. The second explanation sometimes relates

AAVE to creoles of the Caribbean and to Gullah (J. Baugh 1980; Dillard 1972; Holm 1984; Mufwene 1992b, 1994b; Stewart 1968, 1969; Winford 1990, 1992). It has also been argued, however, that insertion of the copula may be independent of any creole origin of AAVE and that even in acrolectal English it may be assumed to have been inserted transformationally in order to meet some surface morphosyntactic peculiarities of the system (Mufwene 1992c).

Whichever explanation is assumed, the surface distributional facts about the presence or absence of the copula remain the same. However, most discussions have focused on the form *is*, with the notable exception of Wolfram (1974) and Rickford et al. Without including other forms (*am, are, was, were*), an incomplete, if not distorted, picture emerges, especially in AAVE. Past tense forms are not absent as often as present tense ones (Labov 1972a). *Are* is more likely to be omitted than *is* (Rickford et al.). Constructions such as **I sick* are not produced at all, although there have been some isolated reports of the **I'm am sick* type of construction.

Lastly, the copula may not be missing in environments characterized by Bickerton as "exposed positions." Examples include infinitival clauses introduced by *to*, as in *Jane wan to be with her mother* (with *want to* often reduced to *wanna*), not **Jane wan to with her mother;* post-modal position, as in *Diane may be sick,* not **Diane may sick;* imperative constructions, such as *Be smart,* not **Smart;* and sentence-final position, as in *I don care who he is,* not **I don care who he.* The copula may not be contracted in these same environments.

Details of the use of the copula in Gullah are still scant. Although observations about the copula in basilectal Jamaican Creole (B. Bailey 1966) generally apply also to basilectal Gullah (Holm 1984), each creole has its own idiosyncrasies. For instance, Gullah uses one copula *duh* or *da* (pronounced with a schwa), as in *Sara duh talk* 'Sara is talking,' *Faye duh she/he chile* 'Faye is her child,' and *Teddy (duh) in the city* 'Teddy is in the city.' On the other hand, Jamaican Creole distinguishes between the locative verb *de* (pronounced [dɛ]) as in *Jaaj de a mi yaad* 'George is at my house' and the copula *a* ([a]) as in *Mieri a mi tiicha* 'Mary is my teacher.'

Gullah, like AAVE, has only one copula; yet the fact that the copulas of Gullah and AAVE differ in form must affect hypotheses about the presence versus absence of the copula in each variety, despite the varieties' similar patterns of verbal and nonverbal predication. There is no reason to assume that the systems of Gullah and AAVE are underlyingly identical. Such an assumption need not be made for any two varieties of a language. Thus the inapplicability of Labov's analysis to Gullah facts does not necessarily invalidate its adequacy for the AAVE copula.

8.2.2.3 Time reference

For Gullah and AAVE it is useful to make a distinction between realis and irrealis tenses. The realis/irrealis distinction is a modal one, which is, however, intimately tied with tense distinctions. The realis tenses refer to states of affairs that have already taken place, and the irrealis to those that have not yet taken place. The latter include the future, which is expressed with the auxiliary verb *go*, as in *I gon/gonna tell Felicia* in AAVE and *Uh go/gwine tell Sara* in Gullah. They also include constructions with English modals such as *would/woulda*, *could/coulda*, and *might/mighta*, in which the second option, derived from the English auxiliary plus the contraction *'ve* (Gilman 1985), is used for reference to the past.

The realis tenses show the most contrasts with other varieties of English. For instance, verb stems, especially but not exclusively nonstative ones, are often used alone for reference to past states of affairs. Thus, *John come* and *Larry tease Tammy* correspond to past or present perfect tenses in other varieties of English, unless the context suggests otherwise. In the sentence *Tracy sick when I come here*, the stative predicate adjective *sick* has past reference because of the interpretation of *come* as past time. This tense, commonly called the unmarked tense in creole studies, contrasts with the second realis tense called "anterior," which is marked with the auxiliary verb *bin*, denoting a state of affairs that took place before the reference time. The anterior tense often corresponds to the past perfect in other varieties of English: *Larry bin gone when I come* 'Larry had left when I came.' However, it sometimes corresponds to no more than the acrolectal past tense: *I bin sleeping when you come* (AAVE) and *Uh bin a/duh sleep when you come* (Gullah) 'I was sleeping when you came.' In AAVE, however, *was* is more common than *bin* in the last sentence. On the other hand, the anterior tense is used with the meaning of past perfect much more in Gullah than in AAVE.

Another function is remote phase *bin* (Rickford 1975). This marker, which is typically stressed, refers to the relatively distant past when an event took place or a current state began: *I bin know(in) you* 'I have known you for a long time' and *Larry bin done gone when Uh come* (Gullah) 'Larry had already left (a long time ago) when I came.' A related use of *bin* is the perfect, which is also common particularly in AAVE, as in *I bin home all day* 'I have been home all day' and *We bin talkin about this forever now* 'We have been talking about this forever now.' These uses highlight both how subtly different Gullah and AAVE are and how inadequate it would be to account for the latter's grammar with only a creole model. Alternations of past tense forms with unmarked verb forms, as in *I eat/ate already* 'I ate already' reveal more of this still poorly understood coexistence of creole-like and English-like patterns in AAVE. The nonmonolithic nature of AAVE is further evidenced by occasional alternations between tense concord (which is more common) and its absence, as in *Jawanda was sick when I came/come*.

AAE differs from other varieties of English most obviously in the morphosyntax of its aspectual system. Gullah and AAVE both use the suffix *-in (-ing)* as a durative or progressive marker, as in *How you doin?* Gullah also uses the auxiliary verb *duh* (also spelled *da*), as in *How you duh do?* 'How are you doing?' Or *duh* and the suffix *-in* may cooccur, as in *How you duh doin?* For past time, this marker alternates with *a* after the anterior marker *bin*, as in *Uh bin duh read* or *Uh bin a read* 'I was reading.'

AAE also uses the perfect, marked with *done*, as in *John done eat/ate* 'John has eaten.' Like the durative construction, the perfect is also used for past events, as in *Sharon done leave/lef Boot when Al meet her* 'Sharon had (already) left Boot when Al met her' (cf. *Pat hollerin when he come back* 'Pat was hollering when he came back').

The perfect marker *done* often combines with the anterior marker *bin* in Gullah and apparently the remote-phase *bin* in AAVE to denote remoteness of the event with respect to the reference time, as in *Larry bin done gone when I come*. *Done* and *bin* are used together in either order, though in Gullah *bin done* appears to be more common. *Bin done* may connote more emphasis on remoteness than on perfect, whereas *done bin* connotes the opposite (Pat Wells, private communication). In the sentence *After all we done been through, here it is 1992, and we still ain free* (Smitherman 1994, 11), the sequence *done bin* amounts to a perfect construction.

Gullah has another peculiarity regarding the perfect construction: *done* may also follow the main verb, as in *I talk done*, which denotes more than perfectivity. This construction signals the speaker's unwillingness to talk any more, meaning more or less 'I have said what I had to say.' The possibility of accounting for perfect *done* constructions in AAVE by the deletion of an underlying *have* is disputed by constructions such as *Larry bin done gone*. Neither of the sequences **have bin done* or **bin have done* sounds English-like. Neither has been attested in AAVE. Labov (1972a, 56) concluded that aspectual "*done* has for all intents and purposes become an adverb, functioning sometimes like *already* and *really*, and lost its status as a verb." However, he adduced no morphosyntactic evidence other than the equivalence of its delimitative function with perfect *have*, either against treating it as a verb or for classifying it as an adverb.

AAE has a verb *done* 'finish,' as in *Laysha done her homework* 'Laysha (has) finished her homework.' It is semantically close to aspectual *done* used with nonstative verbs to denote perfect, as in *I done talk(ed) to him* 'I have (just) talked to him' or 'I have finished talking to him.' One is thus tempted to assume a grammaticization process that would be a concomitant of the development of AAE. However, both main and auxiliary verb uses of *done* are attested in white nonstandard vernaculars (Christian, Wolfram, and Dube). Thus the perfect constructions could have been selected from Colonial English.

AAE also has a habitual aspect marker *be* which combines with a nonverbal predicate, as in *I be tired by the end of the day* 'I am [usually] tired by the end of the day' or *He live here but he be at work most of the time* 'He lives here but he is at work most of the time.' When this distributive *be* or invariant *be* is followed by a verb, the verb must be in the progressive, as in *She be talkin every time I come* 'She is [usually] talking every time I come.' Such verbs are usually nonstative, but even when they are stative, they must be in the progressive, as in *I be hatin when I be havin bad dreams* (Richardson 1991, 297) 'I hate it when I have bad dreams' or 'I hate having bad dreams.' The progressive with stative verbs implies transient duration; thus *be hating* denotes repetition of a state over a period of time. The same *be* also combines with a verb modified by perfect *done*, as in *He be done gone every time I get here* 'He has [usually] left every time I get here.' The oldest elaborate study of invariant *be* is by Ralph Fasold (1969). Several interesting studies have been published since, including those by Fasold (1972), John Rickford (1986a, advancing a possible, though not exclusive, connection with Hiberno-English), Guy Bailey and Marvin Bassett (reporting that the feature is also attested in white Southern nonstandard speech), John Myhill (1988, 1991, uniquely suggesting that it connotes disapproval), Carmen Richardson (disputing Myhill's suggestion), Elizabeth Dayton, Lisa Green (1998), William Labov (1998).

Habitual *be* is distinct from the copula in its infinitive form, although their distributions are partly similar: before verbs in the progressive or nonverbal predicates (habitual *be* does not occur at the end of elliptical utterances or after modals). The main distinction is that habitual *be* has a specific meaning, whereas the copula is a semantically empty device used only to fill the surface requirement in English that a predicate phrase be headed by a verb (Mufwene 1990a, 1992c). Also the AAVE copula has a full paradigm, whereas habitual *be* has a single invariant form. Moreover, habitual *be* is negated with *don(t)*, as in *I don't be telling lies* 'I am not (usually in the process of) telling lies,' whereas the copula is negated with *not* (following it) or *ain(t)*, as in *He's not sick* or *He ain't sick*. Unlike the copula, habitual *be* is substituted by *do* in elliptical constructions, as in *Malcolm be tellin lies, and you do [*be] too.* In emphatic contexts and questions, habitual *be,* unlike the copula, may be modified by *do,* as in *Do he be messin with my brother? *Be he messin with my brother?* is ill-formed.

Habitual *be* followed by a nonverbal predicate or a verb in the progressive is different from a habitual sense of the verb in the present or unmarked tense, as in *Yolanda talk too much,* or of a nonverbal predicate without a copula or any aspectual modifier, as in *Shell Shock always with his babe.* The latter constructions mean no more than habit, as repetition of bounded events or states, but their counterparts with invariant *be* mean repetition of unbounded processes or states, as in *Yolanda be talkin too much* and *Shell Shock always be with his babe,* in which the repeated states of affairs are presented as being in process. The following difference in grammaticality also sheds light on the semantic contrast between these alternative habitual constructions: *He don talk, because he's mute* versus **He don be talkin, because he's mute.* This difference explains why the following is not contradictory: *Nate stay here, but he be with his buddies on 47th Street,* meaning 'but you are more likely to find him with his buddies on 47th Street.'

Gullah has still another habitual marker, *does/duhz,* as in *How you duhz fix you hog maw?* 'How do you cook hog belly?' It corresponds to the regular English habitual in the simple present tense, although, because Gullah has a predominantly relative tense system (in which the axis of reference easily shifts from the present to any other relevant point of time in a discourse), *duhz* is also attested in past contexts. Unlike the habitual *be, duhz* seems to combine only with verbs. John Rickford (1974), who first noted it, reports it as falling out of use, although some middle-aged as well as older speakers used it in my field corpus of the 1980s.

AAE also has a past-habit marker *useta* (< *used to*). It occurs in Chicago in the reduced form *sta* (pronounced with schwa), as in *I'sta see that boy everywhere.* Labov (1972a, 56) observed that it "usually does not carry the tense marker" and probably functions as an adverb: *He useta was workin; She useta hadda pick at me;* and *My mother useta wanted me to be a doctor.* As these examples show, the verb following *useta* is in a past tense. *Useta* is more frequent among African-Americans than among whites, at a proportion of 15 percent of past habitual functions (Richardson 292).

Another aspectual marker is *steady,* used for persistence (J. Baugh 1983, 1984). It has a distribution similar to that of habitual *be* and may also combine with it: *Them fools steady hustlin everybody* 'The fools keep/kept hustling everybody'; *She steady with that s.o.b.* 'She [is/was] still with that s.o.b.'; and *Them fools be steady hustlin everybody* 'The fools [usually] keep hustling everybody.' Unless justified by the context, the interpretation of the first two examples is nonhabitual. In the last example, the habitual *be* may also follow *steady*: *Them fools steady be hustlin*, with no apparent change in meaning.

Some regional varieties of AAVE, especially in the American South, have an imminent future marker *fixin to*, contracted to *fi'na* (pronounced with a glottal stop before the /n/) at least in Georgia, as in *You fi'na use those dumb-bells?* 'Are you about to use those dumbbells?' It has been reported as *finta* from Akron, Ohio (by Charles DeBose in an unpublished work). *Fixing to* is used in American Southern English as a modal with a "core meaning" that "(1) indicates future action, (2) [before which] there will be a period of delay, though a relatively short one, and (3) [about which] the speaker feels a sense of urgency or high priority for the future action to be taken" (Ching 333). It often suggests that some preparatory or other ongoing activity is being completed before the one stated may be started. In the first person, it sug-gests that the speaker is determined to execute the action.

AAVE uses *come* as a modal verb that combines with verbs in the progres-sive to connote indignation or resentment (Spears 1982), as in *She come going in my room – didn't knock or nothing* 'She went in my room – didn't knock or any-thing.' The meaning of the modal *come* does not involve motion; this marker can combine with the verb *go*, as in the example, without contradiction.

8.2.2.4   Negation

Both Gullah and AAVE follow virtually the same principles regarding negation, with *ain(t)*, which has the greatest systemic distribution, as the wide-scope negator (associated with predicate phrases) and *no* as the narrow-scope negator (typically in noun phrases, Labov 1972a). When *not* functions as a narrow-scope negator, it is also emphatic, as in *not a/one soul*. *Ain(t)* combines with both verbal and nonverbal predicates, though it is interpreted differently, depending on whether the predicate is stative or nonstative. In nonstative constructions such as *Bill ain(t) come* 'Bill did not come' or 'Bill has not come,' it suggests past-time reference, whereas in stative constructions such as *Al ain(t) like Bill* 'Al is not like Bill' or 'Al does not like Bill,' present time is the most likely interpretation out of context. The past time interpretation is also possible in an appropriate context. Combinations of *ain(t)* with stative verbs are much more common in Gullah than in AAVE.

It is tempting to interpret AAE *ain(t)* in the same way as in colloquial English, especially because of its use with nonverbal and participial predi-cates, as in *Laura ain(t) fat* and *Joe ain(t) gone* and *Bill ain(t) comin*. However, this analysis is precluded by its combination with nonparticipial verbs, as in *Sara ain say nothin* 'Sara did not say anything' (more common in Gullah), which is also attested in at least some nonstandard British varieties (Cheshire).

In addition to *ain(t)*, AAE also uses *don(t)* to negate imperatives, as in *Don(t) say it*, and verb phrases with a habitual interpretation, as in *Jean don tell lies* and *Jean don be tellin lies* 'Jean does not tell lies.' In the right context, these habituative negative constructions may be interpreted as referring to past time, as alternatives of *ain useta* 'didn't used to.' An alternative in Gullah is *ain duhz/does*, with the same meaning as *don*.

In AAVE but not in Gullah, *not* may also be used as a wide-scope negator with nonverbal predicates or verbs in the progressive, as in *Larry not with Sharon* and *They not comin*. However, both varieties use contracted negative auxiliary verbs such as *hadn(t), didn(t), can't* (pronounced [kɛ̃] in Gullah), *won(t)*, and *wouldn(t)*. A peculiarity of AAVE is negative inversion, the optional use of wide-scope negators in sentence-initial position when the subject is indefinite, as in *Didn't nobody see him* 'Nobody saw him' and *Ain nobody talk to you* 'Nobody talked to you.' Inverted negative constructions with a definite subject, such as **Didn John come* 'John didn't come' or **Didn John tell me nothin* 'John didn't tell me anything,' are not well formed.

The etymological connection between negative inversion and contact relative clauses (those not introduced by a relative pronoun or a complementizer) is unclear. *Ain nobody talk to you* may be interpreted as 'There is nobody that talked to you' (Mufwene 1993). A sentence such as *Don't nobody break up a fight* (Labov 1972a, 187) might be interpreted by a hearer unfamiliar with AAVE as a negative imperative: 'Nobody break up a fight!,' a sense it may have in some contexts. It usually has, however, the nonimperative meaning 'Nobody breaks up a fight.'

Multiple negation is characteristic of AAE (Burling; Labov 1972a), as it is of many nonstandard varieties. Two or more negatives may cooccur, as in *I ain't never had no trouble with none of 'em* (Labov 1972a, 177). Among the unresolved questions are whether negative concord applies only rightward and whether the wide-scope negator *ain(t)* is alone responsible for the spread of negatives (Mufwene 1993) or others may trigger the construction.

8.2.2.5 Complex sentence formation

AAE is also distinctive in the way it forms complex sentences. In both Gullah and AAVE, *say* (typically pronounced [sɛ]), is used to introduce subordinate clauses that would be either reported as direct quotations or indirect quotations introduced by the complementizer *that* in acrolectal English: (a) *We tell Bill say Al sick* 'We told Bill, "Al is sick"' or 'We told Bill that Al was sick'; (b) *I think say Mary gone* 'I think that Mary has left'; and (c) *She aks me say where Mary gone* 'She asked me, "Where has Mary gone?"' or 'She asked me where Mary had gone.' In example (a), *say* may be analyzed as a serial verb; in (b), it seems more adequately interpreted as a complementizer; and in (c) either analysis is plausible (Mufwene 1989). *Say* and *that* alternate in some constructions in AAVE but not in Gullah. However, *say* as a complementizer cannot be equated with acrolectal English *that*. It does not introduce relative clauses in AAE. Subordinate constructions introduced by *say* after a higher predicate of saying, are often like direct quotations in that deictics are not reoriented, as in *I aks him say where you goin? He answer say it ain none of your business*. In long and lively narratives, especially in the AAVE genres known as "toasts" (§ 8.2.4), *say* is often the only element marking a change of speakers (Dance cites examples).

Gullah has distinctive patterns for complex sentences (Cunningham; Mufwene 1989; P. Nichols 1975, 1976). It uses *fuh* (< *for*) to introduce subordinate clauses that acrolectal and other varieties of American English introduce with *(for ..) to* or *in order (for ..) to*: (a) *Uh tell um fuh pay me me money* 'I told him to pay me my money'; (b) *He wan (fuh) uh pay um he money* 'He wants me to pay him his money'; (c) *Uh call um fuh come kyah me ta d'hospital* 'I called him (in order for him) to take me to the hospital.' *Fuh* may be omitted, especially after the verbs *wan* and *try*, as in example (b), when its sense is not purposive. As in the case of *say*, it is difficult to assign a single grammatical interpretation to all the above uses of *fuh*.

AAVE is more like other varieties of American English with respect to constructions with *fuh* and serial verbs. It shares with Gullah such serial verb constructions as *I aks him say . . .* and *Come play with us*, in which two verb phrases are sequenced without an intervening conjunction or complementizer. However, Gullah is more like Caribbean English creoles in allowing serial verb constructions such as *Uh run go home* 'I ran home' and *Uh tuhn look up fuh heh* 'I turned [and] looked up for her' (Mufwene 1990b).

On the other hand, AAVE and Gullah are alike in the way they form relative clauses (Cunningham; Mufwene 1986a; R. Smith). They allow an invariant relativizer: *weh* in Gullah and *what* in both, as in *the man what/weh come here with you*. They both also allow contact relative clauses where acrolectal English does not, as in *The man come here yesterday take sick* 'The man who came here yesterday took sick.' Unlike AAVE, however, Gullah does not have relative clauses introduced by *that*, at least not in available texts (L. Turner 1949).

8.2.2.6 Other grammatical features

Other noteworthy features are the following:

(1) Indirect questions in AAVE: According to Burling, indirect *yes/no* questions are often marked by subject-auxiliary inversion, as in *Ask him can you do it?* 'Ask him if you can do it.' This is interesting especially because the subject-auxiliary inversion rule often does not apply in main questions, as in *Why you don't like him?* 'Why don't you like him?'

(2) The pronominal system in Gullah: The pronoun *he* is not necessarily masculine; it can have a feminine referent, although *she* is also often used in this function. The third person objective pronoun *um* is likewise gender-unspecified, as in *Uh like um* 'I like him/her.' The pronouns *you, he, she, we,* and *they* maintain the same form in the possessive function, as in *he/she/we mother* 'his/her/our mother.' (Cunningham, Jones-Jackson 1978, 1986, 1987, Mufwene 1992a, and P. Nichols 1976 have more detailed discussion.)

(3) Predicate clefting in Gullah: The predicate is sometimes clefted in emphatic constructions, as in *duh **talk** he duh talk to dat chile* 'he was **really talking** to that child' (Mufwene 1987a).

(4) Double modals: In both Gullah and AAVE, modal verbs often combine directly with each other as in *I thought they might would give me something to eat* (Butters 1991a).

AAE has not been exhaustively investigated. There may be still other syntactic features that differentiate it from standard English or other dialects. Features that have been unstudied or little studied include adverbs and adverbials, expletives, gapping, particle shift, and dative movement.

8.2.3 Semantic features

The semantics of AAE other than time reference has been little studied (but see Dillard 1977, Major, Smitherman 1977, 1994, 1998). The works by Clarence Major and Geneva Smitherman (1994) are primarily dictionaries, though the latter contains an introduction treating cultural and linguistic matters. Smitherman (1977) first considers terms used since Colonial days to refer to African-Americans and the preferences African-Americans themselves have had among those terms. She then turns to terms used by African-Americans for addressing each other, for acknowledging messages during speech events (especially in church), for identifying physical characteristics and behaviors, for referring to personalities, and so on. Smitherman defines what she calls "Black semantics" as the "Black Americans' long-standing tendency to appropriate English for themselves and their purposes" (58). She discusses words that "have potentially two levels of meaning, one black one white" (59), such as *bad* in *He is a bad dude*, which may be interpreted either negatively for 'a person of undesirable character' or positively for 'a person of highly desirable character.'

Other such terms are *(bad) nigger, clean, cool, hang,* and *attitude.* Thus, irony and sarcasm aside, a statement such as *You look clean, maam* may be interpreted either as an observation that the addressee is literally clean, contrary to her usual appearance, or as a compliment for the addressee's being sharply dressed. Marcyliena Morgan (1989, 1993) uses the term "counterlanguage" for such terms with double entendre, one of whose interpretations is not accessible to outsiders. Both she and Smitherman trace the practice back to slavery, when the intention was to disguise some intended meanings from white masters. Some terms such as *hip* in the sense 'up-to-date on a trend' and *cool* 'acceptable,' which started from AAE, have become part of general, colloquial American English (Dillard 1977). American English has been influenced by African-American speech (Smitherman 1994).

"Counterlanguage" falls into the broader category of "camouflaged" constructions (Spears 1982). Striking examples are from AAE slang. The term *train* in the meaning of 'group rape' has various metaphorical extensions: *train (a victim), (aggressors) get on a train, run a/the train on (a victim), (a victim) goes through a train.* The verb *front* is used intransitively for 'to pretend (something not yet experienced).' *To sneak* means 'to attack (someone) off guard' and *to double-bank* is 'to gang up on (someone).' Familiar idioms such as *give (someone) some sugar* 'kiss' and *give me five* 'slap my hand(s) in greeting' are learned at a very early age. The terms *brother* and *reputation* are commonly used in their abbreviated forms *bro* and *rep.* A corollary of the latter is *to dis,* from *to disrespect,* which is frequently in the progressive form *dissin.*

A concomitant of the peculiar semantics of these terms is their morphosyntax in both the vernacular and slang. Whereas the noun *pimp* denotes, among other things, 'a man who lives off the earnings of a prostitute,' the verb *pimp* denotes 'to dress and walk like a pimp' (the walk called *pimp strut*), as well as 'to exploit someone or something.' The adjective *bad* in the positive sense forms its comparative as *badder* and its superlative as *baddest,* unlike the negative sense, expressed by *worse* and *worst.* Other semantic aspects of AAE grammar are treated above (§ 8.2.2).

8.2.4 Pragmatic features

The most commonly discussed pragmatic aspects of AAE, almost exclusively of AAVE, pertain to its various speech styles and discourse genres.

Most of the examples in the literature come from street language and may unfortunately have helped to foster the misconception that all AAE is vulgar. Those examples reflect the settings and subcultures they have been taken from. In reality, a continuum of styles runs from the serious to play talk (Kochman; Smitherman 1977). Serious talk typically focuses on content, whereas play talk focuses on form and is exhibitionist. Despite this generalization, dexterous serious talk often incorporates some of the skills developed in play talk. It may also contain "dirty language," which is offensive outside the setting of street culture.

AAE has terms for its various speech styles and genres, but none for the basic vernacular itself as used at home. As noted earlier, terms for AAE have typically come from outside the community. There is no term for the unmarked, basic style of communication. Speakers may embellish their speech with wit and humor, especially when the intent is manipulative (as in courtship), for instance in the style called "rappin(g)." It is part of "smart talk," which is meant to impress primarily the addressee and not necessarily any witnesses. It may turn into what is called "signifyin(g)," negative talk intended to "put down" the opponent or a third party, or simply to make a point. This style is particularly indirect, circumlocutory, metaphorical with images from common life, humorous, ironic, fluent, rhythmic, and "teachy but not preachy" (M. Morgan 1989, 1993; Smitherman 1977, 121).

On the other hand, people may just be "honing" or "talking shit" when the main purpose of the interaction seems to be developing verbal dexterity and command of idiomatic ritual formulae and witty speech. Such skills, which may be exploited in serious talk, are highly rated and important for establishing one's "rep" (positive reputation) among peers during youth; they are developed through practice.

One of the best known and, for outsiders, perhaps one of the most shocking kinds of play talk is "playing the dozens" or "sounding." The participants exchange fictional insults about their opponent's female close kin, such as mother, sister, or spouse, and they try to "chop," "cut," or "woof" (outdo) each other with funnier and wittier derisive comments. The game usually involves witnesses, and victory is determined by one of the participants running out of retorts or by the amount of excitement created. The witnesses are usually also quick at stopping the game if it should take a dangerous turn, for instance, if one of the participants resorted to truth in the insults. The language is typically from the streets. On the South Carolina and Georgia Sea Islands, where the game is often played in mesolectal speech by males, not necessarily adolescents, it is either terminated or suspended once women join the gathering. Extensive examples of the game in AAVE have been reported by Burling, Kochman, and Labov (1972a).

Related in its kind of language to sounding is the long narrative or "tall tale" also called "toast." It is a street epic celebrating urban folk heroes or tricksters, generally the weaker, the oppressed, the exploited, or the criminal, at the expense of the powerful, the oppressor, the exploiter, and the law enforcer. It shows how the "baddest dudes," the street-wise, triumph. Examples are given by Burling and more extensively by Dance. This oral literary genre has made its way into the entertainment industry directed primarily to an African-American audience, in which the same stories, such as "The Signifying Monkey" or "Shine," have been retold in various versions. Toasts involving animal tricksters transform animal tales into street epics. Animal tales are most common in Gullah (C. Jones; Stoddard) and are traditionally told at home in the basic vernacular.

Another style is the preacher "talk-singing" style (Smitherman 1977). It shares with some of the above styles the features of wit, fancy talk, indirectness, imagery and metaphors, and even signifying. As the name suggests, the form is partly sung. It is, however, debatable whether it is always in the vernacular. Depending on the level of education and the degree of rhetorical skill of the minister, features associated with AAE may or may not occur in the sermon. As with much other African-American speech, the preacher's style is a matter of degree, and reports of it depend on what feature a researcher considers significant. The same observation about degrees of approximation to the vernacular can be made about the lyrics of rap music, which may or may not contain several of the structural features typically associated with AAVE in the academic literature. The preacher's delivery style is, however, unique and consistently alike in virtually all African-American churches.

In the domain of discourse and style, as in the case of structural features of AAE, most studies have been limited to male speech (M. Morgan 1994). Consequently little is known about female speech.

8.3   The development of AAE

Accounts of the development of AAE have been controversial since the earliest speculations on the subject matter at the beginning of the twentieth century. They reflect general social attitudes toward African-Americans, either by expressing those attitudes or disputing them. The earliest influential account is that of Ambrose Gonzales, which appears in the introduction to his collection of Gullah short stories, *The Black Border*, which is more accessible than the technical literature. Gullah is character-ized as the worst variety of English spoken anywhere because of the alleged inability of its speakers to acquire native English, a failing he attrib-utes to their "fat lips" and "clumsy tongues."

The stereotypes expressed by Gonzales perpetuated an attitude previ-ously stated by John Bennett, who, while reasonably attributing the origin of several lexical and morphosyntactic features of Gullah to British non-standard English (Scotch, Scotch-Irish, Irish, and southwest England English), also associated its prosodic features with the "intellectual indo-lence, or laziness, physical and mental" of its speakers (1909, 40). He pre-sented Gullah as "the natural result of a savage and primitive people's endeavor to acquire for themselves the highly organized language of a very highly civilized race" (1908, 338). This view was inherited from the nine-teenth century, when European linguists such as Lucien Adam, Charles Baissac, and Julien Vinson (1882, 1888) assumed that black Africans were simply inadequately equipped mentally and physiologically to acquire the "fine Indo-European morphology" and the "delicate articulation of French phonetics" (Baissac, my translation).

It is to this background of misconceptions that scholars such as Krapp (1924), Kurath (1928b), G. Johnson, and Crum reacted in stating that "the Negro speaks English of the same kind and, class for class, of the same degree as the English of the most authentic descendants of the first settlers at Jamestown and Plymouth" (Krapp 1924, 190). The gist of their position is that several phonological and morphosyntactic features of AAE may be traced to the vernaculars spoken by the English colonists in North America in the seventeenth and eighteenth centuries. To be sure, the various Colonial English sources were not all equally influential on every variety of early AAE nor has their influence been equally preserved in present-day AAE. That is, today's varieties of AAE represent an unprecedented re-formation of the features into a new system, dictating some necessary adjustments. However, the English origin of the structural features cannot be denied any more than the role of some African linguistic systems in favoring their selection over other competing alternatives (Mufwene 1992d, 1995, 1996), as neither Colonial English nor the African systems represented in North America were homogeneous.

On the other hand, Krapp also started an incorrect stereotype of the African-American as contributing nothing significant to the American melting pot: "The Negroes, indeed, in acquiring English have done their work so thoroughly that they have retained not a trace of any African speech. Neither have they transferred anything of importance from their native tongues to the general language" (1924, 190). This exaggeration led Lorenzo Dow Turner to react in 1949 with an alternative account that supporters of the African substrate hypothesis unfortunately interpreted in its strongest form. Highlighting several phonological and morphological similarities between Gullah and diverse African languages and presenting in about two-thirds of the book a 4,000-item inventory of African words and phrases in Gullah (3,600 of which are proper names), Turner concludes that the "dialect," as he called it, "is indebted to African sources" (254). Turner's statement does not preclude English influence beyond the vocabulary, nor does it claim that African linguistic influence was primary.

Among Atlantic creolist followers of Turner, his position has generally been interpreted as echoing Sylvain's observation that Haitian Creole is Ewe spoken with French words. Turner's work should have been interpreted simply as documenting diverse African influences in Gullah, which should inspire a more eclectic approach to the history of AAE. However, Turner's followers have assumed that much of Gullah's system is essentially African, despite its predominant English vocabulary (98 percent according to Cassidy 1983). Their interpretation of Turner's *Africanisms* has remained controversial, as reflected in critiques and defenses following its publication, as well as more recently (Holloway and Vass), and also in subsequent literature on the genesis of creoles, in which Turner is often cited.

Similarities between Gullah and AAVE (§ 8.2 above) led J. L. Dillard (1972) and William Stewart (1967, 1968, 1974) to hypothesize that AAVE must have started as a Gullah-like creole once widely spoken in the plantation states of North America. A process of decreolization putatively changed AAVE into a resemblance of American acrolectal English. Krapp (1924) had noted similarities between AAE and English pidgins around the world; but he was reluctant to recognize the African linguistic contributions claimed by Stewart and Dillard. The latter may have been encouraged by Beryl Bailey (1965), who pointed out similarities between AAVE and Caribbean English creoles and suggested at least a typological kinship between these varieties. However, no detailed analyses of Gullah's structure either validate the suggested comparison or support the conclusions of Stewart and Dillard.

Ironically, history suggests that AAVE must have started earlier, instead of later, than Gullah, as the colonization of South Carolina in 1670 follows, by fifty-one years, the first importation of African slaves into Virginia in 1619. Slavery in Virginia was soon extended to several northeastern states, although the African presence in the early American North was never as significant as that on the plantations of the Southeast. In the late nineteenth and early twentieth centuries, however, migration from the Southeast increased dramatically the African-American presence in the North, as elsewhere.

The history of the peopling of colonies such as South Carolina and Georgia also suggests that the basilects must have developed later than the mesolects, thus casting doubt on the Stewart and Dillard account of the origin of AAVE. Similarities such as observed by Dillard between AAE and sixteenth-century (more likely seventeenth-century) West African Pidgin English can be interpreted in several ways, the least likely of which is the version of monogenesis advocated.

The creole-origin hypothesis for AAVE has received support of one kind or another from several studies (J. Baugh 1983; Fasold 1976; Holm 1984; Rickford 1977; Winford 1990, 1992). However, it has been strongly disputed by dialectologists in the tradition of George Krapp and Hans Kurath (D'Eloia; Schneider 1982, 1983, 1989), though Edgar Schneider (1993) makes some concessions for African substrate influence. The latter scholars have pointed out that many of the morphemes and morphosyntactic patterns associated with creoles, such as the perfect construction with *done* and *ain(t)* as a general negator, are well attested in British folk speech. They therefore argue that AAVE's sharing features with particular Atlantic creoles does not entail its development from an erstwhile creole. Schneider (1990) joins Holm (1988, 1989, 1991) in calling AAVE a "semi-creole," suggesting that it did not undergo the full restructuring that results in creole varieties. A problem with this position is the assumption that creolization can be measured structurally (Mufwene 1986c).

Refuting the creole-origin hypothesis for AAVE requires a different kind of argument. The fact that British folk speech has lexified both the creoles and AAVE does not require direct influence from British nonstandard English on AAVE, though such influence must have been the case. Several facts could suggest that AAVE developed from a creole, if one did not take all the historical data into account. Such facts include the initial settling of South Carolina by colonists and slaves from Barbados and the importation of the first Georgia slaves from South Carolina, with the much later African-American migrations from the Southeast, both northward and westward between 1890 and World War II.

An important point is that the formation of creoles or of varieties like AAVE does not exclude grammatical influence by their lexifiers. Creoles have too often been described as though their development involved no structural contribution from their lexifiers. Another point is that, despite the Caribbean–North American historical connection, North American language varieties developed independently, even if they were somewhat influenced from the Caribbean. Assuming it makes sense to determine creolization by structure alone, it is possible that AAVE never started as a Gullah-like creole, despite the role of the coastal areas in the development of the American Southeast.

To resolve the creolist-dialectologist debate, what is needed is convincing historical information regarding different kinds of plantations, their settlement history, and the patterns of Anglo-African interaction on them. Although history argues against the creole-origin hypothesis, the literature against it has done a poor job in attempting to refute it. The main exception to this observation is the collection of essays edited by Shana Poplack.

In the meantime, quantitative sociolinguists have focused on accounting for similarities between AAVE and white nonstandard varieties of American English. While conceding that AAVE may have started as a creole, Fasold (1976, 1981) and Labov (1972a, 1982) also argue that its present grammar is essentially English – the normal outcome of the decreolization hypothesis. Labov (1982, 192) states the following position as a consensus:

1. The Black English Vernacular is a subsystem of English with a distinct set of phonological and syntactic rules that are now aligned in many ways with rules of other dialects.
2. It incorporates many features of Southern phonology, morphology, and syntax; blacks in turn have exerted influence on the dialects of the South where they have lived.
3. It shows evidence of derivation from an earlier Creole that was closer to the present-day Creoles of the Caribbean.
4. It has a highly developed aspect system, quite different from other dialects of English, which shows a continuing development of its semantic structure.

Part of the above position has been endorsed by Fasold, as evidenced by the following:

> Accepting Labov's analysis of the modern dialect is not tantamount to a denial of the creole origin hypothesis, but simply to recognize that Vernacular Black English has reached a late post-creole stage. [1976, 79]

> Decreolization . . . seems to have progressed so far as to have obliterated most of the original creole features. [1981, 164]

> Even those who believe that vernacular Black English (VBE) is a separate language from English would be forced to admit that many of its features are the same as those found in English. [1981, 166]

With regard to the statement above referring to decreolization, if a creole is not defined structurally and the term is used historically for a language variety formed by a specific kind of contact between several languages, then there must be something wrong with speaking of decreolization. The beginnings of a language variety do not change even if some of its structural features change over time. As shown below, this is still a misunderstood aspect of the histories of creole language varieties.

On the other hand, Wolfram meticulously highlights both similarities and differences between AAVE and white nonstandard English. He suggests that some of the features of white Southern English, such as the occasional omission of *is*, but not *are*, "may have been assimilated from decreolizing black speech" (1991 reprint, 93). That is, while he accepts the decreolization hypothesis, he also believes in the influence of AAE on the speech of whites who have interacted regularly with African-Americans, especially in the rural South. As in most of the literature on decreolization, no diachronic evidence is adduced to support this diachronic claim.

AAVE and rural white nonstandard varieties such as Appalachian and Ozark English are similar in several ways, especially in their aspectual systems (Christian, Wolfram, and Dube). However, speakers of these white and African-American varieties with common features have not been in regular contact with each other. Thus the question arises of whether it is necessary to assume influence between AAVE and white nonstandard English in the first place. After all, they developed concurrently, following more or less the same language contact equation with, of course, the values of the variables differing from one subcommunity to another (Mufwene 1996).

As suggested above, the decreolization hypothesis itself is problematic. Claims that Gullah has been decreolizing are disputable, for it is likely that Gullah has not changed any more than have other varieties of American English over the past century (Mufwene 1986b, 1987b, 1991a, 1991b, 1994a). The Ambrose Gonzales texts, which have been cited as evidence of the decreolization of Gullah, are not uniform; the earlier texts are closer to today's Gullah than are the later texts. Gonzales may have responded to a public interest in a language variety that the introduction to *The Black Border* calls "quaint," thus making his later texts more basilectal (Mille).

Moreover, AAVE need not be related to a Gullah-like ancestor but may simply have resulted from a less extensive restructuring than that which produced Gullah. This position was termed "half-creolization," but that is an unfortunate term because creolization is best defined sociohistorically, not structurally (Mufwene 1997b). Hence, once the relevant sociohistorical conditions are met, no language variety is less creole than another, regardless of the extent of its restructuring. That is, once the new contact-based variety, appropriated by nonnative speakers and their descendants, functions as their vernacular and has developed its own norms, it can be identified as a creole, regardless of the extent of divergence from the lexifier. This position still recognizes the typological kinship between Atlantic (English) creoles and AAVE, as noted by Beryl Bailey (1965), without assuming a mother-to-daughter relation between them.

Quantitative sociolinguists have also disagreed about the creole ancestry of AAVE. For instance, after comparing AAVE with Samaná English, a variety used in the Spanish-speaking Dominican Republic by African-Americans who sailed from Philadelphia in the 1820s, Poplack and Sankoff and Tagliamonte and Poplack (1988) conclude that the two varieties are still very similar, though a few nonstandard variables appear to be used less frequently in Samaná English. They find Samaná English less close to Caribbean English creoles than it is to AAVE. Their position is at variance with that of DeBose (1983), who finds Samaná English archaic compared to AAVE and assumes that the latter is decreolizing. On the other hand, Rickford and Blake show that the Samaná pattern differs only from Caribbean basilectal creole not from mesolectal patterns. This correction, well supported by Winford's findings (1992, 1993), does not, however, necessarily invalidate Poplack and Sankoff's and Tagliamonte and Poplack's conclusion.

Poplack and Sankoff conclude that AAVE has not decreolized, at least not since the nineteenth century, a hypothesis corroborated by Poplack and Tagliamonte (1991, 1994), who focus on an offshoot of the African-American population in Nova Scotia. Tagliamonte and Poplack (1993) maintain the same conclusion, having extended their diachronic comparison to Ex-Slave Recordings collected in the 1930s by the Work Projects Administration from former slaves born in the mid nineteenth century. They agree with Schneider (1989, 274), who observes that the Ex-Slave Narratives which he studied "do not support the view that modern Black English is the product of a massive decreolization process."

Much of Liberian Settler English (LSE), another offshoot of nineteenth-century AAE, is more creole-like than AAVE (Singler 1991a, 1991b). However, the diachronic evidence, even from LSE alone, is conflicting and "calls into question the use of this metric in the evaluation of the creole-origin hypothesis" of AAVE (Singler 1991a, 157). While Singler (1991b, 268) notes that "the difference between LSE and the ex-slave speech would reflect the ongoing influence – in the late nineteenth and early twentieth centuries – of non-black speech upon A[merican] B[lack] E[nglish]," his (1991a) discussion emphasizes heterogeneity within LSE, which may certainly be traced back to nineteenth-century AAE itself and is consistent with what the socioeconomic history of North America suggests must have been the case. There is no reason to assume that AAE was ever a homogeneous variety of either basilectal Gullah or basilectal AAVE.

The history of other vernaculars suggests that AAE formed its present basilects by merging and consolidating a number of earlier basilectal varieties (Chaudenson; Mufwene 1994a), a process that must have still been going on in the nineteenth century, as competing variants were selected or eliminated in different subcommunities. LSE varieties must have undergone their own developments, just like AAE varieties.

The diachronic evidence has not been as unequivocal as supporters of the creole-origin hypothesis for AAVE have assumed. Questions arise, for instance, regarding the particular sections of the African-American population that left the United States for these other territories. Were the populations that emigrated to Liberia, the Dominican Republic, and Nova Scotia the same in, for instance, their proportions of basilectal and mesolectal speakers? Were the same kinds of competing structural features used by all three founder populations of emigrants? What selective mechanisms and ecological-ethnographic factors in the new settlements affected the data collected from today's descendants of speakers of these offshoot varieties, which were used for comparison with AAVE?

An alternative theory is of a "creole connection," different from the decreolization thesis, according to which AAVE "arose through a process of language shift toward English dialects by speakers of a creole-like variety" (Winford 1993, 348). Further, "the hypothesis of a rapid shift resulting from a close approximation of the target dialects *with significant retention of creole features* seems to explain the emergence of early [AAVE] more satisfactorily than the traditional view that early [AAVE] was itself a creole" (351, emphasis added). This encouraging change of position also affects the debate on the creole-origin or creole-connection hypothesis. Although there were speakers of English creoles among those who developed AAVE, there is no reason for privileging creole contributions to the structure of AAVE over others. The distribution of the copula in AAVE has been attributed to creole influence (J. Baugh 1980, 101), but it may just as well be due to direct African substrate influence instead (Holm 1984, 301).

Debate on the origin of AAVE should recognize that the development of creoles and other contact-based varieties involves a remolding of features, often from diverse dialects or languages, into a new system that is not necessarily monolithic, but allows structural alternatives for more or less the same functions. The similarities between AAVE and Caribbean English creole mesolects are not necessarily evidence for a contribution from those creoles to the AAVE system. They may instead be similar developments in similar contact and ethnographic settings. The structural similarities among varieties of English spoken by descendants of African slaves in the New World are not themselves diachronic evidence to establish later connections between AAE and other varieties or to measure change in AAVE. Next to their basilectal counterparts, the Caribbean mesolectal creole data show that basilectalization (the development of a consolidated basilect) in continental North America did not proceed as far as it did in the Caribbean.

Since DeCamp (1971), it has generally been assumed that the abolition of slavery brought about social integration, socioeconomic mobility, and easier access to public education and the media. These social conditions would putatively have produced decreolization by the loss of basilectal features especially in Gullah and thus led to the development of today's AAVE. However, the Civil Rights movement of the 1960s is evidence that these conditions were not well in place until this late in American history. The Jim Crow laws (passed in 1877) fostered segregated lifestyles that naturally led whites and African-Americans to develop separate, though related, ethnolinguistic identities. The extensive structural similarities noted today between AAE and white Southern English are simply a legacy of the more intimate interactions between blacks and whites for about two centuries before the Jim Crow laws. As argued by Mufwene (1991b, 1994c), there is no evidence that Gullah has been decreolizing (in the sense of losing its basilect) since the abolition of slavery. Decreolization, which would have been more obvious after the Civil Rights movement, is brought further into question now by arguments about the "divergence" of African-American and white vernaculars by quantitative sociolinguists themselves (G. Bailey and Maynor 1987; Butters 1987; Labov and Harris). This does not amount to denying internal developments within AAE, which would have continued to select features from among competing alternatives, a process going on since the seventeenth century.

Claims of increasing divergence between AAE and white English amount to no more than noticing independent developments in these varieties, with occasional mutual influences (Denning; Myhill 1988). In fact, Labov (Butters 1987, 10) confirms this interpretation when he observes that "the more contact blacks have with whites, the more they move away from the vernacular side, and the more contact whites have with blacks, the more we observe borrowings of black forms." This suggests that authentic white and African-American varieties are preserved by those who are under no pressure to switch to another variety. Therefore no change of the kind suggested by claims of decreolization as affecting the structure of AAE in the overall African-American community is taking place, as may be noticed from some discussions of the divergence hypothesis summarized below.

At the center of the debate over whether or not AAVE is diverging from white American vernaculars have been studies by William Labov and also Guy Bailey. A comparison of invariant *be* used by senior African-Americans in their seventies and by twelve- and thirteen-year old children in the Brazos valley, Texas, shows that the teenagers use the feature three times more frequently, especially with a verb in the progressive (G. Bailey and Maynor 1987). Previous studies were on the absence of the present tense agreement marker, of the possessive marker, and of the copula, the form of negation, a lack of liaison of the indefinite article with the follow-ing word (as in *a apple*), the monophthongization of /ay/ (as in *my* [ma:] *book*), and the nasalization of vowels before word-final *n* as in *man* (Labov and Harris; other studies summarized by Labov in Butters 1987). They noted that the nonstandard forms are generally more common among African-Americans who interact little with whites and are at a higher fre-quency than in previous studies of the 1960s and 1970s. All these studies conclude that AAE has been diverging from white vernaculars, particularly because of "increasing residential and economic segregation from the rest of the [American] community" (Labov in Butters 1987, 6), which has affected a large segment of African-Americans.

Although the socioeconomic factors cited in support of divergence are facts, the conclusion itself has been disputed by other investigators (Butters 1987, 1991b), who argue that the limited number of features covered by these studies do not justify the general conclusion and point to several other features that may be interpreted as suggesting convergence. The conclusion may be premature, since very few features of AAE have been identified to date. As a matter of fact, most of the AAE scholarship has focused on the same features and has been criticized (Vaughn-Cooke in Butters 1987, 15) for violating the "critical time depth principle," according to which "two successive generations of speakers . . . of comparable social characteristics" must be identified to represent stages in the evolution of the same speech community (Labov 1972b, 169). Intra-community varia-tion among speakers implies other social reasons for the higher frequency of nonstandard features among teenagers, namely that they "are less assim-ilationist than their parents and especially their grandparents, and more assertive about their rights to talk and act in their 'natural way'" (Rickford 1992, 190; Rickford et al. 119).

The same questions raised about decreolization can be asked about the divergence hypothesis. For instance, there is lack of diachronic evidence for a diachronic conclusion. There has always been variation within the community; so the attrition (not necessarily disappearance) of some of the variants does not amount automatically to systemic change. Since, according to Labov himself, the putative divergence is attested among African-Americans interacting only minimally with whites, that is, the majority, what has been interpreted as convergence amounts to language shift (characterized by various degrees of success), whereas what has been identified as divergence amounts to independent language development.

There is more consensus on AAE as a continuum of English vernaculars spoken by African-Americans and on what features are typical of them than on how they developed. Aside from the scant diachronic evidence, some working assumptions have negatively affected research on the development of AAE. For instance, there is no historical justification for assuming that there was ever a time in the seventeenth or eighteenth century when every African-American spoke the basilect of a Gullah-like variety. Nor is there any particular justification for assuming that AAVE must have developed from a Gullah-like variety and that its speakers must have aimed at speaking like whites. The fact that some African-Americans speak like other middle-class Americans may be tantamount to language shift. The assumption that all speakers of the same language variety use the same monolithic system begs the question. Do we have to stick to Meillet's (1906) slogan that "la langue est un système où tout se tient"? Why cannot a language have drawn materials for its system from diverse languages? What really counts as decreolization and evidence of it?

8.4   Benefits of studying AAE

Although several issues remain unresolved, the benefits from studying AAE undoubtedly outweigh the shortcomings of the studies noted above (§ 8.3). The most tangible contribution of this research to linguistics at large is certainly variation analysis, also known as quantitative (socio)linguistics. Labovianists have been criticized for neglecting the "socio-" part of "sociolinguistics" in that they have not focused on classic sociological correlates of language variation, such as age, gender, and social class (Milroy 1991). However, variationists have successfully shed light on the heterogeneity of language as a communal institution and on the fact that variation is constrained by structural factors. Although they have focused more on differences between speech communities, it is just a matter of time before they pay more attention to inter-individual variation and raise interesting questions on what is meant by "language" and "language or speech community" (Mufwene 1992c, 1994b).

Even so, studies of AAE have raised interesting questions on the nature and role of idealization in linguistic research, for instance, the extent to which introspective data may be considered representative of the language or dialect a scholar speaks. Advocating the "principle of accountability," Labov (1972b) and his associates (such as Rickford 1986b) have exhorted linguists to produce descriptions that represent all alternate forms and constructions used for the same function and to provide distributional information (including statistics) on their use. They have also sharpened field techniques for collecting natural, spontaneous speech data that are representative of the community. Outside sociolinguistics proper, theoretical linguistics has not yet benefited significantly from these developments; the benefits lie rather in the potential to learn from these field techniques and to construe community-based grammars that reflect inter- and intra-individual variation.

Another benefit from studies of AAE is that more interest has been aroused in white nonstandard varieties. This is significant for several reasons: (1) they deserve as much to be understood as standard English; (2) they hold key information to resolving part of the controversy on the development of AAE; (3) they are likely to shed light on the kinds of English spoken by colonists from the British Isles who settled in different parts of North America. In fact, some of the tough questions being addressed about the genesis of AAE could apply to standard American English itself. It would be rewarding to know the mechanics of the complex processes by which it and standard British English have differentiated.

Finally, works by several students of AAE have highlighted the practical role that awareness of the linguistic systems of the underprivileged can play toward schooling their children more successfully. It is very useful for teachers to know how their students communicate in order to teach them standard English more effectively.

8.5   Future studies of AAE

The earliest studies of AAE were on its origin, before scholars had even developed some adequate knowledge of its structures. In recent years, most studies have been in the quantitative (socio)linguistic framework, focusing chiefly on the distribution of variable features and structural factors constraining them. With few exceptions, studying AAE has become tantamount to doing quantitative analysis highlighting differences between white and African-American speech patterns. While all these developments are positive, they remain partial.

Some prerequisites to sound quantitative analysis must be met. For instance, whether or not two linguistic features may be treated as variants of one another (for example, preverbal *done* and *have* as markers of the perfect, or the unmarked verb and the verbal suffix *-ed* referring to past time) must be determined by some traditional sort of descriptive work that legitimizes their status as variants. Although a few quantitative analyses include such descriptive preliminaries, others do not. Overall, more adequate descriptions also aimed at identifying AAE variables are needed (such as L. Green 1992). The same analytical techniques and theoretical assumptions apply to the study of AAE as to other language varieties. Just as the study of AAE has contributed to the development of sociolinguistics, it may also benefit from advances in theoretical linguistics.

AAE has been studied mainly in the extent to which its structural features deviate from those of acrolectal English. Although comparison with acrolectal English and other nonstandard varieties may be enlightening, AAE needs to be studied in the same way languages such as Kiswahili or Japanese are investigated as autonomous systems. Comparison with other systems is warranted for scholars interested in language typology and universals, but such comparisons should follow descriptions of features of AAE that make their genetic ties with English interesting and probably useful, but not necessary, to consider (Mufwene et al.).

Despite the increasing recognition that a variety close to basilectal AAE is spoken by various segments of the African-American population, most studies have been based on the speech of male adolescents. Studies such as those by Mitchell-Kernan and M. Morgan (1989, 1991, 1993), which deal with adult females, and Goodwin, which covers male and female children, are exceptions to the rule. More research in these directions and on all aspects of African-American language should be encouraged. Such research should become easier as more African-American linguists develop an interest in AAE and can observe its speakers uninhibitedly using the range of its varieties. They can draw on insider knowledge of the cultural dynamics of the African-American community to shed light on aspects of AAE that remain elusive to outsiders.

The involvement of such linguists in research on AAE should make it easier to observe, for instance, variation in lects among African-Americans.

At present it is difficult to determine which speech styles or discourse genres are influenced by gender, age group, or gang membership. For instance, how do African-American women participate in discourse genres such as "toasts" and "the dozens"? Much remains to be learned regarding lect and style differentiation. Unfortunately scholarship has fostered a false linguistic stereotype of the African-American community based on gang language, suggesting, for instance, that AAE is typically vulgar (Tolliver-Weddington 1979, 364). The response of many African-Americans to language "vulgarity" is evidenced by phrases such as *hush yoh mouth*.

The interest that some scholars have taken in language acquisition among African-American children (Stockman 1986; Stockman and Vaughn-Cooke 1982; and Wyatt 1991) will not only enrich our knowledge of child language acquisition but also shed light on other current issues. As research into AAE increases, we are likely to learn more about all varieties of English and about language in general from several perspectives: structural, sociolinguistic, ethnographic, and psycholinguistic.

FURTHER READING

For a more extensive survey of topics and issues on AAVE, see *African-American English: Structure, History, and Use*, ed. Salikoko S. Mufwene, John R. Rickford, Guy Bailey, and John Baugh (1998); *Spoken Soul: The Story of Black English*, by John Russell Rickford and Russell John Rickford (2000); and *Sociocultural and Historical Contexts of African-American Vernacular English*, ed. Sonja L. Lanehart (2000). A useful reference on the development of AAVE is *The English History of African-American English*, ed. Shana Poplack (1999). Geneva Smitherman's *Talkin That Talk: Language, Culture, and Education in African America* (2000) is informative on semantic and cultural aspects of AAVE, as well as on issues associated with it in education. In the latter respect, *Beyond Ebonics: Linguistic Pride and Racial Prejudice* by John Baugh (2000) and *The Real Ebonics Debate: Power, Language, and the Education of African-American Children*, ed. Theresa Perry and Lisa Delpit (1998) are useful complements. Regarding Gullah, Lorenzo Dow Turner's *Africanisms in the Gullah Dialect* (1949) is a seminal source. Such earlier references as *Language in the Inner City* and *Sociolinguistic Patterns* by William Labov (1972) and *Black English: Its History and Usage in the United States* by J. L. Dillard (1972) anchor some of the present issues.

9 GRAMMATICAL STRUCTURE

Ronald R. Butters

9.1 Grammatical categories

The term grammar in this chapter includes both what linguists call inflectional morphology and what they call syntax.

Morphology describes the rules that govern the minimal meaningful units of a language, called morphemes, and the way those minimal units are combined to make words. For example, English noun morphemes (e.g., *dog*) permit various suffix morphemes – called inflections – to be appended to indicate plurality (*dogs*), possession (spelled *dog's* but pronounced exactly like *dogs*), and both plurality and possession (spelled *dogs'* and again pronounced the same as *dogs*). Similarly, the verb *bark* is a morpheme that combines with inflectional suffixes to indicate grammatical agreement (spelled *-s*), past tense and past participle (*-ed* in both cases for *bark*), and progressive aspect and gerundive form (for which *-ing* serves a dual role). Prefix morphemes (e.g., *re-* for verbs and *non-* for nouns) will not be treated here, as linguists generally consider them to be features of word formation (termed derivational morphology) rather than features of the grammar of English. In practice, for English, linguists generally restrict the term inflectional morphology to the kinds of suffixes for nouns and verbs already exemplified here; to the various forms of the personal pronouns (e.g., *I*, *me*, *my*, *mine*); and to comparative and superlative forms of adjectives (i.e., *big*, *bigger*, *biggest*).

The distinction between inflectional and derivational morphology is not clear-cut. Generally speaking, inflectional morphemes do not change the part of speech of the word they affect, and they apply globally to all words in the most general classes (i.e., nouns, verbs, adjectives, and adverbs), whereas derivational morphemes may change the part of speech (e.g., *-ness* is a derivational morpheme which, when attached to an adjective, turns it into a noun) or cannot be combined with all words of the class (e.g., *re-* normally may

325

precede the verbs *marry*, *enlist*, and perhaps *turn down*, but not *die*, *seem*, or *take place*).

Syntax is the set of rules for combining words into sentences. For example, the rules of English syntax tell us that, because nouns generally precede verbs in basic English sentences, *dogs* and *barked* may be combined as *Dogs barked* but not **Barked dogs* (the asterisk being used by linguists to mark constructions that violate the rules of the language). Similarly, *Dogs bark* is permissible, but *Bark dogs* is permissible only if the subject *you* is understood – in which case the sentence would be punctuated *Bark, dogs!* to indicate the normal pronunciation. Still other syntactic rules require the presence of an additional word if *dog* is singular: one can say *A dog barks* or *The dog barks* but not **Dog bark(s)*. Moreover, the rules of standard English syntax tell us that *-ing* must be attached to *bark* if some form of *be* precedes *bark*: *Dogs are barking* or *The/A dog is barking*, but not **Dogs barking*. Yet another rule of English syntax tells us that the word *to* must be present in a sentence such as *I allowed him to sing a song*, yet *to* must not be present if the verb is changed to *hear* (*I heard him sing a song* but not **I heard him to sing a song*). With still other verbs, the speaker has the option of using or omitting *to*, for example, *I helped him (to) sing a song*. Morphemes such as *the*, *a*, *-ing*, and *to* are often termed function morphemes to distinguish them from content morphemes such as *dog*, *bark*, *sing*, *song*, and the like.

9.2   American-British grammatical differences

In tracing the history of American grammar, it is important to note that in many instances what might seem to have been a change in American English compared with the standard English of Great Britain is in fact no change at all – it is British English that has changed, not American. For example, eighteenth-century speakers of English generally formed the past participle of *get* 'receive' as *gotten*, as in *Your brother has gotten my mail*. In the nineteenth century, prestigious speakers in England began to drop the *-en* ending: *Your brother has got my mail*. Most Americans, however, continued using the older form *gotten*. Another example of a grammatical innovation in England that did not extend to America is one that arose in the first half of the twentieth century, when British people from the more prestigious classes began adding the word *done* in certain syntactic contexts where their ancestors had formerly been obliged to omit it; thus to the question *Did you leave your gloves behind at the party?* a normal middle-class British response today could be, *I may have done*. However, Americans would be highly unlikely to answer this way; following their colonial ancestors with respect to this minor rule of grammar, Americans would say *I may have* or (more formally) *I may have done so* – but never *I may have done*. There are many such cases in which American English has been conservative, British English innovating.

Moreover, the history of the grammar of standard American English is impossible to separate from the variation found in the social and regional dialects of America on the one hand and, on the other, from the origins of prominent American grammatical variants in the social and regional dialects of Great Britain. Put another way, one can say with very little exaggeration that the vast majority of important changes that have taken place in American syntax and inflectional morphology throughout history are either (1) limited to a nonstandard social or regional variety of American English and have not become the rule in standard American English or (2) can be matched to historical (and often still persisting) features of the regional and social dialects of Ireland and the United Kingdom, from which each change may putatively be derived. Nor are the two types by any means mutually exclusive. Indeed, although some changes in American grammar seem to be totally indigenous developments and although a scant few grammatical changes may be traced to the influences of languages other than English, a great many of the features of all varieties of American English could be plausibly analyzed as deriving from British dialects.

Moreover, we cannot even be sure about most of the changes that arguably may have taken place independently within American English varieties. For example, in the traditional dialect of Ocracoke Island, North Carolina, speakers characteristically use the present-tense verbal suffix *-s* with certain types of plural noun subjects, especially compound subjects, as in *She and the boy goes fishing*, and collectives, as in *People likes to fish* (Wolfram, Hazen, and Schilling-Estes). On the other hand, Ocracoke-dialect speakers delete the *-s* when the subject is a plural pronoun, e.g., *They like to go fishing* but not **They likes to go fishing*. For 300 years, before very recent times, Ocracoke-dialect speakers were generally isolated from speakers of other dialects. Did Ocracokers evolve their unusual syntactic rule for *-s* throughout their separate 300-year linguistic history? Or is the linguistic rule a survivor of earlier peculiar rules brought to Ocracoke by early settlers from Ulster – where a similar pattern is reportedly found in Scotch-Irish dialects? It is probably impossible to determine which scenario is the right one – or, indeed, if both might not have been to some extent responsible for the way traditional Ocracokers use *-s*.

Given the disparate ways in which various British dialects handled verb morphology and agreement, and given the heterogeneity of the immigrant population, the melting-pot of spoken English during the settlement period would have been itself extremely heterogeneous and unstable. It is not surprising that various, relatively isolated, communities would have leveled out the heterogeneity with results that differed significantly from the speech of aristocratic Britain and from the evolving standard dialects of the emerging United States. These results need not have been solely modeled on any particular English dialect. The same processes that brought forth the original English dialect features in the first place would certainly have been available to work independently in America.

This point can be illustrated with another example, the past tense and past participle of the verb *bring*. In Modern English, the standard past tense and past participle have always been *brought*. One can, however, find ample attestations in dialects on both sides of the Atlantic of the forms *brang* and *brung*. Certainly there must have been settlers throughout the Colonial period who said *brang* or *brung* instead of *brought*. These speakers doubtless influenced the younger people with whom they came into contact, thus promoting *brang* and *brung* at the expense of *brought*. However, there are strong independent linguistic reasons why *brang* and *brung* would have arisen even if all of the original settlers said only *brought*. *Brought* is a highly irregular form – almost no verbs in English change so drastically between the present-tense form and the past and past participle. Furthermore, there are other, phonologically very similar verbs which pattern in almost exactly the way that *bring/brang/brung* do: *ring/rang/rung*, *sing/sang/sung*, *swim/swam/swum*, and *drink/drank/drunk*. Analogy is a powerful force for linguistic change, and highly irregular forms are extremely likely to change, often as the result of child-language-acquisition processes having nothing at all to do with dialect borrowing. In the end, one must say that the original dialect forms *brang* and *brung* persisted in the New World but that both the original forms and the normal processes of linguistic change must have contributed to this persistence.

The remainder of this chapter presents examples of the two types of linguistic change in American English discussed above, concluding with a third, necessarily brief, section on some of the apparent exceptions to the rule that standard American English has had few totally independent grammatical changes.

9.3   American nonstandard grammatical features

This section examines only some of the major features of some of the major dialects of American English. The reader is referred for discussion in greater detail to the appropriate other chapters of this book, especially the two immediately preceding ones "Dialects," by Lee Pederson, and "African-American English," by Salikoko Mufwene.

A number of important examples of nonstandard grammatical differences are features of African-American Vernacular English (AAVE). One such example involves the verb-phrase structure known as invariant *be*. Increasingly since the 1960s, speakers of AAVE have employed the word *be* before progressive forms of verbs: *I (he, she, we, they,* etc.) *always be playing basketball* instead of the standard *I am (he is,* etc.) *always playing basketball*. Often, the invariant *be* seems to be an aspect marker with a specialized connotation indicating that the action of the verb is no mere point in time; sentences with the invariant *be* thus contrast with sentences with inflected copulas – or no copula at all – which have the meaning that the action expressed is immediate: *He('s) playing basketball right now*. Clearly, this development within AAVE has taken place independently of British English (and, for that matter, independently of other dialects of American English).

It is true that an invariant *be* has always existed in the most formal varieties of standard American English, where it is a relatively rare (and waning) form of the subjunctive (e.g., *If this be in error* rather than *If this is in error*). It is also true that invariant *be* is used in other ways in other nonstandard dialects on both sides of the Atlantic. For example, Guy Bailey and Natalie Maynor (1985, 213) found eleven possible examples of invariant *be* in their entire corpus of 1885 instances of some form of the present tense of *be*. Their corpus represents the speech of elderly white Texans. Typical examples are *In the winter time when I get there, that's where they be at* and *I just don't be worried about finding help, you know*.

Scholars have suggested that the ultimate origins of the form (if not the meaning) of AAVE invariant *be* could be either British dialect use or the original African languages of the first slaves. But the suggestion of British historical origins of the form *be* is impossible to prove conclusively; moreover, citing analogous constructions in African languages and Caribbean creoles, many scholars have also proposed that the meaning of the AAVE invariant *be* goes back to seventeenth-century slave language – and ultimately to African languages.

At any rate, the recent development of *be* in AAVE appears to be so widespread, so highly visible, and so different in meaning from the surrounding non-AAVE vernaculars and standard American English that it seems clear that the AAVE development has gone significantly beyond whatever British dialect antecedents it may have had and has taken place independent of the influence of (or to date any influence upon) standard American English. Though most Americans today are aware of the AAVE invariant *be* and are likely even to use it when imitating AAVE, it has not spread into other varieties of American English.

A second example of type-one grammatical "change" in American English is the dialect intensifier *done*, which is commonplace in AAVE and in many other dialects of the American South. The form is fairly heavily stigmatized among educated speakers, though the proscription normally does not show up in usage manuals because it is not commonplace in the substandard dialects to which the traditionally white Northern writers of usage manuals would have been most heavily exposed. The meaning of the intensifier *done* is hard to pin down, having much the same function as, say, *ya* in Spanish or the adverbials *really*, *sure*, and *already* in many colloquial varieties of American English. Thus a sentence such as *It looks like you done had a fire up here!* which was actually uttered to the author in the 1970s by a middle-aged white central North Carolina gas-station attendant who was commenting on a burned patch on the hood of the author's automobile, means 'It sure looks like you had a fire up here' or 'Surprisingly, it looks like you had a fire up here.' The history of the construction is obscure. Some scholars maintain that it has its origins in AAVE and Caribbean varieties of English. Others find analogous forms in British dialects. Still others see it as a totally independent change in American English, arising largely from the same normal linguistic processes that underlie the rise of the similar structures in AAVE, Caribbean English, and British dialects.

Another example of type-one grammatical change clearly has its source not in British dialects or in independent innovation but in the language of the non-English-speaking forefathers of the nonstandard dialect in question. It is an established principle of standard English that direct objects of verbs are normally placed after the verb and before any prepositional phrases of direction or location: *Throw Mama a kiss from the train* and *Throw Papa his hat down the stairs*. Influenced by their first-language syntax, German immigrants frequently produced constructions such as *Throw Mama from the train a kiss* and *Throw Papa down the stairs his hat*. Children of such second-language learners in insular communities tended to adopt these syntactic patterns, though the patterns generally have not spread very far beyond the insular communities, certainly rarely, if ever, into standard American. And they seem to be dying out today.

Other highly visible, widespread American dialectal variants may be largely or fully independent developments rather than the descendants of British dialects. One such feature – widespread in the American South and

parts of the eastern Midlands – is the use of multiple modals: construc-
tions of the form *might could, might would,* and *might ought to,* e.g., *The folks might could go fishing if they get off work in time.* Even more exotic forms are found, including *may can, may will,* and *might should ought to.* The sense of *might* in *might could* is virtually identical to that of *maybe* in the same environment. Most users of the construction are barely aware that it is a dialect feature – it even finds its way into unselfconscious regional publications. Usage manuals rarely mention it. Yet the construction sounds quaint and startling to those who come from regions where it is not used.

Are multiple modals independent American innovations, or are they rooted in British dialects? The answer seems to be that both hypotheses are correct. Similar constructions are known in current dialects in Scotland and Northern Ireland, as well as in earlier forms of their dialects ranging back to Middle English. Clearly, some forms of double modals could have been – and probably were – brought to the New World by English-speaking settlers from north of the Humber. At the same time, the multiple modals found in the New World vary considerably in form and use from those found in Britain. The original British double modals – if indeed the characterization "original" is correct – have developed into such different grammatical forms in American English dialects that that very independent development is worthy of note and cause enough to consider the multiple modal in America in great part – if not entirely – an independent indigenous development.

A similar feature of many varieties of American English is positive *anymore,* as in a sentence such as *Anymore, we need to buy our groceries before 10 p.m. because the stores close earlier than they did in the 1980s.* Here *anymore* means 'these days, as opposed to some previous time.' Although there are parts of the United States where the construction strikes native speakers of English as alien and bizarre, it is widespread and commonplace except for the old South and far East. Clearly, positive *anymore* is an extension, by analogy, of the universal negative *anymore* construction, as in *We don't need to buy our groceries before 10 p.m. anymore.*

For some speakers, part of the grammatical bizarreness of some uses of positive *anymore* is the placement of *anymore* at the beginning of the sentence. Such speakers find *We need to buy our groceries before 10 p.m. anymore* much more acceptable than *Anymore, we need to buy our groceries before 10 p.m.* They also find *Anymore, we don't need to buy our groceries before 10 p.m.* extremely awkward if not downright ungrammatical.

The fact that positive *anymore* has also been reported in some dialects of Ulster is difficult to evaluate historically with respect to the American use of the form. On the one hand, it is found in many areas in which Scotch-Irish settlers were prominent (e.g., Ocracoke Island, North Carolina). On the other hand, it is found as well in vast areas of the country in which Scotch-Irish settlers were only a drop in the linguistic bucket. Moreover, the clear opportunity for analogy to have been at work in extending the negative *anymore* to positive *anymore* environments makes a clear-cut, exclusive assignment of the form to the Scotch-Irish antecedents dubious at best.

A final example is quite complex and often remarked upon: the development of specialized plural forms for the second-person pronoun. When *thou*, *thee*, and *thine* dropped out of the language in the early Colonial period on both sides of the Atlantic, speakers felt a need nonetheless to distinguish between singular and plural forms. The earliest attempt was simply to make verb agreement do the work: speakers would say *you was* for the singular and *you were* for the plural. Beginning in the eighteenth century, this sensible solution met with heavy resistance from purists, however, and *you was* became heavily stigmatized by the end of the nineteenth century in America (though it has by no means dropped out of colloquial speech throughout the United States).

The other solution was to create new plural pronouns. The most famous of these is *y'all* (rhyming with *hall*), apparently a contracted form of *you-all*. It contrasts with singular *you* and has the possessive form *y'all's*. It is widespread in spoken English in the American South and appears to be an entirely indigenous form. Very well known, it is not stigmatized – indeed, users seem quite proud of the form, seeing it as a badge of regional good sense and charm, though it is often avoided in formal contexts.

Occasionally, the use of *y'all* as a singular form is reported, though scholars have generally rejected the putative reported examples as mistakes of speaker or interpreter. For example, it is sometimes reported that sales clerks will say to a lone customer in closing a service encounter, "Y'all come back, hear?" Such examples are usually explained as a formulaic utterance, not a true singular, in which the intent of the clerk is to invite the return of the customer and his or her friends and family.

A different form, *yuz* (often spelled *youse*, with the vowel of *book*), is heard in the American Midwest as far east as Pittsburgh. It may be a completely indigenous development, arising by the addition of the regular plural morpheme to the base form *you*, which is then reanalyzed as only a singular. There are, however, reportedly similar forms in Scotland and Ireland. Though *yuz* is considered substandard, it is rarely commented upon in the usage handbooks.

Still another second-person-plural pronoun, *yuns* (apparently from *you* + *ones*, also with the vowel of *book*), appears to have no known antecedents in

British dialects. It is highly stigmatized as Southern, rural, mountain white speech.

The newest form, *you guys*, though widespread in the United States, especially among younger speakers, is not often even thought of as a pronoun, though increasingly it functions that way in actual usage. It is popular among middle-class white speakers throughout the country, and is used to refer to females as well as males (with very little backlash from feminist writers). It seems to be a thoroughly indigenous development, and it is not stigmatized like the analogous British form *you lot.*

9.4   American standard grammatical features

The second type of grammatical features includes two subtypes: changes that standard British English underwent but that also took place in America; and changes in which a nonstandard British variant became the rule in American English.

9.4.1   Standard changes shared with British English

Two important examples of the first subtype of grammatical change are the complete replacement of *thee, thou,* and *thy* by *you* and *your* early in the Colonial period on both sides of the Atlantic and the abandonment of the *-th* ending in favor of the *-(e)s* morpheme for third-person singular verbs. The earliest colonists would have felt that *Then saith he to the disciple, Behold thy mother!* from the seventeenth-century King James Bible (John 19.27) was just as natural as the modern alternative, *Then says he to the disciple, Behold your mother!*

The development of the passive progressive construction likewise took place in both British and American English. Though the change may have been strongly abetted by the occurrence of the form in literary English, the construction is so firmly established today that its progression through spoken English as well seems firmly established. A sentence such as *My strength is slowly being eroded by this disease* would have been heavily stigmatized in the earlier eighteenth century, where pundits would have required an active sentence (i.e., *This disease is slowly eroding my strength*) or a simple passive (*My strength is slowly eroding from this disease*). However, by the mid nineteenth century the same sentence would have gone unnoticed.

One quite recent change in American English appears to have taken place not only in America, but simultaneously in various parts of the English-speaking world. This is the use of what has come to be called quotative *go*, as in a sentence such as *The teacher looks at me and he goes, "Spit out that wad of gum at once, Frank!"* This use of *go* where previous generations would have used the verb *say* has been reported in the colloquial speech of Australia, England, Canada, and the United States, beginning about the 1970s. It is perhaps an example of American influence spread by mass media, since it seems unlikely that such a specialized new form would have arisen simultaneously in so many distant parts of the globe.

The fact that throughout the Colonial period immigrants continued to arrive in America from London and its surroundings certainly helped to preserve the English of southeastern England as the dominant variety of the tongue. Moreover, the influence of written English – which took its grammar (as well as its spelling and vocabulary) predominantly from the varieties of English spoken by the politically most powerful and socially most prestigious classes in the Old World – was a powerful sustainer of the grammar of that particular variety of the language through the Colonial period and to some extent even beyond.

9.4.2   Standard American features from nonstandard British dialects

By no means did all of the early settlers (even the English-speaking ones) come from southeastern England. Immigrants did not settle homogeneously and uniformly in North America; rather, new arrivals tended to settle where their friends, relatives, and co-religionists from the Old World had already settled, thus creating from the beginning something of a heterogeneous patchwork of homogeneous communities in the largely rural, agricultural society of the earlier years, which endured in the industrial society of the later nineteenth century and beyond.

Such a complex pattern of heterogeneity is the source of the second subtype of grammatical change – forms and constructions which were never found in the standard variety of the language as spoken in England, but which spread from nonstandard English dialects to vernacular communities in the New World, whence they then spread into standard American English.

Such linguistic differences are few and tend to be relatively inconsequential, though highly noticeable to the speakers of different varieties. For example, the British frequently use *to* with *different*, and they have done so since before Colonial times: *My gloves are slightly different to yours.* In the United States, however, *to* is unknown with *different*; instead speakers of standard American English often say and write *different than*. Handbooks of standard English in both countries prescribe *different from* as the "preferred" or "correct" usage. All three forms, however, are found in British writers dating back to Colonial times. Clearly, American English changed one way,

British English another, with respect to the use of *different* both in writing and in speaking.

Differences between standard British and American verb morphology tend to be of this second subtype as well. The *Longman Dictionary of Contemporary English* lists the following different developments on either side of the Atlantic:

> *Dive* takes the past tense *dived* in British English but *dove* in America.
>
> *Kneel* takes past tense and past participle *knelt* in Britain, *kneeled* in America.
>
> *Leap* has *leapt* as past and past participle in Britain, *leaped* in the United States.
>
> *Plead* changes to *pled* (past and past participle) in the United States but takes a simple *-ed* ending in Britain.
>
> The past participle of *prove* is *proved* in British English, but may be *proven* in the United States.
>
> The British say *smelt, spelt,* and *spilt,* whereas Americans say *smelled, spelled,* and *spilled* (past and past participle).
>
> British people say *spat* for the past and past participle of *spit,* but Americans tend to use *spit* throughout the paradigm.
>
> British people must say *sprang* where Americans can say *sprung* (past tense; both have the past participle *sprung*).

The differentiation between the standard speech on the two sides of the Atlantic did not come about as the result of the invention of new forms in America (or Britain) after the Americans gained their political independence. On the contrary, all of these variants were present in England from pre-Colonial times and were carried to the New World by Englishmen speaking various social and regional dialects. And though various alternative verb forms were particularly favored on one side of the Atlantic or the other, the nonstandard variants continue generally to be used in various dialects in both the United States and the United Kingdom. Thus while *I dove into the river* may be stigmatized in Britain (where *I dived into the river* is preferred) but not stigmatized in the United States, one can certainly hear *I dived into the river* in the United States and *I dove into the river* in nonstandard speech in Britain. The variants have been used in England since the beginning of Modern English, as they have been likewise in America since the early settlement period.

9.5 Independent changes in standard American English grammar

The exceptions to the rule that standard American English has had few independent grammatical changes are few. One such exception is the syntactically important and complex rule for forming tag questions and simple yes/no questions with *have*. Tag questions are added to the end of a statement to convert it to a question, e.g., *You know the muffin man, don't you?* Yes/no questions are, quite simply, questions to which *yes* or *no* would be appropriate answers, as opposed to content questions, which require an answer which is one or more words other than *yes* or *no*. For example, *Do you know the muffin man?* is a yes/no question; *Who is the muffin man?* is a content question.

In the early Colonial period, the rules for question formation were in the process of change. In the time of Shakespeare and for a generation or two thereafter, speakers of prestigious varieties of English could form yes/no questions in one of two ways: by moving the verb to the beginning of the sentence, as in *Lives there a man with soul so corrupt as Iago?* or by placing a form of the verb *do* at the beginning of the sentence: *Does there live a man with soul so corrupt as Iago?* In English on both sides of the Atlantic, the rule using *do* eventually replaced the rule using inversion, so that *Lives there a man?* sounds archaic or ungrammatical to modern ears. Only two applications of the inversion survive. First, when the main verb is *be*, inversion is mandatory (one must say *Is Richard III a bad guy?* And not **Does Richard III be a bad guy?*); and second, when the main verb is *have*, inversion is optional in standard British English, but it has become ungrammatical in standard American English for most grammatical environments. Thus the British may ask either *Do you have a banana?* or (and this seems to be preferred) *Have you a banana?* With a few explicit exceptions, Americans must say the former. The distinction extends to tag questions as well: Americans say *She has brown hair, doesn't she?* as opposed to British English *She has brown hair, hasn't she?*

If the direct object of *have* is an abstract noun, many Americans have a choice between inverted *have* and *do*-support. That is, *Have you any need for another notebook?* and *Have you any idea how hard I have worked on this project?* are both possible constructions in standard American English, as are their counterparts with *do*-support, i.e., *Do you have any need for another notebook?* and *Do you have any idea how hard I have worked on this project?* According to Traugott (177), British English absolutely disallows *do*-support for *have* questions where possession is inalienable, e.g., *Has she blue eyes?* versus **Does she have blue eyes?* Traugott also reports that "aspect also makes a difference for the presence or absence of *do* with *have* in British, though not American, speech; in British English *When have you to leave?* is a question about an obligation on one particular occasion, but *When do you have to leave?* is a question about a recurrent habit."

Standard American English has also developed a decided preference for singular verbs with collective-noun subjects (such as *team, government*), whereas British English uses either a singular or plural (with perhaps some preference for the plural). Thus Americans must say *Our team wins often*, whereas British English may have either *win* or *wins*.

Similarly, standard American English has evolved its own pattern of the use of definite articles with a few nonconcrete nouns; among the most common Americanisms are *in the hospital, to/at the university* (British English *in hospital, to/at university*); many Americans (particularly in the South) say *in the bed* (British and also American English *in bed*), and *one at the time* (British and also American English *one at a time*).

Another change which has taken place independently in American English is the tendency – noticeable especially since 1800 or so – towards allowing verbs to take direct objects which formerly would have required prepositions. Kirchner (37–8) lists the following as Americanisms (in each case, British English would more comfortably add a preposition before the object noun): *slip one's notice, wonder the same thing, stay the course, fly the Atlantic*, and *walk the street*. The latter expression is said in British English to have only the idiomatic sense of 'be a prostitute.' However, according to Traugott (174–5) the tendency also affects British English as well as American English, but to a lesser extent. Thus both British and American English of the eighteenth century would have had the following as grammatical expressions: **I accept of your offer, *I miss of it, *I consider of the matter.* All are now ungrammatical in both standard American and standard British English.

Historically, when a sentence has both indirect and direct objects, the direct object most naturally immediately follows the verb and in turn is followed by the indirect object: *Frank sent the letter to Jane*. The indirect object may be moved to the position immediately following the verb, with the loss of the preposition: *Frank sent Jane the letter*. However, if both objects are pronouns, in Colonial English the word order did not change, even if the preposition was deleted: *Frank sent it her*. This pattern has been preserved in British English. American English, however, regularized the paradigm, extending the rule for nouns to the case of pronouns as well; thus *Frank sent her it* is the normal pattern for American English. **Frank sent it her* is ungrammatical for Americans, though of course *Frank sent it to her* is acceptable (Traugott 186–7).

According to Algeo (1992a), British syntax and American syntax differ for what are called mandative constructions – finite clauses that occur after certain expressions of will. In standard American English, speakers are more likely to use a subjunctive form of the verb: *I insist that he give you the sugar*. Educated British speakers tend to prefer an expanded auxiliary: *I insist that he should give you the sugar.* Both forms are possible within standard American English, and the two will be understood equally well. According to Algeo, the use of the indicative is also common in Britain: *I insist that he gives you the sugar.* Ann Nichols reports that in America such indicatives are colloquial and stigmatized. Though it is often asserted that the American mandative subjunctive is an anachronism (and that the British use of *should* in such constructions is dictated by considerations of clarity), it seems most likely that all three options have always existed in both British and American English.

English has a usage problem of long standing in the choice of an indefinite singular pronoun for reference to a noun whose gender is not specified. Speakers find themselves in a quandary in deciding what pronoun should substitute for *teacher's* in sentences such as the following: *The teacher must always keep control of the teacher's students.* A frequent colloquial solution, *their,* has been traditionally scorned by prescriptivists on the grounds that *their* violates number agreement. Prescriptivists held out for the use of the masculine *his,* despite the equally plausible grammatical objection that *his* violates gender agreement. (The prescriptivist's argument that, in these circumstances, *his* is genderless is no more plausible than the layman's argument – seldom made but equally sensible – that *their* under these circumstances could be declared grammatically numberless.)

In response to this dilemma, the writers of usage manuals today generally prescribe the use of a compound pronoun, *his or her,* a construction that is used especially in formal writing, though prudent writers tend to skirt the issue by pluralizing generic nouns (i.e., *Teachers must always keep control of their students*). Even so, there are circumstances in which few speakers will use any pronoun other than the plural, for example in tag questions following indefinite pronouns: *Just about everyone likes ice cream, don't they?* is the only real choice for native speakers. The alternative *doesn't he or she?* sounds pedantic; *doesn't he?* sounds unidiomatic; and *doesn't one?* sounds even worse.

Linguistic change continues to take place. An example of what appears to be a syntactic change in progress in current American English is the following sentence from an e-mail message that the author received from one of his former undergraduate students, a talented writer who is currently pursuing a career in journalism: *But, dammit, I, well, the thing is is that I don't think that I WANT to impress Spike because he falls so short in impressing me.* So far as I know, the addition of *is that* after *is* in this sentence presents an entirely new development in American English, where speakers formerly would have written simply *the thing is, I don't think that I want to impress Spike* or *the thing is that I don't think that I want to impress Spike.* Nor is this a mere mistake:

instances of such reduplicative *is* constructions are widespread in speech and writing in America, and have been so for the past decade or so. The meaning of the construction is problematical: it is not clearly different from the construction without the additional *is*. The historical origin, however, seems clear enough: by analogy with what are known as cleft sentences – constructions of the form *What my idea is, is to first kill all the lawyers!* Whether or not such a construction will persist and eventually become acceptable is, of course, unknowable at this time.

FURTHER READING

Pyles and Algeo (1993, 212–36), "Recent British and American English," survey grammatical and other differences between the two varieties; Kirchner (1957), "Recent American Influence on Standard English: The Syntactical Sphere," treats the grammatical influence of American on British; Traugott (1972), *The History of English Syntax: A Transformational Approach to the History of English Sentence Structure*, examines the overall history of English syntax. Specific structures are examined by Algeo (1992a), "British and American Mandative Constructions"; Bailey and Maynor (1985), "The Present Tense of *Be* in White Folk Speech of the Southern United States"; Butters (1983), "Syntactic Change in British English 'Propredicates'"; and A. Nichols (1987), "The Suasive Subjunctive." Wolfram, Hazen, and Schilling-Estes (1999), *Dialect Change and Maintenance on the Outer Banks*, examine a notable American regional variety.

10   SPELLING

Richard L. Venezky

American English spelling began as a set of patterns, rules, and preferences that traveled across the Atlantic from England in the seventeenth century on the *Mayflower*, the *Arbella*, and dozens of other ships bringing people, books, and pamphlets from one continent to the other. From these beginnings the solidly British core was occasionally expanded and less frequently replaced to yield the orthography that prevails today in the American classroom, newspaper office, publishing house, and private home.

At the core of American orthography is a system that is derived from King Alfred and Abbot Ælfric, Chaucer and the Chancery scribes, Shakespeare and Mulcaster, Johnson and Dryden, Murray and Hart and that is shared throughout the English-speaking and -writing world. But intermixed in that core are local preferences and innovations, including variations on specific spellings and spelling rules (for example, *traveled, movable, jail*), graphemic preferences (*encyclopedia, esthetics*), and nonstandard commercial uses of orthography (*Exxon, Chik-n Flav-r*). The origins and evolution of these variations are one concern of this chapter.

No comprehensive history of American English spelling has been written. Krapp (1925, vol. 1) deals almost exclusively with spelling reform and is dated, as is Mencken (1936), which is more comprehensive. Brander Matthews (1892), like Mencken (1936), attempts to contrast American and British spelling, but is no longer current.

Another interest is American orthographic invention that has not resulted in differences between English and American spelling but reflects American attitudes and interests in orthography. American spelling reform movements and attempts to install modified alphabets are one part of this interest. A second part centers on the spelling of Americanisms, words such as *raccoon, Wisconsin,* and *Pittsburgh*, which are examples of words

shared uniformly throughout the English-speaking world but which originated in America and whose spellings changed over time due to American
orthographic manipulations. A final topic is orthographic hegemony, the
shifting centers of control over American spelling.

10.1   From settlement to Revolution

The settlers who came to Jamestown in 1607 had been educated on Sidney,
Bunyan, and Marlowe and on the *Book of Common Prayer* and the English
Bible, and they spoke and wrote the same language as Shakespeare. For
nearly a century and a half the colonies would derive their primary models
for spelling and composition from England. The colonists were, after all,
English men and women, subjects of the Crown. In addition, centers of
language authority from which unique orthographic principles might arise
– printing houses, authors, lexicographers, legal administrators, and the like
– were slow to form in the New World.

Printing in the colonies was first established in 1638–9 in Cambridge; a
second press did not begin operation until 1675 (Lehmann-Haupt,
Wroth, and Silver). Operating under strict censorship and limited by the
high costs of paper and transportation, the Colonial press served primarily a local market. Its main sources of income, particularly in the seventeenth and early eighteenth centuries, came from government work (such
as assembly proceedings and laws) and, particularly in the eighteenth
century, newspapers and almanacs. The printing of English Bibles
required a patent from the Crown (*cum privilegio*), none of which was
issued for the colonies. (The first complete Bible printed in America came
from the press of Robert Aitken of Philadelphia in 1782 and was recommended "to the inhabitants of the United States" by the Continental
Congress.)

Except for the Revolutionary period, books were imported into the colonies on a regular basis from England. Although this trade was "sluggish"
until the middle of the eighteenth century (Botein), it grew substantially in
the decades prior to the Revolution and continued to grow once the peace
treaty was signed (Barber).

After the beginning of the eighteenth century, Dryden, Pope, and
Addison (among other English writers of the period) became well known in
the colonies and their style and vocabulary were frequently imitated
(MacLaurin). Benjamin Franklin, for example, who was representative of
American writers of the eighteenth century, modeled himself on Addison.
He also avoided introducing neologisms, Americanisms, and colloquialisms

and followed the eighteenth-century English writers in all matters of spelling. The regular past tense, for example, was generally written '*d* (*liv'd*, *look'd*, *pull'd*), as in England at the time.

Colonial authors tended to send materials abroad for publication, particularly larger works that the Colonial press could handle only with difficulty. Thus Cotton Mather sent his manuscript for *Magnalia Christi Americana* abroad through a friend in 1699 and waited several years until an accommodating printer was located (C. Mather 1702).

A further connection with English letters was through education, particularly higher education. Although nine colleges were founded in the colonies prior to the Revolution, only three were in existence before 1746 (Harvard, 1636; William and Mary, 1693; Yale, 1701). Wealthy colonists tended to send their children abroad for their education. William Byrd II, for example, received his early education in Virginia but was then sent by his father to Holland and England for college work. He became a Fellow of the Royal Society of London in 1696, but spent most of his adult life as an estate owner in Virginia and on his death (1744) left an important collection of manuscripts covering his travels and explorations (Ames). Many of the ministers in seventeenth-century Virginia were trained at Oxford and Cambridge and thus brought to their writings and to their schoolmaster duties an English orientation to language and orthography.

The progression of Colonial spelling through the seventeenth century shows the same movement toward stability that English writings demonstrate. Cheever's *Journal of the Pilgrims*, written in 1620, treats the members of the pairs *i/j* and *u/v* interchangeably: *Iournall* (journal), *ariuall* (arrival), *vnitie* (unity), *soueraigne* (sovereign). Cotton Mather's *Magnalia*, published in London in 1702, uses *i/j* and *u/v* as they are used today. Most of Cheever's final *-ie* spellings (*vnitie*, *alwaies*, *satisfie*) become *-y* in the *Magnalia* (*publickly*, *loudly*, *agreeably* but *gratifie*, *glorifie*). Most of the extra doubled consonants and added final *e*'s of the early and mid seventeenth century (as in *owne*, *halfe*, *combate*, *behinde*, *evill*, *shopp*, *sonne*, *sentt*, *fitt*) have disappeared by the beginning of the eighteenth century, as have the *-es* endings of forms like *yeares*, *bookes*, *lawes*, *handes*, and *recordes*, which are evidenced late in the seventeenth century. What is remarkable in late seventeenth- and early eighteenth-century Colonial writing is not the archaic spellings but the high percentage of thoroughly modern spellings. Cotton Mather's diary entries for 1698, for example, while presenting an occasional *mee*, *fitt*, *beleef*, and *alwayes*, are better characterized by such spellings as *duties*, *bitterly*, *righteousness*, *measure*, and *marvellous*.

Mather was not orthographically precocious; he simply followed the prevailing English spelling practices, which had stabilized by the beginning of the eighteenth century. "By 1700 stabilisation was complete. The relatively few changes which have taken place in spelling since then have affected only a small number of words, for example, individual cases like *phantasy* becoming *fantasy*... and *controul* becoming *control* (by analogy with French), or minor developments involving a group of words such as the loss of final <k> from <-ick> in such words as *music* and *comic*" (Scragg 74). Contrary to the common view, printers had far less to do with the regularization of English spelling than orthoepists, lexicographers, and orthographers (Brengelman). Printers had more to gain from flexibility, particularly for line justification, than they did from a fixed set of spelling rules.

By the time of the American Revolution, spelling in the colonies had evolved to a nearly modern look, at least among the better educated. As expected, *-our* was favored over *-or* in words like *honour* and *humour*; *-re* was favored over *-er* in *metre* and *centre*; and a number of words like *waggon* and *gaol* were spelled differently from their modern forms. But usage was not totally fixed: *favor* might occur next to *favour*, even in the same document. Older orthographic habits were retained for capitalization and abbreviations, although usage varied widely for both. Benjamin Franklin, who has been described as conservative in language practice (MacLaurin), generally capitalized all important nouns in a sentence and, as noted earlier, spelled the past tense *-ed* consistently as *'d*, as in *enclos'd, reform'd, fix'd, discours'd*. In contrast, Noah Webster's eighteenth-century capitalization practices were the same as those used today and he rarely abbreviated the regular past tense to *'d*. But Webster, like nearly every other educated eighteenth-century writer, did use a variety of word abbreviations characterized by a small superscript replacing the truncated portion of a word; for example, $serv^t$, Rev^d, $Phil^a$ (or $Philad^a$), rec^d, Gen^a. By the end of the century these occurred primarily in headings and closings to letters and in similar positions on business documents: Decr 26. 1793, *your* $Obed^t$ $serv^t$, *Your* aff^{ate} *wife*, Feb^{ry} 10th.

A small number of abbreviations aside from the past tense also occurred occasionally. Benjamin Rush, in a letter to Noah Webster in 1789, abbreviated *enough* as *en'o*; Ezra Stiles, then president of Yale University, wrote in the following year *altho', thoro', h'ble* (humble), and y^r (Ford and Skeel). The coordinating conjunction *and* was frequently written *&*, and eccentric spellings appeared here and there (e.g., *comeing*) but probably no more so than in a representative sample of present-day correspondence (without the benefit of word processing spelling checkers).

10.2 Orthographic authority

Spelling authority in America, the arbiter of what is correct and incorrect, has shifted over time from the spelling book to the dictionary, with the government claiming rights over place names. In the Colonial and early Federal periods, spelling books, and Webster's speller in particular, were the primary sources of authority for spelling. By the nineteenth century, however, printing houses depended upon dictionaries rather than spelling books (Scragg). Spelling bees in the first half of the nineteenth century may have invoked the authority of the speller but by the 1870s, dictionaries (usually those of Webster, Walker, and Worcester) were most often mentioned as authority for correct spellings.

10.2.1 *Dictionaries*

Prior to Noah Webster's 1828 dictionary, British dictionaries (such as those of John Walker, Thomas Sheridan, Todd Johnson, and Scott-Barley) were considered far superior to American products (Friend), yet none of them appeared to have been a major influence on spelling habits. The few that were written and printed in the United States at the end of the eighteenth and the beginning of the nineteenth centuries were not particularly successful publishing ventures. Samuel Johnson, Jr., for example, a Connecticut schoolmaster and son of the first president of Columbia University, published *A School Dictionary* in New Haven in 1796, basically following British spelling preferences, but with a few deviations. Words like *spectre* and *theatre* were spelled with final *-re*, but no preference was made between *-ize* and *-ise*. *Honour* and *odour* existed next to *arbor* and *fervor*. An 1800 revision, compiled by Johnson and the Reverend John Elliott, used nearly the same spellings as the 1796 dictionary, except that *k* was dropped from *-ck* in *hammoc, havoc, music, physic,* and *public* (but not in *hillock*). Another 1800 dictionary, compiled by Caleb Alexander, a Massachusetts schoolmaster and preacher, was perhaps the first to omit *u* from *ou* spellings: *color, favor, honor, savior* (Friend).

Nevertheless, British dictionaries were widely available since they were regularly pirated by American printers and publishers. William Perry's *Royal Standard English Dictionary* appeared in Worcester and Brookfield, Massachusetts, editions of 1788 and 1801, respectively, and Dr. Johnson's dictionary appeared in Boston and Philadelphia editions (1804 and 1805, respectively) to name just a few American reprintings (Tebbel). The lack of an international copyright agreement left American printers free to reprint without paying royalties, a practice that was especially harmful to American writers.

Noah Webster's *Compendious Dictionary of the English Language*, published in 1806, represented a moderate position on orthography, standing between the thoroughly British spellings of Webster's 1783 speller and the radical reforms of his *Fugitiv Writings* (Baugh and Cable; Friend). As in William Perry's *Royal Standard English Dictionary* of 1801, *i/j* and *u/v* were separated. But unlike the *Royal Standard*, the *Compendious* presented in an authoritative lexicographic context many of the spelling changes that have come to distinguish American from British spelling although, as noted above, some had appeared in earlier American dictionaries. Final *-re* was replaced by *-er* (*scepter, theater, meter*), *ou* by *o* (*honor, favor*), *-ence* by *-ense* (*defense, pretense, recompense*), *-ize* was generalized over *-ise* (*methodize, patronize* but *criticise, circumcise*), and final consonants in words like *travel, cancel,* and *worship* were not doubled before suffixes beginning with vowels. In addition, a number of spelling preferences, such as *wagon* over *waggon*, distinguished Webster's American spellings from prevailing British norms. Other changes mirrored reforms already adopted by Perry and by other British and American lexicographers, such as leveling final *-ck* to *-c* in *logic, music,* and *physic*, and converting final *-que* to *-k* in *mask* and *risk*.

It was, however, Webster's 1828 dictionary, *An American Dictionary of the English Language*, that established the majority of American spellings now distinguishing American from British spelling. Webster's success derived first from his ability to select spellings that American printers already favored and second from his widespread influence on the orthographic practices of school teachers, an influence that itself came from the popularity of his revised speller, *The Elementary Spelling Book* (1829), and his common school dictionary (1830), both of which conformed to the spellings of the 1828 dictionary (Monaghan).

> Like Johnson, Webster could record only those spellings already widely used by printers, and, again like Johnson, his greatest influence was upon the private speller who found in his dictionary a reference book to currently acceptable spelling. Unlike Johnson, however, but like Mulcaster two centuries earlier, Webster deliberately chose from the spellings to be found in printed material of his day not simply the commonest spelling of a particular word but the one which accorded best with his orthographic theories.
>
> [Scragg 84]

In the 1828 dictionary, Webster quietly restored to their more acceptable forms some reforms he had advocated in his 1806 dictionary: *definite, fugitive, soup, soot.* Inconsistencies occurred (*traffick, almanack, frolick, havock* alongside *music, physic*), and reforms were advocated that failed to find acceptance (*ake, aker, bild, bridegoom, nightmar, tung, turnep, wo, iland*). But Webster's views on spelling reform, expressed in the introduction, were reasonable for the time: "The correct principle respecting changes in orthography seems to be between these extremes of position [radical reform versus standing pat]" (cited by Friend 21).

In the second edition of the *American Dictionary* (1843), Webster quietly dropped most of the more radical reforms of 1828 in an effort to increase the popularity and authority of the dictionary, and future editors continued to avoid major deviations from accepted practice. Webster's main competitor was Joseph E. Worcester, whose *Comprehensive Pronouncing and Explanatory Dictionary* (1830) and *Universal and Critical Dictionary of the English Language* (American edition 1846) staked out a position somewhere between American and British styles, spelling *labor* without *u* but preferring *-re* in *theatre* and *centre* (Friend). Through the 1850s and 1860s a "Dictionary War" erupted between the publishers of the Webster and Worcester dictionaries, centered as much on spelling as on the other components of lexicography. Writers such as Washington Irving and William Cullen Bryant, as well as the *Atlantic Monthly*, the New York State legislature, and various universities took public positions in the brawl, but in the end Webster won out because of the quality of the 1864 *Unabridged Dictionary* (Warfel).

10.2.2 Academies

Attempts to form an American academy for language refinement and improvement (or preservation) have met with general disinterest, as have attempts to use the Congress or state legislatures for general spelling reform. But individual spellings, particularly place names, have been the subject of territorial, state, and federal legislation or executive order. The earliest American interest in establishing a national language or orthographic standard was expressed by Hugh Jones, a professor of mathematics at William and Mary College, who in 1721 called for a "Publick Standard" of language (Read 1936). Almost sixty years later John Adams, while an envoy in Amsterdam, wrote to the president of Congress (September 5, 1780), urging the creation of a society to be called "The American Academy for Refining, Improving, and Ascertaining the English Language."

An act to incorporate a National Academy for language was brought before Congress in 1806, only to be referred to committee, from which it never emerged. In 1820, however, the American Academy of Language and Belles Lettres was launched in New York City with John Quincy Adams as its president. Among its lofty objectives was the goal "to form and maintain, as far as practicable, an English standard of writing and speaking" (cited by Read 1936, 1152). Other academies have also come and gone, including the American Academy of Arts and Letters that was founded around 1908, but their net effect upon spelling or any other phase of language usage has been imperceptible.

10.2.3   Government

Governmental attempts to regulate orthography have been more successful than those of academies, but still far short of the goals of most spelling reformers. Noah Webster was the first who seriously considered pressing the government to establish spelling reform, but his efforts never proceeded beyond correspondence or conversations with Franklin, Washington, and a few other notables of the 1780s. Several marginal attempts at reform occurred within the executive branch, including a formal request by the Secretary of State in the Pierce administration (William L. Marcy) to United States diplomatic and consular agents in foreign countries, "requiring them to make all communications to his department in the American language" (Schele De Vere 1872, 3). Exactly what qualified in 1854 as the "American language" and what became of Marcy's request is not recorded by Schele De Vere.

Of more lasting effect was the establishment of the Government Printing Office in 1861. Prior to that time, government printing was let by contract to the lowest bidder. Three years later the Superintendent of Public Printing was authorized to determine "the forms and style in which the printing... ordered by any of the departments shall be executed" (cited by Mencken 1936, 393). The first GPO style manual was issued in 1887, reflecting decisions of the GPO itself. Beginning in 1929, representatives of various other governmental departments – state, commerce, agriculture, interior – plus the Smithsonian were invited to participate in the drafting of the style manual. For almost 125 years, successive editions of Webster's dictionary have been the guides for GPO spellings. In general, the GPO spelling choices favor brevity over etymology, for example, *catalog* rather than *catalogue*.

In contrast to the spellings of everyday words, which are difficult to alter without common consent, place names have, for over a hundred years, been regulated by a government agency, the United States Board on

Geographic Names. This agency was created by executive order of President Benjamin Harrison on September 4, 1890, to ensure "that uniform usage in regard to geographic nomenclature and orthography obtain throughout the Executive Departments of the Government, and particularly upon the maps and charts issued by the Departments and bureaus" (US Board 1892, 2). The motivation for the Board came from Professor Thomas C. Mendenhall, Superintendent of the United States Coast and Geodetic Survey Office, who in January of 1890 circulated a letter to various government departments (Geological Survey, General Land Office, Navy Hydrographic Office, Postmaster-General, Smithsonian Institution, Light-House Board, Army Engineers) and the National Geographic Society, suggesting a board for resolving disputed questions of geographical orthography. Receiving favorable responses from most of the departments originally addressed, Mendenhall convened an unofficial board which met through the spring of 1890 and which, upon President Harrison's order later that fall, became the United States Board on Geographic Names.

The problem with place names is exemplified by *Wisconsin*, which, over the 211 years from the time French explorers first visited the area until the Territorial Council and House of Representatives resolved the issue, was spelled *Ouisconsin*, *Wiskonsin*, *Wisconsan*, and a variety of other ways. In the preface to the 1803 revision of his spelling book, Noah Webster referred directly to this problem when he wrote:

> Many of these names still retain the French orthography, found in the writings of the first discoverers or early travelers, but the practice of writing such words in the French manner ought to be discountenanced. How does an unlettered American know the pronunciation of the names Ouisconsin or Ouabasche, in this French dress? Would he suspect the pronunciation to be Wisconsin or Waubash? Our citizens ought not to be thus perplexed with an orthography to which they are strangers.   [cited by Krapp 1925, 1: 337]

An 1822 map of the "Arkansa Territory" used the spelling *Wisconsan* for the Wisconsin region but showed on another plate the spelling *Wisconsin*, which may have been a spelling error (A. Smith). In contrast, a map published in Detroit in 1830 refers to the "Territory of Michigan and Ouisconsin." When the Wisconsin territory was created in 1836, the current spelling was applied to it. However, sufficient disagreement remained that the Territorial Government approved a resolution in 1845 "to declare the name of the Territory 'Wisconsin.'" Even with this resolution, the United

States Board on Geographic Names found it necessary to include an entry in its *Second Report* (1901, 133) on the Wisconsin River: "Wisconsin; river in Wisconsin. (Not Ouisconsin, nor Wiskonsin.)."

During the first ten years of its existence, the United States Board on Geographic Names decided 4,157 cases in addition to approving spellings for all 2,803 counties then in existence in the United States. The origins of spelling differences for place names are discussed extensively in the Board's *Second Report*. One cause was various expeditions giving different names or different spellings in ignorance of what earlier parties had decided. Several hundred cases from Alaska that the Board considered in its first years derived from this cause, which presented an admixture of native, Russian, Spanish, and English nomenclature. The transliteration of American Indian names was a second major source of variation. Then, railroads and post offices would sometimes adopt names for their offices or stations that differed from local usage in spelling (or in the names themselves). Carelessness and ignorance round out the list. On the positive side, the *Second Report* (15) also noted a tendency "toward the discarding of objectionable names and the adoption of pleasing ones, and toward the simplification and abbreviation of names, particularly as shown in the dropping of silent letters."

Among the nomenclature reforms adopted by the Board (16) during this period included the following:

> The avoidance, as far as seems practicable, of the possessive form of names.
> The dropping of the final "h" in the termination "burgh."
> The abbreviation of "borough" to "boro."
> The spelling of the word "center" as here given.
> The discontinuance of the use of hyphens in connecting parts of names.
> The simplification of names consisting of more than one word by their combination into one word.
> The avoidance of the use of diacritic characters.

In 1911, under pressure from various sources, the Board was forced to reverse its decision on *h* and restore it to *Pittsburgh*. By executive order of April 17, 1934, the Board was abolished and its functions transferred to a newly formed Division of Geographic Names in the Department of the Interior. Then in 1947, a Public Law recreated the United States Board on Geographic Names, the title under which it functions today. Under its present structure it operates with a Domestic Names Committee, which operates on the principle of formal recognition for present-day local usage, and a Foreign Names Committee, which deals with such issues as romanization standards.

Although numerous attempts have been made to effect spelling reform through legislative or executive act, none has achieved more than marginal change; and one such act, President Theodore Roosevelt's order to the White House printer to adopt certain simplified spellings, probably did more to set back spelling reform in America than it did to advance it. Perhaps the clearest view of government legislation on spelling was offered by Edgar D. Crumpacker, a Representative from Indiana at the beginning of this century, in response to Roosevelt's Executive Order:

> I do not believe, as a matter of general policy, that the standard of orthography ought to be established by act of legislation. The tendency of a fixed standard is to retard that evolutionary reform in spelling that I think every person acquainted with the language and its orthography should welcome. [cited by Read 1936, 1171]

10.2.4 *Social obligation*

Standard spelling, in spite of the efforts of spelling reformers, remains as a mark of education and general competence, although its true value varies with social class. A recent composition handbook depersonalized the issue by stating: "Learning to spell well is worth the effort because misspelling can make writing seem incompetent or lazy" (H. R. Fowler and Aaron 506). A more direct statement appeared in an earlier writing guide (Perrin 403):

> Mistakes in spelling are easily noticed, even by people who would have difficulty with some of the more complex departures from standard usage. Consequently, spelling has become a convenient test of literacy and even of respectability. The main reason for "learning to spell" is that educated readers expect to see words in the standard forms and are likely to undervalue a person who does not use them. . . . Correct spelling is an important – if superficial – trait of good English.

10.3 Spelling reform

Spelling reform in America began in the latter part of the eighteenth century, perhaps as a consequence of the educational reforms that originated with Locke, Rousseau, and Pestalozzi. By the 1760s, the American colonies were exposed to the children's books of the English printer John Newbery, who was the first in England to replace stern theological dogma with practical moral instruction, embedded within humor and other forms of amusement (Kiefer). With the desire to teach through "innocent amusement" came an interest in simplifying the initial task of reading by making English spelling more regular. Additional motivation may have come toward the end of the century from numerous missionary efforts, particularly in Asia and Africa, that attempted to devise alphabets for preliterate societies so that the Bible could be read in the native tongues. Since roman orthography provided a familiar base for devising new alphabets, a more regular letter-sound system became desirable.

The history of American spelling reform is a progression of sporadic spelling reform proposals, often the crusades of retired philologists and industrialists who found the strains of modern spelling no longer tolerable, against which a small number of sustained spelling reform movements have played out their efforts with varying, but limited, degrees of success (Krapp 1925, vol. 1, and Mencken 1936). The major reform movements, of which only four can be counted up to the present time, strove for permanent alterations in spelling, with or without alteration in the alphabet itself. Within the proposals, however, a variety of goals have appeared. Some, like Edwin Leigh's Pronouncing Orthography, were designed as initial teaching alphabets, from which the abecedarian would be weaned after acquiring proficiency. Others, like the American Phonetic Alphabet, devised by Benn Pitman, the younger brother of Isaac Pitman, offered completely new symbols and spellings to replace permanently the prevailing orthography.

Benjamin Franklin's *Scheme for a New Alphabet and Reformed Mode of Spelling*, first written in 1768 but not published until over a decade later (Franklin 1779), proposed six new letters for the alphabet, gave new names to a number of the existing letters, and reordered the resulting graphemic symbols according to articulatory process. In contrast, the proposals of the Simplified Spelling Board, which came nearly a century and a half later and were embraced (at least in part) by President Theodore Roosevelt, offered only replacements for specific spellings, leaving intact the majority of the orthography and the roman alphabet upon which it rests. Other schemes, like the American Phonetic Alphabet and the Revised Scientific Alphabet (to say nothing of the original Scientific Alphabet), propose abandonment of the familiar twenty-six letters of the current orthography in favor of a collection of more phonologically agreeable symbols. With each proposal, the abominations of modern spelling are recited with the finality of a Greek chorus, and the possibility of faster acquisition of literacy and improved spelling ability reoffered. Yet across the centuries the American reading public has remained particularly loyal to its orthography, yielding neither to philological plea nor presidential writ. With the exception of the moderate simplifications of the place names promulgated by the United States Board on Geographic Names, spelling reform remains more a historical curiosity than a detectable influence on American spelling.

10.4 Present-day American spelling

Present-day American English spelling is not English spelling with minor deviations from the shared canon, but a system unto itself. Both British and American spelling, although sharing a large core, have mobile peripheries that reflect the ordinary changes of everyday language use. In addition, standard spelling, as reflected in press guides and composition handbooks, and common spelling, as reflected in everyday print materials, do not always agree. Differences between American and British spelling practices, therefore, vary to some degree according to their source. For American spelling, one analysis found more than 2,000 words for which four major collegiate dictionaries gave alternative spellings (Deighton). Furthermore, for almost 1,800 of those words, the dictionaries did not agree on which spelling was predominant.

Nevertheless, the differences between American and British spelling practices are not large and, if any direction of change can be detected, it is toward consensus rather than wider differentiation. Summarized below are the major differences between the two systems, based upon dictionaries and usage guides (Deighton; Flexner; Kirkpatrick; Mish 1993; Proctor; Sinclair 1987; Soukhanov; US GPO; Weiner).

10.4.1 Types of American–British differences

With the exception of a few isolated spellings such as *curb* and *jail* (Brit. *kerb*, *gaol*), all of the British–American spelling differences are in medial or final word positions and most of the prominent and consistent differences are in word endings. Not included here are pronunciation differences for shared spellings (*schedule*) and morphological differences (*dreamed*, *dreamt*). The spelling of compounds and word division are also important, but not extensively treated here. American orthography shows a stronger tendency toward solid spellings than does British. Nevertheless, the spelling of many compounds, particularly newer ones, is unsettled in America. *The American Heritage Dictionary*, for example, records all three of the possible spellings *secondhand*, *second-hand*, and *second hand*, while three major dictionaries disagree on the spelling for *fellow-man*, each preferring a different option.

For the division of words at the end of a line, American practice favors dividing according to pronunciation (*knowl-edge*), whereas British practice favors derivation (*know-ledge*). British dictionaries, however, tend to pay less attention to word division than do their American counterparts.

10.4.2 *Specific American–British differences*

Summarized below are the most important current differences between British and American spelling.

10.4.2.1 *o* versus *ou*

Before *r* and *l*, American spelling prefers *o* to British *ou*. Thus, American *honor*, *favor*, and *molt* versus British *honour*, *favour*, and *moult*. The *-ol* spellings are limited to a small group of words: *mold*, *molder*, *molt*, and *smolder* being the only common ones. The *-or/-our* contrast dates to the American Revolution and in particular to the spelling reform efforts of Noah Webster. But neither American nor British usage is totally consistent. American spelling is more so, deviating only on *glamour* and *saviour*. The British, however, in formal usage, prefer *-or* for agent nouns (*actor*) but *-our* for abstract nouns (*ardour*, *favour*, *valour*). Before certain suffixes (*-ation*, *-iferous*, *-ize*), *-our* changes to *-or*, but before others (*-able*, *-er*, *-ful*, *-ite*) it remains. Exceptions abound: *anterior*, *interior*, *saviour*, *error*, *horror*, *pallor*, *stupor*, *torpor*, *tremor*. Samuel Johnson's 1755 dictionary omitted *u* in *anterior* and *interior*, but its exclusion from *emperor*, *orator*, and *horror* is due to later lexicographers (B. Matthews 1892).

10.4.2.2 *-re* versus *-er*

American spelling prefers final *-er* to *-re*: *center*, *fiber*, *liter*, *meter*, *miter*, whereas British spelling has a complementary preference for *-re*. One of the few British exceptions is *meter*, in the sense of a device (and its verbal counterpart). American usage dates mainly to Noah Webster, whereas British usage has developed over the last 350 years. For example, in the 1623 edition of Shakespeare's plays, more *-er* than *-re* spellings occur (B. Matthews 1892). Nevertheless, by the middle of the seventeenth century, *-re* was the majority preference in England.

10.4.2.3 Doubling final consonants

American and British spelling differ in seemingly contradictory ways in the handling of final *-l* before suffixes. Before *-ment* and *-ful*, the American style is to double or to retain a doubled -*l*: *enrollment, fulfillment, skillful, willful,* whereas British style is for a single -*l*: *enrolment, fulfilment, skilful, wilful.* On the other hand, the British prefer to double a final -*l* after a single vowel spelling, even if the final syllable is not stressed, whereas Americans generally double a final consonant only after a stressed, single-vowel spelling: *traveling, marvelous* versus British *travelling, marvellous.* The British doubling of final -*l* extends even to digraph vowel spellings, yielding such forms as *woollen* where American spelling admits only *woolen.* (But note the British preference for *paralleled, devilish.*)

For final -*p* before suffixes, British spelling prefers *kidnapped, kidnapping* and *worshipped, worshipping.* American spelling is more unsettled. The *Merriam-Webster's Collegiate* and *Random House* both give first place to *kidnapped, kidnapping,* but *worshiped, worshiping,* while *American Heritage* gives single *p* first for both.

10.4.2.4   -*ce* versus -*se*

Like several other spellings, final -*ce* and -*se* vary unsystematically between America and England. *License* with *s* and *practice* with *c* are both noun and verb spellings in America; in Britain, the noun spellings are with *c* but the related verb spellings are with *s*: *a licence, to license, a practice, to practise.* Similarly, the nouns spelled in American *defense, offense, pretense* have *c* in Britain.

10.4.2.5   -*yse* versus -*yze*

The verbal ending -*yze* in American *analyze, catalyze, paralyze,* etc., which is part of the Greek stem -*lyse,* is spelled with an *s* in Britain: *analyse, catalyse, paralyse,* etc. Some British usage statements are emphatic: "The spelling -*yze* is therefore etymologically incorrect and must not be used, unless American printing style is being followed" (Weiner 86).

10.4.2.6   -*xion* versus -*ction*

American spelling prefers -*ction* in many places where British spelling prefers -*xion*: *deflection, genuflection, inflection* versus *deflexion, genuflexion, inflexion.* The trend in British spelling, however, appears to be away from the -*xion* spelling.

10.4.2.7   Dropping final -*e*

To drop or retain final -*e* after *dg* when a suffix is added sharply differentiates American and British spelling. In words like *abridge, judge, lodge,* British usage favors retention of *e* before *-ment*, while American spelling prefers dropping the *e*: *abridgment, judgment, lodgment*. Sir James Murray, chief editor of the *Oxford English Dictionary*, had no patience for the American style. "I protest against the unscholarly habit of omitting it from 'abridgement,' 'acknowledgement,' 'judgement,' 'lodgement' – which is against all analogy, etymology, and orthoepy, since elsewhere *g* is hard in English when not followed by *e* or *i*" (cited in *Hart's Rules* 86 n. 1). However, an equally strong, if not stronger argument can be made that *dg* as a spelling unit has only a single pronunciation, which is the so-called soft *g*, and therefore the *e* is unnecessary. *Dg* entered English spelling in the sixteenth century as a replacement for *gg* representing the pronunciation /dʒ/. Similarly, *tch* was adopted as a replacement for doubled *ch*, and *ck* for doubled *k* (Venezky 1999).

For other words ending in silent *-e*, American spelling generally omits the *-e* uniformly before *-able* while British spelling tends to make exceptions for certain words: American *blamable, namable, ratable* versus British *blameable, nameable, rateable*.

10.4.2.8   *æ* and *œ*

At the end of the nineteenth century, American and British spelling retained *æ* and *œ* in classical borrowings, especially for mythological and technical terms (e.g., *anæmia, amœba*). But according to the *Oxford English Dictionary*, there was a tendency, more so in America than in Britain, to simplify the two ligatures in words that became familiar or popular. By the late 1950s the American practice was generally to simplify these spellings. "Words formerly written with a ligature *æ, œ* are now usually written with the two letters separately. . . . There is a tendency in the US to drop the *a* or the *o*, esp. in common nouns *ecology, gynecology*, but since it is by no means universal & and varies in different words, no rule can be given" (Nicholson 537–8). The *Chicago Manual of Style* (209 [§6.61]), however, states that the two ligatures should not be used at all for classical borrowings. Similarly, the United States Government Printing Office *Style Manual* proscribes ligatures in anglicized or Latin words, but suggests following the appropriate national practice for other foreign words. British style also has changed, according to Scragg (85): "In the last twenty years or so, British printers have come to accept the American simplification of the <ae> and <oe> digraphs (or ligatures) in classical borrowings such as *encyclopedia, medieval, fetid*, though many survive, e.g., *archaeology, Caesar*." With the ligatures eliminated, British spellings now have two separate letters in their place while American spellings have replaced both with *e*: American *ameba, diarrhea, gynecology*, British *amoeba, diarrhoea, gynaecology*.

10.4.2.9 Incidental differences

Besides the words covered by the patterns just discussed, a number of individual differences are noted by Mencken (1936), Deighton, and Weiner. Included are such variations as American *aluminum*, *cozy*, *mustache*, *pajamas*, *skeptic*, *sulfur* as compared with British *aluminium* (a morphological rather than only orthographic difference), *cosy*, *moustache*, *pyjamas*, *sceptic*, *sulphur*. What is most noticeable about this list is not how long it is but its shortness relative to the full vocabulary of the English language.

In addition to differences in standard orthography, commercial spellings are a noteworthy field for graphemic imagination (Bellamann 212–14; Jaquith; Mencken 1936, 171–91; Pound 1923, 1925). A few examples out of very many are names and slogans such as *Bake-N-Serv*, *Cheez-it*, *Uneeda Biscuit*, *Exxperience the Freedom* (for Dos Equis XX imported beer), *E. Z. Walker* (shoes), *La-Z-Boy*, *Publick House*, and *U-Haul*.

10.5 Conclusion

American English spelling, although not widely different from that of British English, has a unique history and a distinct style. Some deliberate attempts were made in the late eighteenth and early nineteenth centuries to modify American spelling to distinguish it from British, but in general American spelling did not develop in that direction. Instead, present-day conventional American orthography is a response to a special set of needs and an independent set of selections from existing variants.

As with the development of dialects, lack of continual communication leads to differences, especially when some variation already exits. *Honor* and *honour*, for example, both occurred in seventeenth-century England, with *honor* dominant in the 1623 Shakespeare folio. During the next century and a half, British preference moved to *honour* and American to *honor*. Spelling reform movements attempted to reconcile American–British differences, but their efforts have been singularly unsuccessful thus far. Perhaps the leveling process of electronic mail and fax communication, multinational corporations, and especially multinational publishing houses will increase the uniformity.

FURTHER READING

I am not aware of any attempt at a comprehensive history of American English spelling or of any publications of facsimiles of manuscripts and printed pages from which a history might be developed. The most comprehensive treatment of present-day American English orthography is *The American Way of Spelling* by Venezky (1999). See especially chapter 3, "Creative Spellings," which covers American spelling variations that are devised to make products, business establishments, and personal names more distinct. *The American Language* by Mencken (4th ed., 1936), although eclectic and dated, remains a useful source for examples of Americanisms in spelling. The contributions of Noah Webster to American orthography are covered by Malone (1925) and more recently by Monaghan (1983, ch. 6). Also important is the *Second Report* of the United States Board on Geographic Names (1901), which describes general principles for simplifying the spellings of place names. For analyses of spelling variations in American dictionaries published prior to the early 1970s, Deighton's *Comparative Analysis of Spellings in Four Major Collegiate Dictionaries* (1972) is the best source.

I I USAGE

Edward Finegan

11.1   Introduction

Consider three scenarios. First, a distinguished psycholinguist discussing "language mavens" invites his readers to imagine themselves watching a nature documentary:

> The video shows the usual gorgeous footage of animals in their natural habitats. But the voiceover reports some troubling facts. Dolphins do not execute their swimming strokes *properly*. White-crowned sparrows *carelessly* debase their calls. Chickadees' nests are *incorrectly* constructed, pandas hold bamboo in the *wrong* paw, the song of the humpback whale contains several well-known *errors*, and monkeys' cries have been in a state of chaos and *degeneration* for hundreds of years.
>
> [Pinker 370, emphasis added]

Viewers would be incredulous at such reports, the psycholinguist predicts: "What on earth could it mean for the song of the humpback whale to contain an 'error'? Isn't the song of the humpback whale whatever the humpback whale decides to sing?" The psycholinguist contrasts the predicted rejection of judgments about animal behavior with the ready acceptance of similar judgments about human language: "For human language, most people think that the same pronouncements not only are meaningful but are cause for alarm." He says, "To a linguist or psycholinguist . . . language is like the song of the humpback whale. The way to determine whether a construction is 'grammatical' is to find people who speak the language and ask them."

Curiously and to the detriment of his argument, this psycholinguist admits to chronic disappointment at people's answers when they respond to such questions. He claims that a question asked by a linguist about the use of, say, *sneaked* versus *snuck* "is often lobbed back with the ingenuous counter question 'Gee, I better not take a chance; which is correct?'" He finds the "pervasive belief that people do not know their own language" distressing and "a nuisance in doing linguistic research." Thus, despite his claim to the contrary, he is not fully persuaded that "the way to determine whether a construction is 'grammatical' is to find people who speak the language and ask them." Were he a true believer, he could hardly lament the character of the answers people offer.

Humpback whales and people may both be singing mammals, but, as one can readily infer from the psycholinguist's report, judging acceptability in human speech is an altogether different matter from judging the song of the humpback whale. This psycholinguist – and professional linguists more generally – fret about and regret the influence prescriptive sentiments exert on the way people think about their language and respond to questions about it.

In the second scenario, the Executive Committee of the Linguistic Society of America approves a set of language guidelines that its members are expected to use "for the preparation of written and oral presentations in linguistics." According to the LSA (1995), the guidelines "reflect a growing body of research which indicates that many people find sexist language offensive." Among the guidelines are these prescriptions:

1. Whenever possible, use plurals (*people, they*) and other appropriate alternatives, rather than only masculine pronouns and "pseudo-generics" such as *man*, unless referring specifically to males.
2. Avoid generic statements which inaccurately refer only to one sex (e.g., "Americans use lots of obscenities but not around women").
3. Whenever possible, use terms that avoid sexual stereotyping. Such terms as *server, professor*, and *nurse* can be effectively used as gender neutral; marked terms like *waitress, lady professor*, and *male nurse* cannot.
4. Use parallel forms of reference for women and men; e.g. do not cite a male scholar by surname only and a female scholar by first name or initial plus surname.
5. Avoid peopling your examples exclusively with one sex, or consistently putting reference to males before reference to females.

For the third scenario, consider an introductory linguistics textbook. It advises that prescriptive grammarians "should be more concerned about the thinking of the speakers than about the language they use" (Fromkin and Rodman 17). Granted that this particular "should" is intended for language analysts rather than language users as such, it is nevertheless a bald prescription – and characteristic of how professional linguists view prescriptive approaches to grammar.

The three scenarios – with the psycholinguist, the LSA's Executive Committee, and the authors of a respected introductory linguistics textbook – were all enacted in the 1990s. Remarkably, the prescriptivism they illustrate emanates from observers who would claim a position as staunch descriptivists. Taken together they indicate that, even in staunchly descriptivist circles, linguistic prescriptivism thrives. In quite different ways they underscore the appeal of prescriptivism and the fact that prescriptivism by no means belongs solely to language mavens or traditional grammarians. Prescriptivism is alive and well in descriptivist circles; it would appear to be endemic to discussions of language.

11.1.1   Traditional prescriptivism

Prescriptivism is, of course, more characteristic of those who regard themselves as custodians of the language (the mavens) than of those who regard themselves as descriptive linguists. We can contrast the illustrations above with a more familiar linguistic prescriptivism – the kind that appears in traditional grammars and handbooks of usage. The statements below are taken from *The Elements of Style* (Strunk and White), a popular style guide containing a dictionary of usage. Superficially they resemble the statements of the LSA.

1. Use a singular verb form after *each, either, everyone, everybody, neither, nobody, someone*.
2. Use the proper case of pronouns.
3. Use the active voice.
4. Avoid the use of qualifiers.
5. *While*. Avoid the indiscriminate use of this word for *and, but,* and *although*.
6. *Nature* should be avoided in such vague expressions as "a lover of nature," "poems about nature."

Or consider these, from *A Dictionary of Modern American Usage* (Garner 1998):

1. *waiter*. If women can be actors and sculptors, then surely they can be *waiters*. Yet in looking for nonsexist alternatives to *waitress*, various groups have championed the silly terms *waitperson* and *waitron*. Let *waiter* do for either sex.
2. *irregardless*, a semiliterate portmanteau word from *irrespective* and *regardless*, should have been stamped out long ago. But it's common enough in speech that it has found its way into all manner of print sources. . . . Although this widely used nonword seems unlikely to

spread much more than it already has, careful users of language must continually swat it when they encounter it.

Compared with the advice of the textbook authors cited above – that prescriptive grammarians should be less concerned about the language speakers use – is a comment by a traditional prescriptivist: "The Custodians of Language hold that there is a right and a wrong way of expressing yourself, and that the right way should be prescribed by works of a certain description, chief among them the dictionaries of the language" (Pei 1964, 82). In so writing, this custodian prescribed what he thought lexicographers *should* do when compiling dictionaries.

Finally, in contrast to the implicit recommendations of the psycholinguist not to pass judgment on language, here is an acknowledgment by the author of *A Dictionary of Modern American Usage* (Garner xiii):

> I don't shy away from making judgments. I can't imagine that most readers would want me to. Linguists don't like it, of course, because judgment involves subjectivity. It isn't scientific. But rhetoric and usage, in the view of most professional writers, aren't scientific endeavors. You don't want dispassionate descriptions; you want sound guidance. And that requires judgment.

The traditional job of a usage dictionary is "to help writers and editors solve editorial predicaments," but, the author notes, "somewhere along the line . . . usage dictionaries got hijacked by the descriptive linguists who observe language scientifically. For the pure descriptivist, it's impermissible to say that one form of language is any better than any other: as long as a native speaker says it, it's OK – and anyone who takes a contrary stand is a dunderhead" (Garner xi).

11.1.2   *Linguistic prescriptivism and linguistic descriptivism*

These contrasting views of descriptivism and prescriptivism are at the heart of the study of grammar and usage over the past two centuries. Professional linguists regard language as a natural phenomenon that needs only to be *observed* and *analyzed*. They thus subscribe to the "descriptivist" view of grammars and dictionaries, and in that sense their work may be said to resemble that of naturalists studying the calls of white-crowned sparrows or the songs of humpback whales. Indeed, among descriptive linguists are some whose goal for language analysis is "to observe the way people use language when they are not being observed," a methodological challenge called the observer's paradox (Labov 1972b, 61). This view would hold that asking people directly about their language is likely to invite misleading responses.

Nor are linguistics textbooks completely descriptive. Granted they do not ordinarily prescribe particular points of usage, but they do not shy away from prescribing what prescriptivists should and should not do (and, of course, in their writing linguists honor the LSA's prescriptions). In an important sense, albeit not the precise one they are criticizing, the authors of our model textbook transform themselves into prescriptivists when discussing grammar and usage. They explicitly prescribe how grammarians "should" go about doing grammar.

Needless to say, prescriptive grammarians and other observers of language have little sympathy with the views of linguists. Decrying the "nonscience and non-sense" of descriptive linguists several decades ago, a professor of English found himself appalled by the "decline in reputation of the teaching of grammar in American schools" and laid the responsibility for the decline "chiefly at the door of the linguists themselves":

> By focusing attention on "it is me," "who are you with," "none are,"
> "data is," *shall* and *will*, and similar instances of divided usage, these self-
> called "descriptive" grammarians have hooted at "prescriptive"
> grammars and have created in educational circles a thoroughly
> rebellious attitude toward all formal study of the English language. . . .
> They have done untold harm, and, except as they have added a few facts
> to the record, they have done almost no good. [Warfel 1952, 18]

Another educator, a prominent intellectual, warned against the insidious influence of descriptive linguistics, an approach to language that he viewed as an "intellectual disaster" and characterized as fanatical, self-righteous, and badly reasoned.

> For the state of the language as we find it in the centers of culture,
> certain modern linguists bear a grave responsibility. In wanting to prove
> their studies scientific, they went out of their way to impress the public
> with a pose and a set of principles that they thought becoming: a true
> science, they argued, only records, classifies, and notes relations; it never
> prescribes. [Barzun 1959, 240]

Thus, in the second half of the twentieth century serious disagreement existed about what constitutes an appropriate tack in analyzing language – description or prescription.

> Descriptivists want to record language as it's actually used, and they
> perform a useful function – though their audience is generally limited to

362

those willing to pore through vast tomes of dry-as-dust research. Prescriptivists – not all of them, perhaps, but enlightened ones – want to figure out the most effective uses of language, both grammatically and rhetorically. [Garner xi]

One way to characterize the difference is by noting that the two schools are approaching different problems. But others see the difference as so fundamental that prescriptive and descriptive grammars "really reflect . . . two ways of looking at language, two ideals of language, and perhaps in the end two ways of life" (Sherwood 276). They are right, of course.

Scores of scholarly books signal the robust strength of linguistic attitudes in the English-speaking world. Books by professional linguists carry titles like *Leave Your Language Alone!* (R. Hall 1950), *Good or Bad Scots?* (Sandred), *Who Cares about English Usage?* (Crystal), *Bad Language* (Andersson and Trudgill), *Verbal Hygiene* (Cameron), *Standard English: The Widening Debate* (Bex and Watts), and *Proper English* (Wardhaugh). Their existence indicates that questions of good and bad, proper and improper, continue to enjoy a respectable pedigree, even among professional linguists attempting to debunk or reshape the perennial discussion of value in language use. In more popular channels, titles like *The Elements of Style* (Strunk and White) and *A Dictionary of Modern American Usage* (Garner) have been abundant for more than a century.

11.1.3   Overview

The history of approaches to English usage in the United States since the time of the War of Independence has been a story of judgments, comparisons, increasingly reliable data, and growing analytical sophistication, coupled with persistently strong feelings concerning the character of American English and its dialects, the relationship between speech and writing, and the purpose and content of dictionaries and grammars. The story is suffused with judgments about morality, social groups, and the role of language in daily life and politics. Part of the tale involves attempts to suppress not only individual scholarly projects but also particular views of language and grammar, as well as proposals for the role of grammar in schools. Indeed, some suppression has been directed at language itself, as in recent efforts to prohibit the use of targeted dialects for particular functions in schools and of entire languages in public life. No one familiar with the history of language study in America over the past two centuries can doubt that language is a matter of deep feeling and great importance or that anyone lacks strong feelings and judgments about language and about language analysts.

To greater or lesser degrees the story involves language planning or language engineering. This is true not only of garden-variety prescriptivists but also of such bastions of descriptivism as the Linguistic Society of America. It involves competing forces of description and prescription, and it points to the very different lenses through which observers view language use. While usage has been the primary target of prescriptivists as well as of many professional societies in recent decades, some prescription has to do with the character of grammar itself. Even the most descriptive of linguists have not shied away from prescribing theirs as the only acceptable approach to grammar nor from ridiculing and condemning the prescriptivist statements of others.

To a great extent, this is a story of a contest about who speaks authoritatively about the character of language and the methods for analyzing and describing it. The story reflects a continuing struggle to gain the exclusive right to speak authoritatively about language. The details reveal that prescriptivism remains entrenched in ostensibly descriptive as well as admittedly prescriptive approaches. For one thing, despite a professed commitment to descriptivism, professional linguists sometimes espouse prescriptivist positions, though not often about particular items of style or grammar, such as the "proper" case of pronouns or the indiscriminate use of *while*. Prescriptions about matters of linguistic form in journals and monographs have existed for a long time, and in the 1980s and 1990s even professional societies of linguists prescribed particular linguistic uses for their profession. While these prescriptions rely on principles whose raison d'être differs from those invoked by language mavens, they nevertheless meet any reasonable definition of prescriptivism.

Throughout the story are woven links between language and grammar, on the one hand, and American traditions of idealism and morality, on the other. The tradition originated at Babel, but it surfaced in recent years in matters of social policy and social practice, matters that have been seen by some as related to questions of racism and sexism. And in America the tradition has pervaded discussions of language usage since they began. Besides the intellectual and social issues that surround discussion of "correct" English or "good grammar," a great deal of commercial interest resides in language matters and in authority for determining correctness. Dictionaries and grammars are big business, and, while no truly unabridged "big" American dictionary has appeared since *Webster's Third New International Dictionary* in 1961 (Gove 1961a), bookshops display a broad selection of desk dictionaries and collegiate dictionaries, and many brick and mortar and e-commerce dealers still carry "The Third." Those same bookshop shelves carry armloads of dictionaries of usage and "how to" books for avoiding errors and writing effective English.

11.2   The origins of the study of grammar in America

The initial widespread study of the English language in the American colonies was motivated in part by a desire to make the Scriptures widely available. As a result, until about 1720, English instruction in the New World consisted primarily of reading, with only secondary attention paid to writing and spelling. In the second and third quarters of the eighteenth century, when effective public speaking was manifestly shaping a new world and when other languages were competing for status in North America, instruction in the rudiments of English grammar was increasingly encouraged throughout the colonies.

To meet the demand for classroom materials, some Americans imported textbooks, while others, more enterprising, wrote grammars themselves (Finegan 1980; Lyman). Hugh Jones (1724a) appears to be the first American to compose a grammar, which he published not in Boston or Baltimore but in London, with the only known copy in the British Museum. In widespread American use before the Revolution was Thomas Dilworth's *New Guide to the English Tongue*. Chiefly a speller and reader, the *Guide* was published originally in London but appeared in a Philadelphia edition as early as 1747, making it the first known English grammar sent to press in the colonies. More substantive was Robert Lowth's *Short Introduction to English Grammar* of 1762, which did not see its first American edition until 1775 and was thereafter shamelessly copied and imitated, serving Harvard students into the 1840s. Other grammars available in the colonies were James Greenwood's *Essay Towards a Practical English Grammar* and the philosophical *Hermes* by James Harris, the former largely a translation of the English grammar of John Wallis and the latter influential but unsuitable as a textbook. Also available for classroom use were an anonymous *British Grammar*, probably written by James Buchanan, and John Ash's *Grammatical Institutes*. Ash's "Easy Introduction to Dr. Lowth's English Grammar," as its subtitle characterizes it, was shipped to the colonies until it was published in New York during the Revolution. Its preface implies Ash's desire for increased refinement among the class of people whose children, not destined for divinity or law, had little interest in and no need for classical training:

The Importance of an English Education is now pretty well understood; and it is generally acknowledged, that, not only for Ladies, but for young gentlemen designed merely for Trade, an intimate Acquaintance with *the Proprieties, and Beauties of the English Tongue*, would be a very desirable and necessary Attainment; far preferable to a Smattering of the learned languages. [Ash iii, emphasis added]

From the first, then, the "proprieties" and "beauties" of English attracted the attention of American school grammarians.

At least four Americans wrote grammars before the War of Independence ended. Besides Hugh Jones, Samuel Johnson, the first president of King's College (now Columbia University), wrote *First Easy Rudiments of Grammar*, a mere thirty-six-page pamphlet. Another New York teacher named Thomas Byerley published *A Plain and Easy Introduction to English Grammar*, and Abel Curtis of Dartmouth College wrote *A Compend of English Grammar*. None reached the popularity of Dilworth's *Guide*.

11.2.1   Noah Webster: schoolteacher, grammarian, and lexicographer

Among the Colonial schoolmasters using the *Guide* was Noah Webster (1758–1843), who had studied it himself as a Connecticut schoolboy. A college student during the War of Independence, Webster also studied law but was forced by a dearth of legal customers to teach school. When he found the available textbooks unsuitable, he compiled his own speller, grammar, and reader and then undertook a lecture tour to tout his system of education and lobby for copyright laws that would protect his book royalties. Any modern descriptivist would be pleased with what Webster (1789, vii) told his audiences:

After all my reading and observation for the course of ten years, I have been able to unlearn a considerable part of what I learnt in early life; and at thirty years of age, can, with confidence, affirm, that our modern grammars have done much more hurt than good. The authors have labored to prove, what is obviously absurd, viz. that our language is not made right; and in pursuance of this idea, have tried to make it over again, and persuade the English to speak by Latin rules, or by arbitrary rules of their own.

Favorably impressed by Lowth, Ash, and Buchanan at this stage, Webster adapted much of their grammars to his own needs. Dilworth's treatment, however, he judged "not constructed upon the principles of the English language" but a "mere Latin Grammar, very indifferently translated" (1784, 3).

By contrast, his own grammar was designed upon the "true principles" of English. "Our language has now arrived to a great degree of purity," Webster (1784, 4) wrote, "and many writers of the last and present age, have, both in elegance and sublimity of style, equaled, if not surpassed the Roman authors of the Augustan age. To frame such a Grammar as to instruct our own youth, as well as foreigners, in this purity of style, is the business of a Grammarian." Practically from the start, the "business of a Grammarian" was to instruct youth and foreigners in elegance and sublimity of style.

Teachers liked Webster's primer sufficiently to make it the first American grammar to attain wide circulation (Lyman 77–8). If the recollections of his school days by a turn-of-the-century Connecticut native are representative, however, pupils at that time may have been as befuddled by grammar as their successors in school now often are:

> The grammar was a clever book, but I have an idea that neither Master Stebbins nor his pupils ever fathomed its depths. They floundered about in it, as if in a quagmire, and after some time came out pretty nearly where they went in, though perhaps a little obfuscated by the dim and dusky atmosphere of these labyrinths. [Goodrich 139]

An ardent nationalist, Webster vigorously campaigned for a distinct American language. He tackled orthographical, lexical, and grammatical codification, seeking liberation from England and uniformity throughout the States. "As an independent nation, our honor requires us to have a system of our own, in language as well as government. Great Britain . . . should no longer be *our* standard; for the taste of her writers is already corrupted, and her language on the decline" (1789, 20).

As one basis for uniformity, Webster endorsed the "*general practice* of a nation*,*" claiming it the duty of grammarians "to find what the English language *is*, and not, how it *might have been made*" (1789, 24, ix). "Grammars should be formed on *practice*; for practice determines what a language is. . . . The business of a grammarian is not to examine whether or not national practice is founded on philosophical principles; but to *ascertain* the national practice, that the learner may be able to weed from his own, any local peculiarities or false idioms. If *this means* and *a means* are now, and have immemorially been, used by good authors and the nation in general, neither Johnson, Lowth, nor any other person, however learned, has a right to say that the phrases are not *good English*" (1789, 204–5). Of course, the national practice and usage among good authors showed variation, or Webster would have lacked reason to address particular points; and while he may have claimed tolerance for *this means* and *a means*, he treasured uniformity more, and that entailed decisions about "good English" and "purity of style."

As a second standard for uniformity Webster recommended analogy. With uniformity, analogy is a convenient reformist principle, for uniformity and analogy maximize a reformer's options. By definition, universal practice is undisputed, and appeal to that principle occurred only when a usage was, in fact, disputed. As for analogy, it resolved disputed usages by suggesting that one or another item conformed to an established pattern, but analogy often recommends competing solutions in English. For the past tense of *dive*, for example, analogy would endorse both *dove* and *dived* (compare: *drove, rode, wrote* and *arrived, hired, piled*). Equally troublesome, analogy sometimes yielded a solution unsanctioned by educated custom. For example, with *himself/hisself* and *themselves/theirselves*, the pattern of *ourselves, myself*, and *yourself* would endorse nonstandard *hisself* and *theirselves*. In short, appeal to analogy can be fruitless.

More important, though, the very attempt to decide between usages rests on the assumption that custom provides a sound basis for acceptability only when it recommends a single universal usage. For, if customary usage sanctions alternative forms, a reformer who outlaws either of them paradoxically disregards custom in so doing. The view that, if one among several variant usages is correct, the other usages must be wrong tacitly governed codifiers ill at ease with variant customs, and that included Noah Webster. For example, in discussing whether *European* should be stressed on the second or the third syllable, Webster (1789, 119) lamented, "The standard authors . . . very absurdly give both pronunciations, that we may take our choice. [But] it is a certain way to perpetuate differences in opinion and practice, and to prevent the establishment of any standard."

Despite a professed faith in democratic ideals, Webster (1789, 24–5) anointed himself as the standard of propriety and elegance and judged nonconformists vulgar and ignorant. Discussing *shall* and *will*, he insisted "there is hardly a possible case, in which *will* can be properly employed to ask a question in the first person" (1789, 238). Equally uncompromising with pronunciations, he sought to "annihilate differences" (1789, 19) and said he found nothing "so disagreeable as that drawling, whining cant that distinguishes a certain class of people; and too much pains cannot be taken to reform the practice" (1789, 108–9). Expressing a concern that has continued throughout American history, Webster feared that immigrant groups would "retain their respective peculiarities of speaking; and . . . imperceptibly corrupt the national language" (1789, 19). Indeed, his speller aimed partly to correct "a vicious pronunciation, which prevailed extensively among the common people" (1828, preface).

Though ostensibly descriptive, Webster frequently analyzed not what occurred in usage but what he thought ought to occur. He might have been more tolerant of variant or competing usages had he not been committed to a uniform language throughout the nation, but by one principle or another he attempted to resolve variation. In Webster's (1784, 60) discussion of the use of past tenses and past participles, his biases surface:

> Here let it be again observed that no auxiliaries can with propriety be joined with the past time. The expressions, *I have wrote, I have bore, I have began, I have drove*, &c. which are so much in vogue, are shocking improprieties: The childish phrases, *you am, I is*, &c. are not more repugnant to the rules of Grammar . . . An ancient Roman would be startled to hear a Latin Grammarian use *ille fuit amatus est* . . . and the most unlettered Englishman would laugh to hear another say, *he has went*, or *it will be gave*; and yet, *I have wrote, have drove*, &c. which are quite as improper, have become so familiar to our ears, that we can every hour hear them uttered by some of our best Grammarians without a smile of ridicule. *I have written, have driven*, &c. are as easy to be learned and employed as the past tense *wrote* and *drove*; and it is inexcusable to sacrifice propriety to any consideration whatever.

Webster subsequently accepted these "shocking improprieties," though his endorsement proved insufficient for their survival in standard American varieties.

Again, despite the fact that he found the use of *will* in first-person interrogatives "frequent, both in writing and conversation" in the Middle and Southern states, Webster castigated its "absurdity": "a correct English ear revolts at the practice" (1789, 238). About neglect of the subjunctive mood, he admitted that "Numberless examples" could be found even in "authors of the first rank" (1789, 240–1). Of the "gross impropriety" of pronouncing *once* and *twice* as if they had a *t* at the end, he would have overlooked it "but for its prevalence among a class of very well educated people; particularly in Philadelphia and Baltimore" (1789, 111). He also condemned the common use of flat adverbs in phrases like *extreme cold, exceeding fine*, and *indifferent well*, and did not explain why *news* must take a plural verb – why *What is the news?* is "certainly an impropriety, however authorised by custom" (1784, 64, 12). The ipse dixit of the codifier must suffice.

Clearly, America's pioneer lexicographer did not regard general usage as the supreme arbiter of correctness. In a hierarchy understandably characteristic of American school grammar from the start, Webster valued writing and spelling above speaking, and he had engineered a hierarchy of standards, although not even educated usage wore the crown when particular forms offended his sense of propriety and purity of style. In his practice, America's greatest codifier subscribed to standards of linguistic propriety other than common usage, and he was not so unencumbered by familiarity with Latin as he expected Dilworth to be.

Like many of its predecessors, Webster's *Grammatical Institute* abounds with concoctions to be corrected: *That books are torn, These is a fine day, Virtue is his own reward, The boy, whom loves study, will be beloved by his instructor,* and *Philadelphia are a large city.* Unlike those of his predecessors, Webster's examples were so unidiomatic they did not likely induce imitation. Lowth and others often chose examples from the best writers and may thus have helped propagate the very forms they sought to purge. Webster's fabrications contributed to making grammar arcane, as a commentator recalling the grammar lessons of his own student days around 1790 confirms:

> We did not dream of [finding] anything practical, or applicable to the language we were using every day, till we had "been through the grammar several times," and "parsed" several months. Why? Because we were presented at once with a complete system of definitions and rules, which might perplex a Webster or a Murray, without any development of principles, any illustrations which we could comprehend, any application of the words to objects which they represent. We supposed ... that the dogmas of our "grammar books" were the inventions of learned men; curious contrivances, to carry the words of a sentence through a certain operation which we called parsing, rather for the gratification of curiosity, than for any practical benefit or use.... When we found that the nominative case did indeed govern the verb ... – when we accidentally perceived that the rules did actually apply to sentences, and that to observe them would really make better sense than to violate them – then great was our admiration of the inventive powers of those great men, who had been the lights of the grammatical world. [Rand 161–2]

Like his contemporaries, Webster could generalize about usage on the basis only of his personal observation and reading. Information available to modern analysts from computerized corpora and great dictionaries on saucer-sized CD-ROMs could not have been imagined by Webster. When he quarreled with Lowth's distinctions between modes because they were "not warranted by the present idiom of the language," he relied at best on his own observations, as he makes clear when he claims never to have heard "an improper use of the verbs *will* and *shall*, among the unmixed English descendants in the eastern states" (1789, 240). Indeed, over time, Webster's increasing familiarity with educated practice forced him to modify his judgments. In 1784 he condemned "*Who* did you marry?" but five years later accepted it, acknowledging that *whom* was "never used in speaking, as I can find, and if so, is hardly English at all." He figured that *who* alone had been used in asking questions "until some Latin student began to suspect it bad English, because not agreeable to the Latin rules" (1789, 286–7).

By the time he issued his *Philosophical and Practical Grammar* (1807), Webster had read Horne Tooke and Joseph Priestley and, swayed by their tolerant view of custom and by his own greater knowledge of American practice, showed himself somewhat less prescriptive. Like Samuel Johnson's mature views of linguistic propriety, Webster's are now noticeably distant from his earlier ones, and his commitment to the language of everyday intercourse triumphs (1807, 202):

> It struck me . . . as the most monstrous absurdity, that books should teach us a language altogether different from the common language of life. . . . It was reserved for the classical writers of the eighteenth century to lay aside the pedantic forms, *if he go, if it proceed, though he come,* &c. and restore the native idiom of the language, by writing it as men spoke it, and as they still speak it, unless perverted by Grammars.

Understanding that customary forms may differ from situation to situation, he noted that "in polite and classical language, two negatives destroy the negation and express an affirmative," but "in popular language, two negatives are used for a negation, according to the practice of the ancient Greeks and the modern French" (1807, 191–2). More clearly than Lowth, Webster recognized that acceptable language exists in several styles and that what is acceptable in one may be unacceptable in another. For example, he spoke of separating a preposition from its relative pronoun object (*the horse which I rode on* versus *the horse on which I rode*) or omitting the relative pronoun altogether (*the teacher I told you about* versus *the teacher about whom I told you*) as being "most common and most allowable in colloquial and epistolary language. In the grave and elevated style, they are seldom elegant" (1807, 193).

For his 1807 grammar Webster cited the writings of the learned as grounds for accepting usages he had earlier rejected. Whereas in 1784 he had inveighed against past-tense forms with *have* for verbs with distinct past participles, in 1807 he observes, "The influence of Bishop Lowth has had some effect in preserving the use of the old participles in books, but not in oral and popular usage; and why should we retain words in writing which are not generally recognized in oral practice?" He cites Locke ("having spoke of this in another place"), Milton, Dryden, Hume, Pope, Swift, Gibbon, Prior, Darwin, Bacon, Shakespeare, Burke, Bentley, Johnson, and others in support of the past participles *spoke, wove, broke, hid, shook, begot, forgot, chose, froze, stole, mistook, took, drank, writ,* and past tenses such as *rung, sprung, sunk, sung, bid, forbid, begun,* and *writ* (1807, 186–9). He identifies 177 verbs in which the past-tense and past-participle forms differed (as with *swam/swum* and *shook/shaken*) but, disagreeing with Johnson, Lowth, Priestley, and Campbell, regretted that any verbs at all maintained "one of the greatest inconveniences in the language."

When Webster eventually compiled the dictionaries for which he is best remembered, the first of them, the *Compendious Dictionary* (1806), did not list *bred, tru, tuf, dawter, bilt,* and *arkitect,* spellings he had recommended in 1789. On them he yielded to custom, though not on *doctrin, medicin, examin, determin, disciplin,* and *opak,* and he also recorded *error, favor,* and *honor,* which he had argued against in 1789. He had come to believe that "it would be useless to attempt any change, even if practicable, in those anomalies which form whole classes of words, and in which, change would rather perplex than ease the learner" (1806, x). Critics faulted Webster for including such "vulgar" words as *advisory, presidential,* and *insubordination* and for accepting certain nouns as verbs (*girdle, advocate,* and *test*). They damned the dictionary for accepting *-ize* in words like *demoralize, Americanize,* and *deputize* and railed at *favor, labor,* and *honor* (*-our*) and *music, logic,* and *public* (*-ick*). *Theater* and *center* were deemed perversely inverted variants of the British spellings *theatre* and *centre* (Evans 77, 79).

Two decades after the *Compendious Dictionary,* Webster and his wife Rebecca Webster finished reading proofs for *An American Dictionary of the English Language.* At its publication in 1828 (2: back matter), the aged Yankee remained distraught over the state of grammatical and lexicographic learning in his beloved Republic:

> I am convinced the dictionaries and grammars which have been used in our seminaries of learning, for the last forty or fifty years, are so incorrect and imperfect, that they have introduced or sanctioned more errors than they have amended; in other words, had the people of England and of these States been left to learn the pronunciation and construction of their vernacular language solely by tradition, and the reading of good authors, the language would have been spoken and written with more purity than it has been and now is, by those who have learned to adjust their language by the rules which dictionaries and grammars prescribe.
>
> ["Advertisement" for *A Philosophical and Practical Grammar of the English Language*]

We see here a reformed reformer, finally endorsing a wholly naturalistic view of usage. Reversing his earlier priority, Webster now places speech above writing and considers the "authority of universal colloquial practice . . . the *real* and *only genuine language*. . . . Language is that which is uttered by the tongue, and if men do not write the language as it is *spoken* by the great body of respectable people, they do not write the *real* language."

Not surprisingly, in Webster's preface (1828, iii) a language planner still sought to improve the language he was ostensibly describing:

> It has been my aim in this work . . . to ascertain the true principles of the language, in its orthography and structure; to purify it from some palpable errors, and reduce the number of its anomalies, thus giving it more regularity and consistency in its forms, both of words and sentences; and in this manner, to furnish a standard of our vernacular tongue, which we shall not be ashamed to bequeath to *three hundred millions of people*, who are destined to occupy, and I hope, to adorn the vast territory within our jurisdiction.
>
> If the language can be improved in regularity, so as to be more easily acquired by our own citizens, and by foreigners, and thus be rendered a more useful instrument for the propagation of science, arts, civilization and christianity; if it can be rescued from the mischievous influence of sciolists ["smatterers"] and that dabbling spirit of innovation which is perpetually disturbing its settled usages and filling it with anomalies; if, in short, our vernacular language can be redeemed from corruptions, and our philology and literature from degradation; it would be a source of great satisfaction to me to be one among the instruments of promoting these valuable objects. . . .
>
> I present it to my fellow citizens, not with frigid indifference, but with my ardent wishes for their improvement and their happiness; and for the continued increase of the wealth, the learning, the moral and religious elevation of character, and the glory of my country.

Thus Webster presented his dictionary, and his sentiments were widely echoed in the century that followed.

11.2.2   Nineteenth-century school grammars

It was not Webster but the American expatriate Lindley Murray (1745–1826) who all but cornered the grammar market during the first quarter of the nineteenth century. Initially published at York in 1795, Murray's *English Grammar* had its first American printing in 1800 and within half a dozen years passed through a score of editions in England and twice that number in America (Lyman 79–80). In all, more than 300 editions are recorded (Alston, front matter). Forced by illness to give up a Philadelphia legal practice (Lyman 54), Murray took his loyalist leanings and sailed for England in 1784, the year that saw Webster's first grammar appear. In York, a headmistress invited Murray to tutor her teachers in the rudiments of grammar, and he subsequently committed his lessons to paper. He perused Priestley's grammar and Blair's and Campbell's rhetorics and assimilated Lowth's *Short Introduction*, incorporating whole sections of it nearly verbatim. Lowth's mission ("to teach us to express ourselves with propriety . . . and to be able to judge of every phrase and form of construction, whether it be right or not") found a willing disciple in Murray, and his gospel ("to lay down rules, and to illustrate them by examples . . . shewing what is right and pointing out what is wrong") found a zealous evangelist. Thus the pedagogical heuristic of judging a native phrase or sentence "right" or "wrong," the seeds of which were borrowed from Latin grammars, germinated in Lowth's grammar and were nurtured in Murray's. "From the sentiment generally admitted," Murray (iv–v) wrote, "that a proper selection of faulty composition is more instructive to the young grammarian, than any rules and examples of propriety that can be given, the compiler has been induced to pay peculiar attention to this part of the subject." To argue for his rule legislating that "Two negatives, in English, destroy one another, or are equivalent to an affirmative," he provides half a dozen examples – all, as it happens, carrying clear negative force: *I never did repent for doing good, nor shall not now; Never no imitator ever grew up to his author;* and so on.

Like Webster, Murray was a devout man, and religious sentiment pervades his grammar. He explicitly constructed a bridge between learning and virtue (preface):

> The author has no interest in the present publication, but that of endeavoring to promote the cause of learning and virtue; and, with this view, he has been studious, through the whole of the work, not only to avoid all examples and illustrations which might have an improper effect on the minds of youth; but also to introduce, on many occasions, such as have a moral and religious tendency.

Two things about Murray's work are significant: its excessive employment of "unacceptable" or "wrong" English as a mode of inculcating good usage, and its religious underpinnings and its commitment to illustrations "such as have a moral and religious tendency." As to the first, it molded the attitudes of millions of school children and contributed significantly to the widespread perception that grammar is the art of adjudicating "right" and "wrong" forms. Murray encouraged the practice of error hunting in composition, as well as in grammar and spelling lessons, and error-hunting taints the subsequent history of English teaching until nearly the present. As to the second point, Murray had written that "English grammar is the art of speaking and writing the English language with propriety," and two million copies of his grammar linked linguistic propriety to "moral and religious" rectitude. When one recognizes that the two most prominent school grammars of English in the eighteenth and nineteenth centuries were written by a bishop and a devout amateur theologian, one begins to understand the widespread and long lasting association between "learning and virtue," between good grammar and righteous living. Among many nineteenth-century speakers of English who thought linguistic propriety was next to godliness, Lindley Murray certainly thought it so.

Devoutly religious sentiment influenced two other American school grammarians, who happened to detest one another's grammatical methods and to despise one another personally. The fervent contest between Goold Brown and Samuel Kirkham remains unmatched in the history of English grammar and provides insight into the character of mid-nineteenth-century views of the link between "learning and virtue." Kirkham acknowledged a debt to Murray and, like him, expressly aimed to ennoble his young readers: grammatical study "tends to adorn and dignify human nature, and meliorate the condition of man." It is "a leading branch of that learning which alone is capable of unfolding and maturing the mental powers and of elevating man to his proper rank in the scale of intellectual existence; – of that learning which lifts the soul from earth, and enables it to hold converse with a thousand worlds" (Kirkham 13). Kirkham wanted pupils not to compromise with virtue and to that end urged them to observe grammatical principles: "These considerations forbid that you should ever be so unmindful of your duty to your country, to your Creator, to yourself, and to succeeding generations, as to be content to grovel in ignorance." Cautioning them about grammar, he said, "Remember that an enlightened and virtuous people can never be enslaved. . . . Become learned and virtuous, and you will be great. Love God and serve him, and you will be happy" (15). In nineteenth-century America, Samuel Kirkham's books fostered a connection between religious piety and linguistic purity and gave his dicta the force of evangelical zeal. He did as much as any textbook writer to promote an absolutist view of correct English.

In more practical ways too, Kirkham regarded grammar as an indispensable tool; without it, no one could "think, speak, read, or write with accuracy" (14), and "without the knowledge and application of grammar rules," he warned his readers, "you will often speak and write in such a manner as not to be *understood*" (63). He proposed a new systematic parsing which compelled a pupil "to apply every definition and every rule that appertains to each word that he parses, without having a question put to him by the teacher" (11). Lyman (120) notes that Kirkham's methods carried into the study of English the centuries-old methods of studying Latin: memorizing, parsing, and correcting false syntax. Excessive attention to categories like case, tense, and mood characterized the parsing and focused students' attention on distinctions seldom manifest in English words. The popularity of parsing among schoolteachers helped foster a view of English more suitable to a highly inflected language like Latin.

Kirkham followed Lowth, Webster, and Murray by exercising his readers in correcting false syntax. He packed his books with constructions like *He bought a new pair of shoes and an elegant piece of furniture; Who did you walk with? Five and eight makes thirteen;* and *He would not believe that honesty was the best policy,* sentences whose impropriety he challenged readers to uncover and avoid. Besides such everyday examples, Kirkham, like Webster, invented sentences that students would likely never meet outside the schoolroom, such as *The fields look freshly and gayly since the rain.*

For Kirkham (17) grammar was "the art of speaking and writing the English language with propriety," and his standard was the "established practice of the best speakers and writers," by which, following George Campbell, he meant reputable, national, and present use. Thus, Kirkham got ensnared in the same trap as his predecessors, for the best speakers and writers are "those who are deservedly in high estimation; speakers distinguished for their elocution and other literary attainments, and writers, eminent for correct taste, solid matter, and refined manner." Such definitions are circular. A standard of acceptability is identified by ascertaining the established practice of the best speakers and writers, while the best speakers and writers are chosen by criteria of literary attainment, elocution, correct taste, and refined manner – in other words by a standard of acceptability. Since qualities of literary attainment, elocution, correct taste, and refined manner must be determined by some other reference, Kirkham, like others, often applied his personal grammatical judgments. Despite lip service to Locke's notion of conventional language, he applied external standards in gauging the merits of expressions and found countless anomalies and imperfections: "Our language being *im*-perfect, it becomes necessary, in a *practical* treatise, like this, to adopt some rules to direct us in the use of speech as regulated by *custom*. If we had a permanent and surer standard than capricious custom to regulate us in the transmission of thought, great inconvenience would be avoided" (18). Neither did Kirkham recognize that a usage appropriate in one context could be inappropriate in another. He warned against certain shibboleths (e.g., *Who did you walk with?*) without recognizing that even if they rarely occurred in some written registers, they had been accepted in daily speech for generations, a matter he could have determined from Priestley, Webster, or Lowth.

To Kirkham's rival Goold Brown belongs the distinction of authoring the densest English grammar of the nineteenth century, a colossus called *The Grammar of English Grammars*. Brown studied grammar "with religious fervor" (Genzmer) and, like Murray, was self-righteous and harshly critical of others. Skeptical of the inductive and productive systems of grammar teaching, he crusaded for a return to rules and parsing. He thought the "only successful method of teaching grammar, is, to cause the principal definitions and rules to be committed thoroughly to memory, that they may ever afterwards be readily applied" (87). In an age when pedagogical experimentation was energetically pursued, he set himself staunchly against innovation. So self-righteous was Brown that no grammarian escaped the scourge of his pen, and he took the real and imagined faults of earlier grammars as personal affronts. Referring to Murray's grammar, Brown (25–6) said:

> Were this a place for minute criticism, blemishes almost innumerable might be pointed out. It might easily be shown that almost every rule laid down in the book for the observance of the learner, was repeatedly violated by the hand of the master. Nor is there among all those who have since abridged or modified the work, an abler grammarian than he who compiled it. . . . No man professing to have copied and improved Murray, can rationally be supposed to have greatly excelled him; for to pretend to have produced an *improved copy of a compilation*, is . . . utterly unworthy of any man who is able to prescribe and elucidate the principles of English grammar.

Brown here expressly calls the grammarian's task one of *prescribing*, as well as elucidating, grammatical principles. Characteristically, he selected countless examples of false syntax from the writings of other grammarians. While delight at identifying putative infelicities in the works of others has characterized the musings of traditional grammarians for centuries, Brown (iv) justified his pursuit as an inevitable by-product of sensitivity and insight.

Although Brown did not launch the practice of error hunting, he propagated it and frustrated his own design by parading before readers a colorful line of the very usages he hoped to suppress. Believing that the oft-cited definition of grammar – *recte scribendi atque loquendi ars* (the art of writing and speaking correctly) – "not improperly placed writing first, as being that with which grammar is primarily concerned," he fell victim to the classical fallacy, and he promoted the mistaken view that "over any fugitive colloquial dialect, which has never been fixed by visible signs, grammar has no control" (2–3). He thought it "the certain tendency of writing, to improve speech" and judged local dialects to be "beneath the dignity of grammar" (3). Indeed, he considered "the nations of unlettered men" to be "among that portion of the earth's population, upon whose language the genius of grammar has never yet condescended to look down!" (14).

As to choosing among alternative locutions, Brown acknowledged a limited role for usage but reserved the prerogative of choosing just whose usage he preferred. Unlike most grammar writers, he did not subscribe even in theory to the importance of custom. Insisting that language derived directly from God, he flatly denied the social compact theory and approvingly cited classical authors to the effect that names and words subsist by nature and not from art. He agreed with the sixteenth-century grammarian Sanctius that "those who contend that names were made by chance, are no less audacious than if they would endeavour to persuade us, that the whole order of the universe was framed together fortuitously" (7). Given true meanings and word uses inherent in nature, it followed that more ancient usages were to be preferred: "Etymology and custom are seldom at odds; and where they are so, the latter can hardly be deemed infallible." Brown rejected Kirkham's view that a grammarian "is bound to take words and explain them as he finds them in his day, *without any regard to their ancient construction and application*" (10).

For Brown, as for Kirkham and many other nineteenth-century commentators, "The grammatical use of language is in sweet alliance with the moral" (94). Language had been divinely instituted and humanly perverted, so mere custom could not be authoritative, and he deemed it necessary for a Solomon-like grammarian to resolve points of disagreement among competing interpretations generated by lesser grammarians. He aimed "to settle . . . the multitudinous and vexatious disputes which have hitherto divided the sentiments of teachers, and made the study of English grammar so uninviting, unsatisfactory, and unprofitable, to the student whose taste demands a reasonable degree of certainty" (iv).

11.2.3   *Philologians versus linguists: the confrontation*

In addition to schoolbook writers, two other forces helped to shape American linguistic attitudes: development of scientific linguistics in Europe and writings by American and British amateur philologians – and these forces tugged in opposite directions. As is well known, in 1786 in Calcutta Sir William Jones announced his realization that Sanskrit bore so strong an "affinity" to Latin and Greek "that no philologer could examine them all three, without believing them to have sprung from some common source, which, perhaps, no longer exists" (cited by Lehmann). With this germinal recognition of an Indo-European language family came solid comparative and historical linguistics in whose wake the Tower of Babel began to crumble. Philologists uncovered a good deal about historical relationships among languages, as well as about language structure and principles of language evolution. The conviction grew that linguistic change was natural, inevitable, and followed regular patterns. By 1828, when Webster's *American Dictionary* appeared, European scholars had gained substantial insight into the development of English and the other Germanic languages.

After nearly half a century of comparative linguistics on the Continent, however, little was known of the new science in America or Britain (Edgerton; Read 1966). Ironically, Webster had retained a student of German linguistic science to read proofs for the *American Dictionary* but refused to consider his suggestions for revision in accordance with Grimm's discoveries. In 1830 Webster remained unwilling to read Grimm, as he was then urged to do by an Englishman eager to publish the *Dictionary* abroad (Read 1966, 173). In 1842, two decades after Grimm's work, Webster proclaimed that "my researches render it certain that in etymology the Germans are in darkness." Had he examined Grimm's monumental *Deutsche Grammatik*, he could not have persisted in his belief that all languages derived from Chaldee, as he called Biblical Aramaic (Read 1966). As George Philip Krapp (1925, 1: 365) noted about Webster's etymologies: "It was really spiritual, not phonological truth in which Webster was primarily interested."

As Webster's *American Dictionary* (1828) went to press, knowledge of the new science took root especially at Harvard and Yale, although no major treatise became available in English until the early 1860s, when Oxford's Max Müller published his *Lectures on the Science of Language*. In 1867 the American William Dwight Whitney published *Language and the Study of Language* and in 1875 *The Life and Growth of Language*. The scientific principles Whitney acquired at Yale and in Germany also served as the foundation for his editorship of the great *Century Dictionary* (1889–91). They form the cornerstone of the relativistic position of usage that has been endorsed, elaborated, and refined by succeeding generations of descriptivists. Whitney maintained that "speech is a thing of far nearer and higher importance" than writing (1867, 45), that language is arbitrary and conventional (32, 35), that it changes all the time (24, 32, 34), and that it varies from place to place and from time to time (153). More than 125 years ago Whitney articulated a view to which modern linguists still subscribe. Usage is the supreme authority in ascertaining correctness, and it is so because the speakers of a tongue constitute "a republic, or rather, a democracy, in which authority is conferred only by general suffrage and for due cause, and is exercised under constant supervision and control" (1867, 38).

In a school text, Whitney (1877, 4) wrote, "Grammar does not at all make rules and laws for language; it only reports the facts of good language, and in an orderly way." He discussed items of usage only when they fell within general patterns, as with *shall* and *will* as parts of the verb phrase. He viewed a grammarian as "simply a recorder and arranger of the usages of language, and in no manner or degree a lawgiver; hardly even an arbiter or critic" (1877, v). He opposed the notion that the chief goal of grammar is to inculcate correct use and advised teachers that improvement in writing is only "a secondary or subordinate" purpose in studying grammar (1877, iii). In this, too, he anticipated the views of modern linguistics.

He described good English as "those words, and those meanings of them, and those ways of putting them together, which are used by the best speakers, the people of best education." In terms unusual for the nineteenth century, he defined bad English in reference to those who avoid it: "Bad English is simply that which is not approved and accepted by good and careful speakers" (1877, 3). As unsatisfying and as aristocratic as that definition may strike modern readers, Whitney's failure to identify good and careful speakers is perhaps less noteworthy than the fact that his criterion for "bad" usage is social and not inherently linguistic. For the first time, an American broke free from the circularity of preferring the usage of the best speakers and writers while identifying such speakers and writers by the character of their English.

Even so, a singularly talented nineteenth-century linguist exhibited a distinctly prescriptivist hand when he discussed specific items. Though Whitney acknowledged without regret that "the subjunctive, as a separate mode, is almost lost and out of mind in our language" (1877, 194), he withheld approbation from certain common usages of the future auxiliaries. He accused the Irish and Scots of having "long been inaccurate in their use" of *shall* and *will* and "putting *will* often where the cultivated and approved idiom requires *shall*" and lamented that "the inaccuracy has recently been greatly increasing in the United States" (1877, 120). He suggested that in his native New England "the proper distinction of *shall* and *will* was as strictly maintained, and a slip in the use of the one for the other as rare, and as immediately noticeable and offensive . . . as in the best society of London" (1874, 203). With its regional chauvinism, its discussion of inaccuracies and the elevation of cultivated and approved idiom, the first part echoes Webster, but Whitney's obeisance to "the best society of London" would have appalled the patriotic lexicographer. In principle, Whitney accepted Locke's view of convention, but his talk of "inaccuracy" and "proper distinction" shows that he harbored notions of inherent correctness. It is an incompatibility exhibited by many eighteenth- and nineteenth-century grammarians.

Shall and *will* were not the only usages that irritated Whitney. He deplored still other usages, including "it is *me*," which he acknowledged to be "firmly established" in both colloquial and written usage. Still, he said, "the expression is none the less in its origin a simple blunder, a popular inaccuracy. It is neither to be justified nor palliated by theoretical considerations" (1874, 173). While usage reigned supreme in Whitney's theory, analogy and personal preference sometimes triumphed in his practice. His commitment to scientific observation and his conviction that language is arbitrary and conventional did not inhibit personal judgments about specific points of usage. An accomplished and distinguished theoretical linguist and Sanskritist, Whitney proved an amateur philologian in the realm of English usage. For all that, Whitney's books set out certain fundamental principles of linguistic science and laid a theoretical foundation for basing grammars on current usage appropriate to its situation. The effect of his linguistic science on school grammars was insufficient to overcome the momentum of an eighteenth-century authoritarian approach – even in Whitney's own grammar.

Representing the competing amateur philologian's viewpoint is George Perkins Marsh. Prominent among Americans whose conservative views influenced popular opinion, Marsh delivered a series of postgraduate lectures that demonstrated the total unacceptability of usage as a standard of correctness among prominent Americans in the middle of the nineteenth century. Marsh understood that English had always been changing. He conceded that "our speech must bow" to the law of change, but he bowed reluctantly. Like Dr. Johnson, Marsh hoped that we English speakers would "avail ourselves of a great variety of means and circumstances peculiar to modern society, to retard the decay of our tongue, and to prevent its dissipation into a multitude of independent dialects" (679). Like so many eighteenth- and nineteenth-century observers, he accepted the authority of usage in principle but disregarded it when its conclusions countered his preferences.

In particular, he articulated a chauvinistic view: "The national language is the key to the national intellect, the national heart, and it is the special vocation of what is technically called philology, as distinguished from linguistics, to avail itself of the study of language as a means of knowing, not man in the abstract, but man as collected into distinct communities, informed with the same spirit, exposed to the same molding influences, and pursuing the same great objects by substantially the same means" (221–2). He thought it "evident . . . that unity of speech is essential to the unity of a people. Community of language is a stronger bond than identity of religion or government, and contemporaneous nations of one speech, however formally separated by differences of creed or of political organization, are essentially one in culture, one in tendency, one in influence" (221).

Languages could be corrupted, Marsh believed (645), and he scathingly criticized a British commentator who had confused "the progress of natural linguistic change, which is inevitable, [with] the deterioration arising from accidental or local causes, which may be resisted." The commentator, Robert Latham (in his preface to the 1848 second edition of his book *The English Language*), had proclaimed that in language "not only *whatever is is right*, but also that in many cases *whatever was was wrong*." Latham had already dropped the offending preface from the fourth edition, five years before Marsh berated the second edition, and only a few have since dared to repeat that claim, among them: "Grammar, like botany or mineralogy, is a purely descriptive science. . . . What is true of nothing else is true of language, that whatever is is right" (Ramsey 51); "There can . . . never be in grammar an error that is both very bad and very common. The more common it is, the nearer it comes to being the best of grammar" (Fries 1927, 33–4); "Essentially, in the usage of native speakers, whatever is, is right; but some usages may be more appropriate than others, at least socially" (McDavid 1966, xxi). Marsh scoffed at the notion that whatever is is right and skewered the contradictory logic in the two parts of Latham's claim. For Marsh (649), it was a straightforward equation: "To deny that language is susceptible of corruption is to deny that races or nations are susceptible of depravation; and to treat all its changes as normal, is to confound things as distinct as health and disease."

In the distinction Marsh drew between inevitable and accidental change, between the normal and the depraved, we spy once again the association between morality and grammaticality that has infused American language attitudes from the start. As the fall of Adam inclines us to sin, so the effects of Babel promote language corruption. In varying degrees Webster, Murray, Kirkham, and Brown all subscribed to this belief, though none so harshly and fanatically as Marsh (258), for whom linguistic propriety was principally a moral question: "The wanton abuse of words by writers . . . of popular imaginative literature has been productive of very serious injury in language and in ethics." Concerning simple variant pronunciations like "Ohiuh" and "Mississippuh" for *Ohio* and *Mississippi*, he preached, "To pillory such offences . . . to detect and expose the moral obliquity which too often lurks beneath them, is the sacred duty of every scholar . . . who knows how nearly purity of speech, like personal cleanliness, is allied with purity of thought and rectitude of action" (644–5). Here then is the coin of the realm in American discussion of English usage: moral obliquity versus sacred duty, purity of speech, purity of thought, and rectitude of action. Correct usage – the pronunciation even of a word-final vowel – has moral fabric; and to mispronounce a word threatens nothing less than "moral obliquity." Marsh's fanciful creed is woven into the fabric of American thinking about grammatical correctness, its tone somewhat muted and its terms somewhat altered.

It is not only isolated usages that Marsh condemns. Whole languages can prove themselves unworthy and – in keeping with the spirit of Richard Chenevix Trench's fossilized ethics (Finegan 1998, 564–72) – reveal national depravity. Marsh (278n) admired Trench's work and recommended it to his New York City audience. He refrained from quoting Trench so as not to "diminish the pleasure" to be found in reading his work. It was perhaps a distrust of the lower classes among recent immigrants from such depraved nations that prompted Marsh to deny linguistic conventionality and arbitrariness. His condemnation of Italian – and indeed of its speakers – is revealing. Distinguishing the Italians of his day, about whom he had no ill to say, from the earlier Roman tyrants to blame for the sorry state of Italian, he remarks, about a year before becoming the first United States Minister to Italy (224–5):

> A bold and manly and generous and truthful people certainly would not choose to say *umiliare una supplica*, to humiliate a supplication, for, to present a memorial; to style the strength which awes, and the finesse which deceives, alike, *onestà*, honesty or respectability; to speak of taking human life by poison, not as a crime, but simply as a mode of facilitating death, *ajutare la morte*; to employ *pellegrino*, foreign, for admirable; . . . to apply to a small garden and a cottage the title of *un podere*, a power; to call every house with a large door, *un palazzo*, a palace; a brass ear-ring, *una gioja*, a joy; a present of a bodkin, *un regalo*, a royal munificence; an alteration in a picture, *un pentimento*, a repentance; a man of honor, *un uomo di garbo*, a well-dressed man; . . . or a message sent by a footman to his tailor, through a scullion, *una ambasciata*, an embassy.

383

Rejecting the conventional view of language, Marsh (1860, 37) saw as "a general law" the supposition that there exists "a natural connection between the sound and the thing signified, and consequently, that the forms of language are neither arbitrary or conventional on the one hand, nor accidental on the other, but are natural and necessary products of the organization, faculties, and condition of men." As old as Plato, the dispute between conventionalists and naturalists remained unsettled in 1860. An influential American lecturer and writer on language was propagating views that a linguistically informed contemporary like Whitney regarded as poppycock.

Still, despite such rigid and narrow views, Marsh cannot be easily categorized. He did claim that English had no grammar (that is, no regularity) and that, if only half a dozen persons in Europe knew French, still fewer in America knew English. But, flouting consistency, he also condemned lexicographers who fail to "present the language as it is, as the conjoined influence of uncontrollable circumstances and learned labor has made it," but who instead present their own "crude notions" of what it ought to be (13, 99, 420). Such ambivalence was typical of the age. Probably most grammarians accepted the principles of an emerging linguistic science, but the implications of those principles ran counter to national and class prejudices, and scientific principle urged grammarians to accept what xenophobia and social snobbery prompted them to disdain. Guilt by association contaminated expressions that some observers recognized could have no intrinsic fault. Nor was it uncommon to see an alliance between purity of speech and rectitude of action, as Marsh did. As a consequence, defending language from the onslaughts of impurity became an ethical imperative. Inspired to restore English to an imagined God-given pristine state, many took to noting errors and inconsistencies in the usage of linguistic enemies and social inferiors. Inevitably, the prescriptions of one person became the proscriptions of another, and amateur grammarians and philologians fell to public feuding.

11.2.4   Amateur grammarians feud

Among the best known feuders were the Dean of Canterbury and an American expatriate living in England. In 1863 Henry Alford, Dean of Canterbury, penned "A Plea for the Queen's English" in a series of magazine pieces. Deliberately misconstruing the title, the American George Washington Moon countered with *A Defense of the Queen's English*. Gathering his pleas into a book, Alford retitled them *The Queen's English* (subsequent editions restored the periodical title, 1864), trying to tempt readers to interpret Moon's *Defense of the Queen's English* as support for Alford. The taunt provoked Moon into calling his next edition *The Dean's English*, and in it he yielded to the temptation to ridicule opponents for violating their own rules.

What had initially moved Alford was a conviction "that most of the grammars, and rules, and applications of rules, now so commonly made for our language, are in reality not contributions towards its purity, but main instruments of its deterioration" (xiv). Using a then customary British technique to demonstrate the importance of language purity, he directed attention to American linguistic shortcomings: "Look at those phrases which so amuse us in their speech and books; at their reckless exaggeration, and contempt for congruity; and then compare the character and history of the nation – its blunted sense of moral obligation and duty to man; . . . and . . . its reckless and fruitless maintenance of the most cruel and unprincipled war in the history of the world" (6). How the "amusing phrases" gave rise to or stemmed from the same causes as the Civil War, Alford left to the imagination of his readers.

Alford's fear that the proliferation of Americanisms would ruin English was widely shared in England and not uncommon among the literati in America. Despite that, Alford's frankly prescriptive notes on speaking and spelling are not nearly so dogmatic as others of his day. By contrast with Whitney, who had called *It is me* "a simple blunder, a popular inaccuracy," Alford sanctioned the expression as one that "everyone uses." By contrast, while recommending that people write much as they speak, he also knew that speech and writing must be distinguished (Alford 154, 279, 74).

Besides his skirmishes with Alford, the American Moon also took aim at the linguistic naughtiness of his fellow expatriate Lindley Murray. Indeed, in *The Bad English of Lindley Murray and Other Writers on the English Language*, Moon (1869, xxv) said, "I cannot resist the temptation to take up the pen against him, and to repay him for the terror of his name in my school days, by showing that, in the very volume in which he laid down his rules, he frequently expressed himself ungrammatically." Moon's attack on the usage of Alford, Murray, Marsh, and other purists was a natural result of the kinds of grammar teaching that characterized contemporary schools. Exercises in false syntax fostered an error-hunting disposition.

Interest in the antics of Moon and Alford was eclipsed by the popularity of New York verbal critic Richard Grant White. Like Max Müller and others, White's verbal criticisms appeared principally in venues like the *Galaxy* magazine, the *New York Times*, and the *Nation*, but were subsequently collected as *Words and Their Uses* (1870) and *Every-Day English*

(1880). One chapter of *Words* is a thirty-page denial of Horace's dictum on the authority of usage (*jus et norma loquendi*) and an implicit undermining of Locke's social contract. White flatly denies the authority (though not the force) of general usage and even of great writers: "There is a misuse of words which can be justified by no authority, however great, by no usage, however general" (1870, 24). Like many, he was uneasy with divided usage and precluded the possibility of multiple acceptable usages. Even if fifty instances of *both* applied to three things could be uncovered – in Milton, Shakespeare, Spenser, and Chaucer ('To whom bothe heven and erthe and see is seene') – the usage could not be justified because of the word's etymology and its usage elsewhere (1870, 400). If *both* properly relates two countable items, then it is degenerate to force it to relate more than two – Chaucer, Milton, and Shakespeare be damned: "It is impossible that the same word can mean two and three!"

White lambasted "words that are not words" and thereby demonstrated the futility of opposing usage by logic, etymology, or esthetics. Among many other locutions, he exhorted people to reject the verbs *donate, jeopardize, resurrect,* and *initiate*; the nouns *practitioner, photographer, pants, conversationalist,* and *standpoint*; the adjectives *presidential, gubernatorial, shamefaced,* and *reliable.* He preferred *enthusiasmed* to *enthused, telegraphist* to *telegrapher, washing-tubs* and *shoeing-horn* to *wash-tubs* and *shoe-horn.* He penned a lengthy chapter against the "incongruous and ridiculous" use of the progressive passive verb form (as in *is being done* and *is being built*), which was coming into common usage at the time. With Marsh and others, he favored the more traditional *The house is building* over *The house is being built,* though he rightly surmised that the latter would prevail. White's view represented what Alford had described as the fallacy of believing that "of two modes of expression, if one be shown to be right, the other must necessarily be wrong," which was a prominent view in the nineteenth century.

A decade later, in *Every-Day English*, White (1880, ix) lauds his earlier success:

> That usage, even the usage of the best writers, is not the final law of language; that in the scientific sense of the word it is not a law at all; and that English is, to all intents and purposes, without formal grammar, are truths now perceived by so many intelligent, well-informed, and thinking men, that he who proclaimed them may safely leave them to work out their proper ends without the aid of further advocacy.

Such self-congratulation would wrongly suggest that White's opposition to the authority of usage and his claim that English had no grammar went unchallenged. On the contrary, they were greeted with "cries of defiance" and "sneers of derision" (1880, xi). Among others the views expressed in the earlier book were ringingly condemned by the learned and distinguished Sanskritist and lexicographer Fitzedward Hall (Finegan 1998, 574–5). Unfortunately, like other condemnations of prescriptive verbal criticism, Hall's *Recent Exemplifications of False Philology* did not share a place in the limelight with White's. Perhaps its polemic tone hurt it, as McKnight (1928, 536) suggested, but polemics enhanced other books. More telling may have been Hall's "assemblage of dry facts," as McKnight remarked and as has been remarked recently (Garner) about linguistic descriptivism more generally (including J. L. Hall; Horwill; Jespersen 1909–49; and Curme 1931–5). Without mentioning Fitzedward Hall's name, White (1880, x) seemed to recognize the inefficacy of the philologists' dry facts:

> Men in general are not convinced by arguments, *pro* and *con*, by retorts, by pleas and replications, rejoinders, rebutters, and surrebutters. The world at large learns through direct dogmatic teaching by those who have strong convictions. The doctrines of such men, suiting more or less the temper of their times, are tested by the general sense, and are gradually absorbed or rejected in the progress of years.

Though writing more than a century ago about contemporary grammars, this note of White's (1880, xi–xii) seems somehow prescient:

> People have yet fully to grasp the fact that there really is no such thing as grammar in the English language; that all systems of teaching English-speaking children their mother tongue by rules and exceptions, and notes and observations, and cautions and corollaries, are useless, and not only so, but worse, because such a system naturally leads to the injurious misapprehension that writing or speaking grammatically is something else than writing or speaking naturally, – something else than saying in plain language just what you mean. The new modified and curtailed grammars are the fruits of an absurd notion that to learn to speak and write his own language a man must be taught *some* "grammar" in one shape or another. This is but a natural attempt to break a fall. The struggle will go on until at last the grammarians and the grammar-loving pedagogues, utterly overthrown, will pass peaceably away, and be carried out to sepulture with a funeral service from Lindley Murray read over their venerable remains.

It is not surprising that, in contrast to Hall's polemic, White's verbal criticism was widely – though not universally – appreciated. Leonard Bloomfield (1944) recalled that his undergraduate instructors at Harvard

387

endorsed White's *Words and Their Uses* even four decades after it first appeared.

Nineteenth-century grammarians showed a notable characteristic in their conviction that linguistic expressions possess *inherent* goodness or badness. In remarks that echo those of Plato's Cratylus, Marsh, White, and others all rejected the arbitrariness of linguistic symbols and the conventionality of usage. Cratylus believed that "everything has a right name of its own, which comes by nature, and that a name is not whatever people call a thing by agreement . . . but that there is a kind of inherent correctness in names, which is the same for all men, both Greeks and barbarians." The sentiment was widely shared in nineteenth-century America.

11.3   Closing the gap: scholars face the facts of usage

In the final quarter of the nineteenth century, increasing numbers of scholars and teachers were embarrassed by the disparity between the language portrayed in grammars and taught in schools and the language used by speakers and writers of English. The founding of the American Philological Association in 1869, the Modern Language Association in 1883, and the American Dialect Society in 1889 gave impetus to the pursuit of accurate information about English usage. In the first quarter of the twentieth century the founding of the National Council of Teachers of English in 1911 and the Linguistic Society of America in 1924 further propelled a more realistic approach to the teaching of English grammar and usage. The single most influential force in promulgating a realistic view of correctness among twentieth-century teachers was the National Council of Teachers of English.

Starting about 1875, some scholars had attempted to apply linguistic insights to English teaching and made headway in mapping varieties of English and promoting their recognition. The 1899 presidential address to the Modern Language Association treated "Philology and Purism," and in it President von Jagemann articulated the orthodox scholarly view that "the chief task of philology is to record and explain, not to prophesy or to legislate" (von Jagemann 74). He ventured, "Philology cannot expect to influence contemporary speech without recognition and consistent application of the principle that the living languages are for the living and the usage of each generation is a law unto itself" (88). Because, as he claimed, the authority of writers past and present was overrated, he called for a class of philologist-purists to balance the forces of usage with desirable changes. The questions to be raised should relate to the hold of present usage on speakers and to the advantages and disadvantages of a particular adoption or rejection. His suggestion that particular locutions be evaluated for their utility is rare in discussions of language correctness, where ipse dixit pronouncements or purely descriptive statements predominate. In the 1901 presidential address to the same association, E. S. Sheldon (1902) urged that philologists' views on grammars, dictionaries, and language be made better known, and he endorsed the principle that "good usage is decisive" regardless of its basis in logic or history. He also acknowledged the dilemma of the schoolteacher, who was expected to know and practice the teachings of linguists and yet be responsible for improving students' English. Within two years, then, presidential addresses to the MLA represented differing views of achieving linguistic correctness, with von Jagemann calling for balanced reform and Sheldon advocating laissez faire.

The attention of teachers was increasingly drawn to the importance of basing grammar instruction on actual usage. In the late 1880s the journal *Education* carried a stout condemnation of writers of grammar texts, noting "a real fascination" for surrounding themselves "with a few hundred of the existing grammars and picking about among them for material to arrange in an odd way." Poking fun at the attempts of many grammarians to "fit all English to ingeniously devised diagrams," the author noted little reliance on current usage in their rules. As he argued the case, "language precedes grammar and dictates its laws"; as a consequence, "the facts which the grammarian records [must] be real, such as he sees in language, not such as exist in other languages, and which he imagines must also exist in English" (E. Allen 465).

Thomas Lounsbury (1838–1915) also recognized the chasm between educated usage and the prescriptions of amateur philologians and school grammarians. A mastery of the history of English supplied him abundant examples and saved him from dogmatic condemnations and assertions. Following "all the great authorities who from remotest antiquity have treated this subject," his essays aimed to maintain "the doctrine that the best, and indeed the only proper, usage is the usage of the best, and that any rules or injunctions not based upon the practice of the best speakers and writers neither require nor deserve attention" (viii, vi). He recognized that the chief weakness of grammarians since the mid eighteenth century had been unfamiliarity with the practice of the best writers and ignorance of the history of English. He argued that the rules of the "amateur champions of propriety" generate a "fictitious standard" of correctness and that appeals to reason, etymology, or "universal grammar" are irrelevant: "It is the practice and consent of the great authors that determine correctness of speech." Typically light was his treatment of *manoeuvre*, which "in all its existing senses . . . refers to actions which are the result of the operations of the mind" but etymologically refers only to work with the hand. As though that were insufficient to reveal "the worthlessness of relying upon derivation as a final authority for present meaning," he notes offhandedly that "*manoeuvre* and *manure* are precisely the same word, so far as their origin is concerned" (154).

Like the mature Dr. Johnson, Lounsbury expressed contempt for the hope of fixing the language (71). Because language changes, the best usage of a past generation may cease to be acceptable, and the sole authoritative standard of propriety must be present good usage. He also attempted to delimit whose usage set the standard. Agreeing with Horace that usage is the deciding authority and taking him to mean the usage of the best speakers and writers, he saw Horace's *usus* as "precisely the same as Quintilian's *consensus eruditorum* – the agreement of the cultivated" (89). Aristocratically, Lounsbury (97) defined good usage as that of the "intellectually good," the "cultivated," and the passage that follows shows the influence of Whitney in his characterization of what the "cultivated" shun linguistically:

> Such men are the absolute dictators of language. They are lawgivers whose edicts it is the duty of the grammarian to record. What they agree upon is correct; what they shun it is expedient to shun, even if not wrong in itself to employ. Words coined by those outside of the class to which these men belong do not pass into the language as a constituent part of it until sanctioned by their approbation and use. Their authority, both as regards the reception or rejection of locutions of any sort, is final. It hardly needs to be said that "the man in the street" is not only no dictator of usage, but that he has no direct influence upon the preservation of the life of any word or phrase. This depends entirely upon its adoption by great writers. If these fail to accept a new locution, it is certain to die eventually and as a general rule very speedily.

One acquires good usage "by associating in life with the best speakers or in literature with the best writers."

If we equate Lounsbury's "good" usage with George Campbell's "reputable" usage, we see that his position lacks the refinement of the Scottish rhetorician's. Whereas Campbell had defined standard as *present, reputable*, and *national*, Lounsbury downplayed national usage. More significantly he emphasized the written word more than his predecessors had. As Krapp (1908b) noted, the chief difficulty with Lounsbury's ideas lay in his insistence on calling only literary usage standard: "The imposing of this authority of literary speech upon the actual, living, creating processes of present speech . . . puts the cart before the horse." A literary standard also left little room to recognize the correctness of situationally appropriate varieties of English. It made cultivated written usage the norm for all varieties and risked suggesting that spoken use properly derives from written.

Most directly akin to Lounsbury's approach was that of J. Lesslie Hall (1856–1928). Prompted by Lounsbury's *Standard of Usage*, Hall's *English Usage* (1917) was the product of a determination "to search the literature and see how far some of the disputed words and phrases" had been employed by reputable authors. Initiating a claim still heard, Hall felt that "purists" were putting teachers, students, and the general public in "strait-jackets" (5). In revolt against the "distinguished grammarians and eminent rhetorical scholars" who condemned locutions frequently used by "eminent writers" and "attractive speakers," he gathered from 75,000 pages of English and American literature instances of about 125 usages "condemned more or less vehemently by purists, pedants, verbalists, grammarians, and professors of rhetoric." Devoting a chapter each to such matters as the difference between *continually* and *constantly*, whether *athletics* is singular or plural, and the correctness of *dove* and *dived*, he intended to point out "the authorities *pro* and *con* . . . and leave the reader to draw his own conclusions."

Hall's approach had the dual virtues of recording actual usage and limiting discussion solely to the record. But in implementing a literary standard, it did not avoid the difficulties Krapp had warned about. In the tradition of absolutist approaches, in this instance on the liberal side of the fence, Hall paid insufficient attention to a locution's appropriateness. After determining whether a usage had been employed by respected authors, his judgments implied a simple dichotomy. If he could document use by reputable authors, a locution was good; otherwise, not. Hall missed the crucial distinction between *standard* and *good* usage, which, as we shall see, Krapp had earlier noted. As a consequence, his handbook – more tolerant than any before it – was also misleading. Traditionalists like Richard Grant White, who judged certain usages wrong no matter how employed or by whom, were somehow no farther afield than Hall, who implied that a locution's use by reputable authors made it acceptable in any circumstances. Hall's liberal view flouted the best contemporary insights.

Providing a radically different solution to the question of language standards was Brander Matthews (1852–1929). President of the MLA and chairman of the Simplified Spelling Board, he played a key role in scholarly discussion of linguistic correctness. Casting aside Lounsbury's written standard, Matthews looked instead to speech. "The real language of a people is the spoken word, not the written. Language lives on the tongue and in the ear; there it was born, and there it grows" (1901, 71, prefatory note). As Lounsbury's love had been written history, Matthews's love was theater. He judged most popular books on usage "grotesque in their ignorance," and the only function he allowed guidebook writers was to record usage and "discover the principles which may underlie the incessant development of our common speech" (1901, 212, 221, 220). He provided the most democratic response to the question of whose usage determines correctness – a simple matter of majority rule. His view of usage is extreme in the authority it assigns the ordinary use of English by ordinary users. "In language, as in politics," Matthews wrote, "the people at large are in the long run better judges of their own needs than any specialist can be" (1901, 212). Naturally, he questioned the efficacy of an academy, noting that language is "governed not by elected representatives but by a direct democracy, by the people as a whole assembled in town meeting" (1921, 9, 28).

As is true of nearly all commentators, Matthews's linguistic essays reveal idiosyncratic biases. Despite a personal preference for new, usually shorter, spellings like *tho*, *altho*, *thoro*, *thoroly*, *fonetic*, and *thruout*, for example, he found certain clipped forms like *pants* and *gents* abhorrent and detested back-formations like the verb *enthuse*, which struck him as "vulgar and uncouth, bearing the bend sinister of offensive illegitimacy" (1921, 110). On balance, though, he expressed uncommon tolerance, and personal distaste did not prompt condemnation. Before the American Academy of Arts and Letters, he vigorously disputed charges that English was becoming debased. Echoing Lounsbury, he said that the history of any language is a history of "corruption" and that growth and improvement presuppose change (1925, 91).

Among his contributions to the usage movement was Matthews's influence on his colleague George Philip Krapp (1872–1934). Krapp articulated the first cogent view of the relativity of correctness and delineated an exposition of levels and functional varieties, recognizing popular, colloquial, and formal or literary among the "kinds of English." He explained that several "manners" of formal English exist, including pulpit speaking and public lecturing. Dedicated to Brander Matthews, Krapp's *Modern English* (1909) deserves credit for instigating a systematic understanding of the varieties of English in America. Like Matthews, Krapp (1909, 14) viewed spoken language as of the greatest importance and thought it "a false standard of values to assume that the test of highest excellence is to be found only in printed and written words." With Matthews, he maintained that "the real guide to good grammar, to good English in all respects, is to be found in the living speech" from which literary language derives its vitality. Citing Walt Whitman and echoing the Romantics, he said that language "is something arising out of the work, needs, ties, joys, affections, tastes, of long generations of humanity, and has its bases broad and low, close to the ground. Its final decisions are made by the masses, people nearest the concrete, having most to do with actual land and sea" (1909, 328–9).

Like many grammarians before him, Krapp saw that "the laws of language are not based on theory, but arise from actual use" and that "the grammarian has no more power of legislating in the rules of grammar than the scientist has in the physical laws of nature" (1909, 158–9, 322). Unlike his predecessors, though, he took the challenge of settling on a standard to lie not in deciding between popular, illiterate speech and educated, cultivated speech but "in determining just who are the cultivated and refined speakers whom we are willing to regard as affording the model or laws of the correct or standard speech" (1909, 159–60). He thus addressed a central issue for the doctrine of usage: Whose usage is standard? More important, Krapp identified good English as English that "hits the mark," and he distinguished it from standard, or conventional, English. Laying heavy stress on appropriateness and effectiveness as measures of good English, Krapp (1908a, 24–5) made a case against the very notion of an absolute or uniform standard:

> The only way in which language grows . . . is by the creation of individuals, who thus established a trend or tendency or law of the language. . . . It follows, therefore, . . . that all future progress in language depends upon individual initiative. The conception of society in which there is no differentiation of individual from individual, but an absolute regularity of impulse and achievement, a complacent acquiescence in a codified and established system of human activity, whether possible as an actuality or not, cannot arouse much enthusiasm as an ideal.

Krapp understood that standard or conventional English is not necessarily good English, and the most favorable set of circumstances for a vital and effective language involves the interplay between forces of standardization and the force of inventiveness: "Standard English must continually refresh itself by accepting the creations of good English" (Krapp 1909, 333). "Poets and prose writers, lively imaginations of all kinds, in speech as in literature, are continually widening the bounds of the conventional and standard language by adding to it something that was not there before. They must do so if speech is ever to rise above the dead level of the commonplace" (1909, 333–4).

In his early work (1908a, 1909), Krapp attempted to define levels of usage and sketch the contours of what could be called a doctrine of appropriate usage. He later laid out a program for pursuing American speechways and filling in the outline of "appropriateness." Krapp (1925, 2: 7) argued that "speech is standard when it passes current in actual usage among persons who must be accounted as among the conservers and representatives of the approved social traditions of a community." He emphasized the users rather than the forms of language and defined standard users conservatively. Though much influenced by Brander Matthews, democratic leveling was not part of Krapp's picture.

Given the premise that socially acceptable persons speak in socially acceptable ways, a description of the language of socially acceptable Americans would by definition codify socially acceptable American English. To determine acceptable American English, therefore, one would need only to record the usages of the socially acceptable. To do otherwise, namely to define socially acceptable people by their use of certain predetermined language forms and then produce a grammar of standard English based on the usage of a group so defined, would be circular. As noted, Krapp acknowledged the great difficulty of determining "just who are the cultivated and refined speakers."

In other writings (1927a, 1927b), Krapp continued to stress appropriateness as a requirement but added speaker comfort: "To be good, English must not only meet the practical demands of utility, it must also satisfy the inner sense of goodness of the speaker or writer" (1927a, 178, 182). The major theme of Krapp's program was that mature students should observe for themselves how language is best used. While his *Comprehensive Guide* discusses debatable points of usage and applies labels (including *literary*, *local*, *dialect*, *colloquial*, *low colloquial*, *vulgar*, and *ungrammatical*) and adjectives (e.g., *careful*, *crude*, *incorrect*, *offensive*, *proper*, *feminine*) to classify usage, he aimed primarily "to encourage direct observation of the varied possibilities of English speech as it appears in living use, spoken and written, and, as a consequence of such observation, to enable readers to make for themselves independent and sensible judgments in the practical use of the English language" (1927b, ix). Krapp's call to train people to observe how language functions became a rallying cry of leaders in the teaching profession during the second quarter of the century, though it found little favor among a more insecure rank and file and among professional language guardians.

11.3.1   The OED's influence

In the English-speaking world, the outstanding philological and linguistic event of the second half of the nineteenth century was the launching of the *Oxford English Dictionary*. Under the auspices of the Philological Society of London and the editorship of James Murray, the original *OED* began appearing in 1884 and was completed in 1928 under William Craigie. The *OED* furnished scholars with a wealth of reference to the literature of every age in which a usage had occurred. It held a mirror up to nature, as Krapp observed.

In the first quarter of the twentieth century, general linguistic works (such as those by L. Bloomfield 1914; Sapir; and Sturtevant) gave linguistics a solid foundation in the United States. Though not directly concerned with correctness, they provided a framework for discussion and implicitly affirmed a doctrine of usage by explicitly arguing that linguistic change is natural, speech primary, meaning conventional, grammar dependent on usage, and linguistic correctness relative. Though they directly influenced few teachers, they helped prompt reevaluation of programs among leaders in the teaching profession.

By 1925, publication of the *OED* was nearing completion. Some scholars and teachers had condemned the doctrine of correctness and taken steps to implement a relativistic view in the schools. Some influential linguistic treatises had appeared, and the professional organizations that were to do most to foster a relative view of correctness had been established. Lounsbury, Matthews, Krapp, and others had eloquently argued for the need to base grammar on usage, although they disagreed as to the relative authority of speech and writing. Matthews had voiced the negative implications of a doctrine of correctness for a democratic society, while Krapp had recognized the relevance of usage levels and functional varieties in a pluralistic democracy and distinguished "good" from "standard" English.

During the fifty years surrounding the turn of the century, however, such views had exercised little effect on schoolbooks. Teachers continued drilling the prescriptions of Lowth, Murray, and White, and the error-hunting syndrome still flourished. Between the views of linguists and those of school grammarians, the gap had never been wider. By 1924, when the Linguistic Society of America was founded, so little had been achieved that Leonard Bloomfield (1925, 5) lamented, "Our schools are conducted by persons who, from professors of education down to teachers in the classroom, know nothing of the results of linguistic science, not even the relation of writing to speech or of standard language to dialect." Intermediaries were needed to apply to school grammars the approach that the linguists were developing, and the task fell to the leaders of the National Council of Teachers of English (NCTE), which had been founded in 1911.

11.3.2 Surveys of English usage

With growing unease about the gap between the textbook prescriptions and the actual speech and writing of ordinary educated Americans, the NCTE undertook to provide teachers information about the character of usage and guidance about informed attitudes toward it. In the decade preceding America's entry into World War II, three of NCTE's past or future presidents published influential monographs on usage and grammar. Sterling Leonard sent a ballot of 102 debated items to linguists, businessmen, authors, editors of influential publications, NCTE and MLA members, and speech teachers. He asked them to rate "according to your observation of what is actual usage rather than your opinion of what usage should be." Relying on 229 replies, he labeled the usages *established, illiterate,* or *disputable.* Usages judged to be *illiterate* included "The *data is* often inaccurate" and "John *had awoken* much earlier than usual." Among the disputable were "*Everybody* bought *their* own ticket," "He *dove* off the pier," "It *don't* make any difference what you think," and "Martha *don't* sew as well as she used to." Among those rated established were several widely condemned ones: "*None* of them *are* here," "*Everyone* was here, but *they* all went home early," "It is *me*," "Invite *whoever* you like to the party," "That's a dangerous curve; you'd better go *slow*," and "*Who* are you looking for?" Leonard concluded straightforwardly that educated speech habits change and that grammar books must keep pace.

Six years later Albert Marckwardt and Fred Walcott compared the views of Leonard's judges with actual usage as recorded in the newly completed *OED* and *Webster's New International Dictionary* (Neilson and Knott). Taking issue with Leonard's study, they reexamined his 121 "disputable" items and found fifty of them recorded in literary usage and thirteen more in American literary usage. Another forty-three were recorded in good colloquial usage. Most strikingly, five of Leonard's thirty-eight "illiterate" items appeared in literary or American literary usage, including "John *had awoken* much earlier than usual" and "I enjoy wandering *among* a library." Another eight "illiterate" items appeared in standard colloquial usage, including "A light *complected* girl passed" and "I want *for* you *to* come at once." All told, a mere five "illiterate" items were not recorded in the sources. Contrary to Leonard's supposition, Marckwardt and Walcott concluded that recorded usage in dictionaries outpaces educated opinion about it. Together, the two studies laid bare the conservatism of handbooks, grammars, and ostensibly liberal opinion.

A third influential study was made by Charles Carpenter Fries, who, like Krapp before him, had urged in the 1920s that students be trained to observe the practice of people carrying on the affairs of the English-speaking world. Echoing refrains of John Dewey's progressive education, he stressed that students need reinforcement outside the classroom and that such support would exist only if teaching reflected current informal usage among educated Americans. If the facts of usage were "not in harmony with the rules or generalizations . . . in our grammars," he proposed, "then these rules must be restated and expanded to include all the facts." In a comment that gained notoriety, he added, "There can . . . never be in grammar an error that is both very bad and very common. The more common it is, the nearer it comes to being the best of grammar" (Fries 1927, 33–4).

More sensitive than his predecessors to the necessity of relative standards of linguistic correctness in a democracy, Fries denied outright that only the speech of people categorized as socially acceptable was correct. Instead, he claimed correctness for all social varieties (1927, 132–3), and called for "a grammar that records the facts of the actual usage of those who are carrying on the affairs of English-speaking people and does not falsify the account in accord with a make-believe standard of 'school-mastered' speech" (1927, 44).

Fries enlisted the support of the MLA, LSA, and NCTE in seeking access to a corpus of current English, consisting of correspondence from citizens to the federal government. For all letters in that corpus, he had demographic information about the writers, including their schooling and employment history. In all, he examined 2,000 complete letters and 1,000 additional excerpts, all written by native-born Americans of at least three generations' standing. Only after he had sorted the writers into social groups on nonlinguistic grounds did he examine their linguistic usage, and he thus broke the vicious circle of defining correct English as the usage of the cultured, while defining the cultured by their linguistic practices. He recognized that "the most important facts" about words and constructions are "the circumstances in which they are usually used, because these words, forms, or constructions will inevitably suggest these circumstances," and he set out to identify "the important matters of American English" with "distinct social class connotations" (1940, 24).

Fries categorized correspondents into three groups: speakers of "Vulgar English" (who had not more than an eighth-grade education and were employed in strictly manual or unskilled labor); speakers of "Standard English" (who had a college degree and were engaged in professions); and a middle group who spoke "Common English" (who had between one year of high school and one year of college or technical school and were neither professionals nor strictly unskilled laborers). Excluding all borderline cases, he had about 300 writers in each group. Among many findings, he noted that both Common and Vulgar English groups used *don't* as a third-person singular verb (while the Vulgar English group exceedingly rarely used *doesn't*, the Common English speakers used *don't* on about 30% of the possible occasions). By contrast, third-singular *don't* did not occur even once in the Standard English letters. Another finding was that only one instance of a noun with apostrophe-*s* or *s*-apostrophe occurred before a gerund, whereas just more than half of the pronouns before gerunds in the Standard English corpus were possessive forms. A third finding was that not a single writer in any category used *whom* as an interrogative. Webster (1789, 286) 150 years earlier had observed that interrogative *whom* "was never used in speaking . . . and . . . is hardly English at all." By contrast, Marckwardt and Walcott had identified interrogative *whom* as good colloquial English, and Leonard as acceptable. Standard English letter writers used *whom* as a relative pronoun in only two-thirds of the instances where traditional grammar would call for it (and *who* in the rest). In harmony with both previous NCTE studies, Fries found only twenty cases of a split infinitive in all the letters, eighteen of them in Standard English; 98 percent of all infinitives had the *to*-marker immediately before the infinitive. Fries concluded that "a study of the real grammar of present-day English has never been used in the schools" (1940, 285), and he recommended that teachers base instruction on "an accurate, realistic description of the actual practices of informal Standard English and eliminate from our language programs all those matters of dispute for which there is any considerable usage in informal Standard English" (1940, 290).

In focusing on social groups, Fries followed in the footsteps of virtually all his predecessors. The history of grammar and usage study shows persistent focus on *who* says *what*, with emphasis on the social standing of the *who*. The literature abounds with references to good and best, refined and cultivated, in reference sometimes to language, but usually to speakers: "the best speakers and writers" (Kirkham and Lounsbury), "the best speakers, the people of best education" (Whitney), "the cultivated" (Lounsbury), "the intellectually good" (Lounsbury), and "cultivated and refined speakers" (Krapp), "persons who wish to pass as cultivated" (Leonard), "writings of well-bred ease" (Leonard). Matters of debate have been whether speech or writing ranks higher in determining good English and distinctions of style – for example Webster's "colloquial and epistolary language" and "grave and elevated style." Throughout the history of usage discussion – good and bad, appropriate and inappropriate – users and uses, speakers and styles, have generally been confused.

As commonly employed in discussing good English, the term "levels" merged cultural levels with various functions – a confusion particularly apparent in contrasts between the colloquial and standard or literary levels. The frequent grouping of "levels" like literary, colloquial, and illiterate leads people to suppose that just as illiterate is culturally below colloquial, so colloquial is culturally below literary. Kenyon (1948) recommended a distinction between "cultural levels" (standard, substandard) and "functional varieties" (colloquial, literary, scientific) in order to make clear that different varieties are equally good when used for their respective functions. The functional variety called colloquial might be standard or substandard (like any other functional variety), but the term "colloquial" would not refer to a level.

11.3.3 Triumph of a relativistic view of correctness

The year 1952 can be viewed a benchmark for a half century of growing liberality in attitudes toward usage. That year the National Council of Teachers of English published *The English Language Arts*, embodying ideas promulgated by advocates of a relativistic view of linguistic correctness. While the report covered all phases of the English curriculum, the chapter on "Grammar and Linguistics" achieved some notoriety. In that chapter, the Commission on the English Curriculum recommended five foundational linguistic principles for teaching English, the first three of which especially drew fire: (1) Spoken language is the language. (2) Correctness rests upon usage. (3) All usage is relative. (4) Language changes constantly. (5) Change is normal.

In recommending that "the language of today . . . is to be chiefly found upon the lips of people who are currently speaking it" and not in books, the commission followed the analyses of Whitney, Matthews, Krapp, Leonard, and Fries and positioned itself within the orbit of Dewey's philosophy. Further, it endorsed the position of the contemporary linguist, who uses "good English" and "bad English" only in "a purely relative sense" in that "language is governed by the situation in which it occurs." Hence, good English is defined as "that form of speech which is appropriate to the purpose of the speaker, true to the language as it is, and comfortable to speaker and listener." These notions were familiar since the time of Whitney and were explicitly justified by Krapp.

Attempts to mirror actual usage in school grammars were not an isolated current in American education. Early in the century, educators sought to have the curriculum reflect life. John Dewey's influence in this regard is well known, and the realism of a relativistic doctrine of usage harmonized with his educational philosophy. His stress on correlating school and home, theory and practice, learning and living, parallels the focus on everyday usage by Krapp, Leonard, and Fries (as noted above, §11.3.2). The consonance between Dewey's view and that of supporters of a relativistic approach to good usage is no coincidence. Dewey taught at Michigan from 1884 to 1888 and from 1889 to 1895; at Chicago until 1904; at Columbia until 1930. Fries attended Chicago in 1910 and received his other graduate education at Michigan. Leonard took his doctorate from Columbia while Dewey taught there and headed the English department at a school that operated under the auspices of Columbia University Teachers College. Fred Newton Scott, first NCTE president and one of Fries's teachers, took his degrees from Michigan in the 1880s. Moreover, Krapp, who influenced Leonard, taught at Columbia during Dewey's tenure there. Leonard acknowledged a debt to Dewey, and Fries (1927) cites various works by Dewey. As recently as 1998, the NCTE and Teachers College Press Columbia University jointly published a book called *John Dewey and the Challenge of Classroom Practice* (Fishman and McCarthy).

11.3.4. *Gathering clouds: reactions to* The English Language Arts

If the first half of the twentieth century witnessed vigorous propagation of relativistic views of correctness, the second half witnessed extreme hostility to them. With a torrent of criticism against *Webster's Third New International Dictionary* in the 1960s, a storm of resentment had been signaled by criticism of *The English Language Arts*. Since mid century, teachers and commentators aplenty have vehemently rejected the assumptions of a doctrine of usage. Rather than revealing simple intellectual disagreement about the character of usage, deep-seated social and emotional convictions underlie the bitterness – and they concern politics, morality, and social status.

Dismayed at the "non-science and non-sense" of *The English Language Arts*, one observer asked *Who Killed Grammar?* and in reply blamed the linguists and especially Fries as the "villain" in this "murder story" (Warfel 1952, v). Appalled by the "decline in reputation of the teaching of grammar," Warfel (1952, 59) wrote, "The worst feature of the non-sense of the 'new' linguists is its 'book-burning' quality. By shaking faith in the correctness of a few items in grammars of the English language, these detractors have destroyed faith in every book on the subject." Joining the attack was a distinguished historian: "To appreciate the extent of the intellectual disaster brought on by the liquidation of grammar and to gauge the fanaticism, the bad reasoning, the incapacity to come to a point, the self righteousness of the antigrammarians," he pointed to the commission's report – one long demonstration of the authors' "unfitness to tell anybody anything about English" (Barzun 1959, 243). Imagining that the aim of linguists was "a classless speech corresponding to the usage of the most numerous" (a position Fries had disavowed), Barzun (1959, 244–5) lambasted the notion that students should be taught to observe language customs for themselves (as Krapp, Fries, and other adherents to Dewey's educational philosophy had indeed urged):

> This pseudo scientific pedantry has obscured the important fact of the willful inexactitude of science, that is, its deliberate refusal to grasp the individual and relate him to its models and systems. Not to know this results, for the whole realm of learning outside natural science, in a superstitious reliance on figures, graphs, and labels. Give a man a rating on a scale, call him a something-or-other, and no amount of direct evidence will erase the suspicion that he is what he has "scientifically" been called. Hence the modern abdication of direct, responsible judgment by human beings.

Along with wholesale consternation at the passing of what was perceived as "old grammar," discussion of "new grammar" flourished in the wake of *The English Language Arts*. Traditionalists distrusted its putative objectivity and scientific bias and scoffed at its progressivism and egalitarianism:

> It stands for democracy; for spontaneity, self expression, and permissiveness; for nominalism; for skepticism; for a social scientific view of life; for progress and modernity; for nationalism and regionalism. It is "other directed," seeing the proper standard of conduct as conformity to the mores of the group. It represents a linguistic Rousseauism, a belief that man's language is best and most real when most spontaneous and unpremeditated and that it is somehow tainted by the efforts of educational systems to order and regularize it. Just as the old grammar tried to take its values from above, the new tries to deduce them, in the manner of Dr. Kinsey, from the facts.
> [Sherwood 277]

By contrast stand the glorified tenets of the "old grammar":

> It stands for order, logic, and consistency; for the supremacy of the written language and of the literate classes in setting linguistic standards; for continuity, tradition, and universality – for what is common to older and modern, British and American English, to the

whole body of European languages rather than for what is local and singular; for discipline and self control; for the practice of an art, a system developed by tradition and the authority of masters rather than statistical study. It is aristocratic only in the sense of following Jefferson's "natural aristocracy," valuing the language of the leaders of the community, and accepting the right of these to give the law to those who are less skilled; it is snobbish only as all education must be snobbish, as implying the transmission of wisdom from those who possess it to those who do not. It values the language of momentous and dignified occasions over casual talk, language that comes from premeditation and thought rather than spontaneous expression. It is a grammar for the idealistic, for Ortega y Gasset's "select man," who is willing to live up to higher standards than the generality are willing to impose upon themselves. . . . Loving logic and order, it opposes oddity and irregularity, and at times may have the coldness that goes with order and regularity. It is not resigned to the chaos of experience but wishes to impose its own order upon it; it believes, with Orwell, in man's power to master his linguistic environment. It may recognize . . . language levels but attaches little importance to the lower levels; it attempts to raise the illiterate to the level of the literate, not to average everyone out to a common level. It is best to think of it not as Platonic, dwelling in a realm apart from concrete reality, but as Aristotelian, the "form" of reality, what reality would be shorn of the anomalous and accidental, what reality at its best tends to be. It is usage, but usage ordered by reflection. [Sherwood 276–7]

Echoing familiar refrains are the elitist disdain for democracy and the association of linguistics with moral and political waywardness. The snobbishness and natural aristocracy of "old grammar" is granted a legitimate place in the teaching of English. As for the implied obliquity of "new grammar," the linking of Fries's research on language practices with Kinsey's on sexual ones suggests that linguistic scientists were viewed as urging linguistic abandon. The coupling of "bad grammar" and profligacy survived from the eighteenth and nineteenth centuries into the twentieth. "What the two grammars really reflect is two ways of looking at language, two ideals of language, and perhaps in the end two ways of life," said one author (Sherwood 276).

"New grammarians" refers chiefly to professors of English like Krapp, Leonard, Marckwardt, and Fries, who were influenced by linguistic science and dedicated to importing a realistic view of English usage into grammar books and language teaching. But the attempts of these new grammarians to undermine the time-honored approach to "good grammar" bred strong resentment in the teaching profession and in the world of letters. If by definition old grammarians were prescribers of what is *good* in English, it is not surprising that the NCTE and new grammarians were viewed as traitors to the written word and even as threatening the traditional employment of English teachers.

11.3.5   Webster's Third *fans the flames*

During the decade after *The English Language Arts* appeared, editors at the Merriam-Webster Company in Springfield, Massachusetts, were compiling a new edition of their flagship dictionary. Like NCTE leaders and the authors of *The English Language Arts*, these editors had been influenced by descriptive linguistics and its philosophy of usage, although this philosophy was far from new to Merriam-Webster lexicography. When to great fanfare *Webster's Third New International Dictionary* appeared in 1961, its editor acknowledged the dictionary's indebtedness to descriptivism and proudly announced that the *Third* represented the best description of the contemporary lexicon. Indeed, in its treatment of scientific vocabulary, organization of word senses, citations of actual usage, and in many other ways, the *Third* was an impressive record.

Overlooking its virtues or despite them, many influential critics expressed dismay at the *Third*'s contents. Reviews in respected and highly visible periodicals bristled with indignation, and the sizzling criticism seared Merriam-Webster and editor-in-chief Philip Gove (Sledd and Ebbitt; Morton). As the inheritor of Noah Webster's mantle and as the leading name in American lexicography, Merriam-Webster had been regarded as the ultimate American authority on linguistic matters, including meaning, pronunciation, and usage. To the shock of critics, however, Gove had changed the calibration of usage labels and been too catholic in his inclusion of dubious lexical items. What Goold Brown said in a different context in 1851, many in effect said of the *Third* in 1961: "Barbarisms and solecisms have not been rebuked away as they deserve to be."

After Noah Webster's death in 1843, George and Charles Merriam bought the remaining copies of the *American Dictionary* and the right to publish subsequent revisions. The first Merriam-Webster dictionary appeared in 1847. By 1934, a second edition of *Webster's New International Dictionary* had appeared and earned a reputation as an authoritative source of information about English. Americans widely regarded it as "the authority" on matters of spelling, meaning, and usage. In 1961 a completely revised third edition was invested with three and a half million dollars and the best scholarship of the day. Perhaps hoping to place the new unabridged alongside the Bible in American homes, Merriam's publicists boasted that "special attention was given to the language of tax forms, game laws, insurance policies, instruction booklets for everything from automobile maintenance to the putting together of children's toys, legal contracts and wills, as well as the colorful vocabularies of such fields as show business, sports, retailing, and fashion and the technical terms of science, agriculture, and industry." They touted the fact that, besides admired sources like Conrad and Shaw, the editors had culled passages from the *Annual Report of J. C. Penney Co.*, the *Boy Scout Handbook*, the *Marine Corps Manual*, and the *Ford Times*. If they had been more politic, they might have forestalled censure, as Dr. Johnson had by conceding in 1755 that "some of the examples have been taken from writers who were never mentioned as masters of elegance or models of stile; but words must be sought where they are used; and in what pages, eminent for purity, can terms of manufacture or agriculture be found?"

Meanwhile, for academic audiences, Gove (1961b) described the principles governing production of the *Third*:

> Within the lifetime of nearly all who are teaching today . . . the study of
> the English language has been deeply affected by the emergence of
> linguistics as a science. . . . The fundamental step in setting down
> postulates for descriptive linguistics is observing precisely what happens
> when native speakers speak. This is the essential first step required by
> scientific method. Its obviousness and simplicity are deceptive,
> however, for its application calls for a radical change in analytical
> method. Instead of observing a language in terms of its past,
> specifically in its relations to Latin grammar, the linguist must first
> observe only the relationships of its own elements to each other.

Avoiding the appearance of radicalism, Gove denied that descriptive linguistics had contributed much to the treatment of spelling, etymology, meaning, or vocabulary – though its influence on pronunciation was "profound and exciting." Gove (1961b) continued:

> If a dictionary should neglect the obligation to act as a faithful recorder
> and interpreter of usage . . . it cannot expect to be any longer appealed
> to as an authority. When the semantic center of gravity appears to have
> moved far enough, when the drift of pronunciation is ascertainable,
> when a new science makes new knowledge and new methods available,
> then revision of the affected parts of a dictionary becomes the
> conscientious duty of the lexicographer.

When copies of the dictionary reached reviewers, the gnashing of teeth unequivocally demonstrated that the views expressed in *The English Language Arts* – views that constituted a foundation of American descriptive linguistics – had failed to persuade many influential commentators. Titles like "Sabotage in Springfield," "The Death of Meaning," "Madness in Their Method," "The String Untuned," and "Say It 'Ain't' So!" signal the discordant reception. Writing in the *Atlantic*, Wilson Follett alleged that "it costs only minutes" to discover that the *Third* is "in many crucial particulars a very great calamity." He was aghast at what he saw as the aim "to destroy . . . every surviving influence that makes for the upholding of standards, every criterion for distinguishing between better usages and worse." Small wonder that the new wordbook was viewed in various quarters as a "disappointment" and a "shock," "a scandal and a disaster," "a fighting document."

One hallmark of the hullabaloo was the widespread assumption that the *Third* was a product of modern linguistics. For a generation – since the time of Leonard's monograph – resentment had been building toward the "infection" linguists were viewed as spreading. That the dictionary seemed to approve nonstandard usages found acceptable in NCTE studies helped cement that connection. So did the dictionary's phonetic notation. And, given linguists' claim that spoken language *is* the language, the absence of the label "colloquial" confirmed the link. Some viewed the *Third* as a "hostage" of linguistic science, and Jacques Barzun discovered a "theology" of linguistics in it. Mario Pei (1962, 45–6) voiced a similar suspicion:

> The appearance of the new Webster's International . . . has for the first
> time brought forth, into the view of the general public, those who are
> primarily responsible for the shift in attitude and point of view in
> matters of language – . . . the followers of the American,
> anthropological, descriptive, structuralistic school of linguistics, a
> school which for decades has been preaching that one form of language
> is as good as another; that there is no such thing as correct or incorrect
> so far as native speakers of the language are concerned; that at the age
> of five anyone who is not deaf or idiotic has gained a full mastery of his
> language; that we must not try to correct or improve language, but must
> leave it alone; that the only language activity worthy of the name is
> speech on the colloquial, slangy, even illiterate plane; that writing is a
> secondary, unimportant activity which cannot be dignified with the
> name of language; that systems of writing serve only to disguise the
> true nature of language; and that it would be well if we completely
> refrained from teaching spelling for a number of years.

Editorial condemnations in respected publications like the *New York Times* and *Life* magazine suggest a view of the *Third* as a political document, not a scholarly treatise. Indeed, "When it came up as a subject of interest at a meeting of the board of *The American Scholar*," a member reported, he "was delegated to express the board's 'position'":

> Never in my experience has the Editorial Board desired to reach a position; it respects without effort the individuality of each member and contributor, and it expects and relishes diversity. What is even more remarkable, none of those present had given the new dictionary more than a casual glance, yet each one felt that he knew how he stood on the issue that the work presented to the public.
>
> That astonishing and possibly premature concurrence within a group of writers whose work almost invariably exhibits judicial tolerance and the scholarly temper defines the nature and character of the new Webster: it is undoubtedly the longest political pamphlet ever put together by a party. [Barzun 1963, 176]

In these critiques the fundamental principle of lexicography – that a dictionary's function is to record linguistic practice – bore the brunt of the attack. The premises of a doctrine of usage, outlined by Whitney in the nineteenth century and amplified by Krapp, Leonard, Marckwardt, and Fries in the twentieth, were trashed as detractors berated Gove and lambasted descriptive linguistics for its debilitating influence on lexicography and the language itself. Just how ineffective had been all the attempts to dent popular credence in absolutist views of linguistic correctness was now fully apparent. Virtually everywhere, the authority of usage in determining linguistic correctness was challenged. Commentators believed certain words, meanings, and uses to be absolutely right and others to be absolutely wrong, and they insisted that those "wrong" usages be blacklisted no matter who employed them.

Three themes recur in the antagonistic notices of the *Third*: it was "scientific," "permissive," and "democratic." Opposition had greeted *The English Language Arts* because it stressed a scientific view of language, and on that count even stronger resistance met the *Third*. Scholars, teachers, and journalists who opposed a relativistic view of usage saw linguistics as "nose-counting" and asked how a "geiger counter" could detect education and culture and how an "adding machine" could measure them. Here is Dwight Macdonald (1962a, 185): "As a scientific discipline, Structural Linguistics can have no truck with values or standards. Its job is to deal only with The Facts. But in matters of usage, the evaluation of The Facts is important, too, and this requires a certain amount of general culture, not to mention common sense – commodities that many scientists have done brilliantly without but that teachers and lexicographers need in their work." Traditionalists despised what they correctly viewed as the amoral, unesthetic, nonjudgmental, statistical approach to language study modeled by linguists.

As to permissiveness, detractors reasoned that by including certain usages Gove granted them a Good Housekeeping Seal of Approval and thereby relinquished his mantle of authority. By refusing to decide right and wrong, by failing to legislate correct usage, Merriam-Webster had yielded to the same permissiveness that was injuring art, music, literature, and morals. "This scientific revolution has meshed gears with a trend toward permissiveness, in the name of democracy, that is debasing our language by rendering it less precise and thus less effective as literature and less efficient as communication" (Macdonald 1962a, 166). The *American Bar Association Journal* (January 1962) drew an economic parallel: "Surely opening the floodgates to every word that is used, no matter how or by whom, and regardless of its propriety, is like the printing of paper money backed by no sound value." Editors at the *New York Times* (October 12, 1961) said Merriam-Webster had "surrendered to the permissive school that has been busily extending its beachhead on English instruction." *Life*'s editors lamented that *Webster*'s had joined "the say-as-you-go school of permissive English" and "all but abandoned any effort to distinguish between good and bad usage – between the King's English, say, and the fishwife's."

The *Third*'s permissiveness was perceived as related to egalitarian imperatives – and to other parameters of conflict. Some associated it with a "relativistic philosophy, fully divorced from both ethics and esthetics," a philosophy that concludes "the native speaker can do no wrong" (Pei 1962, 46). Many detested the supposed tenet of linguistics that good English is whatever is popular. Some reviewers betrayed a conviction that distinctions between "better" and "worse" usage, between careful and slipshod writing and speaking, are important for maintaining class differences. "The reason most people value 'good English' . . . is that ours is a class society in which one of the chief differentiations between the top dogs and the bottom dogs is in the use of language" (Macdonald 1962b, 257fn.). Years later in a radio broadcast this same critic said that in teaching and dictionary making the scholarship of linguists is not as important as what "the elite" think the language is. Another critic, author of a successful writing handbook, lamented the *Third*'s "depressingly low intellectual and social horizon" and proclaimed that "Good English has to do with the upper classes – and there's the rub – with the cultural and intellectual leaders, with the life of the mind in its struggle to express itself at its intellectual best. Linguistic relativism has a fervently democratic base. 'Science' is only an antiseptic label for the deep social belief that we ought not to have classes at all, even among our words" (Baker 1965, 530, 525). A professor of Italian noted that "the battle was not merely over language. It was over a whole philosophy of life. Should there be unbridled democracy, with a nose-counting process to determine what was good and what was bad?" (Pei 1964, 82).

Except for the novel prominence of antagonism toward science, twentieth-century objections to a doctrine of usage resemble nineteenth-century views expressed by Marsh and White. Marsh and White viewed linguistic change as corruption and linked language and ethics. Especially for Marsh, correctness was a moral question, and the language of the lower classes and immigrants reflected moral turpitude. The distaste for foreign expressions stemmed partly from a distrust of recent immigrants often forced to occupy the lowest social positions. A general xenophobia and aristocratic aloofness operated in them as well. They denied the conventionality and intrinsic arbitrariness of language forms. For the twentieth-century critics, moral turpitude had become permissiveness, and national chauvinism yielded to disdain for social inferiors. In short, notions of moral and social superiority persisted.

While nineteenth-century and twentieth-century antagonists of a doctrine of usage expressed strikingly similar attitudes, analysis of particular items reveals two principal differences. First, nineteenth-century writers show more wrangling over individual items than reviewers of the *Third*. In fact, earlier critics cataloged "infelicitous slips" and "egregious errors" by the hundreds; one revered guide (Ayres 1881) exhibited more than fifty entries under the letter A alone. By contrast, some detractors belittled the *Third* without reference to a single entry, and among those who did identify unstigmatized usages the same few were cited repeatedly.

Second, except for a handful of perennial favorites, the usages that troubled White and Marsh differ from those that offended critics in 1961. White condemned *donate* and *jeopardize*, *photographer* and *pants*, *presidential* and *reliable*. Ayres objected to *editorial, ice-cream*, and *section* ('this section of the country'). Resurrecting only a handful of the earlier bêtes noires, the *Third*'s critics still disliked the adjective *enthused* and the suffix *-ize* (as in *finalize*) and sustained the aversion to using *lay* for *lie* and *like* for *as*; but most objectionable expressions had not been condemned earlier. Follett objected to the new semantic content of *cohort* and *ambivalence*, censured *different than*, found *center around* an abuse of *center in* or *on* or *at*, and reproached the *Third* for including the conjunction *like*. Among newcomers he denounced *get hep*, *passel, anyplace, someplace,* and *one for the book.* Editors at the *New York Times* objected to *double-dome, yak* (the verb), *finalize,* and *swell* (the adjective). Apparently unaware that the *Third* labeled *irregardless* "nonstandard," *Life*'s editors bristled at the inclusion of this "most monstrous of all non-words" and ridiculed *-wise* in *wisdomwise* and *governmentwise* (neither of which is listed) and *-ize* in *concretize* and *finalize* (both of which are listed). Others deplored the unstigmatized listing of *complected* and lamented the dictionary's recording of the semantic blurring of *subconscious* and *unconscious, nauseous* and *nauseated, deprecate* and *depreciate, disinterested* and *uninterested, infer* and *imply.* Traditionalists reproved Merriam for an assortment of other entries, among them: *shambles, schmaltz, snooty, tacky, to goof, to contact,* plural *each,* adverbial *due to* ('The game was canceled due to inclement weather'), *transpire* ('happen'), *bimonthly* ('twice a month'), and *ain't.* Some reviewers scolded the *Third* for including certain four-letter words, whereas other reviewers scolded the *Third* for omitting certain four-letter words.

Probably the most irritating cause of objection was the paucity of status labels in the *Third.* The editors used temporal, regional, and stylistic status labels. The first two aroused little comment. Not so, the stylistic labels. Apart from branding a number of words "vulgar" and an occasional one "obscene," the editors employed only "slang," "nonstandard," and "substandard" as status labels. Using Kenyon's (1948) distinction between *levels* and *varieties,* they identified two levels of unacceptability (nonstandard and substandard) and left acceptable words and uses unmarked. With the single exception that "slang" was used to characterize a usage limited to circumstances of "extreme informality," appropriate contexts for acceptable uses were suggested not by labels but solely by the character of illustrative citations, a decision even some linguists criticized. James Sledd (1962), for example, asked how readers could reasonably be expected to infer from the few citations in any entry what the editors, with more numerous citations, refused to do.

In at least one sense or use the editors found the following sufficiently informal to be labeled "slang": the nouns *boondocks, broad, bust, cat, clip joint, cornball, fuzz, happy dust, lulu, pig, prod, puss;* the adjectives *cool, fruity, pickled, pissed, pissed off;* and the verbs *knock-up* and *screw-up.* But what raised eyebrows by their unlabeled presence were unbranded entries like the nouns *boozer, flick, slut, prick* ('a disagreeable person'), and *passel;* the adjectives *groovy, pie-eyed, hell-bent, screwy,* and *swell;* the verbs *busted, concretize, enthuse,* and *juice up;* and the conjunction *like,* a matter of some notoriety at the time because of the early 1960s advertising slogan *Winston tastes good like a cigarette should* (Finegan 1980). The label "nonstandard" was applied to "a very small number of words that can hardly stand without some status label but are too widely current in reputable contexts to be labeled *substand*," such as *irregardless* and *lay* (for *lie*). "Substandard" was applied to entries used "throughout the American language community" but differing "in choice of word or form from that of the prestige group in that community" (for example, *ain't* for "have/has not," *drownded, learn* for "teach," *hisself, them* for "those," *youse* or *yous* for plural "you").

Obscene, vulgar, slang, substandard, and *nonstandard* were the five status labels employed, and critics objected that they were too few and too seldom applied. Indeed, Gove had simply discarded "colloquial," the most popular label, and in so doing, critics argued, had overreacted to its misuse. Instead of identifying an acceptable functional *variety* of English, as was intended, "colloquial" had come to be interpreted as designating an unacceptable *level*, but in scuttling the term Gove disregarded what teachers, editors, journalists, and traditionalists recognized as a crucial distinction between the written and the spoken word. He thus reinforced the association between the dictionary and structural linguists, for whom speech is paramount, writing secondary. The significance of this disregard for educated and intelligent dictionary users cannot be overstated. If writers and editors consult an unabridged dictionary more often than nonwriters, Gove's policy slighted the most frequent and responsible readers; it is also perplexing because the *Webster's Third* citations come almost exclusively from written sources. All in all, a wide band of readers found *Webster's Third* too lenient in its labeling of disputed items of usage and too indulgent.

By contrast, linguists regarded the alarm as a false alarm. They generally admired the dictionary and viewed concern about the language going to hell in a handbasket as hysterical. They dubbed the dictionary's detractors or their views unrealistic and illiberal: medieval, rigid, uninformed, Philistine (Dykema 369); dogmatic and authoritarian (Christensen 24); crippling and enslaving (Christensen 24); and obscurantist and uninformed (H. Allen 1962, 431). One dubbed the guardians' approach to dictionaries "lexicolatry" (McDavid 1962, 435) and called the defamers "spokesmen for literary mandarinism and soft-headed gentility" (McDavid in Mencken 1963, 483fn.). Another called them ignorant, sadistic, masochistic, and superstitious (R. A. Hall 1964, 368–9).

11.3.6   The American Heritage Dictionary: *reactionary and influential*

The treatment of usage in the *Third* and the attendant brouhaha goaded one conservative publisher to try buying out the G. and C. Merriam

Company. "We'd take the Third out of print! We'd go back to the Second International and speed ahead on the Fourth," said the president of American Heritage Publishing Company (*Newsweek*, March 12, 1962, 105). Losing its bid for the revered firm, American Heritage resolved instead to produce a new dictionary, one that "would faithfully record our language" but "would not, like so many others in these permissive times, rest there. On the contrary, it would add the essential dimension of guidance . . . toward grace and precision which intelligent people seek in a dictionary" (Morris 1969, vi).

Motivated by a belief that English, already in a precipitous fall from grace, was being abetted by saboteurs in Springfield, the American Heritage executives determined that their dictionary would reflect their "deep sense of responsibility as custodians of the American tradition in language as well as history." Both the executives and the new dictionary's editor felt that Merriam-Webster's *Third* "had failed both press and public by eliminating virtually all usage labels and other indications of standards of usage" (Morris 1969, vi). So as to provide "sensible guidance" about using the language, William Morris, the editor, empaneled a jury of "outstanding speakers and writers" (Morris 1969, vii), including distinguished critics, historians, editors, journalists, poets, anthropologists, professors of English and of journalism, even several United States senators. More than a dozen panelists had taken public stands against the *Third*, among them Mario Pei, Sheridan Baker, Jacques Barzun, Wilson Follett, and Dwight Macdonald. Predictably, then, their digested opinions as presented in more than 200 usage notes manifest a distinctly conservative tenor, and the dictionary's introductory essay on usage concedes that the panelists tended to feel the English language was "going to hell" if they didn't "do something to stop it" and, further, that "their own usage preferences are clearly right" (Bishop xxiii).

On the acceptability of specific items, it turns out, the panelists disagreed more than they agreed. In fact, they rendered a unanimous verdict just once: against *simultaneous* as an adverb ('the referendum was conducted simultaneous with the election'). On a few items they achieved near unanimity: *ain't I* and *between you and I* disapproved for use in writing by 99 percent; *thusly* disapproved by 97 percent; *dropout* as a noun approved by 97 percent; *slow* as an adverb approved by 96 percent; *anxious* meaning "eager" approved by 94 percent; *rather unique* and *most unique* disapproved by 94 percent; and *finalize plans for a college reunion* disapproved by 90 percent. More typical, however, were divided opinions: "*Who* did you meet?" acceptable in speech to 66 percent, in writing to 13 percent; "He wants to know *who* he should speak to" acceptable in speech to 59 percent.

411

By appointing a panel, *AHD* harked back to the functions of word-books in eighteenth-century England, when lexicographers attempted to ascertain and codify the language. Toward the close of the twentieth century, many educated Americans still felt a need to employ only usages whose standing was above reproach, and they expected authoritative guidance from dictionaries. The *Third*'s disregard of those expectations had stirred such a katzenjammer that the sensible commercial (and societal) tack for the reactionary *AHD* was to court favor among conservers of language orthodoxy, and this it energetically did.

Some observers regarded the panel as a kind of academy, as the publishers had intended. Despite repeated proposals for a language academy – John Adams had proposed one as early as 1780 – its achievement had eluded reformers until *AHD* established this one. Geoffrey Nunberg (1992, xxviii), chair of *AHD*-3's usage panel, disavows the notion that the panel may be considered an academy, offering as evidence the fact that its members often hold divided opinions. In an earlier essay, however, he referred to the panel as "an informally constituted academy" (1982, 36).

On the basis of the original panel, editor Morris (1969, vii) asserted that "this Dictionary can claim to be more precisely descriptive, in terms of current usage levels, than any heretofore published – especially in offering the reader the lexical opinions of a large group of highly sophisticated fellow citizens." By one estimation, however, American Heritage failed to establish a fully respectable panel: it was "recondite in its method of selection of items to be evaluated, incautious in its method of presenting them for assessment, probably biased in its selection of 'experts,' and erratic in its editorial handling of the opinions of those experts" (Creswell 1975). Still, *AHD* found a million purchasers its first year and secured a place on bestseller lists.

For the second edition of *AHD* (1982), Houghton Mifflin was the sole publisher, and American Heritage, which had initially copublished *AHD*, had disappeared from the masthead. Freed from its American Heritage ties, Houghton Mifflin expanded the panel and changed its profile. The third edition of 1992 saw further changes. In an ironic turn, Houghton Mifflin appointed as editor of *AHD*-3 Anne Soukhanov, who had trained with Gove at Merriam-Webster. The *AHD*-3 panel included a better representation of women and minority groups, as well as of linguists, along with other distinguished writers, scholars, politicians, and entertainers. Even with Baker and Barzun still on the board, the *AHD*-3 panel (173-member strong) was younger and more diverse than earlier ones (Nunberg 1992). Given the reconfiguration, it is not surprising that on some items the 1992 panel was more accepting than its predecessors, as with *contact* and *intrigue* used as verbs.

Curiously, though, the newer panel's views were occasionally less accepting, as with *hopefully* as a sentence adverb (Nunberg 1992). *AHD*-2 had reported in a note that *hopefully* ('it is to be hoped') is "grammatically justified by analogy to the similar uses of *happily* and *mercifully*" and warned that "this usage is by now such a bugbear to traditionalists that it is best avoided on grounds of civility, if not logic." Similarly, *AHD*-3 advised that "the usage is unacceptable to many critics, including a large majority of the Usage Panel." However, the author of the more recent note (presumably Nunberg) blushes for the panel: "It is not easy to explain why critics dislike this use of *hopefully* [and] increased currency . . . appears only to have made the critics more adamant." The note speculates that *hopefully* "has been made a litmus test, which distinguishes writers who take an active interest in questions of grammar or usage from the great mass of people who keep their own linguistic counsel." Then, provocatively, it adds: "No one can be blamed who uses *hopefully* in blithe ignorance of the critics' disdain for it, since the rule could not be derived from any general concern for clarity or precision." Message to readers: use *hopefully* at your peril! Message to critics: your position cannot be justified by arguments from clarity or precision.

It is informative to compare *AHD*'s treatment of *hopefully* with that in *Merriam-Webster's Collegiate Dictionary* (Mish 1993). *Merriam-Webster*'s tone could hardly differ more from *AHD*-3's:

> In the early 1960s the second sense of *hopefully*, which had been in sporadic use since around 1932, underwent a surge of popular use. A surge of popular criticism followed in reaction but the criticism took no account of the grammar of adverbs. *Hopefully* in its second sense is a member of a class of adverbs known as disjuncts. Disjuncts serve as a means by which the author or speaker can comment directly to the reader or hearer usu. on the content of the sentence to which they are attached. Many other adverbs (as *interestingly, frankly, clearly, luckily, unfortunately*) are similarly used; most are so ordinary as to excite no comment or interest whatsoever. The second sense of *hopefully* is entirely standard.

More interesting, and perhaps more significant, than the difference in tone is the fact that Merriam-Webster follows *AHD*'s lead in providing a usage note in the first place. Merriam-Webster first appended usage "articles" or "paragraphs" (comparable to *AHD*'s "usage notes") in 1983, one year after *AHD*'s second college edition appeared. Dictionaries had earlier routinely incorporated comments about disputed usage into entries, but the introduction of usage articles into Merriam-Webster's dictionary required the editorial director to explain:

> A number of entries for words posing special problems of confused or disputed usage include for the first time brief articles that provide the dictionary user with suitable guidance on the usage in question. The guidance offered is never based merely on received opinion, though opinions are often noted, but typically on both a review of the historical background and a careful evaluation of what citations reveal about actual contemporary practice. [Mish 1983, 6]

AHD was inspired by a reaction against Merriam-Webster's treatment of usage, but its success may have helped prompt the Springfield lexicographers to append usage articles to some entries. Despite that similarity, however, Merriam-Webster continues its descriptive allegiance, *AHD* its prescriptive pedigree; and, it should be noted, Merriam-Webster remains the bestselling collegiate dictionary.

At least partly as a result of public discussion of treatments of usage in the *Third*, *AHD*, and dictionaries of other substantial dictionary publishers, such as Random House and Webster's New World, the topic of usage again became commerce-worthy, if not really big business. In 1983, the *Atlantic* published an analysis of the grammar wars and an argument for sensible language criticism that received widespread attention (Nunberg 1983). In addition, perhaps a score of major large-scale handbooks and dictionaries of usage appeared in America after 1961 (including Bryant; Bernstein; H. Fowler 1965; Follett 1966; Mager and Mager; Copperud; Timmons and Gibney; *American Heritage Book of English Usage* 1996; Garner). Especially noteworthy is *Webster's Dictionary of English Usage* (E. W. Gilman), whose dust jacket, with some justification, calls it the "definitive guide."

Within a few years of *AHD*'s initial appearance, its editor, William Morris, had convened another usage panel for a dictionary of usage (Morris and Morris). The Morrises report that they borrowed the idea of using an opinion panel from Marckwardt and Walcott, but Marckwardt and Walcott did not use a panel and published their monograph partly to prove that educated opinion about usage (as represented by Leonard's 1932 panel) lags behind recorded usage in dictionaries. As much as anything, the new Morris book proffered the nugatory opinions of 136 consultants, including Baker, Macdonald, Newman, and several others implicated in the smearing of the *Third*. The main purpose in this dictionary of usage was "to call attention to such inaccuracies [as merging *infer* and *imply*, *disinterested* and *uninterested*] and thus to correct or eliminate them" (ix). The book reports panel votes – for example, 58 percent reject the disputed sense of *hopefully* in speech, 76 percent in writing – and at some length what panelists say about contested usages. Often the comments are trifling, such as these about *irregardless:* "Never!" "Abominable!" "It sounds dreadful," and "Originated by Amos 'n' Andy"; or these about *hopefully:* "I have sworn eternal war on this bastard adverb," "Strike me dead if you ever hear me using it in this way," "This is one that makes me physically ill," "The most horrible usage of our time," and "Slack-jawed, common, sleazy." Little wonder that professional students of language dismiss such blather. Mere unmitigated objection, such comments fail to constitute analysis or criticism.

11.3.7 Language criticism extended

So far we have discussed familiar matters of debatable usage – the kinds of grammatical and stylistic concerns that have received attention for centuries. Recent decades have seen something of a sea change in the objects of criticism, however. Manifest in *AHD*-3 – and in other dictionaries – is discussion of quite different matters. *AHD*-3's usage notes reach well beyond style and grammar to expressions of gender, ethnicity, and sexual orientation, matters that more generally figured prominently in late twentieth-century discussion. In professional circles they raised sometimes complex questions of linguistic deference, respect, and social justice.

Championing the cultural importance of language criticism was the chair of *AHD*-3's usage panel, Geoffrey Nunberg (1982, 1983). Speaking about gender-related issues, Nunberg (1992, xxx) noted, "These are precisely the kinds of controversies about particular words and principles that ensured the vitality of traditional language criticism in the 18th and 19th centuries. Here as elsewhere, what matters is not that we should expect to achieve uniformity but that we should find in our differences the occasion for lively critical debate." Earlier, Nunberg (1982, 34) had made the same point more generally: "The specific rules that the grammarians insisted on may sometimes have been ill-considered, but that is less important than the general principle that the rules were intended to illustrate: good usage is determined in rational reflection on language."

Illustrative of such changes in the objects of linguistic criticism, *AHD*-3 contains nearly full-column usage notes at *he* and *man*; by contrast, *AHD*-1 offered no note for either. *AHD*-3 provides usage notes at *–ess, gay, lady,* and *Negress; AHD*-1 provided none. Expressions such as *Native American,* which warrants a usage note in *AHD*-3, lacked even its own entry in *AHD*-1. Further, the labeling of certain words and word senses in *AHD*-3 shows increased social sensitivity. Thus, *mick* "Irishman" and *wop* "Italian" are label-free in 1969 (though their respective definitions indicate "used disparagingly" and "offensive term used derogatorily"), but both are labeled "offensive slang" in 1992. In 1969, *Polack* "disparaging term for person of Polish descent" was slang and *redskin* "informal"; in 1992 both are "offensive slang." Curiously, *gyp* "to swindle, cheat, or defraud" is labeled "informal" in 1969 and "slang" in 1992, but its acknowledged derivation from *Gypsy* did not arouse sufficient concern about possible offense to warrant a note or a label. By contrast, *jew down* "to best at bargaining by haggling or shrewd practices," described as "an offensive expression, used derogatorily" in *AHD*-1, is not treated in *AHD*-2 or *AHD*-3. The expressions *dyke* "lesbian," *faggot* "male homosexual," and *queer* "homosexual" are labeled "slang" in *AHD*-1 and "offensive slang" in *AHD*-3.

Not all dictionaries have addressed these social sensitivities so well or to the same degree as *AHD*-3. *Webster's New World Dictionary of American English* (Neufeldt), not a Merriam-Webster dictionary, carries no usage note for *man* and does not alert readers to objections to its being used to refer to the human race as a whole. Neither, however, does *WNWD* alert readers to potential objections to some ordinary items of contested usage such as *hopefully*, even though in the sense "it is to be hoped" it is said to be regarded as "ungainly" in the dictionary's front matter (Algeo 1988b, xix).

By 1992, it is clear, a new form of linguistic criticism had matured. Like the criticism of the nineteenth and much of the twentieth centuries, it was unabashedly prescriptive. Ironically, many traditionalists ridiculed the new prescriptivism, while linguists and other professional societies and many secular publications propagated and enforced it. Of course, the objects of the new and old prescriptivism differed, as did their motivation. The new prescriptivism sought to raise consciousness about the secondary rank that language use accorded women and girls and to help correct their erasure from much English-language writing and speaking. Sexist practices are "those that contribute to demeaning or ignoring women (or men) or to stereotyping either sex," according to the LSA's "Guidelines for Nonsexist Usage." The guidelines themselves are frankly prescriptive: use plurals; avoid generic statements that inaccurately refer only to one sex; use terms that avoid sexual stereotyping; use parallel forms of reference; avoid gender-stereotyped characterizations. Such laudable guidelines make eminently good sense in a society grounded in equality for all persons. It is sobering nevertheless to recognize that some linguistic prescriptions of past generations were likewise spurred by high-minded goals – sometimes social ones, sometimes moral ones – and they were regarded as utterly benighted and stoutly condemned by generations of linguists.

The LSA's endorsement of a set of linguistic guidelines rightly raises questions about the generality of one long-standing principle of scientific linguistics, namely that language expression is arbitrary. Undergirding such guidelines as the LSA's is a growing perception that, if in principle language is arbitrary, in practice arbitrariness has limits. When it comes to language, use and user are indeed connected. Edwin Newman in 1974, Richard Grant White in 1870, G. P. Marsh in 1860, and many others may have been benighted with claims linking language use and social corruption. But their position is similar to the aims of more recent language guidelines intended to minimize sexism. The point is not that Newman or White or Marsh are precursors of views later espoused by many professional organizations. Nothing could be further from the truth. Arguably, though, a prescriptive kinship links those who claim that abuse of language leads to moral corruption (as Marsh, White, and Newman have done) and those who claim that nonsexist language sustains or promotes social justice (as the LSA, MLA, and NCTE now do). The coincidence depends, of course, on one's view of moral corruption and of social injustice, but those notions have encompassed a wide stripe of sins over the centuries.

There appears to be widespread, if not unanimous, sentiment among linguists that traditional language prescriptivism is wrongheaded and intolerable. If one asks linguists whether any items of usage irritate them, some express distaste for this or that item. Not that their preferences should be imposed on others, they may add, but they themselves try to avoid them. When it comes to guidelines for the use of nonsexist language, however, the virtually unanimous view accepts judgment and enforcement as de rigueur. In a sense, then, nineteenth- and twentieth-century prescriptivism now holds a more respectable pedigree and has gained representation in the most highly respected lexicographical circles.

Philip Gove (1961b), editor of *Webster's Third*, wrote, "Lexicography ... is an intricate and subtle and sometimes overpowering art, requiring subjective analysis, arbitrary decisions, and intuitive reasoning." Decades later Geoffrey Nunberg (1992, xxvii) wrote of the importance of language criticism:

> It is never easy to say which group has authority over any given usage, of course. Who owns *disinterested*? Is the word *kudos* by now a common or garden-variety English plural like *peas*, or is it still an elegant borrowing that should be held responsible to its origin as a Greek singular? We will want to take the facts of use into consideration when we approach these questions, but it is the height of scientistic self-deception to suppose

that use provides an objective criterion for resolving them. Lexicographers invariably have to make critical evaluation of the raw facts of use.

In contrast to most professional linguists, he values criticism of language, arguing that scientific linguistics and traditional criticism are not incompatible. Rather, "there is an important place for a 'critical linguistics' in the study of usage" (1992, xxviii). Nunberg is not the first linguist to espouse this view. The great Otto Jespersen (1925, 112) said:

> I am not one of those who recognize the worst usurper as legitimate as soon as he is firmly established on his throne. There is something called political morality which is greater than momentary power. So . . . I dare to declare that there is also a higher linguistic morality than that of recognizing the greatest absurdities when they once have usage on their side.

Likewise, Charles Fries (1927), who became president of the Linguistic Society of America and later was indicted as the "villain" in the grammar murder mystery, voiced the same sentiment:

> Much as we condemn the purist's view and point to the ignorance with which he deals with the language we cannot help feeling that there may be something entirely valid behind his protests.

Like Merriam-Webster, whose recent inclusion of usage articles tacitly acknowledges public concern with language correctness, linguists have also admitted being chafed by public reaction (Moulton et al. 1964, 152–8): "Largely because of the furor over the third edition of Webster's New International Dictionary, a fair portion of highly educated laymen see in linguistics the great enemy of all they hold dear." That sober assessment by the Linguistic Society of America appears in a report from a distinguished committee of six future LSA presidents: William G. Moulton, Archibald A. Hill, Charles A. Ferguson, Eric P. Hamp, Morris Halle, and Thomas A. Sebeok.

11.4   Conclusion

Although the firestorm generated by the usage controversy of the 1950s and 1960s may seem perplexingly inflated, the embers had smoldered for generations, fueled by educational, social, political, and moral timber. In the nineteenth century Kirkham, Marsh, and White had associated "bad grammar" with moral decadence, and similar, if attenuated, associations have continued through the twentieth century. Recall the revealing comment (Sherwood 276–7, cited in §11.3.4) that old grammar and new grammar represent different ways of looking at life. Not language, but life.

"Unless we can restore to the words in our newspapers, laws, and political acts some measure of clarity and stringency of meaning, our lives will draw yet nearer to chaos," warned the socioliterary critic George Steiner (quoted by Manning 4). The editor of the *Atlantic* wrote, "The debasement of language is a major malady, one of the most serious problems of our time" (Manning 4). Political corruption has been linked to language – as, for example, in the comments that ridiculed the enfeebled usage of the Watergate protagonists and the sworn testimony of President Bill Clinton that led to his impeachment. The author of *Strictly Speaking* speculated that "it is at least conceivable that our politics would be improved if our English were, and so would other parts of our national life" (Newman 5), and his conviction that language "sets the tone of society" reveals how enmeshed cause and effect remain in judgments about linguistic and societal mores. Whether redundancy, murkiness, and dense diction prompt chicanery or merely cloak it is an open question for some; but language guardians seem to suggest that using *infer* for *imply*, *disinterested* for *uninterested*, and even *like* for *as* can lead to ambiguity, obfuscation, and eventually the dissipation of the language.

The function of linguistic traditionalists in society is widely regarded as essential to the maintenance of intellectual and moral standards, and the *New Republic* (April 23, 1962) claimed that the *Third*'s compilers had "abandoned a function indispensable in any advanced society, that of maintaining the quality of its language." In a letter to a feuding linguist, Barzun expressed a similar view: "The work of communication in law, politics and diplomacy, in medicine, technology, and moral speculation depends on the maintenance of a medium of exchange whose values must be kept fixed, as far as possible, like those of any other reliable currency" (quoted by Lloyd 282).

Beyond creating an impression of iconoclasm, linguists are perceived as discounting the importance societies attach to good language use – and not only technologically advanced societies. As early as 1927 Leonard Bloomfield professed surprise at finding among the Menomini Indians awareness about who among them were good speakers. Later Bloomfield (1944) acknowledged that besides the kind of statements about language that linguists and grammarians make (called secondary statements) – hostile reactions (called tertiary) can be aroused when accepted views are challenged. Recognizing that tertiary reactions may not always be rational, he implicitly admonished linguists to proceed cautiously when challenging accepted views. Linguists have tended to ignore Bloomfield's advice, flouting traditional views of language and provoking the hostile reactions we have documented throughout the middle of the twentieth century.

Linguists observe and analyze facts of usage; traditional grammarians are pledged to judge those facts, and in the second half of the twentieth century they feared that the academic ascendancy of linguistic science would slight appraisal and depreciate value. But, as one literary scholar at home with linguistics has observed, linguists and traditionalists must both recognize that "embedded in these disputes and complaints is a philosophic problem of the first magnitude. . . . The problem of what to teach youngsters in English is first of all a question of value, not fact. . . . we not only have to find out what are the facts of language but what are the facts of society and man, problems which are difficult and which involve from the very beginning value questions" (M. Bloomfield 1953).

"At present we are at an impasse," Nunberg (1982, 36) has written. "Both sides fulgurate, while in the middle the lexicographers and educators often counsel an enlightened hypocrisy: even if the canons of good usage have no real justification, it is best that people be taught to conform to them so as not to give offense to traditionalists. . . . At the same time," he writes, in a voice all too rare among linguists,

> linguists have not the fondest hope of convincing the public that all widely practiced forms of usage are equally acceptable; if anything, there is more support now for traditional standards than there was twenty years ago. And this is surely good, for if the idea that good usage has a rational justification is abandoned, people will return to the doctrine that the correctness of usage is based entirely on the social prestige of the speaker – the very notion that both the eighteenth-century grammarians and the modern radicals have found intolerable. This has always been the English speaker's attitude toward pronunciation, which has been considered to lie outside the scope of rational justification; if the laissez-faire party had its way, all other aspects of usage would be reduced equally to matters of pure snobbery.

The development of sophisticated corpora of spoken and written English in recent decades will lead to more definitive information about usage – information more reliable and definitive than any earlier dictionary could have accessed. Doubtless, such corpora will lead to better descriptions of the facts of usage. Better descriptions of usage will make it difficult to maintain that a usage is not used by the best speakers or writers or in the standard language if, in fact, it can be illustrated that it is. But even with such ready access to texts and actual usage as we can now expect, if past is prologue, the desire – indeed, the need – to assess English usage will always remain.

FURTHER READING

From John Locke and Samuel Johnson through Noah Webster and John Pickering to Henry Alford, Henry James, and beyond come many important documents in the history of language attitudes; Bolton (1966), Bolton and Crystal (1969), and Crowley (1991) offer convenient collections of original documents. Unger's (1998) biography of Noah Webster is a compelling read and, alongside descriptions of Webster's lexicographical pursuits, recreates the revolutionary times in which Webster matured and worked. Morton (1994) presents an unusually informative treatment of the development of *Webster's Third* and its astonishingly controversial reception. Nunberg (1983) offers a perspicacious view of the importance of linguistic criticism in intellectual life over the centuries. The best single source on the history of hundreds of items of usage is E. W. Gilman (1989). Baron (1982) and Finegan (1980) overview the development of American attitudes toward language correctness. Representing a largely British perspective is Bex and Watts (1999), a collection of essays, many of which are valuable for their focus on the ideology of standard English. Interesting essays on usage appear in many desk dictionaries, and among the better ones are those by Algeo (1988b) and Nunberg (1992). Wardhaugh (1999) is an accessible discussion of myths and misunderstandings about language and language correctness. Also accessible and reflecting a British perspective is Cameron's (1995) *Verbal Hygiene*. No one has surpassed H. L. Mencken's incisive discussions of language correctness, and Mencken (1963) is an excellent place to begin any course of further reading.

12 CANADIAN ENGLISH

Laurel J. Brinton and Margery Fee

12.1 Introduction

Canadian English claims a rather small number of speakers and spans a relatively brief history – the term "Canadian English" was first recorded only in 1854. As a dialect it has typically been described either as an amalgam of British and American features or as a repository of quaint terms such as *moose milk*. However, as Richard Bailey observes:

> Canadian English, though diverse in communities and variable in the speech of individuals, is *not* a composite of archaic or rustic features or a potpourri of British and American speechways but a true national language. [1982, 152, emphasis added]

It is now generally agreed that Canadian English originated as a variant of northern American English (the speech of New England, New York, New Jersey, and Pennsylvania). Throughout its history, it has been influenced by two powerful external norms, those of British English and American English; the relative prestige of these norms and hence their effect on Canadian English have varied according to the social and political conditions. Nonetheless, Canadian English can be seen as pursuing its own course, with the development of distinctive linguistic features and dialectal forms.

Standard (or general) Canadian English, though perhaps a "scholarly fiction" (R. Bailey 1982, 152), has traditionally been defined as a class dialect, namely, the variety spoken by educated middle-class urban Canadians from the eastern border of Ontario to Vancouver Island. There is a remarkable homogeneity in speech over this vast area. The differences that mark the major dialects – the English of the Maritimes (Nova Scotia, New Brunswick, and Prince Edward Island), of Quebec (Montreal and the Eastern Townships), and of the Ottawa Valley – from the minor variants found in the West (British Columbia), the Prairies (Alberta, Saskatchewan,

Table 1 *Uses of languages in Canada, expressed as percentages of population*

Languages	Home language	Mother tongue
English	66.7	59.2
	(19,031,335)	(16,890,615)
English and French	0.4	0.4
	(119,965)	(107,940)
English and another language	1.4	0.9
	(397,435)	(249,545)
English, French, and another language	0.05	0.03
	(14,395)	(9,225)
French	22.3	23.3
	(6,359,505)	(6,636,660)
French and another language	0.2	0.1
	(48,660)	(35,840)
Nonofficial language	9.0	16.1
	(2,556,830)	(4,590,285)

Note: Figures in parentheses are the base number from which the percentage is derived, based on an enumerated population of 28,528,125.
Source: Statistics Canada, from the 1996 Census.

and Manitoba), and the Arctic North are quite insignificant. The Maritimes varieties of English have only one distinctive phonological feature: the treatment of [ɑ] before medial and final *r* (M. Bloomfield 1948). Even the more distinctive variety of English spoken in Newfoundland is moving towards standard Canadian English (Kirwin, ch. 13 in this volume). With the exception of the last, the accents of anglophone Canadians whose parents were born in Canada are nearly indistinguishable across the country (Chambers 1998).

12.2 Speakers of Canadian English

Canada is an officially bilingual country, though the balance is heavily tipped toward English: in 1996, of a population of slightly more than 28 million, 84 percent claimed a knowledge of English, while only 14 percent were exclusively French speakers (97 percent of whom live in Quebec), and fewer than 2 percent knew neither official language. Table 1 gives more specific data on the percentage of Canadians speaking English as either a "home language" or a "mother tongue."

12.3   The study of Canadian English

Good surveys of Canadian English are by Richard Bailey (1982), Margery Fee (1992a, 1992b), and J. K. Chambers (1998). Despite the existence of several bibliographies (Bähr; Avis and Kinloch; Lougheed 1988) and several collections devoted to Canadian English (Lougheed 1985; Clarke 1993; Edwards), the variety remains relatively understudied. However, new interest in world varieties of English, an increasingly multilingual population, and computer technology have all facilitated research into Canadian English. This scholarly attention is demonstrated by the appearance of reference works devoted to Canadian English and its dialects, including dictionaries such as *A Dictionary of Canadianisms on Historical Principles* (Avis 1967), *Dictionary of Prince Edward Island English* (Pratt 1988), *Dictionary of Newfoundland English* (Story, Kirwin, and Widdowson), *Gage Canadian Dictionary* (DeWolf 1997), *ITP Nelson Canadian Dictionary of the English Language*, and *Canadian Oxford Dictionary* (K. Barber), as well as usage and style guides such as *Guide to Canadian English Usage* (Fee and McAlpine), *Canadian Press Stylebook* (Tasko), *The Canadian Style*, and *Editing Canadian English* (Burton).

12.4   Settlement history

The reasons for the remarkable homogeneity of Canadian English over a huge distance can be found in settlement history.

Newfoundland has been continuously occupied by English speakers since the beginning of the seventeenth century. Most settlers came from southwest England and southeast Ireland: those from England settled mainly along the coast; those from Ireland settled the Avalon Peninsula south of the capital, St. John's. Immigration dwindled after the first half of the nineteenth century. A long history, a sparse population, and geographical isolation account for the distinctive features of Newfoundland English, attested to by the bestselling and historically important *Dictionary of Newfoundland English* (Story, Kirwin, and Widdowson) and a body of specialized studies (Paddock 1981; Clarke 1986, 1991; Kirwin 1993). Newfoundland joined the Confederation only in 1949, mainly because of a weak economy, whose persistence has led to considerable out-migration. As a result, most Newfoundlanders were born there; even so, standard Canadian English is now making inroads with younger speakers in St. John's (Clarke 1991).

The territory now consisting of New Brunswick, Nova Scotia, and Prince Edward Island (the Maritimes) changed hands from French to English several times before 1713, when it was ceded to England. Subsequently settlers from a variety of areas, including Gaelic speakers who went to Cape Breton and German speakers who settled in Lunenburg County, produced a complex pattern of rural dialects; however, settlement by British Loyalists after the American Revolution in 1783 tripled the English-speaking population. Although the dialects of the Loyalists were far from homogeneous, the differences between Maritimes English and standard Canadian English have been explained by the argument that most Loyalist settlers in the Maritimes came from New England and seaports in New York State. Those in central Canada came from western New England, New York, and Pennsylvania (McConnell), and their varieties of English evolved into standard Canadian English. These immigrants and their children formed almost 80 percent of the population of Upper Canada by 1813 (the old Province of Quebec, which fell to Britain in 1763, was divided into Upper and Lower Canada in 1791). Subsequent heavy immigration from England, Ireland, and Scotland in the 1830s and 1840s had more influence on political and social institutions than on Canadian English, which to some southern British immigrants sounded unpleasantly "Yankee" (Chambers 1993).

British Loyalists also settled in Quebec after 1783, mainly moving to the Eastern Townships southeast of Montreal, and by 1831 English speakers were the majority in Montreal itself. However, by 1867, francophones again dominated there. Thus, Quebec English is, like Newfoundland English and Maritimes English, somewhat distinct from standard Canadian English (Hung, Davison, and Chambers; Chambers and Heisler). Since 1974, French has been the only official language in Quebec, which has meant that Quebec English has come under increasing influence from French (§ 12.5.4.11).

The uniformity of Canadian English from Ontario west to Vancouver Island is usually explained by the deliberate settlement policy put into place after Confederation in 1867. Impelled by fear of American incursions, the government moved the railway and settlement westward (protested by Aboriginal peoples, including the Métis of French and Cree descent). Those who took up positions of community power as teachers, ministers of religion, bankers, and government officials were primarily from Ontario. Their children and those of immigrants to the prairies (mostly from the Ukraine, Germany, and eastern Europe) thus grew up speaking standard Canadian English. Most pre-World-War-II rural enclaves of speakers of English as a second language have been dispersed by urbanization.

However, the last wave of immigration since World War II has led to the formation in the largest cities of enclaves of speakers of English as a second language. Large percentages (from about 17 to 30 percent) of the populations of Toronto, Vancouver, Winnipeg, and Montreal speak an immigrant language as a first language. Film and print media in immigrant languages are readily available, many immigrants maintain continuing ties to their countries of origin, and Canada actively supports multiculturalism. For those reasons, the retention rate of the first language is quite high, and thus ESL varieties are likely to persist in urban centres and ultimately to modify standard Canadian in the future (Chambers 1998).

12.5   Linguistic features of Canadian English

Although Canadian English is characterized by a small number of distinctive linguistic features, it is more often described in terms of its unique combination of American and British features, primarily phonological and lexical, but also a number of features of syntax and usage. As Richard Bailey (1982, 161) points out: "What is distinctly Canadian about Canadian English is not its unique linguistic features (of which there are a handful) but its combination of tendencies that are uniquely distributed." Studies of the development of the linguistic features of Canadian English over time do not yet exist, but it is possible to glean some idea of the diachronic development of Canadian English from two quite disparate sources. The first is nineteenth-century attitudes towards Canadian English expressed by (primarily) British visitors and immigrants to Canada, who generally found the dialect full of "vulgar and lawless innovations" (Chambers 1993; Avis 1978). The second, and more important, source of diachronic evidence are the sociolinguistic studies that have been carried out in the last twenty-five years in a number of urban centers in Canada. These include Ottawa (Woods, based on 1979 data), St John's (Clarke 1986, 1991), Vancouver (Gregg), and Toronto (Léon and Martin). Further evidence is provided by the Survey of Canadian English, which examined differences in usage between parents and their children (Scargill and Warkentyne). While these studies do not always show consistent developments, they provide some evidence for evolving trends in Canadian English.

12.5.1   Phonology

12.5.1.1   Canadian raising

Undoubtedly the most distinctive phonological feature of Canadian English is the raised onset of the [au] and [aɪ] diphthongs to [ʌu] and [ʌɪ] before voiceless consonants, which provides contrasting vowel sounds in the following pairs:

lout/loud	bite/bide
bout/bowed	fife/five
house/houses	site/side
mouth (*n.*) / mouth (*v.*)	tripe/tribe
spouse/espouse	knife/knives

Raising also occurs before underlying voiceless consonants in words such as *shouted* and *writer*. This phenomenon was termed "Canadian Raising" by Chambers (1973), though it is not limited to Canada in the North American context. These sounds "constitute both stereotypic and actual distinctive features of Canadian English" (R. Bailey 1982, 153) since they often serve as markers by which even quite linguistically naïve speakers identify Canadians.

Raising of these diphthongs occurs elsewhere in the North American context, for example, in eastern Virginia, South Carolina, and Martha's Vineyard, but is not phonologically conditioned in these places. Raised diphthongs are also found in somewhat different distributions in Hiberno-English and in Scots. They are a conservative feature, representing the second step in the Great Vowel Shift diphthongization of [u] and [i], which in other dialects has progressed to [aʊ] and [aɪ]. Their existence in Canadian English is usually attributed to Scottish or northern British settlement in Canada or to an adaptation of the Scots system to the North American system, though Richard Bailey (1982, 155) suggests that they are a distinctive Canadian development.

Evidence for the spread or decline of this feature is contradictory. Gregg found raised diphthongs to be very robust (over 90 percent) in Vancouver in both of the contexts noted above, with no differentiation due to age, sex, socioeconomic class, or style. Woods (119) found use of the raised variants to be slightly lower among young women in Ottawa, suggesting "a general but slight decline of this Canadian marker for all Canadians in the next decades." Léon and Martin found that [ʌʊ] was remaining constant but [ʌɪ] was losing ground in Toronto. Chambers considers raised diphthongs to be in decline since the 1970s. Hung, Davison, and Chambers, as well as Chambers (1991) see a change in progress in Canadian English (more in Vancouver and Victoria than in Toronto) with the diphthong either fronting to [ɛʊ/eʊ] or nonraising to [æʊ/aʊ]; both are considered adaptations to the American model.

12.5.1.2 Merger of [ɑ] and [ɔ]

Most other phonological features show the genesis of Canadian English in northern American English, though often with some distinctively Canadian modifications. The merger of [ɑ] and [ɔ] for most speakers of Canadian English (up to 85 percent) has resulted in homophonous pairs such as the following:

offal/awful	lager/logger
Don/dawn	Otto/auto
hock/hawk	holly/Hawley
cot/caught	tot/taught

This merger is evident in Canadian English as early as the mid nineteenth century (Chambers 1993, 11). Although these vowels are distinguished in certain dialects of American English, the merger is spreading in the United States as well (from eastern New England and western Pennsylvania into the Midwest and West), where the resulting vowel is the unrounded [ɑ]. Authorities disagree as to whether the merged vowel in Canada retains some degree of rounding [ɒ] or is unrounded [ɑ]. One respect in which Canadian English differs from American English is in the preservation of [ɔ] before [ɹ] more consistently, as in *sorry, tomorrow, orange, porridge,* and *Dorothy*.

12.5.1.3 Voicing of intervocalic [t]

Like most Americans, Canadians voice or flap intervocalic [t] to [d] or [ɾ], producing such homophones as:

metal/medal	bitter/bidder
latter/ladder	litre/leader
hearty/hardy	atom/Adam
flutter/flooder	waiting/wading

The context for voicing includes r-V (*party, dirty*) as in American English but in Canadian English has expanded, though less often, to include l-V (*filter, shelter*). It may occasionally occur in the contexts f-V (*after*), s-V (*sister*), ʃ-V (*washed out*), and k-V (*picture*). However, such voicing is clearly a feature of casual speech and is marked socioeconomically. The fact that it is more common with young speakers suggests that it may be spreading. Voicing may occur in the context n-V (*dentist, twenty*) as well, though it is more common in informal speech for the [t] to be deleted, resulting in homophony of *winter/winner*. Preceding syllabic n in the context V-n (*eaten*) and n-n (*mountain*), the [t] is frequently replaced by a glottal stop.

12.5.1.4 Yod dropping

Like Americans, Canadians consistently drop yod in the [ɪu] diphthong after [s] (*suit*) and variably do so after labials and velars, but the retention of yod following [t, d, n] (*Tuesday*, *due*, *new*) is traditionally said to distinguish Canadian English speakers from American English speakers. Studies show, however, that Canadians are increasingly following the American model by dropping yod after alveolar stops and nasals, carrying on a process begun in the eighteenth century, and that glide deletion is now the majority usage even in formal registers. Clarke (1993) argues that competing prestige models exist for Canadians: the British model of glide retention, which also serves to promulgate a distinctively Canadian (nationalistic) pronunciation in the North American context, and the American model of glide deletion, which appears progressive and forward-looking. She sees a "decided tendency away from autonomous Canadian linguistic standard, in favour of increasing North American heteronomy" (105). One also encounters affricativization to [tʃ] in some varieties of Canadian English, though data on the frequency of such cases are scarce. Instances of over-correction by yod-insertion in words such as *moon* or *noon* occur in Canadian English; the common pronunciation of *coupon* [kɪupɑn] is shared with American English.

12.5.1.5 Retention of [r]

Canadian English is a generally rhotic dialect. In this respect it differs both from southern British dialects and, more important, from American dialects of the Atlantic coast from Maine to South Carolina (excluding Philadelphia), though it resembles general American. Richard Bailey (1982, 143) points out that "of all the many linguistic variables that figure in [the development of Canadian English] perhaps none is as significant in distinguishing Canadians from other English speakers along the Atlantic coast as the history of [r] after vowels." It would appear that a nonrhotic dialect was brought to Canada by the Loyalists from New England. In Canada, the loss of [r] was arrested and reversed for some reason. Bailey suggests that this change may have been the result of other (rhotic) British varieties coming to Canada, or of a sense of national identity, or of the further loss of [r] in American dialects after the departure of the Loyalists.

12.5.1.6 *Marry/merry/Mary*

For the *marry/merry/Mary* set, speakers of standard British distinguish all three; so do some Americans, whereas others make no distinction. Canadian speakers, like a third group of Americans, make a two-way distinction between *Mary*, *merry* (with [ɛr]) and *marry* (with [ær]). Furthermore,

Canadian English appears to have a lower, more open [æ] than either British or American in words such as *Barry*, *guarantee*, and *caramel*.

12.5.1.7 Secondary stress

The retention of secondary stress in words ending in *-ory*, *-ary*, and *-ery* (*laboratory*, *secretary*, *monastery*) is standard in Canadian English as it is in American English, thus being distinguished from British English.

12.5.1.8 [hw] versus [w]

Canadian English shares a general North American shift from [hw] or [ʍ] to [w], with such resulting homophonous pairs as *which/witch; where/wear; whale/wail; whet/wet.*

Richard Bailey (1982) notes that [hw] is rare for Canadian speakers even in citation forms, and Léon and Martin claim that it has almost disappeared in Toronto. However, Woods (139) claims that [hw] "is still held as a goal in Ottawa," though he finds that it is used less frequently by young female speakers – a sign that the pronunciation may be on the way out.

12.5.1.9 Individual lexical items

Some lexical items have distinctive pronunciations in Canadian English, pronunciations that are found in neither British nor American English. These include *khaki* [kɑrki], *offense* [oʊfɛns] (also *official*, *opinion*), and *longitude* [lɑŋgɪt(ɪ)ud]. Studies show, however, that the Canadian pronunciation of *khaki* is being replaced by the American [kæki]. Other pronunciations are shared with American English, though they are of limited distribution in the latter, being either socially marked or old-fashioned: *asphalt* [æʃfɑlt], *progress* [proʊgrɛs] (also *process*, sometimes *product*), *vase* [veɪz], *bilingual* [baɪlɪŋgɪuəl], *drama* [dræmə] (also *pasta*, *finale*, *Mazda*, *Datsun*, etc.), *radiator* [rædɪeɪtər], and *tomato* [təmætoʊ].

It is in the pronunciation of individual lexical items that Canadian English shows the continuing influence of a British prestige. In contrast to American pronunciations, Canadians normally pronounce the suffix *-ine* as [aɪn] rather than [ɪn]; the suffix *-ile* as [aɪl] rather than [əl], and prefixes such as *anti-* and *semi-* with the final vowel [i] rather than [aɪ]. Oddly, [aɪn] for *-ine* was thought vulgar in nineteenth-century Canada. The suffix *-ile* often follows the American pronunciation in *missile*, and sometimes *futile;* Canadians and Americans pronounce *gentile*, *exile*, *crocodile*, and sometimes *domicile* with [aɪl].

Other Canadian pronunciations that resemble British pronunciations are, for example, *again* [əgeɪn], *been* [bin], *decal* [dɛkəl], *either* [aɪðər], *herb* [hərb], *lever* [livər], *produce* [prɑdɪus], *root* [rut] (also *hoof, broom*, etc.), *route* [rut], *senile* [sɛnaɪl], and *shone* [ʃɑn] (also *scone*). (Note that, for a number of these words, there is quite significant regional variability in American and British English.) Spelling pronunciations, such as *herb, arctic* [ɑrktɪk], or *often* [ɑftən], seem to be fairly frequent in Canadian English, as they are in British English. Canadian English also differs from American English in the casual pronunciation of *-ing* as [ɪn] rather than as [ən] and of *going to* as [gɔɪntə] or [gɑnə] rather than as [gənə]. The British pronunciation of *schedule* [ʃɛdɪul] has been promoted by the Canadian Broadcasting Corporation, but the American pronunciation seems to be the preferred form for Canadian speakers. The Canadian Survey of English shows that a number of the British pronunciations, such as *lever* and *either*, are slowly falling out of favor with younger speakers, while other British forms, such as *zebra* [zɛbrə], and *lieutenant* [lɛftɛnənt], are already minority use in Canada. Avis (1978) makes the observation that, when there is a clear-cut preference for a pronunciation in Canadian English, the British form is chosen for words of literary import or limited range and the American form when the word is in widespread use.

What perhaps most characterizes Canadian speakers, however, is their use of several possible variant pronunciations for the same word, sometimes even in the same sentence.

12.5.2   Morphosyntax and usage

Very few differences between Canadian and other varieties of English have been identified in the area of morphosyntax or usage, in part because studies have tended to look at common usage and grammar mistakes (*lie* versus *lay, between you and I, who(m) did you ask?*) rather than identifying distinctive grammatical structures in Canadian English. However, a few minor differences have been observed.

In respect to verbal forms, it is traditionally claimed that Canadians use the British past participle *got* and the American past tense *dove*; however, survey evidence shows *got* and *gotten* and *dived* and *dove* almost equally common. Though in the Vancouver survey *gotten* had quite a high rejection rate (Gregg), it is becoming more frequent there as well. Canadians prefer American *raise* to British *rise* but reportedly use *lend* more frequently than *loan*. The "nonstandard" past tense *sunk* and past participle *drank* are quite common in Canadian English, and the strong past tense *snuck* is gaining ground. The weak past tense *treaded* is acceptable in an aquatic context (as in *he treaded water for five minutes*), and surprisingly *trod* is a common present tense form (with *trod* or *tread* as the past tense form). Canadian English shows some preference for the shortened past and past participial forms *spelt/spelled, dreamt/dreamed, leant/leaned, knelt/kneeled,* which are common in British English. The British verbal idiom *bath the baby* is standard, as is *go missing,* but the American and Scots *want out* (for *want to go out*) is gaining ground. While there is some use of the British English constructions *Have you?* and *Have you got?* in Canadian English, survey evidence again suggests that the American *Do you have?* will soon replace these constructions.

Prepositional idioms are likewise split between American and British usage, Canadians preferring (by a large margin) *to* to *of* in expressions of time such as *a quarter to twelve* and *on* to *in* in *live on a street.* As in America, *different than* is more common than either *different from* (the prescribed American form) or *different to* (a common British form). The British *behind* is more frequent than the American *in back of.* And Canadians resemble British speakers in the omission of articles in expressions such as *in hospital.*

A distinctive syntactic construction in Canadian English, common in governmental language, is the noun + attributive order in phrases such as *Air Canada, Revenue Canada,* or *Parks Canada.* Such inverted order is clearly a calque on French word order, and is used to enable these names to "work" in both official languages. Another distinctive usage is sentence-initial *as well* functioning as a conjunctive adverb in Canadian English (e.g., *When I get home, I have to make dinner. As well, I have to do a load of laundry*); other varieties permit only sentence-medial or sentence-final adverbial *as well.* Chambers (1985) cites two constructions of limited geographical distribution in Canada: positive *anymore* in the sense 'nowadays,' as in *He complains a lot anymore,* and *after* + present participle, with the sense of the present perfect, as in *He is after telling me all about it.* He attributes the first to Loyalist influence and the second to Celtic influence. Positive *anymore* occurs regionally with increasing frequency in the United States, and the perfect use of *after* more restrictedly.

Without doubt, the form thought most typical (indeed stereotypical) of Canadian English is sentence-final *eh?* In an important article, Avis (1972) categorizes eight uses of the form, primarily as a tag inviting or soliciting agreement, as a reinforcement, or as a request for repetition. Citing examples from different varieties of English over time, he argues that *eh?* is not an exclusively Canadian feature. Solely on the basis of Canadian oral evidence, Avis identifies the eighth use, which he terms "narrative *eh?*" He notes that *eh?* in this use is "virtually meaningless," is spoken quickly and without its usual rising intonation, and is of high frequency, as in: "That was when we almost intercepted a pass, eh? and Stu Falkner bumped into him, eh?" Survey evidence suggests that this usage is more common in the lower socioeconomic class. Woods found that not only did 47 percent of his informants claim not to use it (as opposed to 6 percent who said they did), but 47 percent said that they had an abhorrence of it. All evidence, therefore, points to a distinctively Canadian, albeit highly stigmatized, use of *eh?* in narratives.

Finally, on questions of usage in Canadian English, we now have a usage guide, the *Guide to Canadian English Usage*, based on a corpus of Canadian material. This gives us a much clearer idea about Canadian usage: for example, Canadian English requires the subjunctive in *if I were you*, even though the indicative, *if I was you*, is common in standard British English (Fee and McAlpine 474–5).

12.5.3   Spelling

Because of the competing influences of Samuel Johnson's 1755 dictionary in Britain and Noah Webster's 1828 dictionary in the United States, Canadian spelling conventions are a mix of those used in both countries: for example, *tire* (*tyre* is never used) and *cheque* (*check* is rarely used in the sense of 'bank draft'). Spelling varies from province to province (with British Columbia, Newfoundland, and Ontario tending toward British spellings and Alberta, Manitoba, and Saskatchewan toward American ones). Spellings also vary from word to word. For example, *neighbour* is most frequent everywhere but Alberta and Manitoba, whereas *odor* is the majority usage in all provinces except Ontario (Pratt 1993, 55). Some British spellings have become almost a symbol of Canadianness, for example, *theatre* and *centre* as part of the name of cultural institutions. The *-our* spelling was readopted in 1990 by the *Globe and Mail* (Toronto) which styles itself "Canada's national newspaper."

Canadians are often consistent in selecting one or the other convention of spelling within a major category: for example, most Canadians, like Americans, choose the *-ize/-yze* ending over *-ise/-yse*, and they double the *l* before suffixes in words such as *equalled*, *traveller*, etc. as do the British. However, they may also be inconsistent even within the same "set," for example, preferring *colour* at the same time as *favorite*. *Editing Canadian English* concludes that although it makes sense to advise against mixing spellings within the major categories, "mixing between categories not only is acceptable, but may well constitute the 'Canadian style'" (Burton 7).

12.5.4   Vocabulary

The usual definition of *Canadianisms* is "words which are native to Canada or words which have meanings native to Canada" (Avis 1967, vii). Some Canadianisms are borrowings from Canadian French (such as *capelin, coulee, shanty*) or from the Aboriginal languages of Canada (such as *kayak* from Inuktitut, *chipmunk* from Ojibwa, *saskatoon* and *muskeg* from Cree, *kokanee* from Shuswap, *sockeye* from Coast Salish, and *skookum* from Chinook Jargon). However, many of the more than 10,000 Canadianisms in the *Dictionary of Canadianisms* (Avis 1967; also Pratt 1988; Story, Kirwin, and Widdowson) are archaic, rare, or rural. For example, *chesterfield* was the standard Canadian term for a large sofa or couch in the 1940s and 1950s, but has now fallen out of general use, as have most of the terms related to the fur trade, transport by canoe, farming with horses, hand logging, smallcraft fishing, and winter travel.

Many other distinctly Canadian terms are current among the chiefly urban population of today (K. Barber has the most complete list). In addition to words for specific holidays (such as *St. Jean Baptiste Day, Victoria Day, Canada Day*) and government institutions or agencies (*Throne Speech, Charter of Rights and Freedoms, CIDA [Canadian International Development Agency]*), other Canadianisms relate to French–English relations, native peoples, government, law, politics, finance, social structures and programs, sports, education, weather, food and drink, and so on, as exemplified below.

12.5.4.1   French–English relations

anglophone English-speaking person
Bill 101 The Charter of French Language, passed in 1977, requiring, among
    other things, that public signs in Quebec be in French only
francophone French-speaking person
language police The officials of the *Commission de protection de la langue française*
Quiet Revolution The period 1960–6 in Quebec, marked by province-wide
    reforms and a growing separatist movement
separatist A person who favors the secession of Quebec (or of the Western
    provinces) from Canada
sovereigntist A supporter of Quebec's right to self-government

12.5.4.2   Native peoples

Aboriginal rights Rights guaranteed in the Charter of Rights and Freedoms to
    those defined as Aboriginal by the Constitution Act, 1982

band council A local form of Aboriginal government consisting of a chief and councillors

First Nation An Indian band or community

land claim A legal claim by an Aboriginal group concerning the use of an area of land

Métis A person of mixed Aboriginal and European descent

Native Friendship Centre An institution in a predominantly non-Aboriginal community to provide social services to Aboriginal people

Status Indian A person registered as an Indian under the Indian Act

treaty rights The rights of Aboriginal peoples, for example, that of holding land on a reserve, granted under the terms of a treaty

12.5.4.3 Government, law, and politics

For historical reasons, because of their similar systems, Canada shares many governmental and legal terms with Britain, such as *Member of Parliament* and *Queen's Counsel*. Other Canadianisms in this field are the following:

acclamation Election by virtue of being the only candidate

article Of a law student, to serve one's period of apprenticeship

bell-ringing The ringing of bells in a legislative assembly to summon members for a vote

chief electoral officer An official appointed to oversee the conduct of federal, provincial, and territorial elections

Confederation The act of creating the Dominion of Canada; also the federation of the Canadian provinces and territories

equalization payment A transfer of payments from the federal government to the poorer provinces

First Ministers The premiers of the provinces and the Prime Minister of Canada

impaired Having a blood alcohol level above the legal limit

leadership convention A convention held by a political party for the purpose of electing a new leader

mainstreeting Political campaigning

notwithstanding clause The section of the Charter of Rights and Freedoms which allows the Parliament and the provincial legislatures to override the Charter

patriation The transfer of the Canadian constitution to Canada from Britain in 1982

postal code Zip code or post code

riding A district whose voters elect a representative member to a legislative body

RCMP A member of the Royal Canadian Mounted Police

transfer payment A payment from the government to another level of government

12.5.4.4 Finance

bank rate The central bank's minimum interest rate

Bay Street and *Howe Street* The stock markets in Toronto and Vancouver, respectively

credit union A banking cooperative offering financial services; a savings and loan institution

GST The goods and services tax; a value-added tax levied by the federal government

harmonized sales tax A combination of the GST and PST

loonie A Canadian one-dollar coin depicting a loon on one side

open mortgage A type of mortgage that permits the principal to be paid off at any time

PST Provincial sales tax

RRSP or *RSP* Registered retirement savings plan

term deposit An amount of money deposited in a financial institution for a fixed term; a certificate of deposit

toonie or *twoonie* A Canadian two-dollar coin

T4 slip A statement issued by employers indicating annual employee salary, contributions, and deductions, used to calculate income tax

12.5.4.5 Social structures and programs

child tax benefit (formerly *family allowance*) A payment made by the federal government to mothers of children under 18, also *baby bonus*

health card or *care card* A card identifying a person as eligible to receive medical treatment paid for by a public insurance plan

heritage language A language spoken in Canada other than French or English

home care Services provided at home by family members or professional caregivers to those who otherwise might require institutional care

multiculturalism An official policy advocating a society composed of many culturally distinct groups, enacted into legislation in 1985

Old Age Security A system of government-funded pensions

social insurance number or *SIN* A nine-digit number used by the government for identification purposes

UIC Unemployment Insurance Commission; also the insurance payment

12.5.4.6 Sports

deke A fake shot or movement in ice hockey done to draw a defensive player out of position

five-pin bowling A variety of indoor bowling in alleys

Jeux Canada Games An annual national athletic competition, with events in summer and winter

murderball A game in which players in opposing teams attempt to hit their opponents with a large inflated ball

Participaction A private, nonprofit organization that promotes fitness

ringette A game resembling hockey, played by girls

Stanley Cup, Grey Cup, Briar, Queen's Plate Championships in hockey, (Canadian) football, curling, and horse-racing, respectively

12.5.4.7 Education

bird course A course requiring little work

bursary A financial award to a university student (also Scottish and English)

French immersion An educational program in which anglophone students are taught entirely in French

intersession A short university term, usually in May and June

March break A school holiday

reading week A week usually halfway through the university term when no classes are held

residence or *res* A university dormitory

separate school A publicly funded denominational (usually Catholic) school

12.5.4.8 Weather

humidex (from *humidity index*) A scale indicating the personal discomfort level resulting from combined heat and humidity

Lotus Land Southern British Columbia

plug in An electrical outlet near a parking space for plugging in a car's block heater

snow route A major road in a city designated for priority snow clearing

12.5.4.9 Food and drink

all dressed A hamburger with all the usual condiments on it
bumbleberry pie A pie made with a mixture of berries
butter tart A small tart filled with butter, sugar, or syrup, and usually raisins
drink(ing) box A small plasticized cardboard carton of juice
matrimonial cake A date square
Nanaimo bar An unbaked square iced with chocolate
screech A potent dark rum of Newfoundland
smoked meat Cured beef similar to pastrami but more heavily smoked, often
   associated with Montreal

12.5.4.10 Miscellaneous

blood donor clinic A blood bank
blue box A blue plastic box used for household recyclable waste
parkade A parking garage
seat sale A promotion by airlines offering discounted airline tickets
splash pants or *muddy buddies* A child's outer garment to protect against rain
   and mud
toque or *tuque* A close-fitting knitted hat

Like all dialects, Canadian English includes certain distinctive clipped forms, such as *emerge < emergency room*, *cash < cash register*, *reno < renovation*, *physio < physiotherapy* or *physiotherapist*, *homo < homogenized milk* (typically with a butterfat content of 3.25 percent), *grad < graduation ceremony* or *graduation dinner-dance*, and *CanLit < Canadian Literature*. It also includes distinctive slang expressions such as *chippy* 'short-tempered,' *hoser* 'an idiot,' *spinny* 'crazy, foolish,' *keener* 'an overzealous student,' *pogey* 'welfare or less commonly unemployment insurance benefits,' *to have had the biscuit* 'to be no longer good for anything,' and *Molson muscle* 'a beer belly.'

12.5.4.11 Quebec English

The Quebec English vocabulary has become somewhat distinct from the English of other provinces since 1974, when French became the only official language of the province. As a result, English speakers have been exposed to French in public institutions and now commonly work in French as well as English. More French words have moved into the English vocabulary, such as *dépanneur* (*dep* for short) 'corner store,' *caisse* or *caisse populaire* 'credit union,' *allophone* 'someone whose first language is neither English nor French,' *autoroute* 'highway,' *poutine* 'a fast food of French fries with melted cheese curds and gravy,' and *tourtière* 'a meat pie traditionally eaten at Christmas.' Such loanwords may compound French and English words according to an English pattern, such as *francization* 'the adoption of French as the official language' (McArthur 8). Some of these words are now part of the wider Canadian English vocabulary (*anglophone*, *tourtière*).

When English and French words are similar but have meanings that have become distinct over time, the current French meaning is sometimes transferred to the English word, a process that McArthur (9) calls "collisions." For example, now Quebec English speakers may use *primordial* to mean 'crucial,' as in this actual example, "Mind you, the quality and freshness of the fish is primordial," or they might talk about having a mechanic *verify*, rather than *check*, the brakes on their car. They might ask you for your *coordinates*, instead of for your name, address, and phone number. Other examples include *annex* 'appendix of a book,' *conference* 'lecture,' *patrimony* 'heritage,' *subvention* 'grant,' and *syndicate* 'labor union.'

Linguistic politics have also left a mark on English vocabulary; *pure laine* 'pure wool, dyed in the wool' and *vielle souche* 'old roots' are used to refer to someone whose ancestry is exclusively Québécois, for example. All of these changes are results of provincial language policies that have changed the linguistic landscape of the province from one where English was the dominant language to a new French reality (McArthur; Fee and McArthur; Fee and McAlpine).

12.6   Conclusion

Canadian English is the outcome of a number of factors. Canadian English was initially determined in large part by Canada's settlement by immigrants from the northern United States. Because of the geographical proximity of the two countries and the intertwining of their histories, economic systems, international policies, and print and especially television media, Canadian English continues to be shaped by American English. However, because of the colonial and postcolonial history of the British Empire, Canadian English is also strongly marked by British English. The presence of a long-standing and large French-speaking minority has also had an effect on Canadian English. Finally, social conditions, such as governmental policies of bilingualism, immigration, and multiculturalism and the politics of Quebec nationalism, have also played an important part in shaping this national variety of English.

FURTHER READING

The most extensive recent collection on Canadian English is *Focus on Canada*, edited by Sandra Clarke (1993), which includes articles on spelling, pronunciation, lexicography, and dialects (Anglo-Irish and African-Canadian English), as well as several comparisons between aspects of American and Canadian English. John Edwards's *Language in Canada* (1998) is a collection of articles, primarily sociolinguistic, on the languages spoken in Canada, with emphasis on French, English, and Aboriginal languages. J. K. Chambers's "English: Canadian Varieties" (1998) in the Edwards volume is a good, up-to-date, short overview. Other useful reference sources are *The Canadian Oxford Dictionary* (K. Barber 1998) and *A Dictionary of Canadianisms on Historical Principles* (Avis 1967).

13 NEWFOUNDLAND ENGLISH

William J. Kirwin

13.1 Early Newfoundland

Varieties of English have been established in Newfoundland since the early seventeenth century, when small numbers of men began to live year-round near the cod fisheries of the island's coastal waters and the adjacent Grand Bank and when scattered families were established in coastal settlements after the arrival of a few women. The first English birth on the island was recorded in 1613. However, annual fishing voyages had brought Englishmen and other European nationalities to the Newfoundland coasts since at least 1497 (Cell 1969). Several adventurers, for example George Calvert, later Lord Baltimore, attempted to plant colonies in the early decades of the 1600s, but as these did not persist as discrete communities beyond the middle of the seventeenth century, there is little firm documentation about colonists who may have become settlers, married, and produced lines of descendants (Cell 1982).

The island of Newfoundland lies in the mouth of the St. Lawrence River, to the south of Quebec and Labrador. It is the size of the state of Tennessee, and coastal Labrador, which falls within its jurisdiction, is nearly as large as Arizona. Basic to an understanding of the establishment of English in the island of Newfoundland is that from the sixteenth to the late eighteenth century, though with interruptions in wartime, it was visited in the summers by thousands of transient fishermen from the southwestern counties of England. At the same time, it was occupied year-round by a strikingly small number of settlers, likewise from the same West Country sources (L. Harris; O'Flaherty; Story).

From the early eighteenth century, single and married fishermen from southern Ireland also began to fish and overwinter in small numbers. Newfoundland's history as an English colony and later a dominion extended to 1949, when the populace voted to become a province of Canada.

441

Labrador was inhabited only by Aboriginal peoples until the Moravian missionaries arrived in the 1760s. Coastal Labrador, which had been visited for many decades by Newfoundland and American seasonal fishermen, slowly became settled after the early 1800s by winter trappers with Eskimo wives and by seasonal migrants, mostly families coming north from Conception Bay for the summer fisheries, who chose to settle in the harbors (Brice-Bennett 103, 313–15).

The statistics of 1996 recorded 522,602 people on the island and 29,190 in Labrador. The development of English in Newfoundland needs to be viewed in the light of the small number of settlers. Average totals of winter settlers for selected dates are 3,506 in 1700, 5,855 in 1750, 12,340 in 1764–74, 15,253 in 1784–92 (O'Flaherty; Prowse 696), 122,638 in 1857 (*Abstract Census* 124), 217,037 in 1901, plus 3,947 in Labrador (*Census*, table 1, 436). The principal economic bases in the province have been cod and other fish, seal pelts and oil, wood products, minerals, and hydroelectric power (McManus and Wood).

From the first, the English and Irish population was divided between a tiny group of entrepreneurs, captains, suppliers, and "masters" and a large number of laborers who signed papers specifying wages, position, duties, and term of contract. Many young workers of the latter group stayed only one summer or two summers and a winter. They were called *servants*, a fisheries term not to be confused with that for household domestics, but referring instead to indentured laborers working under and fed by a *master* and involved with operating small boats and catching, curing, and loading *fish*, that is, codfish.

The men and women who established families, the settlers, were in contrast with the thousands of fishermen arriving each spring and leaving late in the fall, the transients or seasonal workers. In the seventeenth and eighteenth centuries the total number of settlers was small and increased slowly; in 1675 it stood at 1,700 persons, and by 1770 it had risen to approximately 12,000. In the conduct of the fishery, the settlers and the annual transient fishermen were in close contact. In the seventeenth century, the settlers were mainly English, with a few Irish individuals mentioned in the documents from time to time (Handcock; O'Flaherty 47).

Beginning about 1720 the numbers of Irish merchants and servants steadily increased, so that later in the eighteenth century many productive areas in eastern Newfoundland saw a clear division between the small managerial class – English merchants and agents, always from Devon, Dorset, and neighboring counties – and a large majority of laborers, most of them Irish (Head). English speech was transmitted in the families of the three or four emerging towns and the many coves, called *outports*, with infusions every summer of folk speech from England and Ireland. The customary seasonal West Country Newfoundland fishery tapered off before 1800, and so did the close personal contact with the numerous transients from the two source areas.

Explorers from England encountered indigenous peoples in Newfoundland. On the island was a small elusive group of Indians, the Beothuks, also called *Red Indians* from the use of ochre on their bodies, who were never to establish friendly intercourse with the Europeans (Marshall). The tribe became extinct in 1829, their Algonquian language having had minimal influence on the English vocabulary. Groups of the North American Eskimos (now called Inuit in Canada) were encountered along the Strait of Belle Isle after 1500; and in the nineteenth century, the English came in contact with hunting Indians named Montagnais and Naskapi (now known as Innu). Micmac Indians, now centered in Conne River on the south coast, were more widely dispersed on the island in earlier centuries.

13.2   Settlement

In order to control the rich English fisheries off the coasts of Newfoundland, powerful West Country merchants early gained the support of the English navy to provide annual convoy service for the fishing fleets and, in fact, governance of the colony. Supreme command on shore was given to the commodore of the convoy in 1708 (Thompson 9). In addition, small garrisons of the military were stationed in Newfoundland after 1700 and were considerably increased in the 1760s.

During the fishing season, the governor, an admiral, became the focus of a small elite circle in the capital city of St. John's that included naval officers, principal merchants, clergymen, doctors, officials, and a steady stream of educated visitors and scientists (*DNE2*, xxxvi–xxxix). This changing group, with a growing middle class of native-born residents emerging in the nineteenth century, provided a model of educated and cultured English and Anglo-Irish speech which has been influential down to modern times. The first newspaper was established in 1807. Since the 1830s English and Irish teachers have staffed some schools and, along with their curricula and training, exposed the pupils to prestige varieties of speech and usage. Most nineteenth-century Protestant preachers were from England; most Catholic priests were Irish.

This cosmopolitan coterie in St. John's, the economic and mercantile hub of the colony, and the principal people in east coast centers like

Harbour Grace, Carbonear, and Trinity were in marked contrast to the inhabitants of the hundreds of small coastal communities, where perhaps only one or two persons were literate, print was rare, and schools and churches only very slowly became established. Newfoundland has been called an oral, traditional country, and the many travelers' accounts show that to be accurate. The spectrum ranges from St. John's with orators and belletrists to some settlements without any literate inhabitants even in 1900.

English control declined with the increasing number of native politicians, professionals, and civil servants. The island was a colony, under the Colonial and later the Dominion Office, but after 1833 had a local Assembly that could stimulate economic growth and modernization. After 1855 the colony had Responsible Government, which meant virtual autonomy in its internal affairs. Overspending combined with the stresses of the world economy in the 1930s led to financial crisis. Finally facing bankruptcy in 1933, the country gave up self-rule, and officials from England, with a similar number of Newfoundlanders, took over direction in a body called the Commission of Government (1934–49), presided over by a British-appointed Governor.

Economic conditions improved during World War II, but by the late 1940s vocal leaders and partisans were weighing the possibility of becoming part of Canada. In the second of two referendums in the summer of 1948, Newfoundland voters favored by a narrow margin joining the Canadian Confederation, a union that took place on March 31, 1949. Since that time Canadian government agencies, communication networks, and business enterprises have radically shifted Newfoundland society away from its former close ties with the center of culture and tradition in England.

Newfoundland English, especially its common and folk varieties, began its development well before many English speakers had settled in the present area of Canada and at least 200 years before the United Province of Canada was created in 1841 or the Dominion of Canada in 1867. Linguistic relations with mainland Canadian speech since 1949 are difficult to specify (Avis and Kinloch; Bähr; Lougheed 1988; McConnell; *Regional Language Studies*; Schneider 1984). That is, researchers are hard put to identify any distinctive Canadian pronunciations, intonations, grammatical forms, idioms, or regional vocabulary brought from other provinces to Newfoundland either before 1949 or in the immediate post-Confederation period. This is true despite the fact that World War II brought about 16,000 Canadian personnel for several years to Newfoundland locations (MacLeod 2), and before, during, and after the war Newfoundland males moved to mainland Canadian cities to obtain employment (McManus and Wood, plate 9). At the close of the twentieth century, however, Canadian pronunciations and usages had become noticeable in the speech of the young.

Newfoundland has become a part of Canada, although older generations still have strong feelings of independence and local identity. However, social ties with the United States may have somewhat influenced linguistic developments. People have moved from Newfoundland to the Boston area and elsewhere since the mid eighteenth century (Thornton). Some workers, for example steel workers erecting skyscrapers, coal miners, and fishermen on Gloucester ships (Maurer 1930), supported their families in Newfoundland by their stints in the United States. World War II brought to bases in Newfoundland thousands of Americans who took Newfoundland brides home with them and established close ties between families in both countries. The servicemen, with their dances, radio stations, and movies, were models for imitation by thousands of workers on the bases and young people during the war years and afterwards (Cardoulis). Beginning in 1892, the medical and missionary activities in northern Newfoundland and Labrador of the Englishman Dr. Wilfred Grenfell (1865–1940) drew hundreds of American nurses, teachers, and volunteer college students to northern outports, as small fishing villages are called (Rompkey). Possibly it is the personal relations within families that have led to subtle American influences in some Newfoundland areas.

The settlement history of Newfoundland accounted for many linguistic features of the country, at least until the mid twentieth century, when the modernizing of society accelerated. Before that period, Newfoundland English consisted of a number of sometimes interblended varieties derived from the British Isles, slowly but independently evolving on the western side of the Atlantic.

13.3 West Country Newfoundland English

First, a strain of prestige English from England and Ireland, manifest in the large corpus of books and manuscripts still extant, was cultivated by the families of the mercantile, administrative, and professional classes, some coming as transients from the British Isles and others being settled residents in the island (*DNE2* xxxv–xli; Kirwin 1991). Second, an offshoot of the mercantile and seafaring laboring populations from Devon and Dorset and neighboring counties (Handcock) brought various levels of West Country regional speech to the southeast coast and Conception Bay and later to the north and Labrador as well as to the south coast and the rest of the littoral (Head; Mannion 1977), much of the interior of the island being uninhabited. Third, a small but influential group of Irish merchants, together with many fisheries servants hired on contract by both Irish and English masters, congregated in St. John's, Placentia, and the Avalon Peninsula, and in the older towns of Conception Bay and the northeast coast (Mannion 1986; Kirwin 1993).

Except for these larger communities, the ethnic English and Irish in many areas were – and to some extent still are – separated into distinct settlements or portions of the coastline. For example much of the south coast west of Fortune Bay is inhabited by descendants of the English. Dialectally, this pattern of settlement has led to strong concentrations of West Country sounds, forms, and lexis on some stretches of coast, almost unmixed Anglo-Irish in other areas – nearly all of the southern Avalon Peninsula, for example – and further, among mixed populations, types of Newfoundland English have evolved with elements of both strains that have not yet been sorted out by researchers (Paddock 1981).

Newfoundland English has been examined geographically and structurally. Using twenty-one selected features traceable to West Country or to southern Anglo-Irish sources and found in conversations taped in seventy-two communities, Paddock (1982, 86–7) identified communities that are mainly English, mainly Irish, or either mixed or transitional. Paddock's areas generally coincide with the historical settlement areas determined by Handcock as well as Mannion (1974). Eight focal and transitional areas were identified in the narrow populated strip stretching around the coast of the island (Paddock 1982, 74, 83). An earlier investigation (Seary, Story, and Kirwin 54–73), focusing on the Avalon Peninsula only, found three areas in addition to St. John's: the Southern Shoreline, the Northern Shoreline, and, within the latter, the Bay Roberts area.

Another way of looking at the varieties of English concentrates on the features themselves. Evidence of West Country features is found on all levels of language structure in Newfoundland manuscripts and books since 1600 (*EDD*; Kirwin 1991; Kirwin and Hollett; *SED*; Wakelin 1986a).

Southwestern English consonants are more or less obvious in areas of Newfoundland and Labrador. For many centuries in the southwest, initial voiceless fricatives have been recorded as voiced. Although in Newfoundland this phenomenon is not automatic or analogical, initial consonants have been recorded as voiced from speech and tape: *vish*, *vin* or *ven*, and *varket* 'forked' in the place-name *Varket Channel*. *Vir* 'fir' is frequent, but a regional variant is *var*, which in the minds of speakers seems almost unrelated to *fir*.

446

For initial *s-*, an example is *zen(d)*. Voiceless *thr-* is both voiced and stopped in old forms borrowed from western England: *drung* or *drang* 'narrow passage,' *drash* 'shower of rain,' *drashel* 'threshold,' and *droo* 'number of meshes forming a row in a fishnet.'

The use of initial [h] is similar to that in several British dialects at least since the eighteenth century. Many Newfoundlanders do not employ [h-] as a functional element on a par with consonants such as *r-*, *y-*, or *w-* (Kirwin and Hollett 229–32). They do not systematically distinguish pairs like *hen* and *end*. In informal speech they are not aware whether they have uttered an initial [h-] or begun the syllable with a vowel. Dictionary spellings and historical pronunciations are irrelevant. No conditioning factors have been identified to predict the occurrence or nonoccurrence of [h]. Examples from a recorded folktale illustrate this phenomenon: "Anchored out in the middle; hanchors hove down everywhere"; "An hup comes se hice" (Hollett n.d.).

The lateral [l] in English areas contrasts with the Anglo-Irish type discussed below in being typically a dark -*l*, with frequent vocalization in final position to [o] or [u]: *gayoo* 'gale.' As in educated British use, *wh-* is [w] not [hw] as in *wharf*. The retroflex or constricted medial semivowel *r* [ɹ] has long been a stereotypical consonant in the West Country, especially Somerset, and, with some exceptions, occurs in English areas of Newfoundland, as it does in mainland Canada and America outside eastern New England and parts of the South. Inexplicably r-lessness occurs in the bottom arc of Conception Bay (almost the oldest settled coast in the island), paralleling RP and eastern New England, pronouncing [r] only when a vowel follows (Seary, Story, and Kirwin 68).

When the glide [ɹ] occurs after vowels, giving the North American r-coloring, several singularities are noticeable. There is a collapse of the high and mid vowel contrast so that, for example, *beer* is lowered to *bear* and *bare* (or they are neutralized) and, as in RP, *poor* is lowered to *pour* and *pore*. *Car*, *cart*, *barred* have a very fronted vowel, approaching that in *cat*. A noticeably lowered pronunciation of *or* followed by a consonant, which is often mimicked by other Newfoundlanders, as in "Gearge," is paralleled by forms transcribed in the West Country: *forty*, *horse*, *morning*, *north* (*SED* 122–3, 803, 833–4, 887–8). In Dorset *corn* and *barley* have the same r-colored vowel.

Distinctive vowels of the West Country also have reflexes in areas of Newfoundland. The most frequent among older speakers is the [eː] spelled *ea* in English until the eighteenth century and retained in modern *break* and *steak*: *sea*, *heave*, *leak* (with a local anecdote about ponds and lakes: "A lake is in your boot"). The front vowels in *mitt* and *mess* may involve conditioning (the high vowel often seems lowered before [l] and nasals), restriction to particular words, neutralization of the English phonemic contrast, or even a subtle phonetics that deceives the ear of outsiders. Evidence is minimal in the *Survey of English Dialects* (Orton and Dieth), but *pig* is once transcribed with a lowered vowel. Newfoundland examples include *bilt* 'belt,' *kittle, ef,* and *knitting* or *netting* 'making a fishnet.'

The vowel in *eye* and *tide*, final or followed by a voiced consonant, sounds distinctly different from that in *ice*, where it is followed by a voiceless consonant. The *ice* diphthong is a "fast" glide, with a raised first element, typical of the mainland Canadian vowel system and in parts of the eastern United States (Kurath and McDavid, map 27 for *twice* compared with map 26 for *nine*). Since very old Newfoundlanders have this conditioned diphthong, it is probably not directly related to the similar diphthong in the mainland. Transcriptions of raised onsets in this diphthong appear in the *SED* for Somerset, Wiltshire, Dorset, and elsewhere, but before both voiceless and voiced consonants (*SED* 141–2 *knife* and 365 *rind*).

The personal pronoun system recorded in West Country speech for more than two centuries (Wakelin 1986a, 34), which at first strikes outsiders as perverse, has been transported to Newfoundland almost intact. It is not based on the subject-object paradigm but rather on an opposition between strongly and weakly stressed word forms. When strongly stressed, the pronouns are *I, (h)e, she, we, they*, regardless of grammatical function. When weakly stressed, they are respectively *me, un* or *'n, (h)er, us, (th)em* (Paddock 1988, 385–6).

He and *she* refer to both animate and inanimate referents. *It* is restricted to dummy subjects and mass nouns (*fog, weather*). The basis for choosing between *he* and *she* for inanimates is unclear. *He* often refers to machinery or contraptions: "There he is, this [ring] is he"; "He [an anchor] can be used for a small boat"; "Squeeze up through, for to take the next ladder, and when you get up to he, then there was another." On the other hand: "She [a mine shaft] was boarded over, see"; "She [a clock] was goin' on. I let her go on anyway" (Paddock 1988). It would be a mistake to infer that speakers are endowing these referents with feminine or masculine qualities – or personifying them.

Nonpast finite verbs are inflected with *-(e)s* for subjects of all persons and numbers. When indicating ownership, *have* often takes a regular inflection: "Some people haves fish-houses, little small houses made right square." Assimilated or analogous [d] occurs before contracted *-n't* in many auxiliaries: *idn't* (with variant *int it?*), *wadn't, weredn't*.

13.4   Anglo-Irish influence

Ireland, too, has been the source of distinctive features in Newfoundland. The English language was planted in Ireland in the sixteenth and seventeenth centuries, though there were pockets of English even in Norman times. Irish and English coexisted for a time, with English gradually spreading over the island and Irish declining until it became the vernacular only of rural inhabitants in the western areas. Although it is reported that monoglot Irish speakers were among the seasonal workers in the Newfoundland fisheries and a small number settled there, they did not pass Irish on as a living language to their children. By contrast, the Anglo-Irish of both merchant families and medium and small farmers from Kilkenny, Wexford, Waterford, and the nearby hinterland has become the basis of the varieties of Newfoundland English which are traceable to Ireland (Bliss 1984; Kirwin 1993; Mannion 1974, 1986).

Noteworthy Newfoundland consonantal features influenced by Anglo-Irish are a clear [l]; extensive substitution of the stops /t/ and /d/ (or perhaps dental variants of these) for the fricatives /θ/ and /ð/, especially the latter in words like *the, this, that, there, either, other;* no absence of /r/ (of some phonetic quality) in any positions in a word; a slit fricative or breathy stop for word-final *-t;* no aspiration in *wh-* words like *whale, when, wharf;* and palatalization of /t-/ and /d-/ in words where RP might have following [ju]: the effect is like *-ch-* and *-j-* in *Tuesday, tune, duty, stew, student.*

In the vowel system, the mid-central nucleus of *cut, slub, dull* is a backed vowel, often rounded, in effect approaching the area which in some other dialects is occupied by [ɔ]. For some speakers [e:] and [o:] are long monophthongs, without the rising glides characteristic of these vowels in other national varieties of English, and one incidental pronunciation of [e:] parallels the obsolescent West Country class discussed previously: *beak,* pronounced like *bake,* has the specialized sense 'human nose, face.'

One low-central, sometimes fronted, vowel serves where other varieties of English contrast two phonemes: the Anglo-Irish vowel in *cod, John's, fog* is the norm, occurring also in *caught, song, loss, paw, all; Don* and *dawn* are thus homophonous. The Anglo-Irish single vowel in these words has probably developed quite independently of the structurally similar single low-back vowel in mainland Canadian English. The absence of [ɔ] in Anglo-Irish also affects *oy,* which has an onset ranging between low-central and somewhat backed: *tie/toy, lied/Lloyd, buy/boy,* and perhaps *liar/lawyer* are all riming pairs.

Anglo-Irish grammar has a singular-plural contrast for second-person pronouns; singular *you* and *ya* contrast with plural *ye*, with occasional appearances of *yeer* and *yeers*.

For the verb *be*, Anglo-Irish has an aspect called "consuetudinal present" and "generic/habitual category" (Bliss 1984, 143; Kallen 3). *Am, are, is* denote the present moment, whereas invariant *bes* [biːz], *don't be*, and a rarely reported *do(es) be* are employed for continuous duration or repeated action. Typical examples are "He bes in the lower school"; "I don't know whether he's moody, or whether he does be vexed with me"; and the common retort "Don't be talking!"

Past participles are infrequent in conversation. Especially striking is the absence of the English construction "to have (just) ——ed." Instead, Anglo-Irish uses *be after* ——*ing* (Bliss 1984, 144), based on the Irish constructions *i ndiaidh* or *d'éis*. The idiom is copious in Newfoundland writing and speech: "I'm not old enough to be after doin' too much work anywhere"; "There was an island pan [of ice] after drivin' along"; "We were after bein' that way [with coal shifted in the hold] for twenty-two hours"; "The provincial government is after setting up this offshore petroleum impact committee"; "A load of new ones [shoots on a fern] are after comin' out."

Only *will* is used where southern British English may have a *shall/will* contrast. Verbal past tenses often have short vowels: *lie* 'stretch out' /*lid*, *make*/*med*. The past of *freeze* is *frozed*.

13.5 Vocabulary

The characteristic vocabulary of Newfoundland is especially massive because of the flora and fauna, the long history of the active fishery in the surrounding waters, and the twin streams of localized language of the British Isles introduced with the settlers from southern England and southern Ireland.

The *Dictionary of Newfoundland English* (Story, Kirwin, and Widdowson) gives the known etymologies of many Newfoundlandisms, but the following (arranged chronologically) are of unknown or uncertain origin. It is not widely known that *penguin* appeared in Newfoundland writings, for 'great auk,' before it was applied to similar flightless birds near the South Pole. *Garnipper* or *gallinipper* 'large biting insect, mosquito,' appearing in New England first (*DNE2* 625), may have the element *nipper* from English dialects; the dialect *gurt* 'great' (*EDD*) may have developed a variant *gar* (like Newfoundland *var* from *fir*).

Killick 'stone within a wooden cage to form an anchor' has long been very important in the fishery, but its local use is also antedated by an appearance in New England writing in 1630. Another East Coast Colonial term (1758) without a traceable source is *callibogus*, used for 'mixture of liquor and molasses.' *Waterhorse* may be a *horse* 'pile' of fish placed in layers to allow salted water to drain off, but the *horse* element may conceal other similar pronunciations or specialized senses. A 1710 engraving (Prowse 22) shows a wooden cage or trough suspended in salt water to wash fish; a century later its name, *ram's horn*, appears in print – suggesting no connection with the animal or with the religious instrument used in the Old Testament. It is baffling how the Tamil loanword *catamaran* 'raft' surfaced in Newfoundland in 1810 for 'heavy sledge, often with vertical poles called "horns" placed at the four corners.' The spelling has always been the same, and the final syllable at present is stressed. Evidence in manuscripts or naval drawings may be discovered which shows the resemblance of the sledge to a device of warfare (*OED* sense 2) familiar to naval officers serving on the Newfoundland station in the early 1800s.

A tantalizing disparaging term which arose on the West Coast of the island, *jackatar* 'person believed to have mixed French and Indian ancestry,' cannot confidently be traced to French or to the deceptive English parallel *jack tar* 'sailor.' *More* in *tuckamore* 'low stunted vegetation' is an English dialect term for 'root'; but the origin of *tucka-* has not been identified. In the cluster of vocabulary related to the extensively studied Christmas house visits and mummering, *janny* is both a noun 'mummer' and a verb 'to go about with a disguise on.' The link connecting it with a West Country variant of *johnny* is missing; no mummers are called jannies in any English accounts (Widdowson 1969). *Chovy* or *chuffy* 'piece of kindling with sides shaved by a knife' has not yet yielded any plausible source. *Twack* 'a shopper who examines goods but never buys' seems to have an Irish quality, though English and Irish dictionaries list nothing comparable. *Bantam*, in names for 'a rock that is awash,' is a recently discovered toponymic term whose origin is unclear.

The foregoing miscellany of representative items in the Newfoundland vocabulary whose origins have not been tracked down can be set beside the classes of words borrowed from the peoples and nations long associated with Newfoundland and the great numbers connected with the principal economic activities of the country.

Beothuk words have hardly entered the lexicon. The tribal name, meaning 'the people,' is widely known, and popular in the names of commercial organizations. The 'wigwam' of these people, *mamateek*, has some slight currency in children's textbooks and stories. Inuit words related to the Labrador coast include *adikey* or *dicky* 'cloth or skin parka' and *komatik* – the variant *commeteck* indicates the pronunciation – 'long sled.' In *bakeapple* 'cloudberry,' the origin of *apple* is shrouded in the usage of the first Englishmen in Labrador, while *bake* is parallel to the Eskimo term for cloudberry, *appik*. The Micmacs' *babbish* 'hide filling for snowshoes' may be compared to the Montagnais Indians' *tibbage* 'strips of hide in a snowshoe.'

Quintal (that is, *kental*) 'unit of weight, 112 pounds of fish' has always been a pivotal word in Newfoundland, though also found in English economic history. It is ultimately from Latin, via Arabic, but was borrowed into English from Spanish and Portuguese. Another Spanish loan is *bacallao*, once used for 'codfish' and 'Newfoundland' and at present an island name in the form *Baccalieu*. *Mug up* (with stress often on *up*) 'snack' and *high liner* 'best fisherman or boat' are doubtless terms generated in the nine-teenth-century international Bank fishery (Kirwin and Story).

French and Irish provided many loans, of which the following are a sample. Northwestern French vessels have fished in Newfoundland waters since at least the sixteenth century, leaving a layer of French place-names along several of the coasts (Seary). The spelling *barrysway* appears in Newfoundland texts before the standard French *barachois* 'shallow lagoon sheltered by a sandbar' and the *-sway* accurately denotes the eighteenth-century pronunciation; both pronunciations exist at present. *Caplin* 'bait fish like smelts' (the *OED* spelling is *capelin*) have been located principally in Newfoundland waters and consequently have been known by the Spanish and Portuguese fleets. The word is traceable, however, to the French of Provence. *Capillaire* 'creeping snowberry' is from French, as is *soiree* 'community social,' via British English. *Ursena* 'sea-urchin' (1620) may circuitously have evolved into the modern *ose egg*; the unstable Newfoundland [h] and the Conception Bay r-lessness may have produced the form by way of a folk etymological form, *whore's egg*.

A large majority of Irish loans in Newfoundland also exist in other varieties of Anglo-Irish. A *starrigan* is 'a young evergreen' or 'a gnarled or dead tree'; *slob (ice)* is 'floating fields of slushy ice on the sea,' detrimental to shipping at the end of winter; a *gad* 'a forked branch to hang the catch on' is used when trouting. Currently popular terms are *bogger* 'daring competition' (young people do boggers when they follow the leader in dangerous feats); *colcannon* 'at Hallowe'en, hash of various vegetables'; *gatch* 'to behave in a swaggering fashion'; *gig* 'slight sound or movement as in an unconscious person'; *joog, jook* 'drop, slight sign of life'; *scrob* 'to scrape, scratch, as by a cat'; *sleeveen* 'deceitful person, rascal'; *streel* 'a slatternly person, especially female' with the verb meaning 'to drag (clothes) along the ground.' A sample of words praised in the past as "colorful" but fast fading from usage includes *bostoon, crubeen, dudeen, gamogues, to glauvaun, gomm(er)il, spalpeen, spaugs, sugawn,* and *teeveen.* A loan preserved by the folk movement in a music festival is the curious term *angishore* (the *g* may be pronounced) meaning either 'sickly, unfortunate person' or 'worthless fellow, avoiding work.' By coincidence, in areas where [h] can be inserted or omitted, this can be *hangashore,* and thus seems to be a simple English term for 'sluggard.'

Regional vocabulary is especially noteworthy in the main economic ventures that have been carried on since the first English ships sailed to the fishing grounds: the codfishery, Labrador fishery, seal hunting, trapping fur-bearing animals, and cutting timber. The fishery (closed down in the 1990s because of overfishing) was first conducted from *fishing ships,* later from boats and *skiffs* going out from shore-based settlements. *Green fish* could be taken back salted to England, or fish could be landed at the *stage* and then salted and dried on *flakes* 'platforms' on shore. The fish could be caught by hook and line, seines, *jiggers,* or *(cod) traps.* Bait must be caught, first *caplin* in June, then *squids,* and herring (sometimes *sea-birds* and shellfish). The fish could be carried to the West Indies or to Mediterranean countries (*bim, Madeira, merchantable, tal qual*). After drying, fish can be bought as *rounders, tom cods, leggies,* or *watered fish.* The simple word *fish* is 'cod.'

Some early terms for workers are now chiefly historical: *admiral, planter, skipper* 'boss' shifting to 'respected old man,' *servant, youngster* or *green man* 'inexperienced man,' and the specific names of processors – *cut-throat, header, splitter, salter.*

When population increased, seasonal migrants went to the *Labrador fishery* annually. Shore fishermen were *stationers;* ship crews were *floaters;* people establishing families in coves were *livyers,* and offspring of interracial marriages were technically called *settlers.* Fish was dried on flat areas, sometimes spread with rocks, called *bawn,* from Irish. *Labrador fish* varied widely in quality with particular markets in the West Indies, Brazil, and southern Europe. Names of craft in Labrador waters were *barge, batteau,* and *high rat.*

In the eighteenth century, the *seal hunt* began, first off the coast of the island by *landsmen* often using nets and then in sturdy vessels going *to the ice* or *to the hunt.* The vessels had *shears* near the bows for men to stand on, and after leaving the ship, the *swilers, swoilers,* or *soilers* traveled on the *fields of ice* or jumped the *pans* looking for the *main patch* or *scattered* seals. The ages and types of animals were indicated by the terms *pup, white-coat, cat, dog, ragged jacket, turncoat, bedlamer, harp,* and *(old) hood. Pelts* or *sculps* were removed on the ice, piled in *pans* marked by *flags*, and then brought to the ship *laced* together to form *tows*. When they left port the sealers had paid for their *berths*, and when the *voyage* was over they were paid their *shares*.

With the cod-fishery of the summer *clewed up* 'completed,' many *outharbormen* went in the woods to set traps for fur-bearing animals, collectively called *fur*. These *furriers* followed a *fur path* or *trap-line*, one claimed for each trapper, with *tilts* 'shelters' built at convenient distances for spending each night. *Pelts* were stretched on *fur boards* for *curing* and, when delivered to the local *merchant*, produced a little cash in a society largely operating on the *truck* or *credit system*.

A final category of lexical items was less related to obtaining food and supplies for the family than to mere survival in a land covered by snow and ice a good part of each year. Men would go into the *lumber-woods*, a few miles back from the coast, first for timber for constructing ships, boats, *flakes*, *stages*, and houses and then for the annual supply of firewood. Trees were cut in the summer and left until snowfall, and then the men, with horses or dogs, would *haul* the *longers* 'trimmed trees' home on a *catamaran, horse slide* or *dog slide*, or even *on the dead* 'dragging ends on the snow' on the *slide path*. For a periodic rest the men would stop for a *spell* and have a *mug up* 'snack.' For burning, the trees were cut into *junks* or *billets* and to start the fire into *chovies*, *splits*, *bavins*, or *shavings*.

The representative vocabulary sketched out above has long fed the entire cultural life of the people, but many words at present occur only in catch phrases and proverbs. A person's hair may look "like a birch broom in the fits." A makeshift stove in a *tilt* 'shack' may fill the room with smoke; hence a heavy smoker is said to "smoke like a winter's tilt."

13.6   Conclusion

The immediate future of Newfoundland English in the context of varieties of North American English may be a matter of definition. The younger generations acquiring a liberal or technical education, with barely perceptible regional features, are conforming to the cosmopolitan, educated classes in the rest of the continent. The groups choosing or forced into residence near their place of birth and in local occupations have a good chance of transmitting many facets of the regional speech. Of great interest for the historian of regional speech is how the two main strains – the English West Country variety and the Anglo-Irish type – will affect each other when they come into close contact. Perhaps one might predict that the often derided local stereotypes like r-lessness, unstable [h], [d] for *th-*, unstressed *'n* for *him*, and lowered *or* before consonants will not be maintained.

FURTHER READING

A compact narrative history of the formative years of Newfoundland society is *Old Newfoundland: A History to 1843* by Patrick O'Flaherty (1999). Language studies include a community study of an old town, *A Dialect Survey of Carbonear* by Harold Paddock (1981); "Allegro Speech of a Newfoundlander" by Robert Hollett (1982); "The Rise and Fall of Dialect Representation in Newfoundland" and "The Planting of Anglo-Irish in Newfoundland" by William J. Kirwin (1991, 1993); and "Lexical Retention in Newfoundland Dialect" by J. D. A. Widdowson (1991). *The Dictionary of Newfoundland English*, ed. Story, Kirwin, and Widdowson (1990), a comprehensive survey of regional vocabulary and meanings, also contains material of interest for phonetic, morphological, and syntactic study, and extensive quotation from printed sources and recorded speech; a digital version is <www.heritage.nf.ca/dictionary>. Most recent studies of regional language take a sociolinguistic approach, for example, "On Establishing Historical Relationships between New and Old World Varieties: Habitual Aspect and Newfoundland Vernacular English" by Sandra Clarke (1997).

Richard W. Bailey

14.1 Introduction

"You sockdologizing old man-trap" were the last words Abraham Lincoln heard before the assassin's bullet buried itself deep in his brain. Laughter at Ford's Theatre in Washington was suddenly interrupted by the gunshot. A line from a popular British comedy, *Our American Cousin*, these words produced hearty guffaws from the audience; *sockdologizing* was funny because it was an "American" word put in the mouth of an American type, the hearty backwoodsman, whose intrusion into the drawing room of an English country house established incongruity and created humor. Like many American expressions that became known abroad, it was fantastic, improper, and extravagant. As recreated for the London stage, it was also wrong.

The author of *Our American Cousin* was Tom Taylor (1817–80), a brilliant child of a brewing family in the north of England, a gold medalist as an undergraduate at the University of Glasgow, and subsequently a fellow of Trinity College, Cambridge, where he excelled in classics and mathematics. From 1845 to 1847, Taylor was Professor of English Literature and Professor of English Language at the University of London; he then qualified as a barrister and, not long after, accepted an appointment in the newly founded public health service. All the while he was a regular contributor to the daily newspapers and to the humor magazine *Punch*, eventually rising to the position of editor. By mid century, Taylor had become one of the most popular of English playwrights, adapting familiar tales like *Cinderella* and *Whittington and His Cat* for the London stage and recreating in dramatic form such novels as Stowe's *Uncle Tom's Cabin* and Dickens's *Tale of Two Cities*.

Fond of stage dialects, Taylor flavored the speech of his characters with distinctive diction. His most famous creation, Bob Brierly, was the

"Lancashire lad" of *The Ticket-of-Leave Man*. In *The Overland Route*, another of Taylor's popular productions, he presented *sahibs* and *memsahibs* returning to India, *ayahs* and *lascars* as comic servants, and a flavor of the exotic in language. *Our American Cousin* was Taylor's contribution to the transatlantic mockery of British and American English. First produced in New York in 1858, the play was a popular repertoire piece on both sides of the Atlantic. The play's comic Englishman, Lord Dundreary, is a febrile fop with a lisp: "A whime is a widdle, you know" (41), he says to the bemused inhabitants of an English manor. Into their rarefied world comes Asa Trenchard, the cousin, who, having inherited the estate, has come to take possession. On his first appearance, Trenchard introduces himself by bellowing at the butler: "Wal, darn me, if you ain't the consarnedest old shoat I ever did see since I was baptized Asa Trenchard" (45). Trenchard's *wals* and *reckons* and *fixins* impart the American linguistic flavor, as do his extravagant oaths: "Concentrated essence of baboons," he roars, "what on earth is that?" (46). As in much Victorian melodrama, beneath the rough exterior beats the golden heart and the generous impulse. (It is by destroying his father's will that Trenchard makes the dairymaid the residual legatee, thus raising her to the level of the gentry and qualifying her to be his wife.)

Among the schemes to thwart the eventual marriage of the destined couple is one concocted by a dowager with two daughters in want of husbands. The clever Trenchard sees immediately that she intends to ensnare him with one of them, and, as the three women leave the stage, he bursts out with "you sockdologizing old man-trap" (82).

Sockdolager was coined in a particularly fertile period of American word creation, the first quarter of the nineteenth century. In its earliest uses, it meant a knock-out punch, and if Taylor had wanted to represent a London street tough he could have used the similarly vivid local term *ferricadouzer*. But Taylor wanted something American and *sockdolager* supplied his need. Like many other slang terms, the meaning of *sockdolager* wouldn't stay put, and it was soon generalized to mean something tremendous, a "whopper," whether a stone large enough to upset the plow in a newly cultivated field or a patent fishhook with a powerful spring designed to embed hooks in the fish's mouth.

Aside from Taylor's use, no evidence has been found for a verb *sockdologize*, and within *Our American Cousin* there is nothing but context to reveal its meaning – perhaps "cunning" or "scheming" approaches Taylor's intention. It is unlikely that Taylor heard *sockdolager* from an American mouth, but very likely that he knew it from J. R. Bartlett's *Dictionary of Americanisms*, a volume first published when Taylor was serving as Professor of English

Language. (Bartlett's work was repeatedly reprinted and became, at home and abroad, an authority until replaced by more comprehensive works beginning in the 1890s.) Bartlett supplied *socdolager* – it had no settled spelling at first – with a hypothetical connection to *doxology*. Other imaginative etymologists offered comparisons with Italian *stoccado* (Hotten s.v. *stockdollager*), Dutch *zaakdadelyk*, and even Icelandic *saukdolgr* (thought to reach English through Swedes in Philadelphia [Barrère and Leland s.v. *sockdolager*]). Everyone, however, believed it to be an Americanism, and a highly representative one in being a fantastic creation of unknown origin and expressing in hyperbolic form an idea that could not be rendered in so lively a fashion with a respectable English word.

In its small way, *sockdolager* represented a large issue in Taylor's play, for it dramatized the rivalry of Britain and America: the contrast lay between the sickly Dundreary (whose "riddles" derive from tradition or from linguistic micro-nuance) and the youthful and vital Trenchard (whose humor defies propriety and the constraints of dictionary English). Dundreary (as his name implies) manifests a moribund culture; Trenchard, the new transatlantic society of vitality and imagination. The cousin in *Our American Cousin* returns from the American frontier to take possession of the home place in England; he and Mary Meredith, the dairymaid, are unafraid of working with their hands, happy amid the fecundity of the cow barn, indifferent to the disapproval of the well-bred. In the final scene, as the characters break the imaginary window of the proscenium to seek the approbation of the audience, they form a tableau in which the vitality of America is poised to refresh the worn-out spirit of the Old World. Language is not the topic of Taylor's play, but in it he uses English to create comic obstacles. And it asserts that Trenchard's Americanisms qualify him to father the new generation that will revitalize England and English.

14.2   Americanism

The term *Americanism*, like other linguistic *-isms*, denotes peculiarities and characteristics of usage. These *-ism* words were coined in English in the order in which observers – who regarded themselves at the linguistic center – noticed words they believed to be on the linguistic periphery: *græcism* and *latinism* (both appearing in print in 1570), *hellenism* (1609), *atticism* (1612), *gallicism* (1656), *scotticism* (1682). (A similar sequence of creations appeared later in French: in 1704, *anglicisme* was applied to a word, expression, or turn of phrase from English borrowed into French; in 1866, *américanisme* was used to designate "peculiarities" of style or pronunciation in American speech and writing; in 1905, *britanisme* was coined for specifically British usages.) As these terms were created, they came to refer to linguistic forms that were "peculiar"; the words were somehow distasteful, "odd," not in keeping with the "genius" of English (or French).

The word *Americanism* duly appeared in 1781 as the revolutionary sentiment leading to political independence in North America was felt to apply to language as well. The coiner was John Witherspoon (1722–94), who had emigrated from his native Scotland in 1768 to become president of the College of New Jersey at Princeton. Witherspoon was an ardent but apologetic American patriot who believed it would be useful to survey American English and to form "a collection of some of the chief improprieties which prevail and might be easily corrected" (1803, 181; Mathews 1931, 16). He thought that America might someday enjoy its own language, but that day would come only when "in this new empire, some centre of learning and politeness . . . shall obtain influence and prescribe the rules of speech and writing to every other part" (1803, 181; Mathews 1931, 15). Having coined *Americanism* on the model of *Scotticism*, Witherspoon took pains to examine similarities and differences. While Scotland had earlier enjoyed national and cultural autonomy, the creation of a national parliament for Great Britain in 1707 had doomed Scottish English, a once independent branch of the language, transformed in Witherspoon's opinion to "provincial barbarism." Such would not happen in America, he opined: "Being entirely separated from Britain, we shall find some centre or standard of our own, and not be subject to the inhabitants of that island, either in receiving new ways of speaking or rejecting the old" (1803, 183; Mathews 1931, 17–18). The day of an American cultural capital had not yet dawned for Witherspoon, who declared a dozen supposed Americanisms unworthy of educated usage.

What is American about American English is still a staple of criticism for British journalists, and *Americanism* as a term for reprobate English flourishes. A computer-search of the "quality" London newspapers printed in 1992 yielded such phrases as "the usual quota of insidious, unnoticed Americanisms" and "the loose Americanisms of demotic speech." For linguistic pundits in English newspapers, the nature of the argument against "Americanisms" is not in dispute, only which supporting details are most germane to it. "Americanisms" are never praised, though there may be a begrudging suggestion that they are racy, fashionable, and colloquial. But such "Americanisms" are seen as the tailings from the mine, the dross that is left once the enduring and genuine ore has been refined to perfection.

Much of what is noticed as "American" is, however, not American at all, and *Americanism* often applies without regard to origins to innovations disliked by the observer. In 1992, for example, a more learned journalist chided a less learned one for his "xenophobic defense of the English language" in treating *ain't* as an "Americanism" when it had "appeared commonly in 18th century English." The pronunciation of *controversy* with second-syllable stress is now out of favor with an opinionated sector of the English public; according to the director of the BBC Pronunciation unit, "Our people are accused of being American if they say 'conTROVVersy'" (Pointon), although the pronunciation is, in fact, unknown in America.

Much of the squabbling about American English in Britain is built on flimsy and ill-informed speculation. To accept the premise that "Americanisms" are marginal and unimportant to the main development of the language is to ignore the continuity of the language. It suggests that "English" is the property of England with all other forms of the language on the fringe. That perspective is vividly expressed in an anecdote from one of the Oxford senior common rooms. On the publication of William A. Craigie and James Hulbert's *Dictionary of American English*, one don pointed out that the second volume covered the vocabulary from *Corn-pit* to *Honk*. "Naturally it would," replied a second, thereby dismissing both the dictionary and its contents from serious discussion.

14.3   Early American impact abroad

The impact of the Americas on Europe and on the rest of the world has been far more profound than sentiment in England has been prepared to allow. Probing the New World and bringing back fragments of it to the Old World has been by far the most profound cultural change in the last millennium. The European diaspora changed both the rest of the world and Europe itself. "In 1492 America was, from the European standpoint, simply an event," Wayne Franklin points out. "But in 1493 it became a collection of words" (xi). The collection of words burgeoned, but was slow to reach sixteenth-century England, a country on the margins of Europe and, racked by political turmoil, indifferent at first to the new discoveries beyond the western ocean.

14.3.1   *The first American word in English*

Not until 1533 did the first American word come to English attention: *guaiacum* 'a genus of trees and shrubs native to the West Indies and the warmer parts of America; a tree of this genus, esp *Guaiacum officinale* and *G. sanctum*' (*OED*).

Though only by accident the first American word in English, *guaiacum* is culturally emblematic since it is connected with the most important of the new imports, the affliction first called in English the *French pox*. Contracted by Columbus's sailors in the West Indies, the pox had spread rapidly to the French army besieging Naples. After the Neapolitans capitulated in 1495, the disease spread throughout Europe. In 1503, the term *French pox* appeared in England, and by 1507 Scottish writers began to observe "this strange seiknes of Nappilis." By 1510 it had claimed as many as ten million victims throughout the world. In 1533, Thomas Paynell offered to English readers his short work *Of the VVood Called Gvaiacvm That Healeth the French Pockes*. Translating from Latin, the learned language of the day, Paynell argued that medical books should be available in English; the need for this particular book was to him especially persuasive since the pox had become an epidemic: "For almoste into euerye parte of this realme, this mooste foule and peyneful disease is crepte, and manye soore infected therewith" (ii). Paynell's Latin original had been published in 1519 by a "great clerk," Ulrich von Hutten (1488–1523), whose testimony was particularly to be valued "for he hym selfe hath had the verye experience thereof."

Von Hutten was an enthusiastic advocate of the miracle cures wrought by guaiacum. Its power was especially strong, he thought, because it came from the island where the disease originated:

> The vse of this wod was brought to vs out of an ylonde namyd Spagnola, this ilonde is in the west nigh to the contrey of Amerik, set in that place where the length of Amerike, stretchynge into the northe, doth end: and was founde of late dayes amonge the new landes, which were unknowen by the olde tyme. All the inhabytauntes of that ylonde somtyme be diseased with the french pockes, lykewyse as we be with the mesels and small pockes. [10v]

Von Hutten (and Paynell) accepted the paradigm of Renaissance herbal medicine: local diseases could be cured with the products of local plants. Having criticized doctors who tried to keep guaiacum a trade secret and to monopolize its commerce, von Hutten launched into a philological excursion:

> Now I wyl speke of the thyng intended. They haue gyuen it this name Guaiacum. For so the Spaniardes wryte it with latyne letters, folowynge theyr owne maner of sounde, which worde the people of that ylande pronounce with open mouthe Huiacum.

And Paulus Ritius shewed me at the cytie of August, that he harde saye of a Spanyarde, which had ben in that yland, that the fyrste syllable Gua, of this name, was not pronounced of the Spagnolenses with G, but that his owne tonge dydde require it so to be wryten. And they of that Ilande sounde it with, H, puffed out, as though it were Huiacum, a worde of .iii. syllables with theym, and not Guaiacum. We may gyue unto it some excellent name, callynge it lignum vite, as Philo the phisition called his dregges the handes of god: and this daye the phisitions with greatte boste calle their co[n]fections manus Christi, apostolicu[m], gratia dei, Antidotum, Paulium, and many other such superstitious names. [11r–11v]

Von Hutten was quite correct in thinking that guaiacum would receive an elegant name (as can be seen in the species *G. sanctum* 'holy guaiacum').

Ransacking the New World for new words to enrich the Old World was thus an important European intellectual enterprise. As Paynell had implied, difficulties arose from discovery in the "new lands" of things that were unknown in the "old time." What was the right way to name the new, and how should the new names be sounded? Should *guaiacum* be pronounced as the Spanish implied, by forcing the sounds into "Latin letters"? Or did the natives of Hispanola rightly pronounce the name of their restorative tree, and should the Europeans adopt their pronunciation and write *huiacum*? In von Hutten's opinion, creating an elegant synonym from Latin – like *lignum vitae* – would be a trick of the sort usually played by dishonest physicians in advertising their "dregs" and "confections." Von Hutten himself stopped short at authenticity: his book was titled *De guaiaci medicina et morbo gallico*.

Renaissance thinkers were compelled by the authority of the past, the main vindication of present inquiry. About 1530, an Italian physician and poet, Girolamo Fracastoro (1478–1553), addressed himself to the problem of naming the *French pox*. Rendered from Latin into English by Nahum Tate in 1686, Fracastoro's poem was celebrated in a prefatory verse for having addressed "This *Indian Conq'rer's* fatal March." Tate translated: "Dear was the Conquest of a new found World, / Whose Plague e'er since through all the Old is hurl'd" (A4). Fracastoro imitated a Virgilian eclogue. In his imaginary Hispanola, the "ripe blushing Fruits and ponderous Ears of Corn" provided the basis for a feast in the meadow; the discoverers and the natives "sate mingled on the Ground, / With *Indian* Food and *Spanish* vintage crown'd." This pastoral scene was, however, choked with grief, for the crowd "languish'd with the same obscene Disease." In a recapitulation of ancient Roman rites, a "Priest in snowy Robes" came forth to asperse the people with the blood of sacrificial animals by sprinkling them with leafy branches, "Boughs of healing Guiacum" (70–2). The principal shepherd in this pastoral gave not only his name to Fracastoro's poem but to the disease itself – *Syphilis*. The "new found World," just a quarter century after it became known to Europeans, was thus reduced to the classical and familiar, a pastoral world combining innocence with magic. America was interpreted; *guaiacum* was added to the herbals and to the practice of medicine. The translation of American experience to European comprehension had taken place, but what was strange was mostly made familiar – except for the very foreign word *guaiacum*, written in Latin letters and mispronounced by the Spanish but nonetheless retaining the flavor of the exotic and incomprehensible. Von Hutten thought it came from the northern end of America, but what was America was not a tiny island in the western ocean but a great continent still hidden in the distance. Guaiacum lozenges, however, were still administered in the twentieth century, latterly to alleviate the symptoms of gout and rheumatism.

14.3.2   Early words from and for the New World

British ignorance of the New World discoveries remained profound for the first half century after Columbus. By 1555, nearly 1,000 Continental books had appeared with references to America, some of them careful and thorough descriptions. In the same period, only a dozen books with such references were published in England, half of them devoted to the obsession with syphilis and guaiacum (T. Adams 8). English curiosity was more fully satisfied by the publication of Richard Eden's 1555 translation of *The Decades of the New Worlde or West India*. Just below the table of contents, Eden provided "the interpretacion of certeyne woordes."

A commonplace of the early sixteenth century was that English lacked technical vocabulary and was thus inadequate for the expression of profound ideas in science and philosophy. In compiling and translating Continental books of exploration, Eden recognized that English needed words to express the new ideas in geography and navigation. Of the eleven words for which he provides an "interpretacion," almost all – presuming the trustworthiness of the *Oxford English Dictionary* – were new to English: *continent*, *hemispherium* 'the halfe globe of the earth and water' (> *hemisphere*), *clime, parallels* 'lines whereby the sonne passynge causeth variation of tyme,' *schoene* 'a space of xl. furlonges,' *werst* 'an Italian [? Russian] mile' (> *verst*), and *colony*. *Equinoctial* (like *caravel*) was already in English, but Eden gave it a new meaning, equivalent to our modern *equator*. *Pesus* 'a ducate and a halfe' was a monetary unit that did not become fully English; *Gaiti Mammoni* 'monkeys' was reintroduced to English in 1607 as *mammonet*. None of these words was from an American language, but the occasion of their introduction was discourse about America. England needed a vocabulary for talking about the new discoveries.

Following his Latin original, Eden also provided fourteen words from "the Indian language." Of these, only three entered English: *canoa* (> *canoe*) and *caciqui* 'kynges or gouernours' (> *cacique*), and *zemes* 'an Idole' (> *zeme*). All three are the earliest cited instances of these words in English, and the fact that other English writers used them subsequently shows how influential Eden's translations were. "Indian" words appear in the body of his translation for the first time in English: *cassava, guava, iguana, maize*, and *yucca*, for instance. Discourse about the New World required a new vocabulary. Eden and his successors – especially Richard Hakluyt (c. 1553–1616) – filled the gaps in the vocabulary with borrowed words from Continental writers.

Eden and other translators made the process of explanation highly visible to their readers. English *cat's-eye* was introduced by Eden, following his original, by means of a simile: "stones like vnto cattes eyes." Similarly for *ant-bear:* "There is also on the firm lande an other beaste cauld Orso Formigaro, that is, the Ante beare." Most innovations, however, arose from redefining the semantic territory of existing words or from combining established words into new compounds, some of them loan translations, like *ant-bear*, but others by independent compounding, like *cat's-eye*. In these processes, the new and strange was measured against the familiar and domestic. Eden's source bewailed the difficulty of naming the abundance of fish "which have no names in oure language" (Arber 231), and since it was impossible to describe all of these creatures, he chose three, the last of which was the *manatee:*

> Manate therefore, is a fysshe of the sea, of the byggest sorte, and much greater than the Tiburon [shark] in length and breadth: And is very brutysshe and vyle, so that it appeareth in form lyke vnto one of those great vesselles made of goates skynnes wherein they vse to cary new wyne in *Medina de Campo* or in *Areualo*. The headde of this beast is lyke the head of an oxe, with also lyke eyes. And hath in the place of armes, two great stumpes wherwith he swymmeth. It is a very gentle and tame beaste. [231–2]

At the outset, the description depends upon the prior discussion of another word introduced by Eden: *tiburon*, a creature "of suche huge biggenesse that twelue or fyfeteene men are scarcely able to drawe it owt of the water and lifte it into the shyppe" (231). Much more intriguing to the English reader than the borrowings are the similes: a shape like goatskins – and not just any goatskins but those of central Castille – filled with new wine; eyes like an ox; "two great stumpes" in the place of arms. Linguistic innovations emerging from such descriptions work both ways; both the manatee and the goat skins are transformed when one is seen in terms of the other. Yet this transformation was not dramatic or sudden. *Manatee* emerged as a modern American word, and, though it had priority as the first name for the newly encountered animal, it competed with *lamantin* (from French and attested in English in 1666) and the more prosaically English *cow fish* (1634) and *sea cow* (1613).

In the very first instances, writing about America in England seems to have caused some loss of linguistic inhibition and an unleashing of the impulse to provide new language for the New World. In 1577, Richard Willes brought out an expanded edition of Eden's translation, and in his prefatory remarks chastised Eden for "vncleane speache [which] may seeme hardly Englyshed." It was not the many American words that aroused Willes's ire but Eden's creativity in using ones "smellynge to much of the Latine." Willes criticized *dominators, ponderouse, dictionaries, portentouse, antiques, despicable, solicitate, obsequiouse, homicide, imbibed, destructive, prodigious*. In Willes's view, there was nothing to justify the use of these words when good English equivalents were at hand: *Lords, weyghte, subjects, wonderfull, auncient, lowe, carefull, duetifull, manslaughter, drunken, noysome*, and *monstrous*. While only three of the "Latin-smellynge" words appear for the first time in Eden's translation, they were all reflective of the "inkhorn" terms then pouring into English through translations from the learned languages. Willes's criticisms reflect a small skirmish in the war against such words brought by "Saxonists" who believed that good old English was sufficient to express a writer's meaning. Only later did English speakers distinguish the semantic territories for such pairs as *homicide* and *manslaughter*. Despite the Saxonist nostalgia, lexical innovation brought new words into English – many of them as a consequence of American influence.

14.4 Lexical expansion by curiosity and cupidity

If English books about America were designed to feed curiosity in general, they were also aimed at stimulating investment in expeditions. Willes's dedication of his work to the Countess of Bedford captured both motives:

If varietie of matter, occurents out of forraigne countryes, newes of newe found landes, the sundry sortes of gouernement, the different manners & fashions of diuers nations, the wonderfull workes of nature, the sightes of straunge trees, fruites, foule, and beastes, the infinite treasure of Pearle, Golde, Siluer, & ioyes may recreate and delight a mynde trauelled in weighty matters, & weeried with great affayres: credit me, good Madam, in listning vnto this worke, shall you have recreation, you shall finde delight in reading ouer these relations, wherein so newe, so straunge, so diuers, so many recreations and delights of the mynd are expressed. [vii]

Perhaps the most alluring of these recreations and delights were Willes's accounts of the "infinite treasure" to be collected from the New World. By the time he wrote, English people were vividly aware of the vast supply of precious metals imported by England's great rival power, Spain, and Spanish shipyards were already busy building the vessels that would form the Armada for the planned invasion of the British Isles.

Accounts of the Americas made it obvious that in wealth and in military capacity, England was far behind the Continental powers. English sailors were hardly prepared to sail beyond the sight of land, and there were few books useful to navigators. The tireless Eden supplied that lack in 1561 with his translation of Martin Cortés's *The Arte of Navigation*. This and similar works made it possible for mariners from Britain to reach America and, most important, find their way back. Consequently the vocabulary of astronomy and navigation was vastly expanded, some words deriving from native sources – like *tide table* and *great circle* – but most from Continental languages where they had been derived from Latin and Greek: *acronych, apogee, epact, hydrography, parallax, perigee, solstitial,* and *subcelestial,* among many others. Words of this sort did not attract the ire of the Saxonists, apparently because they considered them necessary to the larger purpose of enhancing English power and wealth.

In addition to precious metals, English people were eager to profit from the products of the New World, most particularly medicinal plants. In 1577, John Frampton, a merchant, translated a work by Nicholás Monardes titled *Joyfull News out of the Newe Founde Worlde*. The lengthy subtitle narrowed the joyful news to an account of "the rare and singular vertues of diverse and sundrie hearbes, trees, oyles, plantes, and stones, with their aplications aswell for physicke as chirurgerie." Some of the American words, filtered through Spanish, did not persist in English – for instance, *pinipinichi*. Others were soon abandoned in favor of less exotic English names – for example, Frampton's *guacatane* entered the pharmacopoeia as *pilewort* since it was regarded as a specific for hemorrhoids. However, a surprising

number of innovations did enter English for the first time in his translation
and persisted in medical and botanical discourse: *carana, copal, mechoacan, sar-*
saparilla, sassafras, and *tacamahac.* As in the dispute about the appropriate
spelling for *guaiacum,* Monardes was willing to cede authority to the native
peoples. Thus, of *tobacco,* he wrote: "The proper name of it amongest the
Indians is Pecielt, for the name of Tobaco is geven to it of our Spaniardes
by reason of an Ilande that is named Tabaco" (1: 75–6).

So far, all knowledge of the Americas was theoretical and secondhand
among the English. When regular voyages at last commenced, they
returned words from abroad to England, most of them from European
languages incidentally encountered – for instance, John Hawkins introduced *alcatras* (> *albatross*), Humphrey Gilbert *frete* (> *fret* 'strait'), and Walter
Raleigh *calabaza* (> *calabash*). A central figure in this importation was
Thomas Harriot, whose travels in 1585–6 led to the publication in 1588 of
his *Briefe and True Report of the New Found Land of Virginia* (a volume repub-
lished in 1590 with splendid illustrations by the artist John White). Harriot
had made efforts to learn the Algonquian language spoken by Wanchese
and Manteo, the first Native Americans to visit England – reluctantly and
willingly, respectively. Harriot arrived in Virginia better prepared than any
earlier English traveler, and his *Report* is filled with words unmediated by
Spanish or the other European languages of prior voyagers. A few of these
came into general use – *cushaw* 'crook-neck squash' and *werowance* 'king'
among them. Several dozen others attracted no attention beyond Harriot's:
openavk a kind of potato; *mangummenauk,* a kind of acorn used for food; *sac-*
quenummener 'cranberry.' Like Monardes, Harriot was concerned with
finding right names for new life forms discovered in America:

> There is an herbe which is sowed a part by it selfe & is called by the
> inhabitants Vppówoc: In the West Indies it hath diuers names,
> according to the seuerall places & contries where it groweth and is vsed:
> The Spaniardes generally call it Tobacco. [16]

In the discussion that follows, Harriot celebrates the salubrious qualities of
tobacco: "We our selues during the time we were there vsed to suck it after
their maner, as also since our returne, & haue found maine rare and wonderful experiments of the vertues thereof" (16).

By the end of the sixteenth century, optimism in England about the discoveries in America reached a high pitch, despite the lost colony at
Roanoke and Raleigh's failure to locate El Dorado in Guyana. Michael
Drayton wrote a celebratory poem "To the Virginian Voyage" in which he
addressed "heroique minds" (Rollins and Baker 442):

And cheerfully at sea
Success you still intice,
    To get the pearl and gold,
    And ours to hold
Virginia,
Earth's only paradise

In 1599, the poet Samuel Daniel speculated about the spread of English: "And who, in time, knows whither we may vent / The treasure of our tongue?" (Rollins and Baker 417). He did not realize that the exportation of English would result in the importation of a new kind of English, American English. With the explosion of the new learning, the days of the "Saxon" purist were numbered. Although Alexander Gill, the headmaster of St. Paul's school and Milton's teacher, could still maintain in 1619 that "the purity of our tongue continues undiluted" (1: 83), he was also obliged to recognize that English had been enriched by foreign borrowings. English people, he wrote, only "borrow words . . . out of necessity," even from "the American Indian languages, such as *maiz*, and *Kanoa*, a boat hollowed of a trunk by fire and flint-stones" (1: 108–9). Allen Walker Read (2001) points to this statement as the first to recognize explicitly the influence of the Americas on British English.

The search for precious metals and medicinal plants was not the only source of curiosity about the New World. Native peoples themselves had to be explained in terms of the received wisdom of the age. Their language became the source of speculation about their ancestry in one or another of the ten tribes of Israel. To expedite this inquiry into origins, Harriot and his successors compiled word lists of interest to speculative philologists. John Smith also gathered a long list (135–7) from which, as from others arising from the settlement in Virginia, American words entered the English of Britain during the first quarter of the seventeenth century: *mockasin* (> *moccasin*), *opassom* (> *opossum*), *putchamin* (> *persimmon*), *puccoon* 'an edible root,' *rahaugcum* (> *raccoon*), *tockawhoughe* (> *tapioca*), *tomahack* (> *tomahawk*).

What is striking in the surviving texts from the early period of settlement is the combination of curiosity and linguistic exuberance. Writing in 1634, William Wood reported to his London readers information about the otherness of the New World. In a chapter on "the Beasts that live on the land," Wood broke into verse. (American words are here highlighted by italics.)

The kingly Lyon, and the strong arm'd Beare
The large limbed *Mooses*, with the tripping Deare,
Quill darting Porcupines, and *Rackoones* bee,

Castelld in the hollow of an aged tree;
The skipping Squerrell, Rabbet, purblined Hare,
Immured in the selfesame Castle are,
Least red-eyed Ferrets, wily Foxes should
Them undermine, if rampird but with mould.
The grim fac't Ounce, and ravenous howling Wolfe,
Whose meagre paunch suckes like a swallowing gulfe.
Blacke glistering Otters, and rich coated Bever,
The Civet scented *Musquash* smelling ever.   [21]

Wood allowed that he had seen no lions, but "some affirm" that they had been seen at Cape Anne (only six leagues from Boston) and others reported roarings in the forest "which must eyther be Devills or Lyons." America offered the terrors of the unknown in a land of abundance; the very names of these "irrationall creatures" heightened the sense of the exotic. Like Harriot and Smith, Wood was curious about the ancient Israelite origins of Amerindian languages: "Some have thought they might be of the dispersed *Iewes*, because some of their words be neare unto the *Hebrew*" (102). Lacking an opinion of his own on this question, Wood offered a list of words "whereby such as have in-sight into the Tongues, may know to what Language it is most inclining" (111). The list contained words eventually assimilated into English, among them *pow-wow* 'shaman,' *sagamore* 'sachem,' *wampompeage* 'beaded strings or belts used as currency,' and *wigwam* 'dwelling.'

While exotic borrowings like these were the most apparent signs of American influence on the English of England, more subtle changes were beginning to take place, changes that exploded in number as the colonies in the Americas became established. Failing in the search for precious metals, the colonists began to seek other resources that could be exported and turned into wealth. The smoking of tobacco became a fashion among the wealthy in London society, and addiction to nicotine depended on importing leaves from Virginia. Smith was critical of the zeal for cultivating tobacco, decrying "our men rooting in the ground about Tobacco like Swine" (195) instead of growing crops to make the colony self-sufficient in food. He had no trouble discerning the impetus: tobacco growing, he noted to the London commissioners "for the reformation of Virginia," produced five or six times the annual income to be expected from food crops (257). As greed overwhelmed good sense, the tobacco industry spawned compound phrases that shifted the meanings of their second element. Specimens from seventeenth-century English documents include *tobacco bag, tobacco bills, tobacco cask, tobacco house, tobacco maker, tobacco money, tobacco pipe, tobacco stick,* and *tobacco tongs*. All of these were subject to shortening.

Thus as early as 1599, a London physician could recommend: "The fume taken in a Pipe is good against Rumes, Catarrhs, hoarsenesse" (*OED* s.v. *pipe*, sense 10). These *fumes* consisted of *tobacco fumes* ingested through a *tobacco pipe*, and the meanings of both *fume* and *pipe* were consequently altered.

The same linguistic process appeared when the English wrested control of the sugar industry from the Spaniards in the Caribbean. Borrowings from other languages entered English – for instance, *machete* and *moscovado* 'low-grade sugar' from Spanish; *cassonade* 'unrefined sugar' and *tache* 'evaporating pan' from French. More consequential for English, however, were the new meanings of existing words: *cane* (< *sugar cane*), *house* (< *sugar house*), *trade* (< *sugar trade*), for example.

As British merchants and mariners became increasingly involved in the *slave trade* (a phrase first documented in 1734), the language acquired an elaborate set of terms for degrees of race mixture, most of them derived from continental languages: *griff*, *mestizo*, *mulatto*, *mustechee*, *quadroon*, *sambo*, *terceroon*. These and other words associated with slavery flourished after the assiento, defined by Samuel Johnson in his *Dictionary* of 1755 as "a contract or convention between the king of Spain and other powers, for furnishing the Spanish dominions in America with negro slaves." Existing English words were altered by new applications – for instance *Guinea-man* 'slave ship' (1695) and *airport* 'ventilation hole' between decks of such a ship (1788). Even so long-standing a word as *seasoning* took on a frightful new context when it was adapted from 'training, discipline' to the process by which slaves were inured to their servitude: "At a moderate computation of the slaves who are purchased by our African merchants in a year, surely thirty thousand die upon the voyage or in the seasoning" (1771, *OED* s.v. *seasoning*).

By 1640, there were some 40,000 English-speaking colonists on the continent of North America. Most of them occupied New England and the watershed of Chesapeake Bay, and others were settled in communities from Newfoundland to the Caribbean. By the end of the century, this number had increased to a quarter million, and regional differences were beginning to be established with the principal centers in Massachusetts, Virginia, Barbados, and Jamaica. Because of the diversity of its population and the unfamiliar climate and terrain, the Caribbean was the source of many new words conveyed to England through maps and books as well as by the spoken English of sailors and traders. Some were borrowings from other languages, including those of the African slaves: *bangil* (> *banjo*, 1739) and *nyam* 'to eat' (1788 but probably in earlier oral use). American languages, usually mediated through Spanish, also yielded borrowings: *jerk* 'to preserve pork or beef after the manner of the Quichua Indians by drying it in the sun, originally without salt' (1707; Cassidy and LePage). Others involved sense shift of existing words: *cockpit* 'steep-sided valley' (1683).

Throughout this period, there was in Britain little consciousness of an emergent American English but considerable curiosity about the borrowings coming into the language from afar. Learned, if uninformed, speculation arose concerning the word *cayman,* the term for the large reptile discovered in the New World and first called *cayman* in English as early as 1577. The established term *crocodile* was available for use by English discoverers and was occasionally used for various American saurians; alternately, the Spanish loanword *dante* (in English by 1600) could have served as well. Nonetheless, *cayman* emerged as the usual word. Intellectuals were as interested in words as in things, and early speculation arose about the source of *cayman*. In his description of American fauna, the Dutch writer Georg Marggraf (1610–44) provided a story: "The slaves, on their arrival from Africa, at the sight of a crocodile, gave it immediately the name of cayman. It would appear from this, that it was the negroes who spread this name throughout America where it is employed even in Mexico" (E. Griffith 9: 197). Etymologies that depend upon anecdotes are nearly always suspect, as this one most certainly is, but the force of Marggraf's etymology lies in his belief that both words and their origins were the keys to knowledge. The African slaves in his tale have authority to name and the power to persuade others to follow their example. For Marggraf and his contemporaries, language variety descended from the punishment inflicted on humankind at Babel; no evidence, however slight, for the ideal language spoken before that divine curse could be safely ignored, and no people were untouched by its power. His speculation about *cayman* shows Renaissance curiosity at its best, unconstrained by the limits of ancient authority but, at the same time, mindful of classical and Biblical antecedents.

14.5 Emerging awareness of American English as a distinct variety

Not until a century after the first loanwords from America did American English begin to emerge as a distinct entity. Only when change became noticeable was it possible to consider the influence of that American English on the English of Britain. What changed was not at the periphery of the language but at the very center through the recognition of the otherness of overseas English. To explain the differences that emerged, linguistic historians have elaborated the idea of "colonial lag." Lag views change from the center outward; the concept assumes that the evolution of London English is the norm and departures from it abnormal. As a metaphor, "lag" presumes that colonial varieties are more conservative than the metropolitan one, and this assumption leads, among other things, to the allegation that "Elizabethan English" is still spoken in one or another isolated district. In North America, the locus of such Elizabethan English has often been placed in up-country notches of Appalachia or among the islands of Chesapeake Bay. Of course Elizabethan English ceased when the last Elizabethan went to her grave, and some authors have been far too quick to assume that "lag" exists rather than to test the idea as a hypothesis. Consequently critics of the metaphor have declared baldly that "the term and the phenomenon described by it are largely myths as far as the hard linguistic facts of English are concerned" (Görlach 55). Such a dismissal is, however, no more justifiable in its absolute terms than is the uncritical acceptance of the hypothesis of lag. Linguistic change did take place at different rates as the two kinds of English diverged, sometimes with the colonial variety in advance of the metropolitan and sometimes the reverse.

14.5.1 Divergence in modal use

The English modal verbs have proved to be an especially fruitful domain in which to measure the shifting evolution of British and American English, partly because the modals occur so frequently and are thus subject to easy measurement and partly because their subtleties and shades of meaning make their usage unstable and consequently prone to differentiation. Consider, for instance, the use of *may* and *can* to express possibility, as in the following extract from a late seventeenth-century American letter: "Its best to send a thousand or two of board, shingle, & clabord nayles, so many of each sort; here will be need enough of them; they *may* be paid for after a while, if you *can* not do otherwise" (Wait Winthrop, quoted by Kytö 1989, 182).

Throughout the seventeenth century, both British and American writers were likely to use *can* (rather than *may*) in a clause where there is a negative. In positive clauses – "they may be paid for after a while" – a significant change took place. Both in sixteenth- and early seventeenth-century London English and in the English of the New England colonists of the 1620s, *may*, rather than *can*, was chosen in such sentences around 70 percent of the time (in the Helsinki corpus of early Modern English, n = 1194). By 1640, however, London English had shifted: to express possibility, *may* and *can* were virtually interchangeable (54.4 percent for *can* and 45.6 percent for *may*, n = 160). American writers did not participate in this shift, and in 1670 they continued to make the choice along traditional lines (30.7 percent for *can* and 69.3 percent for *may*, n = 765, Kytö 1989, 211). The shifting London preference in favor of *can* does not appear in contemporaneous American English, thus producing the phenomenon of "lag."

A difference also arose in the use of *will* in the first person to express simple futurity. At the end of the nineteenth century, Henry Bradley described the history of the difference between *shall* and *will* in categorical terms:

> In the first person, *shall* has, from the early M[iddle] E[nglish] period, been the normal auxiliary for expressing mere futurity, without any adventitious notion. (*a*) Of events conceived as independent of the speaker's volition. (To use *will* in these cases is now a mark of Scottish, Irish, provincial, or extra-British idiom.) [*OED* s.v. *shall* 8.b]

Writing in 1965, Ernest Gowers made this "extra-British idiom" distinction more specific:

> In vocabulary this infiltration [of Americanisms] is notorious; in grammar and idiom it is more subtle but hardly less significant. . .: the obliteration of the distinction between SHALL and WILL that the few who understood it used to consider the hall-mark of mastery of the niceties of English idiom. [s.v. *Americanisms*]

Bradley's perception of post-medieval *I will* as a mark of "extra-British idiom" is inaccurate; the distinction he proposes is not observed in either the Authorized Version of the Bible or Shakespeare. Other thoroughly British writers quoted in the *OED* also used *I will* in expressions of "mere futurity": Isaac Walton (s.v. *artist*), Mary Wortley Montague (s.v. *balm*), Samuel Johnson (s.v. *sterility*), Benjamin Disraeli (s.v. *book*), D. G. Rossetti (s.v. *book-post*), and Randolph Churchill (s.v. *draw*).

The rule decreed for the use of *shall* in the first person was framed in 1653 by the grammarian John Wallis, whose edict for *shall* and *will* became normative for his like-minded successors. The degree of grammarians' influence on popular usage is, of course, impossible to determine, but the ideology of correctness that emerged in the eighteenth century undoubtedly made the "correct" use of first-person *shall* well known to the literate. Wallis wrote at an interesting time for *shall* and *will*; according to the quantitative results from the Helsinki corpus, "the use of first person WILL peaks in British English in the 1570–1640 period and decreases again from the 1640s onwards" (Kytö 1990, 292). In the American English portion of the corpus, the "traditional" use of first-person *will* continues in the colonies without responding to the change in London fashion. (By reversing the direction of change from *shall* to *will*, Londoners unconsciously made their English more conservative, a phenomenon that might be called "metropolitan lag.")

Self-appointed arbiters of usage seized upon first-person *will* with a fierce tenacity. Eighteenth-century grammarians found various labels with which to reprobate it, including "improper," "inaccurate," "dialectal," and "bad." The most popular stigma, however, was that first-person *will* was a "Scotticism." Writing in 1796, Peter Walkden Fogg stated that both Scottish and Irish writers were prone to the mistake:

> Our fellow citizens of North-Britain and Ireland, find much difficulty in these auxiliaries. Even such writers as Lord Kaim [Kames], Dr. Goldsmith, and Dr. Blair, are not always correct in them. . . . The main point of their error seems to be putting *will* for *shall* with the first person. [quoted by Sundby, Bjørge, and Haugland 191]

For British writers in the eighteenth century, there was no category of Americanisms to berate – at least by the name Witherspoon had coined during the Revolutionary War.

Once the term *Americanism* became available, it served to denigrate a new form of "extra-British idioms." Caught up in the idea that first-person *will* was the deviant rather than the naturally evolving form, Otto Jespersen (1909–49) wrote that "the Scotch and Irish, hence also the Scotch-Irish parts of the US, use constantly *will* in this way" (4: 260). "*I will* and *we will* may be used in a futuric sense," he declared, "and in spite of the condemnation of grammarians this usage is constantly gaining ground, which cannot be thought unnatural" (4: 256).

Having made first-person *will* a shibboleth within the British Isles, English purists found it natural to extend the criticism to North American usage:

> The English language is spoken over a great part of the civilized world, and the idiomatic use of *shall* and *will* is possessed, in its fulness, by Englishmen alone. The influence of Irishmen, Scotchmen, Americans, and Australians, will be felt more and more every day; and an idiom so subtle and complicated will hardly be able to withstand the opposing force of so many nationalities, which have never accepted it, or even understood it, in the past, and are never likely to understand it, or accept it, in the future. [Molloy 106]

Most of these discussions are cast in a melancholic and nostalgic mode. Deviation from the "idiom so subtle and so complicated" seemed heedless

of the grammarians' remedies. H. W. Fowler (1944) mourned the "inclination, among those who are not to the manner born, to question the existence, besides denying the need, of distinctions between *sh[all]* & *w[ill]*" (s.v.
shall). Fowler's successor, Gowers (1965), used a revealing past tense in his
own description: "the few who understood it used to consider [it] the hallmark of mastery of the niceties of English idiom" (s.v. *Americanisms*). More
recent British usage writers limit the expression of woe but continue the
sense of grief: "This distinction is dying out" (Greenbaum and Whitcut s.v.
shall). "Extra-British idioms" are, however, no longer blamed as the cause
of change, and, despite the shift so worrisome to the London arbiters of
linguistic taste, *shall* is still more frequent in British English than in
American. While the incidence of the modal verbs in the two varieties of
English is "quite similar," *shall* is about 30 percent more frequent in British
English, a result that is statistically significant at the .01 level. *Will*, however,
occurs at nearly identical rates in the two varieties (Hofland and Johansson
36, 529, 542).

Can/may and *will/shall* represent two aspects of "lag." In the former,
London English produced a new distribution of preferences not imitated
in Colonial New England; in the latter, Colonial American English continued a line of development while London reversed a change already in
progress only to conform, slowly but eventually, to the American pattern.
Neither of these separate lines of innovation necessarily shows the impact
of the other, of course. The concepts of colonial and metropolitan lag thus
afford two ways of looking at the same history; these examples show the
same direction of change but different rates of accomplishing it.

14.5.2   *Divergence in shifting lexical meanings*

Such core elements of English as the modals show the diffusion of change
brought about by geographical separation. Other kinds of changes affect
common vocabulary by shifting meanings. Seventeenth-century British
English was nudged into awareness of American English by the elabora-
tion of meanings of familiar words: *cardinal flower* (1698), *Indess* (1672)
'Native-American woman,' *Indianism* (1651) 'advocacy of Native-American
interests,' *plate fleet* (1625) 'Spanish flotilla bearing precious metals,' *redskin*
(1699) 'Native American.' From the Caribbean came the compounds *man
grass* (1672) and *dumb cane* (1696). American words could even displace traditional English ones. In Britain, the fruits of certain species of bog plants
were known as *marsh-worts* or *fen-berries*. When the related North American
fruits were imported from New England in 1686, they were called by the

name given to them in America: *cranberries* (1672). The source of such novelties was the Caribbean and *New England* – especially the speech of *New Englanders* (terms introduced into English in 1637).

Early New England settlers were townsfolk unprepared for the terrifying American wilderness with its immense trees and unfamiliar coastline. As a result of their inexperience, they did not know the right use of topographical terms and so they adjusted them to suit the new world. A *creek*, an inlet from the sea in Britain, became a tributary to any large body of water (1622). *Hole*, a deep place in a stream or pond, became an anchorage along the coast, then a low, wet meadow (1627), then a valley surrounded by mountains (1714). (The first of these American meanings explains Wood's Hole, Massachusetts; the third explains Jackson Hole, Wyoming.) A *clearing* (1678) or an *opening* (1798) was an arable tract of brushy ground or one from which the trees had been removed to allow cultivation. *Intervals* (short for *interval land*) designated potential farmlands between a river bank and adjacent hills (1647), a term that first competed with *bottoms* (1634 – also *bottom ground* 1637 and *bottom land* 1728) – and then fell into disuse. A *bluff* (short for *bluff land*) was no longer a stretch of high ground along the sea but any wooded, steep-sided shoreland (1687) and then any abrupt change of elevation with or without an adjacent watercourse. Most of these shifts in meaning went unnoticed in London, but finally, in 1735, an English visitor, Francis Moore, detected the "new" meaning of *bluff*. "I took a view of the town of Savannah," Moore reported. "It is about a mile and a quarter in circumference; it stands upon the flat of a hill, the bank of the river (which they in barbarous English call a bluff) is steep and about forty-five foot perpendicular" (94).

14.6   Cultural coherence between the colonies and Britain

Sensitivity to "barbarous English" was thoroughly understood in the American colonies, where a declaration of linguistic independence took far longer to proclaim than the political declaration of 1776. Seventeenth-century migrants to America, who often saw themselves as English subjects in exile, had little wish to assert cultural independence. Most Americans professed the same values as Britons, shared the same tastes, despised the same enemies – first the Spanish and then the French. For them, English was one language, and, if any different, American English was distinguished by its greater "purity" since there were no dialects of the sort that disfigured the language of the parent nation. Expressions of this view are to be found in the work of Hugh Jones (c. 1670–1760), a clergyman appointed in 1716 to the chair of mathematics at the College of William and Mary in Williamsburg. In his survey of *The Present State of Virginia* (1724b), he especially emphasized the shared prejudices of Virginians and Londoners:

> The *Habits*, *Life*, *Customs*, *Computations*, &c. of the *Virginians* are much the same as about *London*, which they esteem their *Home*; and for the most Part have contemptible Notions of *England*, and wrong Sentiments of *Bristol*, and the other *Out-Ports*, which they entertain from seeing and hearing the common Dealers, Sailors, and Servants that come from those Towns, and the Country Places in *England* and *Scotland*, whose Language and Manners are strange to them; for the *Planters*, even the *Native Negroes* generally talk good *English* without *Idiom* or *Tone*, and can discourse handsomly upon *most* common Subjects; and conversing with Persons belonging to Trade and Navigation from *London*, for the most Part they are much civilized, and wear the best of Cloaths according to their Station; nay, sometimes too good for their Circumstances, being for the Generality comely handsom Persons, of good Features and fine Complexions (if they take Care) of good Manners and Address. [43]

In his linguistic work, *An Accidence to the English Tongue*, published in the same year, Jones divided the "Principal Dialects and Tones" of English into five: Northern ("which we may call *Yorkshire*"), Southern (or Sussex), Eastern (or Suffolk), Western ("which we may call *Bristol Language*"), and "the *Proper*, or *London Language*" (13). Only two groups had command of this "proper" language: "our *Learned*, *Polite*, and *Gentile People* every where, and the *Inhabitants* of the *Plantations* (even the Native Negroes) may be esteemed the only People that speak *true English*" (14–15).

Jones's reverence for the propriety of American English anticipated a widely held opinion, expressed frequently up to the nineteenth century (for instance, Candler 326–34). Not only did visitors from Britain report a remarkable purity of the language along the Atlantic coast, but Americans themselves were able to make practical use of dialect differences heard in the speech of newly arrived indentured servants. As often happened, these servants decamped before the term of the indenture was complete, and Colonial newspapers carried notices in the hope that they would be apprehended and returned. Thus, from the *Virginia Gazette* of August 8, 1751: "Run away ... a Servant Man, named *William Newberry*, aged about Twenty Years: He is a West-country-Man, and talks like one" (quoted, with many other examples, by Read 1938, 72). Only London and its environs were never mentioned; Ireland, Scotland, the North and Midlands of England were regularly singled out. The British speech of these regions was distinctive to Colonial Americans.

British recognition of a distinctive American English was slower to emerge. Samuel Johnson's *Dictionary*, published in 1755, contained a variety of American expressions: *chocolate, barbecue, moose, squash,* and *tobacco* among them. These are given no special treatment as American words, and the illustrative quotations for plant names are derived from Philip Miller's 1731–9 *Gardener's Dictionary*. In fact, Johnson has fewer words of American origin than his principal source, Nathan Bailey's 1730 *Dictionarium Britannicum*; Bailey provides definitions for *manatee, musquash, muskrat,* and *sachem* – all words ignored by Johnson. The reception of Johnson's work provided an occasion for public reflection about the language. Just a few weeks before it appeared, the Earl of Chesterfield wrote two genial essays in which he congratulated Johnson "for having undertaken and executed so great and desirable a work." At the same time, Chesterfield declared in a patriotic view of the language: "I have therefore a sensible pleasure in reflecting upon the rapid progress which our language has lately made and still continues to make all over Europe" (*World* 2: 297).

Chesterfield's two essays stimulated a third contribution on the subject, this one by Richard Owen Cambridge. He was not eager to welcome "the fixed and permanent standard of our language" that Chesterfield had imagined might be founded on Johnson's *Dictionary*, and for him the spread of English on the continent was not the most interesting development. English responded to the interests of its speakers, he declared, and recent discussions of Asia had led to such loans as *joss, pagoda, nabob, mandarin, junk,* and *sepoy.* He thought further that a "neological" supplement should be provided for "an interpretation of West-India phrases" (*World* 2: 310). The examples he provided included *six nations, sachem, war-kettle, calumet, half-king, speech-belt,* and *wampum.* Many of these words had been long current in Britain but Cambridge provides the earliest quotation known to the *OED* for *war-kettle.* (If he looked to Johnson to define *calumet,* he was disappointed; if he had consulted Bailey's work of 1730, he would have found an encyclopedic entry and a wood-cut illustration.) What pleased Cambridge about English was its openness to innovation. Rather than a permanent standard, he believed, what was wanted was "a Guide to the new English tongue."

However curious English literary observers may have been about the new contributions to English from abroad, departures from the London standard were not a source of pride to literary Americans. What emerged was a new linguistic self-consciousness, pioneered in Scotland, where, as

Witherspoon had observed, a separate and independent variety of English had, as a consequence of economic and cultural dependency, come to be regarded as a "provincial barbarism." Scots were increasingly derided for their English in the course of the century, and London hacks were fond of pointing out Scotticisms that, in their view, disfigured the writing of even the most ingenious and learned writers (R. Bailey 1991a). So wise an author as Benjamin Franklin could not resist adding his voice to these attacks on the Scots. Writing anonymously to the *London Chronicle*, he resented criticism of the colonists and their conduct; if anything, Americans "wear the manufactures of Britain, and follow its fashions perhaps too closely":

> But as to their language, I must beg this gentleman's pardon if I differ from him. His ear, accustomed perhaps to the dialect practised in the *certain northern latitude* he mentions [i.e., Scotland], may not be qualified to judge so nicely in what relates to *pure* English. And I appeal to all Englishmen here, who have been acquainted with the Colonists, whether it is not a common remark, that they speak the language with such an exactness both of expression and accent, that though you may know the natives of several of the counties of England, by peculiarities in their dialect, you cannot by that means distinguish a North American.
> [Labaree 8: 342]

This smug declaration of American linguistic purity – written in 1759 – was a bit of bluster to conceal what in our own century would be called the "colonial cringe," the uneasy apprehension that one's own preferences, being different from those of the metropolis, were faults.

Franklin's private views become clearer in a letter he wrote to David Hume in the following year. Though the great historian of Britain and its most formidable living philosopher, Hume suffered greatly from anxiety that his writings would be derided for their Scotticisms – so much so that he sent manuscripts to English friends who, by identifying offending usages, might help him avoid ridicule. When Franklin sent pamphlets of his own authoring to Hume, the latter could not resist making observations about their English, and Franklin replied:

> I thank you for your friendly Admonition relating to some unusual Words in the Pamphlet. It will be of Service to me. The *pejorate*, and the *colonizer*, since they are not in common use here [i. e., in England], I give up as bad; for certainly in Writings intended for Persuasion and for general Information, one cannot be too clear, and every Expression in the least obscure is a Fault. The *unshakeable* too, tho' clear, I give up as rather low. The introducing new Words where we are already possess'd of old ones sufficiently expressive, I confess must be generally wrong,

as it tends to change the Language; yet at the same time I cannot but wish the Usage of our Tongue permitted making new Words when we want them, by Composition of old ones who[se] Meanings are already well understood. The German allows of it, and it is a common Practice with their Writers. Many of our present English Words were originally so made; and many of the Latin Words. In point of Clearness such compound Words would have the Advantage of any we can borrow from the ancient or from foreign Languages. For instance, the Word *inaccessible*, tho' long in use among us, is not yet, I dare say, so universally understood by our People as the Word *uncomeatable* would immediately be, which we are not allow'd to write. But I hope with you, that we shall always in America make the best English of this Island [i.e., Britain] our Standard, and I believe it will be so. I assure you, it often gives me Pleasure to reflect how greatly the *Audience* (if I may so term it) of a good English Writer will in another Century or two be encreas'd by the Increase of English People in our Colonies. [Labaree 9: 229–30]

Despite Franklin's and Hume's anxiety about them, *colonize, pejorate,* and *unshakeable* had been established in English for more than a century. Johnson had also shunned the word that Franklin wished to employ but could not; *uncomeatable* he described as "a low corrupt word," though Richard Steele had used it, at least humorously, in that model for eighteenth-century linguistic grace, *The Tatler.* Of the words Franklin discussed, only *audience* – in the sense of readers rather than auditors – was a linguistic innovation.

Franklin's hope that the English of southern England would remain a standard was exactly in agreement with his friend Witherspoon's. American English, they thought, should not have influence abroad because it should not exist at home as a separately respectable variety of the language. Even though grammar and usage books began to flood the British market, none published before 1800 singled out American English for reprobation, though Scotticisms and various dialectal usages were censured – for instance, *pled* 'pleaded' and *proven* 'proved,' though used in America, were criticized as Scottish.

Aside from scattered observations, like Francis Moore's criticism of American *bluff*, there was no attempt in England to extinguish American usages. Errors there were aplenty, of course, and linguistic self-improvement became a mania in both Britain and North America by the end of the eighteenth century. That these errors were not "American" is well illustrated by the writings of Helena Wells Whitford (c. 1761–1824). Born in Charleston, South Carolina, to a family of Scottish origin, Whitford emigrated to

England in 1774 when her father's loyalty to the London parliament made him unwelcome in pre-Revolutionary America. Establishing herself as a schoolmistress, Whitford published two works on education: *Letters on Subjects of Importance to the Happiness of Young Females* (1799) and *Thoughts and Remarks on Establishing an Institution for the Support and Education of Unportioned Respectable Females* (1809). In both she expressed an almost fanatical concern with linguistic correctness, and to the former she appended a long list of errors to be avoided, for instance, saying "wich" for *which*, "Lunnon" for *London*, "nothink" for *nothing* (161, 163, 169). None of these mistakes was American. Whitford's views on language were also expressed in her turgid three-volume novel, *Constantia Neville; or, The West Indian* (1800, 1: 77):

> The pains taken to keep Constantia from the negroes (Mrs. Neville always having an English woman in her nursery) added to the society in which she was permitted to mix in her father's house, gave her at twelve years old a fluency of speech, and a correctness of language, which many of her seniors would have been proud to possess.

Set initially in Barbados – the West Indian heiress in London was a familiar fictional figure, and there is no evidence that Whitford ever visited the Caribbean – the novel echoes the prevailing bigotry of American slave-holding society. Whitford finds flaws in London English – schools for young women, she declared in her *Thoughts*, convert children from "tolerably correct" to "all the cockney dialect" (61) – and she presumes that "negroes" will exercise a baleful influence on English, but she has no alarm about "American" mistakes.

Viewed from London, American English was supposed to be different because it was distant. The least informed among the English public supposed that the newly independent Americans spoke Amerindian languages, but the best informed were mystified on encountering Americans. A London shopkeeper, Boswell reports in the *Life of Johnson*, supposed a customer to be an American because "you speak neither English nor Scotch" (quoted by Read 1933, 314). (The customer was, in fact, a Scottish nobleman who had attempted, with some success, to rid his speech of Scotticisms.) Meeting the visiting American artists Gilbert Stuart and Benjamin West, Johnson rudely demanded to know where Stuart had acquired his very good English: "Stuart very promptly replied: 'Sir, I can better tell you where I did not learn it – it was not from your dictionary'" (quoted by Read 1935, 162). American English was often discerned from principle rather than practice. Benjamin Silliman, touring Britain in 1805–6, dined with a learned assembly at a Cambridge college:

Our sitting lasted for hours; my seat was next to Mr. C——, and, in the course of a very free conversation, he took occasion to observe, that it was impossible that any man born and educated 3000 miles from England, should speak the language so perfectly, that even an Englishman could not distinguish the difference between a stranger's speech and his own. This, he was pleased to say, was just the case between us; and he then, with much good nature and urbanity, insisted that I had been all the while amusing him with the story I was an American, when it was so evident that I must be an Englishman, or must, at least, have been educated in England. [Silliman 2: 227]

Educated English was, according to these testimonies, a unified and "refined" version of the language. For the educated, there was nothing especially American about it.

14.7   Rising British anxiety and antagonism

American English, however, did exist and did influence the language as a whole, though the accusation that Americans were corrupting the language of Britain did not arise until much later. British criticisms were sometimes concerned about the loss of linguistic community:

In the style, we observe, with regret, rather than with astonishment, the introduction of several new words, or old words in a new sense; a deviation from the rules of the English language, which, if it continues to be practiced by good writers in America, will introduce confusion into the medium of intercourse, and render it a subject of regret that the people of that continent should not have an entirely separate language as well as a government of their own. [Review 1810, 182]

This observation, from a review of two biographies of Washington, included three instances: *had issued* 'had resulted,' *delinquency* 'tardiness,' and *releasement* 'release.' The last of these had been used by Milton and was to be used by Matthew Arnold – both paragons of English style. Facts have not often clouded the clarity of such critics.

It was not only British writers who were anxious about the development of separate languages from a single tongue. The American John Pickering was the first to publish a book solely devoted to the "*Americanisms* and expressions of doubtful authority" (iii) he had encountered during a visit to London lasting from 1799 to 1801. Often taken as a mere toady to London prejudices, Pickering believed that the outlying regions could nominate usages but not elect them to the standard: "We should hardly be willing to adopt all the words and phrases which the people of Scotland, of Ireland, or of the British Settlements in various parts of the world, should propose to make as part of our common language" (20n). While London remained the source of authority in Pickering's view, he believed that English speakers abroad had something to contribute to the "common language." Pickering's collection, published in 1816, contained both expressions he had noticed during his visit and those he found criticized in reviews of American publications. Through wide reading, he discovered that some expressions alleged to be Americanisms had been used without reproach by earlier British writers – for instance, *domestic* 'servant' had been used by Shakespeare and Addison – but that others were genuine and defensible American inventions – for instance, *backwoodsman* (1774), *prairie* (1682), and *squaw* (1634). He noticed that *to arrive at a place* was a distinguishing usage: British authors (for example, Austen) tended to write *be arrived at* while Americans (for instance, Hawthorne and Emerson) were likely to use *have arrived at*. (The fact that *have arrived at* prevails in modern British English is not so much a matter of American influence as of parallel development.)

What must have disturbed Pickering was the virulence of many of the London attacks on American English, particularly among the anti-republican factions on the British cultural scene. Travelers were especially inclined to angry portrayals of American usage:

> Colloquial barbarisms . . . , among the peasantry of a country, are excusable; but when they are used in composition by writers, they become disgusting. I could collect hundreds of others equally absurd, which have been invented by Americans who are desirous of introducing, what they call, an *American language*; but unless they resort to the *Catabaw*, *Chactaw*, or *Kickapoo* dialects, I am sure they will never accomplish it by *murdering* the English language.   [Lambert 3: 480]

Reviewers of American publications were especially vigorous in their attacks, and Pickering carefully assembled and dispassionately discussed a remarkable array of them. From these emerged in Britain an idea of "American," a kind of English that was subject to amused or passionate comment for the rest of the century. Thus, the *Quarterly Review* – an organ capable of denouncing homegrown radicals for "Americanisms" (26 [1821–2]: 103) – regularly provided lists of despicable usages coming from the United States:

> Nor have there been wanting projects among them for getting rid of the English language, not merely by barbarizing it – as when they *progress* a bill, *jeopardize* a ship, *guess* a probability, proceed by *grades*, hold a *caucus*, *conglaciate* a wave, &c. when the President of Yale College talks of a

conflagrative brand, and President Jefferson of *belittling* the productions of nature – but also by abolishing the use of English altogether, and substituting a new language for their own.   [Review of Ingersoll 523]

Few passages of xenophobic apoplexy could better illustrate the principle that one generation's shibboleth is the next generation's synonym.

Conglaciate and *conflagrative* both illustrate the pedantry, or affected humor, of the learned, a trait that afflicted the pompous on both sides of the Atlantic. "*Conglaciate* a wave" was a swipe at a typically bad line from Joel Barlow's egregious epic, *The Columbiad* (1808), though the sense of the word to mean 'freeze' had prior scientific credentials in England. Both Thackeray and Carlyle would reinvent *conflagrative* 'burning' with a similar wish to achieve Latinate elegance. *Jeopardize* 'threaten' would shortly be used in a serious context by Richard Chenevix Trench (in a work on miracles in 1834), while *guess* 'estimate' was used in so respectable a work as John Gibson Lockhart's *Life of Scott* (1837). *Grade* was taken as a synonym for *gradation* in the *OED* (s.v. *graduated*). The genuine Americanism *caucus* was regularly derided in Britain but, according to the *OED*, "in English newspapers since 1878, [it was frequently but] generally misused and applied opprobriously" to describe what Americans would call a "political machine." In 1886, it appeared in the *New Zealand Herald* in the American sense of a political gathering. It also appeared, famously, in Carroll's *Alice in Wonderland* (1865). *Progress* as a verb was described in the *OED* as "common in England c. 1590–1670" but obsolescent in the eighteenth century; "app[arently] retained (or formed anew) in America." To English derision, Washington had written in 1791 "our country . . . is fast progressing"; W. E. Gladstone, an admirer of Washington, wrote in 1840 that "we are actually progressing in some particulars," and he did so without arousing adverse criticism. *Belittle*, the *OED* grudgingly says, "appears to have originated in the U. S.," and it was the subject of frequent comment by the reviewers early in the nineteenth century. Though it is still possible for British usage writers to bemoan the displacement of "old established" synonyms, the *Pall Mall Gazette* employed *belittle* without comment as early as 1881, and it appears in novels by Thomas Hardy (1891) and Doris Lessing (1970).

Linguistic fastidiousness is often a guise for cultural arrogance, and it is no surprise that abuse of American English was coupled with attacks on the United States. Visitors used moral terms to denounce "spurious" new words and to bewail sense changes that "pervert the meaning" of old ones ("English Language" 1838, 279). Pickering's *Vocabulary* made it possible for British pundits to lambaste American English on the basis of carefully collected information. Thus an anonymous essayist explained to his English readers in 1820 that the Americans had created such terms as *constitutionality*, *deputize*, *governmental*, and *gubernatorial* ("On Americanisms" 630). All of these had a vogue in the United States as the new forms of government were established – though *deputize* had already appeared in Nathan Bailey's *Dictionarium* – and all soon became part of political discourse in Britain, so much so that the *Spectator* in 1980 could yoke together without discomfort "gubernatorial authority and viceregal judgment" (*OED* s.v. *hiding*). As Mencken (1963, 17) explained in his detailed review of the mutual influences of the two varieties of English: "The general tone of English criticism, from the Eighteenth Century to the present, has been one of suspicion, and not infrequently it has been extremely hostile."

Public scorn was probably less common than private disdain, a state of affairs that can be illustrated from the middle years of the 1830s when Victoria became queen. The United States was, at that time, represented diplomatically by Andrew Stevenson, a Virginian and former Speaker of the House of Representatives. His wife Sarah Coles Stevenson (1789–1848) was another Virginian, and together they dined in aristocratic London circles. The diary of one of their hostesses gives an idea of the impression they created:

> We had the American Minister & his wife to dinner. She is rather
> pleasing, but diverted Mr Hallam whom she sat next to at dinner, by
> lamenting that the people in this country do not speak English, only a
> bad jargon. In the meantime she is often herself unintelligible from her
> accent & very strange *locutions*.   [Holland 164]

Sarah Stevenson seems to have been entirely unaware of the impression she created, very likely presuming the essential unity of the English of Virginia and London as celebrated by Hugh Jones a century earlier. When the Stevensons were invited to a state dinner at Buckingham Palace, the grandeur of the occasion – with other members of the diplomatic corps and a band to heighten the ceremony – provided material for a lengthy letter home:

> I determined to take a more particular look at everything than I had
> done before; but when I raised my eyes to look upon all this royal
> magnificence, the thought occurred to me: "If I gaze about, they will
> say, 'Look at that wild American, how she is staring at everything! I dare
> say she fancies herself in one of the enchanted castles of the Arabian
> Nights.'" So with Indian-like caution I only cast furtive glances around,
> and endeavoured to bear myself as though it was all as familiar to me as

my every-day comforts. In consequence of this prudent determination, I cannot tell you much more than I did before. [Boykin 109–10]

Despite her wariness, Sarah Stevenson did not go unobserved. Sitting nearly opposite her, the young Victoria indulged a little Indian-like stealth of her own. To her neighbor at dinner, Victoria spoke censoriously of the American guest:

> She observed in a low voice on the American *tournure* and manners of Mrs. Stevenson, and seemed much diverted with her – and to an observation of mine she replied that she thought the Americans must be a very disagreeable people, and that it was impossible to see any of them without being reminded of the books which had been lately written about them and which she was afraid were all true in the main points. [Oman 253]

Except for a few groveling anglophiles, Americans were mostly innocent of British scorn, or indifferent to it, but the first half century after American independence fostered the enduring idea in Britain that English in the New World had changed in ways that made it "very disagreeable."

14.8 American reaction and British counter reaction

Only a few Americans were afflicted with the cultural cringe when contemplating their own usage and discovering differences between it and London fashion. Writing in the same year that British troops torched the President's mansion in Washington, an American observer attempted to put linguistic criticism in a political context:

> Old nations, like old belles, are naturally inclined to be jealous of young ones, and seldom miss an opportunity of making ill natured reflections on their youth, their manners, or their accomplishments. This jealousy appears more particularly in the affected contempt with which the writers of old England, and especially the critics, who are always the most conceited of the whole tribe of authors, treat every thing written in this new world, except, perhaps, a political pamphlet, or speech, that happens to agree with their opinions. Not content with attacking our books in a body, they have descended even to words, and what is still more insulting, words of our own invention, and therefore deservedly dear to us all. These they are pleased in derision to call Americanisms, as if an Americanism was not as respectable as an Anglicism, a Gallicism, or any other ism whatever. Nothing can be more provoking than to see, when one of these critics encounters a "lengthy" or a "progressing,"

how the wretch begins to grin. He immediately puts it in italics, or posts a tall note of admiration at the end, to allure his readers to come and gaze at this curious transatlantic monster. After thus, as it were, pointing their finger in derision at us, some of these vain, silly fellows will observe, with a deal of liberality, as he thinks, that the people of the new world, for all this, are not quite so barbarous as some people think, but in reality speak nearly as good English as the cockneys; have almost as much refinement as the manufacturers of Birmingham; and are quite as civilized as the Cornish wreckers, or the students of the universities. This attempt to interfere with the privilege of speech, a privilege for which our ancestors left their native country, and afterwards maintained a seven years' war, is, I think, an ungenerous return for the perfect sobriety of countenance with which we are accustomed to listen to their almost irresistible Yorkshire, Somersetshire [sic], and Leicestershire dialects. Neither is it at all analogous to the scrupulous delicacy with which we refrain from laughing at their 'ard hegs,' their 'hadn't oughts,' or to the liberal toleration we give to a vast number of English books, which are bought up in this country for no other reason, I believe, than that they were written in Old England. The truth is, we have a mighty predilection, or rather an indiscriminate admiration, for every thing of foreign growth, and it is, perhaps, this very ignorant and superstitious veneration that encourages foreigners to treat us with such supercilious airs of superiority. [Lengthy 404–5]

"Affected contempt" did not stem the flow of American usage into British English, and, although the authors of the New England "renaissance" watched London prejudices with anxiety, their usage was frequently echoed in Britain. Thus, *lengthy*, apparently a genuine Americanism, formed by analogy with good Old English *weighty*, was used by such articulate Americans as Franklin, Hamilton, Jefferson, Meriwether Lewis, Melville, Zebulon Pike, Safire, Thoreau, and Washington. *Lengthy*, despite the opprobrium of early nineteenth-century British hacks, was appropriated by such British writers as Bentham, Byron, Carlyle, Darwin, Dickens, George Eliot, Hardy, Joyce, C. S. Lewis, and Rossetti.

Not all Americanisms, of course, found immediate echoes in Britain. What did emerge there was the stereotype of American English to which Tom Taylor's *American Cousin* attests. In part, this stereotype was fabricated from the sneers of such British travelers as Frances Trollope, Frederick Maryatt, and Charles Dickens, whose accounts of American linguistic vulgarity and extravagance were widely read. Particularly galling to Trollope were American representations of English speech; her extract from *The American Comic Annual* (1831) suggests that American humorists, like their

British counterparts, drew their ideas of speech not from actual experience but from the usage handbooks that were beginning to appear in both countries. "Among the pleasantries of this lively volume," she wrote, "are some biting attacks upon us, particularly upon our utter incapacity of speaking English. We really must engage a few American professors, or we shall lose all trace of classic purity in our language" (321). Dickens was less offended by American independence but more deeply scornful of the culture he found on his visit and excoriated it in his 1843–4 novel *Martin Chuzzlewit*. While in Boston, he discovered that in American English *right away* can mean 'immediately,' or, as he glossed it, 'directly' (*American Notes* 39), a sense evolution that was first called by the *OED* in 1885 "U. S. and Engl[ish] dial[ect]" but revised in 1972 to "U. S. and Engl[ish] coll[oquial]" after *right away* 'now' had appeared in Britain through a master of the colloquial – not an "American professor" but P. G. Wodehouse.

Transatlantic linguistic warfare continued with increasing vigor for a century and more after the initial volleys of the Federal era in American history. Typical were the comments of Charles Mackay, writing in 1867, who feared "that English in America threatens to become, at no distant day, a very different language from English in England" (402). Mackay observed that, thanks to British interest in the American Civil War and the popularity of American writers, "a large number of words and phrases, that ought not to be admitted into English literature, have been creeping into use amongst us, and exercising an influence upon the style of our popular journalists, our comic writers, and even of our ordinary conversation, that ought not to be encouraged by any one who desires that our noble language should remain undefiled" (402). Like other linguistic prophets, Mackay was an uncertain forecaster. *Walrussia* (a blend of *walrus* and *Russia*) was, he thought, "likely to be [the] permanent" name of the recently acquired territory of Alaska. Dozens of words to which he objected soon became commonplace in London: *lobby* 'to influence politically,' *bogus* 'fake,' and *boss* were typical imports. *Bogus* was soon used by Hardy and Shaw; *boss* by the Australians and by Orwell; *lobby* appeared in domestic political commentary in the *Yorkshire Post* (1894) and *Westminster Gazette* (1898).

Only at mid century did Britons like Mackay begin to be alarmed by American expressions "creeping" into English on its home territory. In 1889, John S. Farmer – an indefatigable collector of out-of-the-way words – published privately a substantial dictionary of *Americanisms – Old and New*. Farmer, who welcomed the "racy, pungent vernacular of Western life," noticed how American usage was becoming increasingly popular in London:

Hitherto, this divergence in speech [between Britain and America] has been of little moment, except to the curiously inclined in matters philological. Latterly, however, for good or ill, we have been brought face to face with what has been grandiloquently called "The Great American Language" oftentimes in its baldest form, and on its most repulsive side. The works, also, of popular exponents of "American Humor" . . . [are] daily gaining ground – books in shoals, journals by the score, and allusions without stint, are multiplying on every hand. American newspapers, too, humorous and otherwise, circulate in England by hundreds of thousands weekly – all this and a good deal else is doing its work in popularising American peculiarities of speech and diction to an extent which, a few years since, would have been deemed incredible. Even our own newspapers, hitherto regarded as models of correct literary style, are many of them following in their wake; and, both in matter and phraseology, are lending countenance to what at first sight appears a monstrously crude and almost imbecile jargon; while others, fearful of a direct plunge, modestly introduce the uncouth bantlings with a saving clause. The phrase, "as the Americans say," might in some cases be ordered from the type-foundry as a logotype, so frequently does it do introduction duty.   [vii–viii]

Farmer's reference to "The Great American Language" alludes to an essay in the *Cornhill Magazine* by Grant Allen. Allen larded his prose with Americanisms, alleging that "the American language, above all others, palpitates with actuality" (364). American English, Allen alleged, spread like a disease: "The prominent citizens who have struck ile, or run a hotel which panned out well, cross the millpond to spend their heap, and introduce into unsuspecting Britain the germs of the new additions to our common tongue" (364). Farmer's moral outrage expresses the contemporary English view of American developments as Londoners became increasingly aware of the impact of the language of the United States on their own. His dictionary, however, is a thoroughly scholarly production containing an abundance of precisely identified quotations from American publications and defending, as legitimate, many of the expressions so documented.

As the detective story became an increasingly popular British genre toward the end of the century, Americans often figured in the intrigue. Arthur Conan Doyle's Sherlock Holmes stories are filled with Americans, most of them villains of a bloodthirsty kind, and Holmes regularly displays his knowledge of the criminals of New York, Chicago, and Detroit. The voices of these characters owe more to Asa Trenchard than to actual Americans, and Doyle's Americans are easily identifiable by commencing sentences with *well* and using *guess* for *suppose*. Nonetheless, Holmes applies his deductive genius to American English in a way that needs to be explained to his baffled sidekick, Watson. Examining a printed document, Holmes asks his friend:

> "Did you notice nothing curious about that advertisement?"
> "I saw that the word 'plough' was mis-spelt."
> "Oh, you did notice that, did you? Come, Watson, you improve all the time. Yes, it was bad English but good American. The printer had set it up as received. Then the buckboards. That is American also. And artesian wells are commoner with them than with us. It was a typical American advertisement, but purporting to be from an English firm."
>
> [2: 651]

Had the insidious influence of American English been better known to English readers, Holmes's interpretation of these details would hardly have seemed an astonishing feat of erudition. Doyle's readers were not prepared to distinguish "bad English" from "good American." In the Holmes stories, American characters are usually crafty, plain-spoken, and stupid; when faced with discovery they confess with disarming simplicity: "Well, you figured it out about right" (1: 518). Such linguistic stereotypes, about as accurate as stage Irish, conveyed the sense of the exotic that was associated with American English while reserving intelligence for the English characters. De Quincey, in 1855, had already encompassed the American shibboleths as seen from London: "Waal, now to speak yankeeishly, I calculate your dander is rising" (*OED* s.v. *Yankee*). Doyle did little to elaborate on the handful of these traits already in widespread use in English drama and fiction.

American English, as perceived from the outside, carried the cachet of novelty and vitality, untainted by intellectual accomplishment. *OK*, the most pervasively influential Americanism of them all, was coined in 1839 in Boston. The earliest known British instance of its use followed in 1864 (in the *Boy's Own Magazine*) and by the end of the century it was used in South Africa. Consciously invoked Americanisms of this sort were particularly popular among groups scornful of London fashions. In Australia, as early as 1855, some convicts and former convicts, known locally as *white-washed Yankees*, were inclined to affect American speech and manners. Such characters even became the subject of song (Cooke, MacCallum, and Eagleson 26):

> I'll sing you quite a novel song, made by a colonial brick,
> Of a thorough white-washed Yankee who was "tarnation slick" –
> Who thought in every movement his imitation fine,
> And aped the manners of the States so truly genuine.

490

"White-washed" or authentic – the rhyme of *fine* and *genuine* is a characteristic touch – American English epitomized the unrestrained, the indulgence of impulse in language. Popular vernacular literature arose first in America and then in Victorian Britain to represent it. Scots writers took the exuberance, if not the linguistic detail, they found in American writers and made it their own. As the historian of this writing explains, "Like the Scots [the Americans] had little desire for incorporation into the periphery of a monolithic London-centred English literary culture, and they too turned to the speech of the common people as the basis for a new literary language" (W. Donaldson 58–9). American English as imagined in Scotland was no more authentic than that represented by London writers, but the idea was the same: the hearty vernacular of the uneducated but down-right citizen.

The substantial influence of American English on other varieties of the world language is not easy to document, and a racy vernacular, whatever its origin, is seldom adequately represented in written form, even close to its source. Some American influence was mediated through Britain; the American word *sassafras*, for instance, was used in English in 1577, and, with the settlement of Australia, the same term was used in 1802 for a tree newly encountered there. Increased travel in the nineteenth century exposed more and more English speakers to new ways of speaking. The search for precious minerals, for instance, helped to spread American English abroad. *Claim-jumper* first appeared in the US in 1839; in 1854, it had reached the gold fields of Australia. Methods of mining produced the word *sluice* for the flume designed to carry gold-bearing water and gravel to a *sluice box* where the gold particles could be gathered. *Sluice* is first attested in a San Francisco newspaper in 1851; in 1855, the miners who used this method in Australia were called *sluicers*, and *sluice box* was recorded in print in 1869 in the Fraser River gold rush in western Canada. A *cradle* used to agitate gold-bearing sand and water was so called in the US in 1824; in Australia, the term was adopted in 1851; in Canada, it was called a *cradle rocker* in 1859. Where gold could be collected by picking small nuggets from the rocks, Californians applied *dry diggings* in 1848; this term spread to Australia in 1851; to Canada in 1858; to New Zealand in 1862; and to South Africa in 1873 (where the valuables included in the matrix mineral were diamonds). Terms like these spread in part through written English, but gold and diamond fever was endemic in the second half of the century, and the eager prospectors, moving from one country to another, took their specialized terms with them.

Even areas geographically remote from the influence of America show the influence of innovations originating here. New Zealand's pioneers used equipment actually or imaginatively connected with American life: *American axe* (1842; see Orsman for this and the following examples), *American pegged boots* (1861), *American stove* (1861), *American waggon* (1865). Parallel development was more likely than immediate influence in the use of *creek* for a body of freshwater (1815) rather than as an inlet of the ocean.

Once it had become clear that linguistic Americanisms were not welcome in Britain, New Zealanders coined the expression *American invasion* (1920) to refer to "the intrusion of American language and ways," a phrase that became far more familiar when the American military visited New Zealand during World War II. Broadcasting, especially television, has made American usages pervasively familiar, particularly when words and images are aggressively marketed. Iona and Peter Opie (118–20) describe the beginnings of the "adult-organized assault on the juvenile imagination" with the international effort by Disney to market *Davy Crockett* in 1956. In data compiled in the 1980s, children younger than eleven offered *zee* as the name of the last letter of the alphabet while all those older than thirty responded with *zed*. In vocabulary, *radio* has usurped the place of *wireless* in New Zealand, but the use of Americanisms in marketing has not affected usage entirely. For instance, *cookies* and *diapers* are both packaged with those words by New Zealand manufacturers but *biscuits* and *nappies* remain the usual spoken terms (Bayard; Leek and Bayard). Deletion of articles in appositional naming is "a hallmark of American journalistic style" (Bell 1988, 326), for instance, *(the) volume editor John Algeo*. A study of news broadcasts in 1974 and 1984 revealed that the British Broadcasting Corporation's overseas service showed no instance of article deletion, while American networks CBS and ABC deleted the article more than 90 percent of the time. In 1974, the publicly owned Community Network of Radio New Zealand showed only 7 percent deletion (n = 60), and private rock-music station Radio Hauraki 21 percent deletion (n = 58). In 1984, these figures had increased to 89 percent (n = 222) and 91 percent (n = 35) respectively. This development is also taking place in Britain, where in 1980 the *Times* omitted the articles 8 percent of the time (n = 20), but the tabloid *Sun* omitted them entirely (n = 35; results reported by Bell 1988, 337).

Pride in local usage is damaged by admiration for overseas varieties. For New Zealanders and others, Allan Bell's (1982, 254) observation is disturbing. He fears that New Zealand may fall "out of the British frying pan into the American fire." Even in Britain the peril lurks. In August 2000, two grandparents in an Essex village were walking along each holding one of the hands of a four-year-old and swinging him upward at intervals. "[ə'gɛn, ə'gɛn, ə'gɛn]," cried the happy child. Saddened, the grandmother told him:

"Don't say [ə'gɛn, ə'gɛn, ə'gɛn]. Say [ə'geɪn, ə'geɪn, ə'geɪn]." The boy did not respond.

14.9   The triumph of American English

With the increased international mobility of population in the twentieth century, more and more English speakers were exposed on their home territory to the American variety of the language. As one historian of the matter explained, "Before the advent of talking films in the late nineteen-twenties the majority of the inhabitants of Britain were unfamiliar with spoken American except insofar as they might hear recordings or broadcasts of American songs, or a few remarks from an American celebrity who had been brought to the microphone" (Foster 329). Even when films were silent, the American English of the captions aroused British anxiety; "it is a *lingua franca*, or a *lingua californica*," bewailed an English purist (Knox 188). A linguistic autobiography published in 1927 provided further details:

> Among the Americanisms which constantly appear in the captions of the films and have – probably more through them than through other means – attained a measure of popularity are uplift, high-brow (intellectual), low-brow, sob-stuff, mush, mushy; guy, stiff, boob, mutt (synonyms for *'person, fellow'*); joint (*public house* or *saloon*); to put wise, get wise; make a get away, beat it for *escape*, especially in the 'crook' dramas, but also in literature. . . .
>
> The newspapers and magazines as well as many popular novels (especially detective stories and authors like Sinclair Lewis) play a great part in familiarising us with Americanisms. We probably do not keep pace with the neologisms, nor do we ever attain to the rich diversity of American slang (in particular we are immune from the slang of the baseball field), but we seem to offer less and less resistance to the new importations. I have in my survey deliberately refrained in many cases from specifying a given expression as American, as I am often unaware whether it is in origin American or not, and was surprised when reading *Mencken* to see how much I had just taken for granted as native English.
>
> [Collinson 114–15]

Talking pictures did even more to popularize and spread American linguistic fashions, and television syndication beginning in the 1960s eventually brought the nuanced English of "Dallas" into Buckingham Palace.

In Britain, and elsewhere, the conscious choice of American expressions has often signaled rebellion against the prestige of RP and its social meanings. Many of the English rock-and-roll groups that achieved international popularity in the 1960s modeled their performances on the recordings they had heard of American rhythm-and-blues and country-and-western music. As with earlier endeavors of this kind, the imitations were not always accurate. In the song "Rocky Raccoon," for instance, Paul McCartney pronounces *raccoon* as [rə'kun] rather than as the typical American [ræ'kun] and says *Gideon's Bible* (for *Gideon Bible*). In a song from the same era, Mick Jagger uses such explicit Americanisms as *drug store* 'chemist' and *parking lot* 'car park'; in the song "You Can't Always Get What You Want," he pronounces *can't* to rhyme with *pant* and *get* to rhyme with *fit* – the accompanying choir, however, pronounces them to rhyme with *font* and *pet*. In conversation, another "jazz enthusiast," Mick Mulligan, used the Americanism *nosh*, a borrowing from Yiddish, in a sentence otherwise distinctively British: "I'd have noshed the lot if I could have done" (quoted in *OED* s.v. *nosh, v.*; Melly 211); translated into American, this sentence would have been rendered: "I would've noshed the whole works if I could've."

The influence of American on the English of British rock stars has occasionally aroused cultural anxiety in Britain. One of the most vigorous of the purists now active has even declared that "country" music may be to blame for changes in the prestige dialect of England: "It may be that one of the main influences on the speech of young people in Britain today, and even possibly an influence on the way RP itself has been changing slightly over recent years, is the 'mid-Atlantic' flavour of the accents to which many pop singers and pop music presenters speak or sing" (Honey 66–7). Such a jeremiad repeats long familiar complaints about the English of youth; a journalist in 1950 complained that "probably half the young people in this country use American forms, phrases, and words as though they were an inevitable improvement on anything that originated in this country" (quoted by Kirchner 29).

The most recent edition of the *Oxford English Dictionary* identifies nearly 4,000 words as originally associated with the United States but now known and used in many parts of the English-speaking world. Many of these have the high-faluting character attributed to American English by nineteenth-century British critics: *bazooka, hornswoggle, hell-bent, gangster, galoot, hotsy-totsy,* and *skedaddle,* for instance. Others have merged into the language without retaining their American connotations: *alibi, commute,* (sports) *fan, escalator, delicatessen,* and *collectable.*

American English has been especially productive in the creation of new compounds, a hallmark of twentieth-century English in general: *back track, bandwagon, checklist, cheesecake, doubletalk, headlight,* and *hot rod.* Combinations with prepositions are another aspect of this impulse: *about face, back up, build-up, by-line, carry-out, give-away,* and *on-deck.* Other phrases arise from American practice: *go back on* (a promise), *cash in on* (an opportunity), *hold down* (a job), *get* (an idea) *across.* English speakers around the world use such expressions as *co-star, chewing gum, public enemy, self-made,* and *tailor-made* without recognizing their American source. Functional shift, another major development in twentieth-century English, is not an entirely American innovation, though in 1925 Helen Buckhurst, writing from St. Hugh's College, Oxford, blamed Americans for "the loose and inaccurate employment of one part of speech for another" (260). Her examples – *function* as a verb and *unconscious* as a noun – are both of British origin.

Self-proclaimed purists still rail against the importation of American into British English. In 1979, in a House of Lords debate on English, a peer declared: "If there is a more hideous language on the face of the earth than the American form of English, I should like to know what it is!" (Hansard 1979, 164). In 1995, the Prince of Wales asserted: "We must act now to insure that English – and that, to my way of thinking, means English English – maintains its position as the world language well into the next century." That it might not do so, he fussed, would be the result of American English, a "very corrupting" influence; "we have to be a bit careful; otherwise the whole thing can get rather a mess" (*New York Times,* March 25, 1–24).

As the Prince's remarks show, despising Americanisms is still a lively part of British linguistic conversations, though the old self-assurance that was so satisfying to critics a century ago is much diminished. As eminent an authority as the retired editor of the *Supplement* to the *Oxford English Dictionary* has even declared that American has become "the dominant form of English" (Burchfield 1989, 67).

FURTHER READING

The collection of essays by Allen Walker Read (2001), *Milestones in the History of English in America,* includes selections devoted to the recognition and evaluation of American English in Britain. While the abridgment of H. L. Mencken's *The American Language* (ed. Raven I. McDavid, Jr., 1963) is commonly consulted, "The Two Streams of English" – the opening section of that book – should be read in full in both the 4th edition (1936) and *Supplement One* (1945). Primary material from early observers is published by M. M. Mathews in *The Beginnings of American English: Essays and*

Comments (1931). Additional and subsequent observations are discussed in *Images of English: A Cultural History of the Language* (1991) by Richard W. Bailey. National studies sometimes treat this subject either historically, as in *Yankees in Canada: A Collection of Nineteenth-Century Travel Narratives,* ed. James Doyle (1980), or linguistically, as in *Social and Regional Factors in Canadian English,* by Gaelan Dodds De Wolf (1992).

GLOSSARY OF LINGUISTIC TERMS

AAE See **African-American English**.

AAVE See **African-American Vernacular English**.

abbreviation A shortened form; sometimes equivalent to **clipped form**, sometimes restricted to a written shortening of a fully pronounced spoken form, such as *Dr.* for "doctor."

abstract noun A noun denoting a quality or concept rather than a physical object: *fear*, *idea*, contrasted with a **concrete noun**.

accent The sum of pronunciation characteristics that identify a particular regional or social dialect. Also **stress**.

acrolect A variety of a language with high prestige.

acronym A clipped form made from the initial letters of the parts of its etymon, sometimes equivalent to **initialism**, sometimes restricted to such a form pronounced by the usual rules of orthoepy, such as *scuba* 'self-contained underwater breathing apparatus' [ˈskubə].

ADS See **American Dialect Society**.

AE See **American English**.

affix A morpheme that occurs primarily not alone but with other morphemes, particularly a prefix or suffix.

affricate A stop with fricative release, such as [č], which can also be written [tʃ].

African-American; Afro-American A black American.

African-American English; AAE; Black English Any variety of English associated with Americans of black African ancestry.

African-American Vernacular English; AAVE Any vernacular variety of African-American English.

agreement See **concord**.

alienable possession The possession of something thought of as temporarily or not essentially belonging to the possessor: "her book," contrasted with **inalienable possession**.

allophone A speech sound (phone) considered as a member of a particular phoneme class, such as aspirated [tʰ] in *till* or unaspirated [t⁻] in *still*, members of the phoneme /t/ in complementary distribution with each other. Allophones are written between square brackets.

alveolar A consonant sound produced with the tongue tip on or near the alveolar ridge.

American Dialect Society; ADS The largest professional association for the study of dialects and other forms of language variation in the United States.

American English; AE The variety of English that developed on the North American continent.

Americanism An expression that originated in America, or an expression characteristic of American English. See also **diachronic Americanism** and **synchronic Americanism**.

American Name Society; ANS The largest interdisciplinary association of students of onomastics in the United States.

analogy A change in language in which the changed part is remodeled in imitation of some other part of the language.

anglicize To alter the pronunciation, spelling, morphology, etc. of a loanword on the model of native English use.

Anglo-Saxon; Old English Of the language and culture of the early speakers of English.

ANS See **American Name Society**.

antecedent A historical source, as "Scottish *pinkie* 'little finger' is the antecedent of the American term"; the noun to which a pronoun refers.

anterior A tense category referring to a past event prior to some other past event; past perfect.

antiphrasis A figure of speech using words ironically or humorously in a way opposite to their literal meaning (*bad* 'good').

antonomasia A figure of speech using a proper name as a common noun (*Romeo* 'a lover') or an epithet in place of a proper name (*the Bard* 'Shakespeare').

Appalachia See **South Midland**.

***a*-prefix** A prefix added to present participles in varieties of Southern English, as in *a-building* and *a-running*, historically derived from the prepositional prefix *on*, occurring also in *afire* and *aboard*.

argot A secret or indecipherable language of any group, especially criminals.

aspiration The production of an aspirate [h] sound, for example after initial voiceless stops before a stressed vowel as in *tea* [tʰi] or in the sequence spelled *wh* as in *whale* [hwel].

assimilation The process by which two items become more alike.

auxiliary A verb that combines with a main verb to make verb phrases, as in *could have been watching*. Auxiliaries are the three full verbs *be*, *do*, and *have* and the modals.

back Of vowels, produced with the high point of the tongue near the back of the mouth.

basilect A variety of a language with low prestige.

BBC English Received Pronunciation formerly associated with the British Broadcasting Corporation.

bilabial Produced with both lips.

bilingual Using two languages.

Black English See **African-American English**.

borrowing The process of imitating in one language the features of another language; a loanword.

Briticism An expression that originated in the British Isles after the separation of English into its two main national varieties of British and American English, or an expression characteristic of British English after that separation.

British English The variety of English that developed in the British Isles, particularly in comparison with American English after the beginning of the divergence between the two varieties.

broad *a* A low-central or back vowel [a] or [ɑ] as in Eastern New England or British *class* and *dance*, contrasted with the usual low-front [æ] in most American dialects.

broken English A register of English used by nonnative speakers who are learning or have imperfectly learned English.

burlesque metaphor A figure of speech using a comparison that is comic, exaggerated, grotesque, mocking, or ridiculing (*Arkansas toothpick* 'hunting knife').

Canadian English The variety of English that developed in Canada.

Canadian raising The pronunciation of the diphthongs /au/ and /ai/ with a higher first element, [ʌu] and [ʌɪ], before voiceless consonants, so that *bout* and *bowed* have noticeably different vowels.

cant Underworld slang; the jargon of a religious sect or an occupation; more generally, language that is trite, affected, sentimental, or insincere.

central Of vowels, produced with the high point of the tongue near the central part of the mouth.

Chancery English The variety of English used in the records of the Courts of Chancery in the fifteenth century, which became the basis of modern standard English in both the British Isles and America.

checked vowel A vowel that occurs only in a closed syllable, i.e. followed by a consonant, contrasted with a **free vowel**.

cleft sentence A sentence in which the meaning of a single clause has been divided into a main and a subordinate clause, with the principal meaning often in the subordinate clause for purposes of highlighting or focusing: "Our team won the game" can be clefted as "It was our team that won the game" or "It was the game that our team won." Pseudoclefting is of the type "What our team won was the game."

clipped form A word made by omitting part of its etymon.

close See **high**.

cluster A sequence of two or more consonants, like [str] in *strong* or [rts] in *hurts*.

collapse See **merger**.

collective noun A noun denoting a group: *club*, *team*, *staff*.

colloquial Of discourse, occurring more often in speech than in writing and in informal than in formal use.

colonial lag The supposed tendency for colonial varieties of a language to change less than the variety spoken in the mother country.

Colonial period The time in the history of American English between the first permanent English-speaking settlement in North America and the American Revolution, 1607–1776.

concord; agreement The overt linking of two forms to show shared grammatical categories, as subject-verb concord in "I see" / "She sees"; and modifier-noun concord in "this book" / "these books."

concrete noun A noun denoting a physical object: *eye*, *rock*, contrasted with an **abstract noun**.

consonant A speech sound produced with closure or some degree of constriction in the mouth and typically serving as the margin of a syllable.

contact language or **variety** A language or language variety used for interlingual communication, such as a pidgin.

contact relative clause A relative clause lacking a relative pronoun in subject function, as in "She is the one *came to see me*."

content or **wh- question** A question, typically beginning with an interrogative starting *wh*-, that requires an informational answer: "Who's there?" "Why do you ask?" Contrasted with a *yes/no* **question**.

content, lexical, or **full morpheme** or **word** A morpheme or word whose important function is to represent cognitive meaning, such as *laugh*, *moon*, *quick*, *tall*, and *type*, contrasted with **function morpheme**.

copula The verb *be* in its function of linking a subject and a subject complement, as in "She is a computer programmer."

creole A language that was originally a pidgin but has become the mother language of a speech community and consequently broadened its linguistic features and uses.

creole-origin hypothesis The proposal that African-American Vernacular English is a development of an earlier creole.

creolization The process of making a creole, as by converting a pidgin into a mother language of a community.

decreolization The process of assimilating a creole (or some creole feature) into a variety (or a feature) of the language that is the base of the creole.

dental A consonant sound produced with the tip of the tongue behind the upper teeth.

derivational morphology The formal changes that construct one word out of another: *skill, skillful, unskillful, unskillfulness.*

descriptivism An approach to usage study emphasizing observation, analysis, and description of the observed facts, contrasted with **prescriptivism**.

diachronic Historical, of the changes that affect a language system or units through time, contrasted with **synchronic**.

diachronic Americanism An expression that originated in America, whatever its subsequent history, such as *lengthy* and *OK*, which have spread throughout the English-speaking world.

dialect The language characteristics of a particular group of persons as contrasted with those of other groups using the same language.

dialectology The study of the dialects of a language.

digraph A sequence of two graphs functioning as a unit, such as *th* in English *thin* or *then*.

diphthong A vocalic nucleus consisting of two vowels, the second of which is typically an off-glide.

dissimilation The process by which two items become less alike.

distributive See **habitual**.

double negation See **multiple negation**.

dozens, playing the; sounding An African-American verbal game consisting of an exchange of escalating fictional insults about the opponent's female relatives (mother, sister, wife), ending when a participant runs out of insults, loses his temper, or resorts to truthful insults.

drawl A popular term for the impression of slow speech given in some varieties partly by the diphthongization of simple vowels, as in the Southern pronunciation of *head* as [hɛəd].

drift A gradual change over time, especially in a particular direction. See also **semantic drift**.

Dutch See **Pennsylvania Dutch**.

Ebonics One of several alternative names for **African-American English**.

elocution The art of effective public speaking.

elocutionist One who teaches elocution.

ESL English as a Second Language.

etymology The history of a linguistic form.

etymon (pl. **etyma**) The source form of a word in the same or a different language.

external history Changes in the communal lives of the speakers of a language that affect the language they speak.

eye dialect A nonstandard spelling suggesting dialect or uneducated use although it represents a standard pronunciation, such as "sez" for *says*.

family A set of related "sister" languages derived from the same "parent" whose "relationship" is shown by a "family tree" diagram. The metaphor is graphic and useful, but the analogy is imperfect.

flap A consonant sound produced by a quick flip of the tip of the tongue against the alveolar ridge, like the /t/ in *matter*.

folk etymology The modification of a form through a misinterpretation of its meaning or the misidentification of its etymon, for example *woodchuck* from Cree *wuchak* by association of the latter with English *wood* and *chuck*; a form so modified. There are also learned equivalents of folk etymology, such as *comptroller* from *controller* by association with Latin *computare*.

formal Of a stylistic variety characterized by conservative usage, full statement, dignified presentation, objectivity, and distance.

free vowel A vowel that can occur in an open syllable, i.e. not followed by a consonant, contrasted with a **checked vowel**.

fricative; spirant A consonant made by constricting the flow of air to produce an audible friction.

front Of vowels, produced with the high point of the tongue near the front of the mouth.

function morpheme or **word** A morpheme or word whose important function is to signal grammatical categories or relate constituents within a syntactic structure, such as *and*, *-ed*, *-ing*, *'s*, *the*, and *to*, contrasted with **content morpheme**.

general American This term is often avoided by American dialectologists because of its ambiguity and misleading implications. It is often misunderstood as denoting the American analog of **Received Pronunciation**, for which there is, in fact, no analog. It is sometimes used (though not generally by dialectologists) as a term for the variety otherwise called *Inland Northern*. It is also sometimes used to denote features of American English that are not regionally limited but are generally distributed over the land.

glide A semivowel, especially when pronounced as part of a diphthong.

glottal A consonant sound produced by constriction of the vocal cords.

grammar The syntax and inflectional morphology of a language; the features of a language that can be described by general rules.

graph A written symbol used in an orthography: "a" and "ɑ" are different graphs of the same grapheme.

grapheme A class of written symbols (graphs) that is the smallest functional unit in a system of orthography, such as a letter of the alphabet. Graphemes are written between angled brackets: <a>, <b>, <c>.

graphemic Of graphemes or spellings.

Great Vowel Shift A systematic change of the qualities of English long vowels mainly between the late Medieval and the earlier Modern English periods.

Gullah; Sea Island Creole An English-based creole with elements from various African languages, spoken by American blacks on the coast and off-shore islands of South Carolina, Georgia, and northeast Florida.

habitual; distributive Of verbs, an aspect denoting regularity, as in "He be there every day," contrasting with "He (is) there now."

high; close Of vowels, produced with the jaw relatively closed and the tongue near the roof of the mouth.

homophone One of two or more units identical in sound.

homophony Identity of sound.

hyperbole A figure of speech using words in a highly exaggerated sense (*annihilated* 'drunk').

idiolect The speech characteristics of a particular person as contrasted with those of other persons speaking the same language.

inalienable possession The possession of something thought of as a natural part of the possessor: "her eyes," contrasted with **alienable possession**.

Indo-European Of the language and culture from which developed many of the languages and cultures of Europe and South Asia; that language and culture; a speaker of that language.

inflection A morpheme added to the stem of a word to mark grammatical categories; the process of adding such morphemes.

inflectional morphology The formal changes words undergo to mark grammatical categories, such as noun number (*house/houses*), pronoun case (*he/him/his*), verb person, number, tense, and finiteness (*walk, walks, walked, walking*), and adjective comparison (*tall/taller/tallest*).

informal Of a stylistic variety characterized by liberal usage, condensed statement, relaxed presentation, subjectivity, and familiarity.

initialism A clipped form made from the initial letters of the parts of its etymon, sometimes equivalent to **acronym**, sometimes restricted to such a form pronounced with names of the letters of the alphabet, such as *SRO* 'standing room only' ['ɛs 'ɑr 'o].

interdental A consonant sound produced with the tip of the tongue between the upper and lower teeth or behind the teeth.

internal history Changes over time in the pronunciation, vocabulary, and grammar of a language.

International period The time in the history of American English after the beginning of the nation's active engagement as a world power.

intonation The pitch, stress, and timing patterns of a language variety.

invariant *be* The verb form *be* used in finite constructions without concord with its subject, as in "I be trying."

irrealis A category of verbs indicating a state of affairs that has not certainly taken place, as in "It will/could/might be."

isogloss A line on a dialect map that marks the extent of distribution of a regionally limited feature.

jargon The technical terminology and use of a particular group, like computer jargon or medical jargon; a pidgin, like Chinook Jargon, Delaware Jargon, Eskimo Jargon, or Mobilian Jargon; popularly and pejoratively, language that is confused and incomprehensible, strange and exotic, or obscure and pretentious.

jive Slang of African-American origin; hipster jargon; glib, deceptive talk.

juncture A perceived pause or boundary between segments of speech.

koine, koiné A language variety in one region that has become the common or standard variety in a larger area.

koinéization The process by which a regional variety becomes a koiné.

labial A consonant sound produced with the lips.

labiodental A consonant sound produced with the lower lip and upper teeth.

lateral A consonant made by air escaping from the mouth around one or both sides of the tongue, [l].

lax Of vowels, produced nearer the center of the mouth, with less muscular tension.

lect A language variety of any type.

leveling The reduction of two or more different morphological, especially inflectional, forms to one, as in the replacement of several Old English verbal forms (*singan, singe, singest, singath*) by one (*sing*).

lexicographer One who practices lexicography, a dictionary maker.

lexicography The recording of the vocabulary of a language, dictionary making.

lexicon The total stock of morphemes and set combinations of morphemes (idioms) of a language or variety; **vocabulary**.

lexifier A language that supplies the vocabulary of a creole.

lexify To supply vocabulary to a creole from another language (the lexifier).

ligature A linking of two graphs into a single unit, such as "æ" or German "ß" for *ss*.

lingua franca An auxiliary language used for communication between speakers of different languages.

linguistic atlas A work that displays linguistic variants on maps or in some other format that relates them to geographical areas or other social parameters.

Linguistic Society of America; LSA The largest professional association of linguistic scholars in the United States.

linking *r* The sound [r], which would otherwise be nonrhotic, when pronounced between vowels, as in "mother and father" /mʌðər ənd fɑðə/. When linking *r* is nonhistorical, as in "Cuba is" /kyubər ɪz/, it is called intrusive *r*.

literary dialect A convention of nonstandard spellings, vocabulary, and grammar used in literary works to suggest an actual dialect.

loanword; loan A word of one language imitated in another language.

long Of vowels, historically pronounced with greater duration and sometimes by extension the tense or diphthongal development of such a vowel, for example, Middle English *ō* [oː], which became Modern English [ʊu].

low; open Of vowels, produced with the jaw open and the tongue relatively far from the roof of the mouth.

LSA See **Linguistic Society of America.**

macrolinguistics The study of the place of a language within its larger cultural context.

mandative The construction of a verb, adjective, or noun denoting necessity or requirement and followed by a clause whose verb may be variably a modal, indicative, or present subjunctive, according to the language variety: "We ask that he should agree / agree / agrees."

Maritime Pidgin English A language variety used by English seamen and the populations with whom they communicated.

marked Having an overt signal of a grammatical or lexical category, as "*Books* is marked as plural."

marker An overt signal of a grammatical or lexical category, especially a morpheme (such as the **possessive marker**) but also stress, intonation, or word order.

meaning That which is conveyed or is intended to be conveyed by language.

medial Occurring in the middle part of a word, as /k/ is the medial sound in *baker.*

meiosis A figure of speech using words that are understated or disparaging (*tin can* 'naval destroyer').

merger; collapse The loss of distinction between two linguistic units, especially phonemes, such as the merger of the vowels of *cot* and *caught* in the speech of some Americans; the opposite of **split.**

mesolect A variety of a language with middling prestige.

metaphor A figure of speech using an expression that implicitly compares one thing to another because of a perceived similarity between them (*bread* 'money').

metonymy A figure of speech using a word for a thing of which the word literally denotes an associated thing or characteristic (*suit* 'business executive').

microlinguistics The study of the system of a language and its units (sounds, morphemes, constructions).

mid Of vowels, produced with the jaw and the tongue in an intermediary position between those for high and low vowels.

Midland One of the principal dialect regions of American English, consisting of two major subregions: **North Midland** and **South Midland**.

MLA See **Modern Language Association**.

modal verb An auxiliary verb without inflection for person, indicating categories of mood or tense: *will, would, shall, should, can, could, may, might, must, ought to,* and in some uses *need* and *dare.*

Modern Language Association of America; MLA The largest professional association of language and literature teachers and scholars in the United States.

monolingual Using only one language.

monophthong A vocalic nucleus consisting of a single vowel, such as the Southern pronunciation of *nice* as [na:s].

morpheme A class of the smallest meaningful sequence of sounds, as *backwoodsiness* is constructed of five morphemes: {back} + {wood} + {s} + {y} + {ness}, in a hierarchical relationship. Morphemes are written between curly brackets.

morpheme boundary The point preceding the first sound of a morpheme or following its last sound.

morphology The system of variations in the form of a word to mark either grammatical categories (inflectional morphology), as in *song/songs,* or semantically related words (derivational morphology), as in *glee/ gleeful/gleefully/gleefulness.*

morphosyntax Inflectional morphology and syntax, grammar.

multiple modals The use of two or rarely more modals in the same verb phrase: *may can, might should ought to.*

multiple negation The occurrence of two (double) or more negative signals within the same grammatical scope, as in "I ain't never had no trouble with none of them."

narrative *eh?* The particle *eh* used in Canadian English as a marker of narrative segments: "That was when we almost intercepted a pass, eh? and Stu Falkner bumped into him, eh?"

narrow-scope Of negation, applying to only a limited construction, such as a noun phrase, like *no* in "I see no possibility."

nasal A sound made by allowing air to come out through the nose and, for consonants, by stopping the air at some point in the mouth.

National Council of Teachers of English; NCTE The largest professional association of teachers of English on all educational levels in the United States.

National period The time in the history of American English between the establishment of an independent country and the beginning of its international involvement, 1776–1898.

national variety The language characteristics of a particular nation (independent political entity) as contrasted with those of other nations using the same language.

NCTE See **National Council of Teachers of English**.

negative concord The requirement of negative marking of all morphemes capable of it within the domain of a wide-scope negative. Such concord was normal in earlier English, as in Chaucer's description of the Knight in the "General Prologue" of *The Canterbury Tales* (70–1): "He nevere yet no vileynye ne sayde / In al his lyf unto no maner wight" 'He never yet didn't say no villainous thing in all his life to no sort of person.' It survives only in nonstandard use as **multiple negation**.

negative inversion The shifting to initial position of a wide-scope negative marker, as in "Didn't nobody see him."

neologism A word or use introduced recently.

New England short *o* A lax monophthongal vowel occurring in parts of New England in words like *road, home, stone,* and *boat.*

Newfoundland English The variety of English that developed in Newfoundland and neighboring Labrador.

nonrhotacism The omission or conversion to a vocalic element of historical [r], particularly between a vowel and a consonant or pause.

nonrhotic Characterized by nonrhotacism.

nonstandard In language, of a variety or of characteristics restricted to a particular region or social group, used by speakers of low prestige, or not regarded as a norm.

Northern; the North One of the principal dialect regions of American English, consisting of New England, New York State, westward through northern Ohio, Indiana, and Illinois, and Michigan, Wisconsin, Minnesota, Iowa, the Dakotas.

North Midland One of the two major subdivisions of the Midland dialect, extending from western Pennsylvania through Ohio, Indiana, Illinois, Missouri, and Kansas.

nucleus The vocalic center of a syllable or of a diphthong.

obstruent A stop or fricative.

off-glide The second, subordinate element of a diphthong, such as the [ɪ] of [aɪ] and [ɔɪ] and the [ʊ] of [aʊ] in *buy, boy,* and *bough,* respectively.

Old English See **Anglo-Saxon**.

onomatopoeia A figure of speech using words whose sound suggests the metaphorical tenor (*buzz* 'telephone call').

onset The beginning part of a phonological element, such as a syllable or diphthong.

open See **low**.

open *o* The vowel [ɔ].

orthoepist One who studies orthoepy.

orthoepy The system of pronouncing the orthography of a language; the study of that system.

orthography The system of recording a spoken language in writing; the study of that system; spelling.

Oxford English Received Pronunciation associated with the old universities, especially Oxford.

palatal A sound produced with the blade of the tongue on or near the hard palate.

paradigm A set of related inflectional (or less usually derivational) forms, used, when regular, as a model for the construction of other sets and, when irregular, to display the variations from the pattern. Examples are the conjugation of verbs (*sing, sings, sang, sung, singing*), the declension of pronouns and nouns (*we, us, our, ours, ourselves; book, books*), and the comparison of adjectives (*cool, cooler, coolest*).

Pennsylvania Dutch The language spoken by German settlers in Pennsylvania; the settlers themselves (an anglicization of *Deutsch*).

perfect A tense category referring to a past event with continuing relevance to the present.

periphrastic *do* The auxiliary verb *do* used in questions, negatives, and emphatic assertions: "Do you see?" "I don't see." "Now I dó see."

personification A figure of speech using words that represent the metaphorical tenor as a person (*Uncle Sam* 'the United States government').

phatic communion Language used, not for its cognitive content, but for the purpose of establishing social contact and promoting cooperative interaction.

phone A sound used in speech. Phones are written between square brackets.

phoneme A class of speech sounds (**phones**) that, contrasted with other such classes, is capable of making a difference in meaning, such as /t/ contrasted with /d/ in *at* and *ad*. Phonemes are written between virgules (slashes).

phonemic Of phonemes, pertaining to the distinctive sounds of a language.

509

phonetic Of phones, pertaining to speech sounds.

phonology The sound system of a language; its study.

pidgin A language that is a mixture of features from two other languages, used by speakers of those languages to communicate with each other, not the native language of anyone, and having restricted grammatical structure, vocabulary, stylistic ranges, and applications.

pitch The perceived degree of highness of the voice, especially in describing the intonation patterns of utterances.

plosive See **stop**.

positive *anymore* The use of *anymore* 'nowadays' in an affirmative statement: "They all say that anymore."

possessive marker A signal of the genitive relationship, specifically the morpheme usually spelled *'s*.

postvocalic /r/ The sound spelled *r*, historically expected between a vowel and a consonant or pause.

pragmatics The relationship of language to its uses, especially the choices to be made for styles, registers, and rhetorical purposes, also **usage**; the study of that relationship.

predication; predicate One of the two major constituents of a clause, that which makes a statement about the **subject**.

prefix An affix that occurs at the front part of a word, like *co-* in *cooperate*.

prescriptivism An approach to usage study emphasizing the identification of what is appropriate or correct with respect to options, contrasted with **descriptivism**.

principal parts Of a verb, the basic forms from which other forms can be predicted, specifically for most verbs in the historical strong class, the infinitive, preterit, and past participle (*sing, sang, sung*).

pronunciation The manner of producing the sounds of a language by the vocal organs.

pseudocleft sentence See **cleft sentence**.

Public School English Received Pronunciation associated with the English public schools such as Eton, Harrow, and Westminster.

pull-chain Of the tendency of a particular change in language to cause other changes by creating a "hole" in the system that consequent changes fill.

push-chain Of the tendency of a particular change in language to cause other changes by "crowding" a part of a system that consequent changes expand.

quotative *go* The use of *go* in the sense 'say': "He sits down and goes, 'What now?'"

rapping An African-American style of fast, witty talk intended to impress the addressee.

realis A category of verbs indicating a state of affairs that has taken place, as in "It is/was/has been."

Received Pronunciation; RP The prestigious accent of standard British English.

reconstruction The postulation of a hypothetical historical form or use on the basis of compared forms or uses attested in related languages (comparative reconstruction) or within a single language (internal reconstruction); a form or use so postulated. Reconstructed forms or uses are indicated by a preceding asterisk: pre-Old English *manniz 'men.'

reflexive pronoun A pronoun ending in *-self* or *-selves* that refers back to the subject of its clause, as in "They surprised even themselves."

regional dialect A variety of a language associated with a particular geographical area.

regionalism A linguistic form or use restricted to or characteristic of a particular geographical region.

register A variety of language according to the situation of its use, for example, church ritual, computer manuals, or restaurant menus.

relic Of a form that is obsolescent or obsolete in the standard language but survives in a nonstandard dialect.

remote phase A tense category referring to an event in the distant past with continuing relevance to the present.

resonant Any nonobstruent: a vowel, semivowel, lateral, or nasal.

retroflex Of a sound, produced with the tip of the tongue bent back.

r-fulness See **rhotacism**.

rhotacism The pronunciation of [r] where it is historically expected and is represented in the orthography, particularly between a vowel and a consonant or pause.

rhotic Characterized by rhotacism.

r-lessness See **nonrhotacism**.

rounded Of a sound, especially a vowel, produced with the lips pursed and the space between them more or less round in shape.

RP See **Received Pronunciation**.

Scotch-Irish The Protestant population of Ulster, mainly of Lowland Scottish origin, but more generally including northern British; their language variety.

Sea Island Creole See **Gullah**.

segmental Of the consonant and vowel units of a language, in contrast with **suprasegmental**.

semantic drift The process of a gradual change in meaning of a form by which it eventually comes to mean something quite different from its earlier sense, for example, the first name of *Guy* Fawkes, executed for his part in the Gunpowder Plot, was used for a grotesque effigy, then a man of grotesque appearance, next any man or fellow, and recently any person, male or female (as in the second-person plural pronoun substitute *you guys*).

semantics The study of meaning.

semivowel A speech sound made like a vowel but functioning like a consonant, [y], [w], and [r].

sense The meaning of a **morpheme** or a combination of morphemes.

shift A change of sounds, especially affecting a system, like the early Modern English Great Vowel Shift and the First Germanic Consonant Shift (or Grimm's Law).

Ship English A variety of English recorded in logbooks and other records of transatlantic vessels.

short Of vowels, historically pronounced with lesser duration and sometimes by extension the lax development of such a vowel, for example, Middle English *ŏ* [ɒ], Modern English [ɒ] or [ɑ].

sibilant A fricative made with the sides of the tongue higher than its center, creating a grooved channel that produces a hissing-like effect.

signifying An African-American style of ironic, figurative, rhythmic talk intended to put down someone or score points of one-upmanship.

sign language A system of communication by hand gestures used, for example by the deaf or for purposes of interlingual communication, such as Plains Sign Language.

slang An informal, nonstandard, nontechnical vocabulary of novel-sounding synonyms for standard words, associated with youthful, raffish, or undignified speakers, implying impertinence or disrespect for the established culture.

smart talk An African-American style of speech intended to impress the addressee.

social dialect A variety of a language associated with a particular social group or class. Principal broad social dialect groups of American English are Anglo (of European extraction), Black (of African extraction), and Hispanic (of Central American and Caribbean extraction).

sociolinguistics The relationship between language and society; the study of that relationship.

sounding See **dozens, playing the**.

Southern; the South One of the principal dialect regions of American English, also called Lower South, consisting of the Atlantic coastal areas from Virginia to Georgia and the Gulf Coastal areas from West Florida to Texas.

South Midland One of the two major subdivisions of the Midland dialect, sometimes analyzed as a subregion of the South, also called **Upper South** or **Appalachia**, consisting of the interior mountainous regions of Virginia, West Virginia, the Carolinas, and Georgia, and westward through Tennessee, Kentucky, northern Alabama, Mississippi, and Louisiana, southern Missouri, Arkansas, and east Texas.

Spanglish A mixture of Spanish and English uses.

speech community A group of persons who talk together in the same language or language variety.

spelling pronunciation An untraditional pronunciation based on the spelling of a word, like ['for,hɛd] instead of historical ['fɔrɪd] for *forehead*.

spelling reform A proposal to change the details, application, or system of an orthography, usually to bring it into closer alignment with pronunciation or international usage.

spirant See **fricative**.

split The introduction of a distinction between two linguistic units, especially phonemes, such as the split of Middle English /n/ (with allophones [n] and [ŋ] into Modern English /n/ and /ŋ/).

spread See **unrounded**.

stage dialect A synthetic dialect used in play performances to suggest an actual dialect.

standard In language, of a variety or of characteristics that are widely used by influential members of a speech community and are regarded as a norm.

stock A set of languages descended from a common source, generally larger than a family of languages and sometimes including several families.

stop; plosive A consonant made by complete blockage of the flow of air.

stress The prominence of a syllable or word perceived as loudness of utterance.

style The choices to be made by a user according to the relations among the participants in a language event and the register, especially degrees of formality.

subject One of the two major constituents of a clause, that about which the **predication** (or predicate) makes a statement.

substandard In language, of a nonstandard variety with low prestige.

substrate; substratum A language variety that influences a dominant language variety.

suffix An affix that occurs at the back part of a word, like -*ive* in *operative*.

suprasegmental Of the intonational units of a language, in contrast with **segmental**.

synchronic Of a system or units existing at a particular point in time, contrasted with **diachronic**.

synchronic Americanism An expression characteristic of American English, in contrast with standard British English, whatever its origin or earlier history, such as *fall* 'autumn' and the pronunciation of *path*, etc. with [æ].

synecdoche A figure of speech using words that represent a part by the whole, the whole by a part, a species by the genus, the genus by a species, or a thing by the material of which it is made (*wheels* 'automobile').

syntax The system that combines words and morphemes into such structures as phrases and clauses.

tag question A short expression at the end of a statement converting it into a question: "You understand, *don't you?*" or similarly "*right?*" and "*eh?*"

tall talk A style of discourse associated with the West and characterized by extreme exaggeration, boasting, far-fetched metaphors, long words, and boisterousness.

tautosyllabic Occurring in the same syllable.

tense Of vowels, produced near extreme positions of the mouth, with greater muscular tension.

toast An African-American street-culture tall tale celebrating heroes of the underclass who outwit the powerful.

toponym The name of a place, proper or generic.

transplantation The introduction of a language from one region to another. The language so introduced is called "transplanted," but the metaphor ceases to be appropriate after the language has taken root in the new region.

unmarked Lacking an overt signal of a grammatical or lexical category, as "*Sheep* is unmarked as plural."

unrounded; spread Of a sound, especially vowels, produced with the corners of the lips drawn back and the space between them more or less of a slit shape.

unstressed Lacking the prominence of stress.

514

unvoiced See **voiceless**.

Upper South See **South Midland**.

Urheimat The original homeland of the Indo-Europeans.

usage The speech and writing patterns of a linguistic community, and the responses of members of that community to choices between options among those patterns; the study of those patterns and responses; **pragmatics**.

velar A sound produced with the back of the tongue on or near the velum or soft palate.

vernacular A nonstandard, regional, or informal spoken variety of a language.

vocabulary The stock of words in a language; **lexicon**.

vocalize To change a consonant into a vowel, as some dialects vocalize postvocalic [r] to [ə] in *dear* [diə].

voiced Of speech sounds, produced with vibration of the vocal cords and a consequent auditory buzz.

voiceless; unvoiced Of speech sounds, produced without vibration of the vocal cords and lacking the auditory buzz of voice.

vowel A speech sound produced without constriction in the mouth and typically serving as the center of a syllable.

vulgate The speech of ordinary and especially uneducated people.

Western; the West One of the principal dialect regions of American English, extending from the Mississippi Valley westward across the Great Plains and Rocky Mountains to the Pacific Coast.

wide-scope Of negation, applying outside the construction of which it is an immediate constituent, such as the contracted negative in "I don't see any possibility," whose scope requires *any* rather than *some* in the object noun phrase.

word geography A description of dialect boundaries based on vocabulary differences.

yes/no **question** A question that requires *yes* or *no* as an answer: "Did you hear that?" Contrasted with a **content question**.

yod glide The semivowel [y].

zero The lack of a formal signal for a linguistic category, sometimes represented by a zero symbol (∅), as in the plural of *deer* as *deer-∅* or the past tense of *put* as *put-∅*.

BIBLIOGRAPHY

Abbott, Orville Lawrence. 1957. "The Preterit and Past Participle of Strong Verbs in Seventeenth-Century American English." *American Speech* 32: 31–42.

Abstract Census and Return of the Population. &c. of Newfoundland 1857. 1858. Appendix. *Journal of the House of Assembly for the Year 1858.* Saint John's: E. D. Shea.

Adam, Lucien. 1883. *Les idiomes négro-aryens et malayo-aryens: essai d'hybridélogie linguistique.* Paris: Maisonneuve.

Adams, Michael. 2000. "Lexical Doppelgängers." *Journal of English Linguistics* 28: 295–310.

Adams, Thomas R. 1992. Introduction to the facsimile of *The History of Travayle in the VVest and East Indies* (1577). Delmar, NY: Scholar's Facsimiles and Reprints.

Ade, George. 1960. *The America of George Ade (1866–1944): Fables, Short Stories, Essays.* Ed. Jean Shepherd. New York: Putnam's.

AHD = American Heritage Dictionary. AHD1, see Morris 1969. *AHD2,* see Morris 1982. *AHD3,* see Soukhanov 1992.

Alexander, Edward P. 1971. "An Indian Vocabulary from Fort Christanna, 1716." *Virginia Magazine of History and Biography* 79: 303–13.

Alexander, Henry. 1925. "Early American Pronunciation and Syntax." *American Speech* 1: 141–8.

—— 1928. "The Language of the Salem Witchcraft Trials." *American Speech* 3: 390–400.

Alford, Henry. 1864. *A Plea for the Queen's English: Stray Notes on Speaking and Spelling.* Reprint of 2nd London ed. New York: Dick and Fitzgerald.

Algeo, John. 1986. "The Two Streams: British and American English." *Journal of English Linguistics* 19: 269–84.

—— 1988a. "British and American Grammatical Differences." *International Journal of Lexicography* 1: 1–31.

—— 1988b. "The English Language: Variation, the Dictionary, and the User." In *Webster's New World Dictionary of American English,* 3rd college ed., ed. Victoria Neufeldt, xvii–xxiv. New York: Webster's New World.

1989a. "Americanisms, Briticisms, and the Standard: An Essay at Definition." In *Standardizing English: Essays in the History of Language Change in Honor of John Hurt Fisher*, ed. Joseph B. Trahern, Jr., 139–57. Knoxville: University of Tennessee Press.

1989b. "British-American Lexical Differences: A Typology of Interdialectal Variation." In *English across Cultures; Cultures across English: A Reader in Cross-cultural Communication*, ed. Ofelia García and Ricardo Otheguy, 219–41. Berlin: Mouton de Gruyter.

1990. "American and British English: Odi et Amo." In *Papers from the 5th International Conference on English Historical Linguistics, Cambridge, 6–9 April 1987*, ed. Sylvia Adamson, Vivien Law, Nigel Vincent, and Susan Wright, 13–29. Amsterdam: Benjamins.

1990–5. "The Briticisms Are Coming! How British English Is Creeping into the American Language." *Journal of English Linguistics* 23: 123–40.

1991. "Language." In *The Reader's Companion to American History*, ed. Eric Foner and John A. Garraty, 637–40. Boston: Houghton Mifflin.

1992a. "British and American Mandative Constructions." In *Language and Civilization*, ed. Claudia Blank, 2: 599–617. Frankfurt-on-Main: Peter Lang.

1992b. "What Is a Briticism?" In *Old English and New: Studies in Language and Linguistics in Honor of Frederic G. Cassidy*, ed. Joan H. Hall, Nick Doane, and Dick Ringler, 287–304. New York: Garland 1992.

1995. "The American Language and Its British Dialect." *SECOL Review* 19: 114–25.

1996. "American and British Words." In *Words: Proceedings of an International Symposium, Lund 25–26 August 1995, organized under the auspices of the Royal Academy of Letters, History and Antiquities and sponsored by the Foundation Natur och Kultur*, ed. Jan Svartvik, 145–58. Stockholm: Kungl. Vitterhets Historie och Antikvitets Akademien.

Algeo, John, and Adele S. Algeo. 1991. *Fifty Years among the New Words: A Dictionary of Neologisms, 1941–1991*. Cambridge University Press.

1993. "Among the New Words." *American Speech* 68: 253–62.

Allen, Edward A. 1887. "English Grammar, Viewed from All Sides." *Education* 7: 460–9.

Allen, Grant. 1888. "The Great American Language." *Cornhill Magazine* 58: 363–77.

Allen, Harold B. 1962. "Webster's Third New International Dictionary: A Symposium," ed. R. G. Gunderson. *Quarterly Journal of Speech* 48: 431–40.

1973–6. *The Linguistic Atlas of the Upper Midwest*. 3 vols. Minneapolis: University of Minnesota Press.

1977. "Regional Dialects, 1945–1974." *American Speech* 52: 163–261.

Allen, Irving Lewis. 1994. "Slang: Sociology." In *The Encyclopedia of Language and Linguistics*, ed. R. E. Asher and J. M. Y. Simpson, 7: 3960–4. 10 vols. Oxford: Pergamon Press.

Alston, Robin Carfrae. 1968. Note in the front matter of the Scolar Press facsimile of Lindley Murray's *English Grammar* (1795). Menston: Scolar.

Amastae, Jon, and Lucia Elias-Olivares, eds. 1982. *Spanish in the United States: Sociolinguistic Aspects*. Cambridge University Press.

The American Heritage Book of English Usage. 1996. Boston: Houghton Mifflin.

American Heritage Dictionary. See Morris 1969, 1982, Soukhanov 1992.

American Speech. 1925–.

Ames, Susie M. 1957. *Reading, Writing and Arithmetic in Virginia, 1607–1699*. Williamsburg, VA: Virginia 350th Anniversary Celebration Corporation.

Andersson, Lars-Gunnar, and Peter Trudgill. 1990. *Bad Language*. Oxford: Basil Blackwell.

Arber, Edward. 1885. *The First Three English Books on America*. Birmingham: Edward Arber.

——— 1910. ed. *Travel and Works of Captain John Smith*. 2 vols. Edinburgh: John Grant.

"The Argot of Vaudeville." 1917. *New York Times* (Dec. 16), 4–7.

Ash, John. 1763. *Grammatical Institutes*. 4th ed. London. Reprint English Linguistics 1500–1800, no. 9. Leeds: Scolar, 1967.

Atwood, E. Bagby. 1953. *A Survey of Verb Forms in the Eastern United States*. Ann Arbor: University of Michigan Press.

Avis, Walter Spencer, ed. 1967. *A Dictionary of Canadianisms on Historical Principles*. Toronto: Gage.

——— 1972. "So *Eh?* Is Canadian, Eh?" *Canadian Journal of Linguistics / La revue canadienne de linguistique* 17: 89–104.

——— 1978. "Canadian English in Its North American Context." In *Walter S. Avis: Essays and Articles*, ed. Thomas Vincent, George Parker, and Stephen Bonnycastle, 25–49. Kingston, ON: Royal Military College of Canada.

Avis, Walter Spencer, and A. Murray Kinloch. 1979. *Writings on Canadian English 1792–1975: An Annotated Bibliography*. Toronto: Fitzhenry and Whiteside.

Ayres, Alfred. 1881. *The Verbalist: A Manual Devoted to Brief Discussions of the Right and the Wrong Use of Words and to Some Other Matters of Interest to Those Who Would Speak and Write with Propriety*. Rev. ed. New York: Appleton, 1897.

Babbitt, Eugene Howard. 1900. "College Words and Phrases." *Dialect Notes* 2: 3–70.

Bache, Richard Meade. 1869. *Vulgarisms and Other Errors of Speech*. Philadelphia: Claxton, Remsen, and Haffelfinger.

Bähr, Dieter. 1977. *A Bibliography of Writings on the English Language in Canada from 1857 to 1976*. Anglistische Forschungen 116. Heidelberg: Carl Winter.

Bailey, Beryl. 1965. "Toward a New Perspective in Negro English Dialectology." *American Speech* 40: 171–7.

——— 1966. *Jamaican Creole Syntax: A Transformational Approach*. Cambridge University Press.

Bailey, Guy. 1997. "When Did Southern American English Begin?" In *Englishes around the World I*, ed. Edgar W. Schneider, 255–75. Amsterdam: Benjamins.

Bailey, Guy, and Marvin Bassett. 1986. "Invariant *Be* in the Lower South." In *Language Variety in the South: Perspectives in Black and White*, ed. Michael Montgomery and Guy Bailey, 158–79. Tuscaloosa: University of Alabama Press.

Bailey, Guy, and Natalie Maynor. 1985. "The Present Tense of *Be* in White Folk Speech of the Southern United States." *English World-Wide* 6: 199–216.

1987. "Decreolization?" *Language in Society* 16: 449–73.

Bailey, Guy, Natalie Maynor, and Patricia Cukor-Avila. 1989. "Variation in Subject-Verb Concord in Early Modern English." *Language Variation and Change* 1: 285–300.

Bailey, Guy, and Gary Ross. 1988. "The Shape of the Superstrate: Morphosyntactic Features of Ship English." *English World-Wide* 9: 193–212.

Bailey, Nathan. 1730. *Dictionarium Britannicum*. London: J. Cox.

Bailey, Richard W. 1982. "The English Language in Canada." In *English as a World Language*, ed. Richard W. Bailey and Manfred Görlach, 134–76. Ann Arbor: University of Michigan Press.

1991a. *Images of English: A Cultural History of the Language*. Ann Arbor: University of Michigan Press.

1991b. "Scots and Scotticisms: Language and Ideology." *Studies in Scottish Literature* 26: 65–77.

1992. "The First North American Dialect Survey." In *Old English and New: Studies in Language and Linguistics in Honor of Frederic G. Cassidy*, ed. Joan H. Hall, Nick Doane, and Dick Ringler, 305–26. New York: Garland.

1996. *Nineteenth-Century English*. Ann Arbor: University of Michigan Press.

Bailyn, Bernard. 1986a. *The Peopling of British North America: An Introduction*. New York: Random House.

1986b. *Voyagers to the West: A Passage in the Peopling of America on the Eve of the Revolution*. New York: Knopf.

Baissac, Charles. 1880. *Etude sur le patois créole mauricien*. Geneva: Slatkine.

Baker, Sheridan. 1965. "The Art and Science of Letters: *Webster's Third New International Dictionary*." *Papers of the Michigan Academy of Science, Arts, and Letters* 50: 521–34.

Bakker, Pieter J. 1992. "'A Language of Our Own': The Genesis of Michif, the Mixed Cree-French Language of the Canadian Métis." Ph.D. diss., University of Amsterdam.

Barber, Giles. 1976. "Books from the Old World and for the New: The British International Trade in Books in the Eighteenth Century." *Studies on Voltaire and the Eighteenth Century* 151: 185–224.

Barber, Katherine, ed. 1998. *The Canadian Oxford Dictionary*. Toronto: Oxford University Press.

Barnhart, David K., and Allan A. Metcalf. 1997. *America in So Many Words*. Boston: Houghton Mifflin.

Barnhill, Viron L., and George F. Reinecke. 1989. "Indian Trade Languages." In

Encyclopedia of Southern Culture, ed. Charles R. Wilson and William Ferris, 787–8. Chapel Hill: University of North Carolina Press.

Baron, Dennis. 1982. *Grammar and Good Taste: Reforming the American Language*. New Haven: Yale University Press.

Barrère, Albert, and Charles G. Leland. 1897. *A Dictionary of Slang, Jargon and Cant*. 2 vols. London: George Bell & Sons.

Bartelt, Guillermo. 1991. "American Indian English: A Phylogenetic Dilemma." In *Development and Structures of Creole Languages: Essays in Honor of Derek Bickerton*, ed. Francis Byrne and Thom Huebner, 29–39. Amsterdam: John Benjamins.

Bartlett, John Russell. 1848. *A Dictionary of Americanisms: A Glossary of Words and Phrases Usually Regarded as Peculiar to the United States*. New York: Bartlett and Welford. 2nd ed., Boston: Little, Brown; London: Trübner, 1859; 3rd ed., 1860; 4th ed., 1877.

Barzun, Jacques. 1959. *The House of Intellect*. New York: Harper and Row.

1963. "What Is a Dictionary?" *American Scholar* 32: 176–81.

Baugh, Albert C., and Thomas Cable. 1993. *A History of the English Language*. 4th ed. Englewood Cliffs, NJ: Prentice-Hall.

Baugh, John. 1980. "A Reexamination of the Black English Copula." In *Locating Language in Time and Space*, ed. William Labov, 83–106. New York: Academic Press.

1983. *Black Street Speech: Its History, Structure, and Survival*. Austin: University of Texas Press.

1984. "Steady: Progressive Aspect in Black Vernacular English." *American Speech* 59: 3–12.

1991. "The Politicization of Changing Terms of Self-Reference among American Slave Descendants." *American Speech* 66: 133–46.

2000. *Beyond Ebonics: Linguistic Pride and Racial Prejudice*. Oxford University Press.

Bayard, Donn. 1989. "'Me Say That? No Way!': The Social Correlates of American Lexical Diffusion in New Zealand English." *Te Reo: Journal of the Linguistic Society of New Zealand* 32: 17–60.

Bee, Jon [pseudonym of John Badcock]. 1823. *Slang*. London: T. Hughes.

Bell, Allan. 1982. "'This Isn't the BBC': Colonialism in New Zealand English." *Applied Linguistics* 3: 246–58.

1988. "The British Base and the American Connection in New Zealand Media English." *American Speech* 63: 326–44.

Bellamann, Henry. 1929. "Robots of Language." *Yale Review* 19: 212–14.

Bennett, Jacob. 1985. "The Folk Speech of Maine: Clues to Colonial English." In *American Speech: 1600 to the Present*, ed. Peter Benes, 27–34. Boston University.

Bennett, John. 1908–9. "Gullah: A Negro Patois." *South Atlantic Quarterly* 7: 332–47, 8: 39–52.

Bernstein, Cynthia, Tom Nunnally, and Robin Sabino, eds. 1997. *Language Variety in the South Revisited*. Tuscaloosa: University of Alabama Press.

Bernstein, Theodore. 1965. *The Careful Writer: A Modern Guide to English Usage*. New York: Atheneum.

Berrey, Lester V. 1940. "Southern Mountain Dialect." *American Speech* 15: 45–54.

Berrey, Lester V., and Melvin Van den Bark. 1942. *The American Thesaurus of Slang*. New York: Crowell. Supplemented ed., 1947; 2nd ed., 1952.

Berthoff, Roland. 1980. "Welsh." In *Harvard Encyclopedia of American Ethnic Groups*, ed. Stephen Thernstrom, 1012–17. Cambridge, MA: Harvard University Press.

Bex, Tony, and Richard J. Watts. 1999. *Standard English: The Widening Debate*. London: Routledge.

Bickerton, Derek. 1973. "On the Nature of a Creole Continuum." *Language* 49: 640–69.

Bickerton, Derek, and William H. Wilson. 1987. "Pidgin Hawaiian." In *Pidgin and Creole Languages: Essays in Memory of John E. Reinecke*, ed. Glenn G. Gilbert, 61–76. Honolulu: University of Hawaii Press.

Bigelow, Gordon E. 1955. "More Evidence of Early Loss of [r] in Eastern American Speech." *American Speech* 30: 154–6.

Bishop, Morris. 1969. "Good Usage, Bad Usage, and Usage." In *The American Heritage Dictionary of the English Language*, ed. William Morris, xxi–xxiv. Boston: American Heritage and Houghton Mifflin.

Blair, Hugh. 1783. *Lectures on Rhetoric and Belles Lettres*. Ed. Harold F. Harding. Carbondale: Southern Illinois University Press, 1965.

Blake, Norman. 1981. *Non-standard Language in English Literature*. London: Andre Deutsch.

Bliss, Alan J., ed. 1979. *Spoken English in Ireland, 1660–1740: Twenty-Seven Representative Texts Assembled and Analysed*. Dublin: Cadenus.

1984. "English in the South of Ireland." In *Language in the British Isles*, ed. Peter Trudgill, 135–51. Cambridge University Press.

Bloomfield, Leonard. 1914. *An Introduction to the Study of Language*. New York: Holt.

1925. "Why a Linguistic Society?" *Language* 1: 1–5.

1927. "Literate and Illiterate Speech." *American Speech* 2: 432–8.

1944. "Secondary and Tertiary Responses to Language." *Language* 20: 44–55.

Bloomfield, Morton. 1948. "Canadian English and Its Relation to Eighteenth Century American Speech." *Journal of English and Germanic Philology* 47: 59–66.

1953. "The Problem of Fact and Value in the Teaching of English." *College English* 15: 33–7.

Bolton, Whitney French, ed. 1966. *The English Language: Essays by English and American Men of Letters 1490–1839*. Cambridge University Press.

Bolton, Whitney French, and David Crystal, eds. 1969. *The English Language*. Vol. 2, *Essays by Linguists and Men of Letters 1858–1964*. Cambridge University Press.

Boorstin, Daniel J. 1958. *The Americans: The Colonial Experience*. New York: Random House.

1965. *The Americans: The National Experience*. New York: Random House.

1973. *The Americans: The Democratic Experience*. New York: Random House.

Botein, Stephen. 1983. "The Anglo-American Book Trade before 1776: Personnel and Strategies." In *Printing and Society in Early America*, ed. William L. Joyce, David D. Hall, Richard D. Brown, and John B. Hench, 48–82. Worcester, MA: American Antiquarian Society.

Boykin, Edward, ed. 1957. *Victoria, Albert, and Mrs. Stevenson*. New York: Rinehart.

Boyle, Kay. 1943. *American Citizen*. New York: Simon and Schuster.

Bradford, William. 1622. *Of Plymouth Plantation [1620–47]*. Ed. Samuel E. Morison. New York: Knopf, 1952.

Bradley, Henry. 1911. "Slang." In *Encyclopaedia Britannica*. 11th ed. Cambridge University Press.

Braidwood, John. 1969. *The Ulster Dialect Lexicon*. Queen's University of Belfast.

Brasch, Walter. 1981. *Black English and the Mass Media*. Amherst: University of Massachusetts Press.

Brengelman, Fred H. 1980. "Orthoepists, Printers, and the Rationalization of English Spelling." *Journal of English And Germanic Philology* 79: 332–54.

Brice-Bennett, Carol, ed. 1977. *Our Footprints Are Everywhere: Inuit Land Use and Occupancy in Labrador*. Nain: Labrador Inuit Association.

Bridenbaugh, Carl. 1963. *Myths and Realities of the Colonial South*. New York: Atheneum.

Bridges, Robert. 1925. "Anglo-American Vocabulary." *S. P. E. Tract* 22: 58–62. Oxford: Clarendon.

Bright, William, ed. 1992. *International Encyclopedia of Linguistics*, 4 vols: New York: Oxford University Press.

Brooks, Cleanth. 1935. *The Relation of the Alabama-Georgia Dialect to the Provincial Dialects of Great Britain*. Baton Rouge: Louisiana State University.

1937. "The English Language in the South." In *A Southern Treasury of Life and Literature*, ed. Stark Young, 350–8. New York: Scribner's.

1985. *The Language of the American South*. Athens: University of Georgia Press.

Brown, Calvin S. 1889. "Dialectal Survivals in Tennessee." *Modern Language Notes* 4: 205–9.

Brown, Goold. 1851. *The Grammar of English Grammars*. New York: Wood.

Brown, Vivian. 1991. "Evolution of the Merger of /ɛ/ and / ɪ / in Tennessee." *American Speech* 66: 303–15.

Bryant, Margaret M., ed. 1962. *Current American Usage*. New York: Funk and Wagnalls.

Buchanan, James. 1760. *British Grammar*. Reprint of 1762 ed. English Linguistics 1500–1800, no. 97. Menston, Yorks.: Scolar, 1968.

Buckhurst, Helen McM. 1925. "Some Recent Americanisms in Standard English." *American Speech* 1: 159–60.

Buckley, Richard Lord. 1960. *Hiparama of the Classics*. San Francisco: City Lights.

Burchfield, Robert. 1985. *The English Language*. Oxford University Press.

1989. *Unlocking the English Language*. London: Faber and Faber.

Burke, W. J. 1939. *The Literature of Slang*. New York Public Library.

Burley, Dan. 1944. *Dan Burley's Original Handbook of Harlem Jive*. New York: Dan Burley.

Burling, Robbins. 1973. *English in Black and White*. New York: Holt, Rinehart and Winston.

Burroughs, Edgar Rice. 1916. *Return of the Mucker*. Reprint New York: Ace Books, n.d. [ca 1967].

Burt, N. C. 1878. "The Dialects of Our Country." *Appleton's Journal*. n.s. 5: 411–17.

Burton, Lydia. 1987. *Editing Canadian English*. Prepared for the Freelance Editors' Association of Canada. Vancouver: Douglas and McIntyre.

Bushman, Richard L. 1991. "Revolution." In *The Reader's Companion to American History*, ed. Eric Foner and John A. Garraty, 936–46. Boston: Houghton Mifflin.

Butters, Ronald R. 1983. "Syntactic Change in British English 'Propredicates.'" *Journal of English Linguistics* 16: 1–7.

1987. ed. *Are Black and White Vernaculars Diverging? Papers from the NWAVE XIV Panel Discussion* [by Ralph W. Fasold, William Labov, Fay Boyd Vaughn-Cooke, Guy Bailey, Walt Wolfram, Arthur K. Spears, John Rickford]. *American Speech* 62.1.

1991a. "Multiple Modals in United States Black English: Synchronic and Diachronic Aspects." In *Verb Phrase Patterns in Black English and Creole*, ed. Walter Edwards and Donald Winford, 165–76. Detroit: Wayne State University Press.

1991b. *The Death of Black English: Divergence and Convergence in Black and White Vernaculars*. Frankfurt am Main: Peter Lang.

Byerley, Thomas. 1773. *A Plain and Easy Introduction to English Grammar*. New York.

Cameron, Deborah. 1995. *Verbal Hygiene*. London and New York: Routledge.

Campbell, George. 1776. *The Philosophy of Rhetoric*. Reprint, ed. Lloyd F. Bitzer, Carbondale: Southern Illinois University Press, 1963.

The Canadian Style: A Guide to Writing and Editing. 1997. Toronto: Dundurn Press for the Public Works, Governmental Services, Canada, Translation Bureau.

Candler, Isaac. 1824. *A Summary View of America*. London: T. Cadell.

Cardoulis, John N. 1990. *A Friendly Invasion: The American Military in Newfoundland 1940–1990*. Saint John's: Breakwater.

Carey, Henry. 1735. "The Honest Yorkshire-Man." In *The Dramatick Works of Henry Carey*. London: S. Gilbert, 1743.

Carlyle, Thomas, and Jane Welsh Carlyle. 1970–95. *The Collected Letters of Thomas and Jane Welsh Carlyle*. 24 vols. to date. Ed. Charles Richard Sanders, Kenneth J. Fielding, and Clyde de L. Ryals. Durham, NC: Duke University Press.

Carnes, Mark C., and John A. Garraty, with Patrick Williams. 1996. *Mapping America's Past: A Historical Atlas*. New York: Holt.

Carver, Craig M. 1987. *American Regional Dialects: A Word Geography*. Ann Arbor: University of Michigan Press.

1992. "The Mayflower to the Model-T: The Development of American English." In *English in its Social Contexts: Essays in Historical Sociolinguistics*, ed. Tim William Machan and Charles T. Scott, 131–54. New York: Oxford University Press.

Cassidy, Frederic G. 1978. "Another Look at *Buckaroo.*" *American Speech* 53: 49–51.

1981. "OK – Is It African?" *American Speech* 56: 269–73.

1983. "Sources of the African Element in Gullah." In *Studies in Caribbean Language*, ed. Lawrence Carrington, 75–81. St. Augustine, Trinidad: Society for Caribbean Linguistics.

Cassidy, Frederic G., and Joan Houston Hall, eds. 1985–. *Dictionary of American Regional English*. Vols. 1–. Cambridge, MA: Belknap.

Cassidy, Frederic G., and R. B. LePage. 1980. *Dictionary of Jamaican English*. 2nd ed. Cambridge University Press.

Cell, Gillian T. 1969. *English Enterprise in Newfoundland 1577–1660*. University of Toronto Press.

1982. ed. *Newfoundland Discovered: English Attempts at Colonisation, 1610–1630*. London: Hakluyt Society.

Census of Newfoundland and Labrador 1901. 1903. Saint John's: J. W. Withers.

Chambers, J. K. 1973. "Canadian Raising." *Canadian Journal of Linguistics / La revue canadienne de linguistique* 18: 113–35.

1975. ed. *Canadian English: Origins and Structures*. Toronto: Methuen.

1985. "Three Kinds of Standard in Canadian English." In *In Search of the Standard in Canadian English*, ed. William Clinton Lougheed, 1–15. Strathy Language Unit Occasional Papers 1. Kingston, ON: Queen's University.

1991. "Canada." In *English around the World: Sociolinguistic Perspectives*, ed. Jenny Cheshire, 89–107. Cambridge University Press.

1993. "'Lawless and Vulgar Innovations': Victorian Views of Canadian English." In *Focus on Canada*, ed. Sandra Clarke, 1–26. Varieties of English around the World 11. Amsterdam: John Benjamins.

1998. "English: Canadian Varieties." In *Language in Canada*, ed. John Edwards, 252–72. Cambridge University Press.

Chambers, J. K., and Troy Heisler. 1999. "Dialect Topography of Quebec City English." *Canadian Journal of Linguistics/La revue canadienne de linguistique* 44: 23–48.

Chapman, Robert L. 1986. *New Dictionary of American Slang*. New York: Harper and Row.

Chaudenson, Robert. 1992. *Des îles, des hommes, des langues: essais sur la créolisation linguistique et culturelle*. Paris: L'Harmattan.

Cheever, George B., ed. 1848. *The Journal of the Pilgrims at Plymouth, in New England, in 1620: Reprinted from the Original Volume*. New York: Wiley.

Cheshire, Jenny. 1991. "Variation in the Use of *Ain't* in an Urban British English Dialect." In *Dialects of English: Studies in Grammatical Variation*, ed. Peter Trudgill and J. K. Chambers, 54–73. London: Longman.

Chester, Joseph L. 1865. "The Influence of the County of Essex on the Settlement and Family History of New England." *Transactions of the Essex Archaeological Society.* o.s. 3: 37–47.

Chicago Manual of Style. 1993. 14th ed. University of Chicago Press.

Ching, Marvin K. L. 1987. "How Fixed Is *Fixin' To?*" *American Speech* 62: 332–5.

Chomsky, Noam, and Morris Halle. 1968. *The Sound Pattern of English.* New York: Harper and Row.

Christensen, Francis. 1962. "A Case for *Webster's Third.*" *The USC Alumni Review* (November), 11–3. Reprint in *The Role of the Dictionary*, ed. Philip Babcock Gove, 22–5. Indianapolis, IN: Bobbs-Merrill, 1967.

Christian, Donna, Walt Wolfram, and Nanjo Dube. 1988. *Variation and Change in Geographically Isolated Communities: Appalachian English and Ozark English.* Publication of the American Dialect Society 74. Tuscaloosa: University of Alabama Press.

Clapin, Sylva. 1902. *New Dictionary of Americanisms: Being a Glossary of Words Supposed to Be Peculiar to the United States and the Dominion of Canada.* New York: Weiss.

Clark, Thomas D. 1944. *Pills, Petticoats and Plows: The Southern Country Store.* Indianapolis: Bobbs-Merrill.

Clark, Thomas L. 1987. *The Dictionary of Gambling and Gaming.* Cold Spring, NY: Lexik House.

Clarke, Sandra. 1986. "Sociolinguistic Patterning in a New-World Dialect of Hiberno-English: The Speech of St. John's." In *Perspectives on the English Language in Ireland*, ed. John Harris, David Little, and David Singleton, 67–81. Dublin: Trinity College.

1991. "Phonological Variation and Recent Language Change in St John's English." In *English around the World: Sociolinguistic Perspectives*, ed. Jenny Cheshire, 108–33. Cambridge University Press.

1993. ed. *Focus on Canada.* Varieties of English around the World 11. Amsterdam: John Benjamins.

1997. "On Establishing Historical Relationships between Old and New World Varieties: Habitual Aspect and Newfoundland Vernacular English." In *Englishes around the World: Studies in Honour of Manfred Görlach.* Vol. 1, *General Studies, British Isles, North America*, ed. Edgar W. Schneider, 277–93. Amsterdam: Benjamins.

Cobb, Collier. 1910. "Early English Survivals on Hatteras Island." *University of North Carolina Magazine* (Feb.), 3–9.

Cohen, Gerald Leonard. 1982. *Origin of the Term "Shyster."* Frankfurt: Lang.

1985–97. ed. *Studies in Slang.* 5 parts. Frankfurt: Lang.

1991. *Origin of New York City's Nickname "The Big Apple."* Frankfurt: Lang.

2000. "*Jazz* Revisited: On the Origin of the Term." *Comments on Etymology* 30.2-3: 3–72.

Colby, Elbridge. 1942. *Army Talk.* Princeton University Press. 2nd ed., 1943.

Coleridge, Samuel Taylor. 1818. *The Friend.* 4 vols. Ed. B. E. Rooke. London: Routledge and Kegan Paul, 1969.

Collinson, W. E. 1927. *Contemporary English: A Personal Speech Record.* Leipzig and Berlin: Teubner.

Combs, Josiah H. 1916. "Old, Early and Elizabethan English in the Southern Mountains." *Dialect Notes* 4: 283–97.

Combs, Mona R. 1958. "Archaic Words Used in Northeastern Kentucky." M.A. thesis, Morehead State College.

Conway, Jack. 1926. "Why I Write Slang." *Variety* (New York, Dec. 29), 5, 7.

Cooke, Elizabeth A., Susan E. MacCallum, and Robert D. Eagleson. 1966. *Early Goldmining Terms and Popular Collocations.* Occasional Paper 10. Sydney: Australian Language Research Centre.

Cooley, Marianne. 1992. "Emerging Standard and Subdialectal Variation in Early American English." *Diachronica* 9: 167–87.

———. 1997. "An Early Representation of African American English." In *Language Variety in the South Revisited*, ed. Cynthia Bernstein, Thomas Nunnally, and Robin Sabino, 51–8. Tuscaloosa: University of Alabama Press.

Copland, Robert. 1535–6. "The Hye Way to the Spytell Hous." Reprint in *The Elizabethan Underworld*, ed. A. V. Judges, 1–25. London: Routledge, 1930.

Copperud, Roy H. 1980. *American Usage and Style: The Consensus.* New York: Van Nostrand Reinhold.

Craddock, Jerry R. 1981. "New World Spanish." In *Language in the USA*, ed. Charles A. Ferguson and Shirley Brice Heath, 196–211. Cambridge University Press.

Craigie, William A. 1926. *The Relationship between British and American English. S. P. E. Tract* 27, Oxford University Press.

Craigie, William A., and James R. Hulbert. 1938–44. *Dictionary of American English.* University of Chicago Press.

Crawford, James M. 1978. *The Mobilian Trade Language.* Knoxville: University of Tennessee Press.

Creswell, Thomas J. 1975. *Usage in Dictionaries and Dictionaries of Usage.* Publication of the American Dialect Society 63–4. Tuscaloosa: University of Alabama Press.

Crockett Almanac 1839. 1838. Nashville, TN [prob. Boston, MA]: Ben Harding.

Crowley, Tony. 1991. *Proper English? Readings in Language, History and Cultural Identity.* London: Routledge.

Crozier, Alan. 1984. "The Scotch-Irish Influence on American English." *American Speech* 59: 310–31.

Crum, Mason. 1940. *Gullah: Negro Life in the Carolina Sea Islands.* Durham, NC: Duke University Press.

Crystal, David. 1984. *Who Cares about English Usage?* Harmondsworth, UK: Penguin.

Cunningham, Irma Aloyce Ewing. 1992. *A Syntactic Analysis of Sea Island Creole ("Gullah").* Publication of the American Dialect Society 75. Tuscaloosa: University of Alabama Press.

Curme, George Oliver. 1931–5. *A Grammar of the English Language.* 2 vols. Boston: Heath. Reprint Essex, CT: Verbatim, 1977.

Curtis, Abel. 1779. *A Compend of English Grammar*. Dresden, VT [Hanover, NH]: Dartmouth College.

Custer, Elizabeth. 1887. *Tenting on the Plains: or, General Custer in Kansas and Texas*. New York: Charles L. Webster.

DA = Dictionary of Americanisms. See Mathews 1951.

DAE = Dictionary of American English. See Craigie and Hulbert.

Dalby, David. 1972. "The African Element in American English." In *Rappin' and Stylin' Out: Communication in Urban Black America*, ed. Thomas Kochman, 170–86. Urbana: University of Illinois Press.

Dalzell, Tom. 1996. *Flappers 2 Rappers: American Youth Slang*. Springfield, MA: Merriam-Webster.

Dana, Richard Henry, Jr. 1840. *Two Years before the Mast: A Personal Narrative of Life at Sea*. New York: Harper.

———. 1968. *The Journals*. Ed. R. F. Lucid. 3 vols. Cambridge, MA: Belknap.

Dance, Daryl Cumber. 1978. *Shuckin' and Jivin': Folklore from Contemporary Black Americans*. Bloomington: Indiana University Press.

DARE = Dictionary of American Regional English. See Cassidy and Hall 1985–.

DAS = Dictionary of American Slang. See Wentworth and Flexner 1960.

Davie, G. E. 1961. *The Democratic Intellect*. Edinburgh University Press.

Dayton, Elizabeth. 1996. "Grammatical Categories of the Verb in African-American Vernacular English." Ph.D. diss., University of Pennsylvania.

DeBose, Charles. 1983. "Samaná English: A Dialect That Time Forgot." In *Proceedings of the Ninth Annual Meeting of the Berkeley Linguistics Society*, ed. Amy Dahlstrom, Claudia Brugman, Monica Macaulay, Inesse Cirkulis, Michele Emanatian, Donna Sakima, and Ragnel Texerira, 47–53. Berkeley Linguistics Society.

DeCamp, David. 1971. "Toward a Generative Analysis of a Post-Creole Speech Continuum." In *Pidginization and Creolization of Languages*, ed. Dell Hymes, 349–70. Cambridge University Press.

Deighton, Lee C. 1972. *A Comparative Analysis of Spellings in Four Major Collegiate Dictionaries*. Pleasantville, NY: Hardscrabble Press.

de Klerk, Vivian. 1990. "Slang: A Male Domain?" *Sex Roles* 22: 589–606.

D'Eloia, Sarah. 1973. "Issues in the Analysis of Negro Nonstandard English." Review of *Black English: Its History and Usage in the United States*, by J. L. Dillard. *Journal of English Linguistics* 7: 87–106.

Denning, Keith. 1989. "Convergence with Divergence: A Sound Change in Vernacular Black English." *Language Variation and Change* 1: 145–67.

De Quincey, Thomas. 1821. *Confessions of an English Opium Eater*. Ed. R. Garnett. New York: White and Allen, n.d.

De Wolf, Gaelan. 1992. *Social and Regional Factors in Canadian English: A Study of Phonological Variables and Grammatical Items in Ottawa and Vancouver*. Toronto: Canadian Scholar's Press.

———. 1997. ed. *Gage Canadian Dictionary*. Rev. ed. Toronto: Gage.

Dial, Wylene. 1969. "The Dialect of the Appalachian People." *West Virginia History* 30: 463–71.

Dialect Notes. 1890–1939. 6 vols.

Dickens, Charles. 1842. *American Notes*. Gloucester, MA: Peter Smith, 1968.

Dickson, Paul. 1989. *The Dickson Baseball Dictionary*. New York: Facts on File.

Dickson, R. J. 1966. *Ulster Emigration to Colonial America, 1718–1775*. London: Routledge.

Dictionary of American History. 1976. Revised ed. New York: Scribner's.

Dietrich, Julia C. 1981. "The Gaelic Roots of *A*-prefixing in Appalachian English." *American Speech* 56: 314.

Dillard, Joey Lee. 1972. *Black English: Its History and Usage in the United States*. New York: Random House.

1975. *All-American English*. New York: Vintage.

1977. *The Lexicon of Black English*. New York: Seabury Press.

1992. *A History of American English*. London: Longman.

Dilworth, Thomas. 1740. *A New Guide to the English Tongue*. Reprint of 1751 ed. English Linguistics 1500–1800, no. 4. Leeds: Scolar, 1967.

DNE2 = *Dictionary of Newfoundland English*. See Story, Kirwin, and Widdowson 1990.

Dobson, Eric John. 1957. *English Pronunciation 1500–1700*. 2 vols. Oxford: Clarendon. 2nd ed. 1968.

Dohan, Mary Helen. 1974. *Our Own Words*. New York: Knopf.

Dolan, Terence Patrick, ed. 1998. *A Dictionary of Hiberno-English*. Dublin: Gill and McMillan.

Donaldson, Gordon. 1980. "Scots." In *Harvard Encyclopedia of American Ethnic Groups*, ed. Stephan Thernstrom, 908–16. Cambridge, MA: Harvard University Press.

Donaldson, William. 1986. *Popular Literature in Victorian Scotland*. Aberdeen University Press.

Dorian, Nancy C. 1990. "Linguacentrism and Language History." In *The Influence of Language on Culture and Thought*, ed. Robert L. Cooper and Bernard Spolsky, 85–99. Berlin: Mouton de Gruyter.

Dorrill, George. 1986. "A Comparison of Stressed Vowels of Black and White Speakers in the South." In *Language Varieties in the South: Perspectives in Black and White*, ed. Michael Montgomery and Guy Bailey, 149–57. Tuscaloosa: University of Alabama Press.

Douglas, Ann. 1995. *Terrible Honesty: Mongrel Manhattan in the 1920s*. New York: Farrar, Straus, and Giroux.

Doyle, Arthur Conan. 1967. *The Annotated Sherlock Holmes*. Ed. William S. Baring-Gould. 2 vols. New York: Clarkson N. Potter.

Doyle, David. N. 1981. *Irish, Irishmen and Revolutionary America 1760–1820*. Dublin: Mercier.

Doyle, James, ed. 1980. *Yankees in Canada: A Collection of Nineteenth-Century Travel Narratives*. Downsview, ON: ECW Press.

Drake, Glendon F. 1980. "The Social Role of Slang." In *Language: Social Psychological Perspectives*, ed. Howard Giles, W. P. Robinson, and P. M. Smith, 63–70. Oxford: Pergamon.

Drechsel, Emanuel J. 1976. "'Ha, Now Me Stomany That!' A Summary of Pidginization and Creolization of North American Indian Languages." *International Journal of the Sociology of Language* 7: 63–81.

1996. *Mobilian Jargon: Linguistic and Sociohistorical Aspects of an American Indian Pidgin*. Oxford University Press.

Duggan, George Chester. 1937. *The Stage Irishman: A History of the Irish Play and Stage Characters from the Earliest Times*. London: Longmans, Green.

Dulles, Foster Rhea. 1959. *The United States since 1865*. Ann Arbor: University of Michigan Press.

Dumas, Bethany K., and Jonathan E. Lighter. 1978. "Is *Slang* a Word for Linguists?" *American Speech* 53: 5–17.

Dykema, Karl W. 1963. "Cultural Lag and Reviewers of *Webster III*." *AAUP Bulletin* 49: 364–9.

Eble, Connie C. 1984. "Slang: Variations in Dictionary Labeling Practices." In *The Eleventh LACUS Forum 1984*, ed. Robert A. Hall, Jr., 294–302. Columbia, SC: Hornbeam Press, 1985.

1985. "Slang and Cultural Knowledge." In *The Twelfth LACUS Forum*, ed. Mary C. Marino and Luis A. Perez, 385–90. Lake Bluff, IL: Linguistic Association of Canada and the United States, 1986.

1987. "Slang as Poetry." In *The Fourteenth LACUS Forum 1987*, ed. Sheila Embleton, 442–5. Lake Bluff, IL: Linguistic Association of Canada and the United States, 1988.

1989. *College Slang 101*. Georgetown, CT: Spectacle Lane Press.

1996. *Slang and Sociability: In-Group Language among College Students*. Chapel Hill: University of North Carolina Press.

EDD = *English Dialect Dictionary*. See J. Wright 1898–1905.

Eden, Richard, tr. 1555. *The Decades of the Newe Worlde or West India*. Ann Arbor, MI: University Microfilms, 1966.

Edgerton, Franklin. 1943. "Notes on Early American Work in Linguistics." *Proceedings of the American Philosophical Society* 87: 25–34.

Edwards, John, ed. 1998. *Language in Canada*. Cambridge University Press.

Egan, Pierce, ed. 1823. *Grose's Classical Dictionary of the Vulgar Tongue*. Rev. ed. London: Sherwood, Neely and Jones.

Eggleston, Edward. 1894. "Folk-Speech in America." *Century Magazine* 48: 867–75.

Eliason, Norman E. 1956. *Tarheel Talk: An Historical Study of the English Language in North Carolina to 1860*. Chapel Hill: University of North Carolina Press.

Ellis, Alexander John. 1869–89. *On Early English Pronunciation, with Especial Reference to Shakspere and Chaucer*. 5 vols. London: Asher.

Ellis, Elmer. 1941. *Mr. Dooley's America*. New York: Knopf.

Ellis, Michael E. 1984. "The Relationship of Appalachian English with the British Regional Dialects." M.A. thesis, East Tennessee State University.

1992. "On the Use of Dialect as Evidence: Albion's Seed in Appalachia." *Appalachian Journal* 19: 278–97.

Elting, John R., Dan Cragg, and Ernest Deal. 1984. *A Dictionary of Soldier Talk*. New York: Scribner.

Emerson, Oliver Farrar. 1890. "The Ithaca Dialect." *Dialect Notes* 1: 85–173.

"The English Language as Spoken in the United States." 1838. *Penny Magazine* 7: 278–9.

Evans, Bergen. 1962. "Noah Webster Had the Same Troubles." *New York Times Magazine*, 13 May, 11, 77, 79–80.

Farmer, John Stephen. 1889. *Americanisms – Old and New: A Dictionary of Words, Phrases and Colloquialisms Peculiar to the United States, British America, the West Indies, &c.* London: Thomas Poulter & Sons.

Farmer, John Stephen, and William Ernest Henley. 1890–1904. *Slang and Its Analogues Past and Present*. 7 vols. Reprint in one vol. New York: Arno, 1970.

Fasold, Ralph. 1969. "Tense and the Form of *Be* in Black English." *Language* 45: 763–76.

1972. *Tense Marking in Black English: A Linguistic and Social Analysis*. Arlington, VA: Center for Applied Linguistics.

1976. "One Hundred Years from Syntax to Phonology." In *Papers from the Parasession on Diachronic Syntax*, ed. Sanford Steever, Carol Walker, and Salikoko Mufwene, 79–87. Chicago Linguistic Society.

1981. "The Relationship between Black and White Speech in the South." *American Speech* 56: 163–89.

Father Tammany's Almanac for . . . 1792. 1791. Philadelphia: John M'Culloch.

Feagin, Crawford. 1979. *Variation and Change in Alabama English: A Sociolinguistic Study of the White Community*. Washington: Georgetown University Press.

Fee, Margery. 1992a. "Canadian Dictionaries in English." In *The Oxford Companion to the English Language*, ed. Tom McArthur, 178–9. Oxford University Press.

1992b. "Canadian English." In *The Oxford Companion to the English Language*, ed. Tom McArthur, 179–83. Oxford University Press.

Fee, Margery, and Janice McAlpine. 1997. *Guide to Canadian English Usage*. Toronto: Oxford University Press.

Fee, Margery, and Tom McArthur. 1992. "Quebec." In *The Oxford Companion to the English Language*, ed. Tom McArthur, 831–3. Oxford University Press.

Fennell, Barbara A., and Ronald R. Butters. 1997. "Historical and Contemporary Distribution of Double Modals in English." In *Focus on the USA*, ed. Edgar W. Schneider, 263–86. Amsterdam: Benjamins.

Fenton, James, ed. 1995. *The Hamely Tongue: A Personal Record of County Antrim*. Newtownards: Ulster-Scots Academic Press.

Fickett, Joan G. 1970. "Aspects of Morphemics, Syntax, and Semiology of an

Inner-city Dialect (Merican)." Ph.D. diss., State University of New York at Buffalo.

Finegan, Edward. 1980. *Attitudes toward English Usage: The History of a War of Words*. New York: Teachers College Press, Columbia University.

1998. "English Grammar and Usage." In *The Cambridge History of the English Language*. Vol. 4, *1776–1997*, ed. Suzanne Romaine, 536–88. Cambridge University Press.

Fink, Paul M. 1974. *Bits of Mountain Speech*. Boone, NC: Appalachian Consortium.

Fischer, David Hackett. 1989. *Albion's Seed: Four British Folkways in America*. New York: Oxford University Press.

Fisher, John Hurt. 1946. "Primary and Secondary Education and the Presbyterian Church in the United States of America." *Journal of the Presbyterian Historical Society* 24: 13–43.

1996. *The Emergence of Standard English*. Lexington: University Press of Kentucky.

Fishman, Joshua A., Michael H. Gertner, Esther G. Lowy, and William G. Milán, eds. 1985. *The Rise and Fall of the Ethnic Revival: Perspectives on Language and Ethnicity*. Berlin: Mouton.

Fishman, Stephen M., and Lucille McCarthy. 1998. *John Dewey and the Challenge of Classroom Practice*. New York: Teachers College Press; Urbana, IL: National Council of Teachers of English.

Fiske, John. 1889. *The Beginnings of New England*. Boston: Houghton Mifflin.

Flexner, Stuart B. 1987. *The Random House Dictionary of the English Language*. 2nd ed. New York: Random House.

Flink, James J. 1991. "Automobiles." In *The Reader's Companion to American History*, ed. Eric Foner and John A. Garraty, 64–8. Boston: Houghton Mifflin.

Folb, Edith A. 1980. *Runnin' Down Some Lines*. Cambridge, MA: Harvard University Press.

Follett, Wilson. 1962. "Sabotage in Springfield." *Atlantic* (January), 73–7. Reprint in *Dictionaries and THAT Dictionary*, ed. James Sledd and Wilma R. Ebbitt, 111–19. Chicago: Scott, Foresman, 1962.

1966. *Modern American Usage: A Guide*. Ed. Jacques Barzun. New York: Hill.

Foner, Eric, and John A. Garraty, eds. 1991. *The Reader's Companion to American History*. Boston: Houghton Mifflin.

Fonzari, Lorenza. "English in the Estonian Multicultural Society." *World Englishes* 18: 39–48.

Foote, Samuel. 1762. *The Orators*. London: J. Coote.

Ford, Emily Ellsworth Fowler, and Emily Ellsworth Ford Skeel, eds. 1912. *Notes on the Life of Noah Webster*. 2 vols. New York: Privately printed.

Foster, Brian. 1955–6. "Recent American Influence on Standard English." *Anglia* 73: 328–60.

Fowler, H. Ramsey, and Jane E. Aaron. 1989. *The Little Brown Handbook*. 4th ed. Glenview, IL: Scott, Foresman.

Fowler, Henry Watson. 1944. *A Dictionary of Modern English Usage.* New York: Oxford University Press.

1965. *A Dictionary of Modern English Usage.* 2nd ed. rev. and ed. by Sir Ernest Gowers. Oxford University Press.

Fracastoro, Girolamo. 1686. *Syphilis; or, A Poetical History of the French Disease,* trans. Nahum Tate. London: Jacob Tonson.

Frampton, John, trans. 1577. *Joyfull Newes out of the Newe Founde Worlde.* 2 vols. Reprint London: Constable; New York: Knopf, 1925.

Francis, W. Nelson. 1959. "Some Dialect Isoglosses in England." *American Speech* 34: 243–57.

1961. "Some Dialectal Verb Forms in England." *Orbis* 10: 1–14.

Franklin, Benjamin. 1722. "To the Author of the *New-England Courant.*" In *The Writings of Benjamin Franklin,* ed. A. H. Smyth, 2: 40–3. New York: Macmillan, 1905–7.

1737. "The Drinkers Dictionary." *Pennsylvania Gazette* (Philadelphia, Jan. 6), 1–2.

1779. *Political, Miscellaneous and Philosophical Pieces.* London: J. Johnson.

Franklin, Wayne. 1979. *Discoverers, Explorers, Settlers: The Diligent Writers of Early America.* University of Chicago Press.

Friend, Joseph H. 1967. *The Development of American Lexicography 1798–1864.* The Hague: Mouton.

Fries, Charles Carpenter. 1927. *The Teaching of the English Language.* New York: Thomas Nelson.

1940. *American English Grammar.* National Council of Teachers of English Monograph 10. New York: Appleton-Century-Crofts.

Fromkin, Victoria, and Robert Rodman. 1998. *An Introduction to Language,* 6th ed. Fort Worth, TX: Harcourt Brace.

Frost, William Goodell. 1899. "Our Contemporary Ancestors." *Atlantic Monthly* 83: 311–19.

Garner, Bryan A. 1998. *A Dictionary of Modern American Usage.* New York: Oxford University Press.

Garraty, John A. 1991. "Colonial Wars." In *The Reader's Companion to American History,* ed. Eric Foner and John A. Garraty, 205–7. Boston: Houghton Mifflin.

Gaston, Thomas E. 1973. "Slang: The Poetry of Group Dynamics." Filmstrip. Peoria, IL: Thomas S. Klise.

Genzmer, George Harvey. 1930. "Brown, Goold." In *Dictionary of American Biography,* ed. Allen Johnson and Dumas Malone. Vol. 2. Reprint. New York: Scribner's, 1958.

Gibson, Martha Jane. 1933. "Early Connecticut Pronunciation: Guilford, 1639–1800; Branford, 1644–1800." Ph.D. diss., Yale University.

Gilbert, Glenn G. 1986. "The English of the Brandywine Population: A Triracial Isolate in Southern Maryland." In *Language Variety in the South: Perspectives in Black and White,* ed. Michael B. Montgomery and Guy Bailey, 102–10. Tuscaloosa: University of Alabama Press.

Gill, Alexander. 1619. *Logonomia Anglica*. Ed. Bror Danielsson and Arvid Gabrielson. 2 vols. Stockholm: Almqvist & Wiksell, 1972.

Gilman, Charles. 1985. *"Hadve*: A New Auxiliary." *SECOL Review* 9: 9–23.

Gilman, E. Ward, ed. 1989. *Webster's Dictionary of English Usage*. Springfield, MA: Merriam-Webster. Reprint as *Merriam-Webster's Dictionary of English Usage*, 1993.

Gilyard, Keith. 1991. *Voices of the Self: A Study of Language Competence*. Detroit, MI: Wayne State University Press.

Giner, Maria F. Garcia-Bermejo, and Michael Montgomery. 1997. "Regional British English from the Nineteenth Century: Evidence from Emigrant Letters." In *Current Methods in Dialectology*, ed. Alan S. Thomas, 167–83. Bangor: University of Wales.

Goddard, Ives. 1977. "Some Early Examples of American Indian Pidgin English from New England." *International Journal of American Linguistics* 43: 37–41.

Goffman, Erving. 1959. *The Presentation of Self in Everyday Life*. Garden City, NY: Doubleday.

Gold, David L. 1981. "The Speech and Writing of Jews." In *Language in the USA*, ed. Charles A. Ferguson and Shirley Brice Heath, 273–92. Cambridge University Press.

Gold, Robert S. 1964. *A Jazz Lexicon*. New York: Knopf.

1975. *Jazz Talk*. New York: Bobbs-Merrill.

Goldfarb, Jeffrey C. 1991. *The Cynical Society*. University of Chicago Press.

Goldin, Hyman, Frank O'Leary, and Morris Lipsius. 1950. *Dictionary of American Underworld Lingo*. New York: Twayne.

Gonzales, Ambrose. 1922. *The Black Border: Gullah Stories from the Carolina Coast*. Columbia, SC: State Co.

Goodrich, Samuel G. 1863. "Schools As They Were Sixty Years Ago: Recollections of Peter Parley." *American Journal of Education* [new series, no. 5] 30: 123–44.

Goodwin, Marjorie H. 1990. *He-Said-She-Said: Talk as Social Organization among Black Children*. Bloomington: Indiana University Press.

Gordon, George S. 1943. *The Letters of George S. Gordon, 1902–1942*. Oxford University Press.

Görlach, Manfred. 1987. "Colonial Lag? The Alleged Conservative Character of American English and Other 'Colonial' Varieties." *English World-Wide* 8: 41–60.

Gove, Philip Babcock, ed. 1961a. *Webster's Third New International Dictionary*. Springfield, MA: Merriam.

1961b. "Linguistic Advances and Lexicography." *Word Study* 37 (October): 3–8.

Gowers, Ernest. 1965. *A Dictionary of Modern English Usage by H. W. Fowler*. Oxford University Press.

Graham, Ian C. C. 1956. *Colonists from Scotland: Emigration to North America, 1707–1783*. Ithaca, NY: Cornell University Press.

Grandgent, Charles H. 1899. "From Franklin to Lowell: A Century of New England Pronunciation." *PMLA* 14: 207–39.

1920. "Fashion and the Broad A." *Old and New*. Cambridge, MA: Harvard University Press.

Grant, William, and David Murison. 1931–75. *Scottish National Dictionary*. 10 vols. Edinburgh: Scottish National Dictionary Association.

Green, Bennett Wood. 1899. *Word-Book of Virginia Folk-Speech*. Richmond: Wm. Ellis Jones.

Green, Lisa. 1992. "Topics in African American English Syntax: The Verbal System Analysis." Ph.D. diss., University of Massachusetts.

1998. "Aspect and Predicate Phrases in African-American Vernacular English." In *African-American English: Structure, History, and Use*, ed. Salikoko S. Mufwene, John R. Rickford, Guy Bailey, and John Baugh, 37–68. London: Routledge.

Greenbaum, Sidney, and Janet Whitcut. 1988. *Longman Guide to English Usage*. Harlow: Longman.

Greenberg, Joseph. 1987. *Language in the Americas*. Stanford University Press.

Greenough, James Bradstreet, and George Lyman Kittredge. 1901. *Words and Their Ways in English Speech*. New York: Macmillan.

Greenwood, James. 1711. *An Essay towards a Practical English Grammar*. Reprint English Linguistics 1500–1800, no. 128. Menston, Yorks.: Scolar, 1968.

Gregg, Robert J. 1992. "The Survey of Vancouver English." *American Speech* 67: 250–67.

Griffith, Edward. 1827–32. *The Animal Kingdom*. 15 vols. London: Whittaker, Treacher.

Griffith, Francis. 1988. "Irish Usage in American English." *Irish America* (Nov.), 34–5.

Grimm, Jacob. 1822–37. *Deutsche Grammatik*. 4 vols. Göttingen: Dieterichsche Buchhandlung.

Grose, Francis. 1785. *A Classical Dictionary of the Vulgar Tongue*. London: S. Hooper. 2nd ed., 1788. 3rd ed., 1796.

1790. *A Provincial Glossary: With a Collection of Local Proverbs, and Popular Superstitions*. 2nd ed. London: Hooper.

Guy, Gregory. 1980. "Variation in the Group and the Individual: The Case of Final Stop Deletion." In *Locating Language in Time and Space*, ed. William Labov, 1–36. New York: Academic Press.

1991. "Explanation in Variable Phonology: An Exponential Model of Morphological Constraints." *Language Variation and Change* 3: 1–22.

Haertzen, C. A., F. E. Ross, and N. T. Hooks, Jr. 1979. "Slang Knowledge as an Indicator of a General Social Deviancy Subcultural Factor." *Perceptual and Motor Skills* 48: 1235–40.

Hall, Benjamin H. 1851. *A Collection of College Words and Customs*. Cambridge, MA: John Bartlett. 2nd ed., 1856.

Hall, Fitzedward. 1872. *Recent Exemplifications of False Philology*. New York: Scribner, Armstrong.

Hall, John Lesslie. 1917. *English Usage*. Chicago: Scott, Foresman.

Hall, Joseph Sargent. 1942. *The Phonetics of Great Smoky Mountain Speech*. American Speech Reprints and Monographs no. 4. *American Speech* 17.2, part 2.

Hall, Robert Anderson, Jr. 1950. *Leave Your Language Alone!* Ithaca, NY: Linguistica. 1964. *Introductory Linguistics*. Philadelphia, PA: Chilton.

Hamilton, Anne-Marie. 1998. "The Endurance of Scots in the United States." *Scottish Language* 17: 108–18.

Hancock, Ian F. 1980. "Texan Gullah: The Creole English of the Bracketville Afro-Seminoles." In *Social Perspectives on American English*, ed. J. L. Dillard, 305–33. The Hague: Mouton.

1984. "Shelta and Polari." In *Language in the British Isles*, ed. Peter Trudgill, 384–403. Cambridge University Press.

1994. "Componentiality and the Creole Matrix: The Southwest English Contribution." In *The Crucible of Carolina: Essays in the Development of Gullah*, ed. Michael Montgomery, 95–114. Athens: University of Georgia Press.

Handcock, W. Gordon. 1989. *Soe Longe As There Comes Noe Women: Origins of English Settlement in Newfoundland*. University of Toronto Press.

Hansard. 1979–80. "The English Language: Deterioration in Usage." *The Parliamentary Debates: House of Lords*, 5th ser., 403 (4th vol. of Session 1979–80): 131–95.

Harriot, Thomas. 1590. *A Briefe and True Report of the New Found Land of Virginia*. Facsimile ed. New York: Dover, 1972.

Harris, James. 1751. *Hermes*. Reprint English Linguistics 1500–1800, no. 55. Menston, Yorks.: Scolar, 1968.

Harris, Joel Chandler. 1883. *Nights with Uncle Remus: Tales and Myths of the Old Plantation*. Boston: Houghton Mifflin.

Harris, John. 1986. "Expanding the Superstrate: Habitual Aspect Markers in Atlantic Englishes." *English World-Wide* 7: 171–99.

Harris, Leslie. 1979. "Newfoundland." In *Encyclopædia Britannica Macropædia* 12: 1084–8. Chicago: Encyclopædia Britannica.

Hart's Rules for Compositors and Readers at the University Press, Oxford. 1983. Oxford University Press.

Hauer, Stanley. 1983. "Thomas Jefferson and the Anglo-Saxon Language." *PMLA* 98: 879–98.

Hayakawa, S. I. 1941. *Language in Action*. New York: Harcourt.

Head, C. Grant. 1976. *Eighteenth Century Newfoundland: A Geographer's Perspective*. Toronto: McClelland and Stewart.

Hewitt, Ryland H., Jr. 1961. "The Pronunciation of English in the Province of Maine, 1636–1730." Ph.D. diss., Cornell University.

Higginson, Thomas Wentworth. 1886. "English Sources of American Dialect." *Proceedings of the American Antiquarian Society*. n.s. 4: 159–66.

Hoar, George F. 1885. "The Obligations of New England to the County of Kent." *Proceedings of the American Antiquarian Society*. n.s. 3: 344–71.

Hodge, Frederick W. 1907–10. *Handbook of American Indians.* Bureau of American Ethnology Bulletin 30. Washington, DC: Government Printing Office.

Hofland, Knut, and Stig Johansson. 1982. *Word Frequencies in British and American English.* Bergen: Norwegian Computing Centre for the Humanities.

Holbrook, Dick. 1973. "Our Word *Jazz.*" *Storyville* 50 (December): 47–58.

Holland, Elizabeth Vassall Fox. 1946. *Elizabeth, Lady Holland, to Her Son, 1821–1845,* ed. the Earl of Ilchester. London: John Murray.

Hollett, Robert. 1982. "Allegro Speech of a Newfoundlander." In *Languages in Newfoundland and Labrador,* 2nd version ed. Harold J. Paddock, 124–74. St. John's: Memorial University of Newfoundland, Department of Linguistics.

n.d. "Some Uses of [h] in Varieties of Newfoundland English." Typescript.

Holloway, Joseph E., and Winifred K. Vass. 1993. *The African Heritage of American English.* Bloomington: Indiana University Press.

Holm, John. 1984. "Variability of the Copula in Black English and Its Creole Kin." *American Speech* 59: 291–309.

1988. *Pidgins and Creoles.* Vol. 1, *Theory and Structure.* Cambridge University Press.

1989. *Pidgins and Creoles.* Vol. 2, *Reference Survey.* Cambridge University Press.

1991. "The Atlantic Creoles and the Language of the Ex-Slave Recordings." In *The Emergence of Black English: Text and Commentary,* ed. Guy Bailey, Natalie Maynor, and Patricia Cukor-Avila, 231–48. Amsterdam: Benjamins.

Holmes, Oliver Wendell. 1858. *The Autocrat of the Breakfast Table.* Reprint London: Dent, 1965.

1870. "Mechanism in Thought and Morals." Address to the Phi Beta Kappa Society of Harvard University, June 29. In *Pages from an Old Volume of Life,* 260–314. New ed. Boston: Houghton Mifflin, 1891.

Honey, John. 1989. *Does Accent Matter? The Pygmalion Factor.* London: Faber.

Horwill, Herbert William. 1935. *A Dictionary of Modern American Usage.* Oxford: Clarendon.

Hotten, John Camden. 1859. *A Dictionary of Modern Slang, Cant, and Vulgar Words.* London: Hotten. 2nd ed., 1860. 3rd ed., 1865. 4th ed., London: Chatto and Windus, 1874. Also published as *The Slang Dictionary: Etymological, Historical and Anecdotal.* London: Chatto and Windus, 1882.

Hughes, Arthur, and Peter Trudgill. 1979. *English Accents and Dialects.* London: Arnold.

Humbug, Henry [pseudonym]. 1758. "A Plan and Proposals for an Hospital, or Public Asylum, for Decayed and Infirm Thief-Takers." In *The History of the Life of Jonathan Wild, the Great,* by Henry Fielding, lxxiii–lxxx. Reprint "To which is added a contemporary life of Jonathan Wild. Also, J. W.'s advice to his successor; and proposals for an hospital for decayed and infirm thief-takers. With illustrations by 'Phiz.'" London: C. Daly, 1840. This ed. provides the only available text of "A Plan."

Humphreys, David. 1815. *The Yankee in London.* N.p.

Hung, Henrietta, John Davison, and J. K. Chambers. 1993. "Comparative

Sociolinguistics of (aw)-Fronting." In *Focus on Canada*, ed. Sandra Clarke, 247–68. Varieties of English around the World 11. Amsterdam: John Benjamins.

Hunter, Edwin Ray. 1925. "The American Colloquial Idiom 1830–1860." Ph.D. diss., University of Chicago.

Ihalainen, Ossi. 1994. "The Dialects of England since 1776." In *The Cambridge History of the English Language*. Vol. 5, *English in Britain and Overseas: Origins and Development*, ed. Robert Burchfield, 197–274. Cambridge University Press.

Irving, Washington. 1807–8. *Salmagundi*. London: T. Davison, 1824.

ITP Nelson Canadian Dictionary of the English Language: An Encyclopedic Dictionary. 1997. Toronto: ITP Nelson.

Jackson, Elizabeth H. 1956. "An Analysis of Certain Colorado Atlas Field Records with Regard to Settlement History and Other Factors." Ph.D. diss., University of Colorado.

Jagger, Mick. 1969. *Let It Bleed* [audio recording]. New York: ABKCO Music and Records.

Jaquith, James R. 1976. "Diagraphia in Advertising: The Public as Guinea Pig." *Visible Language* 10: 295–308.

Jefferson, Thomas. 1798. *Essay on the Anglo-Saxon Language*. Reprint in *The Complete Jefferson*, ed. Saul K. Padover, 2: 855–82. New York: Duell, Sloan, and Pearce, 1943.

Jespersen, Otto. 1909–49. *A Modern English Grammar on Historical Principles*. 7 vols. Reprint London: Allen and Unwin, 1961.

  1921. *Language: Its Nature, Development, and Origin*. London: Allen and Unwin.

  1925. *Mankind, Nation and Individual from a Linguistic Point of View*. Reprint Bloomington: Indiana University Press, 1964.

Johnson, Ellen. 1996. *Lexical Change and Variation in the Southeastern United States, 1930–1990*. Tuscaloosa: University of Alabama Press.

Johnson, Falk S. 1956. "Phonetic Alphabets and Phonetic Texts as Evidence of American Pronunciation before 1850." Ph.D. diss., University of Chicago.

Johnson, Guy. 1930. *Folk Culture on St. Helena Island, South Carolina*. Chapel Hill: University of North Carolina Press.

Johnson, Paul. 1998. *A History of the American People*. New York: HarperCollins.

Johnson, Samuel. ["Dr. Johnson" of England] 1755. *A Dictionary of the English Language*. 2 vols. London.

Johnson, Samuel. [of America] 1765. *First Easy Rudiments of Grammar*. New York: J. Holt.

Jones, Charles C. 1888. *Negro Myths from the Georgia Coast*. Boston: Houghton.

Jones, Daniel. 1962. *An Outline of English Phonetics*. 9th ed. Cambridge: Heffer.

Jones, Hugh. 1724a. *An Accidence to the English Tongue*. Facsimile ed., English Linguistics 1500–1800, no. 22. Menston, Yorks.: Scolar Press, 1967.

  1724b. *The Present State of Virginia*. London: J. Clarke.

Jones-Jackson, Patricia. 1978. "The Status of Gullah: An Investigation on Convergent Processes." Ph.D. diss., University of Michigan.

1986. "On the Status of Gullah on the Sea Islands." In *Language Variety in the South: Perspectives in Black and White*, ed. Michael Montgomery and Guy Bailey, 63–72. Tuscaloosa: University of Alabama Press.

1987. *When Roots Die: Endangered Traditions on the Sea Islands*. Athens: University of Georgia Press.

Journal of English Linguistics. 1967–.

Joyce, Patrick W. 1910. *English As We Speak It in Ireland*. London: Longmans.

Joyner, Charles. 1999. *Shared Traditions: Southern History and Folk Culture*. Urbana: University of Illinois Press.

Kahane, Henry. 1982. "American English from Colonial Substandard to Prestige Language." In *The Other Tongue: English across Cultures*, ed. B. B. Kachru, 229–36. Urbana: University of Illinois Press.

Kallen, Jeffrey L. 1989. "Tense and Aspect Categories in Irish English." *English World-Wide* 10: 1–39.

Kelly, Douglas F. 1998. *Carolina Scots: An Historical and Genealogical Study of over 100 Years of Emigration*. Dillon, SC: 1739 Publications.

Kennedy, Billie. 1995. *The Scots-Irish in the Hills of Tennessee*. Belfast: Causeway.

Kenyon, John Samuel. 1924. *American Pronunciation*. Ann Arbor, MI: Wahr. 12th ed., expanded, ed. Donald M. Lance and Stewart A. Kingsbury, 1994.

1948. "Cultural Levels and Functional Varieties of English." *College English* 10: 31–6.

Kenyon, John Samuel, and Thomas Albert Knott. 1944. *A Pronouncing Dictionary of American English*. Springfield, MA: Merriam.

Kephart, Horace. 1913. *Our Southern Highlanders*. New York: Macmillan.

Kiefer, Monica. 1948. *American Children through Their Books*. Philadelphia: University of Pennsylvania Press.

Kirchner, Gustav. 1957. "Recent American Influence on Standard English: The Syntactical Sphere." *Zeitschrift für Anglistik und Amerikanistik* 5: 29–42.

Kirkham, Samuel. 1829. *English Grammar in Familiar Lectures*. New York. Reprint of 1843 ed. American Linguistics, 1700–1900, vol. 438. Delmar, NY: Scholar's Facsimiles and Reprints, 1989.

Kirkpatrick, E. M., ed. 1983. *Chambers 20th Century Dictionary*. New ed. Cambridge University Press.

Kirszner, Laurie G., and Stephen R. Mandell. 1989. *The Holt Handbook*. 2nd ed. Fort Worth, TX: Holt, Rinehart, and Winston.

Kirwin, William J. 1991. "The Rise and Fall of Dialect Representation in Newfoundland Writings." In *Studies in Newfoundland Folklore: Community and Process*, ed. Gerald Thomas and John David Allison Widdowson, 227–44. Saint John's: Breakwater.

1993. "The Planting of Anglo-Irish in Newfoundland." In *Focus on Canada*, ed.

Sandra Clarke, 65–84. Varieties of English around the World 11. Amsterdam: Benjamins.

Kirwin, William J., and Robert Hollett. 1986. "The West Country and Newfoundland: Some *SED* Evidence." *Journal of English Linguistics* 19: 222–39.

Kirwin, William J., and G. M. Story. 1986. "The Etymology of *High Liner:* Problems of Inclusion in *The Dictionary of Newfoundland English.*" *American Speech* 61: 281–4.

Klemola, Juhani. 2000. "The Origins of the Northern Subject Rule: A Case of Early Contact?" In *Celtic Englishes II,* ed. Hildegard Tristram. Heidelberg: Winter.

Knox, E. V. 1930. "Cinema English." *Living Age* 338: 187–9.

Kochman, Thomas. 1981. *Black and White Styles in Conflict.* University of Chicago Press.

Kökeritz, Helge. 1953. *Shakespeare's Pronunciation.* New Haven, CT: Yale University Press.

Krapp, George Philip. 1908a. *The Authority of Law in Language.* University Studies, series 2, vol. 4, no. 3. University of Cincinnati.

1908b. Review of *The Standard of Usage in English,* by T. R. Lounsbury. *Educational Review* 36: 195–200.

1909. *Modern English: Its Growth and Present Use.* New York: Scribner's.

1924. "The English of the Negro." *American Mercury* 2: 190–5.

1925. *The English Language in America.* 2 vols. New York: Century.

1927a. *A Comprehensive Guide to Good English.* Chicago: Rand McNally.

1927b. *The Knowledge of English.* New York: Holt.

Kraus, Michael. 1959. *The United States to 1865.* Ann Arbor: University of Michigan Press.

Kretzschmar, William A., Jr., ed. 1998. *Journal of English Linguistics* 26.2 (Special Issue: Ebonics).

Kretzschmar, William A., Jr., Virginia G. McDavid, Theodore K. Lerud, and Ellen Johnson. 1993. *Handbook of the Linguistic Atlas of the Middle and South Atlantic States.* University of Chicago Press.

Kretzschmar, William A., Jr., and Edgar Schneider. 1996. *Introduction to Quantitative Analysis in Linguistic Survey Data.* Thousand Oaks, CA: Sage.

Kurath, Hans. 1928a. "American Pronunciation." *Society for Pure English Tract* 30: 279–97.

1928b. "The Origin of Dialectal Differences in Spoken American English." *Modern Philology* 25: 285–95. Reprint in *A Various Language: Perspectives of American Dialects,* ed. Juanita V. Williamson and Virginia M. Burke, 12–21. New York: Holt, 1971.

1939. *Handbook of the Linguistic Geography of New England.* Providence, RI: Brown University.

1939–43. *Linguistic Atlas of New England*. 3 vols. in 6. Providence, RI: Brown University and American Council of Learned Societies.

1949. *A Word Geography of the Eastern United States*. Ann Arbor: University of Michigan Press.

1964. *A Phonology and Prosody of Modern English*. Ann Arbor: University of Michigan Press.

1965. "Some Aspects of Atlantic Seaboard English Considered in Their Connections with British English." In *Communications et rapports de Premier Congrès International de Dialectologie Générale, Troisième Partie*, 236–40. Louvaine: Centre Internationale de Dialectologie Générale. Reprint in *A Various Language: Perspectives of American Dialects*, ed. Juanita V. Williamson and Virginia M. Burke, 101–7. New York: Holt, 1971.

1972. *Studies in Area Linguistics*. Bloomington: Indiana University Press.

Kurath, Hans, and Guy S. Lowman, Jr. 1970. *The Dialectal Structure of Southern England: Phonological Evidence*. Publication of the American Dialect Society no. 54. Tuscaloosa: University of Alabama Press.

Kurath, Hans, and Raven I. McDavid, Jr. 1961. *The Pronunciation of English in the Atlantic States*. Ann Arbor: University of Michigan Press.

Kytö, Merja. 1986. "On the Use of the Modal Auxiliaries 'Can' and 'May' in Early American English." In *Diversity and Diachrony*, ed. David Sankoff, 123–38. Amsterdam: Benjamins.

1989. " 'Can' or 'May'? Choice of the Variant Form in Early Modern English, British and American." In *Synchronic and Diachronic Approaches to Linguistic Variation and Change*, ed. Thomas J. Walsh, 163–78. Washington, DC: Georgetown University Press.

1990. " 'Shall' or 'Will'? Choice of the Variant Form in Early Modern English, British and American." In *Historical Linguistics 1987: Papers from the 8th International Conference on Historical Linguistics*, ed. Henning Andersen and Konrad Koerner, 275–88. Amsterdam: Benjamins.

1991. *Variation and Diachrony, with Early American English in Focus*. Bamberger Beiträge zur Englischen Sprachwissenschaft 28. Frankfurt am Main: Peter Lang.

1993. "Third-Person Present Singular Verb Inflection in Early British and American English." *Language Variation and Change* 5: 113–39.

Kytö, Merja, and Matti Rissanen. 1983. "The Syntactic Study of Early American English: The Variationist at the Mercy of His Corpus." *Neuphilologische Mitteilungen* 84: 470–90.

1987. "In Search of the Roots of American English." In *Ten Years of American Studies: The Helsinki Experience*, ed. Markku Henriksson, 215–33. Helsinki: Societas Historica Finlandiae.

Labaree, Leonard W., ed. 1959–. *The Papers of Benjamin Franklin*. New Haven: Yale University Press.

Labov, William. 1972a. *Language in the Inner City*. University of Pennsylvania Press.

1972b. *Sociolinguistic Patterns*. University of Pennsylvania Press.

1973. "Some Features of the English of Black Americans." In *Varieties of Present-Day English*, ed. Richard W. Bailey and Jay L. Robinson, 236–57. New York: Macmillan.

1982. "Objectivity and Commitment in Linguistic Science: The Case of the Black English Trial in Ann Arbor." *Language in Society* 11: 165–201.

1998. "Co-Existent Systems in African-American Vernacular English." In *African-American English: Structure, History, and Use*, ed. Salikoko S. Mufwene, John R. Rickford, Guy Bailey, and John Baugh, 110–53. London: Routledge.

Labov, William, and Wendell Harris. 1986. "De Facto Segregation of Black and White Vernaculars." In *Diversity and Diachrony*, ed. David Sankoff, 1–24. Amsterdam: Benjamins.

LAE = Linguistic Atlas of England. See Orton, Sanderson, Widdowson 1978.

Laird, Charlton. 1970. *Language in America.* Englewood Cliffs, NJ: Prentice-Hall.

Lambert, John. 1810. *Travels through Lower Canada and the United States of North America in the Years 1806, 1807, and 1808.* 3 vols. London: Richard Phillips.

LAMSAS = Linguistic Atlas of the Middle and South Atlantic States. See Kretzschmar, McDavid, Lerud, and Johnson 1993.

Landau, Sidney. 1984. *Dictionaries: The Art and Craft of Lexicography.* New York: Scribner. 2nd ed., Cambridge University Press, 1989.

LANE = Linguistic Atlas of New England. See Kurath 1939–43.

Lanehart, Sonja L., ed. 2000. *Sociocultural and Historical Contexts of African American Vernacular English.* Amsterdam: John Benjamins.

Lass, Roger. 1987. *The Shape of English: Structure and History.* London: Dent.

1990. "Where Do Extraterritorial Englishes Come From? Dialect Input and Recodification in Transported Englishes." In *Papers from the 5th International Conference on English Historical Linguistics*, ed. Sylvia Adamson, 245–80. Amsterdam: Benjamins.

Latham, Robert Gordon. 1848. *The English Language.* 2nd ed. London: Taylor and Walton.

Leap, William, ed. 1976. *Studies in Southwestern Indian English.* San Antonio: Trinity University Press.

1981. "American Indian Languages." In *Language in the USA*, ed. Charles A. Ferguson and Shirley Brice Heath, 116–44. Cambridge University Press.

Lear, Daniel J. 1991. "Movies." In *The Reader's Companion to American History*, ed. Eric Foner and John A. Garraty, 754–8. Boston: Houghton Mifflin.

Leechman, Douglas, and Robert A. Hall. 1955. "American Indian Pidgin English: Attestations and Grammatical Peculiarities." *American Speech* 30: 163–71.

Leek, Robert, and Donn Bayard. 1995. "Yankisms in Kiwiland, from Zed to Zee: American Lexical and Pronunciation Incursions in Dunedin (1984–1985) and Auckland (1990)." *Te Reo: Journal of the Linguistic Society of New Zealand* 38: 105–25.

Lehmann, Winfred, ed. 1967. *A Reader in Nineteenth-Century Historical Linguistics.* Bloomington: Indiana University Press.

Lehmann-Haupt, Hellmut, Lawrence C. Wroth, and Rollo G. Silver. 1925. *The Book in America: A History of the Making and Selling of Books in the United States.* 2nd ed. New York: Bowker.

Lengthy, Lemuel [pseudonym]. 1814. "Americanisms." *Analectic Magazine* 3: 404–9.

Léon, Pierre R., and P. Martin, eds. 1979. *Toronto English: Studies in Phonetics.* Studia Phonetica 14. Ottawa: Marcel Didier.

Leonard, Sterling A. 1932. *Current English Usage.* National Council of Teachers of English Monograph 1. Chicago: Inland.

Leonard, Thomas C. 1991. "Magazines and Newspapers." In *The Reader's Companion to American History,* ed. Eric Foner and John A. Garraty, 689–92. Boston: Houghton Mifflin.

Lerner, Max. 1957. *America as a Civilization.* New York: Simon and Schuster. 2nd ed. New York: Holt, 1987.

Lewin, Esther, and Albert E. Lewin. 1988. *Thesaurus of Slang.* New York: Facts on File. 2nd ed. 1994.

Lexicon Balatronicum: A Dictionary of Buckish Slang, University Wit, and Pickpocket Eloquence. 1811. "Compiled originally by Captain Grose. And Now . . . Enlarged . . . By a Member of the Whip Club." London: C. Chappel.

Leyburn, James G. 1962. *The Scotch-Irish: A Social History.* Chapel Hill: University of North Carolina Press.

Library of Congress. 1998. *American Memory: Historical Collections for the National Digital Library.* <http://memory.loc.gov/ammem/ammemhome.html>.

Lighter, Jonathan E. 1994–. *The Random House Historical Dictionary of American Slang.* Vols. 1–. New York: Random House.

Linguistic Atlas of Scotland. See Mather and Speitel 1975–8.

Linguistic Society of America. 1995. "LSA Guidelines for Nonsexist Usage." *LSA Bulletin* (each issue).

Lippi-Green, Rosina. 1997. *English with an Accent: Language, Ideology, and Discrimination in the United States.* London: Routledge.

Lloyd, Donald J. 1951. "Snobs, Slobs and the English Language." *American Scholar* 20: 283–9.

Loflin, Marvin. 1970. "On the Structure of the Verb in a Dialect of American Negro English." *Linguistics* 59: 14–28.

London, Jack [pseudonym of John Griffith Chaney]. 1909. *Martin Eden.* Reprint New York: Macmillan, 1912.

Longman Dictionary of Contemporary English. 1995. 3rd ed. Harlow, Essex: Longman.

Lougheed, William Clinton, ed. 1985. *In Search of the Standard in Canadian English.* Strathy Language Unit Occasional Papers 1. Kingston, ON: Queen's University. 1988. *Writings on Canadian English, 1976–1987: A Selective, Annotated Bibliography.* Strathy Language Unit Occasional Papers 2. Kingston, ON: Queen's University.

Lounsbury, Thomas Raynesford. 1908. *The Standard of Usage in English.* New York: Harper.

Lowell, James Russell. 1848. *The Biglow Papers.* Cambridge, MA: Nichols.

Lowry, Thomas P. 1994. *The Story the Soldiers Wouldn't Tell.* Mechanicsburg, PA: Stackpole.

Lowth, Robert. 1762. *A Short Introduction to English Grammar.* London. Reprint English Linguistics 1500–1800, no. 18. Menston, Yorks.: Scolar, 1967.

Lucke, Jessie R. 1949. "A Study of the Virginia Dialect and Its Origin in England." Ph.D. diss., University of Virginia.

Lyman, Rollo LaVerne. 1922. *English Grammar in American Schools before 1850.* Department of the Interior, Bureau of Education Bulletin 12. Washington, DC.

Macafee, Caroline I., ed. 1996. *The Concise Ulster Dictionary.* Oxford University Press.

Forthcoming. "Scots and Scottish English." In *The Legacy of Colonial English: A Study of Transported Dialects,* ed. Ray Hickey. Cambridge University Press.

MacDonald, Donald F. 1965. "Gaelic with a Dixie Accent!" *Grandfather Mountain Highland Games Handbook.* N.p.

Macdonald, Dwight. 1962a. "The String Untuned." *New Yorker* (March 10), 130–4, 137–40, 143–50, 153–60. Reprint in *Dictionaries and THAT Dictionary,* ed. James Sledd and Wilma R. Ebbitt, 166–88. Chicago: Scott, Foresman.

1962b. "Three Questions for Structural Linguists, or Webster 3 Revisited." In *Dictionaries and THAT Dictionary,* ed. James Sledd and Wilma R. Ebbitt, 256–64. Chicago: Scott, Foresman.

MacDonald, James R. 1993. "Cultural Retention and Adaptation among the Highland Scots of North Carolina." Ph.D. thesis, Edinburgh University.

Mackay, Charles. 1867. "Inroads upon English." *Blackwood's Magazine* 102: 399–417.

MacLaurin, Lois M. 1928. *Franklin's Vocabulary.* Garden City, NY: Doubleday, Doran.

MacLean, John Patterson. 1900. *An Historical Account of the Settlements of Scotch Highlanders in America Prior to the Peace of 1783.* Cleveland: Helman-Taylor.

MacLeod, Malcolm. 1986. *Peace of the Continent: The Impact of Second World War Canadian and American Bases in Newfoundland.* Saint John's: Harry Cuff.

MacNiece, Louis. 1938. *Modern Poetry.* Oxford University Press.

Mager, Nathan H., and Sylvia K. Mager. 1974. *Prentice Hall Encyclopedic Dictionary of English Usage.* Englewood Cliffs, NJ: Prentice Hall. 2nd ed., 1993.

Maitland, James. 1891. *The American Slang Dictionary.* Chicago: privately printed.

Major, Clarence. 1994. *Juba to Jive: A Dictionary of African-American Slang.* New York: Penguin.

Making of America. 1996. University of Michigan Digital Library. <http://moa.umdl.umich.edu>.

Making of America. 1999. Cornell University Digital Library. <http://cdl.library.cornell.edu/moa/>.

Malone, Kemp. 1925. "A Linguistic Patriot." *American Speech* 1: 26–31.

Manning, Robert. 1971. "The Editor's Page." *Atlantic* 227 (May): 4.

Mannion, John J. 1974. *Irish Settlements in Eastern Canada: A Study of Cultural Transfer and Adaptation*. University of Toronto, Department of Geography.

1977. ed. *The Peopling of Newfoundland: Essays in Historical Geography*. Saint John's: Memorial University of Newfoundland.

1986 "Irish Merchants Abroad: The Newfoundland Experience, 1750–1850." *Newfoundland Studies* 2: 127–90.

Marckwardt, Albert H. 1958. *American English*. New York: Oxford University Press.

Marckwardt, Albert H., and Randolph Quirk. 1964. *A Common Language: British and American English*. London: BBC and Voice of America.

Marckwardt, Albert H., and Fred W. Walcott. 1938. *Facts about Current English Usage*. National Council of Teachers of English Monograph 7. New York: Appleton-Century-Crofts.

Marsh, George Perkins. 1860. *Lectures on the English Language*. New York: Scribner.

Marshall, Ingeborg. 1996. *A History and Ethnography of the Beothuk*. Montreal: McGill-Queen's University Press.

Martin, Terence. 1961. *The Instructed Vision*. Bloomington: Indiana University Press.

Mather, Cotton. 1702. *Magnalia Christi Americana*. Reprint ed. Kenneth B. Murdock, with the assistance of Elizabeth W. Miller. Cambridge, MA: Belknap, 1977.

Mather, James Y., and Hans H. Speitel, eds. 1975–8. *Linguistic Atlas of Scotland*. 3 vols. London: Croom Helm.

Mathews, Mitford McLeod, ed. 1931. *The Beginnings of American English: Essays and Comments*. University of Chicago Press.

1936. "Notes and Comments Made by British Travelers and Observers upon American English, 1770–1850." Ph.D. diss., Harvard University.

1951. *Dictionary of Americanisms*. University of Chicago Press.

Matthews, Brander. 1892. *Americanisms and Britishisms*. New York: Harper.

1901. *Parts of Speech: Essays on English*. New York: Scribner's.

1921. *Essays on English*. New York: Scribner's.

1925. "The English Language and the American Academy." In *Academy Papers: Addresses on Language Problems by Members of the American Academy of Arts and Letters*, 63–93. New York: Scribner's.

Matthews, William. 1935. "Sailors' Pronunciation in the Second Half of the Seventeenth Century." *Anglia* 59: 192–251.

1937. "Sailors' Pronunciation, 1770–1783." *Anglia* 61: 72–80.

Maurer, David W. 1930. "Schoonerisms: Some Speech-Peculiarities of the North-Atlantic Fishermen." *American Speech* 5: 387–95.

1940. *The Big Con*. Indianapolis, IN: Bobbs-Merrill. Rev. ed. as *The American Confidence Man*. Springfield, IL: C. C. Thomas, 1973.

1955. *Whiz Mob*. Publication of the American Dialect Society 24. Gainesville, FL: American Dialect Society.

1974. *The American Confidence Man*. Springfield, IL: Thomas.

1981. *Language of the Underworld*. Ed. A. W. Futrell and C. B. Wordell. Lexington: University Press of Kentucky.

McArthur, Tom. 1989. *The English Language As Used in Quebec.* Strathy Language Unit Occasional Papers 3. Kingston, ON: Queen's University.

McConnell, Ruth E. 1979. *Our Own Voice: Canadian English and How It Is Studied.* Toronto: Gage.

McCrum, Robert, William Cran, and Robert MacNeil. 1986. *The Story of English.* New York: Viking Penguin.

McDavid, Raven I., Jr. 1962. In "Webster's Third New International Dictionary: A Symposium," ed. Robert G. Gunderson. *Quarterly Journal of Speech* 48: 431–40.

———. 1966. "Usage, Dialects, and Functional Varieties." In *The Random House Dictionary of the English Language*, ed. Jess Stein, xix–xxi. New York: Random House.

———. 1967. "Historical, Regional and Social Variation." *Journal of English Linguistics* 1: 24–40.

———. 1979. *Dialects in Culture.* Ed. W. A. Kretzschmar. Tuscaloosa: University of Alabama Press.

———. 1985. "Dialect Areas of the Atlantic Seaboard." In *American Speech: 1600 to the Present*, ed. Peter Benes, 15–26. Boston University.

McIntosh, Angus. 1983. "Present Indicative Plural Forms in the Later Middle English of the North Midlands." In *Middle English Studies Presented to Norman Davis in Honour of His Seventieth Birthday*, ed. Douglas Grey and E. G. Douglas, 235–44. Oxford: Clarendon.

McKnight, George H. 1923. *English Words and Their Background.* New York: Appleton.

———. 1925. "Conservatism in American Speech." *American Speech* 1: 1–17.

———. 1928. *Modern English in the Making.* New York: Appleton.

McManus, Gary E., and Clifford H. Wood. 1991. *Atlas of Newfoundland and Labrador.* Saint John's: Breakwater.

McMillan, James B. 1977. "Naming Regional Dialects in America." In *Papers in Language Variation: SAMLA-ADS Collection*, ed. David L. Shores and Carole P. Hines, 119–24. Tuscaloosa: University of Alabama Press.

McMillan, James B., and Michael Montgomery. 1989. *Annotated Bibliography of Southern American English.* Tuscaloosa: University of Alabama Press.

Meillet, Antoine. 1906. "L'état actuel des études de linguistique générale." *Revue des Idées* 3: 296–308.

Melly, George. 1965. *Owning-Up.* Harmondsworth, UK: Penguin, 1977.

Mencken, Henry Louis. 1919. *The American Language.* New York: Knopf. 2nd ed., 1921; 3rd ed., 1923; 4th ed., 1936. Supplement 1, 1945. Supplement 2, 1948.

———. 1963. *The American Language: An Inquiry into the Development of English in the United States.* The 4th ed. and two supplements, abridged, with annotations and new material, by Raven I. McDavid, Jr., with the assistance of David W. Maurer. New York: Knopf.

Merriam, Alan P., and Fradley H. Garner. 1968. "Jazz – The Word." *Ethnomusicology* 12: 373–96.

Merriam-Webster's Collegiate Dictionary, 10th ed. Ed. Frederick C. Mish. Springfield, MA: Merriam-Webster.

Meyer, Duane. 1961. *The Highland Scots of North Carolina 1732–1776*. Chapel Hill: University of North Carolina Press.

Mezzrow, Milton, and Bernard Wolfe. 1946. *Really the Blues*. New York: Random House. Reprint, New York: Signet, 1964.

Millar, Robert M. 1996. "Gaelic-Influenced Scots in Pre-Revolutionary Maryland." In *Language Contact across the North Atlantic*, ed. Sture Ureland and Iain Clarkson, 387–410. Tübingen: Niemeyer.

Mille, Katherine. 1990. "A Historical Analysis of Tense-Mood-Aspect in Gullah Creole: A Case of Stable Variation." Ph.D. diss., University of South Carolina, Columbia.

Miller, Kerby A. 1985. *Emigrants and Exiles: Ireland and the Irish Emigration to North America*. Oxford University Press.

Miller, Mary R. 1967. "Attestations of American Indian Pidgin English in Fiction and Nonfiction." *American Speech* 42: 142–7.

Miller, Michael I. 1986. "The Greatest Blemish: Plurals in *-sp, -st, -sk*." In *Language Variety in the South: Perspectives in Black and White*, ed. Michael Montgomery and Guy Bailey, 235–53. Tuscaloosa: University of Alabama Press.

Miller, Philip. 1731–9. *The Gardener's Dictionary*. 2 vols. London: Printed for the Author.

Miller, William Davis. 1929. "Thomas Mount and the Flash Language." *Rhode Island Historical Society Collections* 22: 65–9.

Milroy, James. 1991. "The Interpretation of Social Constraints on Variation in Belfast English." In *English around the World: Sociolinguistic Perspectives*, ed. Jenny Cheshire, 75–85. Cambridge University Press.

Mish, Frederick C., ed. 1983. *Webster's Ninth New Collegiate Dictionary*. Springfield, MA: Merriam-Webster.

——— 1993. ed. *Merriam-Webster's Collegiate Dictionary*. 10th ed. Springfield, MA: Merriam-Webster.

Mishoe, Margaret, and Michael Montgomery. 1994. "The Pragmatics of Multiple Modals in North and South Carolina." *American Speech* 69: 3–29.

Mitchell-Keman, Claudia. 1971. "Language Behavior in a Black Urban Community." Monographs of the Language Behavior Laboratory, University of California at Berkeley 2.

Molloy, Gerald. 1897. *The Irish Difficulty: Shall and Will*. London, Glasgow and Dublin: Blackie & Son.

Monaghan, E. Jennifer. 1983. *A Common Heritage: Noah Webster's Blue-Back Speller*. Hamden, CT: Archon Books.

Montgomery, Michael. 1989. "Exploring the Roots of Appalachian English." *English World-Wide* 10: 227–78.

——— 1991. "The Roots of Appalachian English: Scotch-Irish or Southern British?" *Journal of the Appalachian Studies Association* 3: 177–91.

1992. "The Etymology of *Y'all*." In *Old English and New: Studies in Language and Linguistics in Honor of Frederic G. Cassidy*, ed. Joan H. Hall, Nick Doane, and Dick Ringler, 356–69. New York: Garland.

1994a. "An Early Letter in Ulster Scots." *Ullans: The Magazine for Ulster Scots* 2: 45–51.

1994b. "The Evolution of Verb Concord in Scots." In *Studies in Scots and Gaelic: Proceedings of the Third International Conference on the Languages of Scotland*, ed. Alexander Fenton and Donald A. MacDonald, 81–95. Edinburgh: Canongate Academic.

1995. "The Linguistic Value of Ulster Emigrant Letters." *Ulster Folklife* 41: 26–41.

1996a. "David Bruce: Ulster-Scot-American Poet." *Ullans: The Magazine for Ulster Scots* 4: 23–8.

1996b. "The Future of Southern American English." *SECOL Review* 20: 1–24.

1996c. "How Scotch-Irish Is Your English?" *Journal of East Tennessee History* 67: 1–33.

1997a. "Making the Trans-Atlantic Link between Varieties of English: The Case of Plural Verbal *-s*." *Journal of English Linguistics* 25: 122–41.

1997b. "The Scotch-Irish Element in Appalachian English: How Broad? How Deep?" In *Ulster and North America: Transatlantic Perspectives on the Scotch-Irish*, ed. Curtis Wood and Tyler Blethen, 189–212. Tuscaloosa: University of Alabama Press.

1997c. "A Tale of Two Georges: The Language of Irish Indian Traders in Colonial North America." In *Focus on Ireland*, ed. Jeffrey Kallen, 227–54. Amsterdam: Benjamins.

1998a. "In the Appalachians They Speak like Shakespeare." In *Myths in Linguistics*, ed. Laurie Bauer and Peter Trudgill, 66–76. New York: Penguin.

1998b. "John Dinsmoor: Another Ulster-Scot-American Poet." *Ullans: The Magazine for Ulster Scots* 6: 50–4.

1999. "Sierra Leone Settler English: Another Exported Variety of African American English." *English World-Wide* 20: 1–34.

2000a. "The Celtic Element in American English." In *Celtic Englishes II*, ed. Hildegard L. C. Tristram, 231–64. Heidelberg: Winter.

2000b. "The Problem of Persistence: Ulster-Scot-American Poets." *Journal of Scotch-Irish Studies* 1: 105–19.

Montgomery, Michael, Janet M. Fuller, and Sharon DeMarse. 1993. "'The black men has wives and sweet harts [and third person plural -s] jest like the white men': Evidence for Verbal *-s* from Written Documents on Nineteenth-Century African American Speech." *Language Variation and Change* 5: 335–54.

Montgomery, Michael, and John Kirk. 1996. "The Origin of the Habitual Verb *Be* in American Black English: Irish or English or What?" *Belfast Working Papers in Linguistics* 11: 308–33.

Montgomery, Michael, and Margaret Mishoe. 1999. "'He bes took up with a

Yankee girl and moved up North': The Verb *Bes* in the Carolinas and Its History." *American Speech* 75: 240–81.

Montgomery, Michael, and Stephen J. Nagle. 1994. "Double Modals in Scotland and the Southern United States: Trans-Atlantic Inheritance or Independent Development?" *Folia Linguistica Historica* 14: 91–107.

Montgomery, Michael, and Philip Robinson. 1996. "Ulster English as Janus: Language Contact across the North Atlantic and across the Irish Sea." In *Language Contact across the North Atlantic*, ed. Sture Ureland and Iain Clarkson, 411–26. Tübingen: Niemeyer.

Moon, George Washington. 1864. *The Dean's English: A Criticism of the Dean of Canterbury's Essays on the Queen's English.* 2nd ed. London: Hatchards. Originally entitled *A Defense of the Queen's English.*

1869. *The Bad English of Lindley Murray and Other Writers on the English Language.* 3rd ed. London: Hatchards.

Moore, Francis. 1744. *A Voyage to Georgia, Begun in the Year 1735.* Reprint in *Collections of the Georgia Historical Society* 1: 79–152.

Morgan, Lucia C. 1967. "North Carolina Accents: Some Observations." *North Carolina Journal of Speech and Drama* 1.1: 3–8.

Morgan, Marcyliena. 1989. "From Down South to Up South: The Language Behavior of Three Generations of Black Women Residing in Chicago." Ph.D. diss., University of Pennsylvania.

1991. "Indirectness and Representation in African American Women's Discourse." *Pragmatics* 1: 421–51.

1993. "The Africanness of Counterlanguage among Afro-Americans." In *Africanisms in Afro-American Language Varieties*, ed. Salikoko S. Mufwene, 423–35. Athens: University of Georgia Press.

1994. "Theories and Politics in African American English." *Annual Review of Anthropology* 23: 325–45.

Morris, William, ed. 1969. *The American Heritage Dictionary of the English Language.* New York: American Heritage; Boston: Houghton Mifflin.

1982. ed. *The American Heritage Dictionary of the English Language*, 2nd college ed. Boston: Houghton Mifflin.

Morris, William, and Mary Morris. 1975. *Harper Dictionary of Contemporary Usage.* New York: Harper. 2nd ed. 1985.

Morton, Herbert C. 1994. *The Story of* Webster's Third: *Philip Gove's Controversial Dictionary and Its Critics.* Cambridge University Press.

Moulton, William G., Archibald A. Hill, Charles A. Ferguson, Eric P. Hamp, Morris Halle, and Thomas A Sebeok. 1964. "Linguistic Society of America." In *Report of the Commission on the Humanities*, 152–8. New York: American Council of Learned Societies.

Mufwene, Salikoko S. 1986a. "Restrictive Relativization in Gullah." *Journal of Pidgin and Creole Languages* 1: 1–31.

1986b. "Number Delimitation in Gullah." *American Speech* 61: 33–60.

1986c. "Les langues créoles peuvent-elles être définies sans allusion à leur histoire?" *Etudes Créoles* 9: 135–50.

1987a. "An Issue on Predicate-Clefting: Evidence from Atlantic Creoles and African Languages." In *Varia Creolica*, ed. Philippe Maurer and Thomas Stolz, 71–89. Bochum, Germany: Brockmeyer.

1987b. Review of *Language Varieties in the South: Perspectives in Black and White*, ed. Michael Montgomery and Guy Bailey. *Journal of Pidgin and Creole Languages* 2: 93–110.

1989. "Equivocal Structures in Some Gullah Complex Sentences." *American Speech* 64: 304–26.

1990a. "Creoles and Universal Grammar." *Linguistics* 28: 783–807.

1990b. "Serialization and Subordination in Gullah." In *When Verbs Collide: Papers from the 1990 Ohio State Mini-Conference on Serial Verbs*, ed. Brian Joseph and Arnold Zwicky, 91–108. Ohio State University Working Papers in Linguistics 39. Mimeographed.

1991a. "Is Gullah Decreolizing? A Comparison of a Speech Sample of the 1930s with a Sample of the 1980s." In *The Emergence of Black English: Text and Commentary*, ed. Guy Bailey, Natalie Maynor, and Patricia Cukor-Avila, 213–30. Amsterdam: Benjamins.

1991b. "Some Reasons Why Gullah Is Not Dying Yet." *English World-Wide* 12: 215–43.

1992a. "Are There Possessive Pronouns in Atlantic Creoles?" In *The Atlantic Meets the Pacific: Papers from the Society for Pidgin and Creole Linguistics*, ed. Francis Byrne and John Holm, 133–44. Amsterdam: John Benjamins.

1992b. "Ideology and Facts on African American English." *Pragmatics* 2: 141–66.

1992c. "Why Grammars Are Not Monolithic." In *The Joy of Grammar: A Festschrift in Honor of James D. McCawley*, ed. Diane Brentari, Gary N. Larson, and Lynn A. MacLeod, 225–50. Amsterdam: Benjamins.

1992d. "Africanisms in Gullah: A Re-examination of the Issues." In *Old English and New: Essays in Language and Linguistics in Honor of Frederic G. Cassidy*, ed. Joan Hall, Nick Doane, and Dick Ringler, 156–82. New York: Garland.

1993. "Scope of Negation and Focus in Gullah." In *Focus and Grammatical Relations*, ed. Francis Byrne and Donald Winford, 95–116. Amsterdam: John Benjamins.

1994a. "On Decreolization: The Case of Gullah." In *Language and the Social Construction of Identity in Creole Situations*, ed. Marcyliena Morgan, 63–99. Los Angeles: UCLA Center for African-American Studies.

1994b. "Theoretical Linguistics and Variation Analysis: Strange Bedfellows?" In *Papers from the Parasession on Language Variation and Linguistic Theory*, ed. Katie Beals, Jeannette Denton, Robert Knippen, Lynette Melnar, Hisami Suzuki, and Erica Zeinfeld, 202–17. Chicago Linguistic Society.

1994c. "African-American English, Caribbean English Creoles, and North American English: Perspectives on Their Geneses." In *Proceedings of the Mid-America Linguistics Conference*, ed. Frances Ingemann, 305–30. Lawrence: University of Kansas.

1995. "Gullah's Genesis: Myths and Sociohistorical Facts." In *Language Variety in the South II*, ed. Cynthia Bernstein, Robin Sabino, and Thomas Nunally. Tuscaloosa: University of Alabama Press.

1996. "Creole Genesis: A Population Genetics Perspective." In *Caribbean Language: Issues Old and New: Papers in Honour of Professor Mervyn Alleyne on the Occasion of His Sixtieth Birthday*, ed. Pauline Christie, 163–96. Kingston, Jamaica: University of the West Indies Press.

1997a. "The Development of American Englishes: Some Questions from a Creole Genesis Perspective." In *Focus on the USA*, ed. Edgar W. Schneider, 231–64. Amsterdam: Benjamins.

1997b. "Jargons, Pidgins, Creoles, and Koinés: What Are They?" In *Structure and Status of Pidgins and Creoles*, ed. Arthur Spears and Donald Winford, 35–70. Amsterdam: Benjamins.

2001. *The Ecology of Language Evolution*. Cambridge University Press.

Mufwene, Salikoko S., John R. Rickford, Guy Bailey, and John Baugh, eds. 1998. *African-American English: Structure, History, and Use*. London: Routledge.

Müller, Friedrich Max. 1862. *Lectures on the Science of Language*. London 2nd ed., rev. New York: Scribner's.

Munro, Pamela. 1989. *U. C. L. A. Slang*. Department of Linguistics, University of California, Los Angeles.

Murray, James. 1873. *The Dialect of the Southern Counties of Scotland*. London: Philological Society.

Murray, Lindley. 1795. *English Grammar, Adapted to the Different Classes of Learners*. York. Reprint English Linguistics 1500–1800, no. 106. Menston, Yorks.: Scolar, 1968.

Murray, Thomas E., Timothy C. Frazer, and Beth Lee Simon. 1996. "*Need* + Past Participle in American English." *American Speech* 71: 255–71.

Myhill, John. 1988. "The Rise of *Be* as an Aspect Marker in Black English Vernacular." *American Speech* 63: 304–25.

1991. "The Use of Invariant *Be* with Verbal Predicates in BEV." In *Verb Patterns in Black English and Creole*, ed. Walter Edwards and Donald Winford, 101–13. Detroit, MI: Wayne State University Press.

National Council of Teachers of English, Commission on the English Curriculum. 1952. *The English Language Arts*. NCTE Curriculum Series, no. 1. New York: Appleton-Century-Crofts.

Neilson, William Allan, and Thomas A. Knott, eds. 1934. *Webster's New International Dictionary*. 2nd ed. Springfield, MA: Merriam.

Neufeldt, Victoria, ed. 1988. *Webster's New World Dictionary of American English*. 3rd college ed. New York: Webster's New World.

Newlin, Claude M. 1928. "Dialects on the Western Pennsylvania Frontier." *American Speech* 4: 104–10.

Newman, Edwin. 1974. *Strictly Speaking: Will America Be the Death of English?* Indianapolis, IN: Bobbs-Merrill.

Nichols, Ann Eljenholm. 1987. "The Suasive Subjunctive." *American Speech* 62: 140–53.

Nichols, Patricia C. 1975. "Complementizers in Creoles." *Working Papers on Language Universals* 19: 131–5. Stanford University. Mimeographed.

———. 1976. "Linguistic Change in Gullah: Sex, Age, and Mobility." Ph.D. diss., Stanford University.

———. 1983. "Black and White Speaking in the Rural South: Difference in the Pronominal System." *American Speech* 58: 201–15.

Nicholson, Margaret. 1958. *A Dictionary of American-English Usage, Based on Fowler's Modern English Usage.* New York: Signet.

Noel-Armfield, Hoel T. 1893. "The Essex Dialect and Its Influence in the New World." *Transactions of the Essex Archaeological Society* 4: 245–53.

Nordhoff, Charles. 1865. "Thieves' Jargon." *Harper's Monthly Magazine* (New York, April), 601–7.

Norton, Mary Beth, David M. Katzman, Paul D. Escott, Howard P. Chudacoff, Thomas G. Paterson, and William M. Tuttle, Jr. 1990. *A People and a Nation: A History of the United States.* 3rd ed. Boston: Houghton Mifflin.

Nunberg, Geoffrey. 1982. "English and Good English." In *The American Heritage Dictionary of the English Language*, 2nd college ed., ed. William Morris, 34–6. Boston: Houghton Mifflin.

———. 1983. "The Decline of Grammar." *Atlantic Monthly* 252.6 (December): 31–46.

———. 1992. "Usage in *The American Heritage Dictionary:* The Place of Criticism." In *The American Heritage Dictionary of the English Language*, 3rd ed., ed. Ann Soukhanov, xxvi–xxx. Boston: Houghton Mifflin.

OED = Oxford English Dictionary.

O'Flaherty, Patrick. 1999. *Old Newfoundland: A History to 1843.* St. John's, Newfoundland: Long Beach Press.

Ogden, Charles K., and I. A. Richards. 1923. *The Meaning of Meaning.* 10th ed. London: Routledge, 1949.

Oman, Carola. 1968. *The Gascoyne Heiress: The Life and Diaries of Frances Mary Gascoyne-Cecil.* London: Hodder and Stoughton.

"On Americanisms, with a Fragment of a Trans-Atlantic Pastoral." 1820. *New Monthly Magazine* 14: 629–32.

Opie, Iona, and Peter Opie. 1960. *The Language and Lore of Schoolchildren.* Oxford: Clarendon.

Orbeck, Anders. 1927. *Early New England Pronunciation as Reflected in Some Seventeenth Century Town Records of Eastern Massachusetts.* Ann Arbor, MI: Wahr.

Orsman, Harold W., ed. 1997. *The Dictionary of New Zealand English: A Dictionary of New Zealandisms on Historical Principles.* Auckland: Oxford University Press.

Orton, Harold, and Eugen Dieth, eds. 1962–. *Survey of English Dialects*. Part A: Introduction; Part B: The Basic Material, 12 vols. (4 numbered vols. each in 3 parts). Leeds: Arnold for the University of Leeds.

Orton, Harold, Stewart Sanderson, and John David Allison Widdowson. 1978. *The Linguistic Atlas of England*. London: Croom Helm.

Otto, John Solomon. 1987. "Cracker: The History of a Southeastern Ethnic, Economic, and Racial Epithet." *Names* 35: 28–39.

Oxford English Dictionary. 1989. 2nd ed. Oxford: Clarendon Press.

Oxford English Dictionary. 1994. 2nd ed. on CD-ROM. Oxford University Press.

Oxford English Dictionary Online. 2000. Oxford University Press. <http://www.oed.com>.

Paddock, Harold J. 1981. *A Dialect Survey of Carbonear, Newfoundland*. Publication of the American Dialect Society 68. Tuscaloosa: University of Alabama Press.

——— 1982. "Newfoundland Dialects of English." In *Languages in Newfoundland and Labrador*, ed. Harold J. Paddock, 71–89. 2nd version. Saint John's: Memorial University of Newfoundland, Department of Linguistics.

——— 1988. "The Actuation Problem for Gender Change in Wessex versus Newfoundland." In *Historical Dialectology*, ed. Jacek Fisiak, 377–95. Berlin: Mouton.

Palmer, David John. 1965. *The Rise of English Studies: An Account of the Study of the English Language and Literature from Its Origins to the Making of the Oxford English School*. London: Oxford University Press for the University of Hull.

Parker, George. 1789. *Life's Painter of Variegated Characters*. Reprint n.p., n.d.

Parker, W. R. 1966. "Where Do English Departments Come From?" *College English* 28: 339–51.

Partridge, Eric. 1933. *Slang To-Day and Yesterday*. London: Routledge. 4th ed., New York: Barnes and Noble, 1970.

——— 1949. *A Dictionary of the Underworld*. London: Macmillan. 2nd ed., 1961. 3rd ed., 1968.

——— 1984. *A Dictionary of Slang and Unconventional English*. 8th ed. Ed. Paul Beale. London: Macmillan.

Paynell, Thomas, trans. 1533. *Of the VVood Called Gvaiacvm That Healeth the Frenche Pockes*. London: Tho. Bertheleti.

PEAS = *The Pronunciation of English in the Atlantic States*. See Kurath and McDavid 1961.

Pederson, Lee. 1977a. *A Compositional Guide to the LAGS Project*. Atlanta: Emory University.

——— 1977b. "Studies of American Pronunciation since 1945." *American Speech* 52: 262–327.

——— 1978. "Sociolinguistic Aspects of American Mobility." *Amerikastudien/American Studies* 23: 299–319.

——— 1986–92. ed. *Linguistic Atlas of the Gulf States*. 7 vols. Athens: University of Georgia Press.

1996a. "Piney Woods Southern." In *Focus on the USA*, ed. Edgar W. Schnieder, 13–23. Amsterdam: Benjamins.

1996b. "LAMR/LAWS and the Main Chance." *Journal of English Linguistics* 24: 234–49.

Pei, Mario. 1962. "The Dictionary as a Battlefront: English Teachers' Dilemma." *Saturday Review* 45 (July 21): 44–6, 55–6.

1964. "A Loss for Words." *Saturday Review* 47 (November 14): 82–4.

Perrin, Porter G. 1965. *The Writer's Guide.* Glenview, IL: Scott, Foresman.

Perry, Theresa, and Lisa Delpit, eds. 1998. *The Real Ebonics Debate: Power, Language, and the Education of African-American Children.* Boston: Beacon Press.

Pickering, John. 1816. *A Vocabulary or Collection of Words and Phrases Which Have Been Supposed to Be Peculiar to the United States of America.* Boston: Cummings and Hilliard. Orig. pub. as "Memoir on the Present State of the English Language in the United States of America," *Memoirs of the American Academy of Arts and Sciences* 3 (1815): 439–536.

Pike, James. 1865. *The Scout and Ranger.* Cincinnati, OH: J. R. Hawley.

Pinker, Steven. 1994. *The Language Instinct: How the Mind Creates Language.* New York: Morrow.

Plato. *Plato with an English Translation.* Vol. 6, *Cratylus, Parmenides, Greater Hippias, Lesser Hippias,* ed. Harold N. Fowler. Loeb Classical Library. Cambridge, MA: Harvard University Press, 1926.

Pointon, Graham. 1994. "Estuary English the Standard of the Future?" *Cambridge Language Reference News* 2: 4.

Polk, William Tannahill. 1953. "Uncle Remus Spake Queen's English." In *Southern Accent: From Uncle Remus to Oak Ridge,* by W. T. Polk, 57–71. New York: Morrow.

Popik, Barry, and Gerald Leonard Cohen. 1995. "Update on *Hot Dog.*" *Comments on Etymology* 25.3: 7–19.

1997. "More Material for the Study of *Dude.*" *Comments on Etymology* 26.7: 2–12.

Poplack, Shana, ed. 1999. *The English History of African-American English.* Malden, MA: Blackwell.

Poplack, Shana, and David Sankoff. 1987. "The Philadelphia Story in the Spanish Caribbean." *American Speech* 62: 291–314.

Poplack, Shana, and Sali Tagliamonte. 1989. "There's No Tense like the Present: Verbal -S Inflection in Early Black English." *Language Variation and Change* 1: 47–84.

1991. "African-American English in the Diaspora: Evidence from Old-Line Nova Scotians." *Language Variation and Change* 3: 301–39.

1994. "-*S* or Nothing: Marking the Plural in the African-American Diaspora." *American Speech* 69: 227–59.

The Port Folio. 1805. Philadelphia, August 24.

Porter, Glen, ed. 1980. *Encyclopedia of American Economic History.* New York: Scribner.

Pound, Louise. 1923. "Spelling-Manipulation and Present-day Advertising." *Dialect Notes* 5: 226–32.

1925. "The Kraze for 'K.'" *American Speech* 1: 43–4.

Pratt, Terry Kenneth. 1988. *Dictionary of Prince Edward Island English.* University of Toronto Press.

1993. "The Hobgoblin of Canadian English Spelling." In *Focus on Canada*, ed. Sandra Clarke, 45–64. Varieties of English around the World 11. Amsterdam: John Benjamins.

Priestley, Joseph. 1761. *The Rudiments of English Grammar.* London: Griffiths. Reprint English Linguistics 1500–1800, no. 210. Menston, Yorks.: Scolar, 1969.

Primer, Sylvester. 1887. "Charleston Provincialisms." *Transactions of the Modern Language Association* 3: 84–99.

1889. "Pronunciation near Fredericksburg, Virginia." *Proceedings of the American Philological Association* 20: xxv–xxviii.

Prince, John D. 1912. "An Ancient New Jersey Indian Jargon." *American Anthropologist* 14: 508–24.

Proctor, Paul, ed. 1995. *Cambridge International Dictionary of English.* Cambridge University Press.

Prowse, D. W. 1895. *A History of Newfoundland from the English, Colonial, and Foreign Records.* London: Macmillan.

Publication of the American Dialect Society. 1944–.

Pyles, Thomas. 1952. *Words and Ways of American English.* New York: Random House.

Pyles, Thomas, and John Algeo. 1993. *The Origins and Development of the English Language.* 4th ed. Fort Worth, TX: Harcourt Brace Jovanovich.

Raleigh, Walter. 1596. *The Discoverie of the Large, Rich and Bewtiful Empyre of Guiana.* Facsimile ed. Amsterdam: Da Capo Press, 1968.

Ramsey, Samuel. 1892. *The English Language and English Grammar: An Historical Study of the Sources, Development, and Analogies of the Language and of the Principles Governing Its Usages.* New York: Putnam's. Reprint, New York: Haskell House, 1968.

Rand, Asa. 1833. "Lecture on Teaching Grammar and Composition." *American Annals of Education and Instruction* 3: 159–74.

Rath, R. C. 1991. "'What meanes hee may for to gett her over': The Transference of Language and Culture from Old to New England in the 17th Century." M.A. thesis, Brandeis University.

Read, Allen Walker. 1933. "British Recognition of American Speech in the Eighteenth Century." *Dialect Notes* 6: 313–34.

1935. "Amphi-Atlantic English." *English Studies* 17: 161–78.

1936. "American Projects for an Academy to Regulate Speech." *PMLA* 51: 1141–79.

1938. "The Assimilation of the Speech of British Immigrants in Colonial America." *Journal of English and Germanic Philology* 37: 70–9.

1939. "The Speech of Negroes in Colonial America." *Journal of Negro History* 24: 247–58.

1963a. "The First Stage in the History of 'O.K.'" *American Speech* 38: 5–27.

1963b. "The Second Stage in the History of 'O.K.'" *American Speech* 38: 83–102.

1963c. "Could Andrew Jackson Spell?" *American Speech* 38: 188–95.

1964a. "The Folklore of 'O.K.'" *American Speech* 39: 5–25.

1964b. "Later Stages in the History of 'O.K.'" *American Speech* 39: 83–101.

1964c. "Successive Revisions in the Explanation of 'O.K.'" *American Speech* 39: 243–67.

1966. "The Spread of German Linguistic Learning in New England during the Lifetime of Noah Webster." *American Speech* 41: 163–81.

1979. "Milestones in the Branching of British and American English." Lecture presented at Vanderbilt University, Nashville.

2001. *Milestones in the History of English in America.* Ed. Richard W. Bailey. Publication of the American Dialect Society. Durham, NC: Duke University Press.

Reed, Carroll. 1953. "English Archaisms in Pennsylvania German." In *Publication of the American Dialect Society* no. 19, 3–7. Tuscaloosa: University of Alabama Press.

Regional Language Studies – Newfoundland [periodical]. 1968–. Saint John's: Memorial University of Newfoundland.

Reinecke, John E. 1969. *Language and Dialect in Hawaii: A Sociolinguistic History to 1935.* Honolulu: University of Hawaii Press.

Reinecke, John E., and Stanley M. Tsuzaki. 1967. "Hawaiian Loanwords in Hawaiian English of the 1930's." *Oceanic Linguistics* 6: 80–115.

Review of Charles Jared Ingersoll's *Inchiquin* (1810). 1813–4. *Quarterly Review* 10: 494–539.

Review of two biographies of George Washington. 1810. *British Critic* 35: 181–4.

Richardson, Carmen. 1991. "Habitual Structures among Blacks and Whites in the 1990s." *American Speech* 66: 292–302.

Rickford, John R. 1974. "Insights from the Mesolect." In *Pidgins and Creoles: Current Trends and Prospects*, ed. David DeCamp and Ian Hancock, 92–117. Washington, DC: Georgetown University Press.

1975. "Carrying the New Wave into Syntax: The Case of Black English *Bin*." In *Analyzing Variation in Language*, ed. Ralph W. Fasold and Roger W. Shuy, 162–83. Washington, DC: Georgetown University Press.

1977. "The Question of Prior Creolization of Black English." In *Pidgin and Creole Linguistics*, ed. Albert Valdman, 190–221. Bloomington: Indiana University Press.

1986a. "Social Contact and Linguistic Diffusion: Hiberno English and New World Black English." *Language* 62: 245–90.

1986b. "Some Principles for the Study of Black and White Speech in the South." In *Language Varieties in the South: Perspectives in Black and White*, ed. Michael Montgomery and Guy Bailey, 38–62. Tuscaloosa: University of Alabama Press.

1990. "Number Delimitation in Gullah: A Response to Mufwene." *American Speech* 65: 148–63.

1992. "Grammatical Variation and Divergence in Vernacular Black English." In *Internal and External Factors in Syntactic Change*, ed. Marinel Gerritsen and Dieter Stein, 175–200. Berlin: Mouton, De Gruyter.

Rickford, John R., Arnetha Ball, Renée Blake, Raina Jackson, and Nomi Martin. 1991. "Rappin on the Copula Coffin: Theoretical and Methodological Issues in the Analysis of Copula Variation in African-American Vernacular English." *Language Variation and Change* 3: 103–32.

Rickford, John R., and Renée Blake. 1990. "Copula Contraction and Absence in Barbadian English, Samaná English, and Vernacular Black English." In *Proceedings of the Sixteenth Annual Meeting of the Berkeley Linguistics Society*, ed. K. Hall, J.-P. Koenig, M. Meacham, and L. A. Sutton, 257–68. Berkeley Linguistics Society.

Rickford, John R., and Russell J. Rickford. 2000. *Spoken Soul: The Story of Black English*. New York: Wiley.

Risch, Barbara. 1987. "Women's Derogatory Terms for Men: That's Right, 'Dirty Words.'" *Language and Society* 16: 353–8.

Rissanen, Matti. 1985. "Periphrastic 'Do' in Affirmative Statements in Early American English." *Journal of English Linguistics* 18: 163–83.

1994. "'Candy No Witch, Barbados': Salem Witchcraft Trials as Evidence of Early American English." In *Language in Time and Space: Studies in Honor of Wolfgang Viereck on the Occasion of his 60th Birthday*, ed. Heinrich Ramisch and Kenneth Wynne, 183–93. Stuttgart: F. Steiner, 1997.

Rollins, Hyder E., and Herschel Baker, eds. 1954. *The Renaissance in England*. Boston: Heath.

Rompkey, Ronald. 1991. *Grenfell of Labrador: A Biography*. University of Toronto Press.

Russell, Bernie Eugene. 1971. "Dialectal and Phonetic Features of Edward Taylor's Rhymes: A Brief Study Based upon a Computer Concordance of his Poems." Ph.D. diss., University of Wisconsin.

Sala, George Augustus. 1853. "Slang." *Household Words* (London, Sept. 24), 73–8. Reprint in *Living Age* (New York, Nov.), 12.

Samarin, William J. 1986. "Chinook Jargon and Pidgin Historiography." *Canadian Journal of Anthropology* 5: 23–34.

Sandred, Karl Inge. 1983. *Good or Bad Scots? Attitudes to Optional Lexical and Grammatical Usages in Edinburgh*. Acta Universitatis Upsaliensis, Studia Anglistica Upsaliensia 48.

Sapir, Edward. 1921. *Language: An Introduction to the Study of Speech*. New York: Harcourt.

Scargill, Matthew Henry, and H. J. Warkentyne. 1972. "The Survey of Canadian English: A Report." *English Quarterly* 5: 47–104.

Schele de Vere, Maximilian. 1872. *Americanisms: The English of the New World.* New York: Scribner.

Schilling-Estes, Natalie, and Walt Wolfram. 1999. "Alternative Models of Dialect Death: Dissipation vs. Concentration." *Language* 75: 486–521.

Schneider, Edgar W. 1982. "On the History of Black English in the USA: Some New Evidence." *English World-Wide* 3: 18–46.

1983. "The Diachronic Development of the Black English Perfective Auxiliary Phrase." *Journal of English Linguistics* 16: 55–64.

1984. "A Bibliography of Writings on American and Canadian English (1965–1983)." In *A Bibliography of Writings on Varieties of English, 1965–1983,* comp. Wolfgang Viereck, Edgar W. Schneider, and Manfred Görlach, 89–223. Amsterdam: Benjamins.

1989. *American Earlier Black English.* Tuscaloosa: University of Alabama Press.

1990. "The Cline of Creoleness in English-Oriented Creoles and Semi-Creoles of the Caribbean." *English World-Wide* 11: 79–113.

1993. "Africanisms in the Grammar of Afro-American English: Weighing the Evidence." In *Africanisms in Afro-American Language Varieties,* ed. Salikoko S. Mufwene, 209–21. Athens: University of Georgia Press.

1994. "Appalachian Vocabulary: Its Character, Sources, and Distinctiveness." In *Verhandlungen des Internationalen Dialektologenkongresses Bamberg 1990 Band 3,* ed. Wolfgang Viereck, 498–512. Stuttgart: Steiner.

1996. ed. *Focus on the USA.* Philadelphia: John Benjamins.

Schuchardt, Hugo. 1889. "Beiträge zur Kenntnis des englischen Kreolisch I." *Englische Studien* 12: 470–4. ["Notes on the English of American Indians: Cheyenne, Kiowa, Pawnee, Pueblo, Sioux, and Wyandot." In *Pidgin and Creole Languages: Selected Essays by Hugo Schuchardt,* trans. Glenn G. Gilbert, 30–7. Cambridge University Press, 1980.]

Scragg, D. G. 1974. *A History of English Spelling.* Manchester University Press.

Seary, E. R. 1958. "The French Element in Newfoundland Place Names." *Onomastica* 16: 5–13.

Seary, E. R., G. M. Story, and W. J. Kirwin. 1968. *The Avalon Peninsula of Newfoundland: An Ethno-Linguistic Study.* Bulletin 219. Ottawa: National Museum of Canada.

Sechrist, Frank K. 1913. "The Psychology of Unconventional Language." *The Pedagogical Seminary* 20: 413–59.

SED = Survey of English Dialects. See Orton and Dieth 1962–.

Seeber, Edward D. 1940. "Franklin's 'Drinkers Dictionary' Again." *American Speech* 15: 103–5.

Sen, Ann Louise. 1973. "The Linguistic Geography of Eighteenth Century New Jersey Speech: Phonology." Ph.D. diss., Princeton University.

1974. "Dialect Variation in Early American English." *Journal of English Linguistics* 8: 41–7.

1978. "Reconstructing Early American Dialects." *Journal of English Linguistics* 12: 50–62.

Sheldon, Edward S. 1902. "Practical Philology." *PMLA* 17: 91–104.

Sheridan, Thomas. 1762. *A Course of Lectures on Elocution*. London: Millar. Photoreproduction with an introduction by Charlotte Downey. Delmar, NY: Scholars' Facsimiles & Reprints, 1991.

1780. *A General Dictionary of the English Language*. 2 vols. London: J. Dodsley. Reprint Menston, Yorks.: Scolar, 1967. 2nd ed. as *A Complete Dictionary of the English Language*. London: C. Dilly, 1789.

Sherwood, John C. 1960. "Dr. Kinsey and Professor Fries." *College English* 21: 275–80.

Shores, David L. 1985. "Vowels before /l/ and /r/ in the Tangier Dialect." *Journal of English Linguistics* 18: 124–6.

1989a. "Chesapeake Bay Dialect." In *Encyclopedia of Southern Culture*, ed. Charles Wilson and William Ferris, 785–6. Chapel Hill: University of North Carolina Press.

1989b. "Outer Banks Dialect." In *Encyclopedia of Southern Culture*, ed. Charles Wilson and William Ferris, 790–1. Chapel Hill: University of North Carolina Press.

Shulman, David. 1986. "The Earliest Citation of *Jazz*." Reprint in *Studies in Slang, Part II*, ed. Gerald Leonard Cohen. Frankfurt am Main: Peter Lang, 1989.

Siebert, Frank T. 1975. "Resurrecting Virginia Algonquian from the Dead: The Reconstituted and Historical Phonology of Powhatan." In *Studies in Southeastern Indian Languages*, ed. James M. Crawford, 285–453. Athens: University of Georgia Press.

Siegal, Alan A. 1984. *For the Glory of the Union*. Rutherford, NJ: Fairleigh Dickinson University Press.

Silliman, Benjamin. 1812. *A Journal of Travels in England, Holland, and Scotland, and of Two Passages over the Atlantic, in the Years 1805 and 1806*. 2 vols. Boston: T. B. Wait.

Simkins, Francis Butler, and Charles Pierce Roland. 1972. *A History of the South*. New York: Knopf.

Simpson, Claude M. 1936. "The English Speech of Early Rhode Island, 1636–1700." Ph.D. diss., Harvard University.

Simpson, David. 1986. *The Politics of American English*. Oxford University Press.

Sinclair, John, ed. 1987. *Collins Cobuild English Language Dictionary*. London: Collins.

Singler, John Victor. 1990. "On the Use of Sociohistorical Criteria in the Comparison of Creoles." *Linguistics* 28: 645–59.

1991a. "Copula Variation in Liberian Settler English and American Black English." In *Verb Phrase Patterns in Black English and Creole*, ed. Walter Edwards and Donald Winford, 129–64. Detroit: Wayne State University Press.

1991b. "Liberian Settler English and the Ex-Slave Recordings: A Comparative Study." In *The Emergence of Black English: Text and Commentary*, ed. Guy Bailey, Natalie Maynor, and Patricia Cukor-Avila, 249–74. Amsterdam: Benjamins.

Sketches and Eccentricities of Col. David Crockett of West Tennessee. 1832. New York: J. and J. Harper, 1833.

Sledd, James. 1962. "The Lexicographer's Uneasy Chair." *College English* 23: 682–7.

Sledd, James, and Wilma R. Ebbitt, eds. 1962. *Dictionaries and THAT Dictionary.* Chicago: Scott, Foresman.

Smith, Alice E. 1942. "Stephen H. Long and the Naming of Wisconsin." *Wisconsin Magazine of History* 26: 67–71.

Smith, John. 1988. *Captain John Smith: A Select Edition of His Writings.* Ed. Karen Ordahl Kupperman. Chapel Hill: University of North Carolina Press.

Smith, Riley B. 1976. "Interrelatedness of Certain Deviant Grammatical Structures in Negro Nonstandard Dialects." In *Black Language Reader*, ed. Robert H. Bentley and Samuel D. Crawford, 90–7. Glenview, IL: Scott, Foresman.

Smith, William. 1791. *The Confession of Thomas Mount.* Newport, RI: Edes.

Smitherman, Geneva. 1977. *Talkin and Testifyin: The Language of Black America.* Boston: Houghton Mifflin. Reprint Detroit: Wayne State University Press, 1988.

———. 1991. "What Is Africa to Me? Language, Ideology, and *African American.*" *American Speech* 66: 115–32.

———. 1994. *Black Talk: Words and Phrases from the Hood to the Amen Corner.* Boston: Houghton Mifflin.

———. 1998. "Word from the Hood: The Lexicon of African-American Vernacular English." In *African-American English: Structure, History, and Use*, ed. Salikoko S. Mufwene, John R. Rickford, Guy Bailey, and John Baugh, 203–25. London: Routledge.

———. 2000. *Talkin That Talk: Language, Culture, and Education in African America.* London: Routledge.

Sornig, Karl. 1981. *Lexical Innovation: A Study of Slang, Colloquialisms and Casual Speech.* Amsterdam: Benjamins.

Soukhanov, Anne H., ed. 1992. *The American Heritage Dictionary of the English Language.* 3rd ed. Boston: Houghton Mifflin.

Spears, Arthur. 1982. "The Black English Semi-Auxiliary *Come.*" *Language* 58: 850–72.

———. 1988. "Black American English." In *Anthropology for the Nineties: Introductory Readings*, ed. Johnnetta B. Cole, 96–113. New York: Free Press.

Spillane, Mickey. 1947. *I, the Jury.* Reprint, New York: Signet, 1948.

Stanley, Lawrence A., ed. 1993. *Rap: The Lyrics.* New York: Penguin.

Statistical Abstracts of the United States 1991. 1991. Washington, DC: U. S. Department of Commerce, Bureau of the Census.

Statistics Canada. <http://www.statcan.ca>.

Stefánsson, Vilhjálmur. 1909. "The Eskimo Trade Jargon of Herschel Island." *American Anthropologist* 11: 217–32.

Stephenson, Edward A. 1956. "Linguistic Resources of the Southern Historical Collection." *American Speech* 31: 271–7.

1958. "Early North Carolina Pronunciation." Ph.D. diss., University of North Carolina.

Stevens, C. 1954. "Early American Phonology." Ph.D. diss., Louisiana State University.

Stewart, William A. 1965. "Urban Negro Speech: Sociolinguistic Factors Affecting English Teaching." In *Social Dialects and Language Learning: Proceedings of the Bloomington, Indiana, Conference 1964*, ed. Roger Shuy, 10–19. Champaign, IL: National Council of Teachers of English.

1967. "Sociolinguistic Factors in the History of American Negro Dialects." *Florida Foreign Language Reporter* 5.2: 11, 22, 24, 26, 30.

1968. "Continuity and Change in American Negro Dialects." *Florida Foreign Language Reporter* 6.2: 3–4, 14–16, 18.

1970. "Historical and Structural Bases for the Recognition of Negro Dialect." In *Linguistics and the Teaching of Standard English to Speakers of Other Languages and Dialects*, ed. James E. Alatis, 239–47. Washington: Georgetown University Press.

1974. "Acculturative Processes and the Language of the American Negro." In *Language in Its Social Setting*, ed. William W. Gage, 1–46. Washington, DC: Anthropological Society of Washington.

Stockman, Ila. 1986. "Language Acquisition in Culturally Diverse Populations: The Black Child as a Case Study." In *Nature and Communication Disorders in Culturally and Linguistically Diverse Populations*, ed. Orlando Taylor, 117–55. San Diego, CA: College Hill Press.

Stockman, Ila, and Fay Vaughn-Cooke. 1982. "Semantic Categories in the Language of Working Class Children." In *Proceedings of the Second International Child Language Conference*, ed. C. E. Johnson and C. L. Thew, 312–27. Lanham, MD: University Press of America.

Stockwell, Elisha, Jr. 1927. *Private Elisha Stockwell, Jr., Sees the Civil War*. Ed. B. R. Abernethy. Norman: University of Oklahoma Press, 1958.

Stoddard, Albert. 1949. *Animal Tales in the Gullah Dialect*. Record albums and mimeographed texts. Washington, DC: Library of Congress.

Stoddart, Dayton. 1941. *Lord Broadway*. New York: Wilfred Funk.

Story, George Morley. 1969. "Newfoundland: Fishermen, Hunters, Planters, and Merchants." In *Christmas Mumming in Newfoundland: Essays in Anthropology, Folklore, and History*, ed. Herbert Halpert and G. M. Story, 9–33. Reprint, University of Toronto Press, 1990.

Story, George Morley, William J. Kirwin, and John David Allison Widdowson, eds. 1990. *Dictionary of Newfoundland English*. 2nd ed. University of Toronto Press. 1st ed. 1982. Digital version <www.heritage.nf.ca/dictionary>.

Stover, John F. 1991. "Railroads." In *The Reader's Companion to American History*, ed. Eric Foner and John A. Garraty, 906–10. Boston: Houghton Mifflin.

Strunk, William, Jr., and Elwyn Brooks White. 1979. *The Elements of Style by William Strunk, Jr., with Revisions, an Introduction, and a Chapter on Writing by E. B. White*, 3rd ed. New York: Macmillan.

Sturtevant, Edgar H. 1917. *Linguistic Change: An Introduction to the Historical Study of Language.* University of Chicago Press.

Sundby, Bertil, Anne Kari Bjørge, and Kari E Haugland. 1991. *A Dictionary of English Normative Grammar, 1700–1800.* Studies in the History of the Language Sciences 63. Amsterdam: Benjamins.

Surnames in the United States Census of 1790: An Analysis of National Origins of the Population. 1932. *Annual Report of the American Historical Association* 1: 103–441.

Svejcer, A. D. 1978. *Standard English in the United States and England.* The Hague: Mouton.

Sylvain, Suzanne. 1936. *Le créole haïtien: morphologie et syntaxe.* Wettern, Belgium: Imprimerie de Meester; Port-au-Prince, Haiti: Chez l'Auteur.

Tagliamonte, Sali. 1999. "Back to the Roots: What British Dialects Reveal about North American English." Paper presented at the conference on Methods in Dialectology X, St. John's, Newfoundland.

Tagliamonte, Sali, and Shana Poplack. 1988. "Tense and Aspect in Samaná English." *Language in Society* 17: 513–33.

1993. "The Zero-Marked Verb: Testing the Creole Hypothesis." *Journal of Pidgin and Creole Languages* 8: 171–206.

Tagliamonte, Sali, and Jennifer Smith. 1999. "Old *Was*, New Ecology: Viewing English through the Sociolinguistic Filter." In *The English History of African-American English*, ed. Shana Poplack, 141–71. Boston: Blackwell.

Tamony, Peter. 1958. "Jazz – The Word, and Its Extension to Music." *Jazz: A Quarterly of American Music* 1: 39–42.

1964–73. *Americanisms: Content and Continuum.* Nos. 1–33. San Francisco. Dittographed.

Tasko, Patti. 1999. *Canadian Press Stylebook: A Guide for Writers and Editors.* 11th ed. Toronto: Canadian Press.

Taylor, Allan R. 1981. "Indian Lingua Francas." In *Language in the USA*, ed. Charles A. Ferguson and Shirley Brice Heath, 175–95. Cambridge University Press.

Taylor, Anna Marjorie. 1944. *The Language of World War II.* New York: H. W. Wilson.

Taylor, Tom. 1858. *Our American Cousin.* Reprint, ed. Welford Dunaway Taylor. Washington, DC: Beacham, 1990.

1985. *Plays by Tom Taylor.* Ed. Martin Banham. Cambridge University Press.

Tebbel, John. 1972. *A History of Book Publishing in the United States.* Vol. 1, *The Creation of an Industry 1630–1865.* New York: Bowker.

Thernstrom, Stephen. 1980. *Harvard Encyclopedia of American Ethnic Groups.* Cambridge, MA: Harvard University Press.

Third = Webster's Third New International Dictionary. See Gove 1961a.

Thomas, Charles K. 1958. *An Introduction to the Phonetics of American English.* New York: Ronald.

Thomas, Erik. 1993. "The Use of *All The* + Comparative Structure." In *"Heartland English": Variation and Transition in the American Midwest*, ed. Timothy C. Frazer, 257–65. Tuscaloosa: University of Alabama Press.

Thomason, Sarah G. 1980. "On Interpreting the Indian Interpreter." *Language in Society* 9: 167–93.

1983. "Chinook Jargon in Areal and Historic Context." *Language* 59: 820–70.

Thompson, Frederic F. 1961. *The French Shore Problem in Newfoundland: An Imperial Study*. University of Toronto Press.

Thornton, Patricia A. 1985. "The Problem of Out-Migration from Atlantic Canada, 1871–1921: A New Look." *Acadiensis* 15: 3–34.

Thornton, Richard H. 1912. *An American Glossary*. 2 vols. Philadelphia: Lippincott; London: Francis.

Timmons, Christine, and Frank Gibney, eds. 1980. *Britannica Book of English Usage*. Garden City, NY: Doubleday/Britannica Books.

Tjossem, Herbert Karl. 1955. "New England Pronunciation before 1700." Ph.D. diss., Yale University.

Tocqueville, Alexis de. 1835–40. *Democracy in America*. 2 vols. Trans. Henry Reeve, 1838. Rev. Francis Bowen, 1862. Ed. Phillips Bradley. New York: Knopf, 1945.

Tolliver-Weddington, Gloria. 1979. "Introduction" to the special issue on "Ebonics (Black English): Implications for Education." *Journal of Black Studies* 9: 364–66.

Traugott, Elizabeth Closs. 1972. *The History of English Syntax: A Transformational Approach to the History of English Sentence Structure*. New York: Holt.

Troike, Rudolph C. 1986. "McDavid's Law." *Journal of English Linguistics* 19: 177–205.

Trollope, Frances. 1832. *Domestic Manners of the Americans*. Ed. Donald Smalley. New York: Alfred A. Knopf, 1949.

Trudgill, Peter. 1996. "Language Contact and Inherent Variability: The Absence of Hypercorrection in East Anglian Present-Tense Verb Forms." In *Speech Past and Present: Studies in English Dialectology in Memory of Ossi Ihalainen*, ed. Juhani Klemola, Merja Kytö, and Matti Rissanen, 412–27. University of Bamberg Studies in English Linguistics 38. Frankfurt am Main: Peter Lang.

1997. "British Vernacular Dialects in the Formation of American English: East Anglian *Do*." In *Language History and Linguistic Modelling*, ed. Ray Hickey and Stanislaw Puppel, 749–57. Berlin: Mouton de Gruyter.

2000. *Dialects in Contact*. Oxford: Blackwell. 1st ed. 1986.

Tucker, R. Whitney. 1934. "Linguistic Substrata in Pennsylvania and Elsewhere." *Language* 10: 1–4.

Tufts, Henry. 1807. *A Narrative of the Life, Adventures, and Travels of Henry Tufts*. Ed. E. Pearson. New York: Duffield, 1930.

Turner, Frederick Jackson. 1894. "The Significance of the Frontier in American History." *Proceedings of the Forty-first Annual Meeting of the State Historical Society of Wisconsin*. Madison: State Historical Society of Wisconsin.

1920. "The Old West." In *The Frontier in American History*, 67–125. Reprint, Tucson: University of Arizona Press, 1986.

Turner, Lorenzo Dow. 1949. *Africanisms in the Gullah Dialect*. University of Chicago Press.

Twain, Mark [pseudonym of Samuel L. Clemens]. 1872. *Roughing It*. Hartford, CT: American Publishing. Reprint ed. Franklin R. Rogers and Paul Baender. Berkeley: University of California Press, 1972.

1876. *The Adventures of Tom Sawyer*. Reprint ed. John C. Gerber, Paul Baender, and Terry Firkins. Berkeley: University of California Press, 1980.

1883. *Life on the Mississippi*. Boston: Osgood.

Twiggs, Robert D. 1973. *Pan-African Language in the Western Hemisphere*. North Quincy, MA: Christopher.

Tylor, Edward B. 1874. "The Philology of Slang." *Macmillan's Magazine* 29: 502–13.

Unger, Harlow Giles. 1998. *Noah Webster: The Life and Times of an American Patriot*. New York: John Wiley.

United States Board on Geographic Names. 1892. *First Report of the United States Board on Geographic Names 1890–1891*. Washington, DC: Government Printing Office.

1901. *Second Report of the United States Board on Geographic Names 1890–1899*. Washington, DC: Government Printing Office.

United States Department of Commerce. 1976. *Historical Statistics of the United States, Colonial Times to 1970*. Part 1. Washington, DC: Government Printing Office.

United States Government Printing Office. 1973. *Style Manual*. Rev. ed. Washington, DC: Government Printing Office.

Upton, Clive, David Parry, and John David Allison Widdowson, eds. 1994. *Survey of English Dialects: The Dictionary and the Grammar*. London: Routledge.

Van Riper, William. 1973. "General American: An Ambiguity." In *Lexicography and Dialect Geography: Festgabe für Hans Kurath*, ed. Harold Scholler and John Reidy, 232–42. Weisbaden: Steiner.

Van Schaak, Henry. 1842. *The Life of Peter Van Schaak*. New York: Appleton.

Venezky, Richard L. 1970. *The Structure of English Orthography*. The Hague: Mouton.

1999. *The American Way of Spelling*. New York: Guilford.

Viereck, Wolfgang. 1985. "On the Interrelationship of British and American English: Morphological Evidence." In *Focus on England and Wales*, ed. Wolfgang Viereck, 247–301. Amsterdam: Benjamins.

Vinson, Julien. 1882. "Créole." In *Dictionnaire des sciences anthropologiques et ethnologiques*. Paris.

1888. "La linguistique." In *La grande encyclopédie*, ed. M. Berthelot, 22: 286–96. Paris.

von Jagemann, H. C. G. 1900. "Philology and Purism." *PMLA* 15: 74–96.

Wakelin, Martyn Francis. 1986a. *The Southwest of England*. Amsterdam: Benjamins.

1986b. "English on the Mayflower." *English Today* (Oct.-Dec.), 30–3.

1988. *The Archaeology of English*. London: Batsford.

Walker, John. 1775. *A Dictionary of the English Language Answering at Once the Purpose of Rhyming, Spelling, and Pronouncing on a Plan Not Hitherto Attempted.* London.

1791. *A Critical Pronouncing Dictionary and Expositor of the English Language.* London: G. G. J. and J. Robinson.

Wallis, John. 1653. *Grammatica linguae Anglicanae.* Facsimile reprint Menston, Yorks.: Scolar, 1969. Trans. J. A. Kemp as *Grammar of the English Language.* London: Longman, 1972.

Wardhaugh, Ronald. 1999. *Proper English: Myths and Misunderstandings about Language.* Oxford: Basil Blackwell.

Warfel, Harry R. 1936. *Noah Webster, Schoolmaster to America.* New York: Macmillan.

1952. *Who Killed Grammar?* Gainesville: University of Florida Press.

Webster, Noah. 1783–5. *A Grammatical Institute of the English Language, Comprising, an Easy, Concise, and Systematic Method of Education, Designed for the Use of English Schools in America.* 3 vols. Hartford, CT: Hudson and Goodwin.

1784. *A Grammatical Institute of the English Language.* Part 2: *Containing a Plain and Comprehensive Grammar.* Hartford: Hudson and Goodwin. Reprint, English Linguistics 1500–1800, no. 90. Menston, Yorks.: Scolar, 1968.

1787. *The American Spelling Book; or, First Part of the Grammatical Institute of the English Language.* 6th ed. Hartford, CT: Hudson and Goodwin.

1789. *Dissertations on the English Language, with Notes, Historical and Critical. To Which He Added, by Way of Appendix, An Essay on a Reformed Mode of Spelling, with Dr. Franklin's Arguments on That Subject.* Boston: Isaiah Thomas. Reprint, English Linguistics 1500–1800, no. 54. Menston, Yorks.: Scolar, 1967.

1806. *A Compendious Dictionary of the English Language.* Hartford, CT: Hudson and Goodwin; New Haven: Increase Cooke.

1807. *Philosophical and Practical Grammar.* New Haven: Brisban and Brannan.

1828. *An American Dictionary of the English Language.* 2 vols. New York: S. Converse.

1829. *The Elementary Spelling Book, Being an Improvement on the American Spelling Book.* New York: Haven and Lockwood.

1830. *A Dictionary of the English Language.* New York: White, Gallaher, and White.

1841. *An American Dictionary of the English Language.* 2 vols. New Haven: The Author.

1842. Letter dated September 20, 1842, printed in the New Haven *Daily Herald*, October 10, 1842. Cited by Allen Walker Read in "The Spread of German Linguistic Learning in New England during the Lifetime of Noah Webster." *American Speech* 41 (1966): 163–81.

1847. *An American Dictionary of the English Language.* Rev. and enl. by Chauncey A. Goodrich. Springfield, MA: Merriam.

1864. *An American Dictionary of the English Language.* Rev. Chauncey A. Goodrich and Noah Porter. Springfield, MA: Merriam.

Weiner, E. S. C., ed. 1983. *The Oxford Guide to English Usage.* Oxford: Clarendon.

Weingarten, Joseph. 1954. *American Slang Dictionary.* New York: privately printed.

Welland, Dennis, ed. 1987. *The United States.* 2nd ed. London: Methuen.

Wells, John C. 1982. *Accents of English.* 3 vols. Cambridge University Press.

Wentworth, Harold, and Stuart Berg Flexner. 1960. *Dictionary of American Slang.* New York: Thomas Y. Crowell. Supplemented ed., 1967. 2nd supplemented ed., 1975.

Werner, Oswald. 1963. "A Typological Comparison of Four Trader Navaho Speakers." Ph.D. diss., Indiana University.

Wertenbaker, Thomas J. 1942. *The Old South: The Founding of an American Civilization.* New York: Scribner's.

Weseen, Maurice H. 1934. *A Dictionary of American Slang.* New York: Crowell.

White, Kevin. 1993. *The First Sexual Revolution.* New York University Press.

White, Richard Grant. 1870. *Words and Their Uses Past and Present: A Study of the English Language.* 3rd ed., rev. and corrected. Boston: Houghton Mifflin, 1881.

———. 1880. *Every-Day English.* Boston: Houghton Mifflin.

Whitehall, Harold. 1939. *Middle English ū and Related Sounds: Their Development in Early American English.* Language monograph 19. Baltimore, MD: Linguistic Society of America.

Whitford, Helena Wells. 1799. *Letters on Subjects of Importance to the Happiness of Young Females.* London: L. Peacock.

———. 1800. *Constantia Neville; or, The West Indian.* 3 vols. London: T. Cadell.

———. 1809. *Thoughts and Remarks on Establishing an Institution for the Support and Education of Unportioned Respectable Females.* London: Longman, Hurst, Reese and Orme.

Whitman, Walt. 1856–? "The Primer of Words." In *Walt Whitman: Daybooks and Notebooks,* ed. William White, 3: 728–57. New York University Press, 1978.

———. 1885. "Slang in America." *North American Review* (Boston, Nov.), 431–5.

Whitney, William Dwight. 1867. *Language and the Study of Language: Twelve Lectures on the Principles of Linguistic Science.* New York: Scribner's.

———. 1874. *Oriental and Linguistic Studies, Second Series.* New York: Scribner's.

———. 1875. *The Life and Growth of Language: An Outline of Linguistic Science.* New York: Appleton.

———. 1877. *Essentials of English Grammar.* Boston: Ginn and Heath.

———. 1889–91. ed. *The Century Dictionary.* 6 vols. New York: Century.

Whorf, Benjamin Lee. 1956. *Language, Thought, and Reality: Selected Writings by Benjamin Lee Whorf.* Ed. John B. Carroll. Cambridge, MA: MIT Press.

Widdowson, John David Allison. 1969. "Mummering and Janneying: Some Explanatory Notes." In *Christmas Mumming in Newfoundland: Essays in Anthropology, Folklore, and History,* ed. Herbert Halpert and G. M. Story, 216–21. Reprint, University of Toronto Press, 1990.

———. 1991. "Lexical Retention in Newfoundland Dialect." In *Studies in Newfoundland Folklore: Community and Process,* ed. Gerald Thomas and J. D. A. Widdowson, 245–58. St. John's, Newfoundland: Breakwater.

Wiley, Bell Irvin. 1952. *The Life of Billy Yank.* Indianapolis, IN: Bobbs-Merrill.

Wilkinson, Rupert. 1984. *American Tough: The Tough-Guy Tradition and American Character.* Westport, CT: Greenwood Press.

Willes, Richard, trans. and comp. 1577. *The History of Trauayle in the VVest and East Indies.* London: Richard Jugge.

Williams, Cratis D. 1978. "Appalachian Speech." *North Carolina Historical Review* 55: 174–9.

Williams, Hugo. 1987. "Signposting the Taboo." *Times Literary Supplement*, May 8, 493–4.

Williams, Robert L., ed. 1975. *Ebonics: The True Language of Black Folks.* St. Louis, MO: Robert L. Williams.

Williams, Roger. 1643. *A Key into the Language of America.* London. Reprint, Providence, RI: Rhode Island and Providence Plantations Tercentenary Committee, 1936.

Wilson, Charles Morro. 1929. "Elizabethan America." *Atlantic* 144: 238–44.

Winford, Donald. 1990. "The Copula Variability, Accountability, and the Concept of 'Polylectal' Grammars." *Journal of Pidgin and Creole Languages* 5: 223–52.

1992. "Another Look at the Copula in Black English and Caribbean Creoles." *American Speech* 67: 21–60.

1993. "Back to the Past: The BEV/Creole Connection Revisited." *Language Variation and Change* 4: 311–57.

1998. "On the Origins of African American Vernacular English – A Creolist Perspective: Part II: Linguistic Features." *Diachronica* 15: 99–154.

Witherspoon, John. 1781. "The Druid," nos. 5–7. *Pennsylvania Journal, or, Weekly Advertiser* (Philadelphia, May 9, 16, 23, 30). Reprint in *The Beginnings of American English: Essays and Comments*, ed. Mitford M. Mathews, 13–30. University of Chicago Press, 1931.

1803. *The Miscellaneous Works of the Rev. John Witherspoon.* Philadelphia: William W. Woodward.

Wofford, Jean. 1979. "Ebonics: A Legitimate System of Oral Communication." *Journal of Black Studies* 9: 367–82.

Wolfram, Walter A. 1969. *A Sociolinguistic Description of Detroit Negro Speech.* Washington, DC: Center for Applied Linguistics.

1974. "The Relationship of White Southern Speech to Vernacular Black English." *Language* 50: 498–527. Reprinted in *Verb Phrase Patterns in Black English and Creole*, ed. Walter Edwards and Donald Winford, 60–100. Detroit: Wayne State University Press, 1991.

1980. "'A'-prefixing in Appalachian English." In *Locating Language in Time and Space*, ed. William Labov, 107–42. New York: Academic Press.

Wolfram, Walter A., Kirk Hazen, and Natalie Schilling-Estes. 1999. *Dialect Change and Maintenance on the Outer Banks.* Publication of the American Dialect Society 81. Tuscaloosa: University of Alabama Press.

Wolfram, Walter A., and Natalie Schilling-Estes. 1997. *Hoi Toids on the Outer Banks:*

The Story of the Ocracoke Brogue. Chapel Hill: University of North Carolina Press.

Wood, William. 1634. *New Englands Prospect.* Reprint, Burt Franklin Research and Source Works Series, 131. New York: Burt Franklin, 1967.

Woods, Howard B. 1999. *The Ottawa Survey of Canadian English.* Strathy Language Unit Occasional Papers 4. Kingston, ON: Queen's University.

Worcester, Joseph E. 1830. *Comprehensive Pronouncing and Explanatory Dictionary of the English Language with Pronouncing Vocabularies of Classical and Scripture Proper Names.* New York: Collins and Hannay.

1846. *A Universal and Critical Dictionary of the English Language.* Boston: Wilkins, Carter.

The World. 1753–6. 4 vols. Philadelphia: Samuel F. Branford and Joseph Conrad, 1803–4.

Woty, William. 1786. *Fugitive and Original Poems.* Derby: Printed for the author by J. Drewry.

Wright, Joseph, ed. 1898–1905. *English Dialect Dictionary.* 6 vols. London: Frowde.

1905. *English Dialect Grammar.* London: Frowde.

Wright, R. L., ed. 1975. *Irish Emigrant Ballads and Songs.* Bowling Green, OH: Bowling Green University Popular Press.

Wyatt, Toya Annette. 1991. "Linguistic Constraints on Copula Production in Black English Child Speech." Ph.D. diss., University of Massachusetts.

Zwilling, Leonard. 1993. *A TAD Lexicon.* Vol. 3 of *Etymology and Linguistic Principles.* Rolla, MO: Gerald Cohen.

INDEX

Index

as, 191–2, 195; in Civil War and Reconstruction, 201–5; from Civil War to World War II, 209–10; databases, 218; definitions, 185–8; diachronic, xxii, 187; earliest, 19, 187–8, 188–9, 189–91; on environment, 18, 19, 20, 67–8, 69, 93, 137, 195–6 (*see also* fauna; flora; topography); ethnic epithets, 208; on foods, 208, 216; foreign loanwords, 192–3, 193–4, 194–5, 208 (*see also* Amerindian languages, loanwords); frontier, xxii, 198–9, 205–9; governmental terms, 485; initialisms, 196–7, 210–11; inventiveness, 137, 201, 209, 456–8; and isolation from British English, 184, 186; literati and, 341, 385; on music, 214–15; overseas adoption, 490–2; rapid dissemination of recent, 213; regional differences, xxii, 112, 193–5; on religion, 215–16; Revolution stimulates, 196; semantic shifts, 187, 192; slang, 219, 226–7, 240, 243; spelling, 340–1; on sports, 216; synchronic, xxii, 187; and technology, xxii, 209, 211, 213; urbanization and, 208–10; Webster and, xxii, 67–8, 199–200; from westwards expansion, 195–9, 205–8; Witherspoon and, xxii, 61, 66, 68, 69, 185–6, 459; World War II to present, 210–13
American Magazine, 78–9
American Mercury, 43
American Philological Association, 388
American Phonetic Alphabet, 351
American Scholar, 406
American Speech, 240, 248
American Telephone and Telegraph (AT&T), 42
Amerindian languages, xxi, 93, 164–8; and AAE, 160; Algonquian languages, *see separate entry;* British belief that all Americans spoke, 481; calquing, 166; creolization, 157; families, xxi, 155 (*see also* Algonquian family); French contact, 157, 167, 171, 188; *Indian*, compounds with first element, 167–8; koinéization hypothesis, 115; lingua francas, 155–7; loanwords, 92–3, 155, 163–4, 164–8,

188–9, 195–6, 206; —, cultural terms, 15, 164, 166, 167, 195, 196; —, on fauna and flora, 15, 137, 164–6, 167, 188–9, 195–6, 464; —, on foods, 189 (see also *maize*); —, loan translations, 166, 464; —, localized, 163; —, 16th-century, 155, 188, 460–5, 466–7; —, topographical terms, 15, 195; —, transmitted through other European languages, 154, 167, 171, 175, 188, 460–3, 466–7, 470–1; number of languages, 154–5; pidgins, 156–7, 157–62; place names, 166, 349; pre-contact languages, 154–7; semantic shift in borrowings, 167; stereotypes of speech, 166; west, words from, 167, 188, 195–6; word lists, 92–3, 468, 469
Amerindians: boarding schools, 159–60; early contacts, 15, 18–19, 20, 60, 154, 467, 468; forced removal: 155, 255; inquiry into origins, 468, 469; interpreters, 158–9; literary character types, 100; migration from Asia, 4; relations with colonists, 190; slang epithet, 246; underclass, 13. *See also* Aboriginal peoples of Canada
Amish, Old Order, 174
amongst you, 149
Amorous Gallant's Tongue, The (1740), 227
analogical formations, 328, 332, 339, 368, 381
and: introducing elliptical clause without verb, 150; written as &, 343
Anglican Church, 7, 8, 10, 177, 190, 264
Anglo-Irish English. *See* Irish English; Scotch-Irish
Angolan language, 180
animal tales, 311
ant-bear, 464
anterior tense, AAE, 301
Antillean Creole, 215
antiphrasis in slang and poetry, 224
antitrust acts, 34
antonomasia in slang and poetry, 225
anymore 'nowadays,' 150, 331–2, 432
A-OK, 244
Appalachian. *See* South Midland dialects
apple pie, 216–17

Index

Index

Houghton Mifflin, 412
house, 138
Household Words, 233
housing, 49, 54
Houston, Texas, as cultural center, 255
Howells, William Dean, 36
Hudson Bay, 17
Hudson Valley, 77, 170, 267, 269–70, 289
Hughes, Langston, 230
Huguenots, 16, 60, 129, 169, 171, 190
Hulbert, James R., 186–7, 217, 460
humble, 73
Humbug, Henry (*pseud.*), 228
Hume, David, 479–80
humor, 182, 310, 489; comic use of dialects, 72, 108
Humphreys, David, 69
Hungary: immigration from, 48, 49–50; McDonald's restaurants in, 55
hurricane, 176
Hurston, Zora Neale, 230
Hutchinson, Anne, 9
Hutten, Ulrich von, 461–2, 463
[hw], initial. See under *w*
/hy/, reflexes of, 268, 282
hyperbole in slang and poetry, 225
hypercorrection, 295, 429

i: Canadian doubling before suffix, 433; *j* interchangeability, 342, 345; Newfoundland lateral, 447; *pen/pin* merger, 131, 139–40, 276, 296–7
ice diphthong in Newfoundland, 448
-ick reduced to *-ic*, 199, 343, 344, 345, 346, 372
Idaho dialect, 284–5, 286
idealization, linguistic, 322
identity, social; slang and, 221–2, 244, 251
idiolects, xviii, 292, 322
-ie changed to *-y*, 342
iguana, 464
-ile, 78, 430
Illinois: in Civil War, 31; settlement, 49, 50, 54, 271; spelling of state name, 171
immigration and immigrants, 3, 4, 49–50, 89–92, 177–81; British colonial migrations, 7–8, 59–61, 79–84, 113–14;

189–91; to Canada, 423, 425–6, 439; changing patterns, 49–50; ethnic culture, 178, 426; European, three waves of, 32, 162–3; involuntary, 14, 86, 91 (*see also* slaves); language contact, 163, 177–81, 254, 330, 439; later 19th-century, 27, 32; mobility of new settlers, 87; provenance and languages, 89–92; regulation, 41, 49, 50, 177; social class, 86, 383, 408; surname research, 89; to urban areas, 208, 425–6. *See also individual peoples, languages, and regions*
imperatives, AAE, 300, 306
imperialism, 38–40
impressment of Americans by Royal Navy, 25, 240
income tax, 40
indentured workers. *See* servants
Independence, Missouri, 286
independence, political and cultural, 4–5
independent language development, xxv, 93, 321, 327–8, 330–1, 335–9
Indess, 475
India, McDonald's restaurants in, 55
Indian, compounds with first element, 167–8
Indiana, xxiv, 31, 49, 246, 271
Indian Interpreter, 157
Indianism, 475
Indians. *See* Amerindians
Indians, Red, Beothuks known as, 443
indignation, *come* construction to denote, 305
indigo, 190, 274
indirect speech in AAE, 306–7
Indo-European linguistics, 379
Industrial Workers of the World (*wobblies*), 209
industry, 40, 44, 287; Americanisms connected with, 209; 19th-century development, 27, 31, 33, 204, 257
-ine in Canadian English, 430
infinitival clauses with *to*, AAE, 300
infinitives, split, 398
inflation, 202
informal language/slang distinction, 220–1

Pennsylvania (*cont.*)
190; Germans, Pennsylvania Dutch, xxii, 124, 174, 190, 194–5, 271–2; —, loanwords and loan translations introduced by, xxii, 194–5, 214, 271–2; —, Ulster Scots archaisms used by, 134; grammar, 125, 148; immigration patterns, 49, 50, 54; Indian pidgin, 157; Irish-born Indian trader, 125, 140; land granted to Penn, 190; Midland/ Northern dialect boundary, 112, 124, 267; migrations to Midland areas, 124–5, 264, 265, 270–1, 272, 273, 274, 282; mobility of population, 87; phonology, 77, 125, 141, 428; Quaker settlers, 11–12, 60, 81–2, 124, 190, 194, 255; —, Welsh, 92, 164; Scotch-Irish and northern Borderers' migration to, xxii, 13, 60, 82, 91, 124, 125, 134, 189, 190, 194, 265, 266; Scots poetic idiom, 134; and Southern dialects, 274; Swedes, 124; Swiss immigrants, 195; vocabulary, 192, 271–2; —, British and Irish antecedents, 124, 125, 134, 139 (*see also under* Germans *above*); Welsh immigration, 92, 124; and Western dialects, 282, 283. *See also individual cities*
penny press, 28, 52
Penobscot, 155, 164
pen/pin merger, 131, 139–40, 276, 296–7
Penutian languages, xxi, 155
Pequot, 15
Percy, Walker, 57
Perelman, S. J., 249
perfect: AAE, 301, 302, 314, 323; Southern dialects, 275
Perry, William; *Royal Standard English Dictionary* (1788, 1801), 344, 345
persimmon, 155, 164, 188, 468
persistence; AAE *steady* marker, 304–5
personification in slang and poetry, 225
Pestalozzi, Johann Heinrich, 350
petitions, 103
Philadelphia, Pennsylvania: Americanisms, 194; as cultural center, 255; dialect, xxiv; English Academy, 65; Federal Society of Journeymen Cordwainers, 27; Irish

Catholics, 92; literati, 62, 65; Midland dialect influenced by, 270–1, 273; phonology, 76, 369; Presbyterian schools, 65; publishing, 365; Quakers, 92, 124; and Revolution, 21, 22, 24; Scotch-Irish, 13, 82; settlement, 13, 82, 92, 124, 190, 244; Welsh settlement near, 92
Philippines, 5, 38, 39, 50
philologians' confrontation with linguists, 378–84
Philological Society, New York, 61
Philological Society of London, 395
philosophy, 29; cracker-barrel, 35–6
Phoenix, Arizona, 255, 286
phonemes, 254
phonetic notation, xxx–xxxii, 140, 159, 351, 405
phonograph, 33
phonology: American influence on British, 492–3; British and Irish antecedents, 71–8, 79, 84, 90, 93; —, and drawl, 9, 80, 123; —, post-settlement influence, xxi, 79, 85, 143–4; —, super-regional features, 137–44; conservatism, 23; dialects, xxiv, 253, 254 (*see also under individual dialects*); Johnson on, 72, 73; National period, 23; orthoepists, lexicographers and elocutionists, 72–4; pronouncing dictionaries, 98, 101, 102, 141; segmental contrasts, American/British, 74, 75–6, 77–8; sources on 18th-century, 142; spelling pronunciation, 73, 78, 80, 143, 431; standard as nonexistent in America, xxiv, 71; uniformity in Colonial period, 93–4, 97; Webster on, 74–5, 368–9. *See also* Received Pronunciation, *individual words and sounds and under individual language varieties and* class, social
photography, 31
picaresque writing, 243
picayune, 172
Pickering, John; *Vocabulary of Words and Phrases Which Have Been Supposed Peculiar to the United States* (1816), 35, 66, 69, 105, 229, 482–3, 484–5
pidgins and jargons, 157–62; African-

Index

Index

Received Pronunciation, British, xxiv, 71, 72, 73; American dialects influenced by, 73–4, 75, 80, 84–5; characteristics, 75, 76, 80, 84; use of Americanisms as revolt against, 493–4

Reconstruction, post-Civil War, xxii, 32, 82, 203, 204

Reconstruction Issue in dialect research, xxi, 104, 111, 115, 116, 118; AAE, 119; and British and Irish dialects, 94

recording, audio, 117

Redcoats (British soldiers), 17, 18, 241

redemptioners (bound workers), 14

redevelopments, linguistic, 150–1

Red Indians, Beothuks known as, 443

red lead 'ketchup,' 224

Red River basin, 279, 283

Red Scares, 41, 45

redskin, 475

redundancy, semantic, in AAE, 298–9

reduplications, Yiddish, 178

relation of forms, hypothesis to test historical, 119

relative clauses: AAE contact, 306, 307. See also *who*, *whom*

relic forms. *See* archaisms

religion: AAE in church, 308, 311; Americanisms, xxiii, 215–16; Christian fundamentalism, 41, 42; church records, 103, 104, 117; denominational academies, 65, 80–1; and etymology, 379; Newfoundland English in church, 443; preaching, 35, 117, 311, 392; and slavery, 30; societies, National period, 29; toleration, 9, 264; and usage, 374

remote phrase *bin*, AAE, 301

Remus, Uncle (Joel Chandler Harris character), 101, 110

rep (AAE, from *reputation*), 309, 310

repeated action: AAE, 303, 304; Newfoundland English *do* + *be*, 450

research needs: on British and Irish antecedents, 94–6, 151–3; comparative linguistics, 152; demographics, 153; on dialects, 255–6; on 18th century, 152; and koinéization hypothesis, 153; on regionalization of forms, 152

resemblance, standard of, 119

resentment, expression of, 305

reservations, Native American, 155

response to American English abroad, xxvi–xxvii, 456–96; *Americanism*, use and misuse of term, 458–60; awareness of American English as distinct variety, 471–6; early impact of Americas, 460–5; exploration and resources, words connected with, 465–71; influence of American English on other varieties, 491–3; to novelty, 490–1; triumph of American English, 493–5. *See also under* Britain

Revere, Paul, 16

reviews of American publications, British, 483–4

Revised Scientific Alphabet, 351

Revolution, American, 3, 20–3; American English becomes national variety, xviii; Americanisms coined after, 196; British scorn for colonial forces, 18; Canadian English develops after, xxvi, 425; conservatism of consequences, 23; interruption of contacts with British English, 73, 93; Loyalist exodus after, xxvi, 23, 425

rhetoric, study of, 65

Rhode Island, 9, 31, 103, 193

rhotacism, xxi, 23, 75–7; British and Irish influence, 75–7, 111, 135, 138, 140, 449; and class, 76; European immigrants bring, 77; Middle states, 111; Newfoundland, 447, 449, 454; prestige, 77. *See also under* Canadian English *and* Northern, Southern *and* Western dialects

rhymes, poetic, xxi, 97, 101–2, 111

rice cultivation, 16, 274

Richmond, Virginia, 129

right (intensifier), 275; *right away*, 488

rile, 139

ring, 372

risk, 345

Rissanen, Matti, 103, 116, 117, 123

roads, 19, 26–7, 49, 53, 287

Roanoke, Virginia, 159, 163, 467

Robinson, Edward G., 251

slaves and slavery (*cont.*)
location, 7, 9, 10, 14, 129, 274, 313, 314;
language use, 10, 160, 213–14, 309, 314;
migration and emigration of freed, 29,
317–18; occupations, 16, 29–30; *peculiar
institution*, 204; runaways, 14, 25, 99, 160;
vocabulary connected with trade, 470
Slavic languages and peoples, 163, 179, 246
Sledd, James, 409
Slovakia, 55
sluice, 491
smart talk, AAE, 310
smearcase, 170, 208, 272
smell, 335
Smith, James (Col.), 159
Smith, John (Capt.), 93, 164–5, 188, 468
Smith, Joseph, 26
Smith, Seba, 230
Smith, William; *The Confession of Thomas
Mount* (1791), 242–3
Smitherman, Geneva, 308–9
smog, 209
smorgasbord, 169
snafu, 211, 223, 247
sneaked, snuck, 309, 431–2
snobbery and usage, 402, 420
social contract theory of language, 378,
386
social development, 19th/20th-century,
26–9, 32–4, 42–3, 48–50
Social Gospel, 40
social issues: context, and usage, 295, 380;
correctness as, 350; reform, and dialects,
288; sensitivity to, and usage, 415–17;
and slang, 220, 221–2, 238, 244, 249–52;
and usage, 364, 397–8, 400, 402, 406,
407–8, 420
social varieties of language, xviii, xxiii, 136,
254, 397
sociohistorical approach, 116–19
sociolinguistics, xxiii, xxiv, 315, 426
sockdolager, 456–8
soda fountains, 55
soft, 99, 141
softball, 216
Solzhenitsyn, Alexander, 59
Somerset, England; dialect, 10, 81, 105, 192

Somerset (NJ) Messenger, 232
Sorokin, Pitirim A., 3
Soukhanov, Anne, 412
sounding, AAE, 310–11
sources: on African-American English,
121; Colonial period, xxi, 96–104, 121;
—, commentary of grammarians and
lexicographers, xxi, 97, 98–9; —, literary
attestations, xxi, 97, 100–1; —, poetic
rhymes, xxi, 97, 101–2; —, popular
observations by outsiders, xxi, 97–8; —,
texts (original records and manuscripts),
xxi, 97, 102–4; on Lower South, 121,
131; on New England, 121, 122
South Africa, 222, 226, 490, 491
South Carolina: AAE, 292, 310–11, 314,
324; backcountry settlement, 82, 124,
125 (*see also* Scotch-Irish *below*); black
population, 30, 129, 274, 314; British
dialect influence, 129, 255–6; Cavalier
settlers, 10–11, 129; in Civil War, 31;
coastal, 129, 276, 292; colonial lag, 106;
colonization, 10–11, 313; creation, 193;
French settlers, 10, 16, 129, 171, 177;
German settlers, 124; Gullah speakers,
292, 310–11, 324; heterogeneity of
settlers, 129; indigo plantations, 274;
Jewish settlers, 129; Midland dialect,
270–1; mountain speech, Elizabethan
hypothesis, 108–9; past tense, 146;
Pennsylvania migration to, 270, 274, 282;
phonology, 79, 142, 427; piedmont,
270–1, 274; rice cultivation, 16; Scotch-
Irish in, 13–14, 82, 91, 104, 124; Scots in,
129; Upper/Lower South division, 125,
129, 270–1; Virginian settlement of,
10–11
South Dakota, 33, 281
Southern dialects, 262–3, 264–5, 274–80,
289; AAE in relation to white dialects,
divergence, 319–21; —, early African
influence, 128–9; —, similarities, 131,
214, 296, 297, 303, 322; AAVE in
relation to white dialects, 297, 315, 316,
320; air conditioning and settlement
pattern, 54; archaism, 129–30, 132; area,
274–5; *be*, invariant, 147, 329; British and

THE CAMBRIDGE HISTORY
OF THE ENGLISH LANGUAGE

GENERAL EDITOR Richard M. Hogg

VOLUME I *The Beginnings to 1066*
EDITED BY Richard M. Hogg

VOLUME II *1066–1476*

EDITED BY Norman Blake

VOLUME III *1476–1776*

EDITED BY Roger Lass